The Abbot and His Peasants

Katherine Brun

Quellen und Forschungen
zur Agrargeschichte

Herausgegeben von
Stefan Brakensiek
Erich Landsteiner
Heinrich Richard Schmidt
Clemens Zimmermann

Band 56

Dieser Band wurde gefördert und mitherausgegeben von der
Gesellschaft Oberschwaben für Geschichte und Kultur e. V.

Katherine Brun

The Abbot and His Peasants

Territorial Formation in Salem from the Later Middle Ages to the Thirty Years War

Lucius & Lucius · Stuttgart

Author:

Katherine Brun
P.O. Box 1102
Mendocino CA 95460
USA

kbrun@mcn.org

Bibliographic information published by the Deutsche Nationalbibliothek
The Deutsche Nationalbibliothek lists this publication in the Deutsche Nationalbibliografie; detailed bibliographic data are available in the Internet at http://dnb.d-nb.de.

ISBN 978-3-8282-0546-8
ISSN 0481-3553

Gerokstraße 51 · D-70184 Stuttgart · www.luciusverlag.com

Design: Claudia Rupp, Stuttgart
Production: BELTZ Bad Langensalza GmbH, Bad Langensalza
Printed in Germany

Table of Contents

Notes on Usage, Currencies, and Measures

As the first English title to appear in a long-established German series, this book has required certain style choices and compromises with respect to the usual conventions in both languages. I have followed American forms of style, punctuation, and spelling over British or Continental European usage, with the exception of certain house rules in keeping with the series, Quellen und Forschungen zur Agrargeschichte. I thank the publishers for their flexibility and understanding.

English equivalents for German terms have been used wherever practical, and German terms are *italicized* upon first mention. Important terms and those that appear frequently may be found in the glossary, and infrequently encountered terms are italicized throughout the text; all translations are mine unless otherwise noted. Source quotations appearing in the footnotes have been transcribed as closely as possible to the original, with the following minor exceptions. The letters u and v as well as i and j have been transposed so that u and i indicate vowels whereas v and j indicate consonants, according to modern usage. The abbreviated word endings -en and -er are spelled out, but other abbreviations reflect the original spelling. Capitalization and accent marks have been retained to the greatest possible extent, and punctuation has been altered only where necessary to make a passage more readable. German place names are spelled throughout the text according to current local usage, with the exception of a few places commonly known in English by an alternate name or spelling: Constance, Lake Constance, and the Danube, among others. Personal names are spelled for the most part as in the original, though frequently recurring names have been slightly regularized according to modern German usage. This avoids the confusions inherent in multiple spelling variations that are characteristic of the period. Only the names of kings and emperors have been Anglicized.

The territory under study did not possess its own unitary system of weights, measures, or currency.[1] Constance, as the region's leading city and market center, set the primary standards shared by Salem and many of its closest neighbors. Measurements in Überlingen deviated slightly and served in some cases as an alternate regional standard. Ravensburg's measures were customary in the eastern Linzgau.

---

1 On local coinages and other measurements, see Rudolf BÜTTNER, Das Konstanzer Heilig-Geist-Spital und seine Besitzungen im Linzgau, PhD diss., Constance 1986, pp. 569–584; Wolfgang v. HIPPEL, Mass und Gewicht im Gebiet des Grossherzogtums Baden am Ende des 18. Jahrhunderts, Mannheim 1996, p. 211; Meinrad SCHAAB, Münzen und Währung, in: Handbuch der baden-württembergischen Geschichte, vol. 1 part 2, ed. Meinrad Schaab and Hansmartin Schwarzmaier, Stuttgart 2000, pp. 575-585; Glossary by Diethard NOWAK, in: Xavier Staiger, Salem oder Salmansweiler, 2nd ed., Meersburg 2008, pp. 377–382. Also GLAK, 61/13373 1624, 66/10418 1600, 98/2018–2019 1566.

The most common local currency in the period was the *Rheinish Gulden* (fl.), whereby 1 *Gulden* (fl.) = 15 *Batzen* (bz.) = 60 *Kreuzer* (kr.) = 240 *Pfennig* (dn.). Another fairly ubiquitous currency in the region was based on the *Pfund Pfennig*, or pound pence (lb. dn.), an accounting measurement whereby 1 pound (lb.) = 20 shillings (ß) = 240 pence (dn.). Eight gulden were equivalent to seven pounds pence. Another currency found occasionally in the area was the *Reichsthaler*, worth around 1½ gulden. The actual values and weights of the many coins in circulation, especially the smaller ones, fluctuated over time and place. The period experienced a long inflationary trend, which was especially severe in the years 1618–1623.

The *Jauchert* was the most common land measurement used for arable as well as forests. It was roughly equivalent to one acre, or the area an individual could cultivate with a plow team in one day. The Jauchert was known across the German-speaking south, but its exact size varied by region (between 0.3 and 0.6 hectares). In the southern Linzgau, a Jauchert was equivalent to an estimated 4,427 square meters. A *Mannßmad* was a meadow parcel identical in size to one Jauchert. A *Hofstatt,* used for measuring vineyards, was approximately one-sixth of this size.

The usual grain measurement was the *Malter*, a giant sack containing 202 or 493 liters and weighing somewhere between 150-300 kilograms depending on the grain type (in Überlingen). One Malter of the "heavy grain" varieties (wheat, rye, husked spelt and barley) was made up of eight *Viertel* (quarters), whereas one Malter of the "light grain" varieties (oats, unhusked spelt and barley) comprised sixteen quaters. One Viertel, either heavy or light, was equivalent to four *Imi.* The eastern Linzgau used the *Schoffel* as a grain measurement. In 1600 one Malter was roughly equivalent to 2.7 Schoffel.

The *Fuder* was a wine measurement equivalent to a large wagonload, also estimated at a volume of 1,500 liters in the Lake Constance region. One *Fuder* = 30 *Eimer* = 120 *Viertel* = 960 *Maß.*

Maps, Illustrations, and Charts

Maps

Illustrations

Charts

Preface

The initial spark that led to the present book came from my first college history course, an introduction to medieval Europe. Prior to that time I had never been consciously interested in history, probably because I saw the subject as a collection of facts and dates, mostly about important people, battles, and turning points that needed to be memorized but had little to do with my own experience or way of seeing things. Suddenly I became aware that history was fundamentally a collection of narratives told by different people from multiple perspectives and that it contained elements of meaning, levels of interpretation, and even inadvertent biases. Once the horizon expanded beyond rote memorization, I began to see a new relevance in history and experience the thrill of discovery. I felt compelled to contribute a narrative of my own about the things I found most important, things I wanted to know more about and to share.

This study is guided by an interest in the lives of ordinary people and the contributions they make to the historical process, even and especially in situations where the struggle is hard and hardly seems worth the effort. It is concerned with domination and discord but also with negotiation, incorporation, and compromise, with examples of how needs and interests can be expressed in ways that bring about change, and how differences may be reconciled through dialogue. The message is hopeful and hopefully relevant, despite the seemingly remote subject matter, for all of us.

This book would not have been possible without the support of many individuals and groups. Above all, I would like to thank Thomas A. Brady Jr., who supervised the dissertation and whose key insights as well as practical advice and steadfast encouragement have sustained me through many times of uncertainty. Both Tom and Kathy Brady have shown unequalled generosity and fostered a strong sense of intellectual community embracing students, colleagues, and friends. I am also especially grateful to Randolph Head, whose careful reading and thoughtful comments on an earlier version of the manuscript have been most helpful. Peter Blickle and David Sabean have not only had a great influence on my thinking in their own different ways, both have offered their advice and support. Leonard Smith and Valerie Kivelson provided inspiration in the earliest phases, while Thomas Tentler introduced me to the German historical scholarship. More recently, I have benefited from the example provided by Jon Mathieu and from our many conversations about history, writing, and language. Among others who have contributed to this project in one way or another, I would like to thank Jan de Vries, Elaine Tennant, Thomas Robisheaux, Tom Scott, Robert Dees, Elmar Kuhn, and André Holenstein. Michael Jenks, Joan Morton, and Angela Rose Heimann assisted with the proofreading. Emma Tome produced the maps. As the editor, Clemens Zimmermann has been extremely patient, flexible, and congenial to work with. Much appreciated financial support at various stages has come from U.

C. Berkeley, the Mellon Foundation, the German Academic Exchange Service, and the Gesellschaft Oberschwaben. I would especially like to thank the Gesellschaft Oberschwaben for generously underwriting this book project. The staff at the Baden State Archive in Karlsruhe provided a friendly and supportive working environment for my research, and throughout the writing phases, the Mendocino Woodlands and Old Mill Farm have served as inspiring places to live and work and as the settings for my own experiences with local community. Finally, I owe my greatest thanks to Aaron, who has put up with the peasants for so many years now. Though he does not share or understand this particular passion, my husband's constant support and encouragement sustain me and his many willing sacrifices have allowed me to write this book.

Map 1: Salem's Central Territory Under the Hills

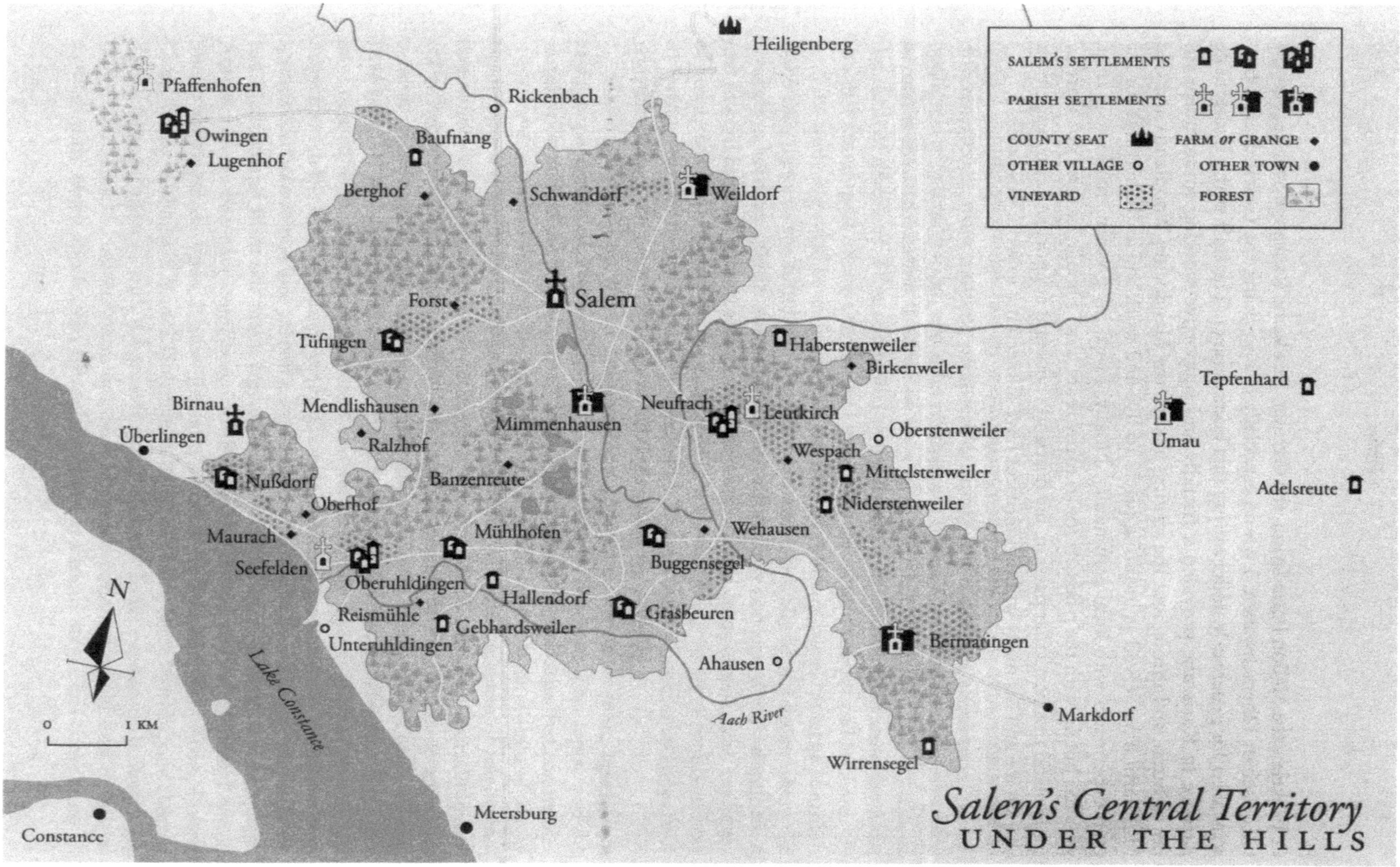

Map by Emma Tome

Map 2: Salem's Regional Networks

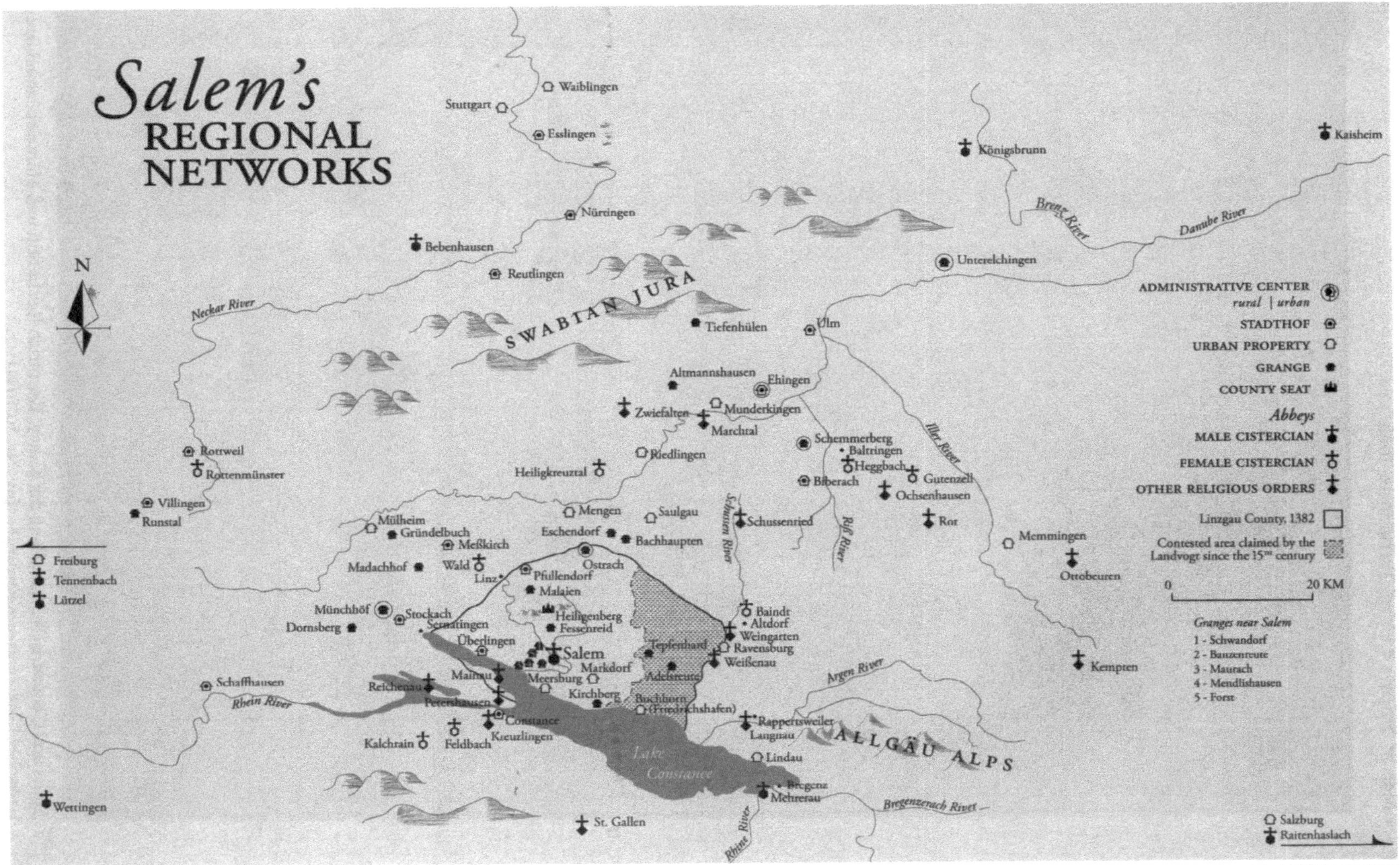

Map by Emma Tome

Map 3: Salem's Central Territory in 1665

Abriss und Geometrische Vorstellung des Königl. Eximirten Reichs Stift und Münsters Salmanßweyler
Badisches Landesmuseum Karlsruhe, Inv.-Nr. 2010/911

im Weingarten

Map 4: Salem's Central Territory in 1765

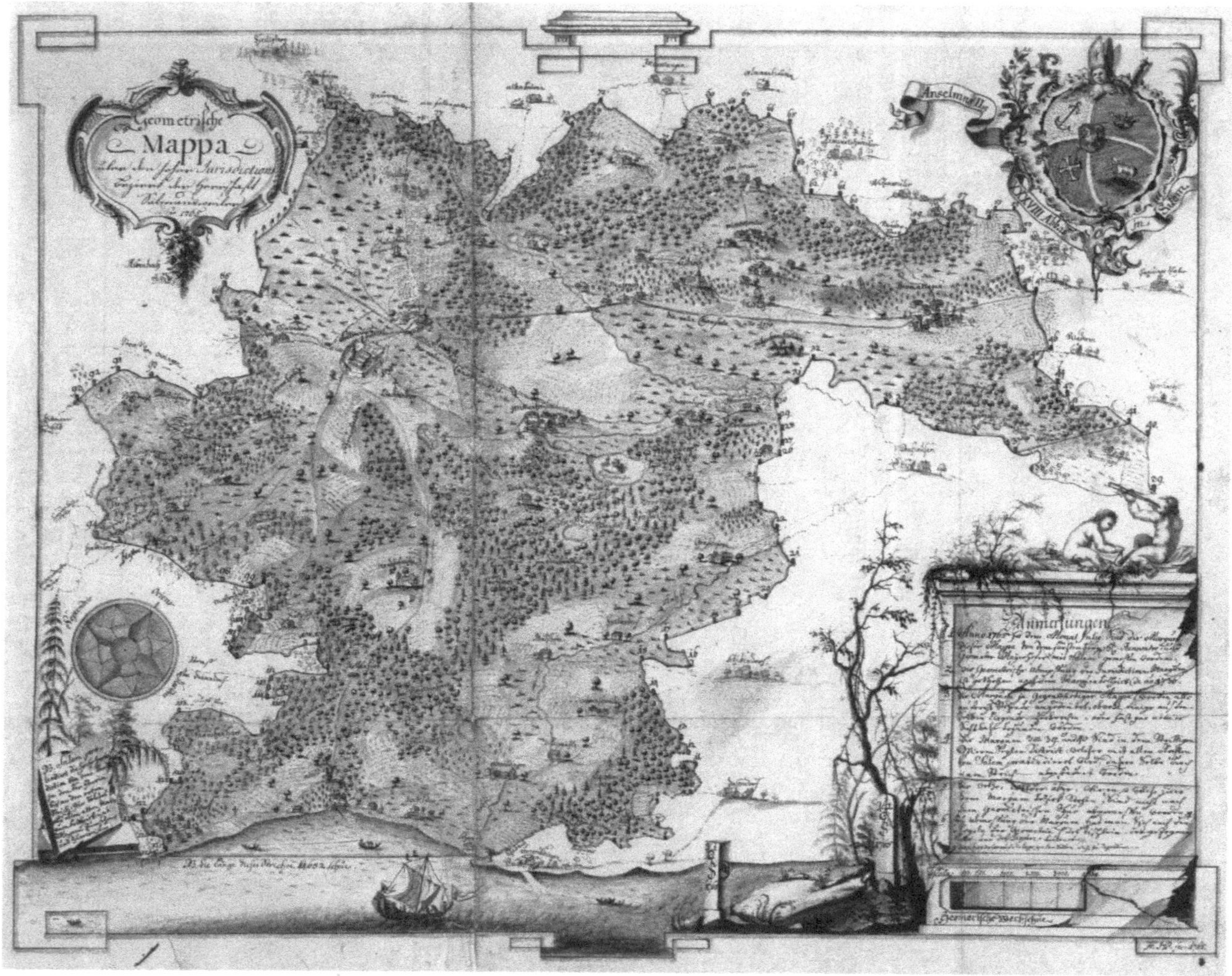

Geometrische Mappa über den hoher Jurisdictions bezierk der herrshaft Salmansweiler de a'o. 1765, by Brother Humbert of Salem

Chapter 1: The Imperial and Cistercian Abbey of Salem and the Political Development of Its Central Territory, 1473–1637

This study investigates how peasant subjects contributed to political development in the South German territory belonging to the imperial and Cistercian Salem Abbey. It proceeds from a central premise, namely, that the demands and actions of ordinary people can and do influence the political process in various ways, even under seemingly adverse circumstances. Here we will explore the relationship between community and lordship in a process of political quickening, characterized by the consolidation of various forms of authority at the territorial level. Two legal treaties frame the period, one from 1473 between Salem Abbey and the subjects of its central jurisdiction and the other in 1637 between the rulers of Salem and Heiligenberg, the abbey's major political adversary and immediate neighbor. Both agreements settled long-standing disputes through arbitration and compromise, and both emphasized the centrality of law in the construction of territorial identity.

The decades around 1600 are characterized by economic stagnation and decline, increasing socioeconomic stratification and competition for resources, and the strengthening of territorial rule at the expense of local autonomy. Yet the conventional view—that the peasantry was pushed to the margins of political life after the German Peasants' War of 1525—is in need of revision. The histories of the imperial and Cistercian Salem Abbey and the subjects of its central territory north of Lake Constance provide a basis for challenging this and other prevailing interpretations. Based on detailed archival research, the following study offers examples of the peasantry's continuing political relevance in the century after 1525. It also argues for broader and more inclusive political models for the early modern period, ones that do not explain historical development in linear or teleological terms, privilege large centralizing states, or assume that some people's claims to political authority are inherently more legitimate, or worthy of attention, than others.

The fascination of history, I find, comes not only from discovering the "facts," though any historian worthy of the name strives meticulously for the greatest possible accuracy. It comes also from the interpretations and narratives presented, for what they reveal about a situation, a people, a way of thinking, or even about ourselves. Histories contain perspective, as do the views of those who write them: no matter how hard we may try, still we see the world and the human past through the filter of our own experience.[1] The

---

1 Wim BLOCKMANS, Citizens and their Rulers, in: Empowering Interactions: Political Cultures and the Emergence of the State in Europe 1300–1900, ed. Wim Blockmans et al., Farnham and Burlington 2009, pp. 281–282.

Illustration 1.1: Earliest Known Depiction of Salem Abbey

By Augustin Hirschvogel, 1536 From the British Museum in London

present study has developed out of my continuing interest in "history from below," the historical contributions of ordinary people. It contains a plea for more emphasis on and recognition of the historical contributions made at the lower end of the social spectrum, for the relevance of everyday life and local experience, and for the broader population of nonelites as a focus of intrinsic interest and as a motor for historical change.

The major actors in this unconventional political narrative fall into roughly two groups: monks and peasants. In the historical literature on early modern German and European state formation, neither one has been viewed as especially competent in political affairs.[2] Yet small, monastic polities were not by definition weak, backward, primitive, or rudimentary. Salem's rule over its tiny rural territory was largely successful by early modern standards. Arguably, this ecclesiastical territory enjoyed certain advantages over the dynastic principalities of its time. The organizational techniques and political principles employed there were well adapted to its situation. The territory's

2 Monks and peasants were not legally incapable of political action, yet they are often perceived as irrelevant to political history. For a plea on behalf of the political significance of these respective groups, see Wolfgang WÜST, Geistlicher Staat und Altes Reich: Frühneuzeitliche Herrschaftsformen, Administration und Hofhaltung im Augsburger Fürstbistum, Munich 2001, p. 1; Peter BLICKLE, Obedient Germans? A Rebuttal: A New View of German History, trans. Thomas A. Brady Jr., Charlottesville 1997, p. 97.

government was certainly more participatory, populist, and negotiated in nature than in many other places. Overall, Salem also enjoyed greater peace, stability, and financial security than did many larger, dynastic states. Because Salem's social and administrative configuration was unusual in certain respects (and perhaps more representative than has been previously recognized), this study offers a new perspective on early modern political development. It highlights the strengths and limitations of ecclesiastical governance and provides new evidence of peasants' long-term political influence over the course of the long sixteenth century.[3] Though political concerns serve as the primary focus, emphasis is also placed on social and economic aspects in the belief that these elements cannot be treated in isolation from one another.

In preparation for what follows, it will be helpful to briefly describe Salem—what it was, what rights and powers it claimed, and in what political and geographical framework it was located. First and foremost, Salem was an abbey of the Cistercian Order, founded in 1134/8 and located a short distance north of Lake Constance, east of Überlingen, in a tiny settlement called Salmansweiler.[4] See Illustration 1.1, Earliest Known Depiction of Salem Abbey. From its modest beginnings, in keeping with the early Cistercian ideals of poverty, humility, charity, and self-sufficiency, the abbey grew in stature to become one of the wealthiest and most powerful ecclesiastical foundations in the southwestern corner of the empire.[5] Already in 1142 it obtained the German king's special and exclu-

---

3 The long sixteenth century refers to the period from the late fifteenth to the early seventeenth century. It emphasizes structural changes in the agrarian economy and social organization, resulting from developments in demography, prices, markets, and productivity. Each of these areas was characterized by expansion until at least mid-century, followed by stagnation in the decades before 1600 and finally by contraction in the early seventeenth century. I use the term long sixteenth century to accentuate the underlying significance of these trends for rural development. See Thomas ROBISHEAUX, Rural Society and the Search for Order in Early Modern Germany, Cambridge 1989, pp. 1, 259; André HOLENSTEIN, Bauern zwischen Bauernkrieg und Dreissigjährigem Krieg, Munich 1996, pp. 44–45.

4 The foundation, granted in 1134, was not confirmed by the order until 1138. According to legend, Salmansweiler (Salomon's villa) was named around the year 630 after the settlement's founder. Later, the name was reported to be a comparison to King Solomon's Temple. The name Salem, a reminder of holy Jerusalem, came from the Cistercians. It derived also from the Arabic and Hebrew terms for peace and greetings (*salaam* and *shalom*) and means "place of peace." Throughout its history the two names, Salmansweiler and Salem, were used interchangeably in reference to the abbey. For more on the date of Salem's foundation as well as the origins of its name, see Werner RÖSENER, Reichsabtei Salem: Verfassungs- und Wirtschaftsgeschichte des Zisterzienserklosters von der Gründung bis zur Mitte des 14. Jahrhunderts, Sigmaringen 1974, pp. 20–24; Xavier STAIGER, Salem oder Salmansweiler, Constance 1863, p. 59; MARKGRÄFLICHE BADISCHE MUSEEN, ed., Kloster und Staat: Besitz und Einfluss der Reichsabtei Salem, Tettnang 1984, p. 62.

5 Hansmartin SCHWARZMAIER, Reichsprälatenklöster, in: Die Territorien im Alten Reich, vol. 2 of Handbuch der baden-württembergischen Geschichte, ed. Meinrad Schaab and Hansmartin Schwarzmaier, Stuttgart 1995, p. 598; Thomas HÖLZ, Krummstab und Schwert: Die Liga und die geistlichen Reichsstände Schwabens 1609–1635, Leinfelden-Echterdingen 2001, p. 127.

sive protection, and by 1354 it could claim the status of a free and unmediated imperial estate, under no political authority other than that of the emperor.[6] Between 1213 and 1331 the abbey acquired lordship rights over its first nine villages, including most of the land and its inhabitants as well as jurisdictional rights and freedom from vassalage (*Vogteirechte*).[7] Through donations and purchases, Salem accumulated other properties in strategic locations surrounding the abbey and throughout the region, including around thirty towns and twenty granges over time. Ownership of land in many of these places was the basis of *Dorfherrschaft*, local lordship over the inhabitants, jurisdiction, regulation of agriculture and trade, parish churches, and many other associated rights.[8] From the late fifteenth century, Salem claimed as its serfs all the dependents of the abbey who lived in the villages of its central territory. In addition, abbey leaders asserted that a central court exercised exclusive jurisdiction over the surrounding countryside, consisting of twenty-some settlements in two administrative districts.

Yet in spite of several imperial privileges and legal charters in support of such pretensions, Salem's claims were contested in the early modern period and subject to overlapping claims, especially those of its closest neighbor to the north, the count of Heiligenberg. During the period 1473–1637, political authority over the people and places in close proximity to the abbey was consolidated in a process of "territorialization," or the strengthening of political authority on a territorial basis.[9] By territory, I

---

6 Salem was the only male Cistercian house in the German Southwest to possess free imperial status in this period; Armgard von REDEN-DOHNA, Die Zisterzienser im schwäbischen Reichsprälaten-Kollegium, in: Rottenburger Jahrbuch für Kirchengeschichte 4 (1985), p. 52.

7 RÖSENER, Salem, pp. 92–94.

8 Werner Rösener has described Salem's early acquisitions, making good use of the abbey's carefully preserved legal charters and medieval copiaries. Many of them are published by Friedrich von WEECH, ed., Codex Diplomaticus Salemitanus: Urkundenbuch der Cistercienserabtei Salem, 3 vols., Karlsruhe 1883–1895. The Leuchtenberg Treaty between Salem and Heiligenberg lists the places belonging to the abbey's jurisdiction in 1390, the same year Bermatingen became the abbey's tenth village. According to the purchase agreement, Salem became the holder of rights in Bermatingen pertaining to "lut und güt, kirchensatz, vogty, vogtrecht, zwing, bann, ehafti, geriht, stura, dienst, tafern, schmid, waid, kelnhof, dinkhof, huser, hofstett, hofraiti, punda, wingarten, holtz, veld, akker, wismad, marka, tratt, waid, pongarten, vischentza, wasserleiti, wasser fluss mit allen nutzin, rehten." RÖSENER, Salem, p. 94.

9 In contrast to the earlier drive to accumulate rights and properties, the new objective was consolidation: to give positive substance to lordly rights the ruler had previously acquired. Territorialization was effected through a two-pronged approach, which on the one hand excluded external lordship claims within a bounded area and on the other hand leveled resident dependents' status and duties, creating a common band of subjects. See Hans-Martin MAURER, Die Ausbildung der Territorialgewalt oberschwäbischer Klöster vom 14. bis zum 17. Jahrhundert, in: Blätter für deutsche Landesgeschichte 109 (1973), p. 157; André HOLENSTEIN, Äbte und Bauern: Vom Regiment der Klöster im Spätmittelalter, in: Politische Kultur in Oberschwaben, ed. Peter Blickle, Tübingen 1993, p. 263; Claudia ULBRICH, Leibherrschaft am Oberrhein im Spätmittelalter, Göttingen 1978, pp. 275–280; Volker PRESS, Kommunalismus oder Territorialismus?

mean a relatively unified political entity defined by supralocal geographical and legal boundaries. A territory, unlike a state, is not an exclusive or sovereign power. Territories such as Salem's grew by pulling together multiple strands of authority under a single ruler, on the basis of integration and exclusion. They developed also by incorporating the needs and interests of their subjects. The primary themes of this study concern the establishment of Salem's territorial governance as well as the interactions among ordinary villagers, local elites, and the abbey's monastic and lay officials who participated in this dynamic process.

In the sixteenth century, Salem exercised petty jurisdiction over a population of around 3,800 inhabitants in twenty or so villages and smaller settlements surrounding the abbey. The area was commonly referred to as "Under the Hills" (*Unter den Bergen*)—that is, the basin between Heiligenberg Palace and Lake Constance.[10] This area is shown in Map 1, Salem's Central Territory Under the Hills. For Salem, low justice was the primary foundation of territorial authority and the basis for additional rights and claims such as labor services, imperial tax collection, military contributions, and the loyalty oath.[11] Jurisdictional authority was central to Salem's status as an unmediated imperial estate as well as to perceptions of its legal and territorial boundaries.[12] Salem's unitary law and its court, established by the fourteenth century if not earlier, possessed enormous influence over territorial development in later centuries.[13] The

Bemerkungen zur Ausbildung des Frühmodernen Staates in Mitteleuropa, in: Die Bildung des Frühmodernen Staates – Stände und Konfessionen, ed. Heiner Timmermann, Dadder 1989, pp. 117–119; HÖLZ, Krummstab und Schwert, pp. 86–87.

10 Under the Hills (*Unter den Bergen*) is a term designating the area between the range of hills to the north and Lake Constance to the south of the abbey, which various sources indicate as the area belonging to Salem's authority. I distinguish this area, defined by shared jurisdiction and early privileges, from a number of outlying administrative districts where Salem's lordship claims were much weaker.

11 Low justice encompassed authority over minor offenses, punishable by fines, as opposed to high justice, which concerned the major and capital crimes including manslaughter, robbery, and arson. The derivation of such rights from low justice was relatively uncommon elsewhere, though it was also prevalent in Franconia, another region characterized by small-scale governance.

12 The significance of the court and its jurisdiction in perceptions of Salem's territorial authority becomes clear when searching any set of records for the word *Gericht* (court). When an individual moved into or out of the abbey's territory, the records speak of the Gericht. When someone was banished from the abbey's lands, they were expelled from the Gericht. The location of land parcels was described with respect to the Gericht. The same was true of property sales, both land and other moveables, which were normally restricted to the Gericht—in other words, straw could not leave the territory and land could be sold only to persons residing within the abbey's jurisdiction.

13 In 1354 a royal privilege mentioned the abbot's court in the context of Salem's imperial status and exemption from overlordship by the counts of Heiligenberg. According to the privilege, the abbey's court settled all worldly disputes involving its dependents, no matter what their status or

court, known as the *Sidelgericht*, was not only the centerpiece of Salem's rule; it was also the heart of the territorial community. Its members were 15 peasant subjects chosen from villages across the jurisdiction. The court served to unify the territory externally and internally but not solely to the abbey's benefit. At the same time, it provided a point for villagers' interests and communal values to enter into a broader political arena.

Communal organization and popular participation characterized territorial development in the region, though not in the same ways as have been demonstrated elsewhere. "Communalism" in Salem took place within territorial rule, interwoven with lordship, rather than in opposition to it.[14] Peasant subjects participated in territorial governance and influenced the direction of political development in many ways. Some of their contributions are surprising, even extraordinary. Besides the Sidelgericht, one of the best examples of popular participation in rule was the election of Abbot Thomas Wunn (r. 1615–1647), a former serf from Salem's village of Grasbeuren. This remarkable man guided his abbey through the difficult times of the Thirty Years War, became the first president of the Cistercians' Upper German Congregation, and signed a momentous treaty with Heiligenberg that substantiated the abbey's claims to free imperial status with full jurisdictional authority inside set physical boundaries. A third area where common subjects had a major influence in territorial decisionmaking was through their presentation of petitions and grievances before the *Verhör* or "Audience," which were formal weekly hearings by a body of the abbey's senior monastic and lay officials. This study suggests that since Salem's peasant subjects performed such a significant role in territorial development, the strengthening and even centralization of authority incorporated their customs and values at a higher level rather than leading to their displacement.

This situation—the communalization of rule and peasants' participation in key areas of governance—could not have happened just anywhere. In addition to the territory's size, location, and social composition, Salem's ecclesiastical identity was an important factor. A working hypothesis is that the lordship's corporate organizational structure and shared monastic values, as a spiritual brotherhood and intentional community of those who lived, worked, and prayed together, had a considerable influence on the development of its territory by providing certain political opportunities while limiting others. The monastery, like the village, employed associative as well as hierarchical principles. The professed monks elected a leader from their own ranks by a majority vote of all members. The abbot, to be sure, cut the figure of an ecclesiastical prince in his representation of the abbey and its lordship, yet he was chosen by his peers and bound to represent their interests. His ability, not his lineage, determined his right to rule.

---

the source of conflict. According to later records, the fifteen peasant judges participated in the creation of the territory's ancient legal customal, the *alte Jarbrief*, in 1301. There are also references from 1224 and 1262 to Salem's jurisdictional rights and its court.

14 Peter Blickle's employment of the term communalism is discussed below.

Because the abbey and its subjects shared certain common interests and had others that were not directly opposed, together they were able to build an effective territorial polity. Furthermore, a greater obstacle to Salem's territorial authority than its peasant subjects was the count of Heiligenberg. With respect to external powers, the abbey found its peasants useful in the augmentation of its authority. For peasants, on the other hand, the greatest concerns in daily life as well as the reasons for political action arose not only from the effects of domination imposed on them from beyond the village but also and especially from the relations between households, kin, and neighbors within the village and across the region. Often, village communities and individual subjects found structures and representatives of rule to be useful in their local or personal struggles. Additionally, since many local and territorial officials were commoners and area residents, the distinction between rulers and ruled was not always clear. The primary intermediaries between the abbey and its villages identified to some extent with both of them, melding elements of lordship and community and softening oppositions between them. Monks and peasants worked together in many cases, not because they agreed or shared identical interests, but because negotiation had its benefits for each side and because a stronger territorial polity served goals that went beyond politics.

Salem Abbey and its territorial rule lasted until the Napoleonic period, though this study ends much earlier. Salem's secularization in 1802/3 resulted not from any political deficiency, but rather, as a consequence of the entire empire's collapse and reconfiguration. Since today's churches no longer exercise direct political authority over bounded territories in Europe (besides the Vatican), some may view Salem as a historical oddity and a dead end. This study takes a different approach. Salem offers a new way of understanding political development in early modern Europe and elsewhere. It presents an alternative to the received political models based on large dynastic states. It shows how the common people in one small German territory contributed to the political process.

1.1 Sources and Methodology

Salem's archive is the most extensive of any Cistercian abbey in South Germany and is indeed among the richest and best-preserved monastic archives in all of Central Europe.[15] Salem's document collection was relocated in the mid-nineteenth century and is housed today in Baden's *Generallandesarchiv* in Karlsruhe (GLAK). The most important sources for this study are listed in the Bibliography. The archive's Section 4 contains Salem's collection of over 8,000 legal charters (*Urkunden*), including contracts, privileges, agreements, and other official, parchment manuscripts. The archive's Section 98 also deals exclusively with Salem and contains an assortment of files that are

---

15 For a description of Salem's archive and its scope, see SIWEK, Zisterzienserabtei Salem, pp. 94–96; GLAK, Abteilung 98 Registerband, Einleitung.

likewise handwritten manuscripts, but these "acts" (*Akten*) possess a less formal nature, lacking the legal standing of sealed charters and agreements. Section 98 includes over 4,500 dossiers, many of them bound volumes that are hundreds of pages long, and the entire collection takes up approximately one hundred meters of shelf space. Sections 4 and 98 each contain two parts, the *Generalia* relating to the abbey overall, and the *Spezialia* with its focus on individual villages or places. Many villages boast extensive records. Besides these two major archival collections, both exclusive to Salem, there are important holdings in the GLAK's Section 62 (account records, 1,000 volumes), Section 65 (manuscripts, 150 volumes), Section 66 (rents, 100 volumes), and Section 67 (copiaries, 110 volumes).[16] Section 229 contains documents from various individual villages. The most useful of all for this study are the contents of Section 61, the minutes (protocols, 350 volumes). These include serial records from the Sidelgericht, Audience, and chancery, each of which begins in the early 1580s and spans thousands of pages, providing volumes of rich material covering the final 50 years of this study and beyond.[17]

This case study is primarily based on archival research. The astounding quantity and quality of documentation have led necessarily to decisions about what to include and how to organize the selected material. In the early stages I chose to focus on Salem's central territory, the lands in the southern Linzgau often referred to collectively as Under the Hills. Since this study aims to describe the participation of peasant subjects in early modern political development, it made sense to concentrate on the major villages and on developments within this domain, rather than the abbey's external relations, general economy, or widely dispersed properties including granges and urban properties beyond its immediate vicinity. Using the selection criteria of location, size, and source coverage, I narrowed the study area to look in greater detail at a dozen or so rural communities within the two centrally located administrative districts, settlements ranging in size from 20 to over 500 inhabitants in the late sixteenth century.[18] I paid somewhat less attention to other tiny hamlets and isolated farmsteads and to the outlying areas where the abbey's political authority was relatively insubstantial.[19] These selection criteria allowed for a concentration on records from a comparable sample of

---

16 SIWEK, Salem, pp. 94–96.

17 Chancery records are found in GLAK, 61/13316–13320 (1582–86, 1587–93, 1604–12, 1612–22, 1632–66); Sidelgericht in GLAK, 61/13322–13329 (1583–87, 1588–92, 1593–97, 1604–11, 1609–24, 1625–31, 1646–48, 1646–54); Audience in GLAK, 61/13369–13488 (1583–1610, 1610–17, 1617–19, 1619–21, 1621–29, 1630–42 and beyond).

18 The study concentrates on the following villages and hamlets: Bermatingen, Buggensegel, Grasbeuren, Leutkirch, Mimmenhausen, Neufrach, Nußdorf, Oberuhldingen, Owingen, Pfaffenhofen, Tüfingen, and Weildorf.

19 Other frequently mentioned villages and hamlets include: Adelsreute, Gebhardsweiler, Mühlhofen, Seefelden, Tepfenhard, Urnau, and (Mittelsten- and Nidersten-) Weiler.

known places in a central area, where we find a greater density of source material and a better opportunity to investigate relations between Salem and its peasant subjects.

It also became necessary to practice selection with regard to the abundant serial records from the Sidelgericht, Audience, and chancery, since it would have taken too much time to read, let alone transcribe and analyze these volumes in their entirety. Instead, I chose a number of years over the period 1583–1635 and did a quantitative analysis of all records from select years.[20] Beyond these samples, I also read and transcribed more broadly from each of the three record sets, searching for information from particular years and about certain topics, including officials, landholding, kinship, communal affairs, and other special interests. Examples throughout the study come from an extensive reading of each series.

1.2 Historiography

Theoretical concerns do not drive this study, and neither does the historical literature, in part because existing models of political development do not lend themselves particularly well to understanding Salem, and in part because Salem is a single, small example from which it is difficult to generalize without in-depth comparisons that are beyond the scope of this study.[21] Salem does, however, provide important points of intersection with several key areas of historiographical debate involving the dynamics of people and politics. The case of Salem, in spite of its tiny size and unusual composition, proves to be a topic of broader significance that will be of special interest for the study of early modern polities, clerical rule, local and regional communities, and rural socioeconomic development.

The Alternative to Statebuilding in Salem

One obvious theme this study shares with larger historical concepts and narratives is the concern with processes of early modern state formation. The concept of the state and views on its development have been heated topics of debate for many generations, and

20 For the court records I chose the first available year and nine subsequent years at five-year intervals: 1583, 1585, 1590, 1595, 1605, 1610, 1605, 1620, 1625, and 1630. From the Audience records I examined the seven years 1584, 1589, 1599, 1600, 1611, 1624, and 1630. The chancery sample includes 1584, 1590–92, 1612–14, 1620, and 1632–35.

21 Though I have consulted and cited many works by other historians, the strength of this project lies in its rich source material. The focus here remains on the details specific to Salem, yet it is hoped that the reader will recognize the contributions and relevance of this narrow case study to major discussions within the field and that the examples presented here may be of service for future research. While revising the manuscript for publication, I have included new references to more recent studies where they seemed especially vital.

for the premodern period they remain controversial issues, particularly in Germany.[22] It is generally acknowledged that within the limitations of the Holy Roman Empire's overarching structures, political development in Central Europe took place primarily at the territorial level.[23] Especially since World War II, the Reformation era has held a prominent position in the view of modern German political development as being characterized by weakness and failure.[24] Recently, however, the interpretation of territorial fragmentation as a major source of Germany's political troubles has come into question. A revitalized image of the empire has emerged, shedding a more positive light on the German territories.[25] Whereas the small-scale polities, once so dominant in the German Southwest, were often viewed as proof of political backwardness, and whereas territorial "particularism" was a term used in the most pejorative sense, it is now possible to see that smaller polities offered considerable political advantages. This becomes especially evident when we view history "from below." Research on governance in regions such as Upper Swabia not only confirms the effectiveness of small-scale polities, it also contributes to a more balanced view of the early modern period.[26]

Though it is widely recognized that the territories were the dynamic element of political formation in the early modern empire, the question remains as to whether the German territories may be considered states, and the answer depends on how we define this term. Especially in Germany, variations and exceptions have thwarted all

---

22 For Germany, where the national state was established relatively late and where the tragedies of the Nazi era have driven the search for historical explanations, the problem of the state has been emotionally charged and essential in importance. See Thomas A. BRADY Jr., Some Peculiarities of German Histories in the Early Modern Era, in: Germania Illustrata: Essays on Early Modern Germany Presented to Gerald Strauss, ed. Andrew FIX and Susan Karant-Nunn, Kirksville 1992, pp. 197–216; idem, Translator's Introduction: A New View of German History, in: Blickle, Obedient Germans, pp. ix–xiv.

23 Karl Siegfried BADER, Territorialbildung und Landeshoheit, in: Blätter für deutsche Landesgeschichte 90 (1953), p. 130; Dietmar WILLOWEIT, Territorialstaat, in: Handbuch der deutschen Rechtsgeschichte, ed. E. Erler and E. Kaufmann, vol. 5, Berlin 1998, p. 147; Ernst SCHUBERT, Fürstliche Herrschaft und Territorium im späten Mittelalter, Munich 1996; PRESS, Kommunalismus oder Territorialismus, p. 117.

24 The Reformation was also at the center of earlier and heroic narratives, above all those of Leopold von Ranke and Heinrich von Treitschke. See BRADY, Peculiarities of German Histories, pp. 199–200; idem, Translator's Introduction, pp. ix–x.

25 BRADY, Pecularities of German Histories, pp. 197–216; idem, German Histories in the Age of Reformations, 1400–1650, Cambridge 2009; James J. SHEEHAN, What is German History? Reflections on the Role of the Nation in German History and Historiography, in: Journal of Modern History 53 (1981), pp. 1–23.

26 Even for the period before the establishment of national states, the focus has traditionally been on the centralizing monarchies such as England and France or the larger principalities such as Prussia and Austria. Upper Swabia, an extremely decentralized region, is generally defined as the area bounded by the Danube River to the north, Lake Constance to the south, the Swabian Jura (or the Black Forest) to the west, and the Iller (or Lech) River to the east.

attempts to produce a common political model or define such terms as state (*Staat*), territorial state (*Territorialstaat*), territorial sovereignty (*Landeshoheit*), or territorial rule (*Landesherrschaft*).[27] According to Ernst Schubert, too many conflicting studies have led to "research confusion" and to more disagreement than ever.[28] One of the biggest challenges for those who would see late medieval and early modern polities as states in Central Europe is that they lacked geographical unity and exclusivity. No village was entirely subject to a single lord, let alone large, bounded areas containing cities and countryside, roads, forests, rivers, and the castles of many minor nobles. In the early modern era, no ruler—not even the greatest princes of the empire—was effectively able to unite all subjects equally under a geographically closed, uniform, exclusive political authority.[29] According to some historians, the very idea of political boundaries was lacking before the sixteenth century.[30]

Another problem with the construction of a general model for premodern statehood is that territorial rule developed from disparate combinations of elements and at different rates.[31] Karl Siegfried Bader questioned whether the description of half a millennium of German constitutional history according to such a concept could further our understanding of the historical process.[32] To define statehood too narrowly based on specific factors would be to disqualify many polities that did not grow out of an identical political medium. To define the concept too broadly, however, leaves it without any real meaning or shared characteristics with which to distinguish it from other political types.

---

27 Peter BLICKLE, Landschaften im Alten Reich: Die staatliche Funktion des gemeinen Mannes in Oberdeutschland, Munich 1973, pp. 30–33; Karl Siegfried BADER, Der deutsche Südwesten in seiner territorialstaatlichen Entwicklung, Sigmaringen 1978, pp. 161–167; BADER, Territorialbildung, esp. p. 110.

28 SCHUBERT, Fürstliche Herrschaft, pp. 51–52.

29 Peter BLICKLE, Bauer und Staat in Oberschwaben, in: Zeitschrift für Württembergische Landesgeschichte 31 (1972), p. 108; SCHUBERT, Fürstliche Herrschaft, pp. 53–55; BADER, Territorialbildung, p. 130.

30 SCHUBERT, Fürstliche Herrschaft, p. 5; idem, Vom Gebot zur Landesordnung: Der Wandel fürstlicher Herrschaft vom 15. zum 16. Jh., in: Die deutsche Reformation zwischen Spätmittelalter und frühen Neuzeit, ed. Thomas A. Brady Jr., Munich 2001, pp. 33, 50–53. Theodor Mayer introduced the idea of "*Flächenstaatlichkeit*," or the geographical concentration of authority, in 1935. For a critical view, see SCHUBERT, Fürstliche Herrschaft, pp. 57–58. On the other hand, patterns of monastic land purchases in the High Middle Ages suggest the intentional consolidation of territories, even if not conceived initially as the basis of political power. See MAURER, Ausbildung der Territorialgewalt, pp. 156–157; RÖSENER, Salem, p. 94; Thomas HÖLZ, Krummstab und Schwert, pp. 85–86; Jürgen SYDOW, Die Zisterzienserabtei Bebenhausen, Berlin 1984, p. 144.

31 BADER, Territorialbildung, p. 129; WILLOWEIT, Territorialstaat, p. 147; HÖLZ, Krummstab, pp. 86–87.

32 BADER, Territorialbildung, pp. 111–112.

A third problem with the concept of the state is that it is a modern term rooted in the national experience of the nineteenth and twentieth centuries. Our view is distorted if we focus only on the political developments of the past that appear to have led in some essential and direct way to the formation or failure to form modern national states as we know them today. To compare the past with our own political experience, and to highlight and value only those forms we recognize as our own, is to reject and ignore those traits that have lost usefulness or value in our own society; it is to view the past through historical blinders. The search for the foundations of the modern state has led back to earlier and earlier points in history until the concept has lost all concrete meaning, so that the particular conditions that distinguish premodern political entities from modern states are all too easily forgotten.[33] Political experience and development is not linear and does not lead always in the same direction. There is therefore no special path, no single path, and political diversity is not tantamount to political failure. This is especially true in the German lands where authority was dispersed. As Immanuel Wallerstein has demonstrated in a broader European context, the success of one polity eliminates opportunity for its neighbors, so that political imitation often fails to achieve its goal.[34]

In the early modern period, diversity and smallness of scale characterized the political experience of Central Europe in general and the German Southwest in particular. By some definitions of statehood, polities such as the one in Salem would be rejected as states based on size alone. This study rejects the notion that strength and stability are directly proportional to size and that small implies political irrelevance or economic weakness. We should view smallness of scale not as the grounds for categorical rejection as something politically insignificant, but rather, as an opportunity to discover alternatives that have been historically neglected due to our own modern biases.[35] The objective here is to understand historical experience in its own terms, not to search out the origins of the modern national state or judge political success by any other single standard.

---

33 SCHUBERT, Fürstliche Herrschaft, esp. pp. 53–55. This point, along with the appeal to avoid modern concepts in favor of period-specific terminology (*geschichtliche Grundbegriffe*), is one of the most important contributions made by Otto BRUNNER, Land and Lordship: Structures of Governance in Medieval Austria, trans. Howard Kaminsky and James Van Horn Melton, from the 4th rev. ed., Philadelphia 1992, p. 97. See also BRADY, Translator's Introduction, p. xi.

34 Immanuel WALLERSTEIN, The Modern World-System, vol. 2: Mercantilism and the Consolidation of the European World-economy, 1600–1750, New York 1980, chap. 5.

35 Armgard von Reden-Dohna presents a strong defense of imperial abbeys against what she perceives as historians' bias in favor of larger polities. In her judgment, "There were indeed problems of smallness. However, these problems did not exactly concern the estates themselves, which enjoyed their secure place in the many-layered structure of the Old *Reich*. Rather, they concern the historian, who was educated within a macrocosm—that is, the large and modern state—and who feels confident in asserting the weakness of the small." Idem, Problems of Small Estates of the Empire: The Example of the Swabian Imperial Prelates, in: Journal of Modern History, supplement vol. 58 (1986), p. 87.

With this in mind, I propose that we consider political development in Salem without relying too heavily on comparisons with "the state." I would even suggest that we try, as Wolfgang Reinhard has argued in a polemical essay against "statebuilding from below," to liberate our discussion of political development in Salem from the domination of this political model, to think instead in terms of the possible alternatives.[36] This is because the state is such a heavily loaded term, carrying with it connotations of modern political experience and based on the assumption of large, centralized, unified, warmaking, national states. To apply the concept of the state to the early modern period may be legitimate, especially if we are primarily concerned with understanding how political development in that period relates to more recent times. It may also be legitimate to employ the state model if we are willing to broaden the definition of the state to include the smaller polities, overlapping competencies, and diverse organizational forms more characteristic of the premodern period. In this study, however, the goals are different. Here the focus is on the political developments of a small abbatial territory in the early modern period, before states as we know them today became the standard political model. In this task, we are better off to take our discussion out from under the long shadow of the state where it is too easy to judge what came before according to modern standards as less unified, less strong, less comprehensive, less politically significant. Some may argue that polities such as the one in Salem are irrelevant to our own experience and therefore not worth taking the time to understand. I strongly advocate the opposite view: by looking at alternative political models, we can perhaps discover some values we have overlooked, which may even provide correctives for the deficiencies of our own political system, in the present and for the future, to see that there are other possibilities besides the "moloch" of the modern national state.[37] Furthermore, it will be argued, smallness of scale is not necessarily a liability or a limitation. For truly, there are cases where less is more, where bigger is not better. As we shall see, governance in tiny Salem was well suited to the needs of the abbey and its peasant subjects. This religious foundation and its political identity evolved over a period of more than 650 years. What state today can boast of such a long and successful history, characterized by peace and prosperity?

Elements of Ecclesiastical Rule in Salem

Territorial authority in the early modern empire was constituted in various forms and in no way derived from a single element or an identical set of building blocks. It evolved through the combination of multiple strands of dominion that varied over space and time. Still, monks typically were and are not viewed as the legitimate bearers of political authority. It is true that the abbot's right to rule was recognized, similar to that of

36 Wolfgang REINHARD, No State-Building From Below! A Critical Commentary, in: Empowering Interactions, ed. Blockmans et al., p. 303.

37 Ibid.

any lord, and that the privileges and protections of corporate legal status the convent enjoyed were not at all unusual at the time. Yet a Cistercian abbey's claim to political authority required noteworthy and unusual modifications to standards of noble rule, for reasons of principle and practice. Several historians have called attention to clerical rule in the German territories and to the characteristics that distinguished this type of polity from its noble counterpart.[38] There are monographs devoted to many individual bishoprics and monasteries of various religious orders, but a general study of ecclesiastical territories in the early modern period, or of monastic lordship as a specific political type, would be a welcome addition to our knowledge. This is not the place to embark on such broad topics, but throughout the following chapters it will be useful to keep in mind some of the peculiarities of ecclesiastical rule in general and of Cistercian rulers in particular, to think about whether and to what degree the clerical nature of Salem's rule played a role in the territory's political development. Here we will consider four important aspects of ecclesiastical rule in Salem: election, economy, peacekeeping, and administrative organization.

Perhaps the most important difference between clerical and aristocratic rulers is that churchmen were elected whereas nobles ruled by hereditary right.[39] Elective rule had several important consequences. First, when an ecclesiastical lord died, the community maintained continuity by choosing his successor from among themselves. As long as there remained a spiritual brotherhood of cardinals, canons, or monks, the ruling line would not die out. Thus, the longevity and alliances of ecclesiastical institutions were based on the social criteria of recruitment rather than the biological limitations of birth and marriage. Second, election provided flexibility in the direction of leadership by allowing members to choose someone whose abilities suited the current needs. They could reinforce or correct previous trends, considering such factors as charisma, skill, age, personal background, networks, prudence, and experience. Third, election relied in principle on cooperative participation among equals. In Cistercian houses, each monk had one vote and each vote carried equal weight in abbatial elec-

---

38 HOLENSTEIN, Äbte und Bauern, pp. 237–262; WÜST, Geistlicher Staat; Lawrence G. DUGGAN, Bishop and Chapter: The Governance of the Bishopric of Speyer to 1552, New Brunswick 1978; SCHWARZMAIER, Reichsprälatenklöster, pp. 546–609; MAURER, Ausbildung der Territorialgewalt, pp. 151–195; Pankraz FRIED, Zur Ausbildung der reichsunmittelbaren Klosterstaatlichkeit in Ostschwaben, in: Zeitschrift für Württembergische Landesgeschichte 40 (1981), pp. 418–435; REDEN-DOHNA, Zisterzienser, pp. 51–58; Katherine BRUN, Ruling Class and Regime in an Ecclesiastical Territory: The Case of Salem, in: Politics and Reformations: Communities, Polities, Nations, and Empires. Essays in Honor of Thomas A. Brady Jr., ed. Christopher Ocker et al., Leiden and Boston 2007, pp. 359–380.

39 The emperor is an important exception to this rule. Yet even the emperor often indicated his choice of successor, and dynastic power certainly played a major role in imperial elections, which was generally not the case in Cistercian abbeys.

tions.[40] The choice of a leader from within was an important reminder of the dualistic nature of rule, a powerful check against absolutist tendencies, and an expression of associative principles.[41]

A second major difference between the territories of nobles and churchmen concerns their properties and wealth.[42] Clerical celibacy and the lack of heirs guaranteed that possessions and lordship rights never split into pieces, never fell to outsiders. There were no younger sons to outfit, no daughters in need of dowries, no noble courtiers to reward for loyal service, and fewer obligations to support a network of kin and followers through favors or patronage.[43] In fact, monks' families often left significant property to the abbey and were thus a source of income, not expenditure.[44] Furthermore, church property and property rights were held in common and could not, in principle, be alienated.[45] This created much greater stability than in most dynastic lordships, not

---

40 According to a papal bull in 1265, the convent alone had the power to elect a new Cistercian abbot. The pope and the abbot of Cîteaux confirmed him, not the bishop. On election practices in Salem, see Reinhard SCHNEIDER, Die Geschichte Salems, in: idem, ed., Salem: 850 Jahre Reichsabtei und Schloss, Constance 1984, pp. 61–63; Walter LEODEGAR, Die Abtwahlen in Salem im 16. Jh. and idem, Die Abtwahlen in Salem im 17. Jh., both in: Cistercienser-Chronik 48 (1936), pp. 98–106 and 321–338.

41 Principles of association and practices of corporate rule were used not only by peasants and burghers but also by nobles, as pointed out by PRESS, Kommunalismus oder Territorialismus, p. 115. Salem's political organization, social composition, and fundamental values as a Cistercian monastery may have made it in some ways more similar, more sympathetic, or at least more open than many other lordships to the social and political norms originating in the villages.

42 REDEN-DOHNA, Small Estates, p. 83.

43 MAURER, Ausbildung der Territorialgewalt, p. 155. This last point is true especially for Cistercians and other religious orders with an emphasis on personal poverty, as opposed to the cathedral chapters and many of the older Benedictine houses, which drew members and support from the nobility and where ties to the regional political elites were much more pronounced.

44 One legal charter describes the rights of Johannes Waybel, a monk, to inherit a share of family property in the nearby village of Lipperatsreute, equal to that of his siblings, with his portion payable to the abbey. Another document mentions land in Bermatingen worth 950 gulden that the abbey had acquired from the parents of one of its monks, P. F. Robert Rueff. GLAK, 4/62; 61/13374; see also SCHNEIDER, Geschichte Salems, p. 57.

45 In practice Salem sold, mortgaged, and traded properties as early as the thirteenth century, but canon law forbade the alienation of church lands (with some exceptions: DUGGAN, Bishop and Chapter, p. 185). Schubert recognized the inalienability of church property as one of four major structural differences between episcopal and noble regimes, citing it as the reason why the territorial foundations of bishops were stronger and more stable than those of secular rulers. Idem, Fürstliche Herrschaft, pp. 6–7. Unlike Benedictines and canons, Cistercians did not distinguish between the property of the abbot and of the convent, and monks held no individual benefices. This strengthened the convent's solidarity. See Hermann TÜCHLE, Süddeutsche Klöster vor 500 Jahren, ihre Stellung in Reich und Gesellschaft, in: Blätter für deutsche Landesgeschichte 109 (1973), p. 112; Cécile SOMMER-RAMER, Einleitung: Die Zisterzienser, in: Helvetia Sacra, ed. Cécile Sommer-Ramer and Patrick Braun, vol. 3/1, Bern 1982, pp. 36, 45.

only in terms of property but also in customs, written records, and relations with subjects.[46] The consumption patterns and financial needs of a monastery were also quite different from those of princely courts. Household expenses including clothing, food, travel, and display were extremely modest in comparison to that of the prince and his court, not to mention military expenditures, and many of Salem's territorial officials were unsalaried monks, laybrothers, or villagers.

Cistercians are well known for their economic prowess, and in terms of landholdings, Salem was among the most affluent abbeys in the German Southwest.[47] Decentralized treasury and accounting records make it difficult to assess the abbey's total wealth, but as for land and other possessions, Salem kept careful records.[48] Even before the order relaxed its property restrictions in the early thirteenth century, lordship rights accompanied the land Salem acquired by donation and purchase.[49] The monks converted some properties into granges and displaced their former inhabitants—at one time Salem had around twenty grange farms—but this strategy proved to be difficult and unpopular with neighbors.[50] Before long Salem had acquired several entire villages, many of them purchased for extremely large sums and located strategically

---

46 This was a definite advantage for territorial residents, who did not have to worry that authority over them would be sold or mortgaged to some overly harsh or less scrupulous lord. See Tom SCOTT, The German Peasants' War and the 'Crisis of Feudalism.' Reflections on a Neglected Theme, in: Journal of Early Modern History 6 (2002), pp. 277–280. In contrast to Salem, rule in neighboring Heiligenberg passed between lines or dynasties in 1277, 1428, 1534, and 1716.

47 According to Schwarzmaier (Reichsprälatenklöster, p. 598), Salem was the wealthiest in this region overall.

48 The lack of centralized accounts may have been intentional, since Salem paid exorbitant taxes to the empire and its wealth was a subject of great envy. On Salem's administrative organization and accounting practices, see Hermann BAIER, Des Klosters Salem Bevölkerungsbewegung, Finanz-, Steuerwesen und Volkswirtschaft seit dem 15. Jahrhundert, in: Freiburger Diözesanarchiv, n.s. 62 (1934), pp. 96–126. For early property acquisitions, see WEECH, Codex; RÖSENER, Salem.

49 Early Cistercian ideals rejected feudal relations and forbade members to exercise authority over villages and subjects or to profit from rents, interest payments, trade, or dependents' labor. Not until 1208 did the order permit certain properties to be rented out, followed by more general permission in 1220. RÖSENER, Salem, pp. 118–123; idem, Entwicklung des Zisterzienserklosters Salem im Spannungsfeld um normativer Zielsetzung und gesellschaftlicher Anpassung während des 12. bis 14. Jahrhunderts, in: Zeitschrift für die Geschichte des Oberrheins 133 (1985), pp. 47–48; Maren KUHN-REHFUS, Konversen und Pfründner in südwestdeutschen Zisterzienserklöstern, in: Das Zisterzienserkloster Bebenhausen: Beiträge zur Archäologie, Geschichte und Architektur, ed. Wilfried Setzler and Franz Quarthal, Stuttgart 1995, p. 105.

50 Salem became embroiled in conflicts with the rural populations it tried to displace in this old-settled region; see Werner RÖSENER, Bauernlegen durch klösterliche Grundherren im Hochmittelalter, in: Zeitschrift für Agrargeschichte und Agrarsoziologie 27 (1979), esp. p. 78; idem, Salem im Spannungsfeld, pp. 48–49. By the sixteenth century many of Salem's granges had been converted to ordinary farms that were rented out to area residents. RÖSENER, Salem, p. 119; SCHNEIDER, Geschichte Salems, pp. 98–99, 117–119.

around the abbey and nearby urban markets. Landed possessions, and the incomes they generated, were among the primary foundations of Salem's political authority and an advantage over neighboring rulers.[51] Salem guarded its property rights fiercely, and in the early modern period, its subjects complained about both the terms of leases (annual renewal, nonhereditary) and the level of rent (including a percentage of the crop rather than a set quantity).

Salem's villages and rent-bearing farms were important sources of income, but they were only one of three pillars in the Cistercian economic system. The second was the aforementioned granges, self-administered monastic farms under the direction of laybrothers, and the third was their urban properties, especially those designated as *Stadthöfe*. These town houses were exempt from the usual taxes, tolls, and military contributions required of all burghers. They provided a residence and guesthouse that could fulfill symbolic functions of display and hospitality, but more importantly, they were storage facilities and marketplaces for the abbey's duty-free produce. They served as access points to the region's most important political and administrative centers and to an extensive trading network of at least 29 cities.[52] Abbey officials stationed in the various granges and Stadthöfe oversaw properties and subjects scattered throughout the surrounding countryside. Map 2, Salem's Regional Networks, gives an idea of the abbey's influence beyond its central territory. Salem is an excellent demonstration of Armgard von Reden-Dohna's argument that many monasteries, Cistercians in particular, were financially powerful and efficient in spite of their small size.[53]

A third characteristic of ecclesiastical rule is routinely described as a limitation, for according to canon law, clerics were forbidden to shed blood. They could not attack, defend, protect, or punish using physical means. They were not allowed to wage wars or seek violent retaliation. In the terms of modern national states, this would certainly be viewed as an impediment, and in the Middle Ages it was perhaps an even greater problem. In a period of noble feuding, when there was literal truth in the saying that "might makes right," this clerical prohibition on violence placed ecclesiastical rulers in a difficult position. Some church leaders, especially bishops and prince-abbots, ignored the sanctions and even came to practice guardianship over their weaker neighbors.[54] Others employed lay officials to carry out the worldly duties of physical defense and legal enforcement on their behalf. In the medieval period, churches normally required a guardian

---

51 REDEN-DOHNA, Zisterzienser, pp. 52–53.

52 These properties varied in privileges and status, not all enjoying the extensive rights of a Stadthof. See RÖSENER, Salem, pp. 130–140; SCHNEIDER, Geschichte Salems, pp. 119–124; MARKGRÄFLICHE BADISCHE MUSEEN, Kloster und Staat, pp. 71–86.

53 REDEN-DOHNA, Zisterzienser, p. 53.

54 Kempten is a good example. See Wilhelm LIEBHART, Die Reichsabtei Irsee im Kampf um die volle Landeshoheit 1551–1692, in: Das Reichsstift Irsee: Vom Benediktinerkloster zum Bildungszentrum. Beiträge zu Geschichte, Kunst und Kultur, ed. Hans Frei, Weißenhorn 1981, pp. 152–167; FRIED, Ostschwaben, pp. 428–429, 433.

(*Vogt*), and the institution of church guardianship (*Kirchenvogtei*) evolved in ways that accommodated the defenselessness of churches by providing them with physical and legal "protection," which at the same time compromised their political autonomy. Church guardians were responsible for the failure of many abbeys to consolidate territorial authority or to achieve the status of unmediated imperial estates.[55] For some, such as those located in Württemberg, it led to secularization in the Reformation period.

Lacking the authority to use force, ecclesiastical lords turned readily to legal arbitration and written records in defense of their rights and properties. Ecclesiastical rulers also joined regional peace associations and defensive leagues in order to protect themselves and their interests. Membership in such groups was especially beneficial in areas of dispersed political authority such as the German Southwest. In comparison to Franconia, another region typified by small-scale governance, the peacekeeping associations in Upper Swabia made feud much less of a problem.[56] Salem belonged to regional organizations including the Knights of St. George's Shield, the Swabian League, the Swabian Circle, the College of Imperial Prelates in Upper Swabia, and the Cistercians' Upper German Congregation. Salem was also a strong supporter of the empire and of the Habsburgs (who held the imperial throne in the early modern period and were simultaneously major landowners and political players in the region), and the abbey was careful to have its privileges confirmed if not extended by each new emperor. The abbey secured its properties and freedoms not through a demonstration of military strength but through these personal relationships, legal charters, regional peacekeeping efforts, and the decentralized, loosely federal superstructure provided by membership in the empire and various regional associations.

Against this nonviolent approach to governance, the objection could be raised that Salem and other tiny rulers in this corner of the empire were extremely fortunate not to have been simply wiped out by larger, stronger neighbors. It is true that the imperial wars in the south and to the east drew militants away from the area, promoting an "oasis of peace" in Upper Swabia.[57] It is equally true that the Thirty Years War (1618–1648) brought total devastation to the region. Yet the Thirty Years War had a similar impact on the larger dynastic territories and in other regions of the empire. The effects of this war, especially for rural populations, were indiscriminately horrific. We must also consider military expenses and their political consequences.[58] Rulers with small terri-

---

55 Maurer, Ausbildung der Territorialgewalt, pp. 173–174.

56 Volker PRESS, Oberschwaben in der frühen Neuzeit, in: Oberschwaben: Beiträge zu Geschichte und Kultur, ed. Peter Eitel and Elmar L. Kuhn, Constance 1995, p. 104.

57 Ibid.

58 The cost of warfare is one of the reasons usually cited for the rise of large national states in the modern period, because wars were becoming so expensive that only larger units possessed the resources necessary to conduct them and to avoid being swallowed up by stronger neighbors. In the early modern period, however, the scale of warefare was much smaller than today, and in Upper Swabia, national states did not provide the model for political formation.

tories and smaller budgets, those with few resident subjects and fewer resources, were limited in the scale and frequency of aggressive acts. Conversely, less warfare required less government expenditure and this made good economic sense, especially from the perspective of taxpayers and subjects.[59] The weakly federal organization of petty rulers in Upper Swabia should not be seen as the consequence of a political vacuum, something cobbled together haphazardly in the absence of "real" power. These petty rulers were in fact the real rulers, and although many of them were small and militarily weak, their regional associations for defense and collective policymaking deserve greater attention. Again, we must be careful not to judge early modern Salem according to modern standards. Applying the criteria of peacekeeping rather than warmongering, Salem turns out to have been a successful polity indeed, as will be demonstrated in the following chapters.

A final difference between clerical and aristocratic rule, though others could be mentioned, concerns their administrative structures. As already indicated, many of Salem's administrative offices were filled by monks or laybrothers, unsalaried members of the abbey who were, at least in comparison to most bureaucrats, extremely loyal to its objectives. The abbey's own subjects, both local elites and other villagers, also carried out many of the tasks associated with Salem's territorial administration. The social origins and professional mobility of abbey officials are discussed in Chapter 6, but here it will be useful to briefly describe the major administrative offices and bodies responsible for territorial decisionmaking and recordkeeping.[60]

The abbot was the head of the monastic community as well as a territorial ruler who represented Salem, both spiritually and politically, to the outside world. Unlike most monks, he was free to leave the cloister and could be absent for long periods during his travels to distant places including Innsbruck, Vienna, Cîteaux, and Rome. Salem's abbot also conducted annual visitations and attended elections at other Cistercian abbeys, including four (male) "daughter" houses and eight subordinate female convents.[61] With the establishment of the Cistercians' Upper German Congregation in 1624, Salem's abbot became the General Vicar over 62 male and female abbeys from Franconia to the

---

59 Franz Quarthal cites this as a major advantage for abbeys, because in the larger secular territories, fifty percent or more of the entire budget commonly went to military expenditures in the eighteenth century. Even though abbeys paid much higher imperial taxes, these were minor in comparison to maintaining a standing army. Idem, Unterm Krummstab ist's gut leben: Prälaten, Mönche und Bauern im Zeitalter des Barock, in: Politische Kultur in Oberschwaben, ed. Peter Blickle, Tübingen 1993, pp. 283–284.

60 For greater detail about these and other administrative positions, see BAIER, Bevölkerungsbewegung, pp. 96–126; Katherine BRUN, The Abbot and His Peasants: Building the Territorial State in Salem, 1473–1637, PhD diss., Berkeley 2008, pp. 606–623; SCHNEIDER, Geschichte Salems, pp. 67–73.

61 The locations of these "daughter" houses (Königsbronn, Raitenhaslach, Tennenbach, and Wettingen) as well as affiliated female houses (Baindt, Feldbach, Gutenzell, Heggbach, Heiligkreuztal, Kalchrain, Rottenmünster, and Wald) are indicated on Map 2.

Swiss Confederation and from Alsace to Bavaria, with the responsibility to visit and oversee them all. The abbot attended imperial and regional assemblies, served on arbitration committees, and maintained correspondence with many other rulers as well as his own administrative officials.[62] No other monk, monastic official, or member of Salem's territorial community had a greater personal impact on its political development than the abbots. More is also known about them than any other group: the biographies of Salem's forty abbots have been written several times, and the abbey's history has been chronicled according to each abbot's challenges and achievements.[63]

The convent consisted of all the professed monks who lived and prayed within the monastery's walls. As an entire body they met regularly for religious services but rarely to make decisions, with the exception of electing the abbot, which was their most significant political activity. The convent did possess its own seal, and many documents refer to the abbot and convent together as the lords of Salem, yet there is little evidence that the monks collectively attended to or participated in the worldly affairs of business, administration, or rule. Individual monks, however, held several of the abbey's highest administrative offices, including the *Großkeller* (grand cellarer), *Pfister* (master baker), and bursar.[64] Salaried employees normally held other administrative positions, such as the many *Hofmeister*, who were responsible for overseeing each of the abbey's

---

62 Salem's abbots attended at least four Imperial Diets (Regensburg 1471, Lindau 1497, Worms 1497, Freiburg 1498) and were members of the Imperial Governing Council (*Reichsregiment*) in 1500 and 1521. Salem's abbots presided over the College of Imperial Prelates in Upper Swabia from 1580 to 1591 and served as assistant directors from 1591 to 1618. See SCHNEIDER, Geschichte Salems, p. 130; Armgard von REDEN-DOHNA, Weingarten und die schwäbischen Reichsklöster, in: Die Territorien des Reichs im Zeitalter der Reformation und Konfessionalisierung, vol. 5, ed. Anton Schindling and Walter Ziegler, Münster 1993, p. 233; HÖLZ, Krummstab, p. 107.

63 See especially Gabriel FEYERABEND, Chronik des ehemaligen Reichs-Stiftes und Münsters Salmannsweiler in Schwaben, von seiner Entstehung bis zu seiner Auflösung, 1833 [unpublished manuscript, Universitäts-Bibliothek Heidelberg]; STAIGER, Salem oder Salmansweiler, pp. 62–189; Gerhard KALLER, Zisterzienserkloster Salem, in: Helvetia Sacra, ed. Cécile Sommer-Ramer and Patrick Braun, vol. 3/1, Bern 1982, pp. 351–375; Alberich SIWEK, Die Zisterzienserabtei Salem: Der Orden Das Kloster Seine Äbte, Sigmaringen 1984, pp. 131–353.

64 The Großkeller was the abbey's chief economic overseer, in charge of granges and farms, land sales, rents, and forests. He also oversaw one of the two central administrative districts (west of the Aach River). The Pfister was initially a laybrother who supervised the abbey's provisions and storehouses. By the sixteenth century it was a monk who held this office, and his expanded responsibilities included supervision of the other central district (east of the Aach). He also oversaw the distribution of bread alms. The bursar handled the abbey's financial affairs including the majority of cash income and expenses (though many district officials reported directly to the abbot, who kept his own separate accounts). In addition, he oversaw tithes, vineyards and wine production, grain storage, and the payment of employees' wages. There was considerable overlap among the competencies of these officials, which underwent significant reorganization during the early modern period. All three officers were among the habitual members of the abbey's small council and Audience.

outlying districts, granges, and urban properties.[65] One senior official who interacted most frequently with territorial subjects was the *Oberamtmann* (called the *Kaufmann* until 1590).[66] The Oberamtmann represented the abbey in its legal prosecutions, mediated disputes, collected fines, witnessed property transactions, and supervised the village headmen. Other hired employees were the secretary and later chancellor, responsible for keeping many of the abbey's records.[67]

The territorial court (*Sidelgericht*) and the Audience (*Verhör*) were two of the abbey's most important decisionmaking bodies; others included the small council (*Rat*), the spiritual council (*Geistlicher Rat*), and the high court of appeals (*Hofgericht*).[68] The various courts, councils, and assemblies met at different frequencies and were composed of different members, but it is significant in each case that they reached their decisions collectively. Later chapters examine the territorial court and Audience, which are of special interest because of their excellent records as well as for their relevance to the politics of everyday village life and local socioeconomic structure.

Communalism

There is a long tradition of interest in the communal element of German history, especially in the later Middle Ages.[69] The legal historian Otto Friedrich von Gierke (1841–1921) developed the influential concepts of association (*Genossenschaft*) and corporate personality (*Verbandspersönlichkeit*) in the framework of medieval Germanic law.[70] In several important contributions focusing on the German Southwest, Karl Siegfried Bader (1905–1998) recognized both the internal political capacity of the vil-

---

65 The typical Hofmeister (alternatively called a *Vogt* or *Pfleger*), who was stationed at a distance from the abbey, was heavily involved in trade and diplomatic activities as well as travel, written correspondence, and recordkeeping. Many Hofmeister were recruited from nearby cities; a few were monks, laybrothers, retired pensioners, or abbey subjects.

66 There was an Oberamtmann for the central territory and another for the northern district surrounding Ostrach. The Oberamtmann usually lived in one of the villages and was often recruited from among the abbey's subjects.

67 Both senior chancery officials kept official records, drafted correspondence, made copies, and supervised lower-ranking scribes. In the early seventeenth century these offices were held by legal doctors recruited from nearby cities who also served as legal advisors and headed Salem's high court of appeals (*Hofgericht*). Employment contracts are found in GLAK, 98/232 and 98/240.

68 An assembly of territorial representatives (*Landschaft*) was notably absent in Salem.

69 For an overview, see Bob SCRIBNER, "Communities and the Nature of Power," in: idem, ed., Germany: A New Economic and Social History, vol. 1, London and New York 1996, pp. 291–325.

70 Otto Friedrich von GIERKE, Das deutsche Genossenschaftsrecht, 4 vols., Berlin 1868–1881. F. W. Maitland translated some of Gierke's major works in 1900 under the title Political Theories of the Middle Ages.

lage commune and the communal influence on small-scale political development.[71] In recent decades, Peter Blickle has been the leading historian associated with the political actions of the common man and with the commune as an organizing principle in the towns and countryside, especially during the period 1300–1800. In his many monographs and essays, collaborative efforts and conference volumes, he has addressed several of this study's central themes. One focal point of Blickle's research is what he calls the *Agrarverfassungsvertrag*, or agrarian constitutional agreement.[72] Such agreements, which resulted from popular resistance against the intensification of lordship as well as the commune's own political self-confidence, took the form of arbitrated settlements and contained important gains for peasant subjects. In Salem, the 1473 settlement between the abbot and the territorial judges is one such agreement. It expresses many of the concerns shared by peasants in other small, ecclesiastical, and South German territories in the years preceding the German Peasants' War, a second major theme of Blickle's research.[73] According to his formulation, the "revolution of the common man" in 1525 exemplified the highest expression of communal principles. Its revolutionary aspect derived from its foundation in godly law, an objective that not only proposed radical change but also united the interests of peasants with burghers, miners, and all common people. Third, Blickle has proposed the term "communalism" as an organizing principle to describe the period 1300–1800 "from below."[74] He sees communalism as the embodiment of political values held by working people, both urban and rural, but not of lords.[75] The collections of studies he has edited, many of them resulting from conferences organized around the themes of communalism, have added

71 See especially Karl Siegfried BADER, Studien zur Rechtsgeschichte des mittelalterlichen Dorfes, 3 vols., Vienna 1957–1973; idem, Der deutsche Südwesten in seiner territorialstaatlichen Entwicklung, Sigmaringen 1978.

72 Peter BLICKLE, Grundherrschaft und Agrarverfassungsvertrag, in: Die Grundherrschaft im späten Mittelalter, vol. 1, ed. Hans Patze, Sigmaringen 1983, pp. 241–261; Peter BLICKLE and André HOLENSTEIN, eds., Agrarverfassungsverträge: Eine Dokumentation zum Wandel in den Beziehungen zwischen Herrschaften und Bauern am Ende des Mittelalters, Stuttgart 1996.

73 Peter BLICKLE, Die Revolution von 1525, Munich 1975, translated by T. A. Brady Jr. and H. C. Erik Midelfort as The Revolution of 1525: The German Peasants' War from a New Perspective, Baltimore and London 1981.

74 Peter BLICKLE, Kommunalismus: Skizzen einer gesellschaftlichen Organisationsform, 2 vols., Munich 2000; idem, Der Kommunalismus als Gestaltungsprinzip zwischen Mittelalter und Moderne, in: Studien zur geschichtlichen Bedeutung des deutschen Bauernstandes, Stuttgart and New York 1989, pp. 69–82; idem, Kommunalismus, Parliamentarismus, Republikanismus, in: Studien, pp. 191–211; idem, Kommunalismus: Begriffsbildung in heuristischer Absicht, in: idem, ed., Landgemeinde und Stadtgemeinde in Mitteleuropa: Ein struktureller Vergleich, Munich 1991, pp. 5–38.

75 See for example BLICKLE, Kommunalismus, vol. 1, p. 131.

immensely to our knowledge of rural life and confirmed many of Blickle's principles through an increasing number of case studies.[76]

Not all historians of the German peasantry have agreed with Blickle. Some critics believe he has romanticized the rural commune as a unity of equals who shared common political goals, ignoring or at least minimizing factional interests, which increased during the early modern period and split the commune internally. This often led to the commune's identification with the interests of local elites or inhibited popular political action altogether.[77] Blickle's use of the term communalism to encompass both urban and rural political traditions in terms of parallel historical developments, structures, and values has also been subject to criticism.[78] Third, some historians object to Blickle's portrayal of communalism as if it were fundamentally opposed to lordship. He recognizes communalism not only as an organizing principle contrary to feudalism and absolutism, he also sees in it the roots of modern political traditions, parliamentary democracy, and republicanism. Here, too, critics suggest that the commune may have been less heroic than he supposes.[79]

In two major areas, this study diverges from the path Peter Blickle has established. First, it argues that Salem's territorial rule developed through the integration of community and lordship, in a negotiated process involving cooperation as well as conflict and a composite of interests rather than a binary opposition between high and low,

---

76 See especially Peter BLICKLE, ed., Aufruhr und Empörung? Studien zum bäuerlichen Widerstand im Alten Reich, Munich 1980; idem, ed., Resistance, Representation, and Community, Oxford and New York 1997; idem, ed., Gemeinde und Staat im Alten Europa, Munich 1998.

77 David Warren SABEAN, Landbesitz und Gesellschaft am Vorabend des Bauernkrieges: Eine Studie der sozialen Verhältnisse im südlichen Oberschwaben in den Jahren vor 1525, Stuttgart 1972; Govind P. SREENIVASAN, The Peasants of Ottobeuren, 1487–1726: A Rural Society in Early Modern Europe, Cambridge 2004; David LUEBKE, His Majesty's Rebels: Communities, Factions, and Rural Revolt in the Black Forest, 1725–1745, Ithaca 1997; Wolfgang KASCHUBA, Kommunalismus als sozialer "Common Sense." Zur Konzeption von Lebenswelt und Alltagskultur im neuzeitlicher Gemeindegedanken, in: Landgemeinde und Stadtgemeinde, ed. Peter Blickle, Munich 1991, pp. 65–91; Tom SCOTT, Society and Economy in Germany, 1300–1600, Houndmills 2002.

78 Thomas A. BRADY Jr., German Burghers and Peasants in the Reformation and Peasants' War: Partners or Competitors?, in: Between the Middle Ages and Modernity: Individual and Community in the Early Modern World, ed. Charles H. Parker and Jerry H. Bentley, London and New York 2002, pp. 33–51; Tom SCOTT, Freiburg and the Breisgau: Town-Country Relations in the Age of the Reformation and Peasants' War, Oxford and New York 1986.

79 David Warren SABEAN, Power in the Blood: Popular Culture and Village Discourse in Early Modern Germany, Cambridge and New York 1984; Volker PRESS, Kommunalismus oder Territorialismus, p. 126; Robert von FRIEDEBURG, Village Strife and the Rhetoric of Communalism: Peasants and Parsons, Lords and Jews in Hesse, Central Germany, 1646–1672, in: Literature and Theology 7 (1992), pp. 201–226; Robert von FRIEDEBURG, "Kommunalismus" und "Republikanismus" in der frühen Neuzeit, in: Zeitschrift für Historische Forschung 21 (1994), pp. 65–91.

center and periphery, ruler and ruled. This ensured that as political authority grew at the territorial level, the village commune did not lose its functions. Peasants retained their influence rather than becoming marginalized. Second, and perhaps because of this difference, political development in Salem after 1550 and the place of communalism in it differed fundamentally from that described by Blickle and others. It was not characterized by peasant revolts and resistance to the tax state, nor did Salem have a representative territorial assembly (*Landschaft*). Blickle does not believe, as did earlier generations of historians, that the German Peasants' War marked the end of peasants' political activities. Yet in each of his major examples of communalism's development after 1550—the village communes, territorial parliaments, and peasant revolts—it appears that the movement began to decline well before the age of absolutism.[80] My modifications of Blickle's concepts with respect to communalism in Salem are not to be seen as a rebuttal, but rather, as new ground for a broader understanding of community and its continuing influence after 1550, through its integration with lordship and in the political growth of the early modern territory.

These concerns bring us back to the earlier discussion of the state as a problematic model for understanding smaller polities in the early modern period. There has been a recent surge of interest in the topic of "policy" (*Policey, Polizei*), and some of the most compelling research in this area has focused on the interactive processes of communication and mediation between center and periphery.[81] As interpretations of political development become more inclusive, less binary, and increasingly informed by the role of local actors and social contexts, the political example of Salem may prove to be less unusual than it had at first appeared.[82]

---

80 According to Blickle, the period between 1550 and 1650 was a second stage in the development of the communal-associative model, in which the German princes posed a challenge to the commune and appropriated the Protestant Reformation. After 1650, he says, communalism was routed by the absolutist state. BLICKLE, Obedient Germans, p. 78.

81 See André HOLENSTEIN, "Gute Policey" und lokale Gesellschaft im Staat des Ancien Régime: Das Fallbeispiel der Markgrafschaft Baden(-Durlach), 2 vols., Epfendorf 2003; idem, Die Umstände der Normen – die Normen der Umstände: Policeyordnungen im kommunikativen Handeln von Verwaltung und lokaler Gesellschaft im Ancien Régime, in: Policey und frühneuzeitliche Gesellschaft, ed. Karl Härter, Frankfurt am Main 2000, pp. 1–46; in the same volume Achim LANDWEHR, Policey vor Ort: Die Implementation von Policeyordnungen in der ländlichen Gesellschaft der Frühen Neuzeit, pp. 47–70; Steve HINDLE, The State and Social Change in Early Modern England, ca. 1550–1640, New York 2000.

82 Contributions pointing in this direction include Sheilagh OGILVIE, The State in Germany: A Non-Prussian View, in: Rethinking Leviathan: The Eighteenth-Century State in Britain and Germany, ed. John Brewer and Eckhart Hellmuth, Oxford 1999, pp. 167–202; Caroline CASTIGLIONE, Patrons and Adversaries: Nobles and Villagers in Italian Politics, 1640–1760, New York 2005; BLOCKMANS et al., Empowering Interactions.

1.3 Physical and Political Geography

Salem Abbey is located in the Aach river valley above the northern shores of Lake Constance, twelve kilometers east of Überlingen, in one of Germany's mildest and most fertile climate regions. The rolling landscape alternates between wide, open valleys and moderately steep, forested hillsides left by retreating glaciers. In many places, the banks north of the lake rise in a band of low hills parallel to the shoreline. Above them, the land continues to slope gently upward in a south-facing basin. From prominent places throughout the region, and all along the lakeshore, the snowy peaks of the Swiss Alps provide the backdrop on a sunny day. The abbey sits in a long valley stretching from northwest to southeast, parallel to the lake and slightly higher in elevation.[83] Meandering through the valley, the Aach River provides a major source of water (with the abbey built directly over its course) and hydropower, which ran several mills in previous centuries. The Aach connected the inland areas with the lake and generally bisected the central territory into its two major districts, the *Großkelleramt* (or *Kelleramt*) to the west and the *Pfisteramt* to the east. The river valley and other flatlands were then and still are well suited for arable, meadows, and orchards. A few villages lie in hilly areas or at the base of steeper inclines. Some of the surrounding slopes were planted with grapes. Others remained forested, and supported grazing, wood harvesting, and other foraging activities. Although it is an old-settled region, parts of the southern Linzgau are still heavily forested to this day. Other areas are low and marshy, most notably the area along the river between Salem and Mimmenhausen.[84]

Two major agricultural products dominated the regional economy in the sixteenth century: wine and grain. Viticulture took on special importance for the area's socioeconomic structure because it required a great deal of labor and relied heavily on markets. The emphasis on arable versus viticulture varied not only among individual households but also by village—for example, the south-facing hills along the lake were unsuitable for grain but produced decent wine. The effects of these differences were evident in local social structure. Textiles and dairying, two major by-employments further east

---

83 Elevation in the southern Linzgau lake basin ranges from 400 meters at the lakeshore in Überlingen to 756 meters at Gehrenberg by Markdorf; Heiligenberg straddles a ridge below a peak at 787 meters. Xavier Staiger provides elevations for Salem and each of its villages (in feet!), ranging from 1,300 feet for Nußdorf to 1,770 feet for Haberstenweiler; Salem sits at 1,485 feet above sea level. See also BÜTTNER, Konstanzer Heilig-Geist-Spital, pp. 22–23; Adolf FUTTERER, Die Geschichte des Dorfes und des Kirchspiels Billafingen im Linzgau, Radolfzell 1970, pp. 1, 4.

84 In the twelfth century, Heiligenberg granted Salem a large wetland along both sides of the Aach between Frickingen in the north and Mimmenhausen in the south. These areas were drained and improved to create meadows, pastures, and fish ponds.

and especially south, never played a major role in the economies of Salem's villages.[85] The abbey was a major employer of both fieldworkers and craftsmen.

Salem's landed possessions resulted from early donations as well as what may be called "acquisition politics."[86] Two historical maps of the central territory, from 1665 and 1765, represent the abbey's lordship as a unified and exclusive whole, downplaying the overlapping claims that characterized our period. Nevertheless, the numbered boundary markers located around the perimeter of both maps (see Maps 3 and 4) had been established much earlier, and the size and shape of Salem's central territory remained essentially fixed over the course of earlier centuries.[87] The carefully numbered stones demarcated the abbey's jurisdictional boundaries. The key feature shared by the villages, hamlets, and isolated farmsteads of the Großkelleramt and Pfisteramt is that they all belonged to the abbey's justice and to its central court, the Sidelgericht.[88]

In addition to this spatially circumscribed area, two outposts east and west possessed special significance and were also part of the core territory referred to as Under the Hills. In the eastern Linzgau, a number of properties in and around Adelsreute and Tepfenhard were among the earliest donations granted by Salem's founder to support the abbey's material needs. Initially converted into granges, they enjoyed legal status and protections equivalent to the abbey itself, and they were specifically mentioned in several royal and papal privileges. For this reason, Salem carefully guarded these early possessions and made them part of the Pfisteramt. To the west, Salem acquired the village of Owingen (including most of the land, jurisdiction, and other rights of lordship) through two costly purchases in 1213 and 1273. This provided convenient access to the region's primary urban market in Überlingen and secured a position on the trade route between that imperial city and Pfullendorf, a route also connecting Lake Constance with the Danube.[89]

---

85 See Peter EITEL, Die Rolle der Reichsstadt Überlingen in der Wirtschaftsgeschichte des Bodenseeraumes, in: Schriften des Vereins für Geschichte des Bodensees und seiner Umgebung 89 (1971), p. 13. Salem lay just beyond the regions of linen production in Upper Swabia and around St. Gallen; see Map 1.2 in Tom SCOTT, Economic Landscapes, in: Germany, vol. 1, ed. Bob Scribner, p. 14.

86 RÖSENER, Salem, pp. 111, 116–118; idem, Salem im Spannungsfeld, p. 52; MAURER, Ausbildung der Territorialgewalt, p. 156.

87 Even in 1240, Salem's possessions were consolidated enough for Rösener to describe them as a roughly bounded, "*zusammenhängenden Komplex.*" Idem, Salem, p. 104. Authority over the maintenance of boundary markers was among the topics of the 1464 Lullin Treaty between Salem and Heiligenberg (GLAK, 67/1431). There were slight fluctuations in the southeastern boundaries around Wirrensegel, and around the hamlet of Oberstenweiler, which became part of the central territory in 1637; previously it had belonged to Heiligenberg.

88 An exception was Bermatingen, which had its own village court and claimed exemption from the Sidelgericht. Still, residents of Bermatingen appeared before the central court and also served among its judges.

89 See Elmar KUHN, Mönche und Bauern: Herrschaften und Untertanen im Mittelalter, in: 1000 Jahre Owingen, 983–1983, ed. Gemeinde Owingen, Owingen 1983, p. 23.

Despite their relative distance, Owingen and its parish hamlet of Pfaffenhofen were attached to the Großkelleramt. Thus the abbey's lordship Under the Hills included not only the consolidated central territory but also a handful of settlements between Adelsreute and Owingen, which were also bound to its jurisdiction. These possessions in the southern Linzgau form the primary focus of this study.

Lake Constance, the major geographical feature in the area, was important not only because of its climate effect.[90] The lake also straddled major trade routes both north-south and east-west, with ports including Bregenz, Buchhorn, Constance, Fußach, Lindau, and Überlingen among others.[91] It served to connect various regions rather than to create boundaries between them, and the Rhine flowed through the lake on its course from the Swiss Alps all the way to the North Sea. Salem did not possess any major harbor along the lake, relying on Meersburg or Überlingen for transportation to Constance and elsewhere. Uhldingen was the most important of several lakeshore communities within the territory, at the mouth of the Aach River.[92]

Salem Abbey sat slightly off the major trade routes but close enough to afford easy access. In addition, Salem enjoyed trade networks far more extensive than its location might suggest, thanks to its possession of numerous Stadthöfe and other urban properties. For Salem and the surrounding region, Überlingen was by far the most prominent market.[93] This imperial city of around 4,000 residents was smaller than Constance, with less extensive trade networks, but it was the primary wine and grain market on the lake and it connected the breadbasket of Upper Swabia with the upland areas to the south, especially St. Gallen, Graubünden, and central Switzerland.[94] Überlingen's close proximity and its specialization in agricultural products secured its position as Salem's primary trading partner. Among the larger cities and for long-distance trade, Constance ranked first in importance.[95] The Stadthof in Ulm provided access to the Danube and to the major east-west route between Augsburg and Lyon.

---

90 The difficulties of overland travel made water routes preferable. Tom Scott points out that all Germany's major wine-producing regions were located along important waterways. Idem, Economic Landscapes, p. 12.

91 Peter EITEL, Handel und Verkehr im Bodenseeraum während der frühen Neuzeit, in: Schriften des Vereins für Geschichte des Bodensees und seiner Umgebung 91 (1973), pp. 67–89.

92 The village of Unteruhldingen is located directly on the lake and it belonged to Heiligenberg's jurisdiction. Oberuhldingen, across the river and slightly upstream, belonged to Salem.

93 By 1211 Salem had established its first Stadthof in Überlingen. It still stands today near the town's Franciscan Gate and next to the old city Hospital of the Holy Ghost.

94 Six times more grain was sold in Überlingen than in Constance. In 1611, between 6,000 and 7,000 tons of grain were sold in Überlingen, enough to feed 20,000 people for a year. See EITEL, Überlingen, pp. 18–19.

95 Hektor AMMAN, Untersuchungen zur Wirtschaftsgeschichte des Oberrheinraumes II. Das Kloster Salem in der Wirtschaft des ausgehenden Mittelalters, in: Zeitschrift für die Geschichte des Oberrheins 110 (1962), pp. 371–404. Salem spent more on purchases in Constance than in Überlingen, though the volume was less.

Illustration 1.2: Salem on the Eve of Secularization

By Johann Sebastian Dürr, 1804
Heiligenberg Palace sits on a hill above and to the right of the abbey.
Generallandesarchiv Karlsruhe B/Salem/2

Politically, Salem and the majority of its possessions lay within the borders of the Linzgau, one of the old Alemannic counties (*Gau-Grafschaften*) named after the Linzer Aach, the river running through the valley past Salem and into the lake. North of the abbey, a range of steep hills divided the central territory from the county's northern districts (hence the names used to distinguish the two regions, Under the Hills and Over the Hills). Today, the imposing Renaissance palace and former residence of the counts of Heiligenberg still sits atop one of these hills, providing an expansive view over the lake, the Aach valley, and the entire southern Linzgau. This symbol of the count's authority could also be seen from the abbey and throughout much of its territory, providing a constant reminder in terms of position as well as proximity of Salem's uphill struggles over the centuries against this neighbor and his superior claims. See Illustration 1.2, Salem on the Eve of Secularization. Yet as we will see, the counts of Heiligenberg possessed a weak central authority with power and lands concentrated in the north rather than the south of the county, where Salem's competing claims to property and rights prevailed. Until 1637, Salem held scattered rights over land and serfs in northern parts of the county just as Heiligenberg did in the south, but in that year the two sides agreed to a regularization of the boundaries between them so that each enjoyed an exclusive geographical sphere.

In contrast to this great and constant rivalry with Heiligenberg, Salem enjoyed relatively peaceful relations and fewer direct conflicts with other neighbors. Überlingen had its own large rural hinterland further west, mostly in the Hegau.[96] Overlapping authority with respect to land and serfs caused only occasional disputes between Salem and Überlingen in villages such as Owingen and Nußdorf. The other major lord in the area was the bishop of Constance, whose authority radiated out from the small towns of Markdorf and Meersburg (where the bishop resided throughout the period). Despite some disputes over spiritual authority, especially resulting from the Council of Trent, Salem's Cistercian privileges exempted it from most of the bishops' claims.[97] In the Linzgau and in the wider region, confessional identity provided a source of unity and alliance—even the county's two imperial cities, Überlingen and Pfullendorf, remained loyal to Rome. Further afield, the Linzgau was bordered to the west by the Hegau county of Nellenburg and to the east by the *Landvogtei* of Upper Swabia, both of which were areas of Habsburg influence belonging to "Outer Austria" (*Vorderösterreich*).[98] Not far beyond Heiligenberg's lands to the north flowed the Danube River, and beyond that was Württemberg. To the south was Lake Constance, and beyond that the Swiss Confederation and its associates.

Salem's location in an area of dispersed authority shaped the nature of its political development to no small degree. The rights and claims of minor nobles, cities and towns, religious foundations, and other diminutive polities overlapped and intermingled with respect to land, justice, and serfs, so that no one power dominated the region

---

96 Überlingen had the fifth-largest territory among imperial cities, including 33 villages and hamlets in five districts. Überlingen did not possess high justice outside the city walls until 1779. BÜTTNER, Konstanzer Heilig-Geist-Spital, pp. 29, 31.

97 In 1540 the bishop attempted to turn Salem into a dependent prebend, but the abbey was able to secure an imperial privilege in 1541 confirming its rights and extending new jurisdictional exemptions, so that a similar attempt in 1562 also failed. SCHNEIDER, Geschichte Salems, p. 133.

98 Salem was loosely surrounded by Outer Austria, yet the regions under Habsburg influence were located just far enough afield that they posed little threat in comparison to other abbeys such as Weingarten. The *Landvogt* of Upper Swabia, the vice-regent who administered the scattered imperial lands, encroached on Heiligenberg's authority and held high justice in the eastern Linzgau where Salem's villages of Adelsreute, Tepfenhard, and Urnau were located. Salem enjoyed generally good relations with the Landvogt, who served as an ally against Heiligenberg. On the dispute between Heiligenberg and the Landvogt in the eastern Linzgau, see Helmut MAURER, Bäuerliches Gedächtnis und Landesherrschaft im 15. Jahrhundert: Zu einer oberschwäbischen "Kundschaft" von 1484, in: Recht und Reich im Zeitalter der Reformation: Festschrift für Horst Rabe, ed. Christine Roll, Frankfurt 1996, pp. 179–198; Max BINDER, Zur staatlichen Geschichte des Linzgaus, in: Badische Heimat 23 (1936), p. 66. For maps of the Outer Austrian lands, see Friedrich METZ,ed., Vorderösterreich: Eine geschichtliche Landeskunde, 4th ed., Freiburg im Breisgau 2000, p. 36; SCHINDLING and ZIEGLER, Territorien des Reichs, vol. 5, p. 256.

or even exercised lordship uniformly over a single village.[99] Upper Swabia's common identity arose in part from the threat that more powerful outsiders such as Bavaria, Württemberg, Austria, or the Swiss might upset the delicate balance. The petty rulers of this region also shared a close relationship to the empire. Salem's geographical location was especially fortunate in this respect, because it sat just beyond Habsburg's predatory reach. Under Emperor Maximilian I (r. 1493–1519), the region was dubbed the turntable of imperial influence, but it was largely freed from Habsburg territorial ambitions once the dynasty acquired the kingdoms of Hungary and Bohemia in 1526 and turned its attention to the east.[100] This simplified Salem's relationship with Austria and the emperor, and the abbey maintained strong imperial ties throughout its history. It is hard to imagine the success or indeed survival of a polity such as Salem's in a region characterized by strong central authority. It is no coincidence that we find it in the German Southwest. This political landscape was built on dense urban networks, proud imperial abbeys, and active rural communes. It was characterized by small-scale self-administration and loyalty to a safely distant Emperor, sustained by common participation in weak federal organizations that kept the peace and maintained balance through mutual aid, councils, courts, and arbitration.[101] A recurrent theme throughout this study is the issue of political geography and landscape: were small size and dispersed, localized authority decisive developmental factors, and if so, were their effects constructive or obstructive in nature?

Abbey, County, Empire: Salem's Struggle for Political Autonomy

For Salem, external relations focused above all on the attempt to define and build territorial authority free from the interference of a single neighbor: the count of Heiligenberg. In fact, centuries of struggle against Heiligenberg as well as the collection of imperial privileges and protections relating to this conflict had a determining impact not only on Salem's external affairs but also on relations with its territorial subjects. This section provides a brief overview of Salem's foundation and early constitutional history, which serves as essential context for the abbey's imperial ties and relations with neighboring rulers in the early modern period. Since these topics have been covered in great detail by Werner Rösener, and because I have also discussed them more fully elsewhere, here we will focus on only a handful of key events, privileges, and legal settlements.[102]

---

99 Swabia was the most politically fragmented region in the empire according to PRESS, Kommunalismus oder Territorialismus, p. 124.

100 PRESS, Oberschwaben, pp. 104, 111.

101 Ibid.; BADER, Der deutsche Südwesten.

102 See RÖSENER, Salem; BRUN, Rulers and Regime, pp. 364–370; BRUN, Abbot and Peasants (2008 diss.), chap. 6.

In 1134 Salem's founder, the nobleman Guntram von Adelsreute, made a modest donation to the Cistercians of a few farmsteads in and around Salmansweiler, Tepfenhard, and Adelsreute, some forests and meadows, and a small chapel.[103] He took great care to have the abbey's foundation and endowment legally recognized and witnessed at a regional court assembly attended by members of the Linzgau's leading noble families. Then in 1140 the new Cistercian house received a privilege from Pope Innocent II, stating: "Since the monks of the Cistercian Order stand under the sole protection of the pope, all others are forbidden to practice or usurp guardianship over Salem."[104] In light of the ongoing dispute between popes and emperors over control of the church during this period, it comes as no great surprise that King Conrad III officially recognized Salem in a privilege granted shortly thereafter, on 19 March 1142. This royal letter proved to be the abbey's most important foundational document. The German king confirmed all Salem's present and future possessions, forbade any person to disturb or molest the abbey in any way, and most significantly, called himself Salem's only protector under God.[105] After securing the king's special protection of his abbey, Guntram von Adelsreute voluntarily renounced his rights as founder and died without a male heir. These actions left Salem free from the influence of a founding dynasty and encouraged a close relationship between the growing abbey and later emperors.[106]

As is already evident in the foundational privileges of 1140 and 1142, the pope and king each laid claim to the same exclusive authority as Salem's sole protector. For the young abbey, continuing struggles between a series of popes and emperors led to even bolder claims and greater privileges, including the offer of special protections and tax exemptions not granted in later centuries or to other religious orders. In 1155 King Frederick I "Barbarossa" granted Salem a privilege in wording based heavily on earlier papal letters (1140 and 1146), except that the new text asserted it was the emperor, and not the pope, who provided exclusive protection to the Cistercians and to the entire

---

103 This donation was admittedly inadequate to support a community, but his offer was accepted and Lützel Abbey in southern Alsace sent the first twelve monks to Salmansweiler in 1137. In 1138 Guntram made a second donation, consisting of the entire village and church in Adelsreute and parcels in several other locations. Some of their place names no longer exist, and they were most likely converted into granges. RÖSENER, Salem, p. 20.

104 "Quia vero fratres eiusdem ordinis sub solius romani pontificis tuicione consistunt, aliquem ibi officium advocatie gerere vel usurpare pariter interdicimus." WEECH, Codex, vol. 1, p. 2 no. 2. With its claim to exclusive protection not only over Salem but also over the entire Cistercian Order, this privilege is among the best examples of papal support for Cistercians' claim to freedom from ecclesiastical guardianship. RÖSENER, Salem, p. 34.

105 "alium Advocatum post Deum praeter Nos non habent." WEECH, Codex, vol. 1, p. 5 no. 3; STAIGER, Salem oder Salmansweiler, pp. 70–73 (full text with German translation); RÖSENER, Salem, pp. 31–34.

106 Since 1356 the German king was chosen by seven electors, and according to tradition he was considered the emperor only after coronation by the pope. Many privileges and confirmations were obtained from a new king before he had been crowned.

Roman Church.[107] After the two sides settled their differences in the 1177 Treaty of Venice, the papacy continued to issue letters of special protection to Salem but dropped the exclusivity of these claims. Salem continued to enjoy imperial protection, and as the Hohenstaufen dynasty strengthened its influence in the regions north of Lake Constance, a close relationship developed that would eventually bolster the abbey's claims to free imperial status and immunity from the authority of its neighbors.[108]

With the Hohenstaufens on the throne, Salem's interests remained secure. During the reign of Louis the Bavarian (1314–1347), however, Salem was "subjected to an infinity of persecutions."[109] Without recourse to imperial favor and assistance, Salem's monks had to accept protection from area nobles where they could, voluntarily or involuntarily, and it was in this period that Salem's political authority sank to its lowest ebb. In 1318 Salem consented, in the first of a series of agreements, to give cash and grain to Count Albrecht of Werdenberg-Heiligenberg in exchange for his protection.[110] Before long, this count successfully used his position to force the abbey under his territorial authority.[111] In 1326 and again in 1332 he was appointed as the Imperial *Landvogt* (vice-regent) in Upper Swabia, and by 1326, Count Albrecht was calling himself "Imperial Landvogt of the Lake." Combining these rights as imperial steward with his exercise of high justice throughout the Linzgau, the count of Heiligenberg effectively achieved full legal guardianship over Salem, in spite of the abbey's earlier freedoms.

Soon after the election of King Charles IV in 1347, Salem's fortunes began to improve. As a result of the abbey's petition, the new king confirmed Salem's freedoms on 27 January 1348. It was the first legal charter since the privilege of 1155 to specifically

107 WEECH, Codex, vol. 1, pp. 11–13 no. 6. Rösener provides sections of both texts for comparison; idem, Salem, pp. 37–38.

108 The privileges of kings and emperors were extremely important to Salem's constitutional development, yet the abbey also maintained good relations with the papacy. Abbot Eberhard I and some of Salem's other early abbots served as intermediaries who sought to establish peace between the two sides.

109 RÖSENER, Salem, p. 71.

110 Between 1318 and 1337 Salem entered at least 21 protection agreements with Heiligenberg. Since most of the abbey's possessions lay within the county, Heiligenberg's prominence in security arrangements comes as no surprise. In addition to Heiligenberg, Salem entered protection agreements with the count of Hohenberg (1317), the count of Werdenberg-Sargans (1323, 1325, 1327), the Vogt of Sigmaringen (1324, 1327, 1329), the count of Nellenburg (1324), the Landvogt (1328, 1331), and the count of Montfort (1343). These letters demonstrate that Salem was not under any one ruler's exclusive protection. The absence of protection letters after 1350 underscores the fragile nature of Salem's relations with its neighbors and the dangers it encountered during King Louis's reign. GLAK, 67/1435; WEECH, Codex, vol. 3, pp. 245–249 no. 1191–1191u; RÖSENER, Salem, pp. 75–77.

111 At a county assembly in 1322, he stated pointedly: "Those abbeys without legal guardians should submit to no one and no law besides ourselves." RÖSENER, Salem, p. 73; Georg GOETZ, Niedere Gerichtsherrschaft und Grafengewalt im badischen Linzgau während des ausgehenden Mittelalters, Breslau 1913, pp. 98–99.

mention royal guardianship (*königliche Vogtei*) in addition to the "special royal protection" (*besonderer Königsschutz*) of more recent confirmations. Three days later, Charles IV recalled Count Albrecht from his position as Salem's legal guardian, declaring: "We have now come to realize that it is damaging and not helpful to the abbey of Salmansweiler or to the empire."[112] In defiance of the new royal order, Count Albrecht continued to interfere in Salem's affairs and extort protection money. This led King Charles to issue a series of four additional protection letters to Salem in 1353–1354, each time sharpening his rhetoric. On 2 October 1353 he called Salem "an abbey of the holy empire" and on 24 February 1354 he stated more explicitly, "We hereby acknowledge that neither this count nor anyone else has any right or lordship over the abbey, since this lordship belongs to us and to the empire without any mediation."[113] This privilege, reproduced in Illustration 1.3, was the most significant acknowledgement of Salem's unmediated imperial status to be produced throughout its history. The privilege also contained the earliest direct reference to the Sidelgericht in the following statement of Salem's judicial immunity: "In all active quarrels, no person of the abbey—wherever they live and however they are called, whether they be of status high or low—is to be invited or forced to appear before any court other than the abbot's own, whose judges traditionally sit at the abbey's Upper Gate. Furthermore, these people of the abbey shall answer in all such disputes only to the abbey's judges at the said location."[114] The privilege of 1354 ended the dispute between Salem and Heiligenberg over guardianship in the sense of physical protection and as a vehicle of territorial overlordship. In later struggles over the division of judicial authority, however, the 1354 privilege continued to serve as a source of disagreement.

For a variety of reasons, Heiligenberg's political grasp began to weaken after 1354 and Salem's abbots took advantage of the opportunity to chip away at the county's rights from below, gradually carving out a separate territorial sphere Under the Hills.[115] Salem expanded its territorial powers mostly through legal suits and arbitration settlements, the investigation of which highlights many of the key elements of territorialization, especially those that were most highly contested. Between 1390 and 1637, ju-

---

112 RÖSENER, Salem, p. 77; GOETZ, Niedere Gerichtsherrschaft, p. 100; WEECH, Codex, vol. 3, p. 351 no. 1296.

113 RÖSENER, Salem, pp. 78–79; WEECH, Codex, vol. 3, pp. 361–362 no. 1311–1312.

114 "Das man alle Leut und diner des vorgen' Closters, wo die wonhaft und gesezzen sind, uf irem gut, Merkten, Dörfern oder Höfen wie die genant sind, sie sein hoch oder nider, umb alle werkliche sache für kein gericht laden oder für treiben sol, wann für des Aptes gericht und richter desselben Closters, der da sitzet gewonlich zu gericht, in der Obern Porten des egenanten Munsters und Closters. Und die sullen umb alle werkliche sache, wie die genant ist, vor demselben Richter und an der vorgen' Stat des Closters antwurten." GLAK, D/305 and 67/1468, fol. 45r. Though the privilege seemed to imply full jurisdictional powers, Salem did not claim or practice high justice until much later.

115 RÖSENER, Salem, p. 81.

Illustration 1.3: Royal Privilege from King Charles IV, 24 February 1354

Generallandesarchiv Karlsruhe, D/305

risdictional issues were the primary source of dispute.[116] The Leuchtenberg Treaty of 1390, the first in a series of legal settlements between the two neighboring rulers, makes clear that Heiligenberg continued to exercise high justice throughout the county in spite of Salem's royal privilege of 1354. The 1390 agreement, frequently cited in later centuries, defined the division of legal authority between Salem and Heiligenberg based on location and the type of offense. In the disputed region, including the abbey

[116] Hermann BAIER, Die Stellung der Abtei Salem in Staat und Kirche, in: Freiburger Diözesan-archiv, n.s. 62 (1934), p. 134.

proper and 17 surrounding settlements, the treaty recognized that low justice, or the authority over minor offenses, belonged to the abbey. High justice, the right to punish crimes involving "manslaughter, robbery, arson, theft, and whatever else may concern a man's life," belonged to Heiligenberg.[117] A middle ground of serious but noncapital offenses, which the sources often refer to as those involving "flowing wounds," were punishable by Salem if they occurred inside settlement boundaries, but Heiligenberg could claim those occurring in uninhabited areas such as forests and fields.

The need to further define the grey area between the two jurisdictional competencies was a common theme in subsequent agreements including the Nellenburg Treaty of 1419, the Lullin Treaty of 1464, the Landau Treaty of 1527, and many others.[118] Over the course of their struggles, each side was quick to point out legal encroachments by the other and to bring seemingly trivial issues before arbitration committees made up of neighboring rulers. In 1502 the two sides submitted a total of 37 grievances to voluntary arbitration.[119] The use of specific examples (no less than twelve complaints cited particular incidents and names) suggests that each lord was keeping close watch over the activities of the other.[120] An agreement in 1509 addressed Heiligenberg's concern that Salem was overstepping its judicial authority. First of all, Salem's ordinances prohibited and stated penalties for manslaughter and feud, both of which belonged to the count's superior jurisdiction.[121] The abbot declared that to his knowledge, the abbey claimed no authority over manslaughter or feud. Nevertheless, the arbitrators sided with Heiligenberg.[122] A second article addressed the appointment of judges to the abbot's court from within Heiligenberg's low jurisdiction. This was unjustified, according to the count, even though he too chose judges for his own court from Salem's jurisdictional sphere. The arbitrators declared that in the future, neither party should use judges living in the lands belonging to the other, even when such individuals were

---

117 GLAK, 67/1431, fol. 19r; 67/1429; 67/1468; 67/1782; WEECH, Codex, vol. 3, p. 399 no. 1361; RÖSENER, Salem, pp. 88–89.

118 There are many copies of these agreements; see the copiaries in GLAK, 67/1431 and 67/1782.

119 GLAK, 67/1431.

120 For instance, Heiligenberg accused Salem of punishing Peter Hell of Wangen with a penalty of two gulden for stealing wine. Salem denied the charges, claiming it had been a repayment, not a penalty for theft. Similarly, Heiligenberg alleged that Salem had punished Hans Bremer for harvesting more than his portion from a shared meadow and removed Bremer from his position as a *Sidelrichter* (judge on the central court) because of the incident. Again, the abbot claimed innocence: officials had never punished Bremer, an honorable man who remained a member of the court.

121 Similar complaints were also raised in 1419, with specific examples. GLAK, 67/1431.

122 In fact, Salem's customary law code did contain articles on feud and manslaughter, though the abbey did not claim exclusive authority to punish these crimes. For example, from the 1470 version: "das ainer den andern zu tod schlug die des closters sind In dem closter oder davor der sol Zechen pfund pfening dem closter verfallen und schuldig on gnad sin … unnserm gnedigen herren von dem hailigen berg Ir Recht unverdingt hin zu geben." GLAK, 4/120, fol. 8r.

bound to them as serfs.[123] Finally, the count objected to Salem's oath formula requiring dependents to swear they would settle all worldly disputes before the Sidelgericht. This clause, derived from the royal privilege of 1354, violated the county court's superior authority in matters of high justice. The abbot responded that the oath in no way diminished Heiligenberg's authority, especially since it contained a clause specifically stating that it did not apply to or infringe upon Heiligenberg's rights of high justice. The arbitrators upheld Salem's right to demand the oath, as long as the abbey did not mean to imply authority over high justice.[124]

By the early sixteenth century, Salem was generally acknowledged to hold a monopoly over low justice within its central territory along with significant derivative rights, such as the loyalty oath, military taxes, and labor services. Salem also claimed other rights one would expect to find associated with county authority, such as those involving weights and measures, tolls, wine presses, trade, tavern and consumption taxes, forestry, and fishing.[125] Salem did not, of course, claim hunting rights, but the abbey was successful in setting limits on the count's hunting parties and their demands for hospitality from its villagers.[126] The ongoing struggle between Salem and Heiligenberg impacted political development within the territory in many ways, and with the growing documentation of the late sixteenth and early seventeenth centuries, it may be observed that many decisions were made in the context of this unneighborly conflict. In some cases, abbey subjects brought petitions before the Audience asking for Salem's intervention against Heiligenberg's demands, as for example in 1596, when the community of Weildorf complained that Heiligenberg forbade them to graze in a field they had customarily used, threatening to imprison anyone found there; in 1599, when Heiligenberg officials came to conduct a mill inspection; and in 1629, when Grasbeuren's *Amtmann* (village headman) received instructions from Heiligenberg's forest warden that all dogs must wear bells to protect wild game. The dispute between Salem and Heiligenberg did not always work in subjects' favor, however. In the 1620s, several

---

123 Apparently they disagreed with the count's argument that there was a big difference between his territorial court and Salem's Sidelgericht. Goetz interpreted this decision as evidence of the county court's decline. Idem, Niedere Gerichtsherrschaft, pp. 85–86.

124 GLAK, 67/1431, fol. 49v. Actually, none of Salem's surviving oath formulas contains a clause mentioning Heiligenberg or authority over high justice, though the oath taken by *Hintersassen* (jurisdictional residents who were not abbey serfs) had a clause limiting their obligations with respect to the (unspecified) claims of their *Halßherren*, other lords who had authority over life and limb.

125 Many of these rights were the subject of dispute and overlapping claims.

126 Hunting rights and hospitality are mentioned in several treaties from the years 1419, 1432, 1445, 1468, 1469, and 1502. GLAK, 67/1431; see also GOETZ, Niedere Gerichtsherrschaft, pp. 109–110. According to Schubert, hospitality for hunting parties was one of the first obligations used by many princes to assert territorial authority. Idem, Fürstliche Herrschaft, p. 40.

manumission requests were denied with the clarification that until Heiligenberg agreed to free his serfs living in Salem's lands, the abbey would respond in kind.[127]

In a settlement of 1577, reached through the mediation of Überlingen's former mayor, Wolffgang Michael Beck, it was agreed that Salem should not demand court penalties of more than ten pounds.[128] This decision was mentioned specifically in the small council minutes on 25 January 1602, where it was stated that the penalty ceiling was suspended, rescinded, and nullified. From that point on, the record declared, the abbot or Audience would freely assign penalties over ten or fifteen pounds, up to twenty, thirty, forty, or more depending on the offense and the situation. Furthermore, any abbey subject who appeared before Heiligenberg's court without permission for whatever reason would face a fine of forty pounds.[129] This decision followed shortly after Salem and Heiligenberg entered a legal suit before the Imperial Chamber Court (*Reichskammergericht*) in Speyer. According to many later descriptions, this was a protracted and extremely costly affair that was never resolved to either side's satisfaction.[130]

Salem took the extreme step in 1615 of revoking all previous treaties and agreements acknowledging Heiligenberg's lordship rights within its lands. Among other documents relating to the oath of allegiance sworn to the newly elected abbot in 1615, following a tirade against Heiligenberg's attempts to control low justice in Salem's territory and failure to honor the abbey's ancient privileges, it was declared that henceforth the abbey would punish all offenses committed in its lands. Major crimes would be judged by the abbey's high court of appeals (*Hofgericht*) and any capital cases referred to Salem's secular officials and counselors. Anyone who disobeyed this ruling would be penalized with banishment from the land and a fine of one hundred gold crowns.[131] Naturally this decision did not sit well with the count, and soon yet another lawsuit began, this time in Prague. In 1616 the abbey's chancellor, Dr. Mattheus Klockh, published a booklet describing the legal arguments each side presented before the imperial arbitrators, along with all the privileges, exemptions, and agreements relating to the dispute from centuries past.[132] Several entries in the small council minutes from 1620 referred to the matter, and the seriousness of the situation is suggested by the fact that the entire convent assembled twice in November of that year to consider an official response to a letter from the count. It was unanimously decided, following each member's stated response

---

127 In response to the manumission request of Marx Rietter in 1624, for example, the Audience declared: "Wan Heiligenberg seine und'thonen, so unter Salem stalten, ledig lasse, wöll man ihn alhie auch ledig geben." Only a few entries later, Agatha Binderin received a similar decision. GLAK, 61/13373.

128 GLAK, 67/1431; 67/1782.

129 GLAK, 67/13315.

130 FEYERABEND, Chronik, pp. 250, 254–255. The suit began in or around 1595.

131 GLAK, 98/1547, fol. 164v–166v.

132 Mattheus KLOCKH, ed., Anticategoriae zwaier Fürnemmer deß Hayl. Röm. Reichsständen Hailgenberg und Salmansweyl wegen ihrer hincinde habenden und praetendirten Privilegien und Verträgen, 1616.

to a formal inquiry (*Umfrag*), that the two sides should meet in order to work out an agreement—as long as it did not infringe on any of the abbey's imperial or papal privileges. In 1625 the small council expressed the desire to purchase all regalian rights the count claimed within the abbey's lordship.[133] In a new ordinance applied that year to the abbey's subjects in the Hegau near Madach, the stated penalties for several offenses were for amounts just slightly over the ten pound limit, a clear assertion of the abbey's claim that its officials could impose whatever fines they felt were necessary.[134] The legal conflict continued throughout the 1620s and 1630s, leaving behind an enormous amount of correspondence and documentation. Finally in 1637, a lasting solution was reached.

The treaty between Salem and Heiligenberg on 15 January 1637 was arbitrated by six mediators in the imperial city of Überlingen.[135] It involved the exchange of properties and derivative rights in a number of locations throughout the Linzgau, which established two separate, bounded spheres to be ruled exclusively by one authority or the other. In the territory Under the Hills, Salem was acknowledged to possess all the superior rights (*Hoheitsrechte*) previously claimed by Heiligenberg, specifically including regalian rights and high justice, along with any other rights possessed or pretended. In return, Salem renounced its claims including property and low jurisdiction in a number of settlements Over the Hills.[136] In the midst of the Thirty Years War, a most terrible and chaotic time, the two rulers and principal parties who entered the agreement were a most curious pair: on one side was Salem's Abbot Thomas Wunn, the abbey's former serf from the village of Grasbeuren. On the other was the widowed countess, Anna Maria of Heiligenberg, who was holding the throne in trust as a guardian for her young sons. Even without regard for the remarkable timing and personal leadership involved, the achievement of this peace was monumental. Salem had claimed the powers of an unmediated imperial estate for centuries, but now the major obstacle was finally cleared and the abbey's many different rights were fully recognized and defined within set boundaries. According to many historians, the compromise agreement in 1637 marked Salem's achievement of full territorial sovereignty (*Landeshoheit*).[137]

1.4 Chronology

The period under investigation is the long sixteenth century, reaching from the later Middle Ages through the early seventeenth century. The endpoints 1473 and 1637

133 61/13315, fol. 47v, 63r.

134 GLAK, 98/396.

135 The originals, as well as many copies, are found in GLAK, 4/1159–1164.

136 For a list of the specific places involved in the treaty, see BAIER, Staat und Kirche, p. 134; STAIGER, Salem oder Salmansweiler, p. 143.

137 BADER, Studien 2, p. 178; BAIER, Staat und Kirche, p. 134; RÖSENER, Salem, p. 80; KALLER, Salem, p. 345.

coincide with two events of political transformation in Salem. In the late 1460s a resistance movement began among Salem's 15 territorial judges, each of them an abbey subject from one of the surrounding villages. This conflict and its resolution in 1473 had much in common with a series of late medieval resistance movements among peasant subjects of other Southwest German abbeys. The arbitrated settlement reached in 1473 between the abbey and its peasants endured as the territory's legal and constitutional foundation throughout the early modern period. It regulated aspects of servility, tenure, inheritance, and other central issues of lordship. The study ends around the time of another legal agreement, the aforementioned treaty between Salem and Heiligenberg. This 1637 treaty acknowledged Salem's fully independent legal authority including high justice over the subjects of its central territory, with defined territorial boundaries and exemption from any claims of political overlordship by the counts.

The reader may be surprised to find that two other events, the Reformation and the German Peasants' War, play a far less significant role in this narrative.[138] Although it is framed by two political events, the organization and analysis of this study are more structural than chronological or episodic. This is based in part on the source material and in part on the recognition that this period of roughly 150 years corresponds not only to political developments and events but also to changes in the agrarian economy and village social life.[139] In these contexts, the period 1575–1625 forms the core of the inquiry.

Starting in the decade after 1580, the density of documentation in Salem's archive increases dramatically. Written records, traditionally a strength of monastic administration, now became a tool that was also used increasingly by peasants to secure their claims with regard to tenure, lawsuits, business transactions, legal status, and many other areas of political and daily life. Not only did the court, Audience, and chancery all begin keeping regular records in the 1580s, their entries contain frequent references

---

[138] The most important result of the Peasants' War was the confirmation and strengthening of pre-established political and social relations rather than any radical change. The evangelical cause had limited influence in the region, especially after 1531, since the region north of Lake Constance remained predominantly Catholic and because Salem did not attempt to impose strict religious reforms on its subjects, even during the confessional period. See Marc Forster, Catholic Revival in the Age of the Baroque: Religious Identity in Southwest Germany, 1550–1750, Cambridge and New York, 2001.

[139] Wilhelm Abel's price and wage shears analogy explains the long sixteenth century as a phase of expansion followed by contraction. His classic work, Agrarkrisen und Agrarkonjunktur, which first appeared in 1966 and was translated by Olive Ordish as Agricultural Fluctuations in Europe: From the Thirteenth to the Twentieth Centuries, London 1980, has come under fire more recently among economic historians. For the most part they agree on what happened and when; their differences focus on the causes and especially on the reasons for the economic stagnation and decline. Also still useful is T. H. Aston and C. H. E. Philpin, eds., The Brenner Debate: Agrarian Class Structure and Economic Development in Pre-Industrial Europe, Cambridge and New York 1985.

to peasants' submission of and requests for written documents. The surge in writing and the ways documents were used in the decades around 1600 highlight the territory's dynamic socioeconomic condition. In another new development, both the abbey and communal representatives expressed growing concern over poverty, begging, and the influx of new residents, and they began to impose stricter restrictions on immigration and housing, especially for territorial outsiders. In a period of tightening resources, servility became a means for denying strangers' access to residence, tenure, office-holding, and spouses, whereas a century earlier servility had been used primarily to bind the population to the soil and increase villagers' dependence and obligations to the lord. Other major issues after 1600 were debt and access to the common lands. In this period written instruments, including legal contracts and the territorial court records, built confidence in regional markets and business transactions. The rise in written records and in territorial regulations signifies not the lord's seizure of power from the commune, but rather, an attempt to provide greater stability on the part of ordinary villagers and their demand for greater accountability from territorial officials in order to promote their own interests and the common good.

In the early seventeenth century, issues of prior concern assumed greater urgency. Subjects, individually and collectively, voiced the expectation that the abbey should extend its aid. The number of petitions villagers brought before the Audience rose dramatically, as did the demand for notarized contracts. Debt was the most frequent topic considered by the court and recorded in the chancery.[140] In addition to greater enforcement of residency restrictions, new property requirements were placed on marriage around 1600. Complaints from villagers about overpopulation demonstrate that these social controls arose from the concerns of certain villagers, not or at least not only from the abbey's senior officials. Villagers increasingly requested alms, firewood and lumber, rent reduction, and debt forgiveness. They also sought assistance with grazing disputes and other local conflicts, sometimes involving divisions between wealthy tenants and poor cottars, other times pitting entire villages against one another. Yet wealthy local elites did not always control communal decisions or have their way. Despite a rising number of petitions brought on behalf of tenants and other groups, shared concerns as well as shifting constellations of interests helped maintain a balance within the community between the haves and have-nots. Failed harvests, troop crossings, tightening resources, and the spread of poverty affected everyone in the village. Issues such as the security of tenure and inheritance, conversion of wastes to vineyards, and the appointment and salary of communal officials affected individuals in various ways, yet all had vested interests in them.

---

[140] Debt is not clear evidence of decline. The land and credit markets suggest that debt was also at least in some cases a useful strategy. The availability of loans, especially from local parishes, allowed peasants to invest in property, settle inheritance portions, and meet various household demands. See Chapter 4.

There were no revolts among Salem's peasants in the early seventeenth century. In 1629–1630, however, the tenants of an entire district organized a movement to demand lower rents and other concessions from the abbey. In this case, the use of formal grievance procedures to resolve the conflict suggests villagers' preference for legal solutions over violent resistance.[141] Audience petitions suggest that peasant subjects were demanding more from their rulers in the early seventeenth century and that the pressure they applied paid off. Political change arose from a dialogue between abbey officials and subjects, and new policies were informed by villagers' concerns, especially in the socioeconomic sphere.

A constellation of factors, not simply a Malthusian ceiling or general market trends, determined Salem's declining economic situation in the early seventeenth century. Changes in land use, social controls, regional markets, and political pressure within the territory and its villages all contributed to the local economy and it was the interconnection between them that affected the situation much more than any isolated factor. The greater density of serial and other records after 1580 coincides with a critical period of socioeconomic restructuring and with a "search for stability."[142] Contrary to the traditional interpretation of increasing documentation, centralization, and regulation as signs of the lord's intrusion within the village, evidence from the economic sphere suggests that peasants' demands fueled the development of governing structures and territorial policy in Salem. The changes they initiated also demonstrate that villagers were not the passive victims of a declining situation.

The 1630s mark a convenient endpoint for the study, in socioeconomic as well as political terms. The Thirty Years War (1618–1648) caused major dislocation, especially in the early 1630s, wiping out rural infrastructure and resources including houses, livestock, grapevines, tools, and grain reserves.[143] In the short term, families and entire communities were devastated by population losses. The war's effects began with the occasional passage of troops, followed by a series of occupations by thousands of soldiers who devastated the countryside and its inhabitants during repeated and months-long winter quarterings. Sebastian Bürster's chronicle vividly portrays the misery of these years in Salem's villages.[144] The abbey's administrative structures survived the

---

141 Nonviolent methods also characterized collective resistance movements in 1473 and 1525. On the juridification of social conflict, see Winfried SCHULZE, Bäuerlicher Widerstand und feudale Herrschaft in der frühen Neuzeit, Stuttgart-Bad Canstatt 1980; idem, Die veränderte Bedeutung sozialer Konflikte im 16. und 17. Jahrhundert, in: Der deutsche Bauernkrieg 1524–1526, ed. Hans-Ulrich Wehler, Göttingen 1975, pp. 277–302.

142 ROBISHEAUX, Rural Society; SREENIVASAN, Ottobeuren.

143 The destruction of vineyards had long-term social and economic implications, since viticulture was the primary basis of the region's market specialization and it provided for a dense population of prosperous smallholders. Viticulture never fully recovered after the war. See EITEL, Überlingen, pp. 13, 21.

144 Friedrich von WEECH, ed., Sebastian Bürsters Beschreibung des Schwedischen Krieges, 1630–1647, Leipzig 1875.

conflict, but the few written records from the 1630s reflect the troubled times. Most of the population fled or perished, and though some remained and others returned after the war, there was also an influx of new residents, especially from the Swiss lands. This study's conclusion in the 1630s coincides with the decline in source material and the abrupt and devastating effects of war on the local population.

1.5 Outline of Chapters

Each of the five subsequent chapters is organized thematically. As a whole, progressing according to a loose chronology, they tell the story of Salem's political development over the long sixteenth century, highlighting the role of rural subjects in that process.

Chapter 2 deals with a dispute between the abbot and his territorial judges in the late fifteenth century. The documentation surviving from this conflict provides an unusual opportunity to view the negotiations between the abbey as lord and the territorial judges who acted on behalf of Salem's peasant subjects. The arbitrated settlement that finally ended the standoff after several failed mediation attempts may be seen as a compromise agreement. It set important ground rules for the territory's legal development and resolved several contested issues of lordship. The agreement of 1473 provided the foundations for the territory's political consolidation and for the participation of peasant subjects. In this sense, it served as a constitutional text throughout the period under study.

Chapter 3 covers a broader set of themes associated with two closely related topics, the German Peasants' War of 1525 and local communal organization. This chapter demonstrates the mobilization of ordinary villagers in mass numbers. Their participation brought a greater awareness of and impact on political formation both local and supralocal. The chapter also examines the village commune as a broadly inclusive form of local political organization. It considers some major challenges the commune faced internally and externally and offers a reassessment of the commune's role, its political capabilities, its leadership, and its relations to lordship in the period after 1525.

Chapter 4 delves more deeply into the socioeconomic structure of villages and households during the late sixteenth and early seventeenth centuries, demonstrating how the material needs and interests of various groups intersected and fueled the demand for regulation. The rise in documentation after 1580 and the picture that emerges from the sources in the decades around 1600—of wealth stratification, competition for land tenure, marriage alliances, inheritance disputes, debt levels, and land sales, among others—suggest that the territory's political development in this period was closely connected to the growing socioeconomic pressures and desire for greater stability felt by all members of the community.

Chapter 5 concerns the territorial court, known as the Sidelgericht, a somewhat unusual institution because of its social composition as well as its central role in substantiating Salem's claim to political autonomy as an unmediated territory within the empire. This chapter explains why the court formed the symbolic center of the territorial polity and how it combined the interests and influences of many territorial actors, resulting in the integration of community and lordship within governance and creating a shared political identity that had obvious benefits for all sides.

Chapter 6 concludes the study by focusing on a series of elements that combined to form the infrastructure of Salem's territorial rule. Some of these components were traditional whereas others were new in the early modern period, but together they served the common purpose of strengthening and consolidating territorial governance. As the points of intersection where the interests of various groups converged and came into conflict, each one provided an avenue for participation, dialogue, and ongoing negotiations. It was in these interactions that the governance of this small territorial polity evolved in the early modern period. Together the strands of political authority combined the influences and addressed the concerns of various groups, clasping them together in a constantly shifting matrix of lordship and community.

Chapter 2: Late Medieval Conflict, Negotiation, and the Foundations of Law in Salem's Land Under the Hills

On 3 September 1470 the abbot and 15 judges of Salem's territorial court, known as the *Sidelrichter*, waited for the bishop of Constance to pass judgment in their legal dispute. The suit had been brought by the abbot against the Sidelrichter, all of whom were his peasant subjects, for acts of resistance begun two years earlier. At issue were many subtleties concerning relations of lordship. Yet the primary question to be resolved was whether abbey dependents, in this case the territorial judges, were justified in their opposition to the lord's actions and commands—whether they were justified in refusing the loyalty oath, alienating themselves from the abbey, and seeking legal counsel and support against their lord—all because, in their view, his actions violated customary law.

This conflict, which unfolded between 1468 and 1473, is the subject of the current chapter. On 21 January 1473, an arbitrated compromise ended the altercation and laid the legal foundations for Salem's early modern political development.[1] The preceding five years of strife, carried out with words rather than violent deeds, provide us with an ideal opportunity to examine each side's views and assertions. Various texts elucidate not only the topics of disagreement but also the more general attitudes of the abbot and his peasants toward law and authority, customary rights and obligations. Perhaps most exciting is the view these texts afford of the negotiation process, the sources of legitimacy and strategies of persuasion each side employed. They demonstrate the complex evolution of legal relations, responsive to pressures from above and below, despite a conservative and traditional framework which purportedly held the law to be firm and unchanging. By listening closely to the arguments these texts contain, we can hear what each side said and even what they chose to leave unspoken. One thing becomes clear upon examination: this group of 15 peasants, the Sidelrichter, were skillful players at the game of politics.

The following investigation relies on a collection of primary sources unique in the documentation of peasant resistance movements. Historians are often aware of late medieval peasant revolts because of documentation arising from their resolution in written legal settlements or more violent conclusions. Such texts, however, cannot answer many important questions about the dispute itself, the ideas behind them, or the process that led to a final decision. Besides the settlement of 1473, Salem's archive contains several letters, receipts, and records from failed arbitration attempts that pro-

1 The text of this settlement is published together with other "agrarian constitutional agreements" from nine South German abbeys in BLICKLE and HOLENSTEIN, Agrarverfassungsverträge, pp. 53–62.

vide details of the conflict's escalation. The aforementioned decision by the bishop of Constance in 1470 is an extremely useful document. The forty pages of text leading up to the bishop's judgment go back and forth between the two sides, describing much of the legal testimony and counterarguments in the first-person plural form. This brings us as close as we will ever come to the peasant judges' own views and expressions. The bishop's 1470 decision is important also because it includes the earliest surviving version of the territory's customary legal code, known as the *alte Jarbrief*.[2] Although the articles of this text were the subject of passionate debate, both sides agreed that the alte Jarbrief had been used in some form since 1302, and according to the abbot, the version recorded in the 1460s was an identical copy of an earlier one from 1401. Other sources relating to the dispute and its evolution include private correspondence between the abbot and his allies, assessments of legal expenses, specifications of court procedure, lists of names, and legal clarifications. From this abundance of documentation, we are able to determine what was at stake and how the disputants supported their positions leading up to the final settlement. The situation in Salem, which pitted the abbot against his peasant judges, appears to have been quite similar to the experiences of many neighboring territories in the later Middle Ages, where conflicts between lords and subjects frequently ended in arbitrated settlements.[3] What sets Salem apart is that

2 The *alte Jarbrief* translates roughly as the "old annual letter," suggesting that it was traditionally read aloud and confirmed each year similar to other customary law codes known as *Weistümer*. Like most Weistümer, it may have originated in oral form. One important characteristic distinguishing Salem's alte Jarbrief from most Weistümer was its validity throughout the territory. A good introduction to the literature is Peter BLICKLE, ed., Deutsche ländliche Rechtsquellen: Positionen und Probleme der Weistumsforschung, Stuttgart 1997. See also Michael PROSSER, Spätmittelalterliche ländliche Rechtsaufzeichnungen am Oberrhein zwischen Gedächtniskultur und Schriftlichkeit: Untersuchungen am Übergang von analphabetischen zu skriptualen Überlieferungsformen im Blickfeld rechtlicher Volkskunde, Würzburg 1991; Gadi ALGAZI, Lords Ask, Peasants Answer: Making Traditions in Late-Medieval Village Assemblies, in: Between History and Histories: The Making of Silences and Commemorations, ed. Gerald Sider and Gavin Smith, Toronto 1997, pp. 199–229; Simon TEUSCHER, Textualising Peasant Enquiries: German Weistümer between Orality and Literacy, in: Charters and the Use of the Written Word in Medieval Society, ed. Karl Heidecker, Turnhout 2000, pp. 239–251.

3 See especially BLICKLE and HOLENSTEIN, Agrarverfassungsverträge; see also MAURER, Territorialgewalt, pp. 151–195; HOLENSTEIN, Äbte und Bauern, pp. 237–262; ULBRICH, Leibherrschaft; SAARBRÜCKER ARBEITSGRUPPE, Probleme der spätmittelalterlichen Leibeigenschaft in Oberschwaben, in: Zeitschrift für Agrargeschichte und Agrarsoziologie 22 (1974), pp. 9–33; Peter BIERBRAUER, Der Aufstieg der Gemeinde und die Entfeudalisierung der Gesellschaft im späten Mittelalter, in: Kommunalisierung und Christianisierung: Voraussetzungen und Folgen der Reformation, 1400–1600, ed. Peter Blickle and Johannes Kunisch, Berlin 1989, pp. 29–56; idem, Bäuerliche Revolten im Alten Reich: Ein Forschungsbericht, in: Aufruhr und Empörung? Studien zum bäuerlichen Widerstand im Alten Reich, ed. Peter Blickle, Munich 1980, pp. 1–68; BLICKLE, Revolution of 1525. The regional context and relevant literature is discussed more fully in BRUN, Abbot and Peasants (2008 diss.), pp. 66–85.

the surviving evidence allows us to contextualize the final agreement and to delve more deeply into the conditions, events, and points of conflict that fueled the crisis and made intervention necessary.[4]

This chapter pursues several objectives. First, it describes the major sources of conflict and escalation. Second, it explores the peasant judges' views on lordship and the law through a closer examination of their demands. Third, it looks at the legitimation strategies and resources they used to bolster their arguments and insist on a leading role in the territory's political policies and practices. Finally, it evaluates the terms of compromise established in 1473.

2.1 Chronology of Dispute and Points of Conflict

The conflict between Salem's abbot and the Sidelrichter began sometime in 1468, but the first written records appear in 1470. Before turning to the causes of controversy, it is worth mentioning a few significant statements on which the parties could agree. First, all adult subjects of the abbey were required to swear an oath, "not to alienate themselves from the abbey, not to seek other or outside protection, to uphold the freedoms and old traditions of the abbey, and to do everything to the best of their ability for the abbey's aid and benefit."[5] Second, there existed an ancient law code known as the alte Jarbrief, with many articles pertaining to the abbey's traditions and customs. Third, the abbey had a central court called the Sidelgericht, composed of 15 peasant subjects, who decided all misdemeanor cases from throughout the territory.[6] These judges, the Sidelrichter, swore an annual oath of office: "To judge and to decide according to freedom, custom, old tradition and statutes, without favoritism or bias, as their predecessors on this same court have also done for longer than anyone can remember."[7] Finally, both sides agreed that until 1468, the 15 territorial judges had sworn these oaths and spoken the law without complaint and without the abbey's interference. In 1468, however, an event galvanized the Sidelrichter to the point that they refused to renew their oaths, resigned from their posts, and left the territory in search of legal counsel.

---

4 Documentation from the negotiations leading to a final settlement also exists for Ochsenhausen; BLICKLE and HOLENSTEIN, Agrarverfassungsverträge, pp. 73–102.

5 "Sich dem gotzhus nit zů empfrembden nit andern oder frembden shirm zu suchen das gotzhus by sinen fryhaitten und altem herkomen beliben zulassen und daby so vil und an Ir ist helffen zu hannthaben." GLAK, 4/120, fol. 1r.

6 In addition to "low justice" (minor offenses), the court had jurisdiction over tenure disputes and certain types of cases involving "flowing wounds," but not "high justice" (capital crimes) or spiritual offences (including marriage disputes).

7 "Nach fryhaitt gewonhaitt altem herkomen und Statuten zůrichten und zů urtailn niemand zů lieb noch zů laid Als das Ir vordern an dem selben gericht och getan habn lennger dann yeman verdenncken mag." GLAK, 4/120, fol. 1r.

The abbot's position was simple. He insisted in each of his statements that the Sidelrichter were disobedient in refusing their duty to speak the law according to the abbey's traditions. More importantly, they had fled the abbey's lands and sought foreign aid and protection against their rightful lord and their oath. These actions were clear violations of the obligations all abbey subjects owed, and they surely deserved to be punished in accordance with the alte Jarbrief. Because the Sidelrichter were territorial officials responsible for maintaining territorial law, their disobedience was particularly reprehensible. As examples for the entire community of subjects, their insubordination caused the abbey great cost and damage and was leading to ever increasing resistance among the rest of the abbey's dependents.

Through their legal spokesman, the Sidelrichter responded that their actions since the conflict broke out were by no means disobedient or in violation of their sworn oath. They explained that they had resigned their posts because of the abbot's obstruction of the legal process. They rejected the charges of oath-breaking and alienation by describing their actions as simply leaving or "going out," as if for a stroll, rather than in terms of estrangement.[8] They asserted that they had simply gone out in search of legal advice, which was an act protected by the ancient traditions of the abbey and their freedoms as territorial judges.[9] They resorted to this action, they added, only after failed attempts to reason with abbey officials and upon the advice of priests and others, who agreed that they had reason to fear for their salvation if they submitted to the abbot's demands.

The Sidelrichter did not limit themselves to defending their own actions. In fact, most of their arguments served to criticize the abbot and show his assertions of authority to be unlawful. According to recent innovations, they protested, the abbot no longer recognized their traditional freedom to seek outside legal counsel. In addition, he expected them to swear an amended oath of office. The new oath explicitly required them to base legal decisions solely on the articles of a revised legal code, deceptively called the alte Jarbrief, that defied territorial custom and prevented them from finding and speaking the law as they had always done before. Should the written law fail to address the issue at hand, or if further clarification were necessary, the abbot demanded that they consult him or his representative and no one else. These innovations were cause for great concern, the Sidelrichter explained, since in the past,

> We often consulted the Jarbrief for instructions concerning judgment, after complaints and responses according to the nature of the case. Yet we also found the law according to our own conscience and knowledge. If a case were ever too difficult to decide, we were not required

---

8 Whereas the abbey used the term *empfrembden* to describe their actions, the Sidelrichter preferred the term *sich ußern*, which meant something like "to go out" or "go abroad" (unlike the modern German verb *sich äußern*, to express oneself).

9 This privilege evidently stemmed from their status as territorial judges, because the abbey's common dependents (or at least its serfs) did not have the right to seek outside advice in legal matters. Since the judges' right to seek outside counsel or the prohibition thereof was undocumented, each side had to rely on oral argument to bolster their positions.

> in any way to follow the abbey's freedoms. That is, we would go to the city of Überlingen, to Heiligenberg's officials, or to others of the abbey's neighbors, in order to seek counsel. Then, after we had found counsel and also according to our best understanding and conscience, the freedoms, good traditions, and old customs of the land, yes then and only then were we able to speak the law.[10]

The Sidelrichter vehemently opposed the so-called alte Jarbrief, a replacement document issued some years earlier and said to be an exact copy of the original text. They contrasted their desire to serve honorably and obediently with the abbot's deliberate introduction of unlawful changes: "What our lord and his officials intended, however, and put to us in words that made their desire unmistakable, was that they wanted us to hear a new roll they had created and written, and they wished to discuss it further with us afterward. At that time we were willing in this and in other matters, and so we listened as the new roll was read."[11] Upon examination, they discovered that the wording of the text was not the same as in previous years. On the contrary, it contained all sorts of new claims in violation of the territory's freedoms and the customs of its inhabitants. After hearing the new roll, they continued, "it was demanded and required that we 15 Sidelrichter should accept and swear the aforementioned oath to this court with the explicit qualification that upon our oath, we would no longer seek or receive any counsel."[12] The Sidelrichter identified the revisions as an effort to curtail their role in the judicial process and monopolize justice in the abbey's own interests. Not only did they oppose the abbot's innovations and interference, they saw it as their moral duty to uphold the law according to tradition and their previously sworn oaths. As the guardians of justice, they emphasized, the abbot's demands burdened their consciences so that they feared eternal damnation. It was for these reasons, the Sidelrichter explained, that they left the territory to seek advice from their neighbors as they had always done in the past.

---

10 "Sonnder habn wir nach clagen anntwurtn offt nach gestalt der clag und sachn, den Jarbrieff fur uns genomen, mochten wir dann In dem Jarbrieff underrichtung des Recht sprechens och nach unnser gewissin recht zusprechen finden, ward zů zitten also Recht gesprochn wolt unns aber ain sach zuswer recht zusprechen sin, So syen wir allweg unverdingt gewesen des gotzhus fryhaitt nachzuvolgn. Das ist also das wir mochten zů überlingen by den Amptlutten der graufschaft zum hailigenberg und andern bysessen des gotzhus Salmenswiler und an söllichen jetzigen enden Rathabn und dann nach der end wir an Rat funden, och nach unnser selbs besten verstentnuss und gewissin fryhaitten gütten lanndsgewonhaittn und altem herkomen, wol recht sprechen möchten." GLAK, 4/120, fol. 2v.

11 "Was aber den vorgenantn unnsern herren von Salmenswiler und sin amptherren genaigt hab ... und an uns mit mercklichen worten begerend gewesen sind, Sy haben ainen nuwen rodel machen und schriben lassen, den wöllen sy uns hörn lassen und dann wyter mit unns reden lassen. Also syen wir willig geweßen An den und andern sachen und haben also den nuwen rodel hörn lesen." Ibid., fol. 3r.

12 "Ward an uns fünffzechen Sidelrichter begert und ervordert, wir solten den aid wie vorlutt zu disem gericht sweren und dartzů In den Aid mit namlichem bedingt nemen und swern das wir an dhainem aid mer dehainen raut suchen noch haben." Ibid., fol. 3r.

The Sidelrichter pressed even further, submitting detailed responses to each of the contested law code's 37 articles and expanding on their grievances.[13] We will return to some of these complaints below, but here one issue deserves particular mention, namely, the Sidelrichter repeatedly asserted in response to several articles that they were the "people of God's house" (*gotzhuslut*) and not the abbey's bondsmen or its serfs (*aigenlut*).[14] This proved to be one of the major points of disagreement. Yet repudiation of the term *aigenlut* and the status it implied was only tangentially related to their defense, as was their lengthy discussion of the alte Jarbrief's articles more generally, since the suit against them made no mention of the abbey's legal code. The peasant judges' response was therefore more than simple justification; they were taking the opportunity to assert their own objections to lordship. The Sidelrichter were on trial for acts of disobedience, but in fact, the charges against them stemmed largely from their previous attempts to press charges against the abbot. These earlier actions had failed when the abbot refused to recognize the authority they allegedly possessed to "seek legal counsel," but now that the two sides had entered legal proceedings on the abbot's terms, the Sidelrichter seized the chance to lay out the grievances that had sparked the conflict in the first place and which had been denied any previous hearing.

The abbot denied the judges' charges in a written counterresponse.[15] He did admit that the document in question was not the ancient, previously used manuscript, but as he explained, this newer copy was an exact duplicate of the alte Jarbrief that was now so badly damaged from centuries of use that it could no longer be read.

> We and our predecessors have established the new roll or Jarbrief according to the exact meaning and contents of an old parchment roll, which the defendants and their predecessors have used and sworn to uphold for the past 60 years. Through such long usage, the writing was almost completely faded, … and its pages needed mending, so eight years ago we had it copied word for word without addition or deletion so that the two copies were identical in wording and

13 A condensed version of this text (from GLAK, 66/7347) is included as an appendix in: Hermann BAIER, Zur Vorgeschichte des Bauernkriegs, in: Zeitschrift für die Geschichte des Oberrheins 78 (1926), pp. 208–218.

14 *Gotzhuslut*, or *Gotteshausleute*, was a term referring to the dependents of a religious foundation, in this case Salem. It was ambiguous with respect to servility status. See Walter MÜLLER, Freie Gotteshausleute: Zur Problematik ständischer Benennungen in Quellen des 14. bis 17. Jahrhunderts, in: Zeitschrift der Savigny-Stiftung, Germanistische Abteilung 92 (1975), pp. 89–104. Claudia Ulbrich (Leibherrschaft, p. 255) demonstrates a connection in this period between the consolidation of territorial authority, tightening restrictions on serfs, and lords' new insistence on terms such as *Eigenleute* and *Leibeigene Leute* to replace earlier designations such as *arme Leute* ("poor folk" or "humble commoners"). Hannah Rabe argued that late medieval peasants used the term *Leibeigene* to emphasize their objections to the oppressive nature of personal bondage in her provocative study, Das Problem Leibeigenschaft: Eine Untersuchung über die Anfänge einer Ideologisierung und des verfassungsrechtlichen Wandels von Freiheit und Eigentum im deutschen Bauernkrieg, Wiesbaden 1977; see also BLICKLE, Revolution of 1525, p. 30.

15 The bishop described his position in GLAK, 4/120.

in every other way ... They [the Sidelrichter] also swore according to their previous oath and upheld this same new copy of the Jarbrief, judging accordingly for six years ... and we hope that this letter, the words of which remain the same even though the parchment has been replaced, should be accepted and referred to not as a new document but rather as the old letter and the old statutes.[16]

The abbot went on to discount the defendants' objections against the preamble to the disputed text. The Sidelrichter had protested that although they had never seen or heard, much less agreed to abide by the document, it named them as participants in the document's creation. Their implication was that the abbot had lied about their inclusion, meaning to trick them and thereby press the judges along with other subjects into submission. The abbot pointed out their misunderstanding while insisting on the document's age in his explanation that the passage in question, along with the entire text, had been written by their predecessors generations earlier. He declined to respond to accusations concerning the specific articles of the alte Jarbrief, insisting that the suit concerned his subjects' disobedience and not the abbey's old traditions. He was the plaintiff in this case, and it was not the defendants' prerogative to bring up impertinent topics.

Now let us return to the bishop's judgment. The question at hand was whether subjects were justified in resisting rulers' commands when they felt their customary rights had been violated. In such a case, could they legitimately refuse the loyalty oath, flee their ruler's lands, and seek counsel and support against him from legal advisors and even neighboring political powers? The authorization of such acts would severely limit the lord's authority to command and prohibit, especially since the abbot's privileges forbade dependents to appear before any court but the lord's own, and because serfs could not move freely or seek outside protection against his demands. Were there standards of law transcending the powers of a lord over his subjects, and did subjects have the authority to hold lords accountable? These questions related in complex ways to the social and political order not only in Salem but also for other territories and the empire as a whole.

After carefully studying the case and considering massive amounts of evidence, the bishop and his advisors reached a decision. They declared: "We recognize ... the Sidelrichter to be released, acquitted, and freed from the claims reported by our friend and lord of Salmansweiler and his convent and to be absolved of all costs and damages.

16 "Wir und unnser vordern haben des nuwen Rodels oder Jarbriefs nach glicher begriffung und Innehaltung ainen alten permetin Rodel gehebt, der by Sechtzig Jarn gebrucht gehalten und gesworn ist, durch die Anttwurter, und Ir vordern an dem Sidelgericht der, was durch söllichn lanngen bruch an der geschrift vast verblichn, ... das man den zůsame näyen must, den haben wir vor acht Jarn lassen abschribn von wort zů wort und nichtz davon noch darzů getan dan dz die zwen brieff noch Ir lutt In allweg gelich gemacht sind ... Sy haben och den selben nuwen Jarbrief sechs Jar gesworn, der by den aiden so sy vor getan hetten, gehalten und darnach geurtailt ... wir hoffen och das durch endrung des berments wann Innehaltung der geschrift belibt, Söllichs nit ain nuwer brieff [b]esonnder der alt brieff und die alten Stattutta genembt und gehaissen werdn und sin söllen." GLAK, 4/120, fol. 13r–v.

Thus ends this court action against the Sidelrichter."[17] The bishop's decision did not end the legal action, however. In fact, it made matters even worse, because its ambiguity allowed for major differences in interpretation. Less than a year later, at both parties' request, the bishop of Constance provided an explanation of his earlier decision. Meanwhile, however, the peasant judges' rejection of the abbot's commands and their collaboration with advisors outside the territory were upheld as legitimate actions. The Sidelrichter were even awarded compensation from the abbey for costs and damages resulting from the suit against them.

The next surviving record in the ongoing dispute comes from 20 March 1471, and it concerns the accounting of legal expenses the abbey owed the Sidelrichter. It takes us back in time, as it describes the judges' actions since the outbreak of hostilities in 1468. We catch a glimpse of earlier court hearings, attempts by several important regional leaders and associations to reinstate peace, the presentation of witness testimony and production of written evidence, contacts with lawyers, innkeepers, and scribes—in sum, every financial expenditure the defendants made during the early stages of the conflict. The measures taken in this period make it even more remarkable that the Sidelrichter were able to convince the bishop and his advisors of their plea: "Venerable prince and honorable gracious lord, if the aforementioned accusations were true and we had acted in such a way, we would be highly deserving of harsh punishment both in and outside the law. Nevertheless, if God wills, it will never again be said that we acted in such a way, because the truth is that we left for a time but we never alienated ourselves from the abbey."[18]

After the Sidelrichter refused the oath in 1468, their very first action was to approach an ecclesiastical ruler who possessed some limited authority over Salem, who had also been in conflict with the abbots over many centuries in matters both spiritual and temporal. The Sidelrichter chose to address the bishop of Constance, they said, because their grievances against the abbey stemmed from moral concern, and because the bishop was the highest spiritual authority in the diocese. The text summarizes their initial actions as follows:

> First, when they were forced to go away and leave their homes, wives, and children, because of the matters described in the suit, they came before our merciful lord of Constance, placed their grievances before him, and called on his grace and on his gracious scholars for help and security against their gracious lord of Salmansweiler. So our merciful lord of Constance wrote to their lord of Salmansweiler of their requests, but the abbot did not respond in a timely man-

---

17 "Erkennen wir ... die Sidelrichter der angezognen anspräch des benempten unßer frunds und herren von Salmenswiler und sins Conuents ledig müssig und unengolten mit ablegung costens und schadens den benanten Sidelnrichtern dis gerichts hanndels halb daruff erganngen." Ibid., fol. 20r.

18 "Hoch wirdiger furst och Erwirdigen gnedigen herren, Zu den obgeschribnen clagenden worten, wann die also an Im selbs waren und wir also gehanndelt hetten, wurde uns In und usserhalb des rechten hoch und swerlich zugemessen das sich aber ob gott wil von unns also gehanndelt oder geschechen niemer ervinden sol und wie sich des sachen begeben das wir unns ain Zit geussert Aber von dem gotzhus nie empfrembdt haben." Ibid., fol. 3r.

ner. Finally, he answered the bishop that according to counsel he could not take it upon himself to respond to such claims.[19]

This passage suggests the underlying tensions between the two spiritual lords. Not only was the abbot unwilling to hear his subjects' grievances, he was also slow to respond to the bishop and loath to submit to his judgment. At the same time, the description is a bold statement of the peasant judges' own asserted liberties, since they freely admitted seeking help and security but at the same time claimed to be loyal subjects who never sought or accepted outside protection.

Since the abbot refused to accept the bishop's mediation, the Sidelrichter left Constance in search of other sympathetic ears, someone who might compel the abbot to hear their grievances.

> So they went to Überlingen, and upon counsel they presented themselves to the Landvogt to petition for an amicable resolution of the dispute. They had to wait for a long time, during which they spent 52 gulden on scribes and messengers. After that, they received a letter of safe-conduct from the Landvogt, but they were unable to come to an agreement with their lord of Salmansweiler before the safe-conduct ran out, so some of them went back to Constance while others went to Überlingen to take counsel. They were advised as before to go back once again to their gracious lord of Constance and appeal to his justice. So they returned to Constance, where a letter from the abbot gave as his answer that upon counsel, he could not find any reason to respond to such claims.[20]

If the initial attempt to secure the bishop's support was a challenge to the abbot's political authority, this visit to the Landvogt was even more so. The Landvogt was not only an imperial governor and neighboring ruler, he was also the abbey's guardian or lay protector *(Schirmherr)*, making him one of the greatest potential obstacles to the full realization of Salem's status as a free and unmediated imperial estate.

---

19 "Des ersten als Sj von der Sachen wegen In den Clagen begriffen von Irm hushaben wyben und kunden ussren und von dannen wychen musten, kommen sy zu unnserm gnedigen herren von Costenntz, Clagten siner gnaden und Rufften sin gnad an umb hilff und Sicherhaitt für sin gnad und siner gnaden gelerten zu Recht gegen Irm gnedigen Herren von Salmenswyler. Also ließ unnser gnediger herr von Costenntz, Ir beger nach, Irm herren von Salmenswyler schryben das Inen guter zyt antwurt nit werden mocht. Zu letst ward unnserm gnedigen herren antwurt gebenn, uff Solch antwurt Sj an Raut nit finden kunden sich haimzefügen." GLAK, 4/121, fol. 1r.

20 "Item darnach kamen Si gen Überlingen und funden an Rat an Iren Herren den Landtvogt Zewerbend umb ainen gütlichen tag und wartetend lanng. Also domals verzerten Sj und gabend den schrybern und botten funfzig und zwen guldin. Item darnach als Inen von Irem herren dem Lanndtvogt ain gelait gegeben ward Und mit Irm herren von salmenswyler nit geainiget werden mochtend, Und das gelait ufgeng, fügtend sich Iro etlich gen Costenntz ain tail gen Überlingen alda Rat Zehabend Wie Sj Zu den Sachen hanndeln solten, funden Sy aber an Rat wie vor noch ainmal Iren gnedigen herren von Costenntz aber umb Recht anzerüffend Das Sj ouch getan haben und ward von Wegen siner gnaden aber geschriben ward aber Antwurt geben Das Sy aber nit an Rat funden kinden sich uff Solch antwurt haym zefügend." Ibid., fol. 1r–1v.

Before long, the abbot filed his own legal action against his peasant judges, first with the Knights of St. George's Shield and later with the bishop of Constance. While they waited for the bishop, who was away on other business, the Sidelrichter decided to seek refuge and counsel from yet another patron, the political significance of which was hard to ignore. According to their testimony, mounting expenses forced them to travel across the lake to the town of Wil in the Thurgau, where they stayed with friends and waited for arrangements in Constance to unfold. These friends explained the legal situation to the mayor and city council, who in turn petitioned their associates, the heads of the Swiss Confederation. "Through much pleading and effort it came about that their lords, the Swiss Confederates, agreed to be present at the upcoming hearing in Constance, to apply all their energy, and to oppose their lords of Salmanswiler insistently and in all seriousness. In these ways, they hoped to bring the matter to justice according to their desire."[21] It is true that the practice of legal arbitration north of Lake Constance had been established largely on the Swiss example.[22] Nevertheless, it was commonly feared among South German rulers that the Swiss political example might well lead their subjects to rebellion, and they expressed great concern over signs that their peasants were "turning Swiss."[23] In this context, it is noteworthy that the abbot first aired his own grievances before the Knights of St. George's Shield.[24] The standoff between the abbot and his judges, supported respectively by the Knights of St. George's Shield and the Wil city councilors, was reminiscent of the situation on the eve of the Appenzeller War only a few generations earlier.

---

21 "Mit vil bitt und arbait ward es darzu gebracht das Ir herren die Aidgenossen zusagtend Das Sy uff dem tag zu Costentz so sin wurde, allen Irn vlysß ton wolten, und drungenlich an Irn herren von Salmenswyler mit ernst ankeren, damit sy hofften und die Sach darzu bringen wolten das die Sach mit Recht nach Irer beger, Wie vor Lut, gehanndelt und von Inen ufgenomen wurde." GLAK, 4/121, fol. 1v.

22 Karl Siegfried BADER, Die Entwicklung und Verbreitung der mittelalterlichen Schiedsidee in Südwestdeutschland und in der Schweiz, in: Ausgewählte Schriften zur Rechts- und Landesgeschichte, vol. 2, Sigmaringen 1984, p. 245. Other models for the arbitration courts in this region were the Roman Church and northern Italian city-states.

23 Thomas A. BRADY Jr., Turning Swiss: Cities and Empire, 1450–1550, Cambridge and New York 1985. According to Philip Robinson, this small territorial town belonging to St. Gallen Abbey may not have been such a threat after all. Wil remained loyal to the abbey during the tumultuous years of the late fifteenth and early sixteenth centuries, he says, as a result of its relatively privileged status compared with the older parts of the territory. Politically, therefore, Wil's position diverged from that of the more rebellious city of St. Gallen. Idem, Die Fürstabtei St. Gallen und ihr Territorium, 1463–1529: Eine Studie zur Entwicklung territorialer Staatlichkeit, St. Gallen 1995, pp. 76–77.

24 This mostly aristocratic society of South German lords formed in 1407 as a regional peacekeeping association in response to the threat posed by peasants from Appenzell and their "League above the Lake." Salem was an occasional member of the society, which had the important function of arbitrating disputes involving its associates. The Knights of St. George were also a precursor for the Swabian League.

After securing Swiss support through their friends in Wil, the Sidelrichter worked to prepare their case and stayed outside the territory despite their loyalty oath and the abbot's command. Several court hearings took place in the months before September 1470, as the list of legal expenses indicates. Not only were there a number of appearances before the bishop, there were at least two apparently unsuccessful mediation attempts at the abbey in Salmansweiler, one by the Landvogt and the other by the Knights of St. George's Shield.

The bishop's judgment in 1470 resulted from a suit the abbot filed against his judges, but this case came in response to the peasant judges' earlier attempts to take legal action and gain support against the abbey. With their overtures to powerful rulers including the bishop of Constance, the Landvogt of Upper Swabia, and the Swiss Confederation, it becomes clear what moved the abbot to bring suit against his subjects on charges of alienation, outside protection, and oath-breaking. For the same reasons, it is clear that the Sidelrichter had much at stake when they argued for their ancient privilege as territorial judges, to consult legal experts and other advisors beyond the territory, in order to find and speak judgments in accordance with the law. In light of their bold and risky actions as well as the prohibitions on mobility and outside protection customary in Salem's villages and elsewhere, it is remarkable that the bishop of Constance ruled in the judges' favor.

This decision, as previously noted, did not diminish the conflict. The bishop's statement left great uncertainty as to which of the abbey's claims and charges against the Sidelrichter had been declared invalid. Moreover, the judges interpreted their victory in the broadest possible way. According to the abbot's later testimony, as well as a report from the archbishop of Mainz, they declared they were not the abbey's serfs and that they were free from the abbot's odious restrictions against their freedoms and traditions. Eight months later, the ailing Abbot Ludwig Oschwald (r. 1458–1471) resigned to be replaced by Abbot Johannes Stantenant (r. 1471–1494), who was previously the abbot in Lützel and possibly Salem's prior before his election.[25] As the Sidelrichter complained, this new abbot enforced the contested Jarbrief and other demands even more harshly than his predecessor, now twisting the bishop's decision in his own favor. Upon their return home, the abbot had the Sidelrichter apprehended and imprisoned. To curb the growing crisis, the two parties asked the bishop to clarify his previous judgment. He did so on 2 August 1471, stating in an official charter: "We did not mean in our former decision to speak, recognize, or decide, nor have we spoken, recognized, or decided on issues of serfdom, death taxes, heritability, the right to command and prohibit, services, freedoms, customs, traditions, or other issues pertaining to the abbey's justice."[26] This

[25] GLAK, 4/755. There is some controversy surrounding Abbot Johann Stantenant's election; see Chapter 6.

[26] "Das wir in sollicher unnser vorgesprochen urtail nit in mainung gewesen sind ze sprechen ze erkennen oder ze urtailen. Haben ouch nit gesprochen erkennt oder geurtailt umb aigenschafft väll läss bott verbott dienst fryhait gewonhaiten harkomen und dieselben des Gotzhuß gerechtikaiten." GLAK, 4/122.

explanation produced no more agreement than before. The abbot expressed satisfaction that the case was finally closed, but the peasants were so outraged by what they saw as an unlawful reversal of the earlier judgment in their favor that they now took their claims before the emperor. He agreed to hear their complaints and gave them a letter of safe-conduct, valid until a settlement could be reached. At first, the emperor authorized an arbitration committee from Constance to speak in his name. Yet both parties refused to accept the commission's powers and the attempt failed. The Sidelrichter again appealed to the emperor. This time they were heard by the Imperial Chamber Court on 25 February 1472.[27] Presiding over the court, the archbishop of Mainz confirmed both the bishop's 1470 decision and his later clarification, saying that the decision had been unnecessarily appealed. The Imperial Chamber Court now declared the Sidelrichter responsible for paying the abbey's legal costs (480 fl., later raised to 556 fl.). Still the dispute remained unsettled, because the Sidelrichter insisted that their original grievances had not yet been addressed. Eleven months passed before there came another, more lasting judgment.

Meanwhile, surviving drafts of the abbot's correspondence reveal a flurry of activity and discussion at the imperial court in Vienna. Both parties had legal representatives there to lobby in their favor as well as to draw up the necessary legal documents. Letters exchanged between the abbot and his supporters during these months reveal a sense of urgency. Not only did the abbot write personally to the emperor, he petitioned his political allies to do the same. Letters from Archduke Sigismund of Austria, the Knights of St. George's Shield, the archbishop of Mainz, and the bishop of Constance implored the emperor to end the safe-conduct and punish the abbey's subjects, citing the threat not only to Salem's authority but also to all the rulers in the empire.[28] The letter from the bishop of Constance is especially noteworthy, since it demonstrates that he was by this point fully behind the abbey. Finally, there came from Vienna a letter to the abbot. It announced that six arbitrators would hear the appeal of the Sidelrichter in the imperial city of Überlingen. The men appointed to this task made their decision on 21 January 1473, bringing five long years of conflict to a close.

2.2 Negotiating Law and Lordship

It is unfortunate that older versions of the contested Jarbrief have not survived for our scrutiny. It is impossible to be certain whether the text disputed in 1468 was worded the same as in the past (whether for 6, 60, or 160 years), or in what specific ways it may have differed. The lack of written documentation about earlier legal customs helps determine the direction of our inquiry. It encourages us to look at the claims each side made and focus carefully on the meanings behind conflicting assertions. We do not

27 GLAK, 4/126.
28 GLAK, 98/1562–1563.

know the legal status of the Sidelrichter in 1460, for example, but we can look at their grounds for saying they were not serfs in 1470 and ask why serfdom was such a central issue at that time. We cannot say for sure if the alte Jarbrief underwent recent or significant alterations, but we can examine what each side said about statutes and traditions and what they thought their respective roles should be in determining, declaring, and maintaining the law. The legal arguments put forward in and around 1470 provide an unusual opportunity to view the attitudes and interests that contributed to political relations between the abbey and its territorial subjects.

Just as it affects our line of questioning, the limited availability of evidence also influenced the disputants' strategies of argumentation. In the absence of written proof, each side had to struggle to support its point of view, defend its actions, and assign blame to the opposing party. The lack of texts allowed much greater room for maneuver within that nebulous body of ideas called "custom," especially for the peasant judges, who were masters of the oral tradition. On the surface, many of the statements the abbot and Sidelrichter made over the course of the dispute addressed particular, alleged acts and abuses by one side or the other, such as whether the Sidelrichter had violated their oath of obedience to the abbot and whether he had obstructed *Recht* ("right," in the sense of both conscience and tradition) through changes to the statutes and the oath. Underlying these immediate accusations existed a much broader dispute involving the limitations on lordship and the sources of legal authority. The arguments expressed by the two parties display a mixture of conviction and strategy. Each side deployed political concepts that were commonly understood and widely acknowledged, but which could also support interpretations by no means acceptable to all. Behind such central words as "custom" or "conscience," complex webs of meaning were woven from different social contexts to promote a variety of different goals. Using shared language, ruler and ruled worked to construct and reconstruct alternative structures of authority and values.

It has been suggested that peasant resistance in the later Middle Ages was largely the result of political experience and self-confidence on the part of the peasant community and not merely a reaction to the intensification of lordship or the result of crushing burdens.[29] Here we will examine the peasant judges' claims in order to demonstrate their understanding of lordship and law as well as their ability to engage the political hierarchy in a discussion of the legal order on their own terms. In an effort to come closer to the peasants' legal mentality, we will pay special attention to the arguments the Sidelrichter put forward. The objectives are twofold: to demonstrate the political efficacy of Salem's peasants in the later Middle Ages and to come out with a better understanding of how the peasant judges viewed the law.

---

29 Karl Siegfried BADER, Bauernrecht und Bauernfreiheit im späteren Mittelalter, in: Ausgewählte Schriften zur Rechts- und Landesgeschichte, vol. 2, Sigmaringen 1984, p. 35; idem, Studien 1, p. 13.

Central to the dispute in Salem was the concept of *Recht*, which could mean law, justice, or right, and often meant all three. Closely linked to claims about Recht were ideas about custom and tradition, because in this period law was by definition old. In their response to individual articles as well as their general defense, the Sidelrichter expressed the common refrain that the abbey's demands went against the old customs and traditions of the land. They rejected the alleged innovations of the new law code but accepted the alte Jarbrief (in its earlier version) on the grounds of tradition, even though they objected to some of its articles: "We have always heard that between two evil things, however bad they both may be, still the one is to be chosen over the other. This is why we have chosen to swear by the old roll."[30] The grounding of Recht in old customs and traditions was not, however, a conception held by commoners alone. The rhetoric of the abbey's legal depositions insisted on this same idea of law as something old and traditional, the main difference being the content of the asserted traditions. Instead of claiming the right to create new traditions when the Sidelrichter accused him of innovation, the abbot maintained that his statutes and oaths, as well as his subjects' dutiful acceptance of them, reached back beyond human memory.

The peasantry's insistence on old law has led many to judge the peasant rebels (as well as church leaders) as reactionary, defensive, and unable to bring change or make new demands of their own. Even Peter Blickle, who has called for more research on the meaning of old law and on the people's understanding of Recht, and who is himself one of the greatest advocates of the common man's political capabilities, has made statements such as "certainly no claims for tomorrow could be made based on a law from yesterday," and "his legal thinking ... could not master the problems of a rapidly changing social and political order, being bound to ancient tradition."[31] In fact, however, oral tradition was quite flexible and could change in barely perceptible ways over time. This is ideally demonstrated in the dispute between Salem's abbot and the Sidelrichter, where in the absence of a comprehensive and written legal code, each side was able to emphasize different aspects of the legal tradition and even assert ideas that were altogether new. According to Simon Teuscher, custom was in fact a rhetorical device especially favored by lords in the later Middle Ages to assert legal claims that were not necessarily old.[32] The arguments presented by the Sidelrichter make clear, however,

30 "Wir haben allweg gehört das under zwain bösen dingen wie wol sy baide bos sind, doch das ain für das ander zuerwöllen ist. So haben wir doch den alten rodel daruff zu sweren erwelt." GLAK, 4/120, fol. 4r.

31 BLICKLE, Unruhen, pp. 59, 65; idem, Revolution of 1525, pp. 89, 92. Blickle's comments are made in the context of the Peasants' War of 1525, which he calls the "Revolution of the Common Man." He contrasts the "old law" with "godly law," which was a major basis of the peasants' demands in 1525 and allowed them to draw more radical conclusions.

32 Simon TEUSCHER, Erzähltes Recht: Lokale Herrschaft, Verschriftlichung und Traditionsbildung im Spätmittelalter, Frankfurt and New York 2007.

that appeals to custom possessed a legitimating function understood and employed not only by powerful rulers. We must be careful not to equate conservative language with conservative ideas.

Customary law, with its strong oral component, was eventually written down for several reasons: to combat the fallibility of memory, to protect against the encroachment of neighboring jurisdictions, to settle disagreements, and to secure the respective traditions of various members. Even peasants supported the introduction of written statutes in certain situations. Still, these were understood to be secondary to the entire body of oral tradition. They were not comprehensive laws but rather aids to preserving the law.[33] The written codes were derived from law, but they were not *the* law. This is what the Sidelrichter meant when they insisted that they spoke the law after consulting many other authorities in addition to the alte Jarbrief, "which is not a matter of law or any of the abbey's rights but a mere provision of statutes."[34]

Although the written formulation was initially secondary to oral customs, it led necessarily to ossification and eventually to the need for new law codes. This was because unlike oral custom, written forms of law could not be changed without notice. Fritz Kern's metaphor is apt when he says that customary law evolves slowly like a primeval forest, while changes to the written law resemble the shock of an earthquake with their sharp and obvious break from the past.[35] Even if commoners could be convinced to make the switch from oral to written forms of law, the lord's real or perceived innovations concerning the community's legal customs were cause for serious resistance. For it was commonly accepted that the lord did not make the law but was subject to it. In Ochsenhausen, where events in many respects paralleled those in Salem, the peasant judges also led a massive protest against the abbot's new law codes. Their oath, they asserted, required them to pass decisions according to tradition and conscience rather than the lord's ordinances, because "law arises not from innovation but from custom."[36]

---

33 This idea began to change, however, as lords began using written law codes as forms of proof in their struggles with other lords and as the bonds between law and custom were loosened; see BURMEISTER, Genossenschaftliche Rechtsfindung, pp. 173, 180; PROSSER, Rechtsaufzeichnungen, pp. 46–47, 175–183.

34 "Den nit gesezt noch dhain gotzhus recht darinne berürt, Sonnder statutten daselbs bestimbt werden." Ibid., fol. 4r.

35 Fritz KERN, Law and the Constitution, in: Kingship and the Law in the Middle Ages, trans. S. B. Chrimes, Oxford 1939, p. 179.

36 Quoted in BLICKLE, Landschaften, p. 114. For background on the situation in Ochsenhausen: idem, Arbeit, Alltag und Recht: Wandlungen in der Ochsenhausener Grundherrschaft an der Wende vom Mittelalter zur Neuzeit, in: Ochsenhausen: Von der Benediktinerabtei zur oberschwäbischen Landstadt, ed. Max Herold, Weissenhorn 1994, pp. 127–138; BLICKLE and HOLENSTEIN, Agrarverfassungsverträge, pp. 63–102.

To the extent that subjects deemed admissible the creation of new written statutes, these required the community's consent.[37] Even Salem's abbot acknowledged the community's representatives in 1468, when he asked the Sidelrichter to hear the law code's articles and discuss them with him before renewing their oaths. The preamble to the alte Jarbrief explicitly cited the involvement of the 15 judges in its creation.[38] The Sidelrichter pushed the idea of popular consent even further when they protested, "And even if we 15 had given such advice that this new roll and its articles should be put in place, still it would have no power, because the people did not command that we enact such a thing and also have given us no power to do so."[39]

The Sidelrichter repeatedly cited conscience as a primary foundation for legal decisions as well as for resistance. They made their own actions out to be deferential and sincere on several occasions while insinuating that the abbot was power-hungry and greedy. In raising moral criticisms they emphasized, too, that they were following the proper channels by consulting their priests:

> After receiving advice from our confessors, we humbly approached our lord the abbot and his district officials and explained earnestly that to judge cases according to the articles alone and without counsel other than his grace would be extremely difficult, especially because no one had more to gain by bringing suits before the Sidelgericht and concerning themselves with the law than the abbey's officials. As the articles themselves will soon make clear, each article would be used to enforce the abbey's commands, prohibitions, fines, penalties, and punishments. Now if we are meant to have no access to counsel other than that of your grace and the officials, and if we must additionally declare each article as valid and just, then this is indeed a difficult task and causes our souls and consciences great worry.[40]

Conscience, they claimed, was the primary reason they decided to leave the territory to consult the bishop when the abbot rejected their pleas, because the abbot's new restrictions and altered law code burdened their sense of morality and because the bishop was the highest spiritual authority in the diocese. "We have always believed and here today still believe that in pastoral issues such as these, there is no proper place to justly

---

37 BURMEISTER, Genossenschaftliche Rechtsfindung, p. 179.

38 According to the alte Jarbrief's preamble, purportedly from 1401: "Allen den die disen brieff lesen oder hörn lesen die sollen wissen das von bevelchens wegen ains herren von Salmenswiler der großkeller und ain koffman mit den fünffzechnen Zůrat worden. Wie sy Irs gotzhus recht satzung für kunftig krieg und stöss die selben fünffzechen och um das gericht gesworn hand und wurdent die gesetzt geoffnet und verkundt an dem Sontag vor Sannt Jacobs tag In dem Schurbuch zů Salmenswiler gelegen ob dem closter nach der fryhaitt und privilegi So sy dann hand von kaisern und von Römischen kungen von ainem an den andern bestätt und Confirmiert ist." GLAK, 4/120, fol. 3r.

39 "Ob wir fünffzechen sollichen Rat geben hetten das diser nuwer brieff und artickel also gestelt wurden das mocht doch Dhain craft dann die lutt unns doch sollichs zusetzen nitt bevolchen und uns och das Zutund dehainen gewalt geben haben." Ibid., fol. 3v.

40 Ibid., fol. 4v.

present one's requests other than your grace, the lord bishop and his scholars, in whose diocese this matter has transpired."[41] The Sidelrichter chastised the abbot for his statutes' imposition of restrictions and penalties on marriage: "Because indeed, each and every entry into the sacrament of holy matrimony should be unconditional."[42] This moral attack was especially acrimonious, as it was leveled against a spiritual leader, and because the judge in this case was the abbot's superior in spiritual matters. Yet even in temporal affairs, conscience and law were closely tied. The Sidelrichter were apparently not alone in believing that conscience was a standard by which justice should be found. When the abbot brought his suit before the Society of St. George's Shield, they referred him likewise to the bishop, since the dispute resulted from moral concerns. Conscience was central to the medieval understanding of Recht, so much so that even the word Recht conveyed both what was right and what was law, and the two meanings were often indistinguishable. Again, Fritz Kern:

> It [Recht] will be found, in the first place, where all morality resides—in Conscience. And, indeed, since law comprises all the rights of the community, it will be found in the common conscience of the people, in their sense of legality, or in that of their representatives, the chosen doomsmen. For them neither learning nor law-books are necessary, but only the possession of the "normal" legal sense of the community, the fact that they are sapientes, prud'hommes, lawful men.[43]

In fact, conscience was such a powerful standard that commands in violation of it were grounds for resistance. The bishop of Constance recognized this right to resist when he declared the Sidelrichter free from the abbey's claims. Subjects not only had the right to resist commands that went against Recht, it was commonly believed that they were obliged to do so. This was the case when the lord's command directly contradicted moral standards and when it repudiated the customs and traditions of the community.

According to medieval perceptions of law, all members of a legal community including its ruler were responsible to God, the law, and good old tradition. The infringement of one member's rights was an infringement of the legal order more generally, which is why it was not only a right but also an obligation to defend against legal violation. With the spread of feudal relations there came the idea of a contract between lord and vassal. According to an oath sworn between the two parties, the lord owed protection and defense in return for his noble vassal's aid and counsel, and the relationship of sworn fidelity could be broken if either side failed to fulfill his obligations. Subjects, too, could claim the right to resist because the lord had broken a contract. This justification is clear

---

41 "Wir Je gemaint hetten und noch hierbitag mainen das umb ain Jeglich derglich sachen die Selsorgen berürend, sind niendert anders zurecht dann für uwer gnad und ain jeden herren und bischoff und sin gelerten In des bistum sich sollich sachen begeben tund Rechtlich und gebürlich erbietung zurecht tun mug." Ibid.

42 "Das doch ain yeglich Ingang zů dem Sacrament der hailigen ee unbedingt sol sin." Ibid., fol. 9r.

43 KERN, Law and the Constitution, pp. 156–157.

in an often-cited passage of the Schwabenspiegel, a thirteenth-century law code that states: "We shall serve our lords so that they must protect us. If they do not protect us we are not bound by the law to serve them."[44] Yet the conflict in Salem was clearly not a result of this form of thinking. The Sidelrichter never questioned the abbot's authority as such, nor did they see themselves as freed from obligation by the lord's infringement of law. The Sidelrichter denied that they were serfs but accepted other responsibilities, even those they disliked. They criticized specific fines and prohibitions they considered too high or contrary to custom while accepting other duties such as the death tax and recognitive fees. They did point out contradictions between the abbot's temporal demands and his spiritual responsibilities, but they never suggested that religious leaders were unfit to rule. There is no sign of the anticlericalism we might expect to find on the eve of the Reformation. The Sidelrichter worked not to abolish the law that oppressed them but to reinstate relations of lordship under the higher order of custom and conscience it was their sworn duty to protect.

Although the Sidelrichter left the abbey's lands, sought outside counsel, and even challenged the abbot's authority by presenting their grievances before several neighboring rulers, they always insisted that they had remained loyal to the abbey and upheld their obligations in every way. Article 16 of the allegedly revised Jarbrief stated that in accordance with imperial privilege, no subject of the abbey could appear before outside courts. The Sidelrichter acknowledged this prohibition in principle, but replied: "Provided that we had been judges without restrictions, we would have sustained this article, because we would have had the authority—even with regard to tenure, tithes, and spiritual matters—to find and state the law for each one according to its proper nature. But now, as you have heard, we have been deprived of these powers by the oath."[45] The Jarbrief stated in Article 36 that any abbey subject who sought foreign citizenship or outside protection would have all his property confiscated. The Sidelrichter responded:

> Yes, we went away, although we took neither outside protection nor citizenship. Yet if we had taken outside protection or citizenship due to the contours of the many issues described above, if necessity and fairness had called for it, ... we would have hoped that we had not forfeited our tenure in any way because of it, nor should it be taken away, as stated above ... therefore we raise our doubts as to whether one's tenure should be forfeited according to the law.[46]

---

44 Quoted by Werner RÖSENER, Peasants in the Middle Ages, trans. Alexander Stutzer, Urbana 1992, p. 212.

45 "Sover und wir unbedingt richter wären gewesen, So hetten wir disen Artickel beliben lassen, dann wir wol macht gehebt hetten, lehen für lehenherrn zehend und gaistlich sach berürend mit Recht gewist yeglich nach siner geburlichait des wir aber nach lutt des aids wie vor gehört ist, abwesen musten." GLAK, 4/120, fol. 7v.

46 "Wie wol wir uns geussert hand und dhainen schirm noch burgrecht an unns genomen haben, und ob wir ander schirm oder burgrecht an uns genomen hetten nach gestalt aller vorgeschribnen sachen, wann die notdurft und billichaitt das gevordert hett, Dann ain yeglicher sol die

The Sidelrichter might have gone much further—they could have used violence to achieve their goals, as did the peasant subjects of other territories. They could have openly violated their duties as subjects with the excuse that the abbot had done so first. Their actions, or at least their arguments, were informed not by the feudal idea that a contract is dissolved once it is violated, but rather, by the idea that all members of a community have the duty to protect the law and to counter any action taken against it.

2.3 Tools of Power—Discourse, Writing, Legal Action, Networking

We must be careful not to confuse legal argument with inner conviction. The statements made by legal advocates for both the Sidelrichter and the abbot were designed to produce a certain effect: to persuade the audience and win a favorable legal verdict. This is not to say the two parties' claims were insincere or deceptive, only that their legal statements were artfully crafted and designed to use resources that worked to their benefit while avoiding and discrediting evidence that weakened their position.[47]

The Sidelrichter interpreted the abbot's own words in ways that implied meanings directly contrary to his original intent. In response to his declaration that the abbey had many freedoms confirmed by kings and emperors, and that the abbey's long tradition of rule over its serfs and other people had been cause for high regard and much praise, the Sidelrichter replied: "We and our predecessors have often rejoiced as well, because of these freedoms and the abbey's high regard, and on many occasions we have enjoyed such freedoms as the people of God's house and not as serfs, in good rule according to the freedoms and good common customs of the land which our lord has mentioned."[48] Certainly the abbot had other freedoms in mind, such as Salem's free imperial status and claims to unmediated authority, or perhaps the right to demand

sinen by billichaitt guter gewonhaitten und rechten beliben lassen, hetten wir das hoffen gehabt dz wir dannocht durch burgrecht oder annemung frombder schirm die lehen In dhainen weg verwurckt hetten, noch also wie obstat vervallen sölten gewesen sin und … mocht dannocht im rechten frag haben ob man sollich lehen vervallen sin solt oder nitt." Ibid., fol. 10r.

47 In his studies of the village of Neckarhausen, David Sabean examines court protocols from a different time period and with a different objective, yet his observations are applicable here. In disputes between kin and members of the household, especially husbands and wives, he found that arguments about the house and about property were chosen both in order to appeal to the magistrates judging the dispute and to describe their actions to their own best advantage. David Warren SABEAN, Property, Production and Family in Neckarhausen, 1700–1870, Cambridge and New York 1990, esp. pp. 76, 79, 113–114 (referred to hereafter as Neckarhausen I).

48 "Darzu geben wir anntwurt das wir sollichs bekennen das das gotzhus zů Salmenswiler wie das In der clag gemelt ist, loblich angesechen und gefreyt sye des wir unns und unnser vordern offt gefrewt und sollicher fryhaitt als gotzhus lutt und nit als aigenlütt mer dann ain mal genoßen haben und In güter Regierung Nach lutt der gemelten fryhaitt und gütten lannds gewonlichen gewonhaiten syen gehalten." GLAK, 4/120, fol. 1v–2r.

taxes, labor, and military services from all those belonging to the abbey's jurisdiction. The Sidelrichter insisted on a wider definition of freedom, maintaining that they, too, had inviolable rights protected by the abbey's ancient privileges and traditions.

On several occasions, the Sidelrichter used arguments that reinforced horizontal rather than hierarchical principles. They implied equality under the law by comparing their actions to those of the abbey:

> That which our lords of Salmansweiler have done and used since the start of this legal process, so we have also done. They chose a speaker with ties to your grace [the bishop], and likewise we also chose a speaker who is related to you in service. They chose nobles and vassals from the knighthood in the Hegau as their advisors ... and because we were unable to use knights and vassals, we chose instead councilors from the cities of Überlingen and Wil who were friends of ours. ... We have not employed any person beyond what was necessary ... In this process and in this matter we have learned from our lord's actions. We have not acted any differently than our lord in our court appearances or in our use of supporters, speakers, and other people.[49]

In some cases, it almost seems as if the Sidelrichter were arguing for some kind of gender equality. In response to the Jarbrief's Article 33, for example, which stated that the woman's bed should fall to the abbey upon her death unless a daughter survived her, they protested: "This article would be hard for us to declare as law, indeed seeing that it would go against nature, kinship, all law, and justice. Why should a son be disinherited from his mother's estate for the reason that he was born a boy and not a girl, especially when it is entirely possible that such a woman's property, with all its accessories, could be worth more than the rest of the estate overall?"[50] We might be tempted to see the peasant judges' insistence on the capabilities of common people and their arguments for the equitable treatment of lords and subjects under the law as indications that they believed all people to be created equal in the sense of natural law or indeed in modern, democratic terms.

---

49 "Wie unnser herren von Salmenßwyler den Ingang und anfanng des Rechten getan und gebrucht, derglichen wir ouch getan haben. Sy haben gehept ain fürsprechen der ist uwer gnad Ampts und Ratshalb gewanndt, desglichen haben wir ouch ainen fursprechen gehept der ist uwer gnaden Ratz und dienstes halb ouch gewandt. Sy haben gehept Edel Ritter und knecht bystander von der veraynung der Ritterschafft im Hegew ... und darumb diewyle wir nu nit Ritter und knecht vermochten, So haben wir zu bystandern by unns gehept Ratzbotten von Uberlingen und von wil In den Stetten etlich under unns angeborn frund haben ... Das wir wider notdurfft dehain person gehept noch gebrucht haben ... und haben unns zu tagen und In der sach uberal nit anders gehalten dann wir uns unnser herren mit Irm tagsüchen bystandern Rednern und andern personen halb gebrucht von Inen gelert haben." GLAK, 4/121, fol. 9r–9v.

50 "Diser artickel were unns hart Recht zusprechen gewesen, dann er doch wider natur die Sipp recht und billichaitt gewesen wär, warumb sölt ain Sun des obgenannd siner mutterlichen gütt enterbt sin umb des willen das er ain knab und nit ain tochter geboren ist, und mag wol komen das sollich frowen gut und zugehorung mer an ainer sum wäre dan des anndern guts uberal." GLAK, 4/120, fol. 9v.

In the examples above, the Sidelrichter clearly used equality as a claim to afford themselves the same legal privileges as the abbot and to deny the abbey's access to peasant property. In other situations, however, their strategies of argumentation demonstrate that the Sidelrichter were not, after all, the champions of equality. They supported the system of estates and privileges just as much as any lord. In their attempts to distance themselves from servility, they insisted on their own privileged position rather than fighting for the rights of abbey dependents more generally. Article 30 of the Jarbrief stated that all abbey serfs owed an annual Shrovetide chicken. The Sidelrichter admitted that they, too, gave an annual chicken, but by no means in recognition of their servility. They clarified: "Our lord of Salmansweiler's traditions with his serfs may be what he will. That we, however, or others of the abbey who are not his serfs, should give an annual chicken, to this we must agree and wish to be found obedient, meaning specifically that as men and women of God's house, we may be responsible to give a Shrovetide chicken as is widely accepted."[51] In matters of serfdom, the Sidelrichter denied any equality in legal status among the peasants. "Now there is a significant difference between serfs and other people of God's house. And we are definitely not your serfs."[52] These statements may be usefully compared to the abbey's own assertion of equality, meant to bolster contrasting claims about serfdom: "Now there is no difference between the people of our abbey in any way, where each one is treated like the other, and where no one is any less or more servile, or free, than the other."[53] These arguments demonstrate the ease with which concepts such as equality could be turned around and used in unexpected ways. The issue of equality demonstrates extremely well how lords and subjects used the same conceptual categories in support of different views. It reminds us that late medieval society cannot be divided neatly between rulers and ruled, groups who held fundamentally different values and expressed them in fundamentally different ways.

The peasants' demands and skilled legal argument made the abbot and his advisors extremely nervous. In an attempt to intimidate his subjects and persuade the judges, the abbot suggested that the Sidelrichter claimed illegitimate and unnecessary legal expenses, were ignorant of court procedure, and had openly flaunted the rules of justice. For example, the abbey's representative objected to the peasants' chosen advocate and spokesman: "Now it may well be true that this Burckhart Rulassinger is an excellent

---

51 "Das unnser herr von Salmanswiler mit sinen aigenlutten Herkomen mag was oder wie er will, das aber wir oder ander sin gotzhus und nit aigenlutt also Jerlich hune geben sollen, mainen wir nain, aber von vastnachthunr wegen zugeben wie das landslöffich und gotzhuslutt, man und frowen, schuldig zugeben syen, darinne wöllen wir gehorsamlich funden werden." Ibid., fol. 9r.

52 "Nu ist mercklicher underschaid unnder gotzhus aigen und sust under schlechten gotzhus luten dero wir aber nit aigen sind." Ibid., fol. 14v.

53 "Nu ist dhain underschaid unnder unnsern gotzhus lutten an dehainen dingen, dann Je ains als dz ander gehalten wirdt es ist och ains nit minder noch me aigen noch fry dann das ander." Ibid., fol. 12r.

speaker and a reasonable man. Nevertheless, he is a layman who is ignorant in the art of letters and who has no authority in matters of life or property outside the city of Constance, nor the right to charge fees for his opinions in such matters."[54] The Sidelrichter replied first of all that they were glad to hear the abbot finally recognizing their right to any legal counsel at all, something he had denied on many occasions. As for lay advocacy:

> We were well instructed by the court about how we should act through advocates and so on, and no such rules were ever applied. The procedural agreement absolutely never forbade us to use lay people, we had the option of taking spiritual or worldly advisors. Now we have chosen to have advocates and spokesmen according to our need and desire, with respect to the nature and content of the suit against us. In this case, it was much more reasonable to use lay people rather than lawyers. The educated ones should take no offense at this, seeing that the complaint against us concerns our honor, oaths, bodies, estates, lives, tenures, customals, and the traditions of the land. In these things, as we have stated elsewhere, those learned in the written law are not as experienced as lay people, having often dealt with such matters.[55]

In another passage, rejecting the Jarbrief as the territory's sole legal authority, they made a jab at legal professionals:

> It is true, we were the Sidelrichter in name. But the fact is, according to their plans, it was the abbey's officials who were both prosecutors and judges, while we were forbidden to declare what we believed to be right or what we had learned from counsel. We were only a mouth, told to speak a truth that had already been set. We would have had a name but no substance. They wanted to make us into jurists—we were supposed to lay the roll open before us and speak the law as whatever its articles said, just as jurists do with the written laws that fill their books.[56]

---

54 "Nun wie wol Burckhart Rulassinger ain Wolredender und vernunfftiger mann ist, So ist er doch ain lay der geschrifft nit gelert und hat In der Sach nit bedorffen usserthalb der Statt Costenntz weder Lib noch gut wagen noch Zerung daruff Legen." GLAK, 4/121, fol. 4v.

55 "So weren wir wol underricht worden, Wie wir durch advocaten und annder solten gehanndelt haben, Das aber In disem Rechten die gestalt niendert gehebt der anlauss unns ouch ganntz nicht verbotten hat dehaynen layen zubruchen Dann wir haben mögen nemen gaistlich oder weltlich Nun haben wir unns furgenomen Advocaten und fursprechen zuhaben nach unnserm gefallen und unnser notdurfft Dann gestalt und Innhalt der Clag So uff unns beschehen ist, die layeschen personen fügklicher dann die Advocaten hierzu zenutzend gewesen, das söllen alle gelerten von unns In argern nit vermercken angesehen das die Clag zu unns getan hat unns berurt unnser Ere ayde lib gut leben lehen offnungen und lanndsgewunhaiten darInne als vorstat die schrifft gelerten nit als geübt als die layen sind die offt und vil In sölhen Sachen zu Recht und tagen gehanndelt haben." Ibid., fol. 8v–9r.

56 "Wie wol wir die Sidelrichter mit Namen gehaissen waren, So waren doch die amptherren nach fürnemen und gestalt diser sachen, cleger und richter dann wir gedorften nit richten was unns recht sin beducht oder wie wir das an Rat funden hetten zůsprechen dann der mund was zu der billichaitt des rechten beschlossen, wir hetten wol ainen namen sine Re und wolt Juristen uß uns gemacht haben, dann wir solten dem rodel für unns gelegt und allweg nach clag und anntwurt

The Sidelrichter used every opportunity to assert the superior authority of commoners in matters both legal and moral. The insistence on the special capabilities of common people could also be used to support other types of argument. Whereas the abbey sought to limit subjects' access to outside sources of information on the basis of servility, the Sidelrichter argued that as common people, this access was all the more necessary. As simple people who needed to take counsel in order to make decisions, they implied that their reliance on outsiders was innocent of strategy or manipulation. Even the choice of vocabulary, playing up their simplicity and openness as humble folk, was a strategy of legitimation. The Sidelrichter emphasized their obedience in order to strengthen their criticisms of the abbot, and their use of politely deferential words of address conveyed the appearance that they knew and accepted their natural place in the social hierarchy, that they were submissive, obedient, sincere, and loyal subjects.

The abbot was not fooled by this act. He emphasized that these men, his serfs, belonged nowhere near the top of the social hierarchy. It was not their place to command, or to interpret:

> Venerable prince and learned, wise lords, we were shocked and displeased when the defendants recently dared to justify, to dispute, and to explain our statutes from one article to the next, and understandably so, since they are in no way entitled to do this, nor does the written law, custom, or proper conduct tolerate or permit such behavior. They are not our lords but our subjects and our own serfs after all, and no one asked them to do any such thing. It is our place to do these things out of imperial and royal privilege, while it is their place to give up the property, death taxes, and inheritance portions that are ours.[57]

Neither should commoners have such ambitions and put on such airs:

> These Sidelrichter who are involved with this thing are simple peasants. For them to live such a high and extravagant lifestyle, or at least to act in such a way—as if they were nobles, burghers, or even lords!—and to expect us to pay the cost of things such as this is against all law and equity, especially when these folks should be happy with plain old fare, vegetables and cheese and garlic and such, as it says in the emperor's book. Besides, there was really no need for every one of them to come to all those court hearings in Constance as they did ... they should have just

den artickel daruff die clag gelutt hat angesechen darus und daruff, das recht gesprochen habn als die Juristen sollichs In Iren büchern den geschribnen rechten tund bruchen." GLAK, 4/120, fol. 4v.

57 "Hochwirdiger furst und hochgelerten wisen herren, Als die anntwurter am letzten In Ir anttwurt sich understand Zuorechtvertigen ze disputtieren und zůerclären unnser Stattutta von ainem an dz ander, Befrombdt uns nit unbillich ser wann doch Inen das In dhainen weg zůstat und weder das geschribner recht gewonhaitt noch billichaitt In das zůtund verhenngt noch zůgibt, dann sy doch nit unnser obern, Besonnder unnser undertan und aigen lutt sind, och das zůtund von niemand gewirdiget. Besonnder wir haben söllichs zůtund uß kaiserlicher und künigclicher fryhaitt dann sölten sy söllichs zůtund haben Besonnder der gutter vall und laß halb So unns zůgehoren." Ibid., fol. 12r.

> sent a couple of attorneys with their spokesman to accept the verdict, which would have saved a lot of unnecessary expense.[58]

Not only were the Sidelrichter effective in their mastery of discourse and the assertion of alternative meanings, they displayed their ability to fight with words in a different sense, through their use of written documents. Steven Justice makes a strong case in his study of the English Rebellion of 1381 for the political nature of writing.[59] He shows that peasants, even those who could not personally read or write, used written documents to assert political claims. They were empowered through the use of messages. The rebels of 1381 also demonstrated their understanding of the ways written documents could be used to perpetuate domination by selectively burning documents in the castles they pillaged. The Sidelrichter of the late fifteenth century, like the English peasants before them, were quite possibly illiterate, but this did not stop them from using written documents or from developing their own arguments based on the alte Jarbrief and other documents the abbey produced. The Sidelrichter challenge our belief, as well as the belief of elites in their own period, that the courts and the written word were tools beyond the peasantry's reach. The Sidelrichter had the advantage of being well acquainted with legal argument, presentation strategy, and court procedures. Perhaps they had more experience with such things because they came from an ecclesiastical territory where violence was forbidden, and where legal documentation was the obvious alternative used by lords and subjects alike. In any case, the Sidelrichter used written documents to their own advantage, even provoking the abbot's objections. They not only produced the written defense statements and counterarguments the court called for, they also requested copies of the abbey's written statements for themselves and submitted written evidence far beyond what the court required.[60] The abbot protested,

> The Sidelrichter demand an enormous sum, which they claim to have given to the chancellor and to other scribes in payment for written documents. Because these costs they name were not required by your princely grace and honor but were used for various and different ends, my lord

58 "So sind ouch die Sidelrichter alle die sollich sach antrifft schlecht purslüt das die so hoh und Costlich Zeren oder Zeren mugen Als ob Sy Edel Burger oder herren gewesen wern und man In sölhen Costen niderlegen sölt, das ist wider alle Recht und billichait. Wann die purslütt söllen schlecht gemüß käs zibillen und knobloch essen als das die keyserlichen buch uswisn das sy ouch alle zu allen ziten so gerichtztag gesetzt sind haben bedurffen gen Constentz kommen ist nit not gewesen … Hetten Si wol und gnugsamlich Iren zwayn gewalt geben Sollich by und endtlich urtailn Zuhörn und zunemen mitsambt Irem fursprechen und nit solchen unzimblichen Costen und schaden uff ditz sach getriben." GLAK, 1/121, fol. 12r–12v.

59 Steven JUSTICE, Writing and Rebellion: England in 1381, Berkeley 1994.

60 According to a document produced on 6 June 1470, the hearing before the bishop of Constance had to be postponed because both sides wanted to introduce more evidence and review the opposing party's testimony. The document set the procedures and time frame for drafting written documents and submitting them to the court. GLAK, 4/119.

and convent of Salmansweiler therefore believe that they are not responsible, since the Sidelrichter have had documents written and spent money in ways that were for their own benefit and not to the benefit of the abbot or of the abbey.[61]

It was in large part because of the peasant judges' mastery over the written word, one of the chief weapons in the abbot's arsenal of domination, that they were able to press their claims successfully. The Sidelrichter challenge the assumption held by many historians that ordinary peasants and subjects no longer had any substantial role to play once written forms of law replaced oral customs.[62]

The political capabilities of the Sidelrichter are also demonstrated by their use of the legal system. Not only did they assert their right to appear in outside courts and take their case all the way to the emperor, they maintained and insisted on their own legal values instead of bowing to the conventions of professionalized justice and the abbot's attempts to exclude them. The abbot denied his subjects access to outside courts, but of course he reserved such rights for himself. He refused to respond to the initial grievances the peasant judges brought before the bishop of Constance but eventually filed his own grievances before the very same authority. The archbishop of Mainz later summarized the abbot's position, that the Sidelrichter had brought an illegitimate suit against him: "The abbot and his convent named herein were not rightfully accountable to such an illegitimate power and court on account of their people, who appeared there entirely improperly and did so completely unjustly against their rightful, natural lords, against the oaths and promises by which they were accustomed and bound, and for no other reason than their wealth."[63] When the Sidelrichter submitted detailed objections to the alte Jarbrief's articles on servility and other burdens, the abbot insisted that the issue under discussion had absolutely nothing to do with serfdom, but as the archbishop described it, "with a punishable offense named in the aforementioned Jarbrief that had been committed and therefore was to be penalized, in that they ran away and became fugitives against the promises and oath by which they were bound to the

61 "Das die Sidelrichter ain treffenlich Sum bestymen dem Canntzler und Sunst umb geschrifften und schrybern geben haben sollen als uwer furstlich gnad und Erwirdigkait das mer dann an ainem end In Irem bestymen, verminet Da min herr von Salmenswiler und der Convent ouch mainen In daby gantz nichtz schuldig sin Dann haben die Sidelrichter Icht umb brief schribern oder anndern ussgeben haben Si zu Irm nutz getan und nit zu ains Abbts oder des Gotzhuß nutz." GLAK, 4/121, fol. 4v. The Sidelrichter responded elsewhere to similar criticisms: "Wir bekennen selbs das die Sum groß aber niemant daran schuldig ist dann unnser herren selbs mit Irem anfang und verzug So sy bisher getan haben." Idem, fol. 9v.

62 As Chapter 5 will show, the peasant court continued to be the very instrument through which the law was interpreted, declared, and preserved.

63 "Der yetzgemelt Abbt und sein Convent wurden durch Ir lewt über die Eide und gelübde damit Sy Ine gewondt und verbunden weren, solichs unbillichen gewalts und gerichts nicht billich beschuldigt, dann Ine daran ganz ungütlich beschehe und tetten das gar unbillichen wider Iren rechten naturlichen herren Beschehe, auch durch dhein annder ursachen dann durch Iren Reichtumb." GLAK, 4/126, fol. 3r.

abbey. They even sought protection and aid in foreign places, in Heiligenberg and in Überlingen, against the same Jarbrief, and unjustly involved the Swiss in their complaints against the abbot."[64] Despite significant hurdles, the Sidelrichter successfully defended themselves against the abbot's attack, using the courts to demand a hearing for their own claims as well.

The Sidelrichter received coaching and strategic support from many parties. At this point, the objection could be raised that it was hired legal advocates and not the Sidelrichter who drafted and presented their case. This argument has been applied to other written statements of peasant demands, such as the Twelve Articles of 1525. Such texts cannot reflect the peasants' true goals, it is said, because they were written and produced primarily by priests, burghers, scholars, or magistrates. The implication is that peasants were unable to make these statements because they lacked the theoretical justification, the vocabulary, the organization, and the technology to formulate and express their own complaints. It is true that the Sidelrichter used outside legal counsel, and although their statements were often written in the first person "we," they were not a pure or faithful reproduction of their own ideas. Their testimony describes the assistance they received from people of many social ranks, including legal advisors and spokesmen, urban magistrates, scribes, messengers, innkeepers, and humble commoners. At the bishop's court alone, 52 witnesses testified in defense of the Sidelrichter, and they came not only from the immediate proximity of the abbey but also from the Hegau and from Heiligenberg, Constance, and Überlingen. These contacts are mentioned in the 1471 list of legal expenses; we can only imagine the extent of undocumented assistance they must have received from friends and associates free of charge.[65]

The territorial judges' legal statements do not display their lack of resources or an inability to state grievances in a convincing and strategic manner. On the contrary, they are evidence that the Sidelrichter commanded resources far beyond what we might expect. Their broad social networks should be interpreted as a sign of their abilities rather than alleged deficiencies in communication and the formulation of ideas, not only because they were able to convince so many others to listen or assist with their concerns, but also because through discussions with others they gleaned many new insights and methods for argumentation. We should not assume that because peasants had contact with members of other social groups, they lacked the capability to act, speak, or think for themselves. There is a tendency to view lords as powerful actors

64 "Sonnder umb einen peenfal in dem vorbestimbten Jarbrief begriffen den Sy verworcht hetten und darein gevallen weren dar Sy auch über gelübde und Eidt damit Sy dem Gotzhauss verbunden außflůchtig weren worden und auswenndigen, und sonndern schirm auch Ratte an frombden ennden zum Heiligenperg und Uberlingen wider Innhalt des obgemelten Jarbriefs gesucht, und den Abbt gegenden Eidgenossen unbillich verklagt hetten." Ibid., fol. 3v.

65 They did not, of course, pay the witnesses; they were mentioned because the court charged a recording fee of 15 kreuzer per deposition. Unfortunately their testimony, if it was ever written down, does not appear to have survived.

with access to vast resources, while their subjects were limited in every sense. We often depict peasants as forced to use outsiders to express their muddled or fragmented ideas in a rational and comprehensive way, while lords are seen to use the same sorts of communication networks as tools of domination. In fact, both groups were practicing the same sorts of behavior. When the emperor provided the Sidelrichter with a letter of safe-conduct and promised that their grievances would be heard, the abbot drew on his own personal networks in an attempt to convince the emperor to retract his protection. The list of financial backers and legal advisers named in connection with the abbey's legal expenses was no less extensive than that of the Sidelrichter. The abbot was well connected and controlled many powerful resources. We must view peasant networks in the same manner. The territorial judges' legal statements were surely not their pure, original, and unmediated opinions, but no one's ideas are produced in a vacuum. Communication generates new ideas and is the product of social experience. One of the most remarkable findings in this case is the peasant judges' ease of access to people and ideas far beyond their home villages.

Throughout the course of the conflict, one tactic was noticeably absent from the methods used by both the Sidelrichter and abbot. Neither side ever resorted to violence. The Sidelrichter resolutely denied seeking outside protection at any time during the dispute, but their actions demonstrate that they were indeed worried about force being used against them. They sought early assurances from the bishop that they would not be harmed, and from the Landvogt they received a promise of safe-conduct. In order to excuse their prolonged absence from the territory, the Sidelrichter portrayed the abbot as a potential threat to their safety and accused him of wishing to do them harm.

> We would have been entirely willing to return home, especially under the security and justice of your princely grace, [but] we did not succeed in this and could not press the matter any further. By this we meant, and still maintain today, that neither we nor any other person should be required to put ourselves at risk, to fear for our bodies and lives, and so we went to your princely grace and humbly called on your grace to write to our lord of Salmansweiler and ask him to guarantee our security.[66]

Later, the emperor offered the Sidelrichter his own personal protection. The abbot protested the imperial letter of safe-conduct, deeming it an unjust threat to the abbey's authority and an unnecessary effort to protect unruly subjects. The archbishop of Mainz seconded this view in a letter he wrote to the emperor in August 1472:

66 "Weren wir zûmal gern willig gewesen anhaim zûwerden, doch uff sicherhaitt und zûrecht fur uwer fürstlichen gnad, hat unns nicht gedichen noch vervolgen mugen uff das wir mainten und noch huttbitag mainen weder wir noch niemand schuldig sye sich unsicherhaitt in sorgsami sins libs und lebens zûgeben, und haben unns zû uwern fürstlichen gnaden gefugt und uwer gnad undertäniclich angerüft unnsern herren von Salmenswiler zûschriben und zûbitten unns sicherhaitt zûgebend." GLAK, 4/120, fol. 15r.

> So then, out of concern that Abbot Johann or his men would desire to use force against them because of these matters and events, your imperial grace granted them—as well as their associates, wives, children, and estates—freedom, security, and safe-conduct in your gracious imperial name and in that of the holy empire, valid until this matter is fully rectified ... in spite of the fact that the aforementioned abbot has never used force against his common dependents in the past, nor has he the intention of doing so in the future.[67]

On the other hand, the potential also existed for an escalation into violence from below. We know that peasant rebels used force to bring attention to their demands in many neighboring territories. This was done, for example, by the subjects of Ochsenhausen, Rot, and Kempten Abbeys.[68] Yet the Sidelrichter eschewed violence. This was presumably not because they lacked the resources to do so but because they, like the abbot, saw force as an extreme measure that would violate the territorial peace and was to be used only when absolutely necessary. Ultimately, they sought to protect their version of Recht from within the legal order rather than by provoking more radical change and repudiating the entire system.

To conclude, the Sidelrichter spoke out against arbitrary rule, insisting that law stood above everyone and was found rather than declared by lords or from books. They refused to be excluded from participation on the grounds of hierarchy or privilege, boldly asserting their rights in a court of law. Theirs was not a defensive, backward-looking, or reactionary struggle. Their initiative and creative use of discourse, social networks, written documents, and the courts actually forced the abbot to act defensively on several occasions. That the Sidelrichter successfully mastered these techniques is demonstrated by the settlements in both Constance and Überlingen.

2.4 A Lasting Settlement

Throughout this chapter, we have focused on the process of negotiations leading up to the settlement of 1473. Now let us turn to the final agreement made in Überlingen and the contents of its specific articles. An undated letter sent by Burckhart Rulassinger from Vienna to Abbot Johann of Salem marked the end of negotiations at the imperial

67 "Syen so dannocht In sorgen das der bemelt abbt Johanns oder die sinen, sollicher Stuck und sachenhalb gewalt wider sy gepruchnd möchten, Darumb so hab E. k. gnad fur sollichen gewalt In und Iren zůgewandter husfrowen kinden haben und gůten E. k. g. und des hailigen richs fry sicherhait und gelait Bis Zů entlichem ußtrag vorgerürter sachen gegeben ... Sich ouch der vorgem' Abbt, gegen sinen armenluten gewaltz Bißher nie gebrucht hat, und ouch furo nit In maynung ist den zubruchen." GLAK, 98/1563.

68 For a more extensive list of peasant revolts, see BIERBRAUER, Forschungsbericht, pp. 62–68; idem, Aufstieg der Gemeinde, pp. 46–47; Peter BLICKLE, Communal Reformation: The Quest for Salvation in Sixteenth-Century Germany, trans. Thomas Dunlap, Atlantic Highlands 1992, p. 169.

court.[69] It explained the procedures for the upcoming arbitration hearings. The panel would sit in the imperial city of Überlingen, and unlike all previous assemblies, it would deal specifically with disputes over territorial custom and the alte Jarbrief. According to the letter, the six arbitrators would include two neutral members assisted by two others of each party's choice.[70] First, the arbitration committee would consider written evidence including the alte Jarbrief, documentation from previous mediation attempts, and "whatever else they otherwise consider necessary." After examining written evidence the court would hear oral testimony, including the territorial judges' charges and the abbot's response. Finally, the arbitrators would attempt to reach a decision amicable to both sides (*gütliche Entscheidung*). If this proved to be impossible, however, the judges had the authority to pass binding legal judgment (*rechtliche Entscheidung*), unanimously or by majority vote. Either way, the disputants would have to abide by the decision; there could be no further hearings or appeals. Additionally, the outstanding assessment of court costs from previous hearings was to be deferred until after the final decision.[71] The representatives of both parties in Vienna evidently approved these guidelines before returning home.

The settlement came on 21 January 1473. See Illustration 2.1, Opening Page and Seals. The written text of the agreement reiterated that its declarations were binding. Any previous discord or related conflicts between the parties were now officially null and void. Following the bishop's decision of 1470, the Sidelrichter were not to be punished for alienation, oath-breaking, or damage to the abbey's honor. They were to

---

[69] GLAK, 98/1562. Burckhart Rulassinger was an advisor at the bishop's court in Constance, as well as the peasant judges' legal spokesman there in 1470. It is unclear by what authority and on what grounds he wrote this letter to the abbot from Vienna, but it shows that he was present at the imperial court and involved in making arrangements for the final settlement. At least one of the provisions mentioned in this letter (the choice of arbitrators, including Rulassinger himself) was abandoned in the final legal process (see footnote below), suggesting that Rulassinger and his letter are not entirely reliable sources of information.

[70] Arbitration committees typically included members chosen by each of the disputants along with one or more neutral members acceptable to both sides; see Karl Siegfried BADER, Das Schiedsverfahren in Schwaben vom 12. bis zum ausgehenden 16. Jahrhundert, in: Ausgewählte Schriften zur Rechts- und Landesgeschichte, vol. 2, Sigmaringen 1984, pp. 195–196. Rulassinger's letter named six men who would settle the dispute but only one of them, Guildmaster Hans Betz, actually took part in the decision. The other five on his list were the former mayor Sailer of Überlingen, Ludwig Appentegg, an unnamed secretary from Constance, Rudolff Giel, and Burckhart Rulassinger. The six actually responsible for the decision were all from Überlingen: Mayor Jos Wanger, Head Guildmaster Lienhart Wingersulg, Councilor Waltz Franck, Guildmaster Hans Betz, Guildmaster Lentz Oswalt, and Councilor Conrat Fundel.

[71] The Sidelrichter were awarded 500 fl. by the bishop of Constance to cover court costs from the abbey's suit against them on 3 September 1470; the abbey was awarded first 480 fl. and later 556 fl. in court costs by the Imperial Chamber Court for the territorial judges' appeal brought in 1471. GLAK, 4/121, 4/126, and 98/1562.

Illustration 2.1: Opening Page and Seals from the Partnership Agreement, 21 January 1473

Generallandesarchiv Karlsruhe, 4/129

return peacefully to the territory and obey their rightful lords, the abbot and his officials, as tradition required. These repeated admonitions to peace were important not only in light of the many previously failed arbitration attempts between the abbey and its Sidelrichter but also because, more generally, arbitration decisions had the weakness that they were difficult to enforce, often lasting only as long as the opposing parties were willing to abide by them.[72] The settlement of 1473 listed members of the two opposing parties by name, including the abbot and Sidelrichter along with an additional seven senior territorial officials and 15 representatives from the village communities. The broadening of participation in the settlement would help ensure that it was upheld

72 BADER, Schiedsverfahren, pp. 193–194, 206; Hans JÄNICHEN, Der Rechtszug im Spätmittelalter am Oberen Neckar und im pfalzgräflich-tübingischen Bereich, in: Zeitschrift für Württembergische Landesgeschichte 15 (1956), p. 217.

in the future. The text also emphasized that the abbey was entering into an agreement not only with the recalcitrant judges but also with the entire community of its territorial subjects.

Article 1 contained a major concession in the abbey's favor. According to the text, "All the people of God's house are to consider themselves and be considered as the serfs of God's house."[73] As such, they were required to swear and promise to perform their servile obligations to Salem's abbot. Mobility and outside protection were not specifically prohibited in this or any later articles, but their restriction was most likely implied and administered through an oath. The recognition of all Salem's dependents as its serfs was an important political gain for the abbey, as this article and its placement at the top of the list makes clear. All abbey subjects were now theoretically equal in legal status; even the territorial judges lost their claim to be free. If this verdict shocked the Sidelrichter, others in positions of authority were probably less surprised. Servility was being resurrected across the region. Precedent had been set in a 1467 decision against the subjects of Montfort who claimed to be free, and Salem's abbot had been among the arbitrators who heard that dispute and declared judgment "that in the Swabian lands, in the diocese of Constance, and anywhere else, a serf is understood to be anyone who owes Shrovetide chickens as well as the best animal as heriot to the lord."[74] Yet even this first article was not without benefit for at least some of Salem's inhabitants. Part of the degrading nature of serfdom was attached to the name itself: who would want to be called a bondsman or a serf, suggesting one's body to be the personal property of another man, when one could be called instead a (free) person of God's house? In a sense, however, if everyone who lived under the abbey's rule was understood to be its serf, the designation would lose some of its denigrating impact. For the many abbey dependents who had formerly been recognized as serfs, this article made them the same as everyone else.

Yet servility was not a burden in name alone with the infringement of honor it implied. There were real political and economic consequences as well, especially where lordship over serfs led to new and arbitrary demands. The bulk of the agreement's articles limited the specific economic burdens associated with servility and provided subjects with powerful checks against the lord's arbitrary exercise of power. First, the heriot was restricted to the best animal or the best garment. Even if there were no

---

73 The entire article reads: "Des ersten von der aygenschaft wegen, das die gotshuslüte sich sollend bekennen und sin aygen gotshuslüte. Und alles das, das aygen gotshuslüte dem gotshuß und einem abt des gotshuß Salmenswil als irm rechten herren schuldig ze tünd sind, tůn sollen mitsampt dem ayd und der trostung, wie dannen derselb ayde gesworn und sölich trostung von alter her bescheen ist." GLAK, 4/129–130; BLICKLE and HOLENSTEIN, Agrarverfassungsverträge, p. 54.

74 "Dass im Lande zu Schwaben, im Bistum Konstanz und sonstwo alle, welche ihrem Herrn Fasnachthünner und nach dem Tode das Besthaupt zu Todfall oder Hauptrecht reichen, … Eigenleute seien." Quoted by ULBRICH, Leibherrschaft, p. 273.

direct heirs, the abbey could no longer claim from the deceased a share of other remaining real and moveable property. In the case of outside marriage, the outside spouse now had a grace period of one year to become the abbey's serf without penalty. Only after a year of noncompliance, the abbey could fine the servile spouse during his or her lifetime or take one-third of moveable property after death (but not freehold land, which was now exempt).[75] As was the case in many neighboring territories, the 1473 agreement limited Salem's ability to increase future revenues based on serfdom. In fact, the financial burdens of servility were reduced in several key areas.

Other major topics of the settlement concerned land tenure and property rights. The abbey lost its control over certain aspects of peasant property relations, to the benefit of parental and communal authorities. Conditions of tenure were improved, if not as much as in some neighboring territories. In principle, it upheld the abbey's claim that leases had to be renewed annually and farms "vacated every year," but the settlement also specified that in the future, tenants could be evicted only for violations of their tenure obligations. The tenant could even pass the lease on to his or her children, so long as they were serfs, though the farm was not to be inherited, sold, or changed in any way without the lord's permission. Regarding alienation from the abbey's lands, the settlement of 1473 was curiously silent. The article from the alte Jarbrief, stating land forfeiture as the penalty for seeking outside protection or citizenship, was dropped entirely in 1473.

On the topic of inheritance and personal property, the new agreement declared that freehold land could be transferred to heirs or others without the previously required permission from the abbey's Kaufmann or Großkeller. Parents could dispose of their own property free from interference, except for widowed spouses, who needed permission from the Sidelrichter (but not the abbey) before selling land held in trust for their children.[76] Finally, all inheritance disputes would now be resolved by the Sidelgericht, which deprived the abbey of yet another way of controlling property.

The 1473 agreement also contained political guarantees for all the abbey's subjects. Several articles concerned the role of the community in future decisionmaking, and for this reason it is entirely valid to call the settlement a partnership agreement. Article 2 yielded important gains. It required the abbot to consult the "Thirty"—the 15 territorial judges and an additional 15 honorable men from throughout the territory—before enacting any future legal amendments or law codes. The agreement also addressed the issue of jurisdiction and outside counsel. Like the alte Jarbrief, it restricted the right of disputing parties to seek protection or legal support from outside the territory, but whereas the alte Jarbrief allowed exceptions to this rule only with permission from the Kaufmann or Großkeller, the 1473 settlement stated that in certain cases such permis-

75 The fine had previously been one-half (for men) or one-third (for women) of the serf's land and moveable property.

76 Additional restrictions were placed on childless widows (but not widowers), who could not dispose of land without approval from their guardians.

sion could be waived. In agreement with the alte Jarbrief, all people of the abbey were required to seek justice from the abbey's court (the Sidelgericht), but appeals were possible; the cost of an appeal rose from two to three gulden. Also in the settlement were limitations on the use of imprisonment, resulting perhaps from the controversial arrest and confinement of the Sidelrichter upon their return home from Constance in 1471, or perhaps in response to their objection to Article 34 of the alte Jarbrief, when they protested that people willing to guarantee their obedience to the court should be punished with fines, not held in custody. According to the new agreement, imprisonment was to be reserved for serious offenses. Such cases would be subject to bail (in exchange for surety) and strict time limits (judgment within one month).

The settlement made no mention of where or to whom exactly its articles applied. We can infer from the treaty participants' places of origin that the articles were valid in the immediate vicinity of the abbey where it held jurisdictional rights but probably not much further.[77] By the early sixteenth century, however, the abbey was gradually extending the provisions of 1473 and other law codes to newer outlying districts, especially in the northern Linzgau villages Over the Hills.

The decision of 1473 was the result of compromise between the abbot and his subjects. Yet considering its insistence on tradition and custom, the immutability of law, and the authority of that which precedes human memory, it is in some sense ironic that the settlement came from outside the territory. The new "partnership agreement" was crafted neither by those responsible for speaking the law, nor by the lord who claimed ultimate authority. It contained some articles that were significantly altered and others that were brand new. It explicitly allowed for the possibility of introducing new law codes in the future. Thus, it recognized the need for change and it established procedures for the evolution of custom and tradition. Medieval legal concepts placed high value on that which was local, communal, customary, and oral. By contrast, early modern law would be based increasingly on written statutes and ordinances set by ruling authorities, which could be used to police even the minute affairs of everyday life. The decision of 1473 heralded the shift from old legal traditions established in customary law codes such as the alte Jarbrief to a newer legal mentality that would soon manifest itself in the ordinances of the sixteenth and seventeenth centuries.[78] The compromise of 1473 was founded primarily on customary relations, but it also recognized the neces-

---

77 The ten (no longer 15) Sidelrichter named in 1473 came from Ahausen, Baufnang, Neufrach, Nußdorf, Owingen, Pfaffenhofen, Rickenbach, Forst, and Wehausen. All these places were near the abbey, but Ahausen and Rickenbach sat just beyond the central territory. The additional 15 abbey subjects named in the agreement were all from within the abbey's jurisdiction and represented the communities of Buggensegel, Grasbeuren, Leutkirch, Mimmenhausen, Mühlhofen, Neufrach, Niderstenweiler, Nußdorf, Oberuhldingen, Owingen, Pfaffenhofen, Tüfingen, and Weildorf. Significantly, no one from Bermatingen took part in the agreement.

78 BLICKLE, Einleitung, in: Blickle and Holenstein, Agrarverfassungsverträge, pp. 5–6; BURMEISTER, Genossenschaftliche Rechtsfindung, p. 176.

sity of creating new laws in the interests of the community as a whole. It is significant with respect to the legislative acts and policies of the following generations that the 1473 settlement named the abbot and the Thirty as joint policy-makers.

2.5 Conclusions

The agreement in 1473 was an important step in the process of "territorialization," the consolidation of the abbey's territorial lordship. It defined jurisdictional rights and obligations, preventing subjects from using outside courts while protecting them from the demands of outside powers. It set standards for declaring and interpreting the law when disputes arose. It protected the abbey's claims to landed property while granting tenants more control over their leases and parents stronger inheritance rights. Most importantly with respect to territorial objectives, Article 1 leveled the legal status of dependents so that all were theoretically equal and all were the abbey's serfs.

The settlement of 1473 strengthened territorial lordship, just as it unified the territorial community. The provision of a new legal code with territorial validity was beneficial to both subjects and the abbey, since it guaranteed that justice would continue to be spoken across the territory by appointees from within the community and according to their own customs. The treaty confirmed subjects' political capabilities by requiring the consent of the Thirty for new territorial policies and by recognizing them as partners in the treaty of 1473. These statements confirmed the community of the territory as a legally competent corporate body and as a collective political actor. Finally, the settlement recognized communal authority over internal affairs such as peacekeeping, property transfers, and inheritance customs.

The fifteenth century has traditionally been seen as the end of an era, a transitional period characterized by weakness and decline. This chapter has demonstrated that for Salem, the period was indeed one of transition, but despite the political instability and even crisis of legal authority experienced in these years, the dispute between Salem's abbot and Sidelrichter and the resolution of conflict in 1473 formed a bridge between old and new. The political developments and conflicts in Salem were a reflection of the times, especially in Upper Swabia and among abbatial lordships. The fifteenth century should be recognized as a crucial period, in which older values were modified and integrated in the service of new demands, both of rulers and of ruled.

The following chapter investigates the immediate outgrowth and efficacy of the 1473 decision over the following decades, as a means of assessing the political evolution of Salem's central territory and the participation of its subjects in that process. So far, the examination of the conflict between Salem's abbot and his peasant judges in the late fifteenth century contradicts the following generalization made by Léopold Genicot about late medieval revolts: "Outside Catalonia, the peasants had nothing to show for their sufferings but failure, and for good reason. They lacked everything: political judgment, sense of proportion, intelligent leaders, financial means, organization. How with these handicaps could they have hoped to impose their demands on the State, or to overthrow the rule of the lords which had already survived plague, famine and total war?"[79] The Sidelrichter did not overthrow their lord, nor was this their goal. They did force the abbey to recognize the community's customs, however, and as a result of the new settlement they were guaranteed a role in future decisionmaking. This chapter has suggested that territorial rule in Salem was a relationship network involving various community members, all with legal rights and responsibilities, many of whom aspired to share in the practice of authority. Rather than increasing their domination over subjects, Salem's rulers were forced to address the needs and demands of all groups within the community, from the abbot down to the landless laborer. The fact that this continued to be the case throughout the early modern period has much to do with the initiative taken by peasant subjects in the fifteenth century and the partnership agreement resulting from their demands.

[79] Léopold GENICOT, Crisis: From the Middle Ages to Modern Times, in: The Cambridge Economic History of Europe, vol. 1, ed. M. M. POSTAN, 2nd ed., Cambridge 1966, p. 739.

Chapter 3: Community, Lordship, and the German Peasants' War

In order to understand political development in Salem's territory and the peasants' place in that process, it makes sense to start in the village. Most historians agree that in the countryside, the village commune was the primary basis for political consciousness, experience, and action.[1] This chapter looks at a series of issues relating to local political life in Salem's villages and its development over the course of the long sixteenth century. It describes the organization, leadership, functions, and activities of the village commune in Salem's territory as well as a related theme, the German Peasants' War of 1525.

One of this chapter's major objectives is to challenge the applicability of two common statements about the German peasantry, at least with respect to the southern Linzgau. The first is that the peasantry's political influence declined over the long sixteenth century along with the deterioration of the village commune. The second is that the German Peasants' War played a pivotal role in that process. This chapter presents a reinterpretation of the commune's historical trajectory and of the Peasant War's long-term significance. It requires a different view of the relationship between community and lordship as organizing principles and between the lord and his subjects as political actors. It downplays binary opposition and conflict in favor of other forms of political influence, namely negotiation, compromise, and even collaboration among various interest groups.

This chapter also contributes to a dialogue between two broad narratives of German agrarian history introduced in Chapter 1. Each of these approaches, which I will call communalism and its critics, has something to offer here, but neither one fully characterizes the situation in Salem. First, let us examine certain assumptions on both sides. Peter Blickle is currently the major figure representing the first approach, though his work must be seen as part of a much longer tradition in German historiography. He describes the village commune as a form of political association built upon horizontal relationships between equal members. Important features of communal decisionmaking included common assembly, election, and consent. The commune served as the primary vehicle for the peasantry's political actions both at the local level and beyond. Central to the commune were the administration of common lands and promotion of the common good. By the later Middle Ages the commune enjoyed corporate legal

1 The village commune refers to local political organization, see below.

status, including the capacity to enter agreements with outside parties and competence over certain areas of self-administration.[2]

In Blickle's view, communal principles were fundamentally opposed to feudal lordship, which was based on hierarchy and inequality, domination and obedience.[3] Blickle and others interpret resistance to lordship and defense of local autonomy as two of the commune's most important functions, which is why the period of revolts culminating in 1525 is seen as the height of communal activity and the German Peasants' War as the decisive turning point. The prevalence of late medieval peasant revolts in the German Southwest resulted not only from the intensification of lordship but also, and perhaps more importantly, from the development of communal institutions, organization, and identity.[4] As Blickle argues, the increasing volume and intensity of resistance movements that culminated in the German Peasants' War presupposes the existence of the village commune, because it was there that political action was organized and awareness fostered.[5] A point of consensus among historians is that the evidence from this period provides a clear connection between communal organization and resistance to lordship.[6] Indeed, the improving economic conditions in this period suggest that peasants' rising political expectations, rather than economic misery, provoked such conflicts.[7]

The German Peasants' War has been seen as a pivotal event for the development of the commune and for peasants' continuing political influence in the early modern period, though here Blickle's view differs somewhat from those of his predecessors. Before Blickle, the West German historiography of the German Peasants' War remained highly dependent on the influential interpretations of Günther Franz, whose

---

2 BADER, Studien 2, chap. 5. Karl Siegfried Bader established that the village commune formed in the period around 1300 and not, as previous generations of historians had assumed, much earlier. He saw the later Middle Ages as no accidental starting point for the study of lordship and rural communities because it is there that the sources first begin to provide evidence of peasant association. Idem, Bauernrecht und Bauernfreiheit im späteren Mittelalter, in: Ausgewählte Schriften zur Rechts- und Landesgeschichte, vol. 2, Sigmaringen 1984, p. 33; idem, Studien 1, chap. 1; idem, Studien 2, chap. 2.

3 See for example BLICKLE, Obedient Germans, p. 36. Bader did not argue for such a fundamental opposition; idem, Studien 1, p. 11; idem, Bauernrecht und Bauernfreiheit, p. 47.

4 BADER, Bauernrecht und Bauernfreiheit, p. 35; Peter BLICKLE, Unruhen in der ständischen Gesellschaft 1300–1800, Munich 1988, pp. 20, 64.

5 Peter BLICKLE, Bäuerliche Erhebungen im spätmittelalterlichen deutschen Reich, in: Zeitschrift für Agrargeschichte und Agrarsoziologie 27 (1979), p. 219.

6 Peter BLICKLE, From the Communal Reformation to the Revolution of the Common Man, trans. Beat Kümin, Cologne 1998, p. 169; idem, Unruhen, p. 20; David Warren SABEAN, The Communal Basis of Pre-1800 Peasant Uprisings in Western Europe, in: Comparative Politics (1976), pp. 355, 357; BRADY, German Histories, p. 185.

7 BADER, Studien 1, pp. 12–13; idem, Bauernrecht und Bauernfreiheit, p. 35; SREENIVASAN, Ottobeuren, pp. 43–45. Blickle's position, that economic decline in the fifteenth century resulted from the intensification of lordship (e.g. Bäuerliche Erhebungen, p. 217) has drawn criticism from SCOTT, Crisis of Feudalism, pp. 265–295.

book Der deutsche Bauernkrieg appeared in nine editions between 1933 and 1972.[8] For Franz, 1525 was primarily a struggle between the local autonomy of the rural commune and the growth of the feudal state. Its result was the lasting political disenfranchisement of the peasantry, a tragedy both for them and for the German people. The German Peasants' War thus represented the high point of the commune's activity as well as its greatest failure. The movement's outcome strengthened princely power, put an end to the people's reformation, and initiated the long decline of the village commune. According to this interpretation the rise of absolutism, built at the expense of local autonomy and self-regulation, resulted directly from the peasants' failure in 1525, never mind the intervening period of roughly 150 years.

In the last generation these attitudes have moderated somewhat, but the narrative of decline after 1525 is still entrenched.[9] One of this study's central objectives is to demonstrate the ways in which Salem's peasant subjects continued to play an important role in political development over the century following 1525. Blickle, the leading advocate for the peasantry's continuing political significance, identifies among the consequences of 1525 certain limited improvements.[10] Yet even he admits that in the end, the peasants were pacified and subjected to the interests of the growing territorial states, in the age of absolutism if not much earlier.[11] Blickle once remarked that the thesis of the peasantry's decline after 1525 could not be reversed without further research.[12] Although his specific examples are not especially well suited to the situation in Salem, his contributions provide several useful suggestions that point toward this goal. Salem had no assembly of territorial representatives (*Landschaft*), but one characteristic it shared with neighbors who did is that communal influence was recognized and integrated at the territorial level, especially in the century after 1525.

---

8 Günther FRANZ, Der deutsche Bauernkrieg, 1st ed., Munich, 1933; idem, 9th ed., Darmstadt, 1972.

9 This despite the exceptional contributions of Winfried Schulze; see for example his comment in idem, Reich und Türkengefahr im späten 16. Jahrhundert: Studien zu den politischen und gesellschaftlichen Auswirkungen einer äusseren Bedrohung, Munich 1978, pp. 271–272.

10 A major contribution is his research on the *Landschaften*, or territorial assemblies, which gave common subjects a voice in territorial decisions and taxation. Blickle sees other areas of improvement including the decline of serfdom and the establishment of hereditary tenure, both of which frequently resulted from agreements similar to Salem's 1473 settlement, though neither one were evident in Salem. Some agreements came after the German Peasants' War (e.g. Kempten and Waldburg), but most settlements preceded it. In many cases the *Landschaften* also grew out of these earlier negotiations—in other words, they were not primarily the result of 1525.

11 BLICKLE, Obedient Germans, pp. 25, 78; he also interprets Winfried Schulze's juridification of social conflict thesis as a negative development for subjects: idem, The Criminalization of Peasant Resistance in the Holy Roman Empire: Toward a History of the Emergence of High Treason in Germany, in: Journal of Modern History, supplement vol. 58 (Dec. 1986), pp. 88–97.

12 Peter BLICKLE, Die politische Entmündigung des Bauern: Kritik und Revision einer These, in: idem, ed., Revolte und Revolution in Europa, Memmingen 1975, p. 302.

A major critique of Blickle's model of the village commune and an alternative interpretation of historical development in the countryside focuses on a second challenge facing the village commune: growing internal stratification and social conflict. This narrative of the agrarian economy emphasizes long-term changes in demography, the availability of resources, and markets as opposed to statebuilding. It sees socioeconomic divisions within the commune as the driving force rather than village unity against outside threats.[13] All the studies in this tradition point out that many villagers were excluded from membership and participation in the commune, which possessed inherent inequalities both politically and otherwise. Even its members, the male householders, did not share identical views or material interests and they were not equally involved in local decisionmaking. The ideology of the commune masked divisions within the village and promoted certain interests over others: those of wealthy farm tenants over cottars and the landless poor, those of fathers over other members of their households.

The German Peasants' War, though a less central topic in this second approach, provides an example of how divisions within the village could manifest themselves in various ways.[14] According to David Sabean's study of Weingarten, the communes provided the organization and initiative in 1525, with an important proviso: they expressed the narrow interests of local elites against the rest of the villagers.[15] The communal movement in 1525 was directed against lords but also against the poor, with the wealthy landholders' bid for control over common lands and communal resources providing a primary motivating factor.[16] After the Treaty of Weingarten, concludes Sabean, the abbot along with other lords throughout the region rewarded local elites for their moderating influence by entering an alliance with them at the expense of poorer villagers. Govind Sreenivasan describes another outcome in Ottobeuren, where the Peasants' War evolved in two distinct phases. The tenant farmers provided leadership for the first and moderate phase, whereas smallholders carried the eventual radicaliza-

---

13 See for example SABEAN, Landbesitz; idem, German Agrarian Institutions at the Beginning of the Sixteenth Century: Upper Swabia as an Example, in: The German Peasant War of 1525, ed. Janos Bak, London 1976, pp. 76–88; idem, Communal Basis, pp. 355–364; SREENIVASAN, Ottobeuren; idem, The Social Origins of the Peasants' War of 1525 in Upper Swabia, in: Past and Present 171 (2001), pp. 30–65; Hermann REBEL, Peasant Classes: The Bureaucratization of Property and Family Relations under Early Habsburg Absolutism, 1511–1636, Princeton 1983; ROBISHEAUX, Rural Society; SCOTT, Freiburg and the Breisgau.

14 John C. STALNAKER, Towards a Social Interpretation of the German Peasants' War, in: The German Peasant War 1525: New Viewpoints, ed. Bob Scribner and Gerhard Benecke, London 1979, pp. 23–38.

15 SABEAN, Landbesitz, pp. 100–113.

16 Ibid.; idem, Communal Basis, p. 361. Sreenivasan agrees: Social Origins, p. 39.

tion.[17] Since the radical phase lacked the support of the commune and its wealthier landholders, the authorities easily quashed the resistance with military force. In Upper Austria, Hermann Rebel has identified a similar division of interests between tenants and smallholders that prevented them, in his view, from joining in any united action. The quarrels among peasant factions explain why they failed to achieve their goals in 1525.[18]

Higher authorities triumphed over radical elements in each of these examples, either with or without the support of peasant elites. The gap between rich and poor widened after the German Peasants' War, and where order and stability were established, it often came at a terrible price.[19] There are obvious merits to such socioeconomic approaches, with their recognition of inherent differences within the village and its households that are partially disguised beneath the cover of the commune.[20] They point to the existence of hierarchy and domination within local politics, not only as the result of the lord's intrusion, but more importantly, in relationships among the villagers themselves. Yet one assumption shared by each of the studies in this group is that wealthy peasants were able to use their influence within the commune to dominate weaker members and nonmembers. The socioeconomic explanation of local political development differs fundamentally from the communalism thesis it rejects, but both interpretations lead to the same basic outcome: the weakness and decline of the village commune after 1525.

Jonathan Dewald describes three major views of early modern community from a French perspective. According to the first, efforts to centralize state power paired with village inequalities led to the destruction of the commune. In the second, the commune remained strong because opposition to feudal lords united villagers despite their very different economic interests. The third explanation is the one Dewald prefers: increasing economic divisions in the village strengthened the commune, because only it could meet the rising demand for social regulations.[21] In addition to these possibilities,

17 SREENIVASAN, Social Origins, pp. 62–3. As he explains, elites had much to gain from the pre-existing agrarian order and recognized that their social status was ultimately guaranteed by the monastery.

18 REBEL, Peasant Classes, pp. 4–5.

19 So concludes Thomas Robisheaux, who also describes divisions in the ranks between tenants and winegrowers as well as between burghers and peasants in 1525; idem, Rural Society, pp. 11, 63–65.

20 Blickle, too, recognizes internal stratification in the villages but downplays its importance, arguing that communalism could not have been an organizing principle for centuries if it served only as a cover for elite interests. He believes that opposition to feudal lords and above all internal solidarity unified the commune despite certain underlying divisions of interest. Idem, Communal Reformation, p. 170; idem, Begriffsverfremdung: Über den Umgang mit dem wissenschaftlichen Ordnungsbegriff Kommunalismus, in: Zeitschrift für Historische Forschung 22 (1995), p. 247.

21 Jonathan DEWALD, Pont-St- Pierre, 1398–1789: Lordship, Community, and Capitalism in Early Modern France, Berkeley 1987, p. 127. He ascribes the first view to Alexis de Tocqueville and the second to Albert Soboul.

André Holenstein contributes a fourth interpretation: that the interactions between community and lordship in both village and territory were a source of strength and stability.[22] They provided for a balance of various groups' changing needs and included their interests in a period of growing economic differentiation, sometimes through conflict but more often through milder forms of negotiation and compromise.

The political web in Salem combined principles of community and lordship in complex ways. Despite obvious contrasts between vertical forms of domination and obedience on the one hand and horizontal forms of equity and inclusion on the other, the two organizational structures were not only interpenetrating but also completely interwoven. The distinction between community as a set of norms and practices supported by subjects, in opposition to lordship as a set of norms and practices supported by rulers, needs to be qualified. This is because the same individuals engaged in both these structures and arguments according to the situation, and neither the actors nor their actions can be neatly divided into two separate groups. Although conflict certainly existed in relations between the abbey and its subjects as well as among villagers, here it is argued that opposition was neither the defining characteristic of such relationships nor the primary instigator of change. It is noteworthy that in each of the three major resistance movements directed by territorial subjects against Salem Abbey during the long sixteenth century, settlements (in 1473, 1525, and 1635) resulted from peaceful negotiation and compromise. Words rather than arms led to the solution.

In the historiography, there continues to be a strong link between the village commune and the German Peasants' War.[23] According to Peter Blickle it is hard to imagine how peasant revolts, let alone the "revolution of the common man," would have been organized in this period if not by the village commune, which he sees as a prerequisite for collective resistance in the countryside. Rebels joined the movement not as individuals but as members of the commune. The major goals stated in many of their political platforms and articles were to strengthen the autonomy of local communes and make communal organization the foundation of a new social order.[24] As already indicated, however, it continues to be a standard narrative that the events of 1525 were not only the high point of the commune's activities but also the start of its decline.[25] This chapter as well as the larger study offers a revision of that view.

---

22 HOLENSTEIN, Gute Policey; idem, Empowering Interactions, pp. 1–31.

23 According to Govind Sreenivasan, "The rural *Gemeinde* is something of a sacred cow in the literature on the Peasants' War; it has apparently become impossible to address the events of 1525 without solemnly proclaiming that the bearer of the resistance was the *Gemeinde*." Idem, Social Origins, pp. 36–37.

24 Horst BUSZELLO, The Common Man's View of the State in the German Peasant War, in: The German Peasant War 1525: New Viewpoints, ed. Bob Scribner and Gerhard Benecke, London 1979, p. 110; Hans-Martin MAURER, Der Bauernkrieg als Massenerhebung: Dynamik einer revolutionären Bewegung, in: Bausteine zur geschichtlichen Landeskunde von Baden-Württemberg, ed. Günther Haselier et al., Stuttgart 1979, p. 272.

25 FRANZ, Bauernkrieg.

Salem's subjects participated in the German Peasants' War with great enthusiasm and in massive numbers. An estimated 10,000 armed rebels assembled in Bermatingen alone, more than twice the total population Under the Hills. Salem's rebel subjects who rallied in Bermatingen also belonged to the Christian Union of Upper Swabia, the federation of three major armies that produced the famous Twelve Articles.[26] In a period of otherwise scarce documentation, the Linzgau peasants' involvement in the German Peasants' War illuminates certain aspects of social and political life and issues of grievance that are hidden from view in ordinary times.[27] This chapter suggests that the German Peasants' War was not a watershed moment in Salem's lands, yet it was a remarkable event. It was fundamentally related to political developments and to socioeconomic conditions both before and after 1525—thus it was not, as Ranke saw it, "the greatest natural event in the history of the German State."[28] Just as the German Peasants' War bridges the chronological gap between the Sidelrichter dispute of 1473 and the comparatively well-documented decades around 1600, this chapter and in particular its interpretations of 1525 provides a link between Chapter 2 and the later chapters of this study.

The following discussion begins by considering three themes, each of which provides essential context for the German Peasants' War in the southern Linzgau. These are the late medieval commune, servility, and local religious foundations. The next section describes the events of 1525 in the region and suggests their broader significance for Salem's political development, especially in terms of relations between the abbey and its subjects as well as between community leaders and other villagers. The second half of the chapter focuses on various aspects of the village commune, both before and especially after 1525. These include its organization and institutions, functions, officials, members, and material resources. It looks at the commune in terms of the mounting challenges posed by external authorities and internal divisions over the course of the period. The chapter ends with two topics that illustrate these issues particularly well: the role of the village headmen (*Amtmänner*) and the use of common lands. In sum, this chapter assesses the importance of the Peasants' War and of the village commune in the territory's political evolution from below.

---

26 The Twelve Articles stated the Christian Union's grievances and objectives, justified in the godly law by specific biblical references.

27 SABEAN, Communal Basis, p. 359.

28 See Kuhn's remarks on why Leopold von Ranke was mistaken on two counts in this famous passage from his Deutsche Geschichte im Zeitalter der Reformation; Elmar KUHN, Der Bauernkrieg am See, in: Seegrunde: Beiträge zur Geschichte des Bodenseeraumes, ed. Dieter Schott and Werner Trapp, Weingarten 1984, p. 20.

3.1 Bermatingen: A Late Medieval Village Commune

The village of Bermatingen is one of the oldest settlements in the Linzgau. The largest village in Salem's territory, it had a population of around one hundred households and 500 inhabitants in 1525.[29] It possessed vigorous communal traditions, strong organization, and an important parish church.[30] Wine and grain production supported a diversified, market-based economy.[31] Located at the eastern edge of the territory near Markdorf, it sat on the major transportation route connecting Salem's territory with places to the east and southeast. Bermatingen has been the subject of several minor studies, and its relatively good source material makes it an obvious choice for closer examination.[32] Bermatingen also holds special interest as the headquarters of the Lake Army's Linzgau regiment in 1525 and as the center of the regional uprising.

In political terms, Bermatingen stands out from neighboring communes in certain key respects. It was not a partner to the agreement of 1473 and was the only village in the central territory to enjoy exemption from the territorial court, the Sidelgericht.[33] Thus, the people of Bermatingen did not identify with the common legal tradition or increasingly uniform legal status shared by other abbey dependents in this period. They did not feel bound by the alte Jarbrief or by the settlement of 1473.[34] Bermatingen had strong political organs of its own, including a local court and a village council with

---

29 Bermatingen was about the same size as the town of Buchhorn (Friedrichshafen). See Elmar KUHN, Der Seehaufen, in: Der Bauernkrieg in Oberschwaben, ed. Elmar Kuhn, Tübingen 2000, p. 111. By 1578, Bermatingen had around 130 households and 552 inhabitants. Population is discussed in Chapter 4.

30 Bermatingen, as the suffix –ingen suggests, was an old settlement, established around the seventh century, and its self-administration predated Salem's authority by several centuries.

31 Extensive winegrowing provided for the livelihood of a large population of smallholders and landless laborers, and as was true of most large villages, Bermatingen had extreme social differentiation. The lack of documentation concerning conflicts within the community suggest that the community was successful in incorporating the needs of its various members, or at least settling its own internal disputes without calling on territorial officials to intervene. That wine was an important economic commodity in the village is confirmed by the many ordinances regulating the sale of wine in the village.

32 Erika DILLMANN, ed., 1200 Jahre Bermatingen, 779–1979, Bermatingen 1979; Vikar DEISSLER, Die Geschichte von Bermatingen, Überlingen 1911; KUHN, Bauernkrieg am See, pp. 19–52.

33 Bermatingen had its own village court with twelve local judges. Residents were not required to appear before the abbey's court, and even in the later period they could request that suits brought against them there be transferred to the local court. Bermatingers did sometimes appear voluntarily before the Sidelgericht.

34 When the partnership agreement of 1473 was confirmed in 1572 at the territorial judges' request, it was stated explicitly that all the people living Under the Hills were bound by it, with the exception of Bermatingen: "ReuerßBrieff Deß Gotzhauß Salmanßweyler Stabhalters, und der Sidelrichtere auch gemeinden Gotzhaußleuthen under den Bergen, (Außgenomen deß Fleckens Bermentingen) Uber die abschrifft deß ernewerten Jarberichts 1473." GLAK, 4/135.

24 members (not to be confused with the village assembly). The "Twenty-Four," both active and large, suggests the broad participation of local householders in political decisionmaking. By the end of the Middle Ages, Bermatingen's local privileges and strong sense of political autonomy set it in opposition to the abbey's efforts to build a unified band of subjects under its undivided territorial authority.

Several documents from the late fifteenth century provide the opportunity to examine the commune's organization, political development, and relations with the abbey on the eve of the German Peasants' War. A 1498 village statute (*satzung*) highlights Bermatingen's communal administration and the regulations in place at that time.[35] The statute's preamble indicates that it had been drafted and produced by the *Amtmann* (village headman), the court, and the Twenty-Four, who had sworn to respect the common good and to defend it against any great damages that might present themselves.[36] Several articles regulating wine appear near the top of the list, an indication of this commodity's economic importance as well as the commune's claim to regulate it.[37] The statute also describes several areas of communal responsibility and fines for personal misconduct. Attendance at communal assemblies was obligatory for all members, with penalties for absence as well as tardiness. Infractions of peace and order were to be reported to the Twenty-Four, and any witness to an assault was authorized to intervene with word or deed, as long as he or she drew no weapons. Certain forests and common lands were off-limits, and fines to the commune for illegal grazing and other offenses increased when not paid by a certain date. Householders were required to attend Mass along with their servants. Lewd behavior (*all unzuchten*) was forbidden. Several articles pertained to the exclusion of nonresident outsiders.[38]

The 1498 statute provides important evidence of the commune's political competence, in terms of both specific regulatory activities and general political awareness. In particular, many of the articles refer to the Twenty-Four as the final authority rather

---

35 GLAK, 67/1484.

36 "Item des Jars do man Zalt … ist ain amman und ain Erber gericht und die vier und zwaintzig habent die satzung by geschworen ayden gesetz und gemacht den gemainen nutz angesächen grössen schaden zů fur komen." GLAK, 67/1484. The text appears in a copiary containing duplicates of important documents.

37 For example, Article 1 states that the innkeeper should not buy wine without permission from the Amtmann and the Twenty-Four, and that in order to determine a fair price he should call the wine assessor and wine taster prior to unloading it into his cellar. According to Article 2, private wine sellers were likewise required to have their wine tasted and assessed. Other articles mention an excise tax and specify profits on wine sales of no more than three pounds per Fuder.

38 Strangers could stay no longer than one night, and servants from outside the village had to register with the Amtmann within one week. New residents including spouses had to pay the commune an entry fee of one pound. Land offered for sale was restricted to buyers within the jurisdiction for a period of one year, after which outside bids required permission from the Amtmann and the Twenty-Four. Manure and wood could not be sold outside the village. Only residents were allowed to grow grapes in the village (*Im Etter oder Im ban*).

than the abbot or his officials. The explicit references to village officials, the lack of acknowledgement for superior or external authorities, and the commune's claim to broad powers of regulation and enforcement all lead to the conclusion that the Bermatingers produced this document to address their concerns rather than those of the abbey. This does not suggest, however, that villagers created the 1498 statute without any reference to lordship. Most likely, it arose as a means of asserting the commune's authority and defending its local customs.

A series of legal conflicts between Bermatingen and the abbey supports this hypothesis. Various disputes between them had been settled by arbitration in 1443, 1457, and 1478. Implicit in each of the agreements was the recognition of Bermatingen as a legally competent corporation, or *universitas*.[39] The agreements were sealed and issued in two copies, one for each side. They required each side to put the dispute behind them and abandon any further claims. In all three cases the primary mediator was the Truchsess von Waldburg, who was also the Imperial Landvogt in Upper Swabia.[40]

The 1443 settlement concerned various unspecified disagreements pitting the abbot and his convent against the "entire common peasantry of the village."[41] The arbitrators declared all past actions and animosities ("*zwytracht spenne vnd misshellung*") between them to be invalid. They instructed the Bermatingers to renew their obedience without any reservation and admonished the abbot and convent to treat the villagers mercifully, "as if these things had never happened."[42]

The agreement of 1457 describes the disputed issues and terms of settlement in comparatively greater detail. As stated in the document's introduction, they concerned "labor services, grazing, the wine tavern, excise taxes, wine presses, and [other] taxes."[43] Labor services, which Salem demanded on the basis of jurisdictional authority, were the first topic of grievance. According to the settlement:

---

39 Bob Scribner (Communities, p. 300) calls this legal-corporative character the bedrock of peasant political and social self-consciousness; see also Peter BIERBRAUER, Freiheit und Gemeinde im Berner Oberland 1300–1700, Bern 1991, pp. 69, 79; BADER, Studien 2, chap. 5.

40 In 1443 Truchsess Jacob von Waldburg was joined as primary mediator (*gemeiner*) by four assistants (*zusätze*), two chosen by Salem and two by Bermatingen. In 1457 the same nobleman headed an arbitration committee including three advisors (*Räte*). In 1478 Truchsess Jorg von Waldburg declared the settlement without mention of additional arbitrators.

41 "Der gantzen gemainen gebursamy des dorffs bermattingen"; elsewhere, "der gemainen geburschafft." GLAK, 4/1769.

42 "Also das der benant unser herr der appt und sin Convent her'en die berürten gebursamy zu Bermattingen des berürten vergangen Handels und unwillens nu furohin in kunfftigen Zyten nit engelten laussen Sunder sy gnediglich halten als ob solichs nie beschehen noch ufferstanden wäre. Es sullen och die selben von Bermattingen dem offtgenanten unserm her'en dem Apptt und sinen Convent her'en gütlich ane wägern gehorsam gewärtig unnd inen von solicher vergangen sachen und unwillens wegen nu furohin och dest unwilliger nit sin. Sunder sy fur ir gnedig her'en halten ane gevärde." GLAK, 4/1769.

43 "Von dienste, Aynungen ettlicher trib und tratt, der win täfrin, des ungeltz, des torggelwins, und der sturen wegen." GLAK, 4/1770.

> Therefore and from now on, the common people (*arme Leute*) of Bermatingen who sit within the court's jurisdiction, no matter who they may claim to be, shall perform for my lord of Salem, his convent, the abbey, and their successors all the services they have performed in the past, both generally and in particular. Moreover, the farm tenants of Bermatingen who are not of the abbey or who do not sit on the abbey's property shall also provide the abbot [etc.] with the four types of plowing services, as the abbey's farm tenants have done until now, without dissent.[44]

The term *arme Leute*, which appears in this context as a reference to abbey dependents and most likely to its serfs, suggests that labor services derived previously from legal status. The article's emphasis on the services owed by farmers who were neither of the abbey nor its tenants, however, made clear that this was no longer the case. Thus, it set an important precedent for the performance of labor services by all residents, regardless of their status. On the topic of grazing, the decision stated that fines collected from certain pastures that were closed to grazing (*den verbannen uchtwaiden*) belonged to the entire village for the maintenance of its paths and byways, as was customary. However, the Amtmann would collect fines from illegal grazing in other rent-bearing fields, meadows, and gardens for the abbey's use. This division of authority recognized both sides' claims to grazing fines but granted neither one a monopoly.[45] Each of three articles relating to wine supported Salem's position on ban rights, including pressing fees and excise taxes.[46] The final topic of the 1457 agreement was "*Sturen*," a likely reference to imperial tax collection. The arbitrators agreed with villagers' claim that they had never paid taxes to Salem in the past and should not be required to do so in the future. This victory turned out to be short-lived, however, since an imperial privilege of 1470 authorized Salem to collect taxes from all inhabitants of its jurisdiction, including Bermatingen.[47]

---

44 "Also das nun hinfur die armmenlute, zů Bermatingen In gerichten zwingen und Bännen gesessen gemainlich ald sonderlich Sy syen wes Si wöllen, dem benanten Minem H'ren von Salmenswyler sinem Convente und Gotzhus, und Iren nachkomen Alle die dienste wie Si die untzher getan hand, tůn sullen und dartzu So söllen die mayer daselbs die nicht des Gotzhus noch uff des Gotzhus gueter gesessen sind demselben meinem Herren von Salmenswiler sinem Convente und Gotzhus und aller Iren nachkomen mit Iren pflügen zů den vier arten dienen als des gotzhus mayer daselbs bißher getan hand ungevarlich." Ibid.

45 The division of such rights can be seen in documentation for other villages as well. See GLAK, 4/4746 (Nußdorf, 1461) and 4/4630 (Neufrach, 1508). Village account records from the late sixteenth and early seventeenth centuries demonstrate the commune's continuing authority over grazing offenses and fines.

46 As previously stated in the Nellenburg Treaty of 1419, Salem claimed half the profits from all wine presses and an excise tax of four pence per Eimer of wine. The amount of an additional consumption tax on drinking establishments was unspecified, but this was a later source of complaint among innkeepers in several villages.

47 GLAK, 4/752.

A third arbitrated settlement in 1478 weighed Bermatingen's customary privileges and exemptions against the more general requirements of all abbey dependents.[48] It addressed just one topic: the loyalty oath. According to villagers, they had never sworn such an oath in the past and had no desire to do so in the future. They called the new oath improper (*unzimlich*) and difficult (*swär*), a violation of their customs and responsibilities. They cited a clause in the settlement of 1443 requiring the abbey to honor their customs and traditions in return for loyalty and obedience. They urged the abbey to uphold ancient practice, whether voluntarily or through legal settlement. Salem's legal advocate referred several times to the "current difficulties" and to the *Berichtsbrief* (the "*neue Bericht*," or settlement of 1473).[49] Though he made no claim that the Bermatingers had sworn an oath in the past, he stated: "No matter what they are called, all his [people] Over and Under the Hills have sworn this oath. For those from Bermatingen to refuse this would bring great future harm. Moreover, my lord of Salem considers it the common practice of the land and not improper."[50] The decision in Salem's favor required all jurisdictional residents to swear an oath according to their status, whether or not they were the abbey's serfs. In other words, the abbey claimed all villagers as its subjects, regardless of their legal status, and they were required as such to uphold certain obligations. Contained in this text are the earliest surviving versions of the two oath formulas sworn by Salem's serfs and jurisdictional residents throughout the early modern period.[51]

The defeat of several of Bermatingen's local privileges and customary claims in each of these three settlements demonstrates both the deterioration of communal autonomy in the generations directly preceding the German Peasants' War and the grounds for mounting opposition to Salem's territorial policies in this period. The Bermatingers were unwilling to accept Salem's introduction of new policies, and they were able to air their collective grievances by way of the village commune, even if many of the decisions were against them. The issues raised in these arbitrated settlements continued to be topics of negotiation and dissent, and the experience of resistance and legal action would serve village leaders in the future, most notably in 1525. Salem's efforts to overrule Bermatingen's local political autonomy and to emphasize instead its inclusion in a broader polity were largely successful in the long term. Yet the abbey's policies in the late fifteenth century help explain why Bermatingen joined the widespread movement

---

48 GLAK, 4/1687.

49 "Der swären löff und hänndel So Jetz Im land vorhannden" was most likely a reference to the Sidelrichter dispute and possibly to lingering disagreements resulting from the 1473 settlement.

50 "Alle die sinen ob und under den bergen wie die gena[n]t sind haben sölh Aid getan und wa das von den von bermatingen nit geschäche möcht Im zû künfftigen Zyten mercklichen schaden bringen und vermaint mein heren von Salmenswiler das syge der gemain landsbruch sye auch nit unzymlich." GLAK, 4/1687.

51 The oath is discussed in Chapter 6.

in 1525 and why it became the center of the Linzgau uprising. Bermatingen's leadership encouraged the participation of surrounding villages in opposition to the abbey and against lordship more generally. As Bermatingen became more fully integrated into Salem's territory, it was not simply on the abbot's terms. Instead, Bermatingen set an example for other communes, as they demanded the inclusion of their interests and customs in the development of territorial rule.

One final text relating to Bermatingen's communal development on the eve of the German Peasants' War is a 1512 agreement concerning use of the commons.[52] This settlement is especially noteworthy because it is the only illustration from Salem in this period of disagreement over the commons between groups within a single village. According to David Sabean, this was one of the primary underlying motivations for Weingarten's farm tenants who joined the movement in 1525. The agreement in Bermatingen, reached by the members of the commune without outside arbitration, offered a creative solution to the problem of land use. The area in question was known as the Brunach, and the settlement describes a compromise of interests according to three distinct seasons and uses. During the first period, from the start of the year until St. John the Baptist's Day (24 June), the farm tenants (*Mayer*) enjoyed exclusive grazing rights. In the second period, from St. John's to St. Michael's Day (29 September), the property was turned over to individual parcel holders for use as gardens. In the third period, from St. Michael's Day through the end of the year, the parcels reopened for grazing, this time by the entire commune. This solution offered a balance of rights to major interest groups within the village, and two unusual stipulations about the garden parcels gave special advantages to the smallholders. Namely, only households without plow teams received parcels at no cost, whereas tenants had to pay a fee for their use.[53] Parcel rights were heritable, but only by members of the commune, and they were redistributed every two years.[54] This periodic redistribution clause provided special protection for smallholders by preventing the accumulation of parcels through sale or inheritance. Yet the agreement also served the interests of farm tenants with their large herds, who enjoyed exclusive grazing rights for half the year. Overall, the settlement was a good compromise in terms of land use and the balance of interests among village households. On one hand, it provides evidence of growing competition within the village for use of the commons before 1525. On the other hand, both the

---

52 GLAK, 67/1484.

53 Anyone with a plow team who inherited a parcel had to give it up or pay a tax. All other married couples or widows were eligible for an equal parcel, subject to redistribution every two years. This suggests that smallholders not only enjoyed rent-free garden plots, they also had preferred access to them.

54 Mimmenhausen followed a similar practice in a commons known as the Mooß. A dozen or so lists from the period 1597–1634 (and others from 1650–1668) name the holders of over one hundred parcels. Many households had the use of more than one parcel, which varied in size and owed land rents ranging from two to twelve kreuzer. The total land rent was just under twenty gulden per year, and parcels appear to have been redistributed annually. GLAK, 98/4419.

compromise of interests struck in 1512 and the lack of similar agreements in this period fail to support the conclusion that internal conflict over the commons was among the central causes of the German Peasants' War. We will return to the commons at the end of this chapter.

3.2 The Bonds of Servility

Servility, as seen in Chapter 2, was a major issue in the Sidelrichter dispute that began in 1468 and in the partnership agreement with which it ended in 1473. The extension of serfdom and opposition to it also provoked conflicts in many other territories, mostly during the century before 1525.[55] Despite the agreements struck in several cases, servility remained a widespread topic of grievance in the very same places, and it served to unite opposition across the region during the German Peasants' War. It ranked high in local and regional articles and came up more frequently than any other issue, except perhaps the godly law.[56] Among the peasant subjects of many Upper Swabian abbeys, serfdom was the number one complaint.[57] Obviously, therefore, the 1473 settlement in Salem and others like it left something to be desired. This section looks at serfdom's social, economic, and political implications in Salem's territory between 1473 and 1525 in order to evaluate its relevance for the region's participation in the German Peasants' War.

As described in the previous chapter, Article 1 of the 1473 settlement stated that all people of the abbey were to consider themselves and be considered as its serfs.[58] This extension of servility to the entire body of the abbey's dependents (despite the fact that such a claim proved impossible to enforce) assisted the abbey in the consolidation

---

55 BLICKLE and HOLENSTEIN, Agrarverfassungsverträge.

56 BLICKLE, Revolution of 1525, p. 215. The Twelve Articles of Upper Swabia as well as the Rappertsweiler Articles list serfdom in third place, following two articles on godly law, tithes, and the election of local clergy by the commune. In the Linzgau, serfdom was mentioned in early March as a source of grievance among Überlingen's subjects. In Markdorf, the mayor explained that so many townspeople joined the peasants because they were serfs and wanted to be free. Hildegard KUHN-OECHSELE and Elmar KUHN, ed., Der Seehaufen im Bauernkrieg: Eine Quellensammlung, vol. 2/2, Friedrichshafen 1982, pp. 71, 79a.

57 HOLENSTEIN, Äbte und Bauern, p. 264, n. 64; BLICKLE, Revolution von 1525, Appendix 2. Holenstein's analysis is based on twenty texts submitted by subjects of various abbeys, three-quarters of which called for the total abolition of serfdom. In six cases serfdom topped the list and in three others it came in second place. This reinforces the conclusion that opposition to serfdom was one of the movement's major issues. Schussenried appears to be an exception in this respect; see the SAARBRÜCKER ARBEITSGRUPPE, Leibeigenschaft, p. 22.

58 "Die gotshuslüte sich sollend bekennen und sin aygen gotshuslüte." GLAK, 4/129–130; BLICKLE and HOLENSTEIN, Agrarverfassungsverträge, p. 54. In fact, not all dependents of the abbey became its serfs. For an interpretation on laws that were not implemented, see Jürgen SCHLUMBOHM, Gesetze, die nicht durchgesetzt werden – ein Strukturmerkmal des frühneuzeitlichen Staates?, in: Geschichte und Gesellschaft 23 (1997), pp. 647–663.

of territorial lordship in two important ways. First, it limited other lords' authority over territorial residents, and second, it strengthened Salem's command over a more uniform group of dependents.[59] The ruling was a major victory for the abbey, since it formed the theoretical basis for residential rather than hereditary serfdom. Yet the imposition of identical and inferior legal status and obligations on all abbey subjects had differing effects for various socioeconomic groups. For the Sidelrichter and others who had previously claimed to be free, it meant a serious deterioration in status.[60] Previously they had distanced themselves from issues of personal bondage, but now they had reason to join the resistance. This energized the communes' political opposition to serfdom and primed them for participation in 1525.

The terms set in 1473 were not the only grounds for opposition to serfdom. During the decade 1476–1486, the extension of the loyalty oath was the subject of three separate agreements. We have already looked at one of them, the 1478 settlement between Salem and Bermatingen requiring all villagers to swear an oath of obedience, regardless of their status.[61] Though serfdom was not its primary issue, this text bears on the current discussion because it contains the earliest surviving oath formulas sworn by Salem's serfs (*aigene Leute*) and other jurisdictional residents (*Hintersassen*) throughout the early modern period. According to the oath formulas, the major restriction specific to serfs involved mobility: serfs could not leave the territory without permission, nor could they seek outside protection or foreign citizenship. Since the 1473 settlement made no mention of mobility restrictions, the timing of this discussion appears to be no coincidence.

The other two documents, statutes from 1476 and 1486, addressed the entire central territory.[62] Each one lists the names of the Thirty (territorial representatives) along with the abbot and other senior administrators who enacted it.[63] According to Article 1

---

59 Hermann Tüchle describes the drive to turn peasants into serfs as a method of territorial consolidation shared by rulers throughout the region, but echoing Hermann Baier, he points to Salem as the harshest and most systematic example among ecclesiastical lords. Idem, Süddeutsche Klöster, pp. 115–116.

60 In 1470 the Sidelrichter claimed repeatedly to be people of God's house and not the abbey's serfs. See Chapter 2; GLAK, 4/120.

61 GLAK, 4/1687.

62 GLAK, 4/131 and 4/363. Both statutes contain four articles and present structural similarities. The 1476 text concerns the political duties and capabilities of male subjects: to swear the loyalty oath, command the peace, evaluate tenure disputes, and certify payments in kind. Control over female serfs and their property appear as the major themes in 1486, with articles on the loyalty oath, death taxes, and limitations on widows' ability to remarry or freely dispose of property. See also BAIER, Vorgeschichte, p. 207.

63 These are the only surviving documents besides the 1473 agreement to mention the collaboration of the Thirty and list them by name. The participation of the Thirty in all new legislation was mandated in 1473, but there is no evidence that the abbot consulted them again after 1486. It appears likely that the 1476 and 1486 statutes resulted from disagreements over the contents and interpretation of the earlier decision, though no specifics are mentioned. The triangular cuts along one side of the 1476 charter reveal that it was one of two copies cut from the same

of the 1476 statute, all men 14 years and older living within the abbey's jurisdiction were required to swear a loyalty oath either as serfs (*aigene Leute*) or as residents (*Hintersassen*).[64] Specifically, they had to promise to uphold both the alte Jarbrief and the settlement of 1473 (*der neue Bericht*). The 1486 agreement extended the same oath to the abbey's female serfs starting at age twelve.

The reference to separate oaths taken by serfs and residential subjects in 1476 raises an interesting point. Even in the years directly following 1473, not all abbey dependents were its serfs. If they had been, there would be no need for an oath specific to nonservile residents. Despite the declaration that all people of the abbey were its serfs, the abbey lacked the power to enforce its will.[65] Later records indicate that universal serfdom was never implemented, though not for lack of trying on the abbey's part. In a 1488 tax list, the names of *Hintersassen* and *aigene Leute* in each village are divided into two separate groups.[66] Tax lists from 1578 and 1593 kept track of the legal status for every male and female householder as well as their children. The percentage of free and foreign serfs increased with distance from the abbey, but even in Neufrach and Mimmenhausen, not all residents were Salem's serfs. In Owingen, abbey serfs accounted for less than half the population in 1578.[67] The fact that some residents continued to be free or foreign serfs, in spite of the 1473 agreement, may have increased opposition to serfdom and the feeling among many abbey subjects that the distinction was arbitrary.

The statutes of 1476 and 1486 suggest an additional reason why servility remained a contested issue on the eve of the German Peasants' War. Namely, the abbey refused to abandon the alte Jarbrief after 1473. Perhaps the new settlement was acknowledged as

---

page; there are two original copies of the 1486 statute. The duplication of these texts in Salem's copiaries indicates that the abbey viewed them as important additions to and clarifications of earlier territorial law codes. See Chapter 6; GLAK, 67/1478.

64 "Das alle und yegclich manns personen, So ... minem gnädigen Herrn von Salem mitt aigenschafft verwanndt oder In siner gnauden Gericht Zwinng und Bann geseßn sind, ... Ainen zimlichn aide sweren solln Mitt namen ain aigenman als ain aigenman und ain hindersase als ain hindersase, Als Irem Rechten naturlichen herrn Doch allweg dem alten Jarbrief ouch dem obvermelten nuwen bericht ... unvergriffenlich und unschadlich." GLAK, 4/131. This passage supports the interpretation of a *Hintersass* as someone living under the lord's jurisdiction who was not his serf.

65 The cooperation of the village headman was crucial, a point we will return to later in this chapter.

66 In Bermatingen, the number of householders who were not Salem's serfs was 38 out of 79 total residents; in Buggensegel it was 3 out of 21, Neufrach 18 out of 87, and Weiler 5 out of 20 residents. GLAK, 98/2007.

67 According to the 1578 list, 78% of all male householders and 74% of female householders in Salem's major villages were its serfs. In Neufrach 94% of men were Salem's serfs compared with 88% in Mimmenhausen, 68% in Bermatingen, and only 45% in Owingen. Buchhorn, Constance cathedral chapter, Heiligenberg, Mainau, Montfort, Petershausen, Radolfzell, Ravensburg, St. Blasien, St. Johann (Überlingen), Tettnang, von Bodman, Wald, Weingarten, Weißenau, and several other lordships had serfs in Salem's territory. GLAK, 98/2024.

the preferred law where it directly contradicted the alte Jarbrief, but even so, it did not address all the older provisions. Where the 1473 settlement did not specifically modify the alte Jarbrief, therefore, the older law code remained (or could be interpreted, at least, as being) in effect. Since the alte Jarbrief was more favorable to the abbey's interests than the new agreement, the abbot continued to insist on it as a foundational legal document alongside the more recent settlement. In addition, the alte Jarbrief was extended to Salem's outlying districts as early as 1500. In a copy of the text produced in that year for use in the district Over the Hills, the preamble explained that the text was an ancient customal, identical in wording to the damaged original. Reminiscent of earlier claims against the Sidelrichter, it asserted that the text had been customary law for centuries. No mention was made of the fact that Salem's fragmented possessions around Ostrach had not been subject to Salem's low jurisdiction or legal statutes until recently. No mention was made of the 1473 agreement either.

In 1493, Abbot Johannes I wrote to Kempten's abbot in reply to a recent inquiry about Salem's customs regarding serfdom. The correspondence between the two abbots provides a good example of lords comparing notes. It also demonstrates their concern about the connection between servility and revolt, as it followed on the heels of an uprising by Kempten's *Freizinser*, dependents who claimed not to be serfs. Salem's abbot answered in detail:

> Our abbey's old traditions, customs, and practices with regard to our serfs are as follows. We do not demand from them any annual taxes except for a Shrovetide chicken from every man of the abbey. They do help carry a portion of the imperial military taxes, however. As for the heriot, a man's moveable wealth and property falls to us when he dies without a widow or unprovisioned child. When a man of the abbey marries a woman or daughter who is not our serf, we penalize him as we wish. When, however, a man of the abbey dies and leaves a widow or unprovisioned child who is also our serf, we take his best animal and his best garment. When the wife dies leaving a husband, we do not take the best animal but only her best dress, and if she leaves neither husband nor unprovisioned child, then we receive all her moveable goods.[68]

This description gives an idea of how the abbot interpreted serfdom and its hallmarks, or at least how he presented them to a peer. Yet it differs in certain respects from the 1473 agreement.[69] It is hard to say whether the abbot knowingly contradicted the earlier compromise or if the abbey actually collected all moveable property in the absence of heirs, but the abbot's statements demonstrate the ambiguous nature and flexible burdens of serfdom. It is surprising and noteworthy that the abbot did not mention mobility, outside courts, or outside protection, focusing instead on marriage fines and

---

68 GLAK, 98/31, 1493.

69 Among the biggest differences, the abbot claimed to inherit all moveable property in the absence of heirs, whereas the 1473 settlement specified a percentage of moveables only in the case of outside marriage. He did not mention the one-year grace period; imperial taxes were collected on the basis of jurisdiction, not servility.

death taxes. This suggests that the economic burdens of serfdom were not irrelevant following the partnership agreement after all.[70]

In sum, there were several grounds for grievance against serfdom in 1525. The settlement in 1473 ameliorated certain burdens, especially relating to property and inheritance rights, but it also sought to extend servility to all abbey dependents including those who claimed to be free. The abbey also required every adult under its jurisdiction to take an oath, regardless of legal status or local privilege. For serfs, the oath emphasized the major burdens left out of the 1473 agreement: they had to swear not to alienate themselves or their property from the abbey or seek outside citizenship or protection. Finally, there are signs that the limited gains of 1473 were eroding even in the years immediately following the agreement. According to the oath formulas and the abbot's personal correspondence, the allegedly ancient customal was still in effect. In this situation there could be no agreement about serfdom, because the two law codes contradicted one another and the meaning and specific burdens of serfdom remained as ambiguous as ever.

3.3 Religious Foundations in the Villages

Godly law was the major slogan in the German Peasants' War as well as the first topic of both the Twelve Articles of Upper Swabia and the Lake Army's Rappertsweiler Articles. No local grievance lists describe the Linzgau peasants' specific demands in 1525, but the rebels in this region clearly supported the godly law. It was, in fact, the only subject mentioned in the oath they forced Salem's convent to swear. Here, in order to contextualize the call for the godly law in 1525, we will examine a group of records that demonstrates the importance of religion in the lives of Salem's late medieval villagers as well as the initiatives taken by village communes to provide for the religious services they lacked at the local level. The funding by local communes for religious services beneath the parish level, known as lesser benefices (*Niederpfründe*), was especially popular in the century preceding the German Peasants' War.

The parish churches of Bermatingen, Leutkirch, Mimmenhausen (since 1630), Pfaffenhofen, Seefelden, and Weildorf were located within Salem's central territory. Urnau, too, was a parish center. Yet parish organization in the Linzgau was extremely old and did not coincide with the political landscape of the sixteenth century.[71] This

70 Lordship over serfs had both political and economic functions, the significance of which changed over time; cf. HOLENSTEIN, Äbte und Bauern, p. 255; ULBRICH, Leibherrschaft, pp. 294–295.

71 The first parishes in the Linzgau formed between the sixth and tenth centuries and most parishes in the region were much older than Salem. The church in Seefelden is mentioned in records from the seventh century, and archeological evidence from Bermatingen dates an altar from the same period. On the early history of Salem's parishes, see STAIGER, Salem oder Salmansweiler;

meant most villages did not have their own parish church (though almost all had a chapel or small church of some kind). It also resulted in parishes composed of settlements both in and outside Salem's territory. Seefelden parish, for example, included the villages and hamlets of Gebhardsweiler, Grasbeuren, Hallendorf, Maurach, Mimmenhausen, Mühlhofen, Nußdorf, Oberuhldingen, and Tüfingen, all within Salem's central territory, plus Deisendorf, Schiggendorf, and Unteruhldingen beyond its borders.[72] Furthermore, not only did the parishioners belong to different lords according to their servility, tenure, and jurisdictional status; the parishes, too, were subject to various divisions of authority. As the church patron over most of the parishes within its central territory (though not Pfaffenhofen or Seefelden), Salem exercised the majority of rights over its churches, but the bishop of Constance and other ecclesiastical authorities also laid various claims including tithe collection, jurisdiction over clergy, and visitation rights. Mainau, a member of the Teutonic Order, was the church patron in Pfaffenhofen, where the division of tithe shares was especially complicated: seven of the sixteen tithe shares went to Mainau, four to Salem, three to the cathedral chapter in Constance, and two to the hospital in Überlingen.[73] With parish incomes split among so many parties, none of them had the incentive to pay parish clergy adequately or maintain local church infrastructure.

Besides this incongruence between political and ecclesiastical organization, there was the basic problem of physical geography. For many villagers, church attendance required an hour's walk or more in each direction, often over difficult terrain and in inclement weather. When an emergency arose and the priest was needed, he did not always arrive in time. This led, especially in the decades before 1525, to the foundation by village communes of lesser benefices. These provided for additional clergy, procedural guidelines, and financial support to guarantee pastoral care at the local level and under local supervision.

There are five letters of religious foundation, written during the period 1448–1532, from four village communities: Bermatingen, Mimmenhausen, Pfaffenhofen, and Un-

---

DEISSLER, Bermatingen; Karl Heinz MINK, Die St-Georgs-Pfarrei, in: Bermatingen, ed. Dillmann, pp. 42–51. Pamphlets available at individual churches provide excellent photographs with overviews of the more recent history, art, and architecture. See, for example, Kirchen und Kapellen der Seelsorgeeinheit Salem, Kunstführer Nr. 2548, Regensburg 2004.

72 STAIGER, Salem oder Salmansweiler, p. 392. Leutkirch parish was similarly large and spatially dispersed. It included the settlements of Neufrach, Haberstenweiler, Birkenweiler, Wespach, Buggensegel, Oberstenweiler, Mittelstenweiler, Niderstenweiler, Rimpertsweiler, and Wehausen.

73 GLAK, 66/10304, fol. 74. The situation was not much different for other parishes. In Bermatingen, for example, a 1529 tithe register describes individual field parcels for over one hundred pages with detailed descriptions of who received what; the parish church in Bermatingen, the abbeys Salem, Kreutzlingen, and Münsterlingen, and the Constance cathedral chapter all claimed tithe shares. GLAK, 4/1810.

teruhldingen.[74] Each foundation provided funds for hiring a chaplain or assistant clergyman and for endowed Masses beyond those the parish priest performed. These documents are excellent sources of information about villagers' expectations of their priests as well as about the religious practices and services they deemed most necessary.[75]

In comparison to parish priests, chaplains and primissaries were subject to less official oversight and greater communal control.[76] The founders in three of the five instances were village communes and not the larger parishes to which they belonged. In Mimmenhausen, which belonged to the distant parish of Seefelden, the founders were the village headman, village treasurers, and the entire commune; in Unteruhldingen, the founders were the churchwardens of Seefelden in addition to the entire commune of Unteruhldingen; in Bermatingen it was the village headman, twelve judges, and the Twenty-Four who acted "in the name of our entire commune." Other groups, however, established the two foundations in Pfaffenhofen: the city magistrates of Überlingen in 1448 and the local confraternity of Our Lady in 1509. In each of the five cases the founders instructed the clergy in their duties, listed the sources of material support, and obtained recognition and confirmation for their foundation from the church patrons, the bishop, or both.

The process of appointment for local priests involved three steps: nomination, presentation, and investiture. Each case differed slightly, but the most usual arrangement was for the commune or other founders to nominate, the church patrons to present, and the bishop to confirm and invest.[77] The appointment of chaplains and primissaries, therefore, required the participation and consent of various interest groups. Since

---

74 GLAK, 229/82293 (Pfaffenhofen, 1447–48); 4/3883 (Mimmenhausen, 1495); 4/5386 (Unteruhldingen, 1505); 98/3499 (Pfaffenhofen, 1509); 4/1776 (Bermatingen, 1532). In addition, documents from Owingen refer to a new altar established shortly before 1528 and to a monk from Salem who served as chaplain there in the 1530s (4/5041–5046).

75 On communal foundations of lesser benefices in this period, see Rosi FUHRMANN, Kirche und Dorf: Religiöse Bedürfnisse und kirchliche Stiftung auf dem Lande vor der Reformation, Stuttgart 1995; idem, Die Kirche im Dorf: Kommunale Initiativen zur Organisation von Seelsorge vor der Reformation, in: Zugänge zur bäuerlichen Reformation, ed. Peter Blickle, Zurich 1987, pp. 147–186; idem, Dorfgemeinde und Pfründstiftung vor der Reformation: Kommunale Selbstbestimmungschancen zwischen Religion und Recht, in: Kommunalisierung und Christianisierung: Voraussetzungen und Folgen der Reformation, 1400–1600, ed. Peter Blickle and Johannes Kunisch, Berlin 1989, pp. 77–112.

76 FUHRMANN, Kirche im Dorf, pp. 152–153.

77 This was straightforward in Bermatingen, where the Amtmann and Twenty-Four nominated the priest in the name of the commune, Salem presented their choice for confirmation, and the bishop or his vicar invested the priest with his office. The foundation in Unteruhldingen followed a more complicated process, with election by ten members representing three interest groups: two votes by the Seefelden churchwardens, four from villagers representing the local commune, and four additional residents of Unteruhldingen who were chosen by the parish priest. The cathedral provost, decan, and chapter presented the committee's choice in a sealed envelope to the bishop for investiture. The Überlingen magistrates elected the primissary in

the communes normally maintained the right of nomination, they played an important role in the selection of their chaplains—as opposed to parish priests, normally chosen by the church patrons.

The founders generally prescribed the priest's duties and required specific services. In some cases, they also claimed the right of dismissal. The most common provisions were for a resident priest in the village, regular Masses (normally four per week), and the administration of sacraments.[78] The Pfaffenhofen primissary had to reside in the village and perform his duties in person, unless he fell ill. He could not exchange benefices without permission from the founders. He was required to perform four Masses per week, at times convenient to the parish priest, and to assist with other Masses and observances. If the parish priest were unavailable, he had to administer sacraments, but he was not to infringe on the senior priest's rights or accept donations for his services. He was expected to set an honorable example and behave as befitting for a priest. He had to maintain church properties. The priest in Bermatingen was additionally required to attend all processions. He could not leave the village without informing the parish priest or churchwardens. If the bishop's court found that he neglected his responsibilities, he could be removed from his post. In return for these religious services, founders provided for the priest's livelihood through a combination of landed property, rents, and moveables. Many lesser benefices were well funded, perhaps better than the salaries of some parish vicars.[79]

Pfaffenhofen and required that their nominee be presented to the bishop within 30 days. Only the founders of the 1509 Pfaffenhofen benefice were without nomination rights; in that case, Mainau nominated and presented the candidate to the bishop.

78 Mimmenhausen's 1495 foundation provided for a chaplain, allowing villagers to hear Mass and receive sacraments in the village even though it remained part of Seefelden parish. Unteruhldingen, another village belonging to Seefelden parish, supported an additional priest of its own with a benefice in 1505. He was required to perform two early morning Masses per week in the village chapel in addition to other special services and Masses for the dead. The 1448 endowment of a primissary (*Frühmeß*) in Pfaffenhofen established an assistant priest responsible to celebrate Mass four mornings per week. The 1509 foundation furnished an additional priest to perform one Mass per week in Owingen and three more in Pfaffenhofen. Bermatingen's chaplain established in 1532 celebrated Mass three times per week in St. Leonhard's chapel and once at the parish church.

79 The Pfaffenhofen foundation of 1448 specified properties in villages throughout the region owing annual land rents of over forty pounds heller. The endowment for Pfaffenhofen's 1509 foundation included a house near the church with orchards, extensive vineyards, arable, meadows, and a cow, as well as ground rent from a smallholding in Daisendorf and interest-bearing loans payable by various villagers. In Mimmenhausen the priest received a salary of fifty gulden in addition to a house and other property. The chaplain in Bermatingen had use of a house near St. Leonhard's chapel, twelve vineyard parcels, several meadows, and annual land rents and interest from various other properties. By comparison, Fuhrmann found that sampled parish priests in the Pfalz and Upper Rhine regions received an average annual income of forty gulden, lesser clergy only thirty gulden. Idem, Kirche im Dorf, pp. 155–56, 164, 174.

Religious practices in Salem's villages were shaped through the interactions of church patrons, parish priests, and various segments of the community. Parish membership did not coincide with the village commune but local residents, especially village officials, worked to shape religious services in their home communities. The major concerns of Salem's villagers, based on their foundations of local benefices, were to provide a resident priest in the village, regular Masses, sacraments, and a spiritual leader who would assume an active role in local traditions.[80] These interests did not directly conflict with those of church patrons and higher ecclesiastical authorities—most were in line with official church teachings. They do suggest the community's desire to maintain control over local church appointments, purse strings, and their priests' behavior. By supporting additional altars, priests, and chapels, villagers filled the gaps in parish organization and created pockets of alternate space at the parish margins, where communal values could thrive under less scrutiny from higher church authorities.[81] These foundations demonstrate the active role peasants assumed in local religious life, in order to provide the basic services they lacked and increase communal control over the church. The timing of their activities suggests the significance of local religious concerns, not only with respect to church reform but also for the formulation of demands in 1525.

3.4 The German Peasants' War of 1525

The settlement of 1473 addressed many issues of lordship including conditions of tenure, servility, inheritance, justice, political representation, and lawmaking. The agreement served as a cornerstone for the territory's legal and political development throughout the early modern period. It did not preclude further negotiations between the abbey and its subjects, however, nor did it satisfy all their concerns. The German Peasants' War of 1525 demonstrates that peasants' demands were still a driving force in relations between the abbey and its subjects some 50 years after the landmark agreement.

The German Peasants' War involved Salem's villagers in a much broader movement. It called on networks among members of the territorial community and neighbors from the surrounding region. The godly law drew support from social groups other than peasants, and according to one estimate, sixty to seventy percent of men who were capable of bearing arms joined the rebels.[82] The Christian Union of Upper Swabia, to which the Linzgau rebels belonged, has been called "the sole large-scale

---

80 Local traditions might include consecration days, saints' days, local festivals, processions, pilgrimages, confraternities, and blessings.

81 FUHRMANN, Kirche im Dorf, p. 185. See also Keith LURIA, Territories of Grace: Cultural Change in the Seventeenth-Century Diocese of Grenoble, Berkeley 1991.

82 Hans-Martin Maurer estimates that in the German Southwest alone there were over 100,000 participants. Idem, Massenerhebung, p. 257.

political creation" of the Peasants' War.[83] This body enacted the famous Twelve Articles, which had a defining influence on the formulation of demands elsewhere in the empire. An estimated 25,000 copies were printed in 25 editions, and this helped spread the movement to new regions where the articles were adopted in whole or in part. Peter Blickle calls the Twelve Articles "a statement of complaints, a programme for reform and a political manifesto in one. [They] held together the revolution of 1525 like a clamp both in terms of matter and in terms of time."[84] Blickle has even described the Christian Union as a model of republican government.[85]

Despite common agreement on the enormous potential of the German Peasants' War, generations of German historians from Friedrich Engels to Günther Franz have shared the view that it was a disastrous failure for the peasantry and for the German nation. Engels and Franz agreed that the peasants' capitulation at Weingarten on 17 April 1525 was a sign and symptom of their general failure to recognize and support a common goal.[86] It is largely because of the intense search in the nineteenth and twentieth centuries for the origins of a German national identity that the consequences of 1525 have been painted in such terms.[87] Most historians continue to link the Treaty of Weingarten, and the Lake Constance peasants who accepted it, to a more general failure of the peasant cause.[88] Alternatively, like Peter Blickle, they have paid little at-

---

83 Tom SCOTT and Bob SCRIBNER, eds., The German Peasants' War: A History in Documents, Atlantic Highlands 1991, p. 18 (referred to hereafter as SCOTT and SCRIBNER, History in Documents). Elsewhere the editors call the Christian Union "the most significant organizational form to emerge in the rebellion in southwest Germany." Idem, p. 128.

84 Peter BLICKLE, Economic, Social and Political Background of the Twelve Articles of the Swabian Peasants of 1525, in: The German Peasant War of 1525, ed. Janos Bak, London 1976, p. 63; idem, Revolution of 1525.

85 Peter BLICKLE, Communalism—Parliamentarianism—Republicanism, in: Parliaments, Estates and Representation 6 (1986), p. 10.

86 Friedrich Engels wrote: "Truchsess' cunning [at Weingarten] saved him here from certain ruin. Had he not succeeded in fooling the weak, limited, for the most part demoralised peasants and their usually incapable, timid and venal leaders, he would have … perished." Furthermore, "the Hegau peasants, though not included in the Weingarten agreement, gave a new example of the appalling narrow-mindedness and the stubborn provincialism which ruined the entire Peasant War." Idem, The Peasant War in Germany, trans. Moissaye J. Olgin, New York 1984, p. 119. According to Günther Franz (Bauernkrieg, 1933, p. 213), "their desire for momentary success led them to sacrifice the entire movement," and "the peasants lacked any consciousness of the interconnectedness of their movement across all of Germany. They failed to recognize that they could achieve victory only by uniting with the other armies." Hans Ulrich Rudolf points out the similarities between these two views in idem, Weingartener Vertrag, in: Der Bauernkrieg in Oberschwaben, ed. Elmar L. Kuhn, Tübingen 2000, pp. 199–200.

87 H. C. Erik MIDELFORT, The Revolution of 1525? Recent Studies of the Peasants' War, in: Central European History 11 (1978), pp. 195–196; STALNAKER, Social Interpretation, p. 24.

88 According to Scott and Scribner, "The Treaty of Weingarten can be seen, in retrospect, as a turning point in the military progress of the war. … The treaty with the peasants freed Truchsess Georg to march away with all his forces intact, on a route which extended from the Hegau

tention to the treaty. Yet a few have begun to question the traditional narrative and neglect of this important event. Hans Ulrich Rudolf points out that Blickle, however indirectly, has made an important contribution to our understanding of the Treaty of Weingarten by questioning the traditional judgment of 1525's outcome on a larger scale as a complete disaster for the peasantry and for Germany. When one "begins to discover positive results" of the Peasants' War more generally, Rudolf reflects, "then the Treaty of Weingarten also begins to fall under a new light."[89]

Among the Christian Union's three great divisions, the least is known about the Lake Army (*Seehaufen*). This army's contribution to the movement has been deemed less significant than those of the Allgäu and Baltringen Armies, and some have even blamed them for the movement's more general failure. Elmar Kuhn, an authority on the Peasants' War in the Linzgau, summarizes:

> In the historical literature, the Lake Army (*Seehaufen*) stands in the shadow of its two neighboring armies, the Baltringers and the Allgäuers. The peasants of the lake joined later in common action, they contributed little to programmatic drafts, their leaders are deemed less distinguished, and they avoided great battles and military actions. Indeed, many authors hold them responsible for the failure of the entire Peasants' War, since the Lake Army shrank from combat at Weingarten and were a party to the treaty there, which Martin Luther later recommended as a model for the peaceful settlement of conflict.

On the other hand, Kuhn reflects, "Seldom considered is the fact that the peasants of the lake remained free from punishment because of their military strength and as a consequence of that treaty, that with the Rappertsweiler Articles they formulated a programmatic document which contradicted the Twelve Articles in certain demands, and that their organization remained intact until the autumn of 1525, even as the executioners roamed the villages all around them."[90] The goal here is not to repeat the major events or review the enormous historiography of the German Peasants' War. Instead, we will focus on the peasants from the southern Linzgau and their actions.[91] Of special interest is how the dramatic events of 1525 fit into the longer trajectory of relations between Salem Abbey and its peasant subjects and how the peasant rebels contributed to the history of lordship and community in Salem's territory.

---

into Württemberg and on to Franconia, during which he was able to defeat a string of smaller and less experienced rebel armies." Idem, History in Documents, p. 58. Sabean writes, "In reality it meant the capitulation of the peasants." Idem, Landbesitz, p. 15.

89 RUDOLF, Weingartener Vertrag, p. 200.

90 KUHN, Seehaufen, p. 97.

91 The sources for this section are all published. They include the anonymous chronicle Bauernkrieg am Bodensee, in: Quellensammlung der badischen Landesgeschichte, vol. 2, ed. F. H. Mone, Karlsruhe 1854, pp. 118–133; KUHN-OECHSELE and KUHN, Seehaufen Quellensammlung; SCOTT and SCRIBNER, History in Documents; Franz Ludwig BAUMANN, ed., Akten zur Geschichte des deutschen Bauernkrieges aus Oberschwaben, Freiburg 1877; Günther FRANZ, ed., Quellen zur Geschichte des Bauernkrieges, Darmstadt 1963.

The first signs of unrest in the region north of Lake Constance were tithe strikes over the New Year in 1525.[92] On 21 February an estimated 8,000 peasants assembled in Rappertsweiler. They chose as their leader Dietrich Hurlewagen, a minor landed nobleman who stemmed from the Lindau patriciate. On 24 February they requisitioned food from nearby Langnau Abbey. In the next few days, they plundered the abbey and formed a sworn union. They also agreed on a list of grievances, known as the Rappertsweiler Articles, written around the same time as the more famous Twelve Articles.[93] By early March, two new regiments had joined them: the Altdorfer *Haufen* and the Bermatinger *Haufen*. The latter comprised the southern Linzgau peasants, including subjects of the Upper Swabian Landvogtei, Heiligenberg, Constance, Überlingen, and Salem. Burghers from Meersburg and Markdorf later joined the rebels, while Überlingen remained hostile and led the opposition against them.

The earliest signs of resistance in the Linzgau were reported in a letter from the city of Ravensburg to Überlingen on 3 March to inquire about rumors that subjects from Salem, Heiligenberg, and Überlingen had gathered in a meadow near Ahausen (by Bermatingen), because "the peasants in our area are absolutely wild, and so we ask you with great seriousness to write to us with any information you may have."[94] Überlingen reported to the Swabian League on 5 March that some of Überlingen's subjects had indeed risen in revolt and were now assembling in large groups, swearing allegiance to the peasants. The letter also explained that the initial assembly place in the Linzgau was being moved from Ailingen (near Buchhorn) to Bermatingen, a better location for many of the regiment's supporters. Überlingen asked for help punishing its subjects; the League wrote back telling Überlingen to wait, that the League would soon have an army ready to deal with them.[95]

By the time the Lake Army joined the Allgäu and Baltringen Armies in Memmingen at a "Peasant Parliament" on 6–8 March, it consisted of as many as 12,000 men.[96] According to the instructions given to the Lake Army's deputies, they were advised to seek an alliance with the other troops and to play a supporting role in the negotiations. The Lake Army submitted articles concentrating on the word of God and on

---

92 SCOTT and SCRIBNER, History in Documents, p. 26.

93 The exact dates for both texts are unknown but the Twelve Articles were written sometime in the week before 3 March, and Elmar Kuhn believes the Rappertsweiler Articles were written around the same period, perhaps even before the more famous Twelve. Idem, Bauernkrieg am See, p. 39; W. VOGT, Die Bodenseebauern und ihr Hauptmann Junker Dietrich Hurlewagen im grossen Bauernkrieg, Augsburg 1892, pp. 12, 15.

94 KUHN-OECHSELE and KUHN, Seehaufen Quellensammlung, p. 22.

95 Ibid., pp. 66–69. Überlingen continued to be the Linzgau peasants' major adversary throughout the war. The Swabian League told the city more than once to exercise restraint, and neighboring lords expressed disapproval at the zeal with which the city punished its subjects. Überlingen's opposition to the peasants was a major obstacle to the union of rebels from the Linzgau and Hegau.

96 SCOTT and SCRIBNER, History in Documents, p. 26.

communal control of the clergy.[97] After just one day of deliberations, the fifty or so representatives in Memmingen established the framework for a "Christian Union of Upper Swabia" and created an interim constitution known as the Federal Ordinance.[98] A list of assembly representatives included the names of three members from the Bermatingen regiment. They were Eitelhans Ziegelmüller, the regiment's captain and a miller from Oberteuringen, Othmar Kleck from Rietheim, and Benedict Aigen, Salem's Amtmann in Bermatingen. The Bermatingen regiment's early participation in the Christian Union built an awareness of the larger struggle and was crucial for its integration into a larger regional federation.

The leaders of the Bermatingen regiment may have attended other meetings of the Christian Union, but their specific contributions to the larger federation and its guiding principles remain unknown. The Bermatingen regiment produced no formal grievances of its own and had no influence over the regional articles it subscribed to, having formed shortly after the drafting of the Twelve Articles and the Rappertsweiler Articles. The Lake Army's Rappertsweiler Articles (also twelve in number) were written by and for members of the eastern regiments, and it is hard to say whether members of the Bermatingen regiment identified more with them or with the widely famous Twelve Articles. According to one analysis of the two manifestos, they corresponded in less than half their content. Still, there was agreement in the first three articles on the most important issues: Articles 1 and 2 of both documents focused on the godly law including the election of priests, use of the tithe, and evangelical preaching. Article 3 in both cases called for the abolition of serfdom. The remainder of the Rappertsweiler Articles focused above all on political and especially judicial abuses, while the Twelve Articles focused more on the use of common lands.[99]

---

97 According to Article 1: "We desire and request that the holy gospel and word of God be preached and proclaimed, and that we be instructed in it, clearly and purely, unobscured and unadulterated by human teachings and opinions, with its fruits, its Christian understanding and implications, by persons learned in holy Scripture, who are virtuous and fit for this task, for the salvation of our souls alone; also that the same, along with all Christian ceremonies and needs, shall be supplied and provided free of charge and not for money, as has occurred hitherto." Ibid., p. 128.

98 The Federal Ordinance and other foundational documents of the Christian Union are translated in SCOTT and SCRIBNER, History in Documents, pp. 128–135.

99 In Kuhn's judgment (Seehaufen, pp. 115, 118–120), the Rappertsweiler Articles did not address Bermatingen's concerns, because the Linzgau peasants had much greater legal (especially judicial) freedoms but carried greater economic burdens than those around Rappertsweiler. Yet the proposed judicial reforms are reminiscent of earlier complaints by Salem's Sidelrichter, especially Article 4, which stated that conscience and knowledge should have priority over legal statutes in the administration of justice. Article 6 demanded term limits for judges and approval of appointments by the communes. The text of the Twelve Articles is widely available, with English translations in BLICKLE, Revolution of 1525, Appendix 1, and SCOTT and SCRIBNER,

The Bermatingen regiment was a considerable distance west of the other lake regiments and the rest of the Christian Union, and in the following phases of the war, it mostly operated alone.[100] An anonymous chronicle, almost certainly written by one of Salem's monks, provides a first-hand account of events in the southern Linzgau.[101] According to the chronicler, a captain and twelve councilors led the rebels in Bermatingen. The regiment expanded quickly in organization, size, and activity. The leaders established an alarm plan, administered an oath, and raised a military tax.[102] After Eitelhans Ziegelmüller established his headquarters at Salem's *Kelnhof* in Bermatingen,[103] he went immediately to Salem with twenty or so supporters to demand that the abbey's servants swear to abide by two articles. The first was to observe the godly law, the second to undertake nothing against the peasant army.[104] After administering the oath, Ziegelmüller returned to his headquarters in Bermatingen. The abbey immediately delivered a gift of bread, wine, and fish.

On 1 April Ziegelmüller marched with 300 men across Salem's territory to Owingen and set up a new subregiment there. On their way, they stopped at the abbey for food and drinks. According to the chronicler, the convent met their demands with relief, since rumor had it that 7,000 soldiers were on their way from the Allgäu to plunder the abbey. They fed the troops at Salem's guesthouse and invited Ziegelmüller and his councilors into the abbey proper. On his way back from Owingen the next day, Ziegelmüller returned to the abbey. This time he bid the entire convent to swear an oath to

---

History in Documents, pp. 252–257. The Rappertsweiler Articles are printed in KUHN-OECHSELE and KUHN, Seehaufen Quellensammlung, pp. 42–43, and described in detail by SABEAN, Landbesitz, pp. 83–85; VOGT, Hurlewagen, pp. 12–14; KUHN, Bauernkrieg am See, p. 40.

100 KUHN, Seehaufen, pp. 100–101. The chronicler's mistaken reference to the Bermatingen regiment as the Lake Army and description of the eastern regiments (Baltringen and Altdorf) as part of the Allgäu Army are indications of the independence with which the regiments operated.

101 Bauernkrieg am Bodensee, pp. 118–133. The author's ties to the abbey are revealed in his report that the rebel captain and his councilors set up headquarters "at our farm" in Bermatingen and that "we all swore" to the two articles.

102 The church bells sounded the call to arms throughout the countryside. The war tax was five gulden from every one hundred men. Ibid., p. 122, chap. 9.

103 The choice of this farm as the rebel headquarters was no accident. By 1525 the *Kelnhof* was leased to a tenant like any other farm in the village, but formerly, this property had been the lord's local administrative center. It was mentioned by name in the 1390 sales contract when Salem purchased the entire village. Low justice in Bermatingen also derived from this farm. On the *Kelnhof* in Owingen, see Kurt-Erich MAIER, Geschichte des Linzgaudorfes Owingen: Eine Heimatgeschichte mit besonderer Berücksichtigung der Sozial- und Wirtschaftsgeschichte, Owingen 1964, p. 105.

104 The two articles are significant because they are among the only recorded statements of demands made specifically by members of the Linzgau regiment. When the members of the convent were forced to swear an oath a few days later, the articles were slightly different (see below).

the peasant cause, as ordered by "the bright army."[105] Upon their request, Ziegelmüller granted time for deliberation and left to join his regiment near Meersburg.

Then the entire convent, young and old, met in an assembly to consider the demand. They sent the prior and bursar to seek the abbot's advice in Überlingen, where he had taken refuge. On 3 April, the chronicler wrote, "the prior called an assembly of the entire convent and revealed to them my lord's counsel, upon which they unanimously decided to swear for the sake of the abbey. So he sent a message to the peasant leader in Meersburg saying he should come, that we would swear."[106] At that time Ziegelmüller was leading an estimated 8,000 men on a march around the Linzgau.[107] Too busy to go in person, the captain sent two of his councilors to receive the convent's oath. One was Benedict Aigen, the Amtmann of Bermatingen. With the entire convent assembled before him, Benedict Aigen instructed the monks to "swear an oath to the two articles alone and nothing more. First, to proclaim the gospel as revealed in scripture, without human addition. Second, to help them implement the godly law. And so we all swore, just to these two articles, first the bursar ... and then the entire convent from the oldest to the youngest."[108] The rebels left three soldiers in charge of the abbey's bells and gates. They warned the convent not to hide its supply of wine and grain, with assurances that nothing would be taken.[109] As Benedict Aigen accepted the convent's oath, the peasant army continued its march across the Linzgau demanding support from any who had not yet joined.[110] They went as far as Buchhorn to the east and Wolmatingen to the west. The only stronghold successful in its resistance to the peasant advance was Überlingen.[111]

---

105 "Da hatt der hoptman an den gantzen convent begert, wir sollen ouch zu in hulden, dan er hab ain befelch vom hellen huffen." Bauernkrieg am Bodensee, p. 122, chap. 13.

106 Ibid., p. 123, chap. 16.

107 The rebels had recently been to Markdorf and Meersburg and both citizenries swore an oath to support them. They had also taken castle Ittendorf, which belonged to Überlingen.

108 Bauernkrieg am Bodensee, p. 123, chap. 16.

109 The chronicler describes Salem's occupation in an article following the convent's oath, but it bears the date 29 March. He may have confused his dates, or the occupation may have taken place earlier. In any case, the convent was treated mildly and not plundered. Ibid., chap. 17.

110 Buchhorn remained neutral but agreed to keep its gates and markets open to the peasants. In a joint effort with the Rappertsweiler regiment (and the Allgäuers, according to the chronicler), the Bermatingen regiment took Montfort's castle in Staufen and the bishop's castle in Meersburg. The bishop agreed to pay a tribute (*Brandschatz*) of 300 fl., six wagons full of wine, and a field gun. Next, Ziegelmüller crossed the lake with 500 men and received the oath from Wolmatingen and other villages outside Constance. They made an agreement with the city council to spare the abbeys Petershausen and Reichenau in return for supplies. In early April the rebels marched on to Heiligenberg, Ramsberg, and Pfullendorf in the northern Linzgau, but sources do not describe the results of this mission. Idem, chap. 21; KUHN-OECHSELE and KUHN, Seehaufen Quellensammlung, p. 82a.

111 Überlingen was well protected by fortifications and its own small army; the city was extremely hostile to the peasants. Many of the area's prelates and noble families took refuge there. According to the chronicler: "All people in the city, clerical and lay, had to prepare themselves with

Meanwhile, other regiments were preparing for battle with the Swabian League. On 26 March, the League Army turned its attention to the Christian Union and marched toward Ulm. That same day, castles and abbeys began falling to the peasants. First to burst into flames was the castle at Schemmerberg, Salem's administrative center near Biberach.[112] The rebels plundered several abbeys in the following days, some of them more than once.[113] Still, the Christian Union's Federal and Military Ordinances strictly regulated violence and plunder.[114] On 31 March, negotiations with the Swabian League broke off when the rebels rejected a proposal that would have amounted to unconditional surrender. Soon after, around the same time Salem's monks swore to support the godly law, the first major battle in Upper Swabia took place at Leipheim (4 April). In this encounter as well as at the battle of Wurzach ten days later, the Baltringen regiments suffered terrible losses. For whatever reason, the Lake and Allgäu Armies failed to come to their aid.[115] For the Baltringen rebels, the battle at Leipheim was such a severe blow to morale that many of them submitted to the League shortly afterward, surrendering their weapons and renewing their oaths as subjects. The unraveling of the Christian Union had begun.

Upon their return from a triumphant conquest of the greater Linzgau, the leaders of the Bermatingen regiment met at Salem Abbey, now under their occupation, to decide what to do next. According to Salem's chronicler an estimated sixty people assembled there, including councilors from Meersburg and Markdorf as well as an envoy from Radolfzell.[116] As they sat in council on the Thursday before Easter, Ziegelmüller

armor and weapons, and together they also swore an oath not to abandon one another and to defend the city with their lives, honor, and property. For a long time they would not open their gates, so no one could enter or leave the city." Bauernkrieg am Bodensee, p. 124, chap. 22.

112 The report by Amandus Scheffer, Salem's administrator at Schemmerberg, is found in FRANZ, Quellen, p. 205 no. 58.

113 According to Salem's chronicler, those suffering damages included Elchingen, Ochsenhausen, Marchtal, Schussenried, Roggenburg, Münchenrott, and Zwiefalten. Idem, p. 121, chap. 6. For a fuller list of events in Upper Swabia, see Petra SACHS-GLEICH, Zeittafel, in: Bauernkrieg in Oberschwaben, ed. Kuhn, pp. 563–572.

114 See the Christian Union's initial proclamation ("it is our intention to do violence to no one"), its Federal Ordinance ("friendly exhortations" to owners of castles), and Military Ordinance ("any spoils shall be placed in the common booty … if we have to plunder our enemy, this shall be done only through the corporals unless permission is given otherwise") in SCOTT and SCRIBNER, History in Documents, pp. 129–135.

115 The Federal Ordinance required regiments to support one another when called. According to the chronicler, the Bermatingen regiment sent 200 soldiers to join the army at Leipheim, but they changed their minds for unknown reasons and returned home before the battle. Bauernkrieg am Bodensee, p. 122, chap. 11.

116 The envoy mentioned in this passage may have come seeking help with the siege of Radolfzell, which began on 18 April and involved an estimated 10,000 rebels. Some Linzgau rebels did join actions in the Hegau, and Hegau rebels were reportedly present at Weingarten on 17 April as well. This is one of several examples of communication and common action between the Lake

received an urgent letter sent in haste by the Rappertsweiler regiment at Langnau.[117] The letter warned that the Truchsess and his army were marching toward Gaisbeuren and planning an attack on the peasants. Within a matter of hours, the entire Bermatingen regiment sprung into action:

> Upon hearing this message, the captain and councilors rode together that same night to Bermatingen and sent out an order to sound the alarm in every village. And so by two o'clock on Good Friday morning, the bells had been rung throughout the valley and along the lake. That morning all the peasants came together at the assembly place in Bermatingen, armed and ready for battle. As the monks sang the office of Christ's passion they could be heard marching from Owingen and neighboring places with cymbals and drums. Others joined them from Markdorf and Meersburg. And so on Good Friday as many as 10,000 men set out for Weingarten.[118]

The next day when the Swabian League Army faced the Bermatingen regiment outside Weingarten, the rebels appeared formidable. According to the Truchsess's intelligence and later reports, the peasant army was at least 10,000 strong with 4,000 muskets as well as many former mercenaries and several cannons. An exchange of fire ended in a draw but left both sides with the impression that a serious battle was yet to come. Unlike the earlier engagements at Leipheim and Wurzach, the peasant gunners demonstrated a steady aim and the infantry stood their ground. That night the League Army made camp in the Altdorf Forest only a short distance from Gaisbeuren, where the peasants held a strategic advantage. The Truchsess ordered his troops to stand ready for battle throughout the night, having heard rumors that the rebels planned to seize the League's field artillery while they slept.[119] They discovered the next morning that the peasant army had moved to join other regiments on a hill overlooking the valley near Weingarten.[120]

On Easter Sunday, both armies rested for tactical as well as religious reasons. Mediation attempts were fruitless, and each side sent out messengers requesting aid. The League soldiers were almost out of gunpowder from the day before and their horses

---

and Hegau Armies. As the western-most regiment of the Christian Union, the rebels of Bermatingen were in a geographical and political transition zone between Upper Swabia and the Upper Rhine.

117 Earlier in March, Hurlewagen acknowledged written communications between the Bermatingen regiment and rebels in Stockach. Their use of letters is noteworthy. KUHN-OECHSELE and KUHN, Seehaufen Quellensammlung, p. 73.

118 Bauernkrieg am Bodensee, p. 124, chaps. 23–24.

119 The Truchsess even sent a foot soldier to set a house on fire in Gaisbeuren so actions within the peasant camp could be observed and a surprise attack prevented.

120 FRANZ, Quellen, pp. 211–15; KUHN-OECHSELE and KUHN, Seehaufen Quellensammlung, p. 92; SCOTT and SCRIBNER, History in Documents, p. 58; Bauernkrieg am Bodensee, p. 124, chap. 24; Manfred BENSING and Siegfried HOYER, Der deutsche Bauernkrieg, 1524–1526, [Berlin 1965], pp. 99–100. Several scenes from the battlefield are depicted in Günther FRANZ, ed., Jacob Murers Weißenauer Chronik des Bauernkrieges von 1525, Sigmaringen 1977.

Illustration 3.1: Scene at Weingarten during the German Peasants' War of 1525

From Jacob Murers Weißenauer Chronik des Bauernkrieges von 1525

were said to be exhausted.[121] Eitelhans Ziegelmüller called out to the Upper Allgäu, Hegau, and Black Forest for "any and all who can carry a spear and a pole."[122] He sent Benedict Aigen to requisition supplies from Salem.[123] The next day the Truchsess marched his army through the Altdorf Forest to face the peasant militia, where they waited as negotiations continued. See Illustration 3.1, Scene at Weingarten. The peasants rejected the demand that they surrender their flags, arms, and leaders to the League. When the Truchsess later spied peasants crossing the river below, he angrily halted the negotiations and rode off to prepare for battle. Eventually the negotiations resumed, and in the end, both sides managed to agree on a set of conditions later

---

121 FRANZ, Quellen, p. 212 no. 62; BENSING and HOYER, Bauernkrieg, pp. 97–99.

122 This call to arms must have been well known afterward, since many contemporaries including Salem's chronicler reported it (Bauernkrieg am Bodensee, p. 124, chap. 26). By the next day, according to the Truchsess's secretary, the peasant army had grown to around 12,000 troops with another 8,000 from the Allgäu stationed half a mile away and 4,000 more rumored to be coming from the Hegau. FRANZ, Quellen, p. 215 no. 62.

123 The peasants intercepted Salem's wagons of bread and wine the next day on the road between Markdorf and Ravensburg. KUHN-OECHSELE and KUHN, Seehaufen Quellensammlung, pp. 72, 130; Bauernkrieg am Bodensee, p. 125, chap. 31.

known as the Treaty of Weingarten (*Weingartener Vertrag*). The oral agreement, made in the field on 17 April, was officially ratified and sealed on 22 April in Ravensburg. This treaty not only called off the battle but also effectively ended the Linzgau rebels' participation in the German Peasants' War.[124]

The agreement now known as the Treaty of Weingarten involved the Swabian League and the entire Lake Army, some regiments of the Lower Allgäu, and one from Baltringen.[125] The treaty required rebels to surrender their flags as well as any written agreements they had made but allowed them to remain armed. They had to disband the Christian Union and any other sworn associations they had made and promise also not to enter any future leagues, agreements, or uprisings. It required them to disperse and return home as loyal subjects, renew their oaths to their rightful lords, and continue paying dues and services as previously required, unless and until these were modified through arbitration. All occupied castles, abbeys, cities, houses, cannons, and other property were to be returned to their rightful owners. In exchange, the treaty guaranteed protection to the rebels against punishment or retribution by their lords and others. They were not required to pay any damages. Local grievances would be settled individually by arbitration, and Archduke Ferdinand was authorized to make the final judgment in cases where no such agreement could be reached.

Wounded relations between lords and subjects did not heal immediately. Obstacles to recovery included mutual distrust and dissatisfaction with the treaty, and peace returned to the Linzgau as elsewhere through a slow, negotiated process. Disagreements not only between the two sides but also among allies led in some cases to factionalism. It took time for the treaty to be circulated, heard, and discussed. In Salem's villages and elsewhere, peasants did not swear the oath or perform other duties for weeks or even months following the agreement.[126] On 4 May, members of the Bermatingen regiment assembled near Salem Abbey and swore an oath to accept the Treaty of Weingarten. Perhaps misinterpreting this event, the district clerk in Ravensburg reported on 5 May that "the peasants at Salem held a commune yesterday and rallied once more in breach of the treaty. What they discussed I cannot tell. I fear terribly another rebellion."[127] Hurlewagen later testified that Ziegelmüller assembled "almost the majority" of his people shortly before 10 May to urge their support for the treaty and explain its stipulations.[128]

---

124 RUDOLF, Weingartner Vertrag, p. 205; BENSING and HOYER, Bauernkrieg, pp. 99–100; FRANZ, Quellen, p. 213 no. 62.

125 See KUHN-OECHSELE and KUHN, Seehaufen Quellensammlung, pp. 125–133; FRANZ, Quellen, pp. 216–233. Representatives of the Upper Allgäu rejected the treaty on 2 May.

126 For Salem, see KUHN, Seehaufen, p. 107. Subjects of Überlingen refused the oath until they had heard the treaty and discussed it among themselves. The abbot of Weißenau had to call in troops to force his subjects to renew their oath. KUHN-OECHSELE and KUHN, Seehaufen Quellensammlung, pp. 227–229; FRANZ, Weißenauer Chronik, pp. 34–35.

127 SCOTT and SCRIBNER, History in Documents, p. 157 no. 53.

128 KUHN-OECHSELE and KUHN, Seehaufen Quellensammlung, p. 231.

Meanwhile, rumors spread on both sides. It was widely believed among the rebels that the written treaty did not reflect the oral agreement made on the battlefield. Lords continued to fear a renewed uprising, and with good reason: rebellion was spreading through the Hegau and Allgäu, and messages to the lake region urged inhabitants to rejoin. Hegau rebels plundered Sernatingen and Sipplingen and destroyed the castle at Heiligenberg in late April.[129] The Rappertsweiler regiment plundered Langnau for a second time on 14 May. Überlingen's stance remained provocative, and for the Linzgau peasants this resulted in one of the war's final, unfortunate episodes.

Soon after the treaty signing, Überlingen raised several thousand troops to fight the rebels in the Hegau. Some of Salem's subjects were compelled to join. Yet when faced with the possibility of fighting against their neighbors and former allies outside Sernatingen (now Ludwigshafen) on 26 May, Überlingen's soldiers refused with the cry: "Our weapons will strike no peasants."[130] When 600 troops rejected a loyalty oath, they were forced to submit at gunpoint. The next day Überlingen rounded up fifty ringleaders of the "mutiny at Sernatingen" and executed many of them, starting with the military sergeant Urban Rest from Owingen, along with Jos Neufrer from Pfaffenhofen and several others from the Linzgau.[131] Salem's abbot expressed some sympathy for the soldiers. Citing his ecclesiastical status, he refused to punish his subjects sent home from Sernatingen.[132] He also denounced Überlingen's cruel retaliation against its mercenaries. Salem's chronicler remarked, "it is a common saying that it is no use hunting foxes with foxes."[133]

---

[129] Edwin Ernst WEBER, Das nordwestliche Oberschwaben, in: Bauernkrieg in Oberschwaben, ed. Kuhn, p. 329. In the village of Herdwangen, near Owingen, dispute broke out between supporters of the treaty and those who wanted to join the Hegau. According to Weber, the regional situation remained volatile.

[130] This cry has been recorded in multiple versions. According to Salem's chronicler they said "ire spyß, die werden kainen puren stechen," and "ire spieß stechen kaine puren" (Bauernkrieg am Bodensee, p. 124, chap. 26). As one soldier later explained, the battle would have forced many of them to fight their own neighbors and kin.

[131] Seven ringleaders were executed on the day of the mutiny and eight others the next day. Kuhn identifies another three from the Owingen area, all from families with large farms: Thoma Bürst, Jakob Moser, and Hans Klenker. A total of forty leaders were reportedly beheaded; others received sentences of imprisonment, fines, and banishment. MAIER, Owingen, p. 71; KUHN, Mönche und Bauern, p. 51.

[132] He avoided responsibility with the excuse that "as a religious leader, he preferred to leave such things to his secular officials." Abbey officials in turn refused to punish the prisoners and sent them back to Überlingen. KUHN-OECHSELE and KUHN, Seehaufen Quellensammlung, p. 248; KUHN, Seehaufen, p. 133.

[133] Bauernkrieg am Bodensee, p. 130, chap. 45. After the events at Sernatingen, Überlingen demanded one-sixth of all property from its subjects who had refused to fight against the Hegau peasants. The city continued to bar peasants from its markets, and in early November, the abbot of Weingarten asked the city council to permit his subjects to trade there. On 14 October it was

This anonymous chronicle is the best and indeed one of the only sources of information about the Peasants' War in the southern Linzgau. Still, like any other account, it should not be trusted as a straightforward and completely factual description. In retrospect, and from the perspective of the cloister, the author was able to emphasize above all the successful cooperation between the abbey and its subjects. In his efforts to praise the restraint on both sides and in an attempt to reconcile differences, he smoothed over any signs of antagonism and made no mention of the peasants' grievances or causes for their actions. For example, he resisted the conclusion that Salem's subjects willingly joined the peasants or had any reason for complaint against the abbey. They joined out of fear, he believed, because of veiled threats from the peasants of Rappertsweiler, who "called upon them in all seriousness to swear to their cause. If they did so, terrific—otherwise, they would just have to wait and see. This of course brought fear to the common man and so, in the end, the entire lake region swore to support the peasants."[134]

The chronicler also emphasized the respect rebel leaders showed for the abbey and its property: "The headman set up on our farm in Bermatingen with twelve or so of his men, yet this was done without any harm to the abbey." Elsewhere he reported that Ziegelmüller treated the convent mildly, even when demanding that the monks swear an oath. The chronicler barely mentioned the abbey's occupation, noting nonchalantly that rebel leaders were holding an assembly there on 13 April when they received the call to Weingarten. The monks complied with every wish, he tells us, feeding troops at the abbey's guesthouse, providing rations for the march, and sending wagons of supplies to the rebels at Weingarten. When peasants threatened damages on their way home, the abbey did not hesitate to appease them with wine. In the weeks before the treaty, the chronicler credited Ziegelmüller with actively protecting the abbey from more radical action on several occasions. The abbey and its property were spared, in his opinion, because "he was a good subject who shielded us loyally. Without this, we might have fared much worse."[135]

Salem's Abbot Jodokus Necker (r. 1510–1529) expressed similar views. On 28 April he wrote in a letter to his procurator in Nuremberg: "Know that all remains well in the abbey; not a heller's worth of damage has been done, beyond wine and bread, which continues to be dispensed to them. Praise God for peace. In truth, it is a wor-

---

reportedly said in the Linzgau: "We don't need the market in Überlingen anyway and would just as happily set up our own in Uhldingen." KUHN-OECHSELE and KUHN, Seehaufen Quellensammlung, pp. 227, 235.

134 Bauernkrieg am Bodensee, p. 121, chap. 8. It is not improbable that some did join the peasants for exactly this reason. SCOTT and SCRIBNER, History in Documents, p. 135 no. 36 and p. 137 no. 38.

135 "Er ist ain gůtter gotzhusman gesin, er hatt hand truwlich ob uns gehept, es wer uns villycht nit wol gangen." Bauernkrieg am Bodensee, 123, chap. 17. The chronicler also praised Ziegelmüller's moderation and protection in chaps. 12, 13, 20, and 21. Other references in this paragraph are to chaps. 9, 23, and 34.

risome time. I believe that for the most part the Lutheran sect is responsible for this; that its doctrine holds a secret poison is fairly obvious. May God bring all things to a good end."[136] Neither the chronicler nor the abbot condemned the peasants for their actions. Instead they painted a rosy picture of the situation at home, contrasting it with the violence abroad. The abbot protected his subjects from retribution where he could, as in the case of Hans Mayer, a rebel from Herdwangen and a major leader of the renewed uprising in the northern Linzgau after Weingarten.[137] Even if the abbot's intention was only to appease rebellious subjects and not to show sympathy for their cause, his conciliatory words and deeds (in contrast to positions taken in Überlingen and Heiligenberg) undoubtedly helped pacify the region.[138]

Writing after the fact made it easy for Salem's chronicler to emphasize cooperation, respect for authority, and the return to peaceful relations. Yet the Linzgau rebels had been on the brink of much more violent action, especially during the tense weeks of April 1525. At that time it was not self-evident that the convent would be able to appease the peasants. Another chronicle, written by Weißenau's Abbot Jacob Murer, presents a completely different perspective on the events of March and April 1525. Murer had been the parish priest for 23 years in Weißenau's village of Ummendorf before the Peasants' War. According to Murer, he had enjoyed good relations with the peasants in those years and settled many of their grievances against the abbey.[139] In early 1525, he remained open to compromise. He even went out to the villages to personally request their loyalty. Weißenau's subjects would not be held back from joining the movement, however, and they came to demand the convent's allegiance just two days after the Linzgau rebels did the same at Salem. This time, when the monks hesitated, Weißenau's peasants ruthlessly plundered the abbey and turned against their former village priest, forcing him to flee. After the Treaty of Weingarten, when Murer finally dared to demand a renewal of the oath, his subjects adamantly refused. They stood openly defiant until League troops forced them to back down. The lessons offered by the chroniclers at Salem and Weißenau are like night and day. There was a fine line between peaceful demands and violent actions, and the experiences at Weißenau raise questions about why Salem's peasants chose not to sack the abbey and why they continued to follow a path of nonviolence.

The peasants' acceptance of the Treaty of Weingarten has long puzzled observers, especially since most have drawn the conclusion that the peasants had a good chance of military victory. Some have accused the peasants at Weingarten of lacking the courage and zeal to fight the Swabian League, or of being tricked by their leaders. The first of these arguments is untenable, however, since the peasant army at Weingarten not only

---

136 KUHN-OECHSELE and KUHN, Seehaufen Quellensammlung, p. 227.

137 WEBER, Nordwestliche Oberschwaben, p. 331.

138 This abbot's outspoken criticism of Überlingen's harsh measures is especially interesting since he was a native of Überlingen and the son of the town secretary (*Stadtschreiber*).

139 FRANZ, Weißenauer Chronik, p. 28.

appeared formidable, it also exchanged fire twice with the League Army. After the first barrage, the League Army was forced to withdraw and wait for fresh supplies of powder and lead. If the Truchsess hoped to test the strength of the peasants' resolve, he must have been disappointed, because these peasants did not run from battle. Indeed, the Lake Army has been seen as one of the strongest and most feared military forces of the entire peasant movement. Balthasar von Wolfstein wrote home to Brandenburg and described the peasant army at Gaisbeuren on 15 April as "around 10,000 men holding a position to great advantage, so well prepared for battle as I have never seen assembled in any war, and they had strong artillery as well."[140] It was the Truchsess known as "Bauernjörg" who feared defeat and admitted as much to the Swabian League in explanation of his actions.[141]

The Treaty of Weingarten was by no means a victory for the larger peasant cause, but it did offer some valuable precedents including the choice of a negotiated settlement over battle.[142] For the area bound by the compromise and for the Linzgau in particular, this treaty offered more direct and concrete benefits. It called off the battle against the Swabian League Army, for one. It also protected villagers from the brutal punishments and reparations that were common elsewhere.[143] In addition, the treaty allowed both sides to save face and offered the possibility of future arbitration.[144] It was a conservative solution to be sure. One of the most striking aspects of the Bermatingen regiment's activities in 1525 is the almost complete lack of violence.[145] The choice of a negotiated settlement over violent rebellion characterized the actions of Salem's peasants on many occasions, not only in 1525.

---

140 KUHN-OECHSELE and KUHN, Seehaufen Quellensammlung, p. 117.

141 Ibid., p. 114 (letter from Gaisbeuren on 15 April); SCOTT and SCRIBNER, History in Documents, p. 157 no. 53.

142 Martin Luther later praised the Treaty of Weingarten as a model solution to differences between lords and subjects and wrote the foreword and postscript to an edition of the treaty published in Wittenberg. See FRANZ, Quellen, pp. 216–223 no. 63. Since Luther opposed the peasant cause publicly and vehemently, many have used his approval of the treaty as proof that it was a bad deal for the peasants. Yet it should not be assumed that Luther was the only one desiring a peaceful solution in 1525.

143 In just the first three months of collections, more than 50,000 fl. was raised from defeated subjects. Thomas SEA, Economic Impact of the German Peasants' War: The Question of Reparations, in: Sixteenth Century Journal 8 (1977), p. 82.

144 The arbitration of grievances promised in the treaty rarely materialized, though lords and subjects came to settlements in a few places. Blickle estimates that various reforms were implemented in around one-third of the affected territories. Idem, Politische Entmüdigung, p. 311.

145 The Lake Army has often been portrayed as militarily strong but idologically weak. Yet Johannes Kessler's later testimony, a major source for this interpretation, may have been politically motivated in order to emphasize the peaceful nature of his own Baltringen regiment. KUHN, Seehaufen, p. 105; VOGT, Hurlewagen, pp. 6–7; Claudia ULBRICH, Oberschwaben und Württemberg, in: Der deutsche Bauernkrieg, 2nd ed., ed. Horst Buszello et al., Paderborn 1991, p. 122.

Another issue that deserves closer attention is the relationship between the movement's leadership and its troops. The Lake Army's Captain Dietrich Hurlewagen has often been accused of intentionally misleading the peasants and bargaining with the League in his own self-interest.[146] In fact, both sides saw him as a traitor. He was forced to flee after the second plundering of Langnau when the Swabian League accused him of inciting violence in order to regain the esteem of his followers. During the same period, rumors swirled about Hurlewagen's actions on the battlefield at Weingarten.[147] It was also believed that Hurlewagen put himself at the head of the rebel army in order to contain its fury and that the Swabian League was paying him 16 fl. per month for his cooperation. All told, the accounts of Hurlewagen's behavior are scathing, yet the disgraced army leader was only distantly involved with the Linzgau rebels. There is no evidence that the leaders of the Bermatingen regiment abandoned the peasant cause or deceived their followers. They may certainly have channeled the movement's energy in ways that promoted their own interests. Yet to interpret this as a sell-out of the peasant cause requires further evidence.[148]

David Sabean and others see growing stratification within the village as the primary motivator in 1525 and not the supposed unity of the commune in the face of feudal domination.[149] Govind Sreenivasan refutes what he calls the "conversion narrative," showing that initial and moderate actions in Ottobeuren were led by the wealthier and conservative peasant leaders, whereas the middling and poorest rebels carried the later, more radical and destructive phases.[150] As for the Bermatingen regiment, though, no such radicalization was reported either before or after Weingarten. Despite repeated

---

146 For an extremely harsh critique of this leader, see VOGT, Hurlewagen. According to Scott and Scribner, "there is more than a suspicion that Hurlewagen had placed himself at the head of the band in order to contain the rebellion and moderate its impact." Idem, History in Documents, p. 26.

147 Many reporters, including Salem's chronicler and Ravensburg's secretary, alleged that Hurlewagen knelt before the Truchsess at Weingarten to plead for a settlement. The Truchsess complained to the Swabian League that the peasants had the story mixed up and were spreading lies throughout the region that it was the Truchsess who knelt to beg for mercy before the rebels. Others accused Hurlewagen of betraying the peasants by encouraging them to leave their strategic battle position on the hill. This has been interpreted as a sign of conspiracy between Hurlewagen and the Truchsess. See KUHN-OECHSELE and KUHN, Seehaufen Quellensammlung, pp. 135–136, 140; Bauernkrieg am Bodensee, p. 125, chap. 30; SCOTT and SCRIBNER, History in Documents, p. 26; KUHN, Seehaufen, pp. 123–124.

148 After the unpopular settlement at Weingarten there were signs of dissatisfaction and division, but for the most part, the southern Linzgau rebels remained outwardly compliant.

149 For the Weingarten region, Sabean draws attention to conflicts over use of the common lands among groups of villagers. Idem, German Agrarian Institutions, pp. 80–81.

150 SREENIVASAN, Social Origins, p. 57. Robisheaux (Rural Society, p. 63) points to similar divisions in the Neckar Valley-Odenwald Army between moderate leaders and a more radical group. See also WEBER, Nordwestliche Oberschwaben, p. 329, describing two factions in the village of Herdwangen near Owingen.

calls for aid from the Allgäu and Hegau Armies, Salem's peasants stayed home in outward support of the treaty.[151] This does not mean, of course, that the Linzgau peasants were happy with the treaty, nor should we assume they were all of one mind. The fact that most Linzgau peasants stayed home after Weingarten does not demonstrate their satisfaction. Still, if Sreenivasan and Sabean are right about the role of conflicting interests within the village, the fact that Salem's subjects complied with the treaty may indicate that local elites had a good deal of influence over their neighbors' actions.

There is no doubt that the leaders of the Lake Army were chosen predominantly from among the wealthier, relatively privileged members of the rural social order. Eitelhans Ziegelmüller, the captain of the Bermatingen regiment, was a wealthy miller and landholder who was both an Amtmann and a district judge for the Landvogtei.[152] Benedict Aigen was a wealthy farm tenant and Salem's Amtmann in Bermatingen who possessed his own seal.[153] The rebel leader in Owingen, named "Velin," was the tenant farmer of Lugenhof, an isolated farmstead just outside the village. The other known leaders of the Bermatingen regiment included Überlingen's administrator in Ittendorf and magistrates from Markdorf, Meersburg, and Tettnang.[154] It is true that the leaders in this movement of the "common man" were not the most common of its members. The question is, how well did these leaders represent the interests and goals of the rebels as a whole, and to what degree were they able to command their obedience and respect? Did the Lake Army's leadership pursue the narrow interests of village elites, and to what extent were these opposed to, or promoted at the expense of, their poorer neighbors and comrades?[155]

One of the major platforms in the German Peasants' War was the community's right to administer its own affairs, including the election of local leaders. The rebel armies chose their leaders, sometimes pressing them into service, because of their

---

151 A few may have joined the Hegau rebels and others from the northwestern Linzgau after Weingarten, but none from Salem's central territory are known. According to one report, the peasants hung three of their members from a tree near the abbey for planning to plunder its church following the treaty. KUHN-OECHSELE and KUHN, Seehaufen Quellensammlung, p. 226.

152 Born a common subject in the village of Unterteuringen, Ziegelmüller was a miller like his father and a tenant of St. John's Foundation in Constance. Shortly before the outbreak of the Peasants' War in Upper Swabia, on 10 February, the Landvogt appointed him as Amtmann and promoted him to head judge over the district court. KUHN, Seehaufen, p. 124.

153 A grazing settlement between Grasbeuren and Hallendorf on 1 July 1528 closes with the following words: "Unnd diewyl wir obman unnd Zusätz unnser aigner Innsigel nit gebruchenn, Haben wir ainhelligclich erbetten den Ersamen Benedict Aigen, der Zit unnsers gnedigern Herren von Salmenschwyler amptman zu Bermatingen, Das er von unnser aller wegen sin aigen Innsigell fur unns, doch Im unnd sinen erben In allweg onschädlich, Zu Urckhundt unnd getzuigknuß aller vorgeschribner dingen, offennlich gehennckt hatt an disen brieff Dero zwen glicher lut gemacht unnd yeder Parthy ainer gegeben ist." GLAK, 4/2734.

154 On the leadership elsewhere in Upper Swabia, see SABEAN, Landbesitz, pp. 107–108; idem, Communal Basis, p. 359; SREENIVASAN, Social Origins, p. 56.

155 SABEAN, German Agrarian Institutions, p. 77; SREENIVASAN, Social Origins, p. 36.

skills as speakers, organizers, and especially negotiators.[156] The army captains knew how to deal with lords, and their experience made them valuable as potential leaders of a new political order. If the movement of 1525 had been the program of the tenant farmers or some other narrow interest group, it could not have won the support of such large numbers of men. As stated in the Christian Union's Military Ordinance, "It is our especially amicable plea that each man in the brotherhood should act fraternally towards everyone, so that the rich should not think that the poor should do as much as they, but they should act equitably, as should be done when a feudal tax is levied, so that there will be fraternity."[157] Moreover, rebel leaders' acceptance of such a visible role in the opposition to regional authorities put them at great risk: retribution against leaders of rebellions tended to be harsh, and they were fully aware of the probable consequences of their actions in the case of defeat. Personal gain could not have been the primary motivator or expected reward for leadership in such an insurrection.

The leaders of the Lake Army may indeed have been among the greatest beneficiaries of the Peasants' War, in both economic and political terms. The best example is Eitelhans Ziegelmüller, who remained the Amtmann and head judge for the Landvogtei until his death in 1545 and even worked for the Truchsess from 1529 to 1531. During the same years he represented his district at Austrian diets in Innsbruck and Linz, and in 1541 he became one of the region's highest administrative officials (*Unterlandvogtverweser*). In addition to the mill, he acquired two other farms in Oberteuringen after 1525 and was "the richest man far and wide."[158] Benedict Aigen, too, remained in office as the Amtmann of Bermatingen after the Peasants' War. He was definitely a Sidelrichter in 1526 and was most likely the court's highest-ranking member.[159] Rent registers indicate he held extensive properties including several farms, and later generations of his family remained involved in local politics.[160]

---

156 SABEAN, Communal Basis, p. 359.

157 SCOTT and SCRIBNER, History in Documents, p. 134.

158 According to his gravestone in Oberteuringen, Ziegelmüller died as a knight with a coat of arms; KUHN, Seehaufen, pp. 123–125 (with illustration); SABEAN, Landbesitz, p. 108.

159 Aigen was probably acting as the court's *Stabhalter* (head judge) when he settled a dispute between Leutkirch and Neufrach over a communal well on 18 October 1526. The legal decision begins: "ICH Benedict aigen Derzit geschworner Sidelrichter Zů Salmanswiler, Von gewaltz unnd befelhens wegen, Des Hohwirdign gaistlichen Mins gnedigen Herren Herren Josen Abbt des gotzhuwß Salmanswiler, Bekenn offennlich mit disem brief ..." GLAK, 4/4429. There are no complete lists of Sidelrichter for the early sixteenth century, so it is unknown whether Aigen was also a judge before 1525, when he was promoted to head judge, or how long he may have served.

160 GLAK, 66/10311–10312, 1501 and 1529/1532; KUHN, Seehaufen, p. 124. Velin of Lugenhof also kept his farm after 1525. It was renewed as an annual leasehold, the most common form of tenure in Salem's villages. KUHN, Mönche und Bauern, p. 50.

The regional authorities' promotion of rebel leaders was further acknowledgement of the power and value of mediation and compromise. Whether we view the conservative resolution of conflict in the region as a sell-out or as a successful compromise, the Treaty of Weingarten and the actions of territorial intermediaries averted violence and paved the way for gradual change through peaceful negotiation. As was also the case in 1473, this treaty ensured that village leaders would continue to play an important role in territorial decisionmaking.

Horst Buszello has shown that the Christian Union provided a political vision rooted in the region's small-scale territorial development and founded on peasant ideals: it associated strong local communities in a loose confederation, much like the Swiss, whose elected leaders worked together to protect common interests while leaving individual members largely in charge of their own affairs.[161] If we interpret the goals of 1525 not in terms of a strong empire or German nation but instead as a call for greater communal autonomy and broader political inclusion, then it becomes clear that the Peasants' War was not such a failure after all. More than any other event, 1525 exemplifies the ability of ordinary subjects in Upper Swabia and other regions to join together across political boundaries, despite numerous obstacles resulting from the regional diffusion of authority and a diversity of local conditions and personal interests. It demonstrated then as now how much they had in common despite their differences and served as a powerful reminder of the common people's capacity for mass action. The movement did not succeed in fulfilling the majority of its stated goals, yet the lessons learned were not that resistance was useless or that the commune was irrelevant. In Salem, territorial authority became stronger after 1525, but not at the commune's expense and not without subjects' continuing participation in the development of political values and practices of rule.

Even as peasants' actions and goals are refracted through the impressions of monks, lords, and other observers, they exhibit a deep understanding of the methods of lordly domination and a remarkable skill in wielding them. The peasants seized the symbols of lordship for their own use and employed them to manipulate the political situation from below, forcing the convent to accept subordination to peasant rule or suffer the consequences. In 1525 Salem's peasants turned lordship upside-down but did not throw it out altogether. The peasants were in charge and the Amtmann was their captain, in a position to make demands and administer the oath. Swearing to do nothing against the peasant cause, the abbey's servants promised their loyalty and obedience; they would not aid the peasants' enemies or seek protection against them. Swearing to uphold the godly law, the monks promised to act according to the legal norms defined by the rebel leaders and the divine order. The bread, wine, and fish sent to peasant headquarters were no inconsequential gift: akin to a tribute, they were symbolic recognition that the peasants had become the lords. Salem supplied provisions to support

[161] Horst BUSZELLO, Common Man's View, pp. 109–122. In contrast to fragmented regions like Upper Swabia, peasants of larger territories such as Württemberg demanded inclusion in political assemblies within the territorial structure.

the war effort, just as subject communities and households normally did. In return, rebel leaders protected the abbey from potential violence. The terms of discourse and use of traditional symbols were familiar to both parties. In their defenselessness, the monks had little choice but to accept the peasants' terms.

Over the long run, 1525 was not a turning point for the agrarian economy, religious practices, or political relations between Salem and its peasants.[162] Instead, it consolidated and reinforced preexisting relationships between the abbot and his subjects. Major alterations to the agrarian order were proposed, considered, and overcome, so that the greatest consequence of 1525 was the lack of dramatic change. It reminded both sides of the power and potential of popular action, but at the same time it demonstrated a preference for nonviolent methods and an understanding, even acceptance, of key principles such as protection, aid, loyalty, and oath-taking. The fact that Salem's subjects remained free from punishment and that village leadership remained intact encouraged stability and continuity. The anonymous chronicler repeatedly praised the restraint practiced by rebel leaders such as Ziegelmüller and Aigen. The abbot's recognition of their ability to direct the peasant troops and to hold more radical actions in check reinforced these leaders' authority after 1525 as the primary mediators and negotiators between the abbey and its subjects. Herein lies the true legacy of 1525.

3.5 Local Communal Organization and Development

Now we turn our attention to the second major topic of this chapter: local politics in the countryside. The village may be understood primarily in a physical sense, as the settlement in which most (but not all) inhabitants of the countryside lived. The village as a physical settlement often coincided with local economic, social, cultural, and political organization.[163] It should not be confused with the rural or village commune, however, which refers to the political organization of a legally recognized corporate group.[164] The members of the commune enjoyed equal political status, at least

---

162 Thomas Robisheaux and Heide Wunder downplay the significance of 1525 as a major turning point in agrarian conditions and in relations between lords and subjects. Much more important, in their accounts, were demographic pressures, economic and social developments, and the agrarian conjuncture of the late sixteenth and early seventeenth centuries. ROBISHEAUX, Rural Society, p. 68; Heide WUNDER, Bäuerliche Gemeinde in Deutschland, Göttingen 1986, pp. 92–93.

163 Roger SABLONIER, Dorf im Übergang vom Hoch- zum Spätmittelalter: Untersuchungen zum Wandel ländlicher Gemeinschaftsformen im ostschweizerischen Raum, in: Institutionen, Kultur und Gesellschaft im Mittelalter: Festschrift für Josef Fleckenstein zu seinem 65. Geburtstag, ed. Lutz Fenske et al., Sigmaringen 1984, pp. 728–729; HOLENSTEIN, Bauern, p. 13.

164 It did not include all residents of the village. On the village commune, see BADER, Studien 2; BLICKLE, Obedient Germans, pp. 11–38; HOLENSTEIN, Bauern, pp. 13–21; Jerome BLUM, Internal Structure and Polity of the European Village Community from the Fifteenth to the Nineteenth Century, in: Journal of Modern History 43 (1971), pp. 541–576.

in theory. They also had a certain degree of collective autonomy in the regulation of internal affairs. One of the commune's central institutions was the assembly of all male householders, who witnessed and ratified laws, elected officials, and made decisions according to majority rule.

The term community (*Gemeinde*) has many meanings and can be understood in more than one sense.[165] In both English and German, community is based on the root-word common (*gemein*). The community is founded on what is held in common, for the good of all. The word Gemeinde appears frequently in the sources, used by lords and subjects alike. As a term with many meanings and generally positive connotations, it has been employed as a rhetorical cloak to support various interests and positions, not only by historical actors but also by the historians who write about them.[166] As an emotionally charged and potentially polemical term, community has been romanticized by some historians and scorned by others, based in part on traditions specific to national historiographies and in part on our own personal experiences and attitudes.[167] Thus, it is imperative to explain what is meant by community rather than taking its existence and form for granted. Here I will focus on two sets of meanings that should not be confused. First, the Gemeinde can be described in its concrete historical form as the village (or rural) "commune," a legal corporation with certain capacities of self-regulation and with a set of institutions for ordering local political activities and other matters of common interest. Second, Gemeinde may be understood in the broader sense of "community," as an ideal for ordering relationships among members with an emphasis on inclusion and equal status. Community is not necessarily local or even spatially restrictive. According to Cynthia Bouton, community designates "networks of individuals, bound together more closely than they are linked to outsiders."[168] The rebel armies in 1525 were a form of community in this wider sense, as were the parishes and the members of the entire territory. When speaking of the territorial community, I am emphasizing this second set of meanings. For the sake of clarity, I will use the term commune when referring narrowly to local self-government. When speaking of personal networks more broadly I will use the term community.

---

165 BADER, Studien 2, pp. 13–18; SCRIBNER, Communities, pp. 294–295.

166 R. W. SCRIBNER, Communalism: Universal Category or Ideological Construct? A Debate in the Historiography of Early Modern Germany and Switzerland, in: History Journal 37 (1994), pp. 206–207; idem, Communities, p. 298; SABEAN, Power in the Blood, p. 29.

167 As Susan Reynolds and Bob Scribner caution, it is especially important not to assign universal qualities to community or assume it had the same or similar meanings and functions as it has in our own time; SCRIBNER, Communalism, p. 207; REYNOLDS, Kingdoms and Communities in Western Europe, 900–1300, 2nd edition, Oxford 1997, pp. xiii–xv. On the historiography of community in Germany, see SCRIBNER, Communities, pp. 291–293; WUNDER, Bäuerliche Gemeinde, pp. 141–152; HOLENSTEIN, Bauern, pp. 75–81.

168 Cynthia A. BOUTON, The Flour War: Gender, Class, and Community in Late Ancien Régime French Society, University Park 1993, p. 168.

It should be noted at the outset that although this section focuses on the village commune, not all inhabitants of Salem's territory lived in large, nucleated villages. There were also a number of smaller hamlets and isolated farmsteads. In some respects, these smaller settlements were treated as extensions of nearby villages: Leutkirch, for example, was considered part of the larger village of Neufrach, just as Pfaffenhofen belonged to Owingen.[169] The same was true for many of the outlying farmsteads, such as Lugenhof (Owingen) and Oberhof (Oberuhldingen). The tax assessment of 1566 lists Schwandorf under Weildorf, Ralzhof under Tüfingen, Banzenreute and Forst as part of Mimmenhausen. The smaller settlements of Seefelden, Gebhardsweiler, and Hallendorf were lumped together in administrative records with the larger villages of Oberuhldingen, Mühlhofen, and Grasbeuren. Yet these smaller settlements differed from the major villages in several key respects. For one thing, local political organization was less developed. There was no communal assembly or council, and usually no Amtmann. Even if the smaller settlements were attached to nearby villages for administrative purposes such as tax assessments, they did not necessarily share a common identity, have a voice in communal decisionmaking, or enjoy the use of common land and resources in the main village.[170] Hamlets and isolated farmsteads were also set apart from the large nucleated villages in a socioeconomic sense. The small number of residents meant less stratification and less interaction, in other words weaker potential for social conflict but also for neighborliness. Without a common herd, common lands, and interspersed field parcels, the smallest settlements required relatively little formal regulation or cooperation.

Though local political development in the smaller hamlets and remote farmsteads was limited, the inhabitants and especially the major tenants in these places were often well integrated at the territorial level. They and their spouses usually came from the same families as in the neighboring villages. Some of them were quite active in territorial politics and justice, such as Conrad Biller from Oberhof, who was the Sidelgericht's head judge (1592–1616), and Hans Dilger from Schwandorf, also a member of the court (1614–1632). The parish was a prominent central place where the community

[169] In various lists for taxation and other purposes, entries for Leutkirch were often included with Neufrach just as Pfaffenhofen was listed as part of Owingen. Mittelstenweiler and Niderstenweiler were almost always listed together as one settlement, though not Oberstenweiler, located above them on the ridgetop and under Heiligenberg's jurisdiction until 1637.

[170] In a dispute between Neufrach and Leutkirch in 1526, the Sidelgericht held Neufrach responsible to help maintain a well in Leutkirch since they belonged to one community: "Diewil die von Nufron unnd Lutkirch ainer gemaind syen, Das dann dieselben von Nufron, Den Insässen zů Lutkirch, an gemeltem Irm costen zů machung unnd bessrung des gedachten brunnens ouch billicherwys Hilff unnd stur thůn, Unnd Hinfuro, mit Stegen wegen unnd brunnen zů machen und zůbessern, ouch Allweg In gemainem Costen, anligen unnd Helffen söllen." GLAK, 4/4429. When Neufrach started construction on a new community building in 1606 and Haberstenweiler residents refused to help, the Audience reminded Haberstenweiler of its duties as part of the commune. GLAK, 61/13369.

gathered regularly on a supralocal basis, because none of the parishes consisted of a single village. Most parish settlements were extremely small, so that the great majority of parishioners traveled to a nearby location for worship along with others from throughout the area. Churchwardens came from the various localities belonging to the parish, not the central place. This promoted a regional understanding of community that included the smaller settlements.[171] Thus, the village commune may be seen as the ideal type of rural community, but it did not typify the experience of all or even most rural communities. The mixture of settlement types in Salem's central territory and the weaknesses inherent in local political structures encouraged communal organization of the entire territory, which coincided with an area of shared legal customs under the jurisdiction of the Sidelgericht. According to Peter Bierbrauer, the neglect of supralocal rural communities and those based on settlement patterns other than large, nucleated villages has led historians to underestimate peasants' political influence beyond the local level.[172] This is a key point for understanding territorial politics in Salem.

The village commune had several political organs responsible for local self-administration. The most important of these was the village assembly.[173] The assembly was a meeting of all the commune's members to discuss and decide on a variety of issues involving the schedule of agricultural labor and direction of economic activities, the election of village officials and employees, the annual audit of village financial records, the use of communal resources, and the declaration of customary laws.[174] At village assemblies in Salem's territory, attendance was required of all male householders and closed to others.[175] This meant that most village inhabitants, including men without property as well as women and household dependents, were excluded from the commune's primary decisionmaking body. Membership in the commune could provide householders with the opportunity to run the village in their own interests. Yet it entailed responsibility as well as privilege. Attendance at assembly meetings was not voluntary, and the ordinances stating penalties not only for absence but also for tardiness suggest that many found participation in village decisionmaking to be burden-

[171] The rural commune is usually described as a local organization based on the village settlement, but in fact it could also form in the absence of nucleated villages. SCRIBNER, Communities, pp. 306–307; SABEAN, Landbesitz, pp. 111–113.

[172] BIERBRAUER, Freiheit und Gemeinde, pp. 70, 72; idem, Ländliche Gemeinde im oberdeutsch-schweizerischen Raum, in: Landgemeinde und Stadtgemeinde in Mitteleuropa: Ein struktureller Vergleich, ed. Peter Blickle, Munich 1991, p. 172; also Randolph C. HEAD, Early Modern Democracy in the Grisons, Cambridge 1995, p. 12.

[173] BADER, Studien 2, pp. 291–297.

[174] BLICKLE, Obedient Germans, p. 17; BLUM, Internal Structure, p. 552.

[175] The communal assemblies in Salem's villages were relatively large. Decisions were made by Umfrag, a structured set of questions and responses used to reach a collective determination. GLAK, 98/233; 98/395; 98/1546.

some.[176] Moreover, the village assembly was not egalitarian in the sense of popular democracy.[177] Members spoke their opinions for all to hear, from the eldest to the youngest, and village magistrates proposed the topics for discussion.[178] Smallholders had an especially strong voice in the assembly, it should be noted, since decisions followed the majority and there were more of them. Communal organization and the village assembly ensured a high degree of local control and spread authority across a broad segment of the population.

The village council in Salem's villages was known as the Four (in Buggensegel), the Fifteen (Mimmenhausen and Neufrach), or the Twenty-Four (Bermatingen) according to the number of its members, as was common throughout Central Europe. The council's large size in the major villages suggests that local decisionmaking involved a broader range of participants than was typical elsewhere.[179] Unfortunately, the scarcity of source references makes it difficult to assess the council's role and its level of involvement in local decisionmaking. Bermatingen's village statute of 1498 was issued by the council along with the village court and Amtmann, and many of its articles invested authority in the council rather than the Amtmann or territorial officials.[180] Yet references to village councils usually arose in the context of exceptional circumstances. The abbey may have played some role in the appointment or at least approval of council members, as suggested in 1583, when Neufrach reported vacancies and asked the Audience that the seats be filled.[181] At the end of this chapter, we will look at a commons dispute from Mimmenhausen that suggests the council did not necessarily represent elite interests and did not exclude modest householders from leadership positions. In any case, it appears that the village councils of Salem's territory were not only large but also relatively inclusive.

---

176 According to one ordinance, anyone absent from the assembly was fined three shillings, and "anyone who has not arrived before the little candle burns [out] shall provide another small candle and be fined two pence." GLAK, 98/1546, first document (undated fragment), fol. 5r–v. According to a 1607 *Memorial* for Mimmenhausen, assembly meetings were held after Mass on Sundays, with fines for unexcused absences. GLAK, 98/4420.

177 On the other hand, Antony Black says, "those who were included could participate more directly and more often, and could exert more power, than the average citizen in a modern democracy." Idem, The Commune in Political Theory in the Late Middle Ages, in: Theorien kommunaler Ordnung in Europa, ed. Peter Blickle, Munich 1996, p. 107.

178 GLAK, 98/4419 and 98/4420. According to Salem's chronicler of the Peasants' War, the convent followed a similar procedure. In both cases age rather than wealth or social status determined rank order.

179 Elsewhere, four was perhaps most common and twelve was considered especially large. BLUM, Internal Structure, p. 561; SCRIBNER, Communities, p. 301.

180 Bermatingen's Twenty-Four is also mentioned in several official agreements and legal charters, such as the religious foundation of 1532 described above.

181 GLAK, 61/13369. On the other hand, records from Mimmenhausen indicate that the commune elected its councilors. GLAK, 98/4419, 1603. Cf. SREENIVASAN, Ottobeuren, p. 44.

Village courts are even less frequently documented in Salem's central territory.[182] One reason for this is the predominance of oral procedures in the villages, but a more important factor is the early development of equivalent institutions at the territorial level. Among villages of the central territory, only Bermatingen and Owingen had their own courts.[183] The few lists of judges and other texts relating to the two village courts suggest that the entire commune assembled at an annual court session (*Jargericht*) to elect communal officials, declare local customs, and swear in new members.

The Amtmann was the most important, most active, and most frequently mentioned local official. He was both the leader of the commune and an appointed abbey official. The Amtmann performed a dual function, acting as both the lord's local steward and the communal spokesperson. He was responsible to report to the abbey's district officials all sorts of specific and detailed personal information about village inhabitants, making him a sort of police officer and agent of the abbey's economic domination in the village. The Amtmann's responsibilities also included settling those petty disputes deemed too insignificant for consideration by the court.[184] Another important duty of the Amtmann was to protect and represent the interests of the commune and its residents. The Amtmann sometimes represented neighbors in court and frequently petitioned on their behalf before the Audience. His political activities and intermediary role are further discussed below.

Each village commune typically had two treasurers (*Dorfpfleger*), responsible for managing income and expenditures and keeping financial accounts. The village treasurers often represented the commune alongside the Amtmann in legal contracts and petitions. They served annual and renewable terms, usually overlapping, so that each year there was one returning and one new treasurer.[185] Most villages had their own church or chapel, in which case two or more churchwardens (*Heiligenpfleger* or *Kirchenpfleger*) held responsibilities parallel to those of the village treasurers.[186] Certain parishes, cha-

---

[182] Even more generally, the functioning of village courts is not well understood because of source difficulties. BLICKLE, Communal Reformation, p. 187 n. 20; BADER, Schriften 2, p. 353. For Owingen, see KUHN, Mönche und Bauern, p. 54.

[183] For Bermatingen there are lists of judges from 1592, 1612, 1613, 1614, 1615, 1629, and 1630; Owingen court lists survive from 1612 and 1614. GLAK, 98/597 and 67/1484. According to these lists, the head judge (*Stabhalter*) was someone other than the Amtmann. Several lists state that the judges were "chosen" (*erwählt*); according to the preamble to a 1501 rent register from Bermatingen, the abbot appointed both the Amtmann and the village judges. GLAK, 66/10311.

[184] GLAK 98/1546, fol. 5v–6r.

[185] Village account records are available for several villages starting around 1590. See BRUN, Abbot and Peasants (2008 diss.), chap. 3; GLAK, 98/4420–4424.

[186] There are account records for a number of village churches, starting as early as 1582. See GLAK, 62/8509–8510, Leutkirch (1617–1620); 62/8589–8591, Mimmenhausen (1589–1632); 62/8599–8601, Mühlhofen (1582–1635); 62/8608, Neufrach (1615–1621); 62/9399, Weildorf (1594–1631).

pels, and local foundations controlled considerable property and endowments.[187] The Leutkirch parish, for example, had extensive vineyards, meadows, and arable worked by peasants in exchange for rents.[188] The parish churches were one of the primary sources of loans, and thus a major factor in the rural economic development of this period. Both village and church account records demonstrate the economic basis of communal organization.

Another local official was the forest and field warden (*Bannwart*), responsible for overseeing the forests, common lands, fields, and firewood distributions. The commune and the abbey both contributed to his salary.[189] The *Untergänger* maintained communal and field boundaries and assisted the Amtmann with property assessments. Some villages had a teacher, whose meager wages came from the lord, commune, and students' families.[190] Other communal employees included herdsmen, midwives, wine tasters and sales inspectors, night watchmen, grave diggers, and even broom makers.[191] Craftspeople and wage laborers such as coopers, carpenters, carters, and field workers were also employed by the commune and often appear in the village account records.

Karl Siegfried Bader called the village a bounded sphere of peace and law and identified one of the commune's primary functions as keeping the peace within its boundaries.[192] A widespread legal custom followed in Salem's villages was the *Fridbot*. This "call for peace" gave any witness to a violent act the right and indeed the responsibility to intervene by ordering others to desist. As the primary means of preventing physical conflict, the Fridbot legally bound all listeners to obey, no matter who had spoken the

---

[187] Local religious organizations owed imperial taxes based on wealth. Listed by tax obligation in 1578, from highest to lowest, they were: St. George's parish in Bermatingen (20 fl. 25 kr.), parish of St. Peter and Paul in Weildorf (10 fl. 30 kr.), Bermatingen priest (8 fl.), Urnau priest (6 fl.), Weildorf priest (6 fl.), St. Sebastian's confraternity in Mimmenhausen (4 fl. 36 kr.), St. Leonard's chapel in Bermatingen (4 fl. 35 kr.), confraternity of Our Lady in Bermatingen (4 fl. 2 kr.), chapel of St. Nicholas in Gebhardsweiler (3 fl.), Bermatingen primissary (3 fl.), parish of Our Lady and the Three Kings in Urnau (1 fl. 45 kr.), St. Pangratz's chapel in Mühlhofen (1 fl. 16 kr.), St. Margaretha's chapel in Buggensegel (1 fl. 15 kr.), another primissary in Bermatingen (1 fl.), and St. Lorenz's chapel in Tepfenhard (15 kr.). Wealth ranged accordingly, from 3,133 fl. for the Bermatingen parish to 30 fl. for the chapel in Tepfenhard. Fourteen churches and priests paid similar amounts in 1603, with another eight churches listed as exempt. GLAK, 98/2024, 98/2007.

[188] GLAK, 4/3401. The 1512 register of Leutkirch parish properties, rents, interest, and tithes is 43 double-sided pages long. The extensive properties, including many vineyards, were located throughout the region.

[189] GLAK, 98/230, 1635.

[190] Village teachers are first mentioned in the late sixteenth century and became fairly common in the larger villages by the early seventeenth century. See Chapter 6.

[191] The broom maker (*Besenmacher*) was listed along with other annually elected officials in Owingen (GLAK, 98/597).

[192] BADER, Studien 1: Das mittelalterliche Dorf als Friedens- und Rechtsbereich.

Illustration 3.2: Owingen and Surrounding Countryside, with Village *Etter*

Unknown artist, early seventeenth century. Generallandesarchiv Karlsruhe, H/Owingen/FN4

command, and the penalty for noncompliance rose sharply each time the spoken command was repeated and ignored.[193]

The physical and legal boundaries of the village proper were maintained and demarcated by the village *Etter*, which could be a fence, hedge, or wall. [194] It is prominent in Illustration 3.2, Owingen and Surrounding Countryside. The *Etter* also reinforced the social boundaries of the village. It was normally required that any house be built inside it, both to limit overpopulation and to protect the fields and common lands from the encroachment of would-be residents. Thus, the village *Etter* separated those who belonged to the village from those who did not. As it displayed in a physical sense, the commune defined itself in large part through the exclusion of outsiders. Residence in the village, even without full membership rights, was subject to strict controls. It required approval by the commune and the abbot and the payment of an entry fee (*Einzug*) to each of them.[195] Permission to join the commune as well as to reside there as a nonmember became increasingly restricted as the pressure on its resources rose in the later sixteenth and early seventeenth centuries.

Even with these restrictions, the level of conflict within the village grew over the course of the sixteenth century alongside demand for limited resources. The village commune was founded on horizontal principles such as household necessity, the common good, and majority rule. Yet community was never based on the ideal of equality with regard to property, use-rights, or social status. It contained many hierarchical relationships including those between members and nonmembers, farm tenants and cottars, propertied and propertyless, men and women, old and young. Although the very name "common lands" suggests that such properties were open to everyone's use, few would have suggested that all should enjoy equal access. Deciding what was equitable was another matter. Thus, another important function of the village commune was to provide for the needs of its various members and to regulate the use of common resources, to which access was never equal but upon which all inhabitants depended. We can be sure that village elites (and others) tried to take advantage of the system where they could, but even where there was corruption or private interest, the commune and its leaders had to solve such conflicts under scrutiny from their neighbors and territorial officials. They were expected to distribute communal obligations, as well as resources, fairly.

---

[193] Statutes mentioning the Fridbot include GLAK, 67/1484 (1498) and 4/131 (1476). Legal suits referring to the Fridbot, mostly in the context of assaults, are found in 1583, 1585, and 1591.

[194] Bader drew attention to the *Etter*'s significance as a legal and symbolic boundary, inside which special rules of peacekeeping applied. It was also a form of real physical protection for the villagers against both human and animal attack. Ibid., pp. 100, 105.

[195] According to a register of entry fees from 1595–1604, the price was ten shillings to the abbey and five to the village, except in Bermatingen. There the price was one pound to each authority; GLAK, 62/9264, 67/1484. It should be noted that these prescriptive measures were not easily enforced and there were many unpermitted residents in the villages. See Chapter 6.

In addition to balancing the needs and claims of competing groups with respect to the commune's material resources, successful leaders were those who were able to diffuse conflicts between village inhabitants. The inequalities within the village rose as population increased, since the large farms were not divisible and their number and size remained constant. This meant that the craftspeople, winegrowers, smallholders, and landless poor were the dynamic element. If the commune or its leaders proved resistant to changing social expectations or land use, especially as local demography shifted toward a larger proportion of smallholders and landless, this could result in a collapse of the commune and an inability to exercise its functions. When villagers could not settle internal problems alone, they sometimes called on territorial authorities or other outsiders to arbitrate or assist them in other ways. Stability in the village depended not only on population size and the level of stratification, but more importantly, on the measures taken to balance their interests and the division of resources between them.

As indicated earlier in this chapter, historians have identified two major factors as the commune's greatest challenges and the reasons for its decline: social stratification and internal division on the one hand, growth of state power and central authority on the other. These issues are not entirely unrelated: under certain conditions, divisions within the commune could play to the ruler's advantage. Yet we should not rush too hastily to the assumption that increasing social differentiation within the village necessarily led to the decline of communal institutions. The rising demand for economic resources and social services, the influx of new residents, and above all the perceived threat to peace, order, and neighborliness, could strengthen the political power of the village commune just as easily as it could strengthen territorial rule. Besides, rising state power did not necessarily weaken local authority. In an attempt to maintain order and stability, the local commune and the territorial government faced many of the same challenges. In practice, the functioning of one depended on the other and the integration of village communes into the territory strengthened authority on both levels. Thus, their relationship should not be interpreted as one of simple opposition or a zero-sum gain. Members of the commune frequently petitioned the abbot or Audience for assistance in local matters and invited them to mediate or decide, indications that they perceived the lord's influence as necessary and even beneficial.[196] The next section takes a closer look at the relationship between community and lordship and at their primary intermediaries, the Amtmänner.

---

196 Caroline Castiglione argues that Italian villagers in Monte Libretti viewed their lords as patrons or as adversaries depending on the situation. Her demonstration of how differently the relationships between lord and community could develop in neighboring localities is especially interesting. She also demonstrates peasants' active and enthusiastic participation in local politics, which she sees as "an ongoing bargaining process."

3.6 The Intermediary Role of the Village Amtmann

The Amtmann was the senior local official in Salem's villages. He was at once the executive officer of the community and the lord's local steward. He was also a householder, often a wealthy farm tenant, engaged in agriculture with a stake in the local economy. He was typically related to many of his fellow villagers by blood, marriage, and a lifetime of experiences. The Amtmann's responsibilities, loyalties, relationships, and interests placed him at the center of local politics. Recent studies of early modern political formation have focused on the interconnections between center and periphery.[197] If we look at the interfaces between the villages and the territory as the essential nodes of political formation, and focus on individual actors rather than institutions as the focal points of communication and exchange, it becomes clear that the Amtmann was involved in the most critical political interactions. The following section explores the Amtmann's position as the central mediator, power broker, buffer, and spokesman who connected the village and the territory. First we will consider his duties as the abbey's local steward, followed by his actions on behalf of the commune and its members.

Several lists of official instructions to the collective Amtmänner provide detailed information about their duties. For example, in 1578 a set of instructions was read aloud to the assembled Amtmänner of the central territory in the abbey chamber, in the presence of the abbot, bursar, Großkeller, secretary, and Kaufmann.[198] First, the Amtmänner were reminded of the oaths they had sworn upon their appointment and of their promises to carry out their duties with all diligence. Then their specific duties were listed in twelve points. In addition to promoting the abbey's honor and interests, they had to report all infractions of the abbey's commands (*Gepott, Verpott, Statuten, Satzungen, und Ordnungen*) and help bring offenders to justice. They were required to respect the abbey's law and justice (*Recht und Gerechtigkaiten*) as well as maintain the commune's good old customs and traditions with respect to grazing, common lands, pathways, and other common interests. In spiritual and worldly matters, they had to defend local customs and make sure no new practices arose without the authorities' prior knowledge and approval. No outsiders should be permitted to reside in the village without permission, and those who were admitted were obliged to swear an oath of allegiance to the abbey. Several points outlined the Amtmann's duty to help the abbey keep track of its serfs. He had to report their names and collect recognitive fees (*Leibrecht*). He was supposed to take special note of those who had died or left the abbey's jurisdiction so that fines could be collected. Likewise, he had to report any outside marriages. Regardless of servility, the instructions emphasized that all subjects or residents of the abbey's jurisdiction were forbidden to appear before outside courts, offer security for a territorial outsider (*Bürgschafft thun*), or submit to any written contract or agreement other

[197] OGILVIE, State, pp. 167–202; HOLENSTEIN, Gute Policey.

[198] GLAK, 98/395. The Amtmänner of Adelseute, Tepfenhard, and Wendlingen were noted as absent.

than through the abbey or with its prior permission. The Amtmänner were ordered not to accept commands from any other lord and to immediately reject and report attempts by outsiders to impose duties on any subject. Finally, the abbey's representatives instructed the Amtmänner to protect the village from strangers such as beggars, highway robbers, and wandering soldiers both day and night. In conclusion, they were reminded to be obedient to any future commands as necessity might require.

The next year, in 1579, the abbot further elaborated the duties of the Amtmänner. Again they were instructed to report on matters of servility and residence either orally or in writing, but this time they were asked to recall all information from the past four years—that is, since the start of the abbot's reign in March of 1575.[199] The abbot repeated his demand for information about serfs who had died, moved away, or married outsiders, as well as about unpermitted residents and offenses against the lord's commands and prohibitions. One detail of special interest relates to the village assembly. First, it stated that only those who owned or rented their own house should attend village assemblies (*Ainungen*), except in special cases. Second, those who did not belong to the assembly should not have a voice or offer their opinion in local elections. These statements may have been prompted by the rising number of smallholder families who sublet or shared houses with others, a practice the instructions strictly forbade with the declaration that multiple couples should not live in the same house except by special permission.[200] Other articles concerned standards of moral behavior. All disreputable women,[201] along with couples who behaved dishonorably and notoriously, should be thrown out of the village—especially if they were not the lord's serfs or resided in the village without permission.

In January of 1594 the recently elected Abbot Peter Müller (r. 1593–1614) issued new instructions, proclaimed yet again in the abbey's great chamber before all the Amtmänner from the two central districts.[202] The 25 articles repeated or expanded on many of those found in earlier instructions. This time he asked the Amtmänner to report

---

199 GLAK, 98/395. Abbot Matthäus Roth's request for information going back to the start of his term in office, as well as a second set of instructions issued so soon after the first, suggests that Abbot Matthäus was an avid reformer with a keen interest in village activities. The repetition of his orders does not indicate, however, that his instructions were carefully followed in the villages.

200 Housing restrictions were mentioned repeatedly in the following decades but apparently they were not well enforced: property transactions from the early seventeenth century mention houses split into halves, thirds, and fourths, and many of the larger tenants rented houses or parts of houses to smallholders. See KUHN, Seehaufen, p. 111; Petra SACHS, Leben und Wohnen in Owingen, in: 1000 Jahre Owingen, ed. Gemeinde Owingen, Owingen 1983, p. 73.

201 "Alle gemaine offentliche, Leichtferttige, Unvershampte, Unzichtige, Ehrvergeßne und beshrayte Weybs personen." GLAK, 98/395.

202 GLAK, 98/395; 61/13369. The title reads: "Dess Gottsshauss Salmenswyler underamptleuths Im keller unnd Pfisterampt seyend uff dem verhörtag dornnstag den 13 January 1594 nachvolgende Articul steiff zu halten mit Ernst furgenomen worden." The Amtmänner had come to deliver the imperial war taxes (*Raißsteur*).

on events over the past eleven years since 1583, including previously disclosed infractions.[203] In addition to the information requested earlier, the new instructions demanded the names of all residents, not only serfs but also free inhabitants, foreign serfs, and anyone who had settled there without permission, so that separate lists could be made and duplicated for the use of various officials.[204] New, stiffer sanctions applied to those seeking outside marriages or entry to the village. The Amtmänner were now required to make sure no new residents were admitted or permitted to marry before they became the abbey's serfs. Also new in 1594 was the introduction of fire regulations, which prohibited the drying of hemp or other products by indoor heat sources. The abbey waived its claim to the fines, "in order to encourage diligent inspections by the Amtmann and village treasurers." The articles about indecent women were repeated in 1594, with the addition that anyone who housed such women would be imprisoned or even banished along with their wives and children. Pregnancy out of wedlock was the subject of two new articles.[205] Another article targeted parents, who were expected to attend church services with their children and servants all the way to the end. It urged parents to take responsibility for their children's moral upbringing, with the reminder that any sins committed by young people were the fault of their parents.

The three texts demonstrate the abbey's dependence on its local officials to enforce its will, suggesting the incomplete nature of the information received from reluctant informants. Without the cooperation of the Amtmänner, the abbot and other administrators found themselves unable to collect fines or even to know who lived in the villages, by permission or otherwise. The fact that these regulations were written as instructions to the Amtmänner and not as general ordinances addressed to the entire population emphasizes the fact that the Amtmann controlled the direction and content of information communicated between the village and the abbey. Although he was the abbot's steward, enforcement was carried out at his discretion.[206] He had the ability to grant or withhold information that was essential to the abbey's practice of lordship within the village.

---

203 The eleven years corresponded to the three short reigns of Vitus Nekher, Johannes Bücheler, and Christian Fürst.

204 There are lists of serfs and nonservile residents for several villages in this period; see GLAK, 98/2300–2303.

205 Unwed couples expecting a child would be punished with two weeks' imprisonment for the man, public humiliation on her wedding day for the woman. If they chose not to marry, the man's punishment increased to eight weeks in the tower and the woman would be immediately banished. GLAK, 98/395.

206 Without motivated and effective monitoring by authorities, says Paul Warde, ordinances were quietly ignored or forgotten. Idem, Common Rights and Common Lands in Southwest Germany, 1500–1800, in: The Management of Common Land in North West Europe, c. 1500–1800, ed. Martina de Moor et al., Turnhout 2002, p. 218. As Schlumbohm argues (Gesetze, pp. 659–660), early modern states passed numerous laws and regulations, yet they were only partially enforced. Furthermore, there are indications that aspects of symbolic representation were often more important than enforcement.

We might assume, since the Amtmann was responsible for reporting on the actions and especially on the financial obligations of his neighbors, that he would be an unpopular man in the village. Since he was a judge, an informant, and the primary local law enforcer all in one, villagers must certainly have guarded their words and behavior in his presence. At the same time, however, the Amtmann was a well-respected leader among the villagers who by no means served only the lord's interests. He was, after all, a member of the community. He prayed at the same church, worked in the same fields, drank at the same inn, knew all the same stories, grew up with the same traditions, and through kinship and sociability he was linked to everyone else in the village.[207] He could adapt the lord's commands and prohibitions to local conditions, modifying their effect. His success as a local leader depended on his ability to balance multiple concepts of order.[208]

According to employment contracts and other official records, the Amtmann was the abbot's appointee.[209] Evidence of villagers' participation in the selection of Amtmänner is lacking, but this does not mean they were without any influence.[210] The

207 The Amtmann was in most cases born and raised in the village where he assumed office, and in three known cases where he was not, he and his family came from the immediate area: Hans Aigen from Markdorf was Bermatingen's Amtmann in 1577–1578. His kinsmen Hermann Aigen (1479–1493) and Benedict Aigen (1515–1532) preceded him in office. Christoph Langenstain, also Amtmann in Bermatingen, was the son of abbey serfs from Kirchberg. Balthas Diem was born in Neufrach and lived in Leutkirch before he married the widow of Mimmenhausen's previous Amtmann. He assumed office there in 1632.

208 Keith WRIGHTSON, Two Concepts of Order: Justices, Constables and Jurymen in Seventeenth-Century England, in: An Ungovernable People, ed. John Brewer and John Styles, London 1980, p. 29; Achim LANDWEHR, Zwischen allen Stühlen: Lokale Amtsträger im frühneuzeitlichen Leonberg, in: Policey in lokalen Räumen: Ordnungskräfte und Sicherheitspersonal in Gemeinden und Territorien vom Spätmittelalter bis zum frühen 19. Jahrhundert, ed. André Holenstein et al., Frankfurt am Main 2002, pp. 108–109. Wrightson contrasts two concepts of order (see esp. pp. 24–25), whereas Landwehr insists on a complex, circular process influenced by various social groups.

209 GLAK, 98/233; 66/10311, 1501, fol. 51r.

210 Johann Schentz replaced Martin Stengelin as Amtmann in 1633 after Stengelin asked to step down. He was appointed with the commune's approval, as the text states: "Freytags den 13ten May Ao 1633, ist In beysein das wolEhrwuerdigen, Andächtigen undt Geistlichen herren P. Thomae Haußers Conventualn undt Großkellers undt Ober Amptmans Lt. Marcelli Ruoff, zu Owingen auß Ihren Gn. das Hochwürdigen unsers Gnedigen herren, gl. befelch, Martin Stengelin uff sein flehenlich underthenig bitten undt Aintfältig anhalten seines Amptmans dienst erlassen undt vor einer gantzen Gemeindt herr Johan Schentz Waldtvogt für einen Newen Amptman Vorgestelt worden, welcher zwar darfür gebetten, doch solches acceptirt, undt weiln man die Ampts sachen, undt den Amptlichen Aydt nit bey der handt, hatt derselb für dißmal nur handttrew geben, undt darmit ist die Gemeindt wol zu friden geweßen; Martin Stengelin der alt Amptman hatt sich der gl. erlassung underthenig bedanckt, undt die Gemeindt, so Er ettwan Jemanden beleidiget, umb verzeyhung gebetten, darauff ettliche dem Newen Amptman gratulirt, unndt sich dißer Actus geendet. Actum ut supra. u." GLAK, 98/216.

Amtmann also spoke on behalf of the village commune and its members in their dealings with the abbey. Besides the evidence from the German Peasants' War, this is clear in legal agreements such as those from fifteenth-century Bermatingen in which the Amtmann, along with other communal officials and the entire village commune, entered legal contracts and settlements ending disputes with their lord. The Amtmann was also the community's major link to territorial decisionmaking. Half of all known Amtmänner were members of the territorial court.[211] At the Audience, Amtmänner often brought petitions in the name of the village commune or on behalf of individual neighbors.

Because the abbey kept such good written records compared to the village commune, it is much more difficult to discover the Amtmann's specific responsibilities and activities on behalf of other villagers than it is to see his duties to the lord. Even the information about his communal involvement, his economic activities, his family, and his participation in local social life must be gleaned from the abbey's records. One of the best sources for discovering the Amtmann's place in the village and his representation of its collective interests vis-à-vis the abbey is the Audience protocol.[212] The Audience records show how villagers and communities called on the abbey for assistance, emphasizing certain elements of lordship to achieve a beneficial result. The Audience and its records are examined in the following chapters, but for our present purposes, we will concentrate on the role of Amtmänner as mediators in the presentation of petitions, especially on behalf of the entire village commune.

Not all Audience petitions mention an Amtmann, but many of them do. The following four political biographies are constructed primarily from a selection of Audience petitions that involve the Amtmann in some way. The participation of Amtmänner in these cases may be classified as petitions on behalf of another individual, on behalf of the commune or another group, petitions made in self-interest, and petitions relating to lordship.[213] The examples are chosen to illustrate the political activities of Amtmänner; in the next chapter, the same source material will be used to highlight their socioeconomic positions and networks.

---

[211] Some Amtmänner held other political offices at the local or territorial level, but no other office was tied so closely to village headmanship as that of Sidelrichter. Among the 122 known Amtmänner in Salem's villages during the period 1472–1648, 60 served concurrently as territorial judges. See Chapter 5.

[212] The Audience members were a fluctuating group of abbey administrators both monastic (Großkeller, Pfister, bursar) and secular (secretary, Oberamtmann, Hofmeister, Amtmann). They met on a regular basis to hear petitions from territorial subjects, both individuals and groups. Petitions involved disputes, grievances, and requests on a range of topics including alms, firewood, rents, residence, manumission, land tenure, marriage, and many others. See Chapter 6.

[213] In a sample of all petitions from seven years, Amtmänner were involved in 171 out of 1,001 cases. Classified by type, these include 57 petitions on behalf of other individuals, 34 on behalf of the commune or other group, 45 personal requests, 23 official reports, and 12 indirect references. GLAK, 61/13369–13374.

1. Blesi Steckborer was the Amtmann in Weildorf (1578–1598) as well as a Sidelrichter (1572–1591) and Wespach hospital warden (1596).[214] Steckborer appeared before the Audience several times during his tenure on behalf of Weildorf, Wespach, and individual villagers. In 1591 he and his commune requested permission to convert a forested hillock above the village into vineyards. They offered to pay a reasonable annual rent. They pointed out that the land was of little use for grazing or timber and that two villagers had already planted there the previous year. The Audience postponed its decision in order to conduct a property inspection.[215] On another occasion, Steckborer reported on behalf of the entire commune that Georg Hergisfelder was collecting manure off the road outside Weildorf. He complained that Hergisfelder should share the manure with others or pay something for the right to take it. The Audience responded that Hergisfelder had permission to clean up the gully and make it passable. Besides, he had a team of horses and was willing to deliver the manure to the abbey's fields. If others wanted to help move it, they were free to do so.[216] In 1595 Steckborer and the village treasurers asked in the name of the entire commune for the construction of a tithe barn in Weildorf. They offered to help with both labor and transport, willingly and in common. The Audience promised an answer in one month but Steckborer repeated his request almost a year later, this time on behalf of the farm tenants (*Mayerschaft*), who were responsible for delivering the tithe to the abbey.[217] Steckborer appeared again in 1596, this time to report in the name of the entire commune that Heiligenberg officials forbade them to graze on some land they had always used in the past, with the warning that next time the count would have them arrested and imprisoned. The Audience replied that Weildorf should continue to use the land since they had done so for longer than human memory. If anyone tried to stop them, the abbey would take legal action on their behalf.[218] That same year, Steckborer requested the commune's exemption from the war taxes, or at least a reduction, in consideration of all their cows that had died. The Audience members declared they would think about it.[219]

   Blesi Steckborer also petitioned on behalf of individual neighbors. In 1591 he asked the Audience to grant benefices to an old potter and the retired abbey gatekeeper, to help them manage in their old age. The Audience denied his request but

---

[214] In addition to significant overlap between the Amtmänner and Sidelrichter, 29 out of 122 Amtmänner held other known offices at the local level: thirteen served as churchwardens, three as village judges (in Bermatingen and Owingen), six as village treasurers, four as hospital overseers, two as forest wardens, and one as a boundary official.

[215] GLAK, 61/13369.

[216] Ibid., 1591.

[217] Ibid., 1595 and 1596. A tithe barn in the village may have been in everyone's interests, but this example provides evidence of village magistrates presenting tenants' interests as the concerns of the entire commune.

[218] Ibid., 1596.

[219] Ibid.

offered weekly bread alms. He made another petition to grant Hans Ruoßmayer's son, who was sick and had an inheritance worth 140 fl., a place in the abbey hospital at Wespach. This request was approved one week later, following a meeting with the bursar. Steckborer testified in support of villagers who needed birth certificates in 1589 and 1595. He petitioned in 1591 on behalf of a young weaver in an inheritance dispute. In 1595 he was involved in a disputed land sale as the guardian of Jerg Hailg, a young man from Weildorf who was studying abroad. In 1589 the Audience rebuked Steckborer for allowing too many unlawful residents in the village. This came as the result of a fight between two of the five men living at the miller's house, against territorial order but with the Amtmann's permission. Steckborer excused himself, saying the previous abbot had granted them residence. The Audience declared that the abbey's customary prohibition remained in effect, threatening punishment for anyone who disobeyed the limit of no more than two (unrelated) residents per household.[220] Overall, the results of Blesi Steckborer's petitions may be regarded as relatively ineffectual. Nevertheless, he actively addressed local concerns and communicated them to the abbey.

2. Andreas Villieber was the Amtmann in Nußdorf (1578–1613) as well as a Sidelrichter and Seefelden churchwarden (both offices 1584–1613). In the sampled Audience records, he presented a few petitions on behalf of the commune and appeared several times as a legal witness or in connection to his neighbors' business transactions.[221] In 1589 he petitioned in the name of the entire commune for the right to choose the village innkeeper, offering to pay the abbey three gulden annually in addition to the normal rent. The Audience consented, emphasizing that the lease was subject to rents and annual renewal. The abbey reserved the right to visit the tavern at any time.[222] In 1591 Amtmann Villieber and the "entire commune" asked the Audience to support them in a tenure dispute with their landlord, Hans Jerg von Bodman. This noble landowner leased his arable and forest parcels to seven tenants, and each time one of them died, the contract between the landlord and all his tenants was renewed. Previously, the leaseholders had paid only for the drafting of a new written contract, but upon one tenant's recent death, von Bodman demanded an entry fine of ten gulden from each of them contrary to custom. The Audience agreed, after consulting the old tenure contract, to write a letter to von Bodman on

220 Ibid., 1589.

221 In his capacity as churchwarden, Villieber lent fifty pounds to the master fisherman of Maurach in 1584, one hundred gulden to the community of Nußdorf in 1587, forty gulden to the former miller of Oberuhldingen in 1590, and fifty gulden to Jerg Pfeiffer of Mimmenhausen in 1591. These and other examples are found in the chancery records. GLAK, 61/13316–13317.

222 GLAK, 61/13369, 1589.

their behalf. In 1595 another tenant died and again the Audience agreed to support Villieber and the commune in their tenure claims.[223]

Like Blesi Steckborer, Andreas Villieber petitioned on behalf of a neighbor for entry to the abbey hospital in Wespach. He also recommended Hans Leub of Nußdorf to take over the vacant mill in Oberuhldingen and offered to pledge security for him. He asked the abbey to rent a vineyard to another neighbor. In 1611 he requested permanent residence for a vineyard laborer from Wintersaulgen who wanted to marry a local girl. Villieber pointed out that this man had worked in the village for several years, owned seventy gulden in property, behaved well, and had the community's support. Each of these requests was approved. Villieber's actions on behalf of his neighbors are also recorded in the chancery protocol: he witnessed a marriage contract in 1582, a retirement contract in 1584, and a manumission in 1604. He served as a guardian in 1584 and pledged security for loans to others in 1587, 1592, and 1605. He was named in a 1585 suit before the Sidelgericht involving a large wine sale he had arranged between Stoffel Schmalzhofen and the innkeeper of Rotenbühl. In 1594 Villieber sought to resign from office, but despite permission from the Audience to do so, he continued as Amtmann and Sidelrichter for another decade until his death in 1613.[224]

3. Hans Villieber, of unknown relationship to Andreas, was Amtmann of Buggensegel during much of the same period (1589–1610).[225] He was a churchwarden for Buggensegel's chapel of St. Margaretha in 1592. His petitions on behalf of the commune are good examples of the range of interests and needs found in one of the smaller villages. The year 1589 was one of economic difficulty across the territory, and the new Amtmann along with the village treasurers arranged for a communal loan of 200 fl. from Salem's legal counselor, Johann Sigmund Hornstain. Later that year he petitioned for an additional loan of 200 fl., so that "in these hard times" the community members could maintain their properties, pay debts, and buy grain. He offered the common lands (*Gemeindt merckh*) as collateral, against which smaller loans would be distributed to individual villagers. The Audience agreed, as long as the loans were made to approved residents, subject to written contract, and repaid within six years.[226] In 1591 the Amtmann and commune complained of field and forest damages caused by excessive runoff from Mimmenhausen's upstream

[223] Ibid., 1591 and 1595. This is another example of a claim being made by and in the name of the entire commune that was in fact in the interests of a narrower group—in this case, the seven leaseholders.

[224] Ibid., 1594.

[225] Hans Villieber was not a Sidelrichter, which may lend indirect support to a kinship link between them, since relatives were not supposed to serve together on the court.

[226] GLAK, 61/13369, 1589.

meadows. The Amtmann and commune of Mimmenhausen countered that the drainage did no harm. If it did, it was only because Buggensegel had not maintained its ditches as was customary. The Audience ordered an inspection of the property.[227] In another dispute, Villieber and the village treasurers brought complaints against Mimmenhausen and Neufrach for refusing to pay impoundment fines for animals grazing illegally on Buggensegel's lands. The Audience made no immediate decision but offered to send someone to hear each side's testimony.[228] Attached to the impoundment petition was Buggensegel's additional request for an ordinance to regulate the foreign poor, who were being driven from place to place.[229] No decision was forthcoming. In 1599, the Amtmann asked the Audience to require the churchwardens to contribute to the costs of a new clock being built in the village. The churchwardens were ordered to help with specific responsibilities.[230] In a subsequent entry, the commune agreed to increase the sexton's wages since he was now responsible for ringing the hours.

4. Mattheus Leub was the Amtmann in Mimmenhausen from 1610 to 1631. He also served as a Sidelrichter (1612–1631) and as a churchwarden for St. Sebastian's confraternity (1611–1613). He was active in the community as a witness for births (1612, 1620) and marriages (1611) and as a guardian for orphans and widows (1608, 1620). He was a boundary guard in 1605 and 1607 prior to his appointment as Amtmann. In 1611 Leub reported the departure of the village teacher and asked for a chaplain to take over the lessons. The Audience offered to think about it. By 1613 there was a new teacher, but the sexton was leaving. With the Amtmann's support, the teacher petitioned for a raise in the form of an additional wagonload of hay from the common lands. The Amtmann and two members of the commune also requested permission to elect a new sexton, rather than transfer his responsibilities to the teacher.[231] Amtmann Leub played a leading role in Mimmenhausen's efforts to obtain a resident priest between 1613 and 1630 and in complaints against

---

227 Ibid., 1591. This dispute reappeared in later Audience records, but no decision is recorded.

228 Ibid., 1596. This dispute also reappeared much later, in 1613, when Mimmenhausen complained against Buggensegel regarding animal impoundment fines. Mimmenhausen's representatives said the fine had been changed from bread to cash according to an agreement involving only some residents, not the entire commune. Since not everyone had consented, they wanted the change rescinded.

229 Ibid. On poor policy and the practice of the "*Bettelfuhr*," see Chapter 6.

230 Ibid., 1599.

231 The request provides evidence of both the lord's and the commune's influence over the appointment of local officials: "Piten demnach Sy von der Gemaindt, ... durch ain Gemaind, wie von Altemheero, einen Anderen Meßmer erwöllen lassen." GLAK, 61/13370.

Seefelden's parish priest, Dr. Birenbaum.[232] Leub's initiative led to the establishment of a new parish in 1630.[233] In another petition, Leub asked for a decision about the watchman assigned to protect moveable property from soldiers. Some members of the commune were complaining against the decision, he explained. The Audience ordered that the guard should proceed with his duties.[234] In 1616, together with the Amtmänner of Neufrach, Buggensegel, and Oberuhldingen, Leub requested a bread inspection. No decision is recorded. Also in 1616 the Audience ordered Leub and the Amtmann of Neufrach to enforce payment of the small tithe, in response to the purchaser's complaint that he was having trouble collecting it.[235]

Mattheus Leub petitioned frequently on behalf of his neighbors.[236] Upon his request in 1611 the Audience agreed to help Catharina Bluemin with an inheritance claim in Württemberg and provided her family with alms. His petition on behalf of Sebastian Spiegelin for a benefice in 1613 was denied, since Spiegelin had insufficient property to pay for the food and other provisions he requested. In 1619 Leub asked the Audience to reduce Thoma Schmidtmaister's heavy fines for insulting the Amtmann of Bermatingen. The Audience was unsympathetic to his appeal that Schmidtmaister had been "full of wine" and had already served his time in

232 In 1613 Mattheus Leub and the village treasurers requested that the abbey send someone to perform Mass every Saturday. The Audience granted the request and renewed it in 1616. In 1618 Mimmenhausen complained to the Audience that they were still without a priest and there was no Sunday Mass either. The many records mentioning the need for a priest in Mimmenhausen are certainly related to complaints from across the entire parish against Dr. Birenbaum of Seefelden. In 1616 the Audience noted that "The entire community of Mimmenhausen complains against Herr Doctor Jos, the lord priest of Seefelden, that he performs the Mass and other duties in the church very poorly and not as he should. They request as subjects that His Grace help them find out if [the priest] might be convinced to put a bit more effort into his work." In 1620 the Amtmann along with the treasurers and the entire commune of Mimmenhausen submitted formal grievances against Jodocus Birenbaum. Their letter stated that he never performed weekly services or holiday Masses in Mimmenhausen as he was required to do. Sometimes he failed to show up for scheduled marriages and funerals and the sexton came to report the priest's excuses only after hours of waiting. The priest also refused to perform baptisms in the village and people had died without last rites because he failed to come. GLAK, 61/13370–13371 and 98/3557. See also Marc FORSTER, Kirchenreform, katholische Konfessionalisierung und dörfliche Religion um Kloster Salem 1650–1750, in: Rottenburger Jahrbuch für Kirchengeschichte 16 (1997), pp. 101–102.

233 Documents relating to the parish foundation are found in GLAK, 98/3432. The Thirty Years War resulted in another period of vacancies, but the parish in Mimmenhausen became firmly established shortly after the war and is still active today.

234 GLAK, 61/13370, 1613.

235 Ibid., 1616.

236 Leub also testified before the Sidelgericht on four occasions in sampled years, twice in 1610 and twice in 1625. He supported two defendants on debt charges, another defendant in a disputed land sale, and the entire commune of Mimmenhausen in a grazing dispute with Mühlhofen.

> the tower.[237] In 1624 Leub reported the deaths of three villagers and petitioned on behalf of their widows for a merciful heriot tax.[238] One was Master Georg Morß, the abbey cook. The Audience agreed to charge his widow only two gulden despite her moderate wealth, since she had three small children and in consideration of her husband's loyal service. Leub reported other neighbors for misbehavior including Martin Bürckh, who was getting along badly with his wife, drinking and swearing, and "stinking like the devil." Bürckh continued with his threats and diabolical speech even when confronted by the Amtmann and higher abbey officials. The Audience sought legal counsel and ordered his arrest.[239] On another occasion, Leub reported Hans Jäger's wife and others for gossiping about the teacher's reasons for leaving and speaking badly about his wife, as well as calling the Kramer girl a whorebag without good reason. A maid, pregnant by the smith's servant, was punished in 1613 as a result of Leub's report.

These examples demonstrate the variety of local issues the abbey's officials were asked to weigh in on. In many cases, it is surprising that an Amtmann or entire commune would want to involve the abbey rather than make the decision on their own. In others, the Amtmann emphasized the protective elements of lordship to obtain privileges or special aid. Not all requests resulted in the desired response, but they show that the Amtmann and other villagers sometimes welcomed and even demanded the lord's assistance in the settlement of internal affairs. Even when villagers were reported for punishment, the petitions indicate that the abbey's involvement was not an unwanted intrusion. Rather, it often resulted from the commune's expectation that the abbey support them in maintaining public order and from their inability to enforce their will over recalcitrant residents.

Not every Amtmann served in office until his death. At least two men, Martin Stengelin of Owingen and Andreas Villieber of Nußdorf, asked to step down.[240] Two others, Jacob Klotz of Weiler and Mattheus Senfft of Mimmenhausen, were removed from office following their denunciations by an Oberamtmann who resided in the same village. In the first case, Salem's former Oberamtmann Michael Walraff com-

---

237 GLAK, 61/13371.

238 In sampled Audience records there are 17 heriot tax petitions by Amtmänner on behalf of their neighbors in 1624, compared to none in most sampled years. What was unusual in 1624 was not the number of reported deaths but the involvement of the Amtmann in presenting such requests. The reasons for this are unclear—perhaps it was a reflection of administrative changes, or of economic decline following the monetary collapse of 1623. Individuals may have hoped that the Amtmann's involvement would lead to a reduction of the tax. In any case, heriot petitions are a good example of intersecting interests and the Amtmann's role in brokering the relationship between lord and subject.

239 GLAK, 61/13370, 1611.

240 GLAK, 61/13369, 1594 and 98/216, 1633. Both resignation requests are described earlier in this chapter.

plained to the Audience in 1624 that Amtmann Klotz and the entire commune had blocked the residence of Georg Weißenkönig over the abbey's approval. Instead of following that decision, Walraff said, Klotz called an assembly of the entire commune (Mittelsten- and Niderstenweiler). Following discussion and a vote, they decided not to admit Weißenkönig. Walraff, furious, accused Klotz of disregarding the abbey's decision and questioning Walraff's authority.[241] The Audience had Jacob Klotz replaced both as Amtmann and as Sidelrichter, positions he held simultaneously.[242]

The other Amtmann involved in a dispute with the Oberamtmann was Mattheus Senfft of Mimmenhausen. Oberamtmann Johann Vögelin, who also lived in Mimmenhausen, submitted a letter to the abbey in 1599, as he explained, to establish his honor and restore order to the village.[243] He requested in addition that everyone in the village submit to questioning. For 14 pages he described a series of incidents involving the Amtmann Mattheus Senfft over the past three years. Vögelin's letter is the only document surviving from the dispute and it is certainly one-sided. Still, it is worth examining more closely. The relationships between the two officials as well as between the Amtmann and other members of the community raise issues about the constellation of personal loyalties and political factions in Mimmenhausen at that time. It offers unusually rich details about the inner workings of the village commune. It also provides context for a dispute in 1603 over the use of common lands in Mimmenhausen, described later in this chapter.

According to Vögelin's letter, problems began in September of 1596 when the Amtmann publicly accused four young men of shaking his fruit trees and stealing fruit

---

241 Walraff was no longer the Oberamtmann when he reported Klotz, having ended his service earlier that month for unknown reasons. He may have been acting out of revenge or in the context of some previous disagreement, of which there were several. Only a week earlier he had complained against Weiler's forest warden for his distribution of vine stakes, drinking, and swearing. Grievances against Walraff by a resident of Bermatingen suggest his unpopularity went beyond the village. In 1625 the abbey offered the former Oberamtmann a position as secretary and he remained in the abbey's service through at least 1626 as an Audience member and councilor.

242 "Gewesster OberAmptman Michael Wallraff clagt wider Amptman [Jacob Klotz], dorffpfleger und Gantze Gemeindt Mettersten- und Niderstenweiler wie das Er, Ihme Amptman und Gemeindt auß empfangnem Gnedigem befelch, den bericht geben, das Ihr Gnaden gnediger befelch seye, Sie sollen den Geörgen Weissenkönig hinfüro in der Gemeindt Passieren lassen und aus der Gemeindt nit aussetzen sollen. Weiln aber sich die Gantze Gemeindt darwider gesezt und ungehorsamblich sich verhalten, beneben aber so vil bericht einkhommen daß diser Amptman, den empfangnenn Gnedigen befelch nit vorgehalten, sonder nach die Gemeindtsleüth durch Umbfragen (was ieder gesint seye) gefasset ... B. Amptman soll hinfüro seiner Amptsglübte und Ampt erlassen sein, auch deß Sidelghts weitter bemüessigen: Nitt weniger wider Ihne und andere mitconsorten gebürende Straff vorbehalten sein." GLAK, 61/13373, 1624.

243 GLAK, 98/4419, fol. 268r–275v.

while a communal procession was underway.[244] At a communal assembly in May of 1597, the Amtmann angrily declared that no one listened to or respected him. Instead, he complained, everyone went straight to the Oberamtmann. At another assembly meeting Senfft exchanged sharp words with Simon Herman, who told the Amtmann he was just another fellow like everyone else. Senfft swore angrily that he would never, not for one thousand gulden, admit to being someone like Herman. Herman asked the Oberamtmann for help, demanding to know what the Amtmann meant by this insult to his honor. Meanwhile rumors about the Amtmann were spreading beyond the village. Veit Lölin, a Heiligenberg subject from Oberstenweiler, commented in June to Hans Ungericht senior of Mimmenhausen: "Hans, what a strange sort of Amtmann you have here, who has the nerve to accuse the community of stealing."[245] Ungericht repeated the comment to the village treasurers and they reported it back to the Oberamtmann—since it concerned the entire commune, Vögelin explained. Though he took the matter to the abbot, no decision had been made.[246]

Vögelin's letter went on to describe more recent problems with the Amtmann, including the time he plowed over his property line into the communal forest and the time he grazed his animals on a cultivated field. He had also taken more than his share of firewood at the annual distribution, not from the place the forest warden had indicated and not for the first time. Vögelin accused Senfft of generally ignoring communal statutes, especially regarding grazing and the use of pathways. Furthermore, the council of Fifteen seldom met and some of them had not been sworn into office. Twice Senfft had spoken inappropriately at the inn about his legal suit with the Schorpps, insulted the Oberamtmann, and complained repeatedly that no one listened to him.[247]

Parts of the description reveal that there were others in the village who opposed the Oberamtmann. Vögelin suspected Senfft of spreading slanderous words not only among his drinking companions, who had reported him, but also to the schoolteacher,

---

244 There had been earlier problems with fruit thieves and Vögelin had recommended to the Amtmann that he raise the fine from one to three pounds. He denied, however, Senfft's claim that he had encouraged the Amtmann to call people thieves in front of the communal assembly.

245 "Hanns Was haben Ir für ain Seltzamen Amptman alhie, dz er ain Gmeind so frevenlich Dieb gehaißen hat." Ungericht, whose son was among the accused, replied that he knew nothing since he was not at the assembly where the words were spoken. GLAK, 98/4419, fol. 269r.

246 "Alß nun hernach vermelter Ungericht dise des Lölins reden baiden Dorffpflegern Marx Maisterhanßen und Lorenz Böshen angezeigt, Seind sie umb Joannis Baptistae gleich zu mir Ober-Amptman komen mich deren Verstendigt bey neben umb Rath gebetten, Dieweil solche reden ain ganze gmeind berüeren thue, weßen sie sich verhalten sollen, Damit Inen kain nachtail darauß entstande. Hab ichs mit dem Beshaid hingewisen das ich dz alles meinem gnedigen Herrn anzeigen und mich hieruber Beshaidts erhoben wolle. Wie Ichs dann den nechsten Verhör tag Hernach Underthenig fürgebracht und dieweil es mein gnediger Herr Domalen in bedenckhen gezogen Ist es bis dato also darbey verbliben." GLAK, 98/4419, fol. 269r.

247 Senfft stated publicly that although the Oberamtmann could have settled his dispute with the Schorpps, Vögelin referred it to the Sidelgericht and failed to offer him any protection.

who had not. Even a stall boy and a carpenter without permission to reside in the village were making false accusations against the Oberamtmann, saying he meddled in the commune's affairs by introducing new customs, punishing communal offenses, interfering with local prerogatives, and playing favorites in the distribution of firewood.

Most recently, Vögelin reported, Senfft had complained to him about people in Mimmenhausen who were ruining his reputation and property even though they themselves were worthless. Vögelin pressed him for names, "so that I should not sit in the commune next to someone who is not worth five batzen." As far as the Oberamtmann knew, he told Senfft, the members of the commune were honorable people. If not, they should be punished. He encouraged the Amtmann to speak up. Senfft refused, saying the people who despised and disobeyed him were Vögelin's favorites, so each one was free to act as he pleased. This accusation cut to the core of the dispute: Senfft felt that Vögelin diminished his authority as Amtmann by encouraging disobedience and favoring those who despised him, while interfering in communal affairs instead of protecting him as he should. Vögelin answered that if these words were true, and if it were found that he was an unworthy Oberamtmann who had encouraged and supported disobedience among the abbey's subjects, then God would find him unfit and he would step down. Vögelin continued to demand the names of the disobedient villagers and called for an assembly of the entire commune to discuss these matters. Again he urged the abbot to question everyone in the village and find out the truth. In closing, he maintained that his intent was to defend himself and his honor, not to shame the Amtmann or anyone else. No further documentation has been found to shed light on the resolution of this struggle in Mimmenhausen, but by 1602, Mattheus Senfft was no longer in office.[248]

To conclude, political development in Salem grew out of both community and lordship. Looking at the Amtmann as the interface between the village and the abbey demonstrates that lordship was not simply hierarchical and the community was not a level playing field. The Amtmann shows that the relationship between lordship and community and the orientation of individuals between these poles was much more complex. Some Amtmänner were closer allies of the central administration than of their neighborhood, and vice versa, but each of them was in a position where many lines of power intersected.[249] Political development in Salem may be seen as a web, with interwoven threads running not only horizontally and vertically but in many different directions.[250] The constellation of political relationships within Salem's territory was not static; it resulted from constant negotiation and movement. The Amtmann,

---

[248] GLAK, 61/13369; see below.

[249] LANDWEHR, Zwischen allen Stühlen, p. 109; SCHLUMBOHM, Gesetze, p. 656.

[250] As Landwehr says, early modern lordship offered a continuously changing field of opportunities to a variety of participants, and the relationships between rulers and ruled should be seen as a "polylectic" rather than a dialectic. Idem, Policey vor Ort, p. 70.

who held the strands in place, shows how adaptable and intricate the web could be.[251] Rather than having different faces, the political practices of lordship and community shared many interfaces.

3.7 Common Lands, Common Resources, Common Good?

The final section of this chapter looks at the common lands, or commons—those areas where resources were used collectively rather than individually. They typically included forests, wastes, and pastures. Vineyards, meadows, and arable parcels were also cultivated collectively in some villages. In addition, most privately owned freehold and tenured fields such as arable and meadows were open to common grazing at certain times of the year when the land lay fallow. The commons could even be divided into individual parcels and distributed among members of the commune in exchange for rent. The extent of the commons varied from one settlement to the next, but everywhere they were an extremely valuable resource subject to increasing pressures, competing claims, and changing uses.

The commons were a place where many interests came into contact. They provided a basis for heated debate but also a material resource that made the difference for many between going hungry and getting by. The management of the commons remained one of the commune's primary functions, and struggles over its use mirrored the struggles within the commune more generally. The commune's administration of its commons is an indication of its ability to regulate and sustain collective resources, impose social order in the village, protect its privileges and boundaries against outsiders, and adapt to new circumstances.[252] The commons are of special interest to this study because they provide an opportunity to examine the history within the village rather than of the village.[253]

As previously mentioned, David Sabean and Govind Sreenivasan see the German Peasants' War not as a conflict between communes and lords but as a conflict sparked by differences between the village elites and an increasing number of smallholders, in which the former used the commune and its organs to promote their own interests at the expense of the latter. Many of Sabean's primary examples come from the commons, which he sees as the key in this struggle for control of local resources. This interpretation is directly opposed to that of Peter Blickle, who does not devote much space to the commons but criticizes Sabean on the basis of his sources and interprets commons disputes in the context of the commune's defense of its autonomy against

---

251 SABEAN, Power in the Blood, p. 16.

252 KASCHUBA, Kommunalismus, p. 72.

253 WARDE, Common Rights and Common Lands, p. 197.

external threats, especially by lords.[254] Sabean's evidence in this case may be thin, but other historians have followed his lead with new examples of the local divisions between rich and poor, in the early sixteenth century and beyond.[255] In Salem, disputes and settlements relating to grazing rights are richly documented. As this section will show, the commons relate to many of the central themes of community, and the picture is more complicated than either Blickle or Sabean suggest.

The commons were crucial to the economies of village and household. They provided many different resources, the most important of which were wood and pasture. Wood was the primary source of heat and building materials in the preindustrial age.[256] In addition, forests offered food, fodder, and fertilizer.[257] Grazing, the other major use of common lands, allowed villagers to maintain the animals that provided so many essentials: food, transport, fertilizer, status, income, and of course, plowing. Under the care of one or more herdsmen, the animals of the entire village went out to graze as large common herds according to livestock type. On the eve of the Thirty Years War there were an estimated 264 cows and horses in Neufrach, 196 in Bermatingen, 133 in Weiler, and 97 in Buggensegel. In 1608 there were 267 cows, horses, and pigs in Mimmenhausen.[258] The herds moved according to a seasonal rotation from stalls in winter to the fallow fields, forests, wastes, common pastures, harvested fields, and back to stalls again.

The commons were also an important source of income for the entire commune. They brought in revenues from the sale of fruit and nuts, parcel rentals, and grazing fines. Wood products could be sold only by special permission from the abbey, but it was not unusual for the commune to pay off debts through wood sales or borrow

---

[254] Peter BLICKLE, Wem gehörte der Wald? Konflikte zwischen Bauern und Obrigkeiten um Nutzungs- und Eigentumsansprüche, in: Studien zur geschichtlichen Bedeutung des deutschen Bauernstandes, Stuttgart 1989, pp. 37–50. Blickle has challenged Sabean's findings repeatedly (Unruhen, p. 72; Communal Reformation, p. 171; Begriffsverfremdung, p. 247).

[255] SREENIVASAN, Social Origins, p. 39: "The *locus classicus* of this practice was the administration of the village lands." Sabean's two volumes on Neckarhausen involve similar themes in a later period and are extremely well documented.

[256] It was used for construction, maintenance and repairs, fencing, vine stakes, firewood, tools, crafts and trades—especially cooperage, wagonry, the smithy, public bathhouse, and bakery. In addition to houses, barns, sheds, stalls, and outbuildings, wood was essential for building wine presses, well houses, boats, and bridges. See WARDE, Common Rights and Common Lands, pp. 200, 210–212.

[257] Fallen leaves and duff were mixed with manure for fertilizer. Edibles for man and beast included fruit and nuts, especially acorns, as well as herbs, mushrooms, grass, and other roughage. The sources rarely mention poaching, perhaps because hunting rights were not a major issue in ecclesiastical lordships.

[258] GLAK, 98/2309; 98/4419, fol. 300r.

money by leveraging the commons against a short-term loan.[259] The commons were also used to support the poor, which provided a social safety net for individual families and simultaneously eased the burden they posed for the rest of the community.[260]

The resources of the commons were meant to support the common good, yet it should be reiterated that access to them was never equal or unrestricted. Certain groups of users enjoyed greater benefits than others, and use rights were not shared by all in theory, let alone in practice. Grazing rights were especially profitable to the wealthy tenants and those with livestock. Since only farm tenants could normally own horses and oxen, plow teams were a defining characteristic of wealth and privilege.[261] Smallholders could benefit from common pasture and grazing rights, though not to the same degree or in the same manner, because of limits on the number and type of animals they could keep.[262] The common lands were perhaps the commune's chief economic resources, yet they were also among its greatest challenges. Disputes over grazing rights and other uses of the commons were prevalent throughout the period. Especially in the decades around 1600, the pressures of demography, land scarcity, and economic decline led to changes in how the land was used and by whom.

Disputes over the commons pitted various interest groups against one another and sometimes fostered surprising alliances. The following discussion examines two major constellations of interests that had an influence on the development of resource management and commons use. They involve disputes between two or more neighboring communes and those between groups within a single village.[263] The decisions and policies resulting from the negotiation of conflicting interests benefited some groups

---

259 For example, Neufrach petitioned the Audience in 1583 for permission to sell wood from the commons to pay its debts. Oberuhldingen was allowed to sell wood from the commons in 1584 to pay for fire buckets. GLAK, 61/13369.

260 The village poor, who were not members of the commune, had permission to glean, forage, and collect deadfall for firewood. Following the harvest they normally had a period of three days to collect the remainder of the chaff before the common herd was driven in, and for this reason landholders were prohibited from cutting stalks down to the ground.

261 In 1492 Peter Kun of Tüfingen was penalized for keeping a horse on his smallholding (*Guetlin*) without permission, as the result of a suit brought against him before the Sidelgericht. GLAK, 4/5692. An exception to the general restriction on draft animals is found in Mimmenhausen, where in 1600 there were 15 households with horses but very few farms (see below).

262 Among the poorest households, animals were a major resource. Having little or no land of their own, they relied heavily on the common lands for fodder. Yet cottars had to overwinter their animals like everyone else, and even a single cow required at least some hay and a small enclosure. These necessities could strain a poor household, putting animal ownership beyond their means. As a result, pasture rights for cows were of limited use to smallholders and they had no interest whatsoever in promoting the horse herd, since it reduced the amount of land available for other uses. See WARDE, Commn Rights and Common Lands, pp. 212, 214.

263 Disputes between the abbey and a commune, as well as between individual users, are not considered here. See BRUN, Abbot and Peasants (diss. 2008), for a fuller discussion.

over others. One thing is clear, however: the commons and their use underwent significant changes during the long sixteenth century. With all the pressures on dwindling resources, with the changing needs of the commune and its growing membership, the commons presented a dynamic issue that could not be handled in the same old way.

Over the course of the fifteenth and early sixteenth centuries, numerous arbitrated agreements delineated the grazing rights of individual communes with respect to neighboring settlements both within and beyond Salem's territory.[264] The agreements from this early period are in most cases the first written descriptions of each side's grazing rights. The profusion of settlements between neighboring communes suggests that grazing was becoming subject to stricter regulation as the needs and practices of each village began to encroach on one another.[265] These early grazing settlements share a number of similarities. First, they typically resulted from voluntary arbitration, initiated at both parties' request. The arbitrators varied from one case to another and could be landlords, territorial administrators, city councilors, guild masters, territorial judges, or even ordinary villagers.[266] The Sidelgericht settled a number of grazing disputes between neighboring communes, especially in the early to mid-sixteenth century.[267]

The settlement of grazing disputes with the help of outside mediators is noteworthy. It demonstrates that communes were not always able to settle commons disputes on their own and that they voluntarily called on neutral outsiders or abbey officials to provide support and assistance. Arbitration as well as legal settlements recognized the legal capacity of village communes and were based on collective memory and custom rather than lordly interference or written statutes. The establishment and documentation of boundaries for grazing and other rights proved useful in later conflicts, as pressures on the commons mounted and as written evidence took on greater authority.

---

[264] On the development and significance of arbitration, see Karl Siegfried BADER, Das Schiedsverfahren in Schwaben vom 12. bis zum ausgehenden 16. Jh. and idem, Die Entwicklung und Verbreitung der mittelalterlichen Schiedsidee in Südwestdeutschland und in der Schweiz, both in: Schriften 2, pp. 157–225 and 226–251.

[265] The archive's Section 4 contains many such agreements, especially from the fifteenth and early sixteenth centuries. See GLAK, 4/1771, 1423 Bermatingen and Ahausen; 4/2731, 1446 Grasbeuren and Ahausen; 4/4744, 1458 Nußdorf and Daisendorf; 4/2127, 1474 Buggensegel and Neufrach; 4/5979, 1479 Oberuhldingen and Grasbeuren; 4/1772, 1479 Bermatingen and Markdorf; 4/6404, 1479 Weildorf and Altenbeuren; 4/2643, 1483 Gebhardsweiler and Schiggendorf; 4/5981, 1490–1491 Oberuhldingen and Unteruhldingen; 4/2732, 1497 Grasbeuren and Schiggendorf; 4/2178, 1503 Buggensegel and Mimmenhausen; 4/4006, 1514 Mimmenhausen and Neufrach; 4/4214, 1516 Mühlhofen, Gebhardsweiler, and Hallendorf.

[266] A few legal doctors served as arbitrators, but professional training was not required; knowledge of local custom was a key qualification. Some arbitration committees had to ask someone else to provide a seal, since none of their members possessed one.

[267] Examples include GLAK, 4/2178, 1503 Buggensegel and Mimmenhausen; 4/4216, 1559 Oberuhldingen and Mühlhofen; 4/4217, 1570 Mühlhofen and Buggensegel; and 4/4219, 1592 Mühlhofen and Mimmenhausen.

In sampled grazing disputes from the fifteenth and early sixteenth centuries, communes normally substantiated their claims through extensive witness testimony rather than written documentation. Witnesses were often named, sometimes with their ages. Details of the testimony were recorded in some cases, as in the 1497 agreement between Grasbeuren and Schiggendorf, which listed the depositions of 35 witnesses.[268] Individual testimony focused on specific boundaries and landmarks and on recalled events, such as the time Michael Urnau helped the herdsman chase cows across the river to avoid impoundment and fines. Some witnesses qualified their statements by saying they did not know each party's legal rights, only what had been done in the past.[269] Yet most of them agreed that members of both villages had cooperated in the past and that their herdsmen had grazed in common without any conflict. Several witnesses had been personally involved in grazing there, others had "always heard" or "heard from the old ones" about the situation; Hans Suter from Ahausen said he had heard from Hans Wern and also seen for himself that the two villages used the disputed area in common without any previous disagreement. According to counsel as well as their own understanding and consciences, the arbitration committee of seven members decided in favor of Schiggendorf, who had presented the better testimony.[270] Copies of the decision were presented to both parties, sealed by the mayor of Markdorf.

The apparent concentration of commons disputes between villages but not within them in the period before 1525 is significant, for two reasons. First, the disagreements over boundaries and use rights pitted entire communities against one another. They appear to have played a role in the establishment and solidification of boundaries between the rapidly growing villages. Second, they lead away from the conclusion that socioeconomic differentiation and tensions within the village were the major cause of the German Peasants' War.

---

268 GLAK, 4/2732. The age, place of residence, relationship to the disputing parties, and approximate date of the recalled information were listed for each witness. None of the 35 witnesses lived in Grasbeuren or Schiggendorf at the time, but most had resided there in the past as children, servants, or herdsmen. Their ages ranged between 30 and 90, and they came from surrounding villages and towns including Ahausen, Baitenhausen, Buggensegel, Constance, Daisendorf, Gebhardsweiler, Meersburg, Neufrach, Seefelden, Stetten, and Uhldingen.

269 In the 1497 dispute, Peter Stebli of Meersburg testified: "Ob aber die von Schigenndorff des Recht hetten gehept zuthun oder nit wißdte er nit." Ulrich Mertz from Neufrach said the two sides had grazed together as good neighbors when he was a servant in Grasbeuren, though he had heard at the time that Schiggendorf had no legal right. In 1458 Hans Han of Überlingen testified in a dispute between Nußdorf and Daisendorf: "Er Aber wisße wer darzu Recht habe wisße er nit." Most of the twelve other witnesses testified similarly. GLAK, 4/2732, 4/4744.

270 The head arbitrator was an administrative official (Vogt) from Hohenbodman, and the others hailed from Altenbeuren, Illwangen, Mainwangen, Mimmenhausen, Mittelstenweiler, and Neufrach. All three arbitrators from Salem's villages were also members of the Sidelgericht.

The second configuration of commons disputes involved neighbors or factions within a single commune. Some conflicts were between the entire commune and an individual member.[271] Others involved larger groups, and for our purposes, these are worth examining more closely. Some complaints were by the tenants against the cottars, or by the cottars against the tenants. For example, the cottars of Weildorf complained to the Audience in 1619 that the farm tenants refused to let them graze on the slope by the brick kiln. The tenants also refused to show a letter in their possession that described use rights in the disputed area. After consulting the letter, the Audience declared that according to customary practice, grazing rights belonged to the tenants alone.[272]

In Buggensegel, the cottars brought suit before the Sidelgericht in 1552 against the farm tenants.[273] Their three grievances involved the tenants' exclusive use of certain grazing areas, including the Lehrholz with its acorns and in fields following the harvest. They also complained against the tenants' custom of assembling without the cottars and deciding according to their own interests on matters that concerned everyone. In their defense, the tenants claimed they had always enjoyed exclusive use of the grazing areas in question and, as in the previous example, they had a sealed letter to prove it. Never in their memories were the cottars entitled to a share of the acorns or grazing rights in the Lehrholz. The cottars protested that they had heard the tenants' letter and it mentioned no such exclusions. They demanded access to the pasture, whether by voluntary agreement or legal settlement. The Sidelgericht postponed its decision to examine witnesses and consider written evidence. Before declaring their decision in a second hearing, the judges focused on the cottars' complaints about the tenants' private assembly (*Ainigung*). The tenants explained to the court that they had always assembled according to necessity, based on their possession of freehold or tenure. It was customary practice, they said, for the landholders to regulate land use on everyone's behalf and for everyone's use.[274] The Sidelgericht declared in favor of the cottars with respect to

---

271 For example, the commune of Oberuhldingen and the miller agreed in 1481 on the number of cows he could graze in the common pasture. Tüfingen came to an agreement with Andreas Leub in 1515 concerning grazing rights and Grasbeuren came to an agreement in 1528 with two individuals from nearby Hallendorf. Neufrach's disputes with Stoffel Scharpfer of Leutkirch were arbitrated in 1564 and again in 1578. The Amtmann and farm tenants of Owingen complained against Conrad Biller and the Hitzlers for keeping oxen against common custom and in competition with their horses. Hans Mussel of Weildorf complained in 1592 that the commune would not let him graze his new horse. Pelagius Lehen, the miller of Mimmenhausen, complained in 1604 that the commune allowed him to keep only three pigs. GLAK, 4/5980; 4/5708; 4/2734; 4/3408; 4/4627; 61/13369 (1583, 1592, 1595, and 1603).

272 GLAK, 61/13373, 1619.

273 GLAK, 4/2179.

274 "Darwider die anntwurter Reden lassenn, das sy die ainigung, unnd alles wie gemellt, Irer notturfft nach, lennger dann Mans verdennckhen, genutzt unnd genossen, dann sy lehens und aigens Inhetten und besessen, darauff Inen auch ainigungen gefiellen, unnd sy anntwürtere

most of their claims. They designated the Lehrholz as a common land (*gemain Merckh*), open to cottars as well as tenants for acorn pannage and other uses. When an adjacent field (the Lehrösh) was used for grazing, it would also be open to both groups. The tenants could graze exclusively in other fields following the harvest until St. Michael's Day (29 Sept), but then everyone could use the fields and the remainder of the chaff, which the tenants were forbidden to mow or sell. Matters of common concern, such as pathways, should be decided by a common assembly that included the cottars, who were obliged to assist according to their sworn duty.[275]

The tenants' use of a private assembly to circumvent the opinions of the entire commune is also documented in Neufrach. In 1590 the Audience cited the Mayerschaft with a stiff penalty of five pounds each, after word reached the abbey that they had met to discuss wage limits without consulting the cottars. When the tenants protested that their meeting was to discuss grazing issues according to their customary right, the Audience dropped the charges but warned them that in the future, matters such as these must be brought before the entire commune rather than settled in private meetings of their own.[276]

Only a few years later, the entire commune of Neufrach created a village grazing ordinance and submitted it to the abbot for ratification.[277] The bulk of the 1596 text concerned the number of animals each household was permitted to graze, with gradations

---

bey Irn ayd pflichten solches alls wol alls sy clegere verbannen müessten, unnd Iren nutz damit schieffen, were auch ain gemainer brauch, Unnd deßhalb guter hofnung, wie von allterher dabei zubeleiben unnd gehanndthabt." Ibid.

275 "Unnd zum dritten unnd ledtsten, das Ermellte clegere, bey Ir Pflicht und glibt, die ainigung In gemain, zu Steg und weg, und alles Jhenigen die notturfft erfordert helffen zuhanndthaben." Ibid.

276 The Audience declared: "Ist Inen solche Ir Frechhait durch mein Gn. hern mit hochsten ungnaden verwisen worden, und dieweil sich aber zimlicher massen verantwurt, das sie des Lohns halb nichts gehandlet, und die zusamenkunfft wie von altem heero wegen der Roß und vichs gehalten haben Seind sie der Straf erlassen. Daneben aber Inen uferlegt und Bevolhen worden hinfüro fir sich selbsten kain Aynung mer zehalten sonder sollen Iro sachen hiefüro vor ainer ganzen Gmaind verrichten." GLAK, 61/13369, 1590.

277 Neufrach petitioned the Audience at least twice for ratification of their grazing ordinance before the document was produced in two sealed manuscript copies, both of which have survived (GLAK, 4/4544 and 4/4628). The ordinance was presented by the Amtmann and four other residents, "uß bevelch und von gwaldts wegen ainer gantzen Gmaindt daselbsten." The Audience's response further demonstrates the abbey's lack of initiative in the matter: "Dieweil sich die Gmeind also mit ain ander Verglichenen und derselbigen in allweg zefriden seyen, So wöllen Ire gl. solche Auch bewilligen und die Brief verfertigen laßen." GLAK, 61/13369. There are later references to similar ordinances passed in Owingen in 1579 and Mimmenhausen in 1603, though the originals have not survived. See GLAK, 61/13369, 1626; 61/13369, 1604; 98/4419, 1609, fol. 291r.

according to the amount of land they cultivated.[278] Other stipulations of the agreement covered fines for grazing offenses, which were collected and used by the commune, not the abbey. Fines were divided according to who committed the offense, into two separate funds: penalties from tenants were returned to the collective farm tenants, who were responsible for paying the warden's salary. Fines from cottars went to the village treasury, to be used for the common good. The usual offenses, subject to a fine of three shillings, included grazing damages, petty fruit theft, and grass collection (*greßen*).[279]

A 1603 grazing dispute from Mimmenhausen provides one final example. This complex local drama demonstrates the centrality of the common lands in discussions about the commune, its practices, and values. It also provides evidence of the abbot's active involvement. Though it leaves several questions unanswered, this dispute illuminates many intersecting layers of lordship and community, showing how alliances formed and reformed and how different groups influenced communal decisions.

On 17 April 1603 Mimmenhausen's Amtmann Marx Maisterhans, village treasurer Bartlin Kraus, and councilor Mattheus Leub brought a petition before the Audience in the name of the village magistrates. Their account began with the previous summer, when they had converted a parcel of common land called the "salt flats" (Salz Egarten) from pasture to arable, following the abbot's well-meaning recommendation and in order to promote the common good (*der Gmeind nutzen*). Now a dispute had arisen over this parcel's use. In an assembly of the entire commune (*ainer gantzen Gemeind*) on 31 March 1603, the council of Fifteen had proposed to continue using the parcel as common arable in accordance with the abbot's recommendation. The Amtmann conducted an Umfrag, an inquiry to determine each householder's opinion, which resulted in three alternatives. The positions were first, to return the land to its customary use as common pasture; second, to continue using the land as common arable following the lord's advice; and third, to split the land into individual, rent-bearing parcels. According to majority opinion the communal assembly agreed on the first proposal, to revert to the land's customary use as pasture.[280] A week or so later the Amtmann met with the Fifteen to discuss various communal matters, and they returned to the issue of the salt flats. The magistrates agreed that common arable would best promote the common good and decided to press for the abbot's plan, despite the full assembly's earlier vote. The next day, hoping to raise support for the idea, they called a meeting of the *Roßler*,

278 Each of the four largest tenants could keep six horses, one foal, eight oxen (*zugvieh*), and as many cows as they could overwinter in stalls. Other farm tenants were allowed six horses and two to six oxen, depending on the farm. The miller could keep only one horse and no more than five or six pigs. One tenant with a small, hereditary farm could keep three horses; most other landed smallholders could have one horse or two oxen, plus cows. Cottars were permitted neither horses nor oxen, but could graze three cows if they had some land or two cows if they did not.

279 Village account records from the 1620s list individual offenses. Many involved grass collection by children and servants. GLAK, 98/4422.

280 "Darauf also Letstlich, durch das mehr uf das Alt heerkomen geshloßen worden, darbey es also verbliben." GLAK, 98/4419, fol. 293r.

or horsemen, who were surprisingly not members of the council.[281] When asked their opinion, the horsemen remained firm in their support of grazing, old custom, and the will of the majority.

It was that evening, following the meeting with the horsemen, that the dispute broke out. According to testimony in support of the village magistrates, an angry discussion began over drinks at the village tavern. The primary instigator was the former Amtmann, Mattheus Senfft.[282] Senfft complained to his drinking companions that the Fifteen were promoting an innovation against common grazing rights. He banged on the table causing glasses to fly through the air and swore a thousand holy sacraments that he would commit his life to seeing that this did not happen. He also claimed to know more than all the councilors put together and said, referring perhaps to his wealth, that he brought more to the abbot than they did.[283] When Martin Hörer tried to calm him down, Senfft continued swearing and told him to shut up, since it was none of his business. Thoma Schmidtmaister rushed to Senfft's support, swearing a hundred thousand holy sacraments and telling Hörer to watch his step. Hörer responded by questioning Senfft's obedience to the abbey: "Didn't you swear to His Grace?" he pointedly asked. "Yes," said Senfft. "Then why are you disobedient?" asked Hörer. "This has nothing to do with His Grace, it's a communal matter," Senfft retorted. Hörer pressed on: "But the commune belongs to His Grace, does it not, so why then are you not obedient?"[284] At this point Jacob Dreer stood up to join them, asking Hörer why Amtmann Maisterhans

---

281 The so-called *Roßler* seem to have been a distinct social category in Mimmenhausen but not in other villages, where only farm tenants were permitted to keep horses. For Mimmenhausen, a quartering list from around 1600 designates an intermediate group of 15 "*ain Roßler,*" those with one horse, in addition to farm tenants and smallholders (GLAK, 98/2305). The households in this group may have been minor landholders, or the ownership of one horse (for riding, not plowing) may have been a sign of higher social status derived from nonagricultural employment. In any case, there were only two farm tenants in Mimmenhausen besides the miller and innkeeper (in addition to 55 smallholders), and the *Roßler* involved in the 1603 commons dispute were among the wealthiest men in the village.

282 He was no longer in office following his earlier dispute with Johann Vögelin, described above. The timing and means of Senfft's departure from office are unknown, but Marx Maisterhans was the Amtmann by at least 1602 if not earlier. Mattheus Leub, who was also involved in the 1603 grazing dispute, was the Amtmann by 1610.

283 "Habe Senfft Hannsen Erharten angefangen zeclagen, die Fünffzehen wollen ain Newerung anfahen, und helffen gemeine Trib und Tratt Einze[ne]men, unnd beyneben uf den Tish geshlagen das die Gleser ufgesprungen, unnd 1000 H. Sacrament geshworen, ehe er das Zuelaßen wolle, mues Ime ehe Leib und Leben Costen, frage den Funffzehnen nichts nach wann shon Iren noch sovil weren, Er wiße mehr dann sie Alle, Wöll auch mehr bey Iren Gnaden ußbringen dann Sie." GLAK, 98/4419, fol. 293v.

284 "Uf dz Hörer Senfften gefragt, ob er Iren G. nit geshworn, er geantwort Ja. Er wider gefragt, warumb er dann nit gehorsam seye. Er geantwort dz treffe Ir G. nit ahn, gehöre auch deren nit zue, Seye der Gmeindt sach. Hörer Abermal gesagt, ob die Gmeindt nit Ir G. gehörig, Er mit Ja gestettigt. Hörer wider geantwort warumb er dann nit gehorsam seye." Ibid., 294r.

had not asked his opinion at the meeting earlier that day. Again, the implication was that it was none of Hörer's business as a smallholder. Nella, the innkeeper's wife, burst in that the officials should have asked everyone's opinion, not just the wealthy horsemen. Then Thoma Schmidtmaister vowed, still swearing, that the officials' plan would be carried out over his dead body. Christa Wuest drew a weapon but innkeeper Galle Nihel held him back, swearing a hundred thousand times on Christ's stigmata that they would have to take his grazing rights by force. Nella stood over Hörer with her fists raised and swore a hundred times on the Lord God that she would really love to punch him in the mouth.[285] Then Hans Leub's wife spoke in her husband's absence and swore a thousand times on the Lord God that Hörer should "hold his cart in check" (*solle nur den Karren still steen laßen*). She declared in support of Senfft that the former Amtmann knew more than any of the others. She reminded Hans Stadler, the sexton, that his wages were paid by the rich and not the beggars. Besides, she said, there was no use in tearing each other's hair out. There was more swearing, and some took the argument out into the street. Later, when Hans Leub heard his wife's account and hurried to the tavern with an axe, the place was empty.

Consulting the imperial tax assessment of 1603, the socioeconomic division between the two sides are clearly visible. The council's critics were the village's wealthiest householders, including Thoma Schmidtmaister in first place with 2,894 fl. in assessed property value and the former Amtmann Mattheus Senfft, the second wealthiest householder with 2,478 fl. Third in household wealth was innkeeper Galle Nihel and his wife Nella with 1,655 fl., and sixth in the village was Hans Leub with 1,070 fl. The only member of the opposition party who was not among the wealthiest villagers was Jacob Dreer, the herdsman and a cottar with moderate wealth (20th in the village with 490 fl.). Evidently, none of these men belonged to the village council. On the other side of the dispute were the three village magistrates who brought the petition with the support of six witnesses. Amtmann Marx Maisterhans ranked fourth in the village with 1,140 fl. The councilor Mattheus Leub was tenth with 805 fl., whereas village treasurer Bartlin Kraus ranked 66th with only 120 fl. The six witnesses included Bartlin Greiß (215 fl., 45th household), Martin Hörer (158 fl., 55th household), the sexton Hans Stadler (154 fl., 57th household), Christa Wuest (80 fl., 74th household), and Wuest's son Claus (no taxable property).[286] This wealth information shows that the division within the commune was between the village magistrates on the one hand, with the support

[285] "Sie hett ain Lust, dz sie Ime die faust in dz maul shliege." Ibid., fol. 294v.

[286] Only the sixth witness, Hans Erhart, was not listed. According to a troop-quartering list from around 1600 (GLAK, 98/2305), Thoma Schmidtmaister and Hans Leub were farm tenants and both the Amtmann and former Amtmann owned one horse (*ein Roßler*). Among 55 smallholders were the herdsman Jacob Dreer and several of the loyalists, the sexton, as well as Johann Vögelin (Salem's Oberamtmann since 1590). Vögelin is never mentioned in connection with the dispute, but he was undoubtably on the side of the loyalists and may have been working behind the scenes to discredit his old enemy, Mattheus Senfft.

of the abbey and some of the cottars, and most of the wealthiest householders on the other, who were not councilors but could initially claim support from the majority.

The formation of an alliance between the abbey, village officials, and poorer householders is suggested especially by Hörer's statement that the commune belonged to the abbey and that in communal matters, villagers should be obedient to both authorities. Senfft's statements present a contrasting view about communal business, the councilors, his superior knowledge, and his worth. Several participants on both sides raised the issue of participation in political decisionmaking. On the one hand, Hörer was told to stay out of a discussion that did not concern him. On the other hand, the innkeeper's wife and the herdsman (according to later testimony) criticized the council's private meeting with the wealthier horsemen. The participation of two women, both of whom swore and made threats in the tavern, is another interesting element in the dispute. Apparently women were not entirely excluded from political discussions within the community.

The magistrates' April petition led to a hearing in the village on 6 May 1603 by Salem's secretary, Großkeller, and the Hofmeister of Constance. According to the opening lines of the text, both parties had asked abbey officials to mediate. On one side were the Amtmann, the Fifteen, and the majority of the commune (*merer tail der Gemeindt*). No mention was made of the fact that the majority had apparently switched sides since the earlier assembly. The opposition was described as a group of horsemen (*ettlich andern uß der Gemeindt so Rosßhallten*). First, the mediators held a private session to hear the case presented by the village officials and communal majority. Their testimony repeated the description of the three opinions expressed at the previous village assembly, with the majority in favor of customary grazing rights. They confirmed the earlier statement that the village officials had decided to push for arable before consulting the opposition (*Ire widertail*), who would neither hear nor consider their proposal. As for the tavern dispute, the new testimony alleged that the conversation involved scorn and insults against the Fifteen, the Amtmann, and the village treasurers. Some had suggested that the magistrates were unreliable and not to be trusted because of their lies and collusion with the abbot. Furthermore, the disagreement went beyond the use of the salt flats. At a recent fence inspection, the Amtmann and village treasurers found that Mattheus Senfft had not maintained his fence. When they demanded a fine, he retorted that it was not his responsibility but eventually gave in, reportedly saying, "I will do it if I must, but this is not right." According to the officials, his words and actions brought further injury to the commune. New difficulties also surrounded the herdsman, Jacob Dreer, who wanted pasture space for oxen. When the Amtmann put his request to the communal assembly in an Umfrag, Thoma Schmidtmaister objected that pasture for the common herd was necessary, regardless of majority opinion. He asserted that the herd would graze on the land whether or not the commune voted for it. In each situation, the officials accused their opponents of acting against the commune's customary practices. They asked the mediators to support them in the name of friendly unity and peaceful coexistence.

Next, the six horsemen gave their response. They agreed with the testimony about the village assembly, emphasizing that the majority supported the land's customary use as a common pasture. As for the tavern incident, they saw the events somewhat differently. They admitted to statements against the abbey and the councilors—Senfft expressed his opinion, when asked, that the abbey cared more about the land than about the peasants, and Schmidtmaister admitted to questioning the reliability of a councilor who favored the abbey over his own community. The innkeeper, too, questioned the council's decision to proceed against the majority. Herdsman Jacob Dreer complained that not everyone's opinion counted because some were consulted while others were excluded from discussion. The horsemen protested, however, that they were not the ones responsible for the tavern incident. It was their opponent, Bartholome Greyß, who first challenged Dreer to explain why he, as a modest herdsman, had sided with the horsemen. It was also Greyß who raised his tankard threateningly in the air, so that the innkeeper's wife had to grab it from him. The cottar Christian Wuest had drawn a weapon and threatened Thoma Schmidtmaister and Galle Nihel, swearing a hundred or thousand times in the name of the holy sacrament. In closing, the horsemen claimed not to have said or done anything wrong. They were trying to promote the old law and only wanted justice. They asked the mediators to consider their customs and means, so they could live together in peace and unity.[287] Although the horsemen were opposed to the land conversion, they told the mediators they would willingly support whatever the abbot ordered. A revealing margin note at the bottom of the document states: "Note. It is deemed necessary that the commune elect a few farmers, or those who own horses, as members of the Fifteen, in order to promote the peace, which they should swear to uphold."[288]

On the same day, Abbot Peter issued a separate decision in response to the officials' report. According to the text, he passed judgment and affixed his seal to the agreement upon the commune's request. Yet the only surviving copy of the decision is an unsealed copy, as it explicitly states on the final page. Since it contains several short, scattered margin notes with words and entire lines crossed out in dark ink, there is reason to doubt whether this document was, or even resembled, the final settlement. In any case, the document outlines the abbot's judgment between the magistrates and horsemen in several articles. [289] The major points in Article 1 were that the Fifteen should

[287] "Waß Nun sie hierundter gethan und gehandelt, Were kheiner andern meinung, Dann die Allten Recht und gerechtigkheiten, wie Auch dz gemacht wer, von der Gemeindt zehandthaben, vermeinen daran weder zevil noch unrecht gethon zehaben, Pitten Auch nichtz anders, dann sie by disen Irn herkhomen und uf mitel zugedenckhen. Dz sie mit ainandern In frid und Ainigkhait leben möchten." GLAK, 98/4419, fol. 281r.

[288] "Nota. Es were Nottwendig dz die funfzechner von der Gemeindt, und zu mererm friden Auch Ettliche Mayer oder so Rosß hallten, darzu Erwällt werden, Daruber beaydigt." Ibid.

[289] The articles in the text are numbered one, two, five, and six. The text appears to be an early and incomplete draft of the abbot's judgment.

be elected annually by the entire commune and that at least three of the seats should be reserved for farm tenants or horsemen. All future councilors would be sworn into office, where they would accept good counsel and advice and promise to uphold the common good and best interests of Mimmenhausen. Article 1 also described how communal decisions should be made. The Amtmann should meet in advance with the village treasurers and the Fifteen to discuss matters relating to the common good, as well as how to avert damages and disadvantages to the same. Then the village officials should call a full assembly of the commune and hold an Umfrag to discover each one's opinion. Decisions would follow the majority, and no one should act against its will. Regarding the salt flats, the abbot ordered in Article 2 that three or four acres of the disputed land should be used in common and planted with grain to support the community's needs. The responsibility to raise and harvest the crop would be a shared duty under the direction of two members of the commune, one farmer and one cottar or vintner. They would undertake the harvest diligently and use the profits to promote the commune's interests. The chaff should be distributed for a fair price among the village poor. The arable parcels would be maintained for as long as they continued to support the common good, and any future disputes or damages should be reported to the abbot for further decision.[290]

These two articles contain obvious contradictions. On the one hand, the abbot described the process of communal decisionmaking as one in which the officials proposed the issues and majority opinion was established based on everyone's response. On the other hand, the abbot's decision concerning the salt flats upheld the plan he and the councilors had advocated all along, against the majority's initial vote. He not only claimed to know what was best for the common good but also reserved the right to intervene in future disputes. The abbot and village officials claimed to favor land conversion in order to promote the common welfare. Still, the question remains: Whose good was the common good? If we pay attention to the arguments on each side, it becomes clear that the common good was a rhetorical phrase used by one party, just as old custom and traditional use rights were used by the other, to frame each side's position in the best possible terms. It is ironic that while village officials stated their desire to promote the commune's best interests, they freely admitted to acting against the majority. Thus, it appears that the entire commune and its opinions were invoked selectively in order to promote certain interests over others.

Both sides claimed to have majority support at some point during the dispute, yet it is doubtful whether either of them trusted the majority to make decisions on the com-

---

290 Article 5 stated that gardens were closed to grazing throughout the year, with fines for noncompliance. Article 6 concerned grazing rights for oxen, and declared that the question should be submitted to an Umfrag. Both articles supported the commune against previous complaints by Mattheus Senfft and Thoma Schmidtmaister respectively. Articles 3 and 4 are not found in the text.

mune's behalf.[291] Again, references to the entire commune's opinion were used as a legitimation strategy. Even though the council sought the assembly's opinion initially, they chose to proceed against its wishes. The following week they consulted only the horsemen, which led to objections by certain villagers. The horsemen, too, had interests that conflicted with the majority, and judging from Senfft's remarks against Hörer, he felt that some opinions were more valuable than others. The opposition party's desire to use all the land for grazing may have been in line with custom, but since most villagers had no horses or oxen, it was clearly not in most people's interests. This is why Thoma Schmidtmaister objected that grazing rights should not be subject to a vote.

The 1603 dispute in Mimmenhausen is probably not a typical case, since the former Amtmann headed the opposition party and none of the village's wealthiest members were among the councilors. For them, the abbot's declaration that the council should include at least three tenants or horsemen was a slight improvement over none, but one-fifth of the seats were not enough to exert major influence over communal decisionmaking. Schmidtmaister's comment that grazing rights should not be subject to a common vote and the margin note suggesting greater council representation for the horsemen in order to promote the peace further demonstrate that in Mimmenhausen, village elites were not in control of the commune around 1600. The divisions and alliances within the village were influenced by a combination of factors including Mimmenhausen's unusual socioeconomic structure, the recent turnover in village leadership, and the village's close proximity to the abbey. Even though the council's composition seems unusual, the exclusion of the wealthiest villagers in this case is an important reminder that the commune did not invariably support the interests of local elites. When it did not, it could lead to unexpected alliances and involve territorial officials in local affairs.

3.8 Conclusions

In sum, this chapter has emphasized the local roots of political action. Villagers took the initiative to provide for the things they found most essential, such as local religious services, and they also made clear that they wanted control over local aspects of decisionmaking, as in Bermatingen's 1498 village statute. The German Peasants' War demonstrated the power of resistance and served as a reminder for later generations

[291] The statement in two of the documents that the majority supported the council is puzzling, since earlier testimony from both sides agreed that the majority had voted for grazing rights. Perhaps the cottars switched sides for economic reasons, since they had more to gain from common arable than common pasture. Or perhaps their reasons were political, since an alliance with the abbot and council could protect their interests against wealthier neighbors. None of the documents provide an explanation, most likely because the disputing parties were not primarily interested in what the majority wanted or why.

that if bargains were not kept and new burdens imposed too severely, subjects were capable of united action that could threaten the entire political and social order. The broad participation evident in 1525 suggests that support for the movement came from a range of social groups including rich and poor, villagers and townspeople. The Treaty of Weingarten was a conservative solution that avoided violence and dramatic changes. It did result in the abbey showing greater respect for its subjects and vice versa. One of the movement's most important consequences was to strengthen the intermediary role of local leaders.

By the decades around 1600 there are increasing signs of strain within the local social fabric, perhaps most notably in disputes over the common lands. Yet we should not conclude that the interests of the "entire commune" were identical to those of the wealthiest villagers or that they favored elites disproportionately. One reason is that the village assembly included all male householders, the majority of whom were not farm tenants. A few village councils had over a dozen members and there is evidence from several villages that local elites tried to circumvent the commune, not always successfully, in order to pursue narrower interests. As local pressure on resources and divisions between rich and poor were felt more keenly, villagers approached territorial authorities for assistance. The Amtmänner played a key role in communications between the center and periphery, especially through Audience petitions, in which local leaders presented diverse requests on behalf of other individuals and groups. Villagers' willingness to involve territorial officials in settling local problems suggests that resistance to lordship in this period was minimal, not because subjects lacked the solidarity to make their voices heard but because the magnitude and type of challenges they faced made them more likely to see the abbey as a possible patron and protector.

In the regulation of use rights and the local enforcement of order, this chapter has demonstrated the interconnections between principles of community and lordship. The relationships between them changed over time and differed from one place to the next. There was a certain level of conflict, and village and abbey officials were involved in overlapping areas of competency. Yet representatives of the commune and the abbey often worked together, and the principles of custom, inclusion, equity, hierarchy, obedience, and the common good were used in complex ways by various individuals and groups when it suited their interests. The evidence does not suggest that the abbey took advantage of local discord to estrange communal competencies for its own uses. On the contrary, the commune or its members often sought the lord's assistance to settle internal disputes or to support local authority. A quickening of political relations may be observed in the decades around 1600, in which the abbot's authority as territorial lord grew, but not necessarily at the expense of the commune. As one became stronger, so could the other. There were certainly elements of lordship and hierarchy in the village, but communal aspects were also intertwined within territorial authority. The argument here is not that the abbey and its villagers were equal partners, far from it. Yet the strengthening of political authority should not be viewed as a zero-sum gain, in which the rise in princely authority resulted in a decline of communal authority. In Salem, territorialization succeeded to the extent that it was able to incorporate the villagers and their interests. It depended on local organization and local officials for information, for the collection of revenue, for policing, and for representation of the lord's authority. Villagers and communities relied on the lord as well, for advice, support, protection, and aid.

Communal organization in Salem did not fade into the shadows of territorial rule in the late sixteenth and early seventeenth centuries. Instead, the organizing principles and structures of the commune were integrated within territorial governance. The community maintained its influence, at the local level but especially at the territorial level, during the century between the German Peasants' War and the Thirty Years War. As for the growing social stratification and search for stability within the villages, these are the subjects of the next chapter.

Chapter 4: The Village Economy and Social Relations

One of this study's major arguments is that social and economic conditions in the countryside were a driving force for Salem's political development and territorial policy. The population and wealth structure of the villages as well as changing relationships among households had both indirect and direct political impacts in a period characterized by the tightening of resources and increasing social stratification. The rise in written documentation in the late sixteenth and early seventeenth centuries not only illuminates the challenges facing individuals and communities in this period, it also demonstrates subjects' attempts to secure or improve their positions, in some cases by soliciting the abbey's assistance.[1] Evidence supports the hypothesis that subjects did not affect territorial policy primarily by resisting the lord's interference in communal affairs, but rather, by pressing for the development of territorial policies that were more responsive to their needs.

Throughout the study I have referred to Salem's villagers, in the most general sense, as peasants.[2] The term peasant is useful for distinguishing members of this group from others such as burghers, nobles, and clergy. Within the village, however, there were in fact many social groups under the rubric of the peasantry. When referring to individual subjects and village communities, it is important to be clear about whom exactly we are speaking. There were major disparities among households, in their socioeconomic positions and access to resources. As indicated in Chapter 3, the commune and its headman (the Amtmann) did not represent all residents' interests equally. This chapter looks at differences between major farm tenants (*Mayerschaft*, or *Bauern*), smallholders (*Seldner*, cottars), and landless laborers (who worked for others and had little or no property). Yet even these categories prove to be overgeneralizations since smallholders, to take one example, could be wealthy or poor, work the land, practice a trade, or labor for others. Over the course of their lifetimes and at different points in the year, many individuals fit into each of these categories.

---

1 This can be seen in the Audience, Sidelgericht, and chancery records.

2 Definitions of the peasantry were a topic of considerable debate in the 1960s and 1970s, especially among anthropologists. I understand peasants to be those who live in the countryside, who work with their hands in predominantly agricultural activities, whose households form the basic socioeconomic unit, and whose surplus is extracted in part through lordly domination. For other definitions, see Teodor SHANIN, Introduction, in: idem, Peasants and Peasant Societies, Harmondsworth 1971, pp. 14–16; Eric R. WOLFF, Peasants, Englewood Cliffs 1966, pp. 2–4; Robert REDFIELD, Peasant Society and Culture, Chicago 1956, p. 19. See also Peasant Studies Newsletter 1–4 (1972–1975).

In some villages where wine rather than grain predominated, smallholders could be relatively prosperous whereas farm tenants were few in number and had less political influence. In the villages closest to the abbey, service opportunities provided an additional factor of differentiation in socioeconomic structure. Millers and innkeepers might hold little or no land, and at the same time achieve high social standing and wealth. Although the categories of tenant farmer, smallholder, and landless laborer are imperfect descriptions of village socioeconomic groups, they are helpful for understanding how various households sustained themselves and interacted with one another. Here we will look at Salem's villagers—their wealth, property, social standing, and relationships—in order to establish the range of experience and interconnections among as well as within households and villages.

The early modern household was not a self-sufficient unit.[3] Village households were interdependent, commonly working for and sharing resources with the members of other households. Craftsmen, vintners, and others who were not primarily engaged in food production relied heavily on market exchange. Tenant farmers, smallholders, and laborers were also market-oriented, however, since the larger households sold their surplus in order to pay obligations to the landlord, field workers, yielding heirs, and other creditors, whereas smallholders and landless laborers sold their labor in order to buy food.[4] The village poor without land of their own depended upon the farm tenants for work, and the farm tenants depended in turn upon day laborers and servants to help maintain their large family enterprises. It is hard to imagine a self-sufficient household in the village, regardless of its composition and social status. Within each household, moreover, members neither pursued identical goals nor had equal access to common resources.[5] As David Sabean has powerfully shown for Neckarhausen, members of different households were bound to one another through complex, interconnecting webs of work, property, kinship, and obligation.

This chapter is driven by data collected from several key sources. Population and wealth information comes from four imperial tax lists compiled between 1566 and 1603, with the 1578 and 1593 lists providing especially comprehensive coverage and detail.[6]

---

3 A.V. Chayanov's classic study, The Theory of Peasant Economy, ed. Daniel Thorner et al., Madison 1986, has been criticized for its claims about the economic self-sufficiency of the peasant household. In contrast, Govind Sreenivasan stresses the strong market-orientation of peasants in idem, Ottobeuren, esp. chap. 5.

4 According to Sreenivasan (Ottobeuren, pp. 263–264), demands from outside the household resulted in its orientation toward the market.

5 Studies challenging the concept of "the whole house" as a cooperative unit (*das ganze Haus*, introduced by Wilhelm Rihel and expanded upon by Otto Brunner) include SABEAN, Neckarhausen I; REBEL, Peasant Classes; ROBISHEAUX, Rural Society; SREENIVASAN, Ottobeuren; Merry WIESNER, Family, Household, and Community, in: Handbook of European History 1400–1600, vol. 1, ed. Thomas A. Brady Jr. et al., Leiden 1994, pp. 51–78.

6 GLAK, 98/2019 (1566), 98/2024 (1578), 98/2050 (1593), 98/2007 (1603). These sources are further described below.

The 1578 record receives major emphasis, while lists from other years provide comparisons over the longer term. These tax lists are also the best starting point for information about farm tenures. Rent registers and individual tenure contracts, as well as lists of various sorts, provide additional details and are especially helpful for reconstructing the early and later periods, for which tax lists are lacking or unreliable. Serial records from the Audience, chancery, and Sidelgericht start in the early 1580s and provide descriptions of property, contracts, disputes, requests, and relationships of all kinds.[7]

Kinship information about Salem's villagers is limited, especially because no parish registers survive for the period before the Thirty Years War. The 1578 and 1593 tax lists provide spouses' names and the number of children in each household, as do several lists of serfs from the decades around 1600. The most comprehensive source of family information is a serf list from circa 1600, which has margin notes describing changes over the next 15 or so years.[8] It gives the names of both spouses and their children (limited to abbey serfs) and in some cases provides information about deceased family members, remarriages, and the whereabouts of children no longer living at home. Relying on this assemblage of sources, the following sections of this chapter illuminate various socioeconomic aspects of village life, including population, wealth, property, tenure, debt, inheritance, and officeholding.

4.1 Population and Wealth Under the Hills

Imperial tax registers provide the best approximation of population and wealth for Salem's territory over the second half of the sixteenth century. In fact, the tax registers are such a valuable source of various types of information that we will return to them repeatedly throughout this chapter and the next. They are not an exact reflection of population or wealth, since they were kept for the purpose of resource extraction. In many ways, they were "strategic representations of social reality."[9] Though we must acknowledge certain limitations in using tax lists as the primary source of population statistics, the four registers from 1566, 1578, 1593, and 1603 are surprisingly consistent, appear quite reliable, and provide a firm basis for tracking the number of households over the second half of the sixteenth century.[10]

---

7 GLAK, 61/13316–13320 (chancery), 61/13322–27 (Sidelgericht), and 61/13369–74 (Audience).

8 GLAK, 98/1568–1569.

9 SABEAN, Neckarhausen I, p. 99.

10 Hermann Baier's pioneering articles on Salem's population and wealth rely heavily on the tax lists; idem, Zur Bevölkerungs- und Vermögensstatistik des Salemer Gebiets im 16. und 17. Jh., in: Zeitschrift für die Geschichte des Oberrheins, n.s. 29 (1914), pp. 196–216; idem, Bevölkerungsbewegung, pp. 57–130. I agree with Baier's judgment that the registers for 1578 and 1593 are of excellent quality. He says of the 1578 and 1593 registers that they make "a very trustworthy impression," allowing the researcher "to ascertain the population in the lordship Under the Hills fairly precisely" in 1578. The 1593 list is less comprehensive but still useful, he says,

The most comprehensive and trustworthy source of household information for Salem's entire territory is the tax register from circa 1578.[11] It lists 823 households in 45 villages, hamlets, and isolated farmsteads of the central territory.[12] In addition to the names of both the householder and his wife (or widow), the record gives the number of children and the servility status of each family member. The servants' tax (three kreuzer each) indicates the number of household servants. Even the destitute with no recorded sources of wealth are listed and they, too, were subject to a minimum tax of ten kreuzer. The tenant households, those in possession of large farms or smaller properties according to various leasehold arrangements, are described in especially full detail. Since Salem claimed the right to collect imperial taxes from all territorial inhabitants regardless of property or legal status, and because this right was an important foundation for Salem's claims to imperial status as well as independence from Heiligenberg, abbey officials had political as well as financial incentives for including as many dependents as possible in what doubled as a type of territorial census.[13] According to the tax list, the entire population of the central territory including men and women, children, servants, and paupers was approximately 3,824 persons.[14]

In addition to total population, the 1578 tax register allows us to examine household size and structure. For the territorial population as a whole, average household size was 4.7 members, including an average of 2.3 children and 0.5 servants. The wealthier households tended to be larger than poorer ones, not only because wealthy families kept more children at home, but also because they employed more servants: farm tenants employed 326 out of 444 servants in 1578, whereas the poorer and destitute households rarely had any.[15] Among 150 farm tenants, average household size was 7.9 persons, including an

---

especially since the similarity between the two sources demonstrates that the 1578 record is not an anomaly that could convey a false impression. Baier did not consult the 1603 list, found in GLAK, 98/2007. My use of the tax registers differs slightly from Baier's, as described below.

11 GLAK, 98/2024.

12 This is according to my count, excluding corporate entries and clergy. (Baier describes 805 separate listings, including 784 "families" in 42 places.) Some of the places listed in the 1578 register were admittedly outside the central territory—17 mostly single adults from Sipplingen, for example, were probably vineyard workers.

13 In addition to peasant households, orphans, teachers, priests, and territorial officials, the tax registers list confraternities, parishes, and entire communes (insofar as they were taxpayers and village property-holders). I have excluded corporate entities, mostly parishes and communes, from household and wealth statistics.

14 According to my count there were 708 men, 763 women, 1908 children (excluding 68 who were married and lived elsewhere), and 444 servants.

15 Wealthier households had the resources to feed and house more people, and their large agrarian enterprises required additional labor—mostly from servants when their children were young, supplemented by family labor as the children grew older. In landless households, children were typically put out to service as soon as they were old enough to work. On differences in the structure of rich and poor households, see Lutz K. BERKNER, Rural Family Organization in Europe: A Problem in Comparative History, in: Peasant Studies Newsletter 1 (1972), p. 145; idem, The

average of 3.9 children and 2.2 servants. Among destitute and poorer households the average was 1.8 and 2.2 children respectively, with no servants. Most households included a husband and wife, but single women (many of them widows) headed 12.2 percent and single men another 5.6 percent of all households. Retirees living with their adult children do not appear in the record as such and were probably listed separately. Orphans appear to have been underreported or listed as members of other households in 1578.

The tax register from 1593 provides comparable demographic information with a total of 869 households in 40 locations and an estimated 3,980 individuals residing in the central territory.[16] Household size averaged 4.6 members in 1593, including 2.6 children and 0.3 servants. In comparison to 1578, the number of households and individuals rose a bit (up by 156 persons in 46 households), whereas the average household size fell very slightly (almost stable at 0.1 persons less on average per household). The number of children rose by one-quarter of one child per household on average, while the average number of servants was one-fifth of one servant lower than in 1578, almost cancelling each other out.

Surrounding tax lists give an overview of population over a longer period. Information about household dependents is not provided in other years, so the number of households must stand as a rough indicator of population size.[17] Chart 4.1 shows the number of households according to tax lists from the period 1488–1603. Surviving lists from the period 1488–1557 are incomplete, but taken as a whole, tax registers show that the number of households reached its peak around 1566.[18] Numbers actually declined between 1566 and 1578, then began to rise again at a much slower rate so that the number of households in 1603 was still less than it had been in 1566.[19] If

---

Stem Family and the Developmental Cycle of the Peasant Household: An Eighteenth-century Austrian Example, in: American Historical Review 77 (1972), pp. 408, 410–416. On households involved in crafts and cottage industry, see Hans MEDICK, The Proto-industrial Family Economy: The Structural Function of Household and Family during the Transition from Peasant Society to Industrial Capitalism, in: Social History 3 (1976), p. 301.

16 The places listed in each tax register differ slightly, resulting in a minor discrepancy between them. In order to account for this difference as well as to focus on a set of known villages over time, I have relied in some cases on samples that exclude places beyond the central territory as well as many of the irregularly appearing isolated farmsteads. The sample of "main villages" for 1578 comprises 753 households in 26 places. For tenants, most comparisons are based on a sample of 13 villages (see below).

17 Based on an average household size of 4.7 in 1578 and 4.6 in 1593, we can assume minimal fluctuation over time and ascertain that households were not increasing in size during the late sixteenth century.

18 Early tax registers, including some fragments and undated lists, are found in GLAK, 98/2007.

19 At no point in Salem's history did the population recover to the record levels set in the mid-sixteenth century. See BAIER, Bevölkerungsbewegung, p. 59. Sreenivasan reaches a similar conclusion for Ottobeuren, where population peaked in 1564 (with some variation among individual villages). Idem, Ottobeuren, pp. 119, 158. This also fits with the more general population trends described by HOLENSTEIN, Bauern, pp. 94–95.

Chart 4.1: Taxpayers in the Central Territory (1488–1603)

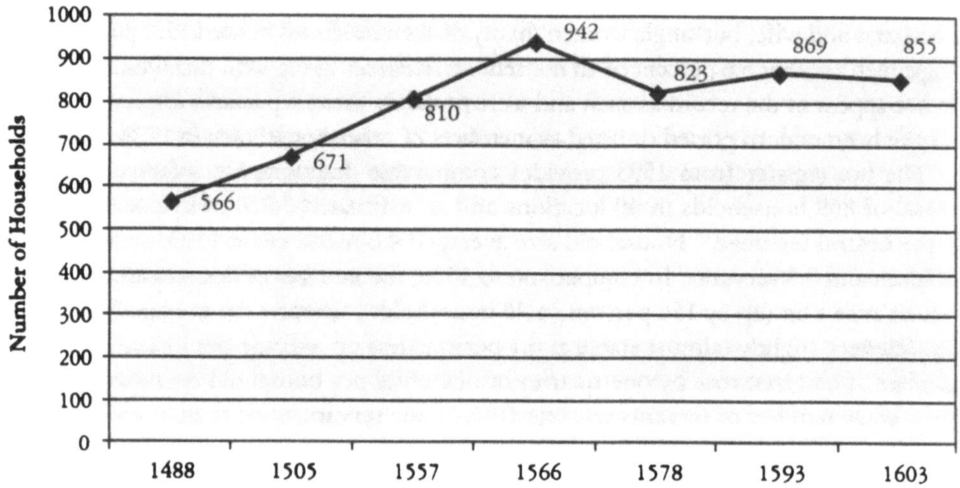

the tax registers are an accurate index, then population reached its highest point in the mid-sixteenth century, well before the onset of economic decline associated with the general crisis of the early seventeenth century.

Household Wealth

Tax registers provide wealth statistics for the same set of years, again with the best information coming from the 1578 and 1593 lists. Household wealth (gross property value) in 1578 ranged from zero to over 5,000 gulden (fl.) with a territorial average of 391.1 gulden (fl.).[20] Chart 4.2 compares average household wealth in all four years. Average wealth remained extremely stable according to all four assessments over the period 1566–1603, and in 1578 and 1603 it was almost identical.[21] Median wealth was

20 For an overview of monetary values and measurements used in this chapter, see the Notes on Usage, Currencies, and Measures.

21 These figures do not account for inflation, and in adjusted terms, wealth may in fact have dropped. On the other hand, reported wealth was based on set values for various commodities that rose little if at all from one tax record to the next. For example, the value of a horse for assessment purposes was 15 lb. dn. in 1566, 15 fl. in 1578, and 20 fl. in 1603; a cow 5 lb. dn., 6 fl., and 7 fl.; an ox 10 lb. dn., 12 fl., and 12 fl.; a pig 2 lb. dn., 2 fl., and 2 fl. respectively. The values for wine, hay, hens, eggs, calves, and sheep were the same in 1603 as in 1578. The standard assessment value for an annual leasehold remained 50 fl. for large farms and 25 fl. for smallholdings. Arable parcels were assessed at a rate of 3 Malter per acre for winter grain and 1½ Malter for summer grain, and grain values rose only slightly according to tax assessment values (in contrast to market values): spelt was worth 4 fl. per Malter in 1578 and 4½ fl. in 1603; rye 3 fl. and 3½ fl.; barley 4 fl. and 6 fl.; oats 3 fl. and 3½ fl. respectively. GLAK, 98/2019, 98/2026, 98/2003.

Chart 4.2: Average Household Wealth in the Central Territory
(according to imperial tax lists)

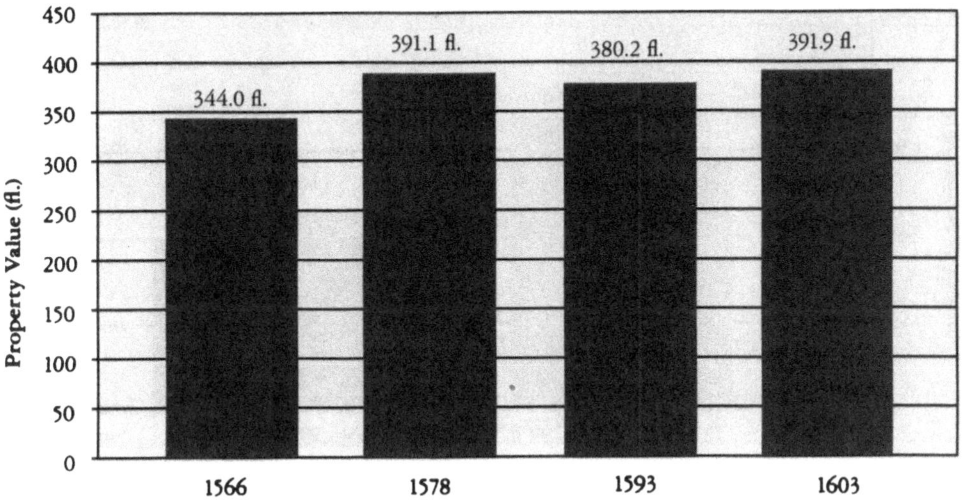

lower than the average, reflecting the large number of poor households, but it was also relatively stable over time.[22]

Household wealth may be further analyzed according to various wealth brackets. I have divided households into six wealth groups, which we will return to throughout the chapter. They are the destitute (with wealth of less than 25 fl.), the poor (with 25–99 fl.), the smallholders (100–299 fl.), the middling (300–499), the prosperous (500–999 fl.), and the very rich households (1,000 fl. or more). Using this classification, we can compare wealth groups in a single year and over time. First, let us consider the wealth data for 1578, displayed in Chart 4.3. In that year more than one in four households were destitute with less than 25 fl., while one in eight was very rich with 1,000 fl. or more.[23] Looking at clusters of wealth groups demonstrates similar results: around half of all households were in the bottom two brackets with 100 fl. or less, while about one-quarter were in the top two brackets with 500 fl. or more. Put simply, the territorial population was bottom-heavy. There were two poor households for each wealthy one, and the largest segment of the population had little or no property. Meanwhile, very few households were at or near the territorial average of 391 fl. Middling households, those with 300–499 fl., comprised

22 Average wealth in 1566 was 344 fl. among 942 households, in 1578 391.1 fl. among 823 households, in 1593 380.2 fl. among 869 households, and in 1603 391.9 fl. among 855 households. Median wealth was 150.3 fl. in 1566, 163 fl. in 1578, 132 fl. in 1593, and 140 fl. in 1603. Baier's wealth figures are higher, but his sample excludes unpropertied households.

23 Out of a total of 823 households, 27.3% of the population was destitute and 12.2% was very rich. Entries for destitute households sometimes provide a property value but more often leave the value blank, perhaps with the added description "pauper," "has nothing," or "less than 25 fl."

Chart 4.3: Wealth Groups among Territorial Households (1578)

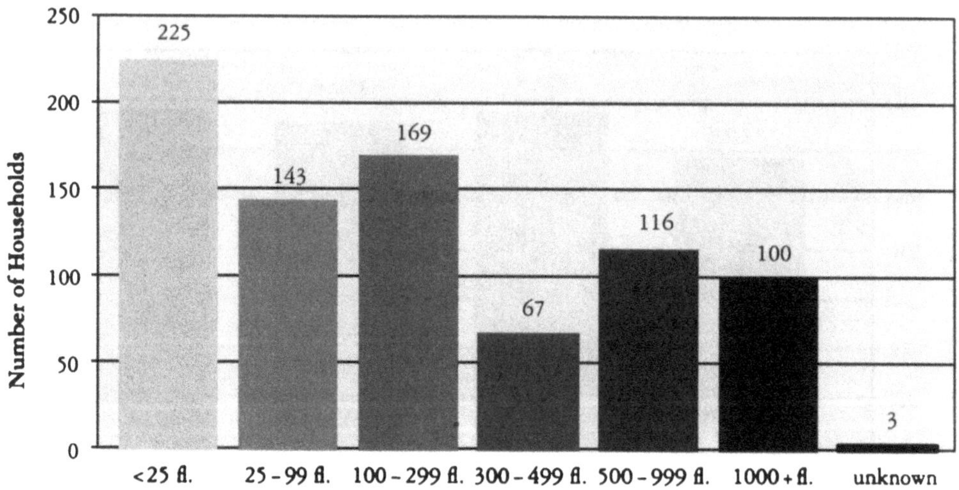

the smallest wealth group with only 8.1 percent of the population. In other words, the great majority of territorial households were at one wealth extreme or the other. We can conclude that the population was relatively polarized in terms of wealth.[24]

Another method of comparing household wealth is to plot a Lorenz curve, which shows the degree of inequality in the distribution of two variables—in this case, the relationship between population and wealth. The Lorenz curve has the advantage of displaying relative inequality in terms of percentiles that can be compared to any other set of data.[25] This not only avoids the problem of adjusting for inflationary values, it means we can relate the wealth structure of Salem's population to other places and time periods. Chart 4.4 shows the Lorenz curve for all territorial households in 1578.[26]

---

24 Of course, all societies contain a certain level of economic inequality. During nationwide protests in the United States in 2011, the wealth gap and especially the wealth of the top 1% of households has drawn outrage and increasing attention. According to current estimates, this group held 34.6% of the country's total wealth in 2007, a number that has been rising since the start of the Great Recession in that year. See Wikipedia, Distribution of Wealth (http://en.wikipedia.org/wiki/Distribution_of_wealth, accessed 7 Dec. 2011), with links to recent estimates by scholars such as Edward N. Wolff and G. William Dornhoff as well as more popular news sources (Vanity Fair estimated in May 2011 that the top 1% controls 40% of wealth in the United States).

25 For comparable information on wealth distribution from other early modern territories, see SREENIVASAN, Ottobeuren, p. 146, and ROBISHEAUX, Rural Society, p. 85, both of which provide Lorenz charts; see also HOLENSTEIN, Bauern, p. 47.

26 The diagonal line at 45 degrees represents the hypothetical condition of full equality, where each household would have identical wealth. The curve shows actual wealth, according to the cumulative percentage of all wealth held by a cumulative percentage of all households. For unpropertied households paying the minimum tax, wealth is assumed to be zero.

Chart 4.4: 1578 Wealth Inequality Under the Hills

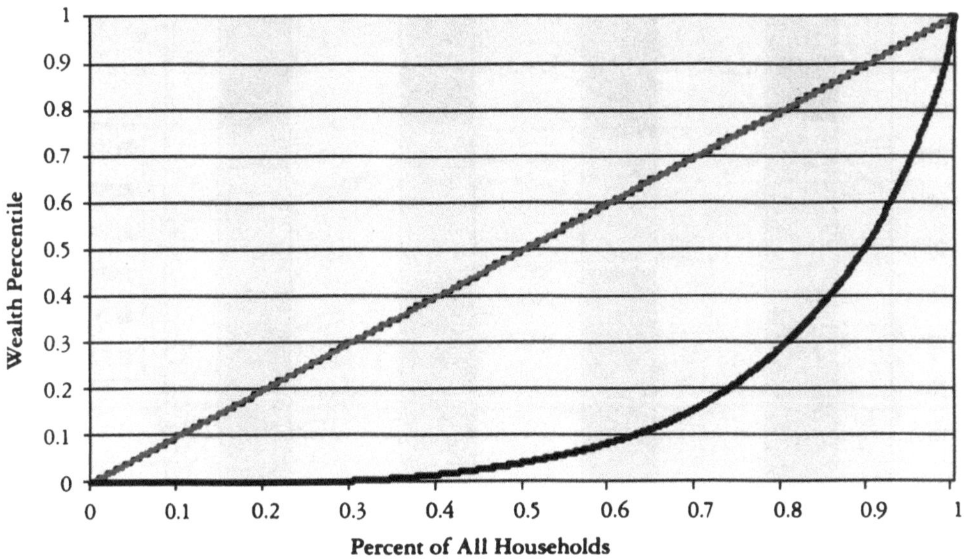

From the Lorenz curve we can calculate the Gini coefficient, a number between zero and one indicating the level of inequality where zero represents absolute equality and one represents absolute inequality.[27] For the entire population in 1578, the Gini coefficient equals 0.690. Using the Gini index for modern nations to provide context (as reported in 2000), the level of wealth inequality in Salem's central territory was much lower than in the United States of America (0.801), much higher than Japan (0.547), and just above modern Germany (0.667).[28]

Next, we can compare the wealth and inequality of households over time using data from the four tax records. Looking at all six wealth brackets in Chart 4.5, we find stability over time. In the highest wealth bracket, the percentage of households fluctuates around 10 percent with no overall trend in either direction. The percentage of households in the top two brackets combined (those with 500 fl. or more) is also relatively stable, fluctuating around 25 percent. Among destitute households the picture is also generally flat, with the percentage almost the same between 1593 and 1603 and declining only slightly over

27 The Gini coefficient is obtained by calculating the area between the Lorenz curve and the hypothetical equality line as a proportion of the entire triangular area below the line. Jan de Vries provided the idea of plotting the Lorenz curve and calculating Gini coefficients, and P. Wessa's Free Statistics Software at http://www.wessa.net/co.wasp facilitated the computations.

28 List of Countries by Distribution of Wealth in 2000, from Wikipedia (http://en.wikipedia.org/wiki/List_of_countries_by_distribution_of_wealth, accessed 6 Nov. 2011); based on research by UNU-WIDER and James B. Davies et al., The Level and Distribution of Global Household Wealth, in: Economic Journal, 121 (2011), pp. 223–254.

Chart 4.5: Wealth Groups among Territorial Households

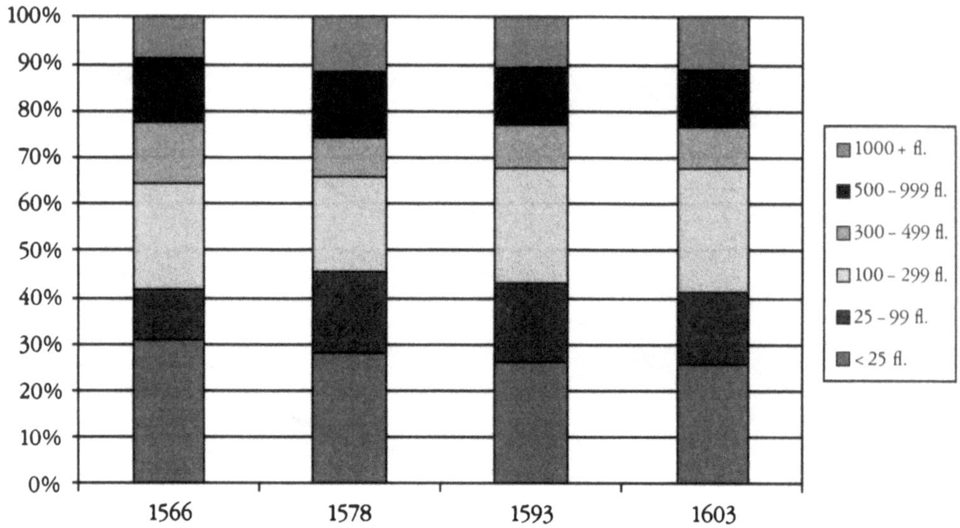

time. When we look at the bottom three wealth brackets combined (those with less than 300 fl.), we notice a contrasting trend: the percentage of households in below-average wealth groups rose slightly over time. Here, too, the percentage of households was almost identical in 1593 and 1603. Finally, we see that middling households remained weak in number relative to all other wealth groups. Though the percentage was smallest in 1578, it was not appreciably larger in any other year. In sum, the number of smallholders with 100–299 fl. rose slightly to compensate for a minor fall in the destitution rate. Over the course of the period 1566–1603, the other wealth groups as well as the overall picture show only slight fluctuations and general stability.

Over the longer term, the Lorenz curve and Gini coefficients confirm the stability indicated by a comparison of wealth brackets. The Gini coefficient was lowest, indicating greater equality in household wealth, in 1566 (0.654). It was highest in 1603 (0.693), indicating greater inequality, but the number in 1578 was almost exactly the same (0.690) and in 1593 it was only slightly lower (0.681). Inequality was increasing over the period 1566–1603, but not by much and not according to any consistent trend with respect to wealth groups or chronology. In all four years, the Lorenz curve indicates that the bottom fifty percent of households held around five percent of the wealth, whereas the top five percent of households held around thirty percent and the top ten percent of households around fifty percent of all wealth. Over time, the very rich were getting slightly richer: in 1566, the top one percent of households held 5.2% of wealth, in 1578 they held 5.4%, in 1593 5.8%, and in 1603 6.4% of all household wealth.

Chart 4.6: Village Households (1488–1603)

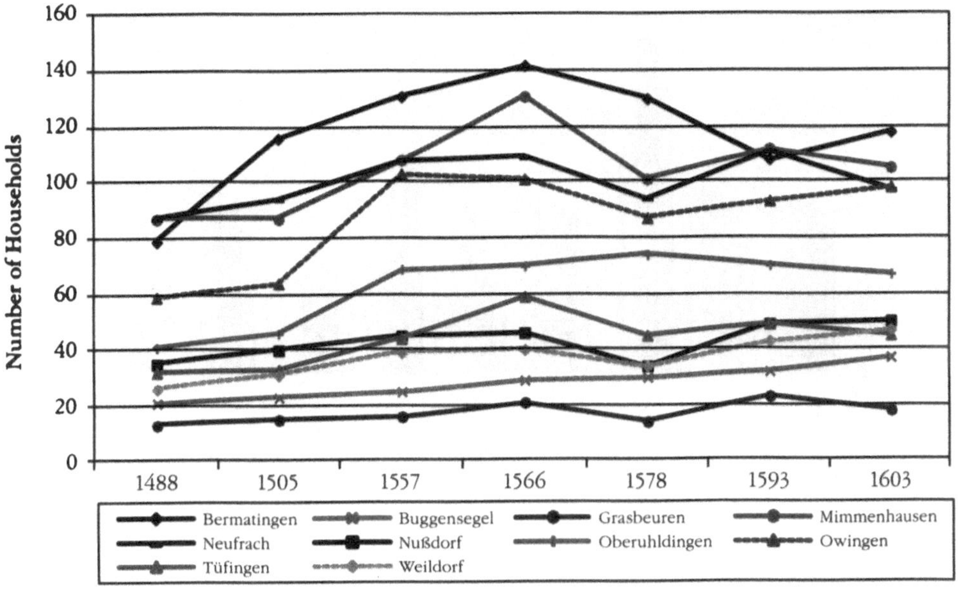

Village Population and Wealth Distribution

Taking our comparisons one step further, we can analyze the households and populations of individual villages. Chart 4.6 shows the number of households in a sample of ten large and middling villages in Salem's central territory. Here we notice that the number of households in Bermatingen, Mimmenhausen, and Tüfingen follow a bell curve similar to the general population. Many of the smaller villages, including Grasbeuren, Buggensegel, Gebhardsweiler, and Mühlhofen experienced gradual growth and relative stability in size. Perhaps smaller communities had lesser opportunity for expansion, with the limited resources there leading to greater restrictions on new household formation.

The village wealth data also show greater fluctuation than for the territory as a whole. Trends are mixed, both between different villages and within individual villages over time. First, Chart 4.7 shows household wealth averages by village over four years. Combining the four averages for each village we find that Grasbeuren (725 fl.) was by far the wealthiest village, followed by Owingen (430 fl.), Buggensegel (421 fl.), Bermatingen (388 fl.), Weildorf (382 fl.), Mimmenhausen (364 fl.), Nußdorf (337 fl.), Neufrach (323 fl.), Oberuhldingen (268 fl.), and Tüfingen (265 fl.). Second, Chart 4.8 shows the 1578 wealth distribution within each village by wealth bracket. Looking at wealth structure for individual places, we notice great variation among the villages. Grasbeuren and Nußdorf represent two extremes, the former with almost no middling households and the latter with almost no very rich or destitute households. In Owingen almost half the households were destitute, and in Tüfingen there were more below-

Chart 4.7: Wealth Averages for Individual Villages

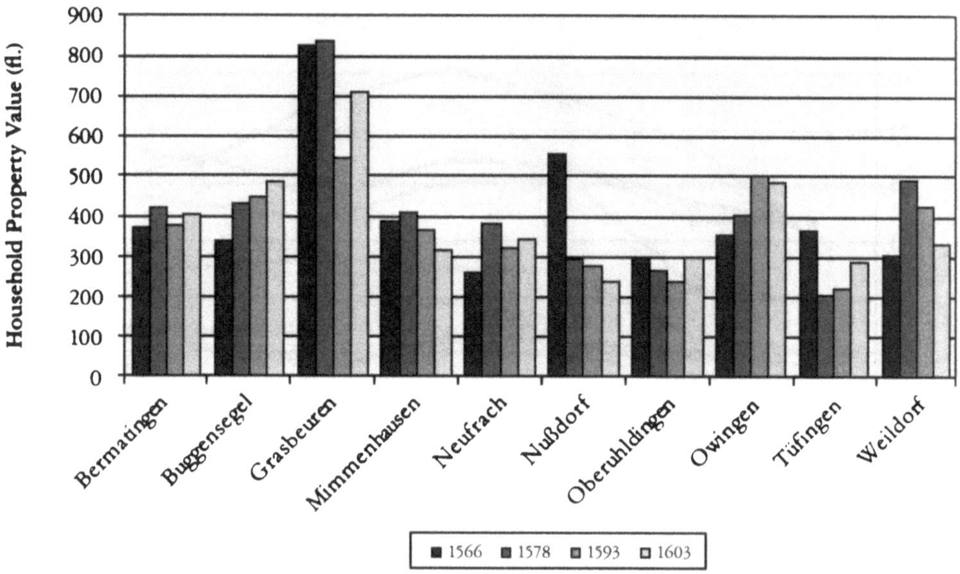

Chart 4.8: Village Wealth Groups (1578)

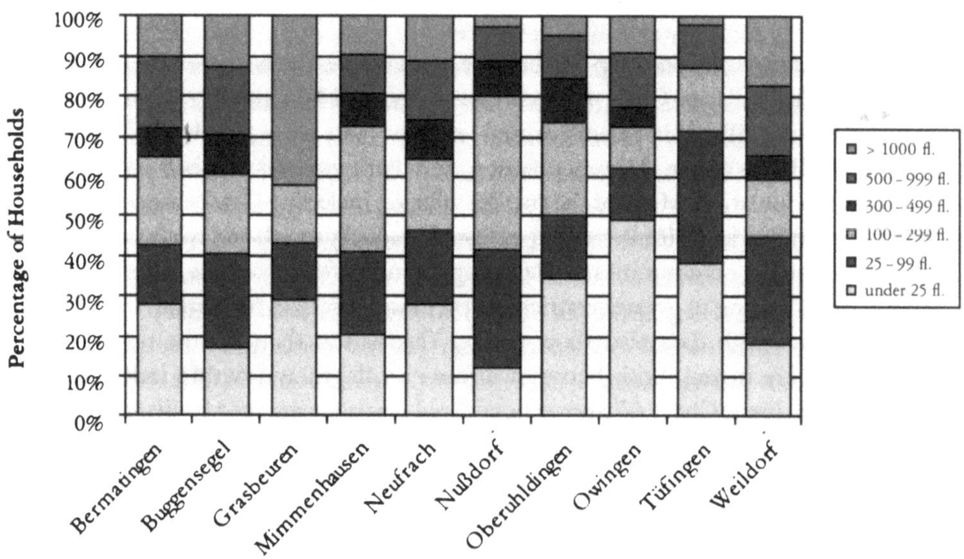

average households and fewer very rich ones than in any other village. Third, using the Gini index, we can compare the relative inequality within each village. From highest to lowest, representing the greatest to least relative inequality among households in 1578, the Gini coefficients are as follows: Owingen (0.802), Tüfingen (0.793), Bermatingen

Chart 4.9: Tenants and Nontenants (1578)

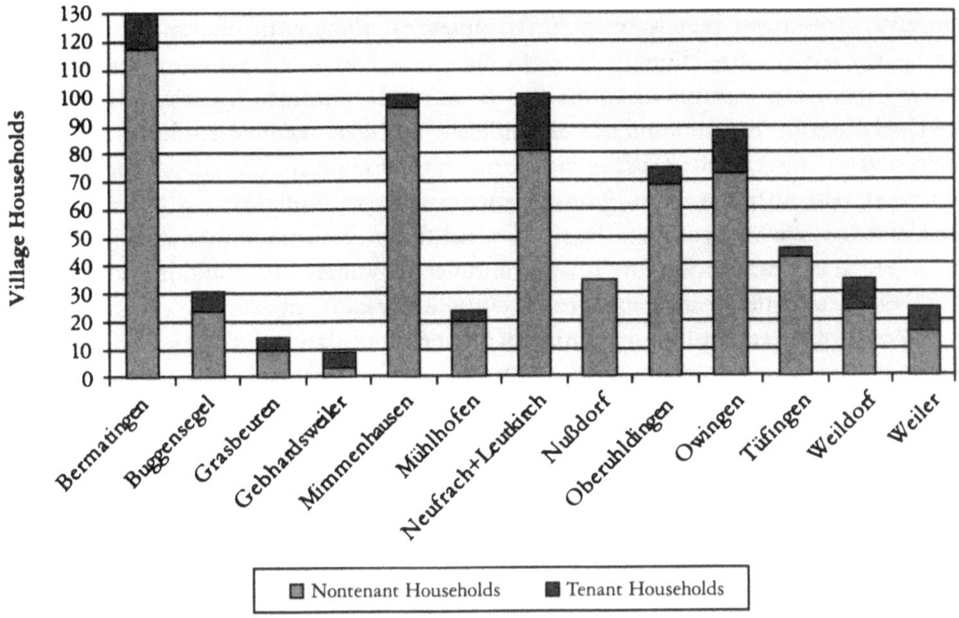

(0.696), Oberuhldingen (0.683), Neufrach (0.662), Mimmenhausen (0.660), Buggensegel (0.628), Grasbeuren (0.627), Weildorf (0.613), and Nußdorf (0.607).[29] It should be noted that there is no correlation between a village's average wealth and inequality. Tüfingen, for example, the poorest village overall, was also one of the least equal, but so was Owingen, one of the wealthier villages. In the wealthiest village of Grasbeuren, wealth was distributed more equally than most (despite very few middling households), and in Nußdorf, one of the poorer villages, we find the greatest level of equality. Despite the statistical problems of comparing such small numbers of households, we may conclude that wealth structure varied significantly among individual villages.

Landholding patterns obviously play a major role in rural economic structure. In general, villages with larger populations also had more farms than hamlets. See Chart 4.9. In Nußdorf and Mimmenhausen, however, the absence of major farms imparted an exceptional economic structure.[30] Nußdorf had neither large farm tenures of any

[29] These coefficients have been calculated using P. Wessa's Free Statistics Software at http://www.wessa.net/co.wasp.

[30] In a list of territorial households used for quartering troops around 1600, households from each village were grouped into the Mayerschaft (farm tenants) and Seldner (smallholders). In Nußdorf there were no farm tenants whatsoever and in Mimmenhausen, where there were only a few small farms, no households were required to house troops. GLAK, 98/2305.

type nor smaller, hereditary properties.[31] The landscape north and east of Nußdorf, as shown in Illustration 4.1, was rural but without significant arable. In addition to forests and meadows there were extensive vineyards along both sides of the road, parallel to the lake. Located directly along the lakeshore, Nußdorf's economy was oriented toward viticulture and the urban market of nearby Überlingen. Locally, this resulted in a high demand for labor and less dependence on Salem or other landlords. Nußdorf demonstrates the commercial alternative to cereal agriculture. The social composition there was also different from grain-producing villages. Nußdorf had fewer wealthy residents than any other village, but it also had fewer destitute households. Its wealth structure was characterized by a large number of poorer and middling households (25–499 fl.) and the greatest equality of household wealth anywhere in the territory.

Mimmenhausen, despite being one of the territory's largest villages, had no large farms and only a few smaller ones.[32] Again, geography helps explain Mimmenhausen's unusual situation. As the closest major village to the abbey, Mimmenhausen was something of a service and administrative center where many of Salem's officials, craftsmen, fieldworkers, and other employees lived.[33] In addition to agricultural labor and craft production, residents of Mimmenhausen provided for the abbey's household needs and looked after its visitors. Most of the abbey's cooks lived in Mimmenhausen, as did its guestmasters. Compared to Nußdorf, Mimmenhausen had a higher average wealth, a number of very wealthy households, broader wealth distribution, and greater economic stability over time.[34]

Bermatingen and Owingen, respectively located at the eastern and western frontiers of Salem's central territory, each had an unusual number of properties leased from outside landlords. This factor, along with the more distant location, proximity to urban markets in Markdorf and Überlingen, and the high percentage of residents who were not the abbey's serfs all contributed to greater economic and political independence

---

31 The noble von Bodman family had seven tenants in Nußdorf. They were most likely winegrowers.

32 In 1578 the properties listed in Mimmenhausen included a hereditary lease from Salem with 23½ Jauchert in two fields, another hereditary lease from Salem with 17 Jauchert in two fields, and a third hereditary lease from Constance with 21 Jauchert in two fields. The mill was a lifelong lease with 23 Jauchert. The inn was not mentioned in 1578 or 1593, but according to a 1577 rent register (GLAK, 66/10378), it had 17 Jauchert in three fields. These were all small farms compared to those found in other villages.

33 Matthias Biderman for example, the abbey's mason from Nußdorf, requested residency in Mimmenhausen because of the distance he had to travel from home to work. His request was approved, pending the community's consent. The Amtmann of Mimmenhausen petitioned the Audience in 1633 as the result of disagreement within the village over the responsibility to quarter troops. The Audience replied that all residents should house soldiers except for the priest and five abbey employees: the Oberamtmann, chamber secretary, organist, cook, and barber-surgeon. GLAK, 61/13370 1616, 61/13374 1633.

34 See Charts 4.7 and 4.8 above.

Illustration 4.1: Landscape with Field Patterns Northeast of Nußdorf

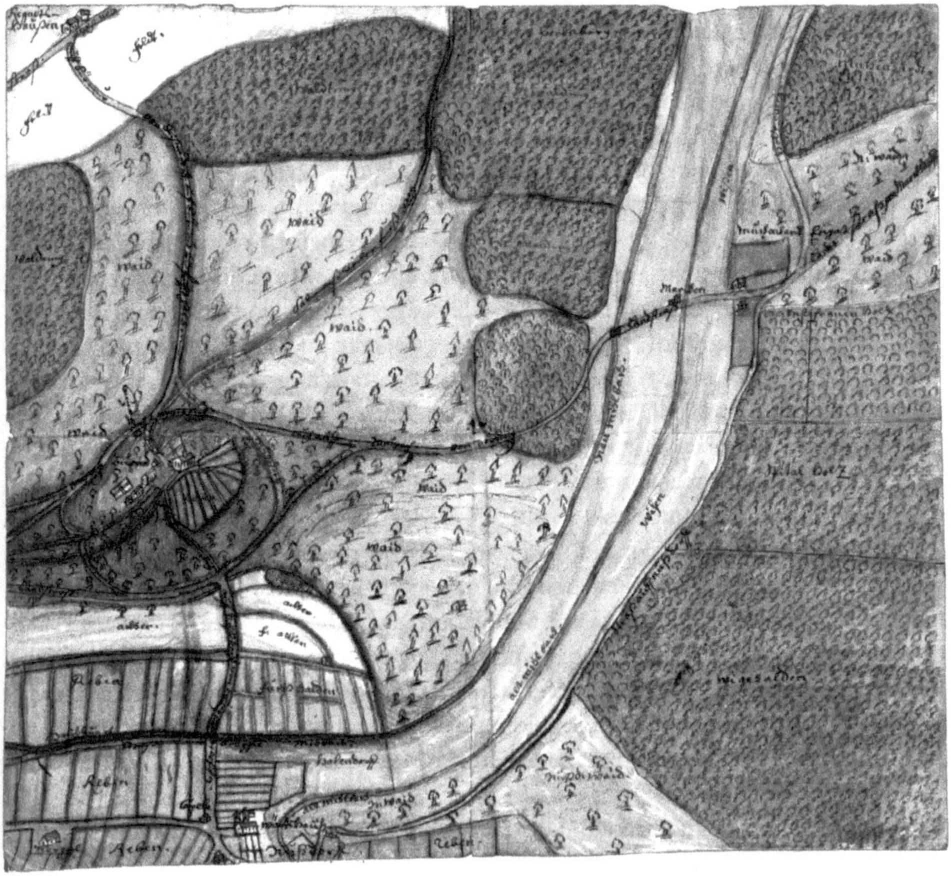

Unknown artist, seventeenth century

Vineyards, forests, and meadows are prominent but there are few arable fields. Also shown are the alt Birnau pilgrimage church, Nußdorf's wine press and inn, the old and new Mühlbach stream-bed, and the road connecting Owingen and Markdorf.

Generallandesarchiv Karlsruhe, H/Nußdorf/FN1

from Salem than in most other villages. In Buggensegel, Neufrach, and Tüfingen, where Salem was the only landlord listed in 1578, Salem's political and economic influence was especially strong. This was the case above all in Neufrach, with its close proximity to the abbey and numerous large farms, all leased from the abbey.[35]

---

[35] There were eleven major farms in Neufrach, all annual leases, with acreage ranging from 18 to 37½ Jauchert in one of three fields according to the 1593 tax list. In addition there were at least two lifelong leases and a number of hereditary leases, many of them smaller, with inconsistent listings from year to year.

Summary of Trends and Seventeenth-Century Outlook

The findings presented thus far are extremely important for our understanding of the territory's population and wealth structure during the second half of the sixteenth century. First, the population as a whole was not rising with the exception of a slight increase between 1578 and 1593. Second, the total number as well as percentage of unpropertied households declined slightly over time. Third, wealth was not significantly consolidated in the hands of the very rich or even prosperous households: the percentage of households in these wealth brackets remained quite stable over time. To summarize, during the period 1566 to 1603, the population declined slightly while experiencing stability in wealth structure. These conditions do not lead to the expectation of an increase in local competition for property and other resources. They do not suggest population or household wealth distribution as grounds for rising conflict between rich and poor villagers (though social controls restricting population growth may have been an issue). If conflict between rich and poor *was* rising during the late sixteenth century, the reasons are not to be found in local demographic change or even in a rising disparity of household wealth.

Still, the lack of a strong middling group suggests there was a divide between those with and without property. Few households found themselves between the two economic extremes. The division of the population into two categories, the wealthy landholders versus the landless poor, is confirmed by the literature. The question is, how did members of these two groups interact and how did they view one another? To what degree was social mobility possible, and how did this affect householders on either side of the divide? Attitudes among villagers in this period are notoriously difficult to discover, but we can observe changes in economic fortunes and interactions between individuals of differing socioeconomic status. By paying attention to villagers' attempts to secure or hold onto land, and looking at the relationships built around property, we may be able to reach some conclusions on issues of social perception and the development of class interests within the village.

Unfortunately, the tax lists do not allow any firm conclusions about population and wealth in the decades after 1603, because the next imperial tax list was not compiled until 1651, after the Thirty Years War.[36] There are rent registers and other lists of householders from the early seventeenth century, but since they exclude some segments of the population and underestimate others, they do not reveal much about overall population and wealth.[37] It seems reasonable to expect that population in Salem's villages

---

36 GLAK, 98/2066, 1651.

37 Rent registers list only those households holding land in tenure from the abbey. A list of households compiled for the purpose of quartering troops around 1600 underestimates the number of smallholders, whereas a report on damages resulting from the Thirty Years War exaggerates the number of households in the period before the war. A list of households owing labor services in 1607 appears more accurate, but again, smallholders are probably underestimated. Lists

was not rising by much, if at all, before the Thirty Years War.[38] As for wealth, the early seventeenth century was a period of general decline, so we might expect that wealth declined as well or at least became more stratified.[39]

The Thirty Years War, which began in 1618, impacted the Lake Constance region in full force during the 1630s. At that point population and wealth dropped off abrubtly, as depicted in Sebastian Bürster's chronicle and other sources describing the war years.[40] Troop quarterings began around 1629 and became frequent starting in 1632, with increasing damages from both armies over time. In 1632, 26 homes were burned to ashes in Neufrach, and the imperial troops stationed in Mimmenhausen and Weildorf in 1633 demanded white bread with milk and butter while behaving themselves worse than any enemy. As monks and peasants fasted during Lent, soldiers quartered in Salem's villages drank wine day and night as if it were carnival, and they took all the livestock and grain they could find, so that before long "there was nothing left to bite or break."[41] The farm tenants were forced to seek alms, but according to Bürster, the abbey had nothing to spare and many starved.[42] Soldiers loaded up wagons with everything worth anything, even roofing tiles, so that houses and churches filled with water when the rains came. Things continued to get worse, so that by 1635 there were only ten or twenty, perhaps thirty survivors left in large villagers where there had once been two or three hundred people.[43] Fields and

---

of households receiving firewood in exchange for manure name only a percentage of the population. These sources are relatively unhelpful for counting the poor and landless households or for tracking the general population over time.

38 Suggestive of population decline in Salem are a plague epidemic in 1611, a series of harvest failures with seed loans distributed in 1614, widespread grain debt in 1625, and stricter social controls in the early seventeenth century that restricted immigration and limited the marriages of poor couples. This hypothesis is also supported by studies of other territories such as Ottobeuren and by broader population trends for Germany described by HOLENSTEIN, Bauern, pp. 48, 94–95; Christian PFISTER, The Population of Late Medieval and Early Modern Germany, in: Germany: A New Social and Economic History, vol. 1, ed. Bob Scribner, London 1996, pp. 41–42. Conversely, the population in Hohenlohe reached a peak in 1630; see ROBISHEAUX, Rural Society, pp. 73, 78.

39 This conclusion is supported by the many alms requests and poor lists as well as reports of food shortages and famines in the early seventeenth century. High grain prices and periodic shortages may have helped the largest farmers, but smallholders had to buy grain and monetary inflation meant that cash wages declined, even if the population remained steady. In addition to greater stratification of wealth, material instability and the lack of security, both physical and emotional, were likely factors in this period.

40 WEECH, Bürsters Beschreibung; Hermann BAIER, ed., Akten zur Geschichte des dreißigjährigen Krieges am Bodensee, in: Schriften des Vereins für Geschichte des Bodensees und seiner Umgebung 44 (1915), pp. 129–162.

41 WEECH, Bürsters Beschreibung, p. 30.

42 In Weildorf parish, around seventy adults and one hundred children reportedly died of starvation in 1634. BÜTTNER, Konstanzer Heilig-Geist-Spital, p. 484.

43 WEECH, Bürsters Beschreibung, p. 91.

vineyards reverted to wastelands, there were no animals, and nothing left to eat. While the convent sought refuge in Constance and Überlingen, the abbey's subjects crowded within the cloister's walls for safety.[44] They searched for grain in rodent caches and ate acorns and tree bark; cats and dogs were no longer safe. The devastation of the war, which literally decimated the population and destroyed entire villages along with their physical and social infrastructures, created a sharp break in the previous continuities of property relations and village life. This is one of the reasons for this study's endpoint in the 1630s, around the height of the war's effects on the region.

In view of the lack of statistical data for the period after 1603, other types of sources are extremely useful. The serial sources from the chancery, court, and Audience all begin in the 1580s and provide insight on villagers' economic activities, relationships, and concerns both before and after 1600. The challenge is to apply what is known for the earlier decades, complemented by serial records that span both periods, to determine how villagers adapted their household strategies and personal relationships to accommodate the socioeconomic pressures that were presumably rising all the way into the 1630s.

4.2 Farm Tenants and Forms of Leasehold

In Salem's villages, the large farms (*Höfe*) as well as many smaller properties (*Güter*) were leased to tenants by Salem or some other landlord. Salem's tenures ranged widely in size and rents, but the makeup of individual farms remained relatively consistent over time.[45] Both large farms and smallholdings included a house, typically surrounded by a farmstead with kitchen garden and fruit trees. It might include various outbuildings such as a shed, barn, stalls, pigsty, or bake house. Land parcels included strips in each of three arable fields, in addition to meadows and occasionally forest and vineyard parcels. There were three major forms of tenure in Salem's villages: annual lease, lifelong lease, and hereditary lease. Salem was the landlord for most properties, and most of the abbey's properties were annual leases that had to be renewed each year.[46]

---

44 Villagers remained within the abbey walls for most of 1636, sleeping in the courtroom (*gerüchtstuben*) among other places. WEECH, Bürsters Beschreibung, p. 99.

45 The number of farms decreased slightly over time according to the tax lists from 1578–1603. This may indicate a gradual consolidation of properties or temporary vacancies, or it may be that the first register was the most complete and carefully recorded of the three.

46 In 1578, Salem was the landlord for 96 properties in a sample of 13 villages, compared with 19 properties belonging to all other landlords. At least 70 of Salem's properties were annual leaseholds, whereas all but 2 properties belonging to other landlords were hereditary leases. Outside landlords had properties in Bermatingen (4), Buggensegel (1), Gebhardsweiler (3), Grasbeuren (1), Mimmenhausen (2), Mühlhofen (1), Oberuhldingen (1), Owingen (2), Weildorf (1), and Weiler (3).

Annual tenures (known variously as *Schupflehen*, *Jahrlehen*, or *Handlehen*) formed the backbone of Salem's landlordship. They comprised not only the majority of farms but also most of the large farms.[47] Salem's law codes, rent registers, legal agreements, and other official documents reiterated the requirement that tenants give up their farms each year on 1 May, "with word and hand," to be renewed by the abbot's grace.[48] Salem took great interest in maintaining the custom of annual leases, as reflected in the ubiquitous use of the phrase *jedes jahr ledig*, or "vacated every year." By denying farm tenants any hereditary right to the land they held, annual leases secured the abbey's control over its properties. In practice, however, tenants were rarely evicted, for custom and written law protected the rights of tenants as well as the lord. According to the partnership agreement of 1473, the abbot could remove a tenant only in cases of extreme debt or mismanagement, not according to his pleasure. As long as the tenant paid the rent and kept the farm in good order, the abbot would continue to lease the property to the tenant and even to his or her children.[49]

When we compare the tax registers of 1578, 1593, and 1603, we find that many of the abbey's large farms remained in the same family for long periods despite the terms of annual lease.[50] This family continuity confirms the suspicion that annual leases did not turn over on a regular basis, let alone annually. When they did, the new tenant was usually a close relative. That so many families were able to hang onto the same farm for 25 or more years suggests that annual lease was not so different from lifelong lease

47 Annual leases comprised 74% of Salem's properties and 61% of tenures from any landlord in 1578. Among 58 annual leases and 14 hereditary leases listing the number of arable parcels in the two productive fields, annual leases averaged 40 Jauchert whereas hereditary ones averaged 29. Only two lifelong leases, both mills, have acreage listed, so their average of 19 Jauchert is neither representative nor statistically significant.

48 "Item zu Bermatingen ... sollend järlich die Höff mit mund und hand uffgeben werden ußgenommen Rümperschwiler welches ein Leublehen ist." GLAK, 66/10418, 1600. Sreenivasan provides the text of a similar requirement for the *Gotteshausrecht* tenures in Ottobeuren. There, too, tenants had to renew their leases every year, receiving them from the lord "with trembling hands," although they enjoyed lifelong tenure. Idem, Ottobeuren, p. 22.

49 Articles 3 and 4: "Von der hof und hůben wegen, das die gotshuslüte das nachgeben, das die järlich ledig syen, doch also, wa da ist, das einr söliche gůt in erbern zitbüwen und in eren helt, och dem gotshuß rent, zins und gült järlich davon git, das dannen unser herre von Salem söliche gůt in und irn kinden wyder lyhe." Blickle and Holenstein, Agrarverfassungsverträge, p. 55. Occasional references in legal suits and Audience petitions confirm that the abbey needed good reason to evict a tenant.

50 Individuals who held annual leases for 25 years or more include: Hans Meßmer of Buggensegel, Franz Dulenkopf and Bernhard Bronner of Gebhardsweiler, Jacob Jörg, Hans Weißenkönig, and Othmar Bommer of Neufrach, Jerg Hitzler, Andreas Burckhart, Mattheus Burst, and Hans Biller of Owingen, Ulrich Lang, Simon Hergisfelder, and Andreas Zäsin of Tepfenhard, Martin Zürckh of Tüfingen, and Bartlin Biller of Weiler. At least seven additional farms remained within the patriline and two or more others passed to female kin in the same period (1578–1603).

or even hereditary lease, especially since a number of hereditary leases passed out of the patriline during the same period.[51] If so many annual leases remained in the same family while some hereditary leases did not, then what was the advantage of hereditary lease, and what real differences distinguished the two types?[52]

The key difference was that for families with annual leases, their future use of the property and its eventual transmission to a child were dependent upon the abbot's grace. When a farm fell vacant and a spouse, child, or other relative took over the lease, they did so with the abbey's permission. And though they might try to influence the lord's decision, it was the abbot or his advisors who ultimately decided who would be the next tenant. Annual leases reinforced the abbey's control over the major farm tenants, reminding them each year that they owed their position directly to the lord. According to abbey policy stated in an instruction manual from circa 1500, "Property shall be leased to a tenant not out of obligation or any legal right but by grace alone, and according to his or her submissive request, petition, surety, and loyalty."[53] Although the abbot normally chose a successor to the farm from among the previous tenant's kin, they had to compete for his favor, knowing full well he had the power to retract his goodwill if they failed to reciprocate through hard work, fiscal responsibility, and obedience to the lord's commands.

Hereditary leases (*Erblehen*, also *Erbzinslehen*) were less common in Salem's villages, and they tended to be smaller than annual tenures. Many hereditary leases had no arable parcels at all, others very few. Hereditary leases offered the tenant better terms for security and transfer, however. Such properties could be sold or, as the name suggests, passed freely to heirs.[54] Perhaps this is why Salem maintained so few hereditary

---

51 No kinship tie is apparent between tenants of a hereditary Gut in Gebhardsweiler held by Stoffel Storch, Hieronimus Villieber, and Michael Schuechmacher; a Hof in Mimmenhausen held by Hans Zürckh and Hans Leub; another Gut in Mimmenhausen held by Bernhard Dreer, Jorg Pfeiffer, and Mattheus Senfft; a Gut in Oberuhldingen held by Hans Hermann and Jacob Dulenkopf; a Gut in Tüfingen held by Christa Hailg and, following a possible vacancy, by Thoma Biller; and a Hof in Weiler held by Hans Klotz and Joachim Haimpel. Several other hereditary leases passed through women out of the patriline. Büttner confirms for the Constance hospital's farms in the Linzgau that the turnover rate for annual leases was comparable to that of hereditary and lifelong leases. Idem, Heilig-Geist-Spital, p. 176.

52 One possibility is that the market price and assessed value of hereditary leases was rising dramatically, while benefits remained the same, so that holders were selling them to outside parties or forfeiting as a result of debt. Another possibility is that widows, daughters, in-laws, and stepchildren took over the farm rather than sons. Baier noted with surprise that hereditary leases changed hands so frequently in the period after 1630. Idem, Bevölkerungsbewegung, p. 79.

53 "Item das Ime das Gůtt, Uß kainer schuld oder gerechtigkaitt, sonder allain auß gnaden, unnd auf sein, oder der seinenn underthenig pitt, firpit, birgschafft, vertreistung u. seyn gelichen worden." GLAK, 98/1987, fol. 3v.

54 This security of tenure carried a high price. Whereas annual and lifelong leases were assessed at 25 to 50 fl. for tax purposes depending on size, hereditary leases were valued at up to 1,000 fl. in 1578 and increased even further over time.

tenures, especially among the largest and most profitable farms. Article 6 of Salem's instructions on leases, cited above, said of such properties: "Lacking a reason of greatest consequence, no tenure shall be made or treated as hereditary unless it was so in the past."[55] Hereditary leases typically owed a small recognitive or renewal fee upon the installation of a new abbot or tenant but not the much larger entry fines associated with lifelong leases.[56] Both hereditary and lifelong leases were subject to a written tenure contract (*Lehensbrief*), an important tool for securing the rights of landlord and tenant alike. The contract secured a fixed rent, specified the conditions of sale and forfeiture, and usually described each individual parcel in great detail.[57] To summarize, hereditary properties were beneficial to tenants because they could be passed down and owed a low, stable rent. Yet with few exceptions, they could not support a large household and were not major sources of income or power in the village.

Lifelong leases (*Leiblehen*) specified terms of one to three lifetimes (for the tenant, tenant and spouse, or tenant spouse and child). These farm returned to the abbey's control after the specified period, and each time the farm fell vacant, rent and other terms were subject to change. One major drawback of lifelong lease was the entry fine (*Erschatz*), which was charged to each new tenant and could be a hefty sum requiring repayment over several years.[58] The amount of the entry fine was negotiable, and it may have risen during the early seventeenth century as lifelong leases became more common.[59] The lifelong tenure contracts are very similar to those for hereditary farms, except that lifelong leases could not be sold or transferred to a third party and they were not subject to recurring recognitive fees. With the exception of mills, lifelong leases were uncommon in Salem's villages before 1600.[60]

---

55 GLAK, 98/1987. By contrast, Büttner found that the Constance hospital improved terms of leasehold in the Linzgau over time. Idem, Heilig-Geist-Spital, p. 178.

56 Recognitive fees varied by farm, generally between five shillings and two gulden.

57 Salem usually reserved the right of first purchase and required that any other buyer be an abbey serf or territorial resident.

58 The entry fine typically ranged from 40 to 200 fl. and tenants normally made a large downpayment the first year, followed by annual payments for several years thereafter.

59 In other territories, entry fines were one of the most important sources of lords' rental incomes during this period. See ROBISHEAUX, Rural Society, pp. 168–169; Robert DEES, Economics and Politics of Peasant Production in South Germany, PhD diss., Los Angeles 2007, pp. 349, 514. Evidence for Salem is limited before 1600, so although entry fines are mentioned more frequently in the seventeenth century, it is hard to say whether the amount increased or by how much.

60 One out of three lifelong leases in both the 1578 and 1603 tax registers were mills. This may be because mills required much greater capital investment and maintenance than an annual lease could bear.

Illustration 4.2: Excerpt from the 1578 Imperial Tax Register

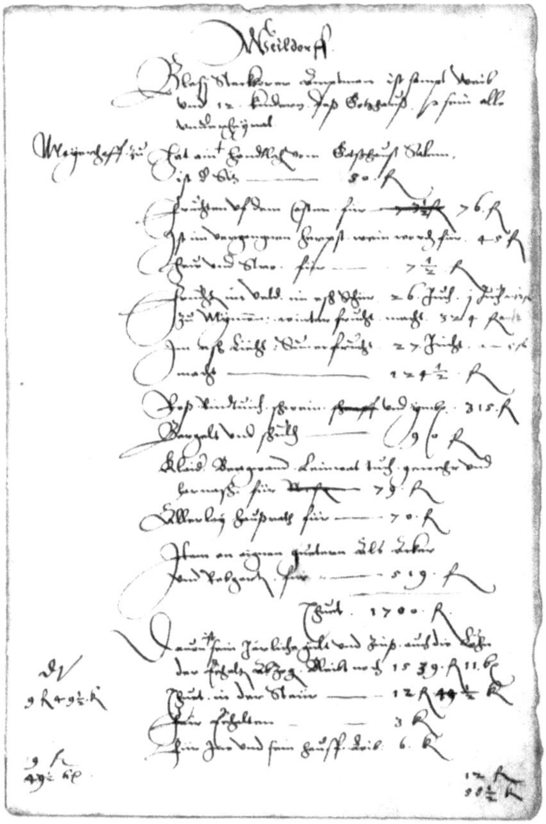

Generallandesarchiv Karlsruhe, 98/2024

Farm Tenants

The 1578 tax register gives the total property value and tax assessment for all households. For the farm tenants, it describes subcategories of property and wealth in greater detail. Illustration 4.2, Excerpt from the 1578 Imperial Tax Register, shows the property assessment for Blesi Steckborer of Weildorf. It lists his farm, an annual lease with 53 one-acre parcels in the two productive fields, along with freehold property (arable and vineyards) worth 519 fl. and moveables including animals (horses, cows, pigs, and bees), stores of grain, wine, straw, and hay, household items, clothing and textiles, armor and weapons, cash and credit. Steckborer's tax of over twelve gulden was based on his net wealth of 1,539 fl., which was in turn derived by subtracting taxes, rents, and wages from 1,700 fl. in gross wealth. Besides twelve minor children who were not subject to any special taxes, Steckborer owed an another three kreuzer for one household servant and three kreuzer each for he and his wife, in recognition of their servility. In order to investigate the farm tenants more closely, I created a sample from the 1578 tax list comprising all households with a farm tenure (*Hof*) or smallholding (*Gut*) in thirteen villages.[61] Including twelve tenants with more than one property and three with only half of one, the sample consists of 104 households with a total of 115 tenures.[62]

Among the 104 tenant households, 91 had arable land with listings for the combined acreage and value of crops in each of the two productive fields.[63] The average and median acreage was 19 Jauchert in the winter field and 18 in the summer field. The maximum in a single field was 42 Jauchert, and the largest combined acreage in two fields was 70 Jauchert. Since the number of parcels in each field varied, we can only roughly estimate the average holdings in all three fields to be around 56 Jauchert. This was a substantial amount of land, compared with subsistence needs or with the landholdings of the territorial population overall.[64] Salem's major farms were also extremely large in comparison to other territories.[65]

Average gross wealth among tenant households in 1578 was 1,215 fl., with a median value of 936.5 fl. and range of 108 to 5,020 fl. As the assessment values for various types of property demonstrate, however, wealth is quite different from income. For tax purposes, all annual and lifelong tenures were assessed at 50 fl. for large farms and 25 fl. for smallholdings. Hereditary leases, on the other hand, were much more highly valued because of the security they provided and because the sale of hereditary properties pushed up their market price.[66] In fact, the possession of hereditary tenures

---

61 Villages in the sample include Bermatingen, Buggensegel, Gebhardsweiler, Grasbeuren, Mimmenhausen, Mühlhofen, Neufrach (with Leutkirch), Oberuhldingen, Owingen (with Pfaffenhofen), Tepfenhard, Tüfingen, Weildorf, and (Mittelsten- and Nidersten-) Weiler.

62 The information listed in 1593 is similar to 1578, with many comparable subcategories of wealth, whereas the 1566 list provides no additional property information and the 1603 list gives details only about farm tenures (lease type and value), freehold property, and the value of all moveable property lumped together.

63 One field was planted with winter grain (most often spelt, sometimes rye), the second with summer grain (usually oats), while the third lay fallow. The fallow field was excluded from the tax assessment. Among thirteen households without arable, three were millers and ten were smallholders.

64 The tax lists do not provide comparable information about the extent of landholding by smallholders and nontenants, but the size of Salem's farms suggests that the abbey's strict control over annual leases resulted in the preservation of extremely large farms. Govind Sreenivasan estimates 6.5 Jauchert as the minimum arable requirement in all three fields to meet subsistence needs for an average household (of 4.7 persons) in Ottobeuren. Idem, Ottobeuren, p. 148.

65 Compare SREENIVASAN, Ottobeuren, pp. 149–150, 208 n. 29; ROBISHEAUX, Rural Society, pp. 88, 244–245; HOLENSTEIN, Bauern, p. 4. According to Sreenivasan, thirty Jauchert in Ottobeuren was enormous.

66 Nonhereditary leases could not be sold or freely alienated, and the assessment value of these farms remained consistent throughout the period. The value of hereditary leases rose with demand and did not reflect their acreage or other physical attributes.

Chart 4.10: Freehold and Wealth among Farm Tenants (1578)

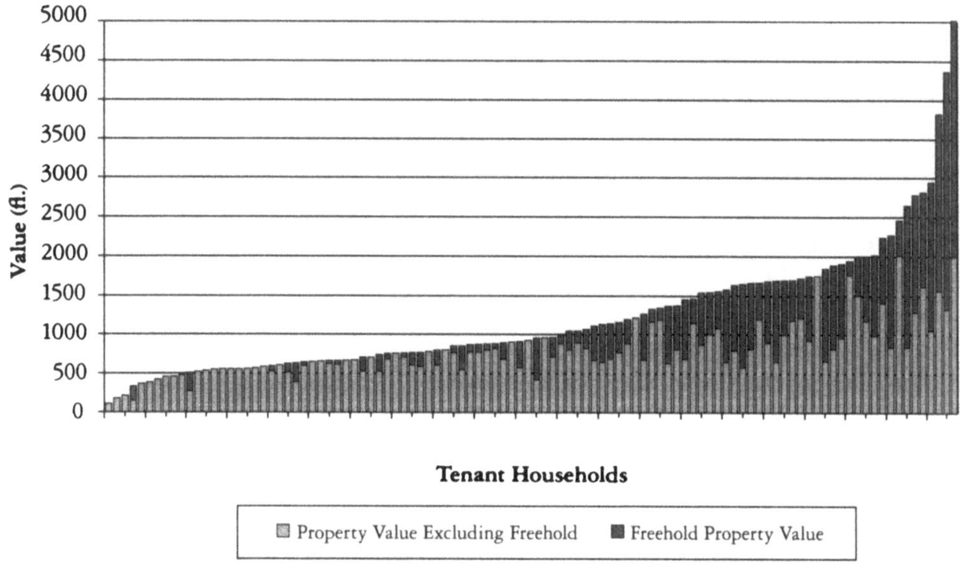

among the wealthiest as well as poorest tenants suggests that hereditary tenures are a poor indicator of household wealth.[67] They correspond even less to household income derived from agriculture, since most of the arable land belonged to the farms held in annual lease.

In addition to their tenures, many households owned freehold property (*Aigengüter*). Freehold land, like hereditary tenures, was assessed at a high value relative to its size. Unlike hereditary tenures, however, freehold property was often a substantial factor in the household economy and a strong indicator of overall household wealth. Chart 4.10 demonstrates this correlation: wealthier tenants had more freehold property. Among the twenty wealthiest tenants, only one held no such property and the average value of freehold among them was 1,225.4 fl. Among the twenty poorest tenants, at least fourteen had no freehold property whatsoever. Among 72 households with freehold

[67] A few of the wealthiest households had highly valued hereditary properties, including Ulrich Meßmer, whose farm lease from Kreuzlingen Abbey was worth 1,000 fl. and whose overall wealth ranked eighth among tenants in the sample. Bernhard Schmidmaister, who ranked tenth in wealth, held a hereditary lease worth 600 fl. from the Constance cathedral chapter. Yet many hereditary leaseholders ranked among the poorest tenants, with few or no arable parcels or much else of value. Anna Denderline held a hereditary lease worth just 60 fl. plus 48 fl. in all other property. Widower Michel Nihel had 332 fl. in total property including a hereditary smallholding worth 150 fl. and other freehold land worth 182 fl. Widow Ursula Biblerin had a hereditary smallholding worth 300 fl. but all her other property was worth only 66 fl.

Chart 4.11: Livestock and Wealth among Farm Tenants (1578)

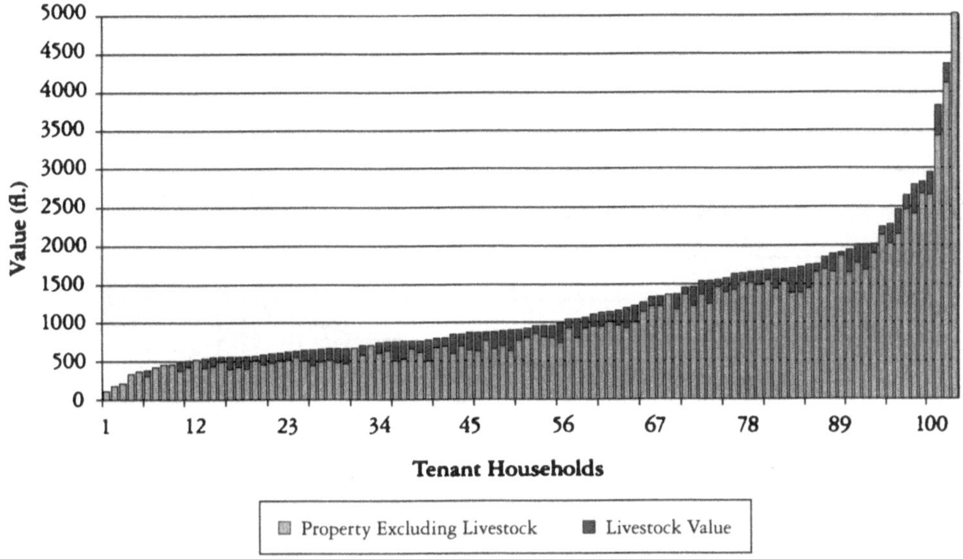

property of known value, the average was worth 604.7 fl.[68] We will return to the significance of freeholdings later in the chapter.

Animals were indispensable for farm tenants, especially for plowing, fertilization, and transport. It comes as no surprise, therefore, that most tenants (90.4 percent) owned livestock.[69] Yet wealthy households did not necessarily report owning more animals than poorer counterparts, and the value of animals was not a major factor for total wealth. As Chart 4.11 shows, the cash value of livestock was low compared to total wealth, and there was no correlation between animals owned and total household wealth. The average value of livestock among all tenant households was 154 fl.[70]

Since the tax lists provide both gross and net wealth for farm tenants, we can assess the debt load of individual households and compare it to total property value. Average net wealth among tenants was 958.3 fl., or 78.9% of gross wealth. In other words, the average household carried debts just over one-fifth of their total estate value. Yet as Chart 4.12 shows, the range of debt from one household to the next fluctuated widely and there is no obvious correlation between wealth and debt levels. For example, Hans Winter's gross wealth was 2,016 fl. while Caspar Schaitteckh's was 1,262 fl. After the

68 Twenty-seven tenants in the sample had no freehold property and five others had freehold of unknown value because their land and moveables were not separately itemized.

69 Ten households, including the five poorest in the sample, had no livestock listed. Three of them are listed with all moveables combined, so the value of animals is unknown.

70 The average among 91 households with livestock of known value was 176 fl. The combined value of all tenants' livestock was 16,043 fl.

Chart 4.12: Tenants' Gross and Net Wealth (1578)

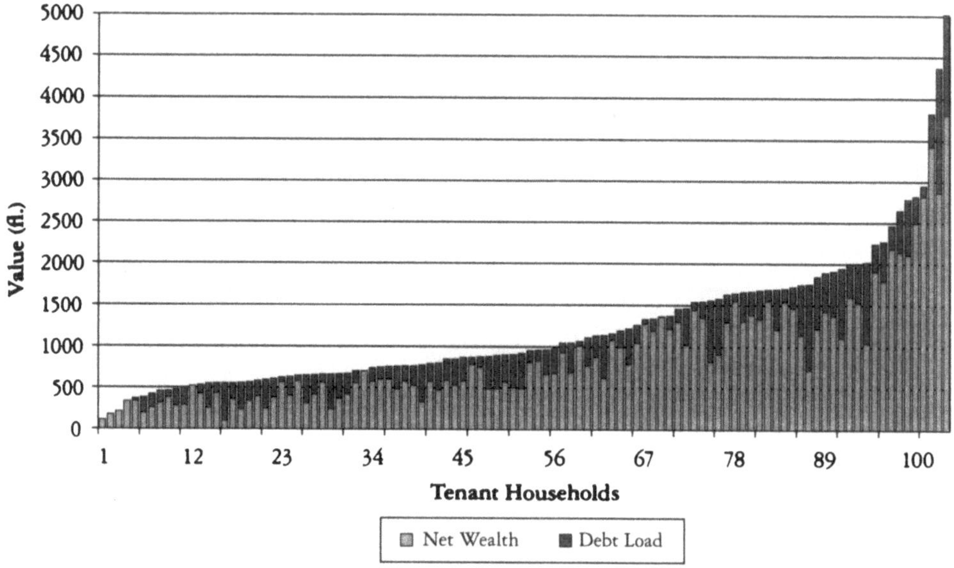

subtraction of debt, however, both householders had the same net wealth of 1,048 fl. In another comparison of extremes, Sebastian Leub and Jerg Rogg each had gross wealth of 554 fl. But while Leub's debt load of 20% left him with 433 fl. in net wealth, Rogg's debt of 82% left him with a remainder of only 100 fl. Such examples caution us against equating gross property value with actual wealth, because variations in debt levels meant that households with similar gross values might not have been similarly wealthy.

Transmission of Farm Tenures

Since most large properties were secured through the abbot's favor and not hereditary right, the petitioning process played an extremely important role in property transfers. The Audience protocol, which is filled with tenure petitions of various types, helps explain how the abbey allocated property among its subjects and what pressures influenced decisions about property distribution. The record shows how tenants and would-be tenants negotiated, for what purpose, and with what success. Although senior abbey officials made tenure decisions, they were not free from the needs and strategies of villagers, expressed above all in the language of kinship. In fact, land tenure provides a good example of how the expectations of kin influenced territorial policy and vice-versa.

Audience petitions reveal how property, even nonhereditary property, passed along family lines with the lord's approval. Widows commonly took over farms formerly held by their husbands. For example, Christa Binder's widow petitioned for and received his farm in Bermatingen as an annual lease. The widow of Neufrach's Amtmann, Hans Utz, was permitted to remain on the farm with her children for life, or until her remarriage. Magdalena Hartmännin received her late husband's farm for life, in return for an entry fine of forty gulden. In Neufrach, Hans Leub's widow secured the inn. The Amtmann Moritz Mayer of Tüfingen made provisions for his wife to receive retirement benefits under the new tenant when he died, including room and board, one or two garden plots, and some animals of her own. Each of these requests, it should be noted, was approved in the period after 1600.[71]

Children, including stepchildren, were also in a good position to assume their parents' farms. Mattheus Biller petitioned for the transfer of his farm in Oberhof to a son in 1630. The abbey agreed and even lowered the rent upon Biller's request.[72] Bastian Ower wanted to pass his farm, an annual lease, to his son Martin in 1600. The abbey postponed its decision in order to inspect the property and its debts. Hans Fünfflin died in 1630, leaving two daughters. The older daughter successfully petitioned for the farm, offering to take care of her younger sister and seek a good marriage with the abbey's approval. The abbey agreed that she should find a husband right away. When Michael Mayer requested a smallholding in Mühlhofen after his stepfather's eviction in 1611, he pointed out that his father and grandfather had managed the property capably before it fell into disrepair. Bernhard Schaitteckh received his stepfather's farm in 1630, on condition that he repair the house and barn.[73]

For the successful farm transfer, timing was essential. Tenures were commonly passed to the younger generation during a parent's lifetime, because if the tenant died without establishing an heir, he or she would no longer be able to influence the lord's decision. Marriage was a popular time for *inter vivos* lease transfers, and a suitable marriage partner was an extremely important component of the successful tenure petition. Mimmenhausen's innkeeper Galle Nihel asked to transfer the inn to his daughter and son-in-law upon their marriage. Veit Burckhart petitioned for his deceased father's farm, but the abbey told him to get married first.[74] A parent might also petition to transfer property to the younger generation upon the death of a spouse, or when old age or poor health forced them into retirement.

When a tenant died or otherwise withdrew his or her property claim, someone often stood ready to petition immediately for the lease. Requests directly following an announcement of death or default suggest that access to information about farm availability must have played a role in many property transfers. In one case, Veit Rueff's

---

71 Examples in this paragraph are from GLAK, 61/13369–13374 1611, 1624, 1630, 1606, and 1611.

72 Rent had been the third or fourth share; it was now lowered to one-fourth across the board.

73 Examples in this paragraph are from GLAK, 61/13369–13374, 1630, 1600, 1630, 1611, and 1630.

74 GLAK, 61/13370, 1611; 61/13373, 1624.

decision to give up the inn in Neufrach started a chain of petitions.[75] That same day his stepson, Hans Leub of Baitenhausen, requested and received tenure to the vacated inn. Then Leub's brother-in-law, Balthas Ower, gave up his farm in Oberuhldingen and requested Leub's now vacant farm in Baitenhausen. Finally, in the fourth consecutive petition before the Audience, the innkeeper Georg Rauch of Oberuhldingen asked for Ower's farm in that village. This series of carefully orchestrated requests indicates that some tenants gave up farms in order to obtain better leases or secure property for a younger relative during their lifetimes. It also shows how tenants moved from village to village, following land opportunities in a supralocal property and information network.

Hopeful tenants often competed for consideration. Conflicting claims of an adult child and his or her stepparent, the surviving spouse, were especially common. For example, Bartlin Hailg of Weildorf died in 1624 leaving a vacant farm. His widow and son from a previous marriage both petitioned for the lease. The widow requested lifelong tenure and offered to pay an entry fine, pointing out that she had invested enormous capital in a newly built house. Her son would help her with the work. The other son, living in Neufrach, said he had the resources necessary to manage the farm. The abbey chose the widow, but offered the farm as an annual lease.[76] After Christa Hailg of Adelsreute died in 1585, a dispute ensued between his widow and children. The Audience told the parties to set a date to divide the estate (which did not include the farm), warning that the abbey was disinclined to throw the widow out. Seven years later, the children's guardians renewed their petition. The Audience responded that the widow had managed her household without any reason for complaint, and therefore the abbey would not dispossess her. Furthermore, they reminded the guardians, the farm belonged to the abbey. In the future, His Grace would lease the farm to whomever he wished.[77] When multiple parties showed interest, the abbey was able to choose the one believed to be the most capable, forcing petitioners to list their qualifications and jockey for the lord's favor. Moreover, the abbey could afford to offer inferior lease terms or elicit extra promises if there was more than one potential tenant.

The abbey was not always in a position to dictate the terms of tenure, however. The lord's interest in farm occupancy and rent collection sometimes gave villagers the opportunity to bargain. Indeed, if the economy were particularly bad, the lease terms too difficult, or the property in disrepair, no one petitioned for a vacant farm and it remained empty. Other times, tenants gave up farms for other opportunities. Georg

---

75 GLAK, 61/13374, 1630. He explained that his wife was old and hoped the abbey would take no offence.

76 GLAK, 61/13373.

77 The 1592 decision was as follows: "Beschaidt. Es habe die Witib bißhero ohn mangel und ohnclagbar Verwalten unnd gehauset, Allso dz Ire Gl. nit bedacht seien sie darvon zetreiben, derwegen sei Ihnen diß Ihr begehren Abgeschlagen und stannde Iren Gl. haim denselben uff künfftigen fahl zuverleihen wen sie wollen." GLAK, 61/13369.

Tumb of Owingen gave up his farm in 1583, explaining that a better situation had come along. In 1589 the abbey pressured Hans Hailg of Bermatingen to state whether he would accept the inn as a hereditary lease. He declined, citing the troubled times, but said he would be willing to manage the inn for two more years. Martin Stett asked for help rebuilding his collapsed roof in 1630. The abbey promised him some wood but denied his request for a loan. When Stett died later that year, the farm fell vacant and the house was uninhabitable. No local residents or kin were interested in the property. When Oswald Stengelin died in 1630, conditions were similar: the farm he vacated in Owingen was in serious disrepair with a burnt-down house. His son Georg secured the lease, along with building materials and a construction loan, but returned one week later to decline the offer, explaining that he could not afford the improvements.[78]

When the Audience asked tenant Jacob Jerg to declare within the week whether he wished to keep his lease according to the offered terms, signs of previous bargaining were obvious. Abbey officials stated that the entry fine could be reduced to 50 fl. and the wine rent to four Eimer, but as for Jerg's other complaints, the terms would remain the same.[79] In 1589 Hans Winter defaulted on his lifelong lease to a mill in Oberuhldingen. Hans Leub of Nußdorf, Winter's brother-in-law, immediately petitioned for the mill as a hereditary lease. When the abbey declined, Leub requested a lease for three lifetimes. Still, Salem refused. Leub told the abbey he was only interested in the mill as a long-term tenure, demanding the same terms as his predecessor. Finally the abbey agreed, subject to one condition: Leub had to assume the previous miller's considerable cash and grain debts.[80] The above examples demonstrate that the abbey's leverage was strong, especially with the rising land hunger after 1600. Yet even as it refused to grant hereditary tenure, the abbey generally acknowledged the claims of kin. This gave peasant subjects significant influence over tenure decisions.

The Shift to Lifelong Leases

Lifelong leases were relatively uncommon in Salem's lands during the sixteenth century.[81] In the 1603 tax assessment, 66 out of 96 properties including most of the large farms in 13 villages were still described as annual leases; only six were lifelong leases. Yet one by one in the following years, peaking around 1613, many farms switched

---

78 When his brother (Amtmann Martin Stengelin) petitioned for the farm, the Audience members seemed relieved if not overjoyed, volunteering to pay for a new roof along with the loan and building materials they had already promised. Examples in this paragraph are from GLAK, 61/13369–13374, 1583, 1589, 1630, 1630.

79 GLAK, 61/13369, 1604.

80 Ibid., 1589. Leub could try to collect payment from Winter if he chose. Hans Winter's son of the same name later acquired the mill and briefly served as Amtmann. The Winters also held mills in Neufrach and Urnau.

81 For the entire century there are only 16 known lifelong lease contracts, most of them for mills.

from annual to lifelong leases, so that between 1603 and 1620 at least 44 lifelong lease contracts were sealed.[82] The shift from annual to lifelong leases was the result of deals struck between the abbey and individual tenants, with the initiative in most case coming from below. This section examines how and why this occurred.

The shift in lease terms after 1600 is demonstrated by individual tenure contracts (*Lehensbriefe*) and property descriptions (*Renovationen*).[83] For example, a 1608 description of Moritz Bronner's farm in Gebhardsweiler explicitly stated that he held the farm as an annual lease (*Schupflehen*). On the last page of the document, the list of rents and dues was entirely crossed out with a note below, stating Bronner's request for a lease of two lifetimes. One year later, Bronner and the abbey entered a new, lifelong lease contract. The description of parcels was exactly the same as before, but the cash rent more than tripled in addition to new poultry and wine rents.[84] A tenure contract for Veit Langenstain of Buggensegel specified annual lease terms in 1603, but sections were modified in a second hand, probably around 1610. The phrase *järlich ledig* was crossed out, with Veit's name replaced by Georg Langenstain and wife Margaretha Schreiberin. A note at the bottom amended the rent. The crop share remained the same, but poultry dues of six chickens were added on top of six pounds cash, up from two and a half.[85] Michel Stett of Tepfenhard entered a lease of two lifetimes in 1605, on the farm his mother held previously as an annual lease. The farm description gave both the old and new rent. As in the previous examples, the rent rose significantly, and the entry fine was an additional one hundred gulden.[86] The new leases were clearly accompanied by higher rents, with the greatest increases in cash and poultry.[87] Salem took advantage of the demand for lifelong leases to raise rents, which tenants were in a position to pay because

---

82 The repetition of dates is noteworthy: Adelsreute 1603, 1612; Bermatingen 1613, 1613, 1615; Buggensegel 1610, 1612, 1613, 1613, 1618, 1618; Gebhardsweiler 1604, 1609; Grasbeuren 1613; Mimmenhausen 1617; Neufrach 1603, 1607, 1609, 1610, 1612, 1612, 1612, 1613, 1613, 1613, 1618; Oberuhldingen 1613; Owingen 1608, 1615, 1617; Tepfenhard 1609, 1609, 1609, 1609, 1609, 1613, 1613; Urnau 1612, 1615; Weildorf 1612, 1613, 1618, 1619; Weiler 1605. Tenure contracts may be found in GLAK, Section 4, by village.

83 The title *Renovation* is itself an indication of the change in property relations.

84 Whereas the 1608 description specified the rent as 19 shillings (house and hay rent), 60 eggs, 4 cartloads of manure, and one-quarter of the grain, the 1609 contract specified the rent as 3 pounds cash, 6 chickens, 60 eggs, 3 Eimer of wine, 4 cartloads of manure, and one-quarter of the grain. GLAK, 4/2637, 4/2622.

85 GLAK, 4/2153.

86 The grain rent, a set amount rather than a share of the crop, went from 7 to 12 Schoffel for spelt and from 4 to 9 Schoffel for oats. The cash rent went from 16 ß 2 dn. to 5 lb. dn. The farm now owed 5 hens and 120 eggs, whereas none were previously given. GLAK, 4/5616.

87 The increase in cash (house and hay) rents was exorbitant in many cases. Mattheus Heß paid 1 lb. 9 ß dn. in 1603 but 8 lb. dn. for the same farm in 1612, now a lifelong lease. Even the smallholdings paid a much higher rent than before. When Hans Hilbin of Neufrach received a Gut with 10½ acres as a lifelong lease in 1611, his cash rent (8 lb. dn.) and manure tax (6 cartloads) were higher than what most large farms paid at the time. GLAK, 4/4321.

they, too, were profiting handsomely from grain sales.[88] With the high rate of default and mortality in the early seventeenth century, entry fines provided the abbey with a major new source of income.

Audience petitions from the early seventeenth century demonstrate that the switch from annual to lifelong leases came in many cases as the direct result of a tenant's request. In 1605 Jos Vogler asked for the mill in Owingen as a lease for three lifetimes. The Audience agreed, noting he would owe an entry fine and higher rent. In 1619 Jacob Ehinger asked the Audience to change his annual lease to a lease for three lifetimes, pointing out that he had spent 600 fl. on property improvements. The abbey granted two lifetimes as a compromise, waiving the entry fine in consideration of his efforts. In 1624 Jacob Weißenkönig petitioned to convert his annual lease in Neufrach to a lease for two lifetimes. His request was denied, probably because his wife was a foreign serf from Württemberg.[89] These requests, brought by tenants in the early seventeenth century, demonstrate their desire for longer leases, even if it meant paying higher rent. The abbey's refusal to grant some requests provides further evidence that it was peasants who initiated the change in terms.

The timing of these tenure conversions is noteworthy, since they came a century or so after similar changes in neighboring territories and under very different circumstances. What we know about general conditions in the early seventeenth century suggests some possible explanations. Motivating factors for tenants probably included local population pressure, social stratification, and tightening resources. The number of people in the village may not have been rising but the villages were busting at the seams. The lack of space to support new households, the visibility of the poor, and the high price of grain made secure farm tenures all the more desirable. With the successive harvest failures and recurrent plague epidemics, the situation certainly felt unpredictable. Just as tenants were attempting to attain longer leases, new limits were being placed on marriage and household formation, primarily to restrict new residents. In the exact same years as the switch to lifelong leases, marriage contracts specifying the right of a surviving spouse to remain on the farm for life were becoming popular and widows frequently petitioned the Audience, as already mentioned, for permission to take over their former husbands' annual tenures. There was also a spike in arable land prices around 1613, and both arable and house prices remained high in 1620.[90] In a period of uncertainty and scarce resources, these factors provide the context for tenants' drive to create a feeling of greater security, gain control over the land, and make

---

88 Tenants' willingness and ability to pay a much higher cash rent and entry fines in exchange for greater security of tenure demonstrates the profitability of grain in this period. Notably, the abbey did not demand higher grain rents from farm tenants who already owed one-third to one-half of the crop.

89 Hans Schaitteckh's request for a lifelong lease in 1624 was similarly denied. Examples are from GLAK, 61/13369 and 61/13373.

90 See Chart 4.15 below.

sure their farms remained among kin rather than falling to outsiders. It is noteworthy that they were willing to pay more, in some cases much more, to obtain greater security of tenure. The established families briefly strengthened their hold on village property, only to lose it again during the Thirty Years War.

To conclude, the transmission of farms to kin was not a right but a privilege. By granting favors selectively, the Audience reminded tenants that their position depended on the abbot's grace. By refusing petitions implying hereditary rights and granting most farms on a short-term basis, the abbey maintained greater control over its land and tenants. The choice of a new tenant was not completely one-sided, however: villagers influenced the decision in various ways. Outgoing tenants tried to help their kin by giving up the farm when an heir was in a good position to manage it, or by making future provisions for their widows. Hopeful candidates emphasized their strengths and qualifications. The abbot or Audience made the final decision, though based on information circulating in the community about who would be the best tenant. The shift from annual to lifelong leases on many individual farms and in several villages after 1600 was an important form of negotiation between abbey and tenants that transcends issues of land tenure. It may be interpreted as an adaptation to new socioeconomic conditions on the eve of the Thirty Years War. Despite some drawbacks as well as benefits for both sides, Salem and its tenants each supported the shift to lifelong leases. Tenants must not have been happy to pay higher rents, especially when the cash obligation rose fourfold in many cases on top of entry fines. Still, it was usually the tenant who initiated the change.

Tenants are easier to track than other villagers because they were wealthier on average and had control of the most important farms. This gave the abbey greater incentive to record their activities. They are worth emphasizing, too, because tenants were among the local elites with social and political leadership positions corresponding to their landholdings. Yet we want to know something about the others, those without the largest properties and the most influence. Though information is comparatively thin, let us turn to some other segments of the population: widows, craftsmen, and winegrowers.

4.3 Widows and Female Householders

Not all household heads were men. Widows and unmarried women feature prominently among householders in each of the tax registers. They are worth examining more closely as a group not only because they offer a rare look at the intersection between socioeconomic status and gender but also because widows shared certain social characteristics that set them and their interests apart from other individuals, householders, family members, and economic groups. Widows appear in many of this chapter's later sections, but here we will consider their wealth and status as householders.

In the 1578 tax register there were one hundred households headed by single or widowed women, a little over twelve percent of all households in the territory. Among female householders without husbands, 65 are called widows. Although age and marital status are not mentioned for the others, 18 out of 35 women not designated as widows had children and all appear to have been adults.[91] Almost half of female householders had no property listed and were among the poorest households. Among the 52 with some property, however, several were quite wealthy. In fact, Lucia Neuffrin of Owingen headed the wealthiest household in the entire territory in 1578 with 5,020 fl. in all property, including the freehold mill.[92]

Widows were on average much wealthier than other female householders. Among 39 propertied widows, wealth averaged 724 fl. Including the unpropertied, widows' average wealth was 434 fl., still higher than the territorial average. Among the other 35 women who headed households in 1578, average wealth was much lower, suggesting that the two groups were in fact distinct social categories. Among the 13 propertied women who were not widows, average wealth was 317 fl. Including 22 single women without property, average wealth was only 118 fl. Besides the miller in Owingen, eight women (all widows) held large farms or hereditary smallholdings in Boshasel, Buggensegel, Hederstenweiler, Neufrach, Weildorf, Weiler, and Wendlingen. Since six of these farms were annual leases, the abbey must have viewed at least some widows as acceptable tenants. Among all female household heads in 1578, average wealth was 324 fl., somewhat lower than the territorial average of 391 fl.

In the 1593 and 1603 tax lists, female householders made up a similar proportion of all households but with lower average wealth than in 1578. There were 117 women including 97 widows and 20 others listed in 1593, comprising 13.5 percent of all territorial householders.[93] Average wealth among all female household heads in 1593 was only 163.8 fl., about half that of 1578. Not only were half of female householders unpropertied in 1593, few were very rich.[94] Widows were still wealthier than nonwidows,

---

91 The 1593 and 1603 tax lists designate many single male and female householders as unmarried (*noch ledig stands*), but this term does not appear in 1578. In some cases it is difficult to distinguish widows and unmarried adults from orphans and children.

92 Other wealthy widows were Anna Villieberin of Nußdorf (2,551 fl.), Margaretha Mattheißin of Neufrach (1,708 fl.), Barbara Wagnerin of Weildorf (1,544 fl.), Appolonia Schaitteckhin of Neufrach (1,540 fl.), and Madalena Rockhin of Boshasel (1,002 fl.).

93 The twenty women not called widows include seven with children, two wives (without husbands listed), two pensioners, and nine designated as "still single" (*noch ledig*).

94 There were 57 women with property worth less than 25 fl. The wealthiest widows in 1593 were Katharina Renawerin of Adelsreute (1,407 fl.), Madalena Hauserin of Owingen (1,255 fl.), Elisabetha Lentzin of Mimmenhausen (1,251 fl.), and Barbara Storchin of Seefelden (1,114 fl.). No other women had over 1,000 fl.

but they were less distinctive as a powerful economic category than in 1578.[95] Seven women (all widows) held farm tenures, yet none of them were exceptionally wealthy.[96]

In 1603 there were 106 female household heads, including 51 widows and 55 other women, comprising 12.4 percent of all territorial households. As an entire group their average wealth was 257.1 fl., about midway between the averages of 1578 and 1593. In other respects, however, the distribution of women and their wealth in 1603 was quite similar to 1578. Over half of all widows (59 percent) had property, averaging 622.7 fl. in value, whereas the average among all widows was 336.3 fl. Among 55 other women, including three pairs of sisters and 13 who were designated "still single," half had some property with an average value of 306.2 fl.; the average for all nonwidows was 155.9 fl. Another commonality is that a woman again headed the wealthiest territorial household in 1603: Margaretha Dilgerin of Bermatingen had 7,345 fl., including two farms and additional freehold property worth 5,500 fl. Several other women, both widows and nonwidows, were very rich householders, though only one was a farm tenant.[97]

According to the tax lists we find that female householders were poorer than men on average, but not by far. A higher percentage of widows and single women were destitute than married couples, but there were also some who controlled significant property including mills, farms, freehold, credit, and other moveables. The widows in 1578 and 1603 were significantly wealthier as a group than other single women, and it is noteworthy that widows in both years headed the wealthiest household in the entire territory. The finding that women headed over twelve percent of households in each tax register as well as a number of major farms confirms their importance as a socio-economic category. Their ability to run households and to hold significant property without husbands may be interpreted as a sign of relative independence, something women were rarely afforded in this period. Yet female householders were by no means free from the influence of men and other relatives, especially since so many of them were either very rich or very poor. On both ends of the spectrum, their economic situation was precarious and their status could be contentious, so that relationships with kin and neighbors as well as guardians and officials were crucially important. We will return later to the economic roles of women and especially widows with respect to land sales, moneylending, and inheritance.

---

95 Average wealth was 367.2 fl. among propertied widows and 179.5 fl. among all widows, compared with 128.7 fl. for unmarried women with property and 87.3 fl. for all who were not widows.

96 Widows held annual tenures on major farms in Adelsreute, Hederstenweiler, Tepfenhard, and Weildorf as well as hereditary tenures in Mimmenhausen and Seefelden. Widows also held two properties in Urnau, one of them a lifelong lease and the other, belonging to the local parish, of unspecified type.

97 Those with property worth over 1,000 fl. were Hans Mayer's widow in Bermatingen (3,260 fl.), Appolonia Nabhölzin in Bermatingen (1,910 fl.), Hans Müller's widow in Mimmenhausen (1,132 fl.), and Margaretha Pfannenstilin in Neufrach (1,115 fl.). Katharina Detschlerin of Tepfenhard (894 fl.) held a large farm as an annual lease.

4.4 Crafts, Trades, and Viticulture

Craftsmen—along with other trades such as millers, innkeepers, butchers, and barbers—formed an occupational group that was for the most part distinct from the farm tenants. Occupational information is not noted in tax and rent registers, with the exception of milling and occasionally innkeeping, and most craftsmen are difficult to identify or track over time. Some of the best sources for their names are the Audience and chancery protocols, where they appear as petitioners or contracting parties. Chart 4.13 lists the villages where crafts and trades were practiced in the period 1575–1635.[98] In addition to village craftsmen, Salem employed its own masters in many of the same professions: bakers, blacksmiths, cabinetmakers, carpenters, cooks, coopers, millers, saddlers, tailors, and wagonwrights. The variety of crafts and number of known craftsmen in the territory suggest a high demand for specialized goods from both villagers and the abbey, with that demand satisfied in large part by local craftsmen.[99] The scarcity of references to occupations in textile production (with the occasional exception of weavers) and other protoindustrial employments is conspicuous. Unlike much of Upper Swabia, Salem's territory never became a center of textile production.[100]

The tax lists provide information about wealth and household structure for a number of craftsmen, some of them over extended periods. The number of villagers by occupation is too small for statistical analysis but the data suggest a range in wealth, even within a single profession. Among coopers, for example, Conrad Haimpel of Weiler (1605–1608) had property worth 120 fl. in 1603 and Hans Storch of Oberuhldingen (1587–1610) had 135 fl. according to the same list. Michel Zürckh of Mimmenhausen (1591–1600) had 440 fl. in 1593 with a wife, child, and one servant; Peter Seissing of Neufrach (1590–1615) had 478 fl. in 1593 including 385 fl. in freehold property, a wife, five kids, and one servant. By 1603 he had seven children and 366 fl. Finally, the master cooper Wilhelm Pfannenstil of Leutkirch (1573–1590) was extremely wealthy. In 1578 he had 1,906 fl. in property including a hereditary lease, 950 fl. in freehold property, and 70 fl. in wine. In 1593 his wealth had increased to 2,600 fl. including 2,000 fl. in freehold land. In both lists he had a wife, three children, and two servants. By 1595

98 The known craftsmen in this period, probably only a fraction of those practicing in Salem's villages, include 56 millers, 39 innkeepers, 26 blacksmiths, 19 coopers, 19 bathhouse managers and barbers, 14 shoemakers, 12 cabinetmakers, 12 carpenters, 11 bakers, 10 tailors, 10 saddlers, 9 butchers, 8 wagonwrights, 6 potters, 5 cooks, 5 weavers, 4 locksmiths, 4 stonemasons, 3 brickmakers, 2 midwives, and 2 tanners. These include masters employed by the abbey.

99 Craft production in Überlingen was primarily for local consumption. Specialization there was low relative to other imperial cities, and many of Überlingen's guilds were related to agriculture, especially viticulture and garden production. See EITEL, Überlingen, p. 19.

100 Wine production largely explains the lack of protoindustry and textile work in the region, in contrast to neighboring areas to the south and east. See EITEL, Überlingen, p. 13; SCOTT, Economic Landscapes, p. 14.

Chart 4.13: Craftsmen in Select Villages

Occupation	Neufrach	Mimmen-hausen	Berma-tingen	Owingen	Weildorf	Oberuhl-dingen	Nußdorf	Tüfingen	Buggen-segel	Gras-beuren
Innkeepers	●	●	●	●	●	●	●	●	●	●
Blacksmiths	●		●	●	●	●		●		●
Coopers	●	●	●	●		●	●			
Millers	●	●	●	●	●	●			●	
Carpenters	●		●				●	●	●	
Bathhouse/ Barbers	●	●	●				●	●		
Cabinetmakers	●	●	●	●		●				
Shoemakers	●	●	●	●		●				
Tailors	●	●	●		●					
Bakers	●	●	●	●						
Butchers	●	●	●		●					
Saddlers	●	●		●	●					
Wagonwrights	●			●		●				●
Weavers	●	●			●					
Brickmakers	●				●					
Locksmiths	●					●				
Potters		●			●					
Tanners		●		●						
Midwives		●								

he was retired, but in 1603 he was still listed with 1,200 fl. and no farm. This range in wealth was similar in other professions. Among blacksmiths, for example, wealth ranged from 84 to 2,416 fl.[101]

Craftsmen were primarily involved in nonagricultural labor. They supported the needs of their local communities and depended on them in turn for their livelihoods, which meant they were heavily involved in market exchange. With their energies focused in the workshop rather than the fields, the organization and division of labor in these households was obviously different than for many villagers.[102] There is some evidence of intermarriage among craftsman households, and those offering specialized skills had a greater opportunity to marry into and become new residents of villages where there was a high demand for their services.[103] Apprentices from outlying villages, such as the smith's assistant Galle Kramer, made an effort to move closer to the abbey; in 1594 he received permission to reside in Mimmenhausen "as long as he behaved himself."[104]

Mills were extremely important to local economic infrastructure and could be found in most villages.[105] Millers were often quite wealthy, one of the reasons they turn up so frequently in the sources, though some were poor and others were heavily indebted. Among twenty millers identified in tax lists, wealth ranged from 150 to 5,020 fl.[106]

---

101 Georg Zembroth of Neufrach (1593–1614) took over the smithy from his father-in-law Georg Bart around 1593, when he was listed with 84 fl. in all property and a wife, two children, and one servant. By 1603 he had seven children and 215 fl. Steffan Muettinger of Oberuhldingen (1588–1600) had 457 fl. in 1578 with a wife and two kids; by 1593 his wealth had increased to 2,416 fl. though he had no farm or servants. Around 1600 he became the Amtmann and passed the smithy to his son Jorg; Steffan was also a Sidelrichter since 1589.

102 Hans Medick's discussion of protoindustrial household structure and labor can also be applied to artisans; idem, Proto-Industrial Family, pp. 304, 309.

103 Both above-mentioned smiths came from outside the village and married the previous smith's daughter. The cabinetmaker's assistant in Owingen, Hans Bregenzer from the Swiss lands, married his master's widow in 1630 with the abbey's approval. In Mimmenhausen, the bathhouse manager's stepdaughter received permission in 1583 to marry a barber from outside the territory. Many craftsmen were granted residency, even in years such as 1624 when most outsiders were denied entry. When the baker Jacob Spett from Hofen was approved as a new resident of Bermatingen in 1630, the need for a baker was specifically mentioned. On the other hand, outsiders hoping to practice their craft in Salem's villages were rejected if they would compete with another resident's established business. See Chapter 6.

104 GLAK, 61/13369, 1594.

105 There were grain mills in Bermatingen, Buggensegel, Mimmenhausen, Mühlhofen, Neufrach, Oberuhldingen, Owingen, Tepfenhard, Urnau, and Weildorf. Sawmills were also mentioned in conjunction with the grain mill in Mimmenhausen (1604), Oberuhldingen (1595), Owingen (1606), and Urnau (1605). Petitions for building materials suggest that many sawmills resulted from the initiative of millers in this period.

106 Examples of the wealthiest millers include Lucia Neuffrin of Owingen with 5,020 fl. in 1578, her son Jos Vogler with 3,855 fl. in 1603, Georg Rogg of Buggensegel with 2,818 fl. in 1603, Hans Mussel of Weildorf with 2,266 fl. in 1593, and Bernhard Baumann of Oberuhldingen

Lease terms for mills varied from place to place and even from one tenant to the next, but many were held as lifelong tenures and rarely, in contrast to the abbey's large farms, was a mill subject to annual lease.[107] The expenses associated with operating the mill, repairing equipment, and investing in improvements made it unlikely that any tenant would be willing to accept a mill on such inferior terms. As it was, millers frequently petitioned for wood and building materials and new tenants often complained about the state of decline or accepted responsibility for improvements as a condition of their lease contracts.[108] Hans Leub of Oberuhldingen and Pelagius Lehen of Mimmenhausen each bargained for an increase in the length of their leases from two to three lifetimes.

Not all mills included land parcels. In the 1578 tax list the mills in Neufrach and Bermatingen had no arable, which helps explain why these millers were poorer than many others. Because mills required much greater capital investment and maintenance than a farm, millers without skill, wealth, and luck were susceptible to failure. The Hartmanns in Weildorf are a good example. Father Michael held the mill in 1578 along with a large farm (with 63 Jauchert in two fields), both hereditary leases. His gross wealth was 1,753 fl. but his net wealth was only 724 fl., he had few animals and no freehold property. His son Andreas Hartmann was the miller in 1603 with a total of only 331 fl. in property value, and he almost lost the mill in a default settlement before the abbey agreed to his plea in 1613 for a new lease contract. Several other millers were in serious debt, including Lorenz Buechmüller of Urnau whose gross wealth was 445 fl. and net wealth only 148 fl. Georg Rogg (or Rockh) of Buggensegel similarly had 554 fl. gross and only 100 fl. net in 1578 (though his situation later improved). In 1589 the formerly wealthy Hans Winter went bankrupt and was evicted from the mill in Oberuhldingen. The miller Pelagius Lehen of Mimmenhausen, finally ready to enjoy retirement, petitioned several times in 1611 to secure succession for his son. Only a

---

with 2,205 fl. in 1603. Among the poorest were Bartholome Abler of Neufrach with 150 fl. in 1593, Mattheus Weissenrieter of Bermatingen with 295 fl. in 1603, and Mattheus Müller of Mühlhofen with 316 fl. in 1578.

[107] According to the 1578 tax list, two mills were freeholdings—the Owingen mill worth 1,200 fl. and the Buggensegel mill worth 445 fl. Mills in Mimmenhausen, Neufrach, Oberuhldingen, and Urnau were subject to lifelong leases and those in Bermatingen and Weildorf to hereditary lease. None were annual leases in 1578.

[108] The new miller in Mimmenhausen asked for help rebuilding the waterworks in 1592, and in 1613 wood was again required to improve this mill. Also in Mimmenhausen a new miller in 1604 was required to build a house as part of his tenure agreement; the miller in Oberuhldingen agreed to similar terms in 1594, yet eight years later he was replaced and charged sixty gulden for the decline of buildings during his tenure. The new miller in Neufrach received wood in 1606. In Oberuhldingen, wood was granted for a variety of building projects. Jacob Menner's widow petitioned the Audience in 1633 for permission to keep the mill in Mimmenhausen, citing the fact that she had invested 1,500 fl. in repairing the waterworks. Her request was approved, "*uff Ihr wolverhalten*." The Owingen commune requested repairs to the village sawmill in 1636 because they were unable to obtain lumber or rebuild their houses without it. These examples are from GLAK, 61/13369–13374.

few months after the transfer, the son died. Pelagius lost the mill and his retirement as a result, even though he had recently built a new house and sawmill and provided his son with a marriage portion and entry fines.

Several families controlled mills for more than one generation.[109] Millers also tended to marry one another.[110] When Hans Winter defaulted in 1589, his wife's brother took his place. Cecilia Bronnerin, who married two millers and survived them both, operated a mill in Oberuhldingen together with her son until he was ready to manage it himself. Kinship linked millers to one another much more than to office-holders and other local elites. A vacant mill was more likely to pass to a widow or outsider with some experience than to another villager with no technical training or skill.[111]

Innkeepers were central figures in the local communities and in supralocal personal networks, in part because the village inn was the social meeting place where people relaxed, sat with friends, discussed news and gossip, conducted business, verbally abused, and sometimes physically assaulted one another. Innkeepers were familiar with everyone in the village and their relationships, words, and deeds. A search for their names in the Audience and court records leaves the impression that male and female innkeepers alike were heavily involved in local affairs and personal disputes with their neighbors.[112] Travelers brought information that made innkeepers a source of news and broadened their connections throughout the region.

Innkeepers were also central figures in the village because of their wealth. Among 15 innkeepers found in tax lists, nine had over 1,000 fl. and they were wealthier on average than either millers or farm tenants.[113] Some innkeepers held tenure on farms with

---

109 Milling families including the Buechmüllers in Bermatingen, Buggensegel, and Urnau, the Winters in Oberuhldingen, Neufrach, and Urnau, the Stetts in Tepfenhard, the Roggs in Buggensegel, the Trautmanns in Mimmenhausen, and the Hartmanns in Weildorf and Oberuhldingen. Many passed from father to son.

110 In 1606 Bartholome Abler's widow in Neufrach married the miller's assistant, Hans Winter, who was the cousin of another miller in Oberuhldingen. The miller's daughter in Oberuhldingen also married a miller's assistant who came from outside the territory. Christa Buechmüller, the miller in Urnau, married Waldpurga Rockhin while Martin Krueg, the miller in Neufrach, married Katharina Voglerin; both women were millers' daughters from nearby villages.

111 Millers from outside the territory included Bartholome Abler from Bregenz, Hans Winter from Constance, and Pelagius Lehen, who paid to become a territorial resident in 1595.

112 Nella, the innkeeper's wife in Mimmenhausen, was punished in 1595 for stirring up trouble between two spouses. Bermatingen's innkeeper sued on his wife's behalf for slander in 1611, for it was said she did not use correct measurements. There were several accusations reported between the innkeeper and miller of Oberuhldingen, and between the innkeeper and Amtmann in Neufrach. Innkeepers frequently offered legal testimony for incidents they had witnessed or statements they had heard.

113 Hans Hailg of Bermatingen (1589–1592) was the wealthiest householder in the entire territory with 6,724 fl. in 1593; other wealthy innkeepers included Hans Leub of Neufrach (1593–1604) with 3,003 fl. in 1593 and 4,474 in 1603, Hans Vogler of Owingen (ca. 1600–1605) with 2,906 fl. in 1603, Simon Mußel of Mimmenhausen (1581–1590) with 1,535 fl. in 1578 and 2,993 fl. in

large acreage, either attached to or separate from the inn. Nußdorf's inn had no land, and innkeepers there complained repeatedly about the high rents and fees. The poorest innkeeper in the sample was Hans Scheck from Nußdorf, with 295 fl. in 1603.[114]

There was a tendency for inns to stay within the family, but not to the extent seen for mills. Jacob and Georg Knecht both held the inn in Bermatingen, Jerg and Veit Resstlin held the inn in Mimmenhausen, Hans Jerg, Christoph, and Hans Rauch held the inns in Weildorf and Oberuhldingen, and Simon and Lorenz Mußel of Mimmenhausen both served as Salem's guestmaster. Compared with millers, innkeepers tended to be more closely related to the farm tenants and political elites. Innkeepers and their wives included members of several leading families: the Claußmars, Dulenkopfs, Hailgs, Leubs, Schaitteckhs, Senffts, and Villiebers.

Winegrowers

Wine production was a major activity and source of income in Salem's territory, and innkeepers were not the only ones who sold wine.[115] Vineyards were extensive in most villages, especially along the lake and on south-facing slopes. Approximately one-quarter of the productive land in Bermatingen was devoted to grapes.[116] Some vineyards were leased from Salem, the village commune, or other landlords, while others were peasant freehold. Numerous sales contracts and probate inventories suggest that freehold vineyards were prevalent and that they were owned or leased by households be-

---

1593, and Jacob Knecht of Bermatingen (1599–1608) with 1,527 fl. in 1603. The least wealthy were Hans Scheck of Nußdorf (ca. 1600) with 295 fl. in 1603 (down from 493 in 1593), Simon Scharpfer of Tüfingen (1595) with 562 fl. in 1593, and Hans Schnabel of Oberuhldingen (1595–1618) with 736 fl. in 1603.

114 Nußdorf's innkeeper Jerg Ulmer complained in 1606 that business was slow, he had paid a lot of money for the lease, and the rent was too high. The Audience told him the abbey could rent the inn to someone else if he no longer wanted it. In 1619 the innkeeper Jerg Holl complained similarly: "Weyl er nunmehr vollig 14 Jahr die wirtshafft besessen, alles uf sein khosten erhalten miessen unnd vom Gotshaus weder wisen noch Äckher wie andere deß Gotshaus wurt, niehmahlen zuenuzen gehapt, auch vor der Zeit in dz GroßkellerAmpt Järlich allain 2 lb. 10 ß dn. Tafern gelt geraicht unnd geben worden, an Jezo aber dz gewohnliche Umbgelt erstaten muesse." GLAK, 61/13369 and 61/13371.

115 Territorial statute allowed individuals to sell up to one Fuder of wine they had produced. Others sold wine by permit: Michael Claußmar of Grasbeuren paid 20 fl. in 1624 for the right to sell wine for one year. In 1605 the farmers of Tüfingen asked for a reduction of fines resulting from illegal wine sales, citing the fact that the inn was vacant. GLAK, 61/13373, 1624; 61/13369, 1605.

116 KUHN, Seehaufen, p. 111. Kuhn also discusses winegrowing in his earlier articles on Bermatingen and Owingen, pointing out that viticulture was the reason why there were so many smallholders in Salem's villages in proportion to the tenant farmers. Kuhn also suggests a connection between bad wine years, discontent among poor vineyard workers, and their participation in the German Peasants' War.

longing to various economic strata, not just the wealthy. A variety of sources indicate the extent of wine production in Salem's villages. A register of winegrowers from 1614 lists a total of 154 sharecroppers who held vineyards from the abbey. A similar register lists the vineyard tenants in 1625.[117] Another document from 1657 describes the abbey's vineyard parcels under production before the Thirty Years War in comparison with that year. Prior to the devastation, the number of parcels in select locations was listed as follows: Bermatingen 222, Buggensegel 42, Leutkirch 57, Mimmenhausen 66, Neufrach 93, Nußdorf 139.5, Oberuhldingen 41, Salem 151, Tüfingen 67, Weildorf 24, and Weiler 88.[118] An employment contract for Hans Strobel of Bermatingen, Salem's vineyard inspector in 1605, gives a comprehensive list of places where he visited the abbey's vineyards three times per year.[119]

Many of Salem's villages had their own communal vineyards as the result of land clearance projects after 1550, with parcels distributed among individual households. The conversion of forests, wastelands, hillsides, and other less productive areas to vineyards was in most cases the result of communal initiative, with permission granted by the abbey. Some vineyards were built on the commons, others on land belonging to the abbey. In one of the earliest agreements, a legal charter from 1561, the abbot agreed to let Mimmenhausen convert a hill of about ten acres to vineyards.[120] The parcels could be inherited or sold, but any that fell to outsiders had to be sold back to a member of the commune. Each parcel-holder owed the tithe to Salem but land rents, payable in wine, went to the commune along with any fines for offenses committed there. The agreement was produced in two copies, one for the abbot and one for the entire commune of Mimmenhausen along with its Amtmann, village treasurers, and council. The abbot entered a similar agreement with Buggensegel in 1567, granting permission to turn four acres of hillside arable into 25 vineyard parcels.[121]

The entire commune of Neufrach petitioned in 1596 to convert a section of its common forest into vineyards. At first there was no decision, but upon their repeated request in January 1597, the Audience finally agreed. [122] Abbey officials stipulated that for five or six years the land would owe the tithe only, but when the vines reached

---

117 Both lists are found in GLAK, 98/1671. Vineyard locations included Bermatingen, Leutkirch, Mimmenhausen, Neufrach, Nußdorf, Oberuhldingen, Weildorf, and Weiler among others.

118 GLAK, 66/11285.

119 The places were listed as: "Alhie zu Salem im Closter garten, Krauttgarten, Mümmenhausen, In den halden, Schnellenberg, Müchratt, unnd Bergkhouer newsatz, zu Neüfra, Im Weingarten, Tobel, unnd Newsatz, sampt Leükürch, Achhausen, Bremgarten, Oberuldingen, in den halden unnd Kalchbronen, Maurach, Nußdorff, Uberlingen, Sipplingen, Frückhingen, Bufflang unnd Weildorff, Bermatingen, uff Rothshalden, In Weilern, Raderach, Illmasee, Hagnaw, Imenstad, den Hoppen weiler gartten, Kürchberg, Kippenhausen, unnd Costantz." GLAK, 98/216.

120 GLAK, 4/3892. The Berghof, as the land was formerly known, had been used for grazing but was said to be of little value. The new vineyard was called the Newsatz.

121 GLAK, 4/2116.

122 This followed three unsuccessful petitions in 1591. GLAK, 61/13369.

maturity, land rents would be split equally between the abbey and the commune. Neufrach's Amtmann returned in May to ask the Audience how the commons should be divided, since there was some disagreement. The Audience gave its decision that everyone who lived in the commune and participated in communal work projects should receive an equal parcel.[123] An agreement from 2 June 1597 lists the names of all 99 parcel-holders.[124]

Similar requests to construct vineyards soon followed in Buggensegel (1601), Tüfingen (1602), and Weildorf (1603).[125] The Audience granted permission for Buggensegel to convert a hill called the Elsenberg into 28 vineyard parcels. Tüfingen's request, presented by the Amtmann and village treasurers, was likewise approved, but with the stipulation that like other villages, Tüfingen must now provide manure in exchange for firewood. Three weeks later the Audience gave permission to start clearing the land and warned village officials to be mindful that the new vineyard was on the abbey's land and not the commons. Once the grapes were established, the land rent would be half the harvest. Buggensegel petitioned to convert more land to vineyards in 1618, as did Nußdorf in 1619.

The timing of vineyard conversions appears as no coincidence. Vineyards not only turned marginal lands to more intensive uses and greater profits, they also employed greater man power: as much as eight times the labor required for arable, with work distributed throughout the year.[126] This meant vineyards could support a larger population and one that was different in socioeconomic structure from areas devoted to cereal agriculture, among other reasons because vineyard parcels were relatively small and affordable to modest households and because larger-scale viticulture depended so heavily on markets and on hired, seasonal labor.

4.5 Freehold Property

Freehold properties (*Aigengüter*) were privately owned lands that were freely transferable. They were widespread in Salem's territory and were important for several reasons to peasant households and the local economy. First, freehold property was one of the major sources of household wealth. Second, freehold property was not subject to a landlord's control and it therefore provided a degree of independence. One major advantage was that unlike annual tenures, freehold could be bought and sold without the lord's permission. Third, it could be divided among heirs, providing for children who did not acquire a farm. Whereas tenures were impartible and mostly nonhereditary,

---

123 GLAK, 98/4421.

124 GLAK, 4/4258.

125 These petitions and decisions are copied down together in GLAK, 98/4421. See also GLAK, 61/13369.

126 SCOTT, Society and Economy, p. 178.

freehold provided flexibility and gave parents the opportunity to transfer some land to each child, securing for them a place in the village. Fourth, and as a consequence of their divisibility, most freehold properties were small and therefore not beyond the reach of modest households. Fifth, freehold property was used as security for loans, and it was the most important basis of creditworthiness. This allowed smallholders as well as major tenants to borrow money.

Freehold property ownership was extensive in Salem's lands. As already indicated, there is a strong correlation between the value of tenants' freeholdings and their overall household wealth. According to tax lists, freehold land not only made up a significant proportion of tenant households' total wealth (32–40.8 percent), it was even a major percentage of territorial wealth overall (17.6–20.9 percent).[127] This does not account for the additional freehold property belonging to nontenants, which the tax registers do not itemize. Yet as records of property sales, debts, and probate inventories demonstrate, freehold was an important factor and source of wealth for a broad spectrum of households with and without tenures.[128]

Some freehold parcels in Salem's territory owed the tithe only, and a few paid nothing at all. For example: "From this property absolutely nothing is owed, as it is rent-free, unencumbered, unmortgaged, unencroached, legal freehold."[129] Yet small land rents or interest payments (*Bodenzins*) were fairly common. Some freehold properties were subject to land rents just like other leasehold property. In the chancery records describing land sales and mortgages, many contain notes similar to the following: "This parcel owes annual rent in the amount of three shillings plus the tithe and is otherwise free and unencumbered legal freehold." The payment of rent suggests that freehold in Salem's lands was not equivalent or comparable to rent-free peasant freehold in places like the Allgäu.[130] In some cases the dues associated with freehold may have derived from something other than rent, such as interest on a mortgage or payment for some

---

127 In 1578, 101 households had freehold property valued at 58,219 fl., and the total wealth of 823 territorial households was 331,260 fl. In 1593, 102 households had freehold property valued at 64,843 fl., compared with 330,514 fl. in total wealth among 869 households. In 1603, freehold property in 106 households was worth 69,554 fl., compared with 332,175 fl. in total wealth among 855 households. The number of households with itemized freehold as well as the property value for the entire territory are surprisingly consistent over time, while the value of freehold rose slightly.

128 There were on average twenty land sales per year listed in sampled chancery records (see below).

129 "Darab geth überal nichts, besonnder ist Zinßfrei ledig unversetzt unnd unverkümbert recht aigen." GLAK, 61/13317, 1588.

130 Blickle does not see rent-paying *Eigen* as true peasant freehold, and freeholdings in the Allgäu did not owe rents. Idem, Bäuerliches Eigen im Allgäu, in: Zeitschrift für Agrargeschichte und Agrarsoziologie 17 (1969), p. 57. According to Baier it is completely unfounded to claim that there was no peasant freehold in Salem, although they did pay rent. Idem, Bevölkerungsbewegung, pp. 77–78.

benefit, such as firewood.[131] Or perhaps the status of freehold land rights was deteriorating over time. Whatever rents or other encumbrances freehold property had to bear, however, it was in many respects preferable to leasehold.

The widespread ownership of peasant freehold in Salem's villages had great political as well as economic significance. It meant that peasant households were less reliant upon Salem and other lords for farm tenures. It also limited the population's accountability to laws and local customs established on the basis of landholding. Most importantly, the widespread ownership of freehold property made landlordship an imperfect tool for establishing and strengthening territorial rule. Looking again at the Allgäu, where peasant freehold made up around seventy percent of all land, Blickle has convincingly shown that landlordship could not provide the basis for territorial rule. As a result, the structures of domination there were totally different from other regions. The primary basis of territorial rule was lordship over serfs, which made the Allgäu's agrarian and political structures unusual if not unique.[132] In Salem, too, it appears quite possible that there was a connection between the abbey's claims over its serfs and the extensiveness of peasant freehold.[133] The weakness of landlordship as a unifying factor also underscores the importance of the Sidelgericht. Salem's central court provided a stronger basis for territorial unity than lordship rights over land or serfs.

Salem's territory Under the Hills was located in a fertile winegrowing region, and many freehold parcels were vineyards.[134] Freehold vineyards were the major source of wealth for many households, including some of the wealthiest. The probate inventories for Amtmann Christoph Langenstain and Sidelrichter Severinus Rueff, for example, each contain dozens of vineyard parcels.[135] Hans Hailg of Bermatingen headed the territory's wealthiest household in 1593 and he had no farm, but he did have freehold property valued at 4,600 fl. and an additional 700 fl. in wine. Most vineyards were not large, however. Smaller parcels sold for as little as 13 fl. in the 1590s and 18 fl. in the period 1612–1614.[136] For modest households with only a few strips of land, vineyards were especially valuable because of the intensive nature of cultivation and high market value. On the south-facing slopes north of Lake Constance, terraced vineyards were an obvious choice.

---

131 In 1584 the chancery protocol describes a mortgaged house as owing four shillings and four cartloads of manure to Salem in exchange for firewood, which was otherwise free (*sonst frei und aigen*).

132 BLICKLE, Bauer und Staat, p. 109.

133 Baier's comment (Bevölkerungsbewegung, p. 59) that no lord other than perhaps the prince-abbot of Kempten was more ruthless than Salem's abbot in driving his population into serfdom is especially interesting in the context of this comparison between Salem and the Allgäu.

134 In a sample of chancery records from 15 years, there were 76 vineyard sales for an average of five sales per year.

135 GLAK, 98/3204, 98/4402.

136 Chart 4.15 below provides the range of values from a sample of vineyard sales.

Freehold land was put to a variety of uses. There were arable parcels, meadows, houses, gardens, orchards, woodlands, workshops, mills, and so on. Even in households with significant freeholdings, properties were described as a collection of separate parcels, not consolidated farms. Their small size was most likely the result of subdivision down to the smallest possible strips. The availability and partibility of freehold property was an advantage for heirs who were not slated to inherit a large leasehold, allowing poorer householders to buy and sell small chunks of land. There were certainly households that assembled significant landholdings over the course of a lifetime. Yet freehold did not contribute to the consolidation of land within a lineage. The large number of small freehold parcels and the ease with which they could be transferred fueled an active land market. It also enabled even modest households to borrow money, because freehold land was the most acceptable form of surety for debt. In fact, records of land sales and debt provide good sources of information about freehold property, and it is to these subjects that we turn our attention next.

4.6 Land Sales and Debt

The chancery records, starting in 1582, provide evidence of a brisk market in land sales and credit circulating among Salem's territorial residents. This section looks at village land sales, followed by borrowing activity, as seen through the record of notarized contracts. Territorial residents used the chancery to notarize and seal documents of various sorts in exchange for a small fee, in addition to which the office kept its own records. This provided greater security for business transactions, and was especially useful in the case of later disagreements over repayment or other specific terms. The multivolume chancery registers, containing abbreviated versions of all documents drawn up by that office, are among the best sources of information about property transactions.[137]

The two topics, sales and debt, are linked by the source material but also, as it turns out, by other similarities. The monetarization of the economy fueled sales as well as credit, and the two types of transaction were often directly interrelated. In a sample of 15 years between 1584 and 1635, the number of recorded sales ranged from 1 to 49 with an average of 20 transactions per year. In the same years, credit notes ranged from 8 to 84 with an average of 35. In both cases the highest number of transactions came in 1613 and the lowest in 1634, with the trends mirroring one another over time, as shown in Chart 4.14. The topics of sales and debt are also linked by a common line of inquiry. More than the property itself, we would like to know about the individuals involved in the transactions—about their economic backgrounds, household status, and any relationships between them.

---

[137] GLAK, 61/13316–13320. Chancery records survive from the years 1582–1593, 1604–1622, and 1632–1666.

Chart 4.14: Sales and Debt in Chancery Records (select years)

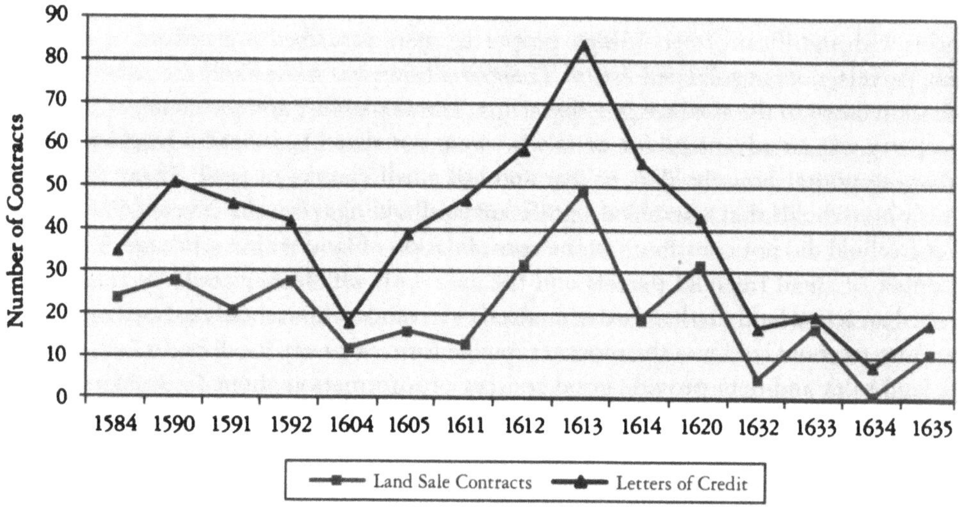

Most property sales involved small parcels of freehold property such as arable, vineyards, meadows, and forests. Sales of houses and half-houses, with gardens and orchards attached, were common. Larger collections of parcels and workshops sold less often and sales of hereditary farms, large or small, were rare.[138] On the one hand, land prices varied widely from one sale to the next. For example, houses sold in 1620 for 90 to 600 fl.; in 1612–1614, vineyards sold for 18 to 770 fl. On the other hand, average prices do not appear to have risen or fallen dramatically over time. See Chart 4.15. The great variation in prices within a single year suggests a wide range in values for similar types of properties—then as now, one house is not equivalent to another in size, location, and value.

By searching the tax lists for names of buyers and sellers, we can discover something about their wealth. In some cases, tax lists also provide information about household structure and relationships between buyers and sellers. In order to study the backgrounds of buyers and sellers including wealth, kinship, and place of residence, I collected the names of all buyers and sellers for three sample years: 1584, 1592, and 1605. I

---

[138] The largest and most expensive properties sold in sampled years include some vineyards worth 825 fl., six vineyards for 515 fl., a collection of 18½ individual parcels for 547 fl., a house with a small meadow for 600 fl., and six vineyards for 450 fl. In 1584 the widow Elisabeth Hermännin sold the smithy in Oberuhldingen to her son-in-law for 100 fl. In 1620 the commune of Neufrach sold its smithy to Thoma Mayer for 378 fl., reserving buy-back rights. Michel Duler, Neufrach's innkeeper, sold the local bathhouse to Michel Amman for 260 fl. in 1589. One farm in Weiler, a hereditary tenure from St. Johann's in Constance, sold several times.

Chart 4.15: Land Prices according to Chancery Sales (in fl.)

	1583–1589	1590–1592	1604–1605	1612–1614	1620	1632–1635
Houses, whole and half						
Sample size	19	14	10	13	6	9
Maximum	304	380	500	320	600	410
Minimum	86	68	107	100	90	100
Average	163	171	211	157	288	210
Median	142	139	158	128	183	150
Arable, one acre						
Sample Size	10	11	10	14	8	4
Maximum	79	66	81	120	130	80
Minimum	29	20	34	33	40	30
Average	46	36	62	80	86	60
Median	40	32	69	100	89	65
Vineyards, any size						
Sample Size	10	16	9	23	6	12
Maximum	825	695	745	770	330	450
Minimum	75	13	60	18	76	50
Average	201	173	183	188	158	181
Median	115	178	120	120	117	173

then compared the list of names from a total of 67 transactions against tax registers and serf lists from the surrounding years: 1578, 1593, 1603, and ca. 1600–1614.[139]

First, let us consider the 67 buyers. All came from within the territory and most were individuals; wealth information can be found for 55 buyers in corresponding tax lists.[140] Looking at buyers by wealth bracket, each group is well represented in the sample with the exception of the destitute, who bought no properties in the sample. The most active purchasers of land were the very rich and the middling householders (25.5% each), followed by the smallholders (20%), the prosperous (16.4%), and finally the poor (12.7%). It comes as no great surprise to find the wealthiest householders as

139 Since household wealth is a dynamic factor, the information from surrounding years must be considered approximate. I compared 1584 sales to the 1578 tax list, 1592 sales to the 1593 tax list, and 1605 sales to the 1603 tax list where available, also searching the other lists to assess changes over time. For a few names not found in the adjacent tax list, I estimated wealth using the next available list.

140 Buyers without available wealth information include five individuals, Salem Abbey (3), the Seefelden priest (2), Leutkirch churchwardens (1), and Mimmenhausen commune (1).

major land purchasers, but it is noteworthy that the middling households were involved in just as many sales, especially because this group made up the smallest proportion of the territorial population overall.[141] It suggests that this group was dynamic in economic terms and upwardly mobile. Sreenivasan's study of Ottobeuren confirms that there, too, middling families were prominent among land buyers.[142] For Salem, I suspect that the high number of purchases within lower and middling wealth brackets also reflects the availability of freehold property and the small size and price of individual freehold parcels.[143]

Going beyond wealth, occupational information is provided in several cases. Among the 67 buyers, nine were millers (including five purchases by the same person, Salem's master miller); there were also three priests, two smiths, a baker, butcher, chamber servant, cook, saddler, and stonemason. One buyer was an orphan (represented by guardians) and none were widows. At least nine individuals (13.4 percent) bought land on credit, borrowing from the seller or a third party.

Moving on to the sellers, 46 names appear in corresponding tax lists.[144] Prosperous householders made up the largest group (34.8%), followed by middling ones (23.9%), and then the smallholders and very rich (17.4% each). Only two poor and one destitute individual sold property (4.3% and 2.2% of sales respectively). Compared with buyers there were fewer known craftsmen (two carpenters and a baker) but many more widows (10) and orphans (8). There are several possible explanations for why widows and orphans sold so many properties. They may have inherited parcels they were unable to manage or farm by themselves, or they may have acquired a house larger than their needs.[145] In the case of widows, they may have had to sell off land in order to satisfy younger heirs.[146]

---

141 The middle wealth bracket was the smallest group of households in the territory, with 8.1% of the population in 1578 (compared with 12.2% very rich, 14.1% prosperous, 20.5% smallholders, 17.8% poor, and 27.3% destitute households).

142 SREENIVASAN, Ottobeuren, pp. 198–199, 202.

143 The properties in the sample include 36 small land parcels, 14 houses and half-houses, 13 vineyards, a smithy, a bakery, one collection of assorted parcels, and one hereditary farm.

144 Among 21 sellers not found in any list, three came from outside the territory and three were the priest in Leutkirch. There were also a large number of orphans and widows, some of whom could not be identified.

145 For example, in 1605 the guardians of orphan Michael Habnichts sold his house to a neighbor (no known relation) with a wife and two children for 180 fl. In 1584 the guardians of Mattheus Hermann sold his vineyard to the abbey for 260 fl.

146 In 1592 the widow Barbara Schmalzhafin of Mimmenhausen sold four small parcels, one to the kinsman of her deceased husband and the others to neighbors of no known relationship. The value of parcels ranged from 27½ to 46 fl. That same year another widow, Anna Reichartin of Neufrach, likewise sold four parcels, all to Salem's master miller Jacob Ruess (whose wife shared a surname with Reichartin's deceased husband). The parcels ranged in value from 20 to 52 fl. Both widows were propertied (with 350 fl. and 541 fl. respectively) and neither one had young children, whereas each of the buyers was married with children.

Whatever the reason in each particular case, the fact that widows and orphans collectively sold over one-quarter of properties in the sample and bought just one stands out as an important finding.

Out of 67 sales, 37 involved buyers and sellers from the same village. That over half of sales involved residents of the same village is not surprising. What demands explanation is the fact that 30 sales were supralocal, especially because Salem required that property be offered for sale first within the local community and only then to outsiders.[147] Despite these restrictions, some transactions involved property located in a village where neither the buyer nor the seller lived. In 1592, for example, Hans Claußmar of Grasbeuren sold Thoma Biller of Mendlishausen six vineyard parcels (*Hofstätte*) in Nußdorf for 695 fl. Yet it stands out that all buyers lived within the territory. Only three sellers, and no buyers, were territorial outsiders. It appears that limitations on sales to outsiders were selectively enforced to restrict unwanted residents, absentee landlords, and foreign property-holders. There were two distinct types of outsiders, those from beyond the local community and those from beyond the territory, and whereas sales to locals were preferred, territorial residents were an acceptable second choice. Clearly, the land market in Salem was supralocal but restricted to members of the territorial community. Villagers were aware of and involved in land sales throughout the surrounding area. Some individuals moved from one village to another, while others held property in a village where they did not reside. Land transactions and sales restrictions built a common territorial identity and strengthened territorial boundaries.

We would certainly like to know what relationships existed between buyers and sellers, both in the context of this study's larger themes and in comparison to other studies that have discovered a strong link between kinship and land sales.[148] Though we might expect to find that kinship played an important role in land sales within Salem's territory, such relationships are in fact difficult to establish because relevant details are usually lacking. Among the 67 sales, only four specified a kinship tie, and

---

147 Communal lands, especially vineyards and pastures, were subject to similar rules. Many Audience petitions mention the requirement that land be offered first for sale within the community, typically for one year. Only then, if there were no local buyers, could it be offered to outsiders. In one case, Salem effectively nullified an unpermitted sale to the Poor Claires of Pfullendorf by refusing to issue a sales contract. The Audience told the seller, Conrad Haimpolt of Weiler, that he should have first offered the vineyards for sale to community members for one full year. GLAK, 61/13369, 1591. The Audience rarely rejected requests for ratification of sale by sellers and buyers from different villages within Salem's central territory.

148 According to Govind Sreenivasan, land sales to a single heir replaced partible inheritance in Ottobeuren during the late sixteenth century, typifying major changes in property and social structure there. David Sabean argues that as land markets became more competitive, kinship became more rather than less important as a means of securing access to resources in Neckarhausen. SREENIVASAN, Ottobeuren, p. 157; SABEAN, Neckarhausen I, pp. 36–37, 365.

two others involved parties with a shared surname. A comparison of wives' names over the period 1578–1614 yields an additional eleven sales among affines, for a total of 17 sales. Though only one-quarter of sales can be identified as involving kin, we should not assume that the other parties were unrelated. It does appear that land sales occurred more frequently among in-laws than within the direct line, which makes sense if parents transferred property to their children through inheritance rather than sale.

The search for relationships between buyers and sellers turns up a number of interesting details beyond kinship ties. Some cases suggest the possibility of a social relationship, clientage, or affinity based on friendship. For example, the sale of a meadow in Mimmenhausen linked two households with similar structure and wealth. The seller, Bartlome Höltzlin, was married with six children and no servants and had 462 fl. in total wealth. The buyer, Hans Nickh, was married with three children, no servants, and 523 fl. Both households were well established in the village, listed consistently over the period 1578–1614. What is most interesting is that both families had a son living in Hungary. Perhaps this commonality created a bond between them. In two other examples, there is a possible link between buyer and seller on the basis of clerical profession. In one case the priest in Leutkirch, Bernhard Ill, sold property to Bartlome Kraus of Mimmenhausen, whose son was also a priest. In the other example Jerg Restlin, Salem's guestmaster from Killenberg, sold property to the abbey. In addition to his own professional link to the abbey, one of his sons was a monk and another later became the court bailiff for the Sidelgericht. These kinds of details may be small and sporadic but they do seem significant. They suggest that relationships were a factor behind economic transactions, that the land market was not completely blind to family, friendship, geography, and other personal factors, and that sales in turn could cement future relationships.[149]

To conclude, the data show that individuals from various wealth groups not only sold but also bought property. This is worth emphasizing because poorer householders might be expected to sell property under duress, in order to feed themselves or pay off debts. The fact that poorer householders bought as well as sold land demonstrates that not all were forced into the land market through financial weakness. Some were able to use the land market to achieve their goals and accumulate property, and modest householders were not excluded from participation. We might also expect to find wealthier householders taking advantage of the land market to buy up land at the expense of the poor, resulting in the increasing consolidation of property. Yet this was not the case, perhaps because the small size and modest price of freehold parcels meant that the wealthy had no particular financial advantage over others. In fact, it makes sense that

[149] As mentioned earlier, nine buyers in the sample purchased property on credit, which established a long-term economic bond between the buyer and the lender (usually the seller, another neighbor, or local charitable institution). Then as now, sales allowing the purchaser to put no money down and secure the loan using the newly acquired property allowed modest families to acquire property.

smallholders would be heavily engaged in transactions involving small land parcels. Craftsmen were well represented, especially among buyers, with a total of 16 out of 67 purchases.[150]

Credit and Debt

Debt was extremely common among peasant households in the decades around 1600. This topic raises a number of important issues, only a few of which can be considered here.[151] Using the same block of chancery records described above, with data collected from a sample of three years, this section concentrates above all on the relationships mediated by credit, the possibilities for borrowing money, and the ways debt could function as an economic strategy as well as an economic burden for individual households. The credit notes (*Schuldbriefe, Zinsbriefe*) recorded by the chancery provide the names of both parties, the amount borrowed, any special conditions of repayment, and a description of the property used to secure the loan. There are a total of 106 debt records in the three sample years 1584, 1592, and 1605. This sample, as well as debt records from the longer period 1583–1635, provide for an analysis of the socioeconomic backgrounds as well as relationships among lenders and borrowers.

All 106 debtors in the three-year sample came from Salem's villages and 95 can be found in the tax records.[152] By wealth bracket, the highest percentage of debtors were the smallholders (27.4%), followed by the prosperous (21.1%), the very rich (17.9%), the middling (16.8%), the poor (14.7%), and finally, the destitute (2.1%). Many of the poorer borrowers secured small sums from local churches: Georg Guettman of Mühlhofen borrowed 5 fl. from St. Pangratz of Mühlhofen, Simon Strasser of Urnau borrowed 10½ fl. from the local churchwardens, and George Kraus of Neufrach borrowed 15 lb. dn. from St. Marx of Neufrach. Each of these borrowers, and several others, had wealth of less than 100 fl. according to tax records from the same period. Other poor borrowers secured larger loans with assistance: Bastian Weißenkönig borrowed 180 fl. from Salem's secretary, mortgaging the house he shared with his father-in-law. Michel Schneider's father helped him secure an 80 fl. loan from a burgher in Überlingen. Gallin Waibel of Neufrach and his neighbor borrowed 50 fl. from an orphan. Martin Gaist's father-in-law sold him a house and carried the loan of 200 fl. The fact that

150 Audience requests for ratification of sale confirm the high representation of craftsmen among buyers and sellers. In 1630, nine out of thirty requests for ratification of sale involved at least one craftsman, miller, or innkeeper.

151 For a fuller discussion of debt among Salem's villagers, using a larger variety of sources, see BRUN, Abbot and Peasants (2008 diss.), pp. 378–395. Two in-depth studies of debt, offering contrasting interpretations, are SREENIVASAN, Ottobeuren, chap. 4 and DEES, Peasant Production, chap. 4.

152 Besides 97 individual men, debtors in the sample include two individual women, five groups of two or more local householders, and two village communes.

not only the wealthy but also poor and even destitute households were able to borrow small sums of money is an important finding.[153] The main factor for creditworthiness in Salem seems to have been the availability of land to secure the loan's repayment, and the widespread ownership of freehold parcels meant that even poorer households often had something they could mortgage. Sometimes, instead of specific parcels, a borrower pledged all his or her land and moveable property to secure the loan, or a relative offered to guarantee repayment. The participation of poorer householders among borrowers could be interpreted as a result of their economic necessity, and in many cases debt was the negative effect of poverty. Yet the ability to borrow money could be used as economic strategy and even the poor may have occasionally used debt to their advantage.[154] As previously indicated, land buyers sometimes borrowed the entire purchase price from the seller or other lender.

Wealthy householders often owed money to widows and orphans. Among debtors with wealth of over 1,000 fl., Claus Haimpolt owed 40 fl. to some orphans with the same surname. The miller Georg Spett owed 30 fl. to a widow of no known relation. Lorenz Bürster likewise owed 30 fl. to a widow, who appears to have been a wealthy moneylender (with 1,708 fl., no debt, and 1,540 fl. in freehold property and credit notes). Hans Schaitteckh also borrowed from a wealthy widow. Veit Dulenkopf borrowed 70 fl. from an orphan and another 30 lb. dn. from his village chapel in the same year.[155] Wealthy householders in the sample did not borrow small consumption loans of less than 30 fl., but neither they did not borrow large amounts—the largest loan to a wealthy borrower was 133 fl. from Salem's bursar.[156]

Groups of prominent villagers borrowed substantial amounts of grain from outside sources on several occasions during the period 1587–1592, but rarely in other sampled years.[157] Millers were among the borrowers in many of these cases, which makes sense when we consider their source of livelihood. Amtmänner were also heavily represented among joint borrowers of grain. Group borrowers were usually, but not always, from the same village, whereas grain lenders were almost always burghers from the surrounding towns. Why were large grain loans to groups of villagers common in this brief period? One possibility is that the borrowers were speculating on grain for profit, selling it to neighbors at high prices. Another is that wealthy villagers borrowed grain to help the community through hard times, bearing the responsibility for repayment voluntarily or out of obligation. In any case, the period in question coincided with widespread sick-

153 This is in contrast to Neckarhausen, where a committee of villagers determined creditworthiness and the process of loan approval. SABEAN, Neckarhausen I, p. 365.

154 SREENIVASAN, Ottobeuren, p. 202.

155 Several wealthy householders borrowed from local churches and abbey officials, but this did not distinguish them from other borrowers.

156 Only three loans to individual borrowers were for amounts over 200 fl., and none of these were to households in the top wealth bracket.

157 There was one similar joint grain loan in 1632.

ness and possibly a plague epidemic.[158] Group grain loans in this period suggest local grain shortages, during which the lack of outside assistance or reserves led villagers to unusual measures in order to stave off hunger and supply the village.[159]

Two village communes in the sample borrowed one hundred gulden each, Weiler from an outside lender and Mimmenhausen from the Großkeller, who was acting as a churchwarden for St. Antony's Altar in Salem. In the second case, the reason for the loan is provided in the directly preceding entry, a sales contract in which the commune purchased two vineyard parcels for 185 fl. The money was used to purchase land.

Turning now to the 106 lenders in the sample, some were village householders but the majority were not. Instead of relying on the six wealth brackets, lenders are best classified according to four major groups: individual villagers (34), individuals from outside the territory (18), Salem and affiliated officials (15), and all other religious organizations or clergymen (39).

The largest group of lenders includes all church-affiliated lenders other than Salem—local parishes, chapels, priests, confraternities, and churches from the surrounding region. Most of them were local, including 26 from Salem's villages.[160] For borrowers who secured loans in their own parishes, it was their neighbors who kept the accounts, controlled church property, and made lending decisions as the churchwardens. The amount of credit offered to individuals was typically low, but so were the underwriting criteria. In some cases, villagers were clearly using church funds to loan money to one another.[161] Other villagers borrowed from a neighboring parish or some other church, 13 of which were located beyond the territory.[162] Religious organizations, both local and regional, played an extremely important role in supplying credit to villagers, acting as

---

158 The Audience hardly met at all in the years 1586–1588, and the record notes that meetings were suspended for the better part of a year because of illness.

159 Villagers commonly owed grain to the abbey in the early seventeenth century as the result of borrowing or unpaid rents, and in that period grain loans to groups of villagers are unknown. Perhaps the abbey was unwilling, or not in a position to lend grain to hungry villagers in the years 1587–1592, but later took on this responsibility as the situation became more serious. In 1614, for example, the abbey made substantial seed loans to a majority of its tenants, distributing over 64 Malter of barley, 26 Malter of oats, and 17 Malter of peas. GLAK, 98/1729.

160 Local churches included St. George of Bermatingen, St. Martin of Seefelden, St. Marx of Neufrach, St. Sebastian of Mimmenhausen, Our Lady of Leutkirch, Our Lady of Urnau, Our Lady of Bermatingen, St. Pangratz of Mülhofen, St. Margaretha of Buggensegel, and the parish assistant in Leutkirch. Wespach hospital is also counted among local churches since it was a charitable organization overseen by local wardens, usually villagers from Weildorf or Weiler.

161 The churchwardens in Buggensegel took turns loaning money to one another in three sequential chancery records. GLAK, 61/13317, 1592.

162 Abbeys Schussenried and Wald, a chaplain in Beuren, priests from Hofkirch and Meßkirch, convents Beche and Pfullendorf, the Linzgau rural chapter, Überlingen and Constance hospitals, and Bettenbronn foundation all extended credit to Salem's villagers in sampled years.

early lending institutions.[163] More than any other group, churches made it possible for villagers to borrow money for various purposes. Religious lenders fueled rural markets and provided economic opportunity to individual households.

A second category of 15 loans came from the abbey or its affiliates: the prior, bursar, secretary, Großkeller, Oberamtmann, herb gardener, Hofmeister of Maurach, and St. Antony's Altar in the abbey church. These lenders could be considered alternatively as private individuals or religious organizations, except that they were also closely identified with territorial lordship, and this necessarily affected the relationship between creditor and borrower. Such lending activity may have been intended as a form of charity, and perhaps the abbey and its officials felt a special obligation to assist villagers seeking credit. Yet such lending was backed by a political force that created an additional layer of dependence not found in loans from local parish churches or other private persons. It seems significant, in any case, that the abbey and its officials offered fewer loans on the whole than other neighbors and religious organizations. It is also interesting that three individual monks extended loans to peasants.[164]

The third group of creditors included 18 individuals from outside the territory, mostly representing urban areas.[165] No personal relationships could be discovered between this group of lenders and their borrowers, and most likely these transactions represented a standard form of investment. In the court records, discussed in Chapter 5, burghers sometimes appeared as plaintiffs in suits involving debt. These lending activities explain why. Credit offered by burghers to villagers from the surrounding region also provides important evidence of regional markets, often involving small sums, which are easily overlooked in studies of large-scale market activity. Letters of credit such as those involving Salem's villagers could contribute to a better understanding of urban investments in the countryside and the regional integration of markets.

Finally, the fourth group of creditors were local villagers. Thirty-four lenders, roughly one-third of those sampled, belonged to this category. Widows and orphans, 14 in all, formed an important subgroup. Many of them could not be identified in tax records, but a few widows were among the wealthiest villagers. These widows and

---

163 The savings bank (*Sparkasse*) in Salem claims to be the first institution of its type in Germany (see their publication: 225 Jahre Bezirkssparkasse Salem, 1749–1974). It was founded under Abbot Anselm II to care for orphans. Sreenivasan says churches were the major rural lenders in Ottobeuren, and from their perspective, loans to peasants were a good investment that yielded a steady cash flow. Idem, Ottobeuren, p. 180.

164 If the prior, bursar, and Großkeller lent money from their own pockets, which the record leaves unclear, this would raise questions about the Cistercian Order's commitment to individual poverty and the lack of personal property. In at least one case, the Großkeller lent money from the funds of St. Antony's Altar. In the others, too, abbey officials may have been acting on the abbey's behalf.

165 These included Altdorf, Beuren, Constance, Hausen am Andelsbach, the Klettgau, Obersiggingen, Ostrach, Ravensburg, Stetten, and Überlingen.

some others may have lent money to reinvest a cash inheritance or other savings.[166] For others, the credit note probably represented an inheritance not yet distributed by a senior relative who controlled their share. In such situations the widow or orphan was waiting to get paid rather than voluntarily lending the money. Either way, the discovery of so many widows and orphans among creditors confirms the importance of kinship and inheritance in the transfer of property and circulation of credit.

Among village lenders, 13 came from extremely wealthy households with over 1,000 fl. in property. The very rich had the resources available to invest; moreover, lending to neighbors was a form of patronage that strengthened social relationships. It may have even served as a tax shelter.[167] Seven local lenders had wealth below the average: five were smallholders, one had less than one hundred gulden, and one paid the minimum tax of ten kreuzer. These lenders from the lowest wealth brackets indicate that not all credit came from wealthy investors. Debts within the village could involve extremely modest households including laborers, craftsmen, and yielding heirs both as borrowers and as lenders. What is perhaps more surprising is that such debts also resulted in written contracts.

A broader look at chancery records over the period 1582–1633 reinforces many findings from the core sample. It continued to be common practice in later years to buy freehold property on credit, which made it possible even for poorer individuals to purchase land and borrow money.[168] Parish churches, chapels, and local confraternities continued to provide the primary sources of credit, followed by fellow villagers, abbey officials, and burghers.[169] Some parishes had large endowments, and the churchwardens who oversaw their finances were members of the community where the money was invested. Thus, local churches functioned as a type of credit union and source of self-help. By contrast, village communes were more likely to borrow money to fund projects and pay off debts, rarely lending voluntarily to their members (though many individuals owed them money). Loans from fellow villagers as well as outsiders demonstrate the economic networks connecting households across the territory and the wider region. The records yield very little information about kinship or other social relationships, though the prominence of widows and orphans among lenders is suggestive.

---

166 Hermann Rebel has shown that moneylending was a high-status activity pursued by wealthy retirees. Idem, Peasant Stem Families in Early Modern Austria: Life Plans, Status Tactics, and the Grid of Inheritance, in: Social Science History 2 (1978), pp. 273–274.

167 Interest-bearing loans were rarely reported in personal tax assessments.

168 St. Margaretha of Buggensegel sold seven parcels in a row to local villagers in 1613 and lent money to six of them.

169 I counted 520 debt records in a sample of chancery protocols from 15 years (see the breakdown by year in Chart 4.14). About 20% of lenders in the sample were local parish churches, another 20% were nonlocal churches, 17% were outside individuals, 13% were Salem abbey or territorial officials, 12% were neighbors from the same village, 8% were individuals from nearby villages, and 8% were individuals whose place of residence is unknown.

In summary, villagers in the decades on either side of 1600 were heavily engaged in borrowing and to a lesser extent in lending activities. Credit was an essential ingredient in the economic development of households and villages, and debt could be a sign of economic decline but it was not necessarily so. Borrowing helped individual families and entire communities through lean times. Not only wealthy households but also poorer ones were among the borrowers and buyers, indicating a high accessibility of credit. Anyone with unencumbered freehold property was eligible to borrow money, and the widespread ownership of land bolstered the credit market. Sales and debt were often interconnected and the relationship between them worked in both directions: property ownership allowed individuals to borrow money, whereas land was often purchased on credit.

Debt involves a relationship between creditors and borrowers. The patterns of credit circulation as revealed in the chancery records indicate strong ties between villagers as well as beyond the local community. The security of the loan's repayment is always a factor in the availability of credit, just as the security of title is important for land sales. One form of guarantee was the written record itself. Borrowers and lenders as well as buyers and sellers had an interest in recording transactions in order to limit their liabilities, protect their rights, and set the parameters for future repayment. The large number of entries in the chancery protocol involving sales and debt confirms villagers' interest in the written record, just as it demonstrates the widespread use of financial transactions in the villages around 1600. These contracts were drafted upon the initiative of peasants, not the abbey, and parties were willing to pay a fee to acquire them.[170] This, too, ensured a stronger market network and a greater availability of land and loans.

4.7 Inheritance

Inheritance was among the major methods of property transfer in Salem's villages (the others being tenure and sale). Inheritance practices provide special insight on family and social structure, within households and between them.[171] Within the household, inheritance affected family roles, decisionmaking, and the division of authority. Control over and access to family resources, or lack thereof, was often a factor in the ability

[170] As Sreenivasan argues for Ottobeuren, such documents were notarized as the result of peasant demand. Idem, Ottobeuren, p. 184.

[171] The scholarship on inheritance is quite large and cannot be listed here, but David Sabean's Neckarhausen volumes provide the best study of a partible inheritance region in Upper Germany. See also Hermann REBEL, Peasant Classes; MEDICK and SABEAN, Interest and Emotion; ROBISHEAUX, Rural Society; Lutz BERKNER, Stem Family, pp. 398–418; Jack GOODY et al., eds., Family and Inheritance: Rural Society in Western Europe, 1200–1800, Cambridge 1976; David Warren SABEAN, Simon TEUSCHER, and Jon MATHIEU, eds., Kinship in Europe: Approaches to Long-Term Development (1300–1900), New York and Oxford 2007.

to find a spouse and establish a new household.[172] Inheritance practices also bound the members of different households and communities together, and could promote common interests as well as conflict among kin. These conflicts, when recorded, show how families were structured and how family members related to one other. Inheritance practice was an important factor for gender, generational, and sibling roles and relationships, the documentation of which can bring these relationships to light.[173] The distribution of family resources through inheritance not only affects relationships within the household or among kin. It is also central to population growth, property-holding, social structure, and political relations.[174]

Inheritance has often been classified as either partible or impartible, depending on whether family property (the farm) is divided or kept together. At one end of the spectrum, a few households might control almost all the land in the village while the rest would have close to nothing. At the other extreme, land and resources might be divided into such small pieces that although economic disparities would be lessened, no household would have the resources necessary to sustain itself. Most societies seek to achieve a balance between the two, and the classification of inheritance as partible or impartible should not be viewed in terms of stark contrast. There are variations within each general type—for example, impartible inheritance includes primogeniture, which favors the eldest son, and ultimogeniture, which favors the youngest son. Stem families (multiple generations) and joint families (multiple siblings) allow more than one married couple to live together under the same roof. Partible inheritance, involving the division of land among heirs, varies according to who may inherit (all sons or sons and daughters) and the type of property each heir receives (pieces of the farm, other parcels, or moveables). In fact, inheritance practices often combine different elements or fall between the two major types.[175] Whether partible or impartible, another impor-

---

172 Delayed marriages and a high proportion of adults who remained single are the primary characteristics of the European marriage pattern, which imposed preventative checks on population growth, largely through social controls. See Jan de Vries, The Economy of Europe in an Age of Crisis, 1600–1750, Cambridge 1976, pp. 9–12; Pfister, Population, pp. 43–48.

173 In light of the lack of information about marriage partners and kinship before the Thirty Years War, the sources relating to inheritance are especially useful for examining family relationships and the role of women in social structure and property relations.

174 This is one of David Sabean's major arguments. He demonstrates that kinship was extremely important for property relations and social structure in a period of growing market integration and monetarization. Noteworthy is the shift in emphasis over time toward certain family relationships at the expense of others. Idem, Kinship in Neckarhausen, 1700–1870, Cambridge and New York 1998 (hereafter referred to as Neckarhausen II).

175 See Sabean's discussion of Martine Segalen's research in Neckarhausen II, p. 422; also Zvi Razi, who found that sixty percent of landholders shared land with siblings in one impartible region. Idem, Family, Land and the Village Community in Later Medieval England, in: Past and Present 92 (1981), p. 7. In Hohenlohe, compact farms were normally impartible whereas the rest of the patrimony was divided up according to a practice Robisheaux calls "preferential partibility"; idem, Rural Society, p. 128.

tant variable is the timing and speed of transfer from one generation to the next.[176] In terms of social structure and property relations, it makes a great difference whether daughters as well as sons receive an equal share, whether yielding (landless) heirs are permitted to marry and remain in the community, whether large farms are divided or kept in one piece, and at what point in the family life-cycle property devolves.

Inheritance customs are of special interest in the late sixteenth century, because population had already reached its peak and competition for land and resources was extremely high; changes such as increasing geographic mobility, monetarization, and market integration were additional factors. Inheritance practices changed over time, and the interconnections between family, land, property, and social structure suggest a multidirectional process whereby inheritance practices not only influenced the broader social structure but were also modified in turn. For Ottobeuren, Govind Sreenivasan identifies the final third of the sixteenth century as a key period of transformation in property relations.[177] In that territory the shift from partibility to impartibility and the expulsion of yielding (noninheriting) heirs from the village helped preserve the integrity of the large farms. Under the new system, the main heir in Ottobeuren's villages bought the others out, leading to a rise in land sales and especially debt, which was possible by the late sixteenth century because of the greater availability of credit and monetarization of the rural economy. David Sabean, too, demonstrates that in Upper Swabia, inheritance customs and social structures affected one another and changed over time.[178]

In Salem's inheritance practices, we find a blend of partible and impartible aspects. On the one hand, inheritance in Salem was partible in the sense that all daughters and sons inherited property of equal value, and the family's freehold land was distributed among them in separate parcels. Among propertied families, it was common for each child to receive freehold strips of arable, meadows, or vineyards as inheritance portions. It was also common practice to partition houses among two, three, or even four heirs. As a result of partible inheritance, freehold properties around 1600 were small,

---

176 Delayed partition increased the dependence of children on their parents, as Sabean demonstrates, citing the old proverb "don't put young bees in a full hive." Delayed partition also resulted in later marriages, a higher celibacy rate, and slower population growth. David Warren SABEAN, Young Bees in an Empty Hive: Relations between Brothers-in-law in a South German Village around 1800, in: Interest and Emotion: Essays on the Study of Family and Kinship, ed. Hans Medick and David Warren Sabean, Cambridge and New York 1984, p. 183.

177 SREENIVASAN, Ottobeuren, chap. 4.

178 David Warren SABEAN, Family and Land Tenure: A Case Study of Conflict in the German Peasants' War (1525), in: Peasant Studies Newsletter 3 (1974), pp. 1–8. A more recent collection of essays argues that a major shift may be observed in the meanings assigned to kinship at the beginning and end of the early modern period. The processes associated with statebuilding, market growth, and modernization did not lead to a decline in the relevance of kinship, but rather, to a reorientation and establishment of new relationships. See SABEAN et al., Kinship in Europe.

and no effort was made to preserve the integrity of family lands. Abbey officials did not interfere in this process of parcelization and recombination. On the other hand, Salem's major farms were neither heritable nor divisible. As previously indicated, Salem's custom of annual leases meant that the distribution of farms was subject to the lord's will and not hereditary claims. Only in the case of hereditary leases could an heir expect to take over the farm, and only then did all the heirs hold a claim to the (still impartible) property.[179] Salem's practice of partible inheritance, paired with the exclusion of major farm tenures from hereditary claims, distinguishes it from neighboring territories. This section highlights the specific configuration of inheritance customs in Salem, which had a major influence on social and political relations.

Parents enjoyed relative freedom to adapt partition to their own unique family circumstances, because territorial law provided few guidelines for inheritance beyond stating that each child should be provided for and that parents, especially widows, should not squander their property to the children's detriment.[180] Property transfers through inheritance came gradually, not all at once. Children typically received an "advance" (*Voraus*) upon majority, consisting of a small cash payment, clothing, (and for girls) a bed and a cow. The advance was typically not enough to set up an independent household, but for some children, majority coincided with marriage and the promise of additional property from both families.[181] Later occasions for the transfer of property might include a parent's retirement, remarriage, or death. A final estate division usually occurred after the death of both parents, though the claims of stepparents and their spouses could postpone full partition even longer. The prolonged and flexible practice of distributing family property kept the younger generation dependent upon their parents and uncertain about their eventual shares. Parents could use the timing of partitions to maintain control over property, establish children favorably, or both. Marriage contracts, retirement agreements, and probate inventories are three types of

---

179 Hereditary leases were theoretically impartible in the sixteenth century, but their small size indicates that they may have been divided in the past. Because hereditary leases tended to be very small and were rarely the household's sole economic resource, their impartibility did not create a major burden for the main heir.

180 According to Article 8 of the 1473 partnership agreement: "Item war sach, das ein vatter, der ein gotshusmann ist, einen tail siner kind mit varendem gût berauten und usgestürt hett und die andern sine kind mit sovil varendem gût nit beraten möcht, hat er dann eigen und ligend gût, damit sol und mag er dieselben kind beraten, das sy och versehen und versorgt, das yegclichem mit der somm ein glicher tayl verlangen werden ungevarlich." Article 30: "Item welher mann oder frow ir eins vor dem andern mit tode abgat und aigen ald ligend gût verlaust, das dannen dasselb gût iren elichen kinden belibe. Und das dannen dasselb beliben egemachyt sölich gût weder versetzen noch verkoffen möge one der kind gunst und willen, es erschine dann sinr lipsnoturft und derselben notturft nach." BLICKLE and HOLENSTEIN, Agrarverfassungsverträge, pp. 57, 60.

181 Estate partition documents show that the advance and marriage portion were two separate property transfers and that a child did not have to marry in order to qualify for the advance.

documents that served to regulate the claims of various heirs and reduce the possibility of future conflict over the use and division of family property. A brief discussion of each type illustrates key points in the gradual transmission of family property and the possible variations in its distribution.

Marriage contracts (*Heiratsabreden*) were legal documents containing special provisions to protect the future interests of the surviving spouse, any children, and in some cases, other kin following one partner's death. These written agreements, registered and recorded with the chancery, became increasingly popular over the sample period (1580s–1630s).[182] Marriage contracts were exceptional agreements, the provisions of which went beyond the ordinary inheritance customs of the territory. They were most often made when there were preexisting children or when the spouses brought property of unequal value, and wealthy families were more likely than poorer counterparts to utilize them. Despite their exceptional nature, the provisions of marriage contracts offer useful information about family relationships—such as the care of elderly parents and stepparents, the division of resources among siblings from different marriages, property relations between spouses, and the expectations of other kin.

The primary objective of many marriage contracts was to provide for preexisting children.[183] Such documents were designed on the one hand to ensure that minor children eventually received a proper share, but on the other hand, they often allowed widowed spouses to delay partition and maintain usufruct of the marital property after they remarried. This was achieved through the stipulation of an advance on the inheritance from the deceased parent's estate, to be distributed to each child upon majority.[184] Even contracts providing an advance to preexisting children tended to treat all children equally, specifying that all heirs would receive equivalent portions upon the estate's final division.[185]

---

182 In my sampling of chancery records I have come across 48 marriage contracts. Ten are from the 1580s, two from the 1590s, four from 1600–1609, twenty from 1610–1620, and twelve from the 1630s. No chancery records have survived from the decade after 1622, but it appears that such contracts became increasingly popular over the course of the period.

183 Most agreements make reference to children from prior marriages involving one or both spouses, suggesting that these children's interests were the primary reason why couples entered such contracts. Marriage contracts in the sample mention children's inheritance claims three times more often than those of a spouse, and children's claims are always listed first.

184 The advance was normally a small sum of 10–15 fl., but in some wealthy families it could be several hundred gulden.

185 For example: "Jedem der 6 kinder, wan es zu seinen manbaren Jharen kombt unnd heurathen wirdt, solle 150 fl. mit hochzeitlicher ehrlicher klaidung, unnd darzu jedem der vier mägdlin ein bettstatt unnd khue gegeben werden. Doch wan er Hans Dilger bey seiner haußfrawen mher kinder erzeugen und bekommen wirdt, sollen die eltere kinder so von Frantz Schaideggen herboren so lang stillstehen, bis der jungeren kinder auch jedes 150 fl. empfangen hatt. Was dan darüber bei künfftiger verlasßenschafft vorhanden sollen die eltere und jungere kinder aichelenwis thailen." GLAK, 61/13319, 1613.

The marriage contract's provision of an advance in place of full and immediate partition is a good example of why equal portions were not truly equal. Often the substitution of an advance meant that some heirs had to postpone or subordinate their plans until the retirement or death of a parent, stepparent, or sibling. The practice did require the consent of children or their guardians, each of whom witnessed the marriage contract. For example, Salem's chamber servant Jacob Dreer of Mimmenhausen was engaged to be married in 1589. His daughter from a previous marriage complained to the Audience that the advance her father offered, in place of the customary partition of her mother's estate, was too small. The Audience responded that a partition should take place unless both sides agreed to other arrangements. Dreer clarified that the child wanted an advance of 600 fl., but he was willing to offer only 300 fl. The Audience repeated that they should follow the abbey's custom unless they could agree otherwise. A chancery record from later that year indicates a compromise of 500 fl. This case confirms that an estate partition was customary upon the remarriage of a widowed parent but also that an immediate partition could be avoided with the consent of those concerned.[186]

After describing the claims of any children, the marriage contract went on to describe the eventual rights of the surviving spouse. He or she received at the very least a child's portion, that is, a share in the estate equal to that of each child (excluding any stated advance).[187] According to some contracts the couple held all marital property in common, but others specifically reserved for the surviving spouse the exclusive use of their marriage portion or other specified property, in addition to a child's share.[188] Sometimes the surviving spouse was accorded use rights to the house and other property for life, whether or not they remarried. This was more frequently provided for widows than for widowers, but surviving husbands occasionally received lifelong benefits on property held by their wives.[189] Such examples are a reminder that women, even married women, controlled property that did not pass automatically to their husbands. Alternatively, the contract could specify retirement benefits for the parent, provided

---

186 GLAK, 61/13369, 1589; 61/13317, 1589. Indeed, delayed partition was often in the abbey's interests, because it avoided the parcelization of land, limited population growth, and provided stability if the yielding heirs were minors who could not maintain the property themselves.

187 Inheritance custom in Salem did not provide the widower with a larger portion of the estate than the widow as was the case in some other territories, such as Hohenlohe, where widowers claimed two-thirds and widows only one-third of marital property. See ROBISHEAUX, Rural Society, p. 128.

188 For example, Abraham Fimppel of Bermatingen reserved the right to leave his vineyards in Bermatingen to anyone he wished. GLAK, 61/13374.

189 "Jerg Millern, wan er sein haußfrawen uberlebt, bewilligt und versprochen, daß er nach ihren ableiben herberg in ihrer behausung haben sollen und darvon er heurate gleich wider oder nit, nit außgetriben werden, jedoch, wan er die andere frawen nemen oder bekomen solt, solle nach seinem absterben sye der herberg und behausung nichts genießen, sonder allein er und solang er mit ihr seiner anderen haußfrawen in ehestand leben wurd." GLAK, 61/13319, 1616.

by one or more children. Amtmann Martin Richel's marriage agreement with Agatha Wiererin stated that one of the children from his first marriage would eventually take over the farm (held in lifelong lease), but with the stipulation that he or she must provide lifetime maintenance for the stepmother, even if she remarried.[190]

A 1633 decree, issued by the abbot with the approval of the prior and entire convent, suggests an additional reason for the popularity of marriage contracts in the early seventeenth century: it substantiated the widow's claims to a farm held in annual lease by her deceased husband. The decree, citing the problems caused for a new tenant by the previous tenant's widow and children who had nowhere else to go, was an attempt to curtail the widow's claims and free the new tenant from the obligation to provide for her. It stated: "Following the eventual death [of a tenant], that which is beyond the personal freehold property or, in the case of the lease, that which is not reserved through a proper marriage contract with the prior permission of the authorities, shall not be claimed or demanded [by the heirs] at the expense of the authorities or the new tenant."[191] The decree was meant to protect the new tenant, his ability to pay the rent, and the abbot's right to distribute farms as he saw fit, but the text described a loophole, one which was not new in 1633. The marriage contract, subject to ratification by the abbey, allowed tenants to secure for their spouses a place on the farm after their death, even if the farm was an annual lease and even if it would eventually pass to a tenant other than the widow. The marriage contract was yet another way that tenants and their families exerted influence over the abbey's control of property.

A second type of contract, the retirement agreement (*Leibgeding*), described the property a retiree offered in exchange for lifelong maintenance, which varied according to his or her needs and the value of the property. The benefits normally included room and board, with food and drink described in great detail. Also included might be the exclusive use of certain areas of the house, certain fruit trees or garden plots, the right to graze an animal with other household livestock, or personal allowances of cash, grain, wine, firewood, and clothing.[192] Retirement could be contracted with a son or daughter (and son-in-law), a stepchild, more distant relative, or even nonkin. For various reasons, retirement agreements tended to favor the youngest child, but there was no strict rule.[193] Some retirees chose more distant kin or even wealthier neighbors,

---

190 GLAK, 61/13319, ca. 1615. The widow did remarry, resulting in a dispute with stepson Lorenz Richel over other hereditary property she controlled.

191 GLAK, 98/331.

192 The retiree did not necessarily hand over all his or her property. Some was usually reserved for personal use and for later partition among heirs.

193 The youngest child was more likely than older siblings to be living at home under the parents' authority. The youngest child also offered the best possibility of long-term care based on age. Unmarried children who remained at home were less independent and might be easier to live with, lacking material possessions and experience living in other households; their loyalties were not yet divided by the demands of spouses, in-laws, and their own children. Strict ultimogeniture, or the designation of the youngest child as the main heir, was not customary in Salem's ter-

perhaps because of their greater ability to provide stability and comfort, or because the retiree had no direct heirs.[194] Other retirees purchased benefits from the abbey, with care to be provided in the Wespach hospital or elsewhere.[195] If the caretaker and retiree were not direct kin, or even if they were, the retirement contract could be attached to a property sale rather than an outright grant.

When a parent retired, he or she gave up the role of primary decision-maker within the household, passing authority to the younger generation.[196] In addition to the transfer of household leadership and use-rights over specific property, this usually established the child (or caretaker) as a householder with full membership rights in the commune. This shift in the relationship between parent and child was not always easy or free from conflict. For example, a dispute broke out in 1596 between the retiree Anna Rosenboshin, her son Hans Fünfflin, and his wife. The wife was sentenced to public humiliation for calling her mother-in-law a demon (*Unhold*). Rosenboshin demanded that her son keep better order in the household and asked the authorities to punish him unless he returned the money she had paid for retirement benefits.[197] Retirement contracts sometimes provided for the possibility that the caretaker might not uphold his or her responsibilities to the parent or retiree's satisfaction, or for the possibility that things simply did not work out as planned. When his wife died in 1624, Michael Waibel of Owingen requested permission to pass his smallholding on to a stepson. In case relations deteriorated, Waibel reserved the right to demand 35 fl. in compensation so he could move back to his village of origin. If the retirement went well, the stepson could expect to assume all Waibel's property when he died.[198]

---

ritory, but there is some evidence to suggest that the youngest child may have had a better claim to family property (see below). On the practice of modified ultimogeniture in Upper Swabia, see SABEAN, Family and Land Tenure, pp. 4, 6.

194 Anna Jägerin of Oberuhldingen arranged for retirement in the household of the village Amtmann. She paid for her maintenance with 40 fl. in cash, two beds, and several interest-bearing credit notes worth a total of just under 200 fl. plus interest. Christian Betzlin of Weildorf paid 110 fl. to Gallin Bach of Neufrach (of no specified relationship) for lifelong benefits, including the same food enjoyed by the rest of the household, with meat at least twice per week. Betzlin would provide for his own clothing, except that Bach should give him one shirt per year and help him with the mending. GLAK, 61/13320, 1635; 61/13319, 1616.

195 See BRUN, Abbot and Peasants (2008 diss.), chap. 7; Claudia SCHOTT, Armenfürsorge, Bettelwesen und Vagantenbekämpfung in der Reichsabtei Salem, Bühl 1978, pp. 45–57.

196 Retirees retained certain rights within the household, however. According to Hermann Rebel, retired parents did not subordinate themselves to their children or the interests of the household. Instead they maintained a degree of economic independence, guaranteed by lifelong benefits and the reservation of property for personal use or investment. Rebel found that retired parents were heavily involved in moneylending, an activity associated with high social prestige. See REBEL, Peasant Classes, pp. 211–214; idem, Stem Families, pp. 273–274.

197 GLAK, 61/13369, 1596.

198 GLAK, 61/13373, 1624. See similar examples in SABEAN, Neckarhausen I, p. 344; SREENIVASAN, Ottobeuren, pp. 201, 232–240; BERKNER, Stem Family, p. 402.

The details of retirement contracts varied widely, and the use of property could be subject to conditions that limited the caretaker's enjoyment of them, not to mention the challenging personality conflicts such agreements between generations often entailed. Hans Herman, for example, drove a hard bargain. In exchange for retirement benefits, he agreed to sell his hereditary farm to a son for 300 fl., which was certainly below market price. Yet in addition to food and supplies and his own private quarters, the father reserved extensive property for his own use and expected the son to manage them as well as provide most of the labor. He had to work his father's six arable acres and vineyards at his own expense. He also had to deliver four wagonloads of manure to his father's parcels annually and feed the laborers during harvest season (the father would pay their wages). If the son preceded his father in death, his wife and children would have to leave unless they were able to honor the agreement. When the father died, his considerable remaining property would be divided equally among all his heirs.[199] In comparison, Martin Bronner secured a much better deal with his mother-in-law Catharina Langenstainin. He received 16 parcels of land without having to pay for them, in addition to all her remaining land and moveable property upon her death. She made no specific demands on the household, though he was expected to provide her with food and plenty of wine according to her wishes.[200]

Perhaps in an attempt to provide equally for each child and avoid conflicts among them, some retirement contracts named multiple heirs as a parent's caretakers. For example, Ursula Hergotzfelderin of Weildorf contracted for lifelong care with all three of her sons, who were to divide her property (including house, arable, meadow, and forest parcels) among themselves. She reserved the right to quantities of spelt, oats, barley, white flour, peas, hemp seed, lard, eggs, salt, and four gulden in cash, to be distributed along with whatever else she might need on a quarterly basis. In 1615 the widow Anna Lienhardtin contracted with two sons-in-law, who divided her house and shared responsibility for her lifelong care.[201]

The third type of document relating to inheritance was the probate inventory. These post-mortem property descriptions (*Verlassenschaft*) listed both property and debts, followed by details of the estate's division among heirs. They were produced by a senior abbey official in the presence of witnesses representing each heir. Probate inventories survive in small numbers for Neufrach, Owingen, and Grasbeuren, starting in the late sixteenth century.[202] These documents provide information about the division of property through inheritance as well as the types of property and debt found in various individuals' estates.

199 GLAK, 61/13317, 1591.
200 GLAK, 61/13318, 1612.
201 GLAK, 61/13319, 1613 and 1615.
202 GLAK, 98/3475 (Neufrach, earliest from 1594); 98/3502 (Owingen, from 1599); 98/3310 (Grasbeuren, from 1597). There are a few scattered inventories from other villages, including those of Christoph Langenstain and Severinus Rueff fromBermatingen.

It was not unusual for siblings or half-siblings to share a joint inheritance. For example, when Georg Miller of Owingen died in 1633, he left property including a house and several vineyards to four children, three from his first marriage and one from his second. Instead of splitting the estate into four parts, half-brothers Hans and Martin shared half of the house and a share of other property as a single portion while siblings Jerg and Catharina shared the other half of the house and the remaining property in common.[203] Jacob Beckh's probate inventory from 1611 illustrates the situation of another modest household, in which several siblings had to share property in common. The partition among his eight children left each with a portion of 57 fl. The house in Neufrach was divided among four of them. Another two daughters shared a vineyard worth 100 fl., and two eventually moved away with cash portions.[204] The individual shares were evened out using petty credits and debts.[205]

Agatha Müllerin of Owingen died a wealthy woman in 1634. She was survived by her second husband, Martin Stengelin, and six children including four from her previous marriage to Georg Schreiber. Both her husbands were village headmen in Owingen and members of the territorial court; Stengelin had been the head judge since 1631. Since Müllerin was survived by her husband, the inventory clearly describes her property and not that of her husband. Müllerin's gross wealth was 3,562 fl. and her net wealth was 2,587 fl., leaving 369 fl. to each of seven heirs. Her property included a house and farmstead worth 200 fl., 14 vineyards (*Hofstätte*), a few parcels of arable and meadow, several wine casks and trunks, some grain, harnesses, silver, and a box of letters (*Brieftröglin*).[206] Her debts included 203 fl. in wine rents to Salem and small sums to various workmen and servants including a bricklayer, carpenter, smith, and baker. She also left money for religious purposes: 3 fl. to the sexton in Überlingen for Masses, 50 fl. to a roadside shrine outside the village, and 20 fl. to the local confraternity. She had already paid an advance to three children from her first marriage as well as marriage portions ranging from 140 fl. to 300 fl. Although these portions had not been equal, the final partition reflected prior payments so that in the end, each heir received an equal share. Under Salem's inheritance practice, sisters received shares equal to their brothers and wives controlled property separate from their husbands.

When Martin Krueg of Grasbeuren and his wife Katharina Voglerin died in 1597, a daughter inherited the farm over three sons.[207] Besides the small farm there were several credit notes for loans to local villagers, and the total property value was 1,016 fl. The daughter Ursula and her husband Matheis Meßmer received the farm, a hereditary

203 GLAK, 98/3502.

204 Agatha lived in Constance by 1614 and Anna paid for her manumission and birth certificate in 1617.

205 GLAK, 98/3475.

206 No animals, beds, clothes, textiles, or other moveables are listed.

207 GLAK, 98/3310.

tenure worth 700 fl.[208] As the only heir to receive real property, she was responsible to pay shares in cash to her brothers Michel and Martin. The third brother, another Matheis, had to collect his portion from twelve petty debtors owing money to the estate. Ursula, the main heir, was the only sibling to remain in the village. Matheis collected his portion from the many debtors sometime before 1604, when he moved to Meersburg and became a miller. Martin's career path is unknown but he, too, left the village with his portion by 1604. In 1606 or perhaps earlier, Michel entered Neuenburg Abbey in Alsace and became a monk. We could infer that Ursula received the farm because she was the only married sibling and thus in a position to manage it. Yet according to tuition receipts, brothers Michel and Martin each attended school in the early 1590, before their parents' deaths.[209] Their education and cash portions prepared them for careers beyond the family farm, so that each was provided for and able to find opportunities elsewhere.

Adolescent children and young adults left their parents' households for various reasons. Wealthier villagers typically employed one or more servants, and many came from local families.[210] Other young people moved out of their parents' households with a marriage portion or the promise of one.[211] Among those who left the village or territory, many were young and single. We can call them yielding heirs, since they did not have land in the village, yet evidence does not suggest they were forced out.[212] As the above example of the Krueg siblings reminds us, we should not assume that yielding heirs were sacrificed for the good of the line, nor should we assume that parents did not do their best to provide equally for all children. Among both men and women who left, marriage was probably the most common reason.[213] Still others, including those

---

208 The farm included a house with garden and orchard plus twelve assorted land parcels (including vineyards and woodlands), two cows, three calves, two pigs, four beds, three trunks, some linens, and other moveables.

209 Tuition receipts (*schuelgelt*) from 1590 and 1592 totalled 13 fl.

210 A list of Oberuhldingen's residents from ca. 1600 lists 371 individuals including 144 children living at home, another 44 children serving in other households, and 38 "foreign" servants and maids. GLAK, 4/5852. According to Sreenivasan, households traded children to acquire better service from a child who was not the heir. Idem, Ottobeuren, pp. 225–226.

211 Couples from poorer as well as wealthier families managed to set up new households by combining their marriage portions, perhaps working for others until they were able to acquire parcels of their own through purchase or inheritance.

212 I agree with Sreenivasan when he says that equal shares are not equal. Evidence does not suggest, however, that stability in Salem's villages was achieved through the expulsion of the young, or that yielding heirs were recognized as the necessary victims. See SREENIVASAN, Ottobeuren, pp. 228, 278.

213 Manumission requests often name the outside spouse and give their place of residence or lordship. Since manumission and exit taxes depended on the individual's wealth, and were more likely to be recorded for wealthier individuals, the emigrant children of village elites are especially visible in the Audience records. Despite some Audience records suggesting that wives customarily joined their husbands, men moved quite often for reasons of marriage.

without land or a spouse, left to pursue work prospects in the cities, vineyards, crafts, or in service to some household or territorial administration. Some completed apprenticeships, with certificates provided for local journeymen leaving the territory.[214] One baker's marriage contract promised financial support to his children from a previous marriage, including a daughter, to learn a trade of their own choice.[215] Sons sometimes went away for education or training and a few are known to have served in positions of high status afterward.[216] The departure of heirs from the village eased pressure not only for individual households but also for the community as a whole. Geographical distance may have weakened local ties for those who left, yet preexisting personal networks were not completely severed. Having kin in neighboring villages or nearby cities could be advantageous to both sides, especially for the circulation of information about the availability of land, business opportunities, and spouses.

When an inheritance dispute could not be settled amicably, the best option for a legal settlement was to bring suit before the Sidelgericht. The partnership agreement of 1473 not only diminished the abbey's claim to a portion of its serfs' post-mortem estates, it also established that disputes over such property should be settled by the Sidelgericht, not the abbot or his representative.[217] Perhaps as a result of this legal agreement, or perhaps because territorial officials did not want to become involved in such disputes, the Audience often referred subjects' inheritance petitions to the court.[218] The Audience did occasionally offer decisions in inheritance disputes, with some overlap in the material the two bodies considered. Both series of records are

---

214 The chancery certified, with the master's approval, that the apprentice had studied for the requisite number of years and behaved honorably during that time. Chancery records from sampled years between 1604 and 1620 contain an average of one or two apprenticeship certificates per year, including six in 1611, four in 1620, three in 1606 and 1614, two in 1612, and one each in 1604, 1605, 1607, 1608, 1613, 1615, 1616, and 1619. I found no apprenticeship certificates in sampled years from the 1590s or 1630s, and only one from the 1580s; no records survive from the decade after 1622. Since apprenticeship certificates were necessary only for those going abroad, these records indicate that young people with specialized job skills were leaving the villages, especially after 1600.

215 GLAK, 61/13317, 1620.

216 The guardians of one orphan boy were required to pay 19 fl. to an Augsburg master for his apprenticeship. The boy was admonished to work diligently. Caspar Widenmayer, who borrowed money from a sister for his education, became a court secretary in the bishopric of Speyer. GLAK, 61/13369, 1596; 61/13373, 1624.

217 Article 8: "Und soverr die fründ sich sölicher taylung nit zû einigkeit betragen möchten, das sy dann darum zû erkantnüß der fünfzehen sydelrichtere kommen und derselben erkantnüß des tails halb nachkommen." BLICKLE and HOLENSTEIN, Agrarverfassungsverträge, p. 57.

218 While figures are not available for the total number of inheritance disputes referred by the Audience to the Sidelgericht, there were many such referrals in 1613 including seven inheritance disputes.

good places to find evidence of the parties involved, the reasons for disagreement, and the type and value of the property in question.[219]

The dispute between two brothers over hereditary tenure rights to the mill in Münchhöf is one of very few examples to assert the superior inheritance claims of the youngest child. In an Audience petition from 1589, Georg Renner complained that upon his father's death, brother Michel was designated as the new tenant, "which gave him reason for the utmost grievance, since he was the youngest and should be favored according to abbey custom."[220] Michel countered that Georg had operated the mill previously, during their father's lifetime. Georg did such a poor job and piled up so many debts that the father was forced to oust Georg and put Michel in his place, despite the fact that Michel had a good service appointment elsewhere at the time. The Audience ruled, "out of special and moving circumstances," that the elder brother Michel should continue to hold the mill. Although Salem's inheritance customs and territorial law codes do not specify which child should be the main heir in the case of hereditary tenures and other large properties, this petition suggests that younger siblings may have had a better claim to family property and that a modified form of ultimogeniture may have been favored in Salem's villages.[221]

Inheritance disputes might center on the equity of portions, the assessed value of properties, or the timing of their distribution. When Stephen Stett sold a meadow for 40 fl. more than its assessed value in an earlier property division, other heirs complained he had received more than his share. In 1599 the sons of Anna Eitlerin submitted complaints against their stepfather, the widower Jerg Hitzler. The sons demanded their portions as promised in the marriage contract between Hitzler and their mother, but Hitzler countered that this would ruin him and make him unable to maintain his farm. The Audience ordered him to honor the agreement. Sometimes the issue of conflict was not the division of property but limitations on its use. For example, two brothers inherited a house in Oberuhldingen. One brother wanted to rent his half to a third party, but the brother intending to live there opposed him. The court ruled that if the resident brother wanted to live alone, he should pay rent to the absentee brother. There were also disputes over inherited debts. Thomas Heßler complained that he had

---

219 In a ten-year sample of all civil suits brought before the Sidelgericht, 9.9% involved inheritance disputes. In a seven-year sample of Audience petitions, inheritance is mentioned in 5.8% of all requests.

220 "Thue er sich aines solchen zum Höchsten beschweren uß der sonndern ursachen Dz er Unnder den gebruedern der Jüngste sei unnd Ime nach gebrauch deß Gotshauß der Vorgang gebüre, bitt man Wolle Ime bei demselben gebrauch Handthaben." GLAK, 61/13369, 1589.

221 Sabean describes modified ultimogeniture as inheritance by the youngest capable heir rather than the youngest overall. As he points out, ultimogeniture works best in societies where elder siblings leave the farm at an early age and where all sons can be provided with the means adequate for their independence. Where economic competition was great, however, positions for older siblings were harder to come by and conflict was the result. Idem, Family and Land Tenure, pp. 4, 6.

promised as a child at his father's deathbed to take over the debts along with half of the house, leaving the other half to his stepmother and younger sister debt-free. He had been young at the time, he explained, and had not understood the implications of his promise or the level of debt until much later. He asked that the debts, as well as the property, be split equally among the heirs.[222]

The switch from annual to lifelong leases in the early seventeenth century brought new complications. In 1606, for example, the miller in Neufrach was recently deceased. His widow still held the lease, which had a term of three lifetimes. Hans Winter wanted to marry her, but only if he could take over the mill.[223] The problem was, the lease contract designated one of the deceased miller's young children as the next tenant. The mill was already heavily indebted, and the widow could hardly manage without a husband. Her remarriage and the solvency of the abbey's property depended on revising the previous contract to make room for a new tenant. The solution was to grant Winter permission to marry the widow and take over joint tenure with her for the next 18 years or until her death, whichever came first. After that, a child of the first marriage would be given the opportunity to take over the mill, if he or she was in a position to do so.[224]

To conclude, the flexibility in Salem's practice of partible inheritance made various arrangements possible. Partibility encouraged the redistribution of property among individuals and families over the generations. Inheritance was a means for the gradual transfer of property, with many stages between the advance and the final, post-mortem partition. Yet the major drawback of partible inheritance, the impoverishment of a growing population through the fragmentation of land, was largely avoided by the exclusion of farm tenures from the process of parcelization. This exclusion had another important consequence: among wealthy tenants, the amount of property to be inherited was low compared to the total value of household property and this alleviated tensions among the heirs. Still, the property subject to inheritance was by no means trivial. The ability of young people to marry and establish new households was often tied to the property they received and the timing of its distribution. Houses and vineyards were especially valuable in this respect, because they were freely alienable, divisible, and readily available on the land market. Their low value and small size compared to farm tenures made them affordable, enabling new couples to set up modest households without endangering the major farms. The availability of freehold land, sources

222 The Amtmann Georg Langenstain complained similarly in 1605 that the house he received from his father as part of a retirement agreement was loaded with undisclosed debts. Examples in this paragraph are from GLAK, 61/13327, 1625; 61/13369, 1599; 61/13322, 1585; 61/13322, 1585; 61/13369, 1606.

223 He was a kinsman of the bankrupted former miller from Oberuhldingen with the same name.

224 The new agreement, an *Eventualleben*, is found in GLAK, 4/4533–4534. The child never got the chance to take over the mill, however. In 1609 a new lease contract named Hans Winter and a different wife, Barbara Richlerin (the niece of Amtmann Martin Richel), as lifelong tenants. GLAK, 4/4535.

of credit, and the ability to buy, sell, borrow, or leave allowed the recombination of parcels to continue without overburdening the local population or limiting the options of smallholders. Partible inheritance, the shuffling of land parcels, the development of secondary sector employment, and market integration cannot be understood in isolation from one another.

4.8 The Amtmann in Social Context

The Amtmann, or village headman, was the central figure in relations between the abbey and its subjects. His actions had an enormous impact on territorial governance and the direction of its development. The official duties of the Amtmann as the highest local representative, spokesman, and intermediary between the territorial lordship and the village commune are described in Chapter 3. Here we investigate the Amtmann's property, wealth, kinship, and interactions with neighbors in order to illuminate the socioeconomic underpinnings of his political involvement and the interests he represented.

Concluding with the Amtmänner fulfills another purpose, namely, to bring together the various elements of everyday life and property relations explored in earlier sections of this chapter. Because the activities of Amtmänner are recorded more commonly than those of other villagers, many of their personal histories can be reconstructed in greater detail. As much as we would like to know about the lives of ordinary villagers, the poorer folk and those who were not householders, we are able to examine the Amtmänner as individuals in a way that is not possible for most of their neighbors. A closer examination of the Amtmänner is not only easier, it is also further justified by their political significance. These men demonstrate how authority was practiced and negotiated in the village and between the center and various regions of the territory. Their personal backgrounds provide insight about the types of people who were in a position to lead, decide, and communicate issues of local importance, even suggesting what made them successful and why they may have been chosen as political mediators between the abbey and their neighbors.

There are no comprehensive lists of Amtmänner from Salem's territory or its individual villages, but a total of 116 individuals can be identified as holders of this office during the period 1472 to 1648.[225] Their names and dates of office are found in Appendix 4.1. Since the data are concentrated in the decades after 1575, the fifty years straddling the turn of the century and the 58 Amtmänner from this period receive primary attention.

---

225 Over the course of my research, I have collected the names of Amtmänner and their dates in office from every possible source and entered them in a database along with other pieces of personal information. Audience and Sidelgericht records are especially good sources for names.

Property and Wealth among Amtmänner

The imperial tax registers are once again the best sources of economic data for the late sixteenth century. We will first consider the 15 Amtmänner listed in 1578 and then compare them as a group to the listings for 1593 and 1603. Average household wealth among 15 Amtmänner in 1578 was 1,711 fl.[226] Compared with the territorial average of 391 fl., these men were wealthy indeed. Ten were tenants, nine of them with a major farm (*Hof)* in annual lease, their acreage in two fields ranging from 19 to 70 Jauchert. Three households held more than one tenure, with a total of 14 properties among ten households. Just one was a hereditary lease and three were lifelong leases (all three belonged to one household).[227] All ten tenants had livestock (ranging 138–372 fl. with an average of 242.8 fl.) and eight owned freehold property (ranging 178–1,894 fl. with an average of 682.4 fl.) Net wealth among the ten tenants averaged 1,314 fl., which was 65.3 percent of gross wealth among these same households. The five remaining Amtmänner were without farm tenures. This group included Hans Aigen of Bermatingen, the wealthiest Amtmann in the sample with 4,342 fl., as well as Laux Leub of Weiler, who was the least wealthy with 264 fl.

The tax lists from 1593 and 1603 present several similarities and a few important differences. First of all, all three lists include 15 men who were Amtmänner at the time of the assessment and nine of them held farms in annual tenure. In 1593 there were ten tenants and five nontenants, and in 1603 there were nine tenants and six nontenants. Besides the annual leases, there was one hereditary property in 1593 and in 1603 there was one hereditary and one lifelong lease, with two households in possession of more than one farm. Another interesting finding is that the nontenured Amtmänner in all three years included the wealthiest as well as poorest households in the sample.[228] This confirms that many wealthy households and even wealthy office-holders did not rely on large-scale farming or have the abbey as their landlord. It also indicates that there were Amtmänner with very little property, whose wealth was below the territorial average. The three lists show almost identical structures of land tenure among a constant number of current office-holders.

---

226 Excluded from the sample are an additional nine households headed by men who were Amtmänner in some other year, as well as four households headed by the parents of future Amtmänner. These listings are useful for understanding the family origins, life-cycle, and household development of Amtmänner over a longer period, but here the focus is on the property and wealth of these men while in office.

227 Jacob Hailg of Neufrach had a hereditary lease worth 800 fl. in addition to a farm held in annual lease. Michael Urnau of Oberuhldingen had a smallholding and a farm, both annual leases. Christa Buechmüller held the mill and two smallholdings in Urnau, all lifelong leases.

228 Amtmänner without farm tenures in 1593 included Andreas Villieber of Nußdorf, who was the wealthiest in the sample (2,205 fl.), as well as Christoph Langenstain of Bermatingen, who had the highest net wealth (2,050 fl.). The poorest in 1593 was Martin Stett of Oberuhldingen (314 fl.). In 1603 Christoph Langenstain was the wealthiest (4,775 fl.) and still he had no farm; the poorest that year was Balthas Sixt of Mühlhofen (630 fl.).

A comparison of the three lists shows that the Amtmänner were wealthiest on average in 1578. Whereas average wealth in that year was 1,711 fl., in 1603 it was 1,686.3 fl. and in 1593 only 1,326.7 fl. Barring some major inaccuracy in the record, the Amtmänner were significantly less wealthy in 1593 than in other sample years. At the same time their debt-level was also much less. Whereas net wealth among the tenants was 65.3% in 1578 and 64.3% in 1603, net wealth in 1593 was 78% of gross, leaving an average of 1,055 fl. per household (slightly higher than the average net wealth of 996.4 fl. in 1603). Freehold property ownership also declined, down from an average of 682.4 fl. in 1578 to 451.3 fl. in 1593 and 501 fl. in 1603. Animals are not itemized for 1603, but in 1593 their value sank from 242.8 to 195.4 fl. on average and the range in values (113–286 fl.) was also much lower than in 1578. In terms of wealth, including freehold, moveables, and debt, village office-holders were better off in 1578 than in 1593 or in 1603. We can conclude from this comparison that the wealthy were not becoming wealthier and that top local officials were not consolidating economic power at the expense of their neighbors during the late sixteenth century.

Whereas the imperial tax lists provide detailed economic data for a few fixed points in time, additional sources including rent registers and tenure contracts provide glimpses of the period after 1600 and offer a long-term perspective. During the half-century from roughly 1575 to 1625, records are dense enough to track the property and economic activities of many Amtmänner over the course of their adult lifetimes and beyond. This allows us to examine changes in property and wealth over time and look for patterns between property and officeholding. For example, how did an Amtmann's wealth during his time in office compare with his wealth before and afterward? Was he a tenant long before he became Amtmann, did he attain office and tenure at once, or did he become a tenant after assuming office? Did he remain in office until his death, and if not, then why?

It comes as no great surprise that the majority of Amtmänner became more wealthy over time. Among the 26 Amtmänner named in more than one tax list, the wealth of 19 Amtmänner rose while that of five others sank and only two remained essentially the same.[229] Some men were tenants or headed wealthy households for several years before they assumed office, as in the case of Christoph Rauch, who was the innkeeper of Weildorf for a decade before he became Amtmann in 1611. Others, however, be-

229 Among the most dramatic increases were Solomon Mayer of Mühlhofen with 700 lb. dn. in 1566 and 2,269 fl. in 1578, Jacob Schreiber of Owingen with 1,200 lb. dn. in 1566 and 2,191 fl. in 1578, Adam Ower the elder of Grasbeuren with 1,060 lb. dn. in 1566 and 2,945 fl. in 1578, Andreas Mayer of Tüfingen with 1,583 lb. dn. in 1566 and 2,782 fl. in 1578, Andreas Villieber of Nußdorf with 777 fl. in 1578 and 2,205 fl. in 1593, and Mattheus Burst of Owingen with 794 fl. in 1578 and 1,341 fl. in 1593. Declining in wealth were Bernhard Höltzlin of Mimmenhausen with 721 lb. dn. in 1566 and 428 fl. in 1578, Laux Leub the elder of Weiler with 1,061 lb. dn. in 1566 and 264 fl. in 1578, and Hans Waibel of Nußdorf with 1,302 lb. dn. in 1566 and only 286 fl. in 1578.

came tenants late in their careers or headed modest households only shortly before or even during their years in office. One Amtmann who became a major property-holder late in life was Georg Schreiber of Owingen (1612–1618). His father Jacob had been Amtmann before him (1578–1588) and was a man of considerable wealth, though not an abbey tenant. Georg, who had a wife and two children around 1600, remained modest by the standards of other Amtmänner until shortly after he assumed office in 1612. In 1603 his property value was 616 fl., and he was listed as a smallholder in 1607. In that year he is found toward the end of the list of those owing labor services. It was in 1613, the year after he became Amtmann as well as village judge and Sidelrichter, that the Audience approved his petition for the inn as a lifelong lease.[230] Suddenly he was at the center of local social and political activity, with a lucrative business and one of the largest farms in the village. This achievement came near the end of his life, after at least a dozen years as a smallholder. He died in 1618.

Georg Hailg of Urnau (1600–1616) is the best example of an Amtmann whose economic fortunes declined. It was not that his property holdings were insufficient: his gross property value was 1,137 fl. in 1603 and he had a major farm, freehold property worth 255 fl., and moveables worth 832 fl. The problem was his debts. Already in 1603 they were up to almost half his entire property value (his net wealth was 620 fl.). Eventually he became so heavily indebted that he lost his office and then the farm. The last time Georg Hailg was called the Amtmann was in 1616. In that year the Pfister complained to the Audience that Hailg had borrowed 18 measures of spelt in 1614 and another 21 in 1615 for a total of 39 Schoffel.[231] At the time of the Pfister's complaint, Hailg had repaid only seven Schoffel toward the debt, but he promised to deliver the remainder shortly. The Audience told the Pfister to collect as soon as Hailg was able to pay, but things continued to get worse. In 1620 Hailg sold 5½ acres worth 285 fl. to Hans Speckher, who had replaced him as the Amtmann. By 1624 he owed the abbey 46 Schoffel, and as the Pfister told the Audience, it would be impossible for him to get out from under such a debt load. Besides, Hailg had already failed to fulfill his earlier promise to pay off a portion of the debt, and by now his son Balthas Hailg also owed a substantial 28 measures. The Audience agreed to evict both Hailgs. Outside creditors started to bring claims against the former Amtmann before the Audience and the court. The marriage portion he had promised his daughter was six years past due. In 1624 a burgher from Ravensburg asked for help collecting the 340 fl. Hailg owed him

---

230 Though he asked for a lease period of three lifetimes, the Audience granted him only two in 1613. In 1617, the year before his death, the lease was extended to include his son and the new lease contract described the parcels attached to the inn as 49½ acres of arable and 10½ parcels of meadow. The timing was extremely fortuitous for his son Georg, who became the innkeeper after his mother's death despite her remarriage.

231 A Schoffel ("shovel") was the grain measurement used in the eastern Linzgau. Salem's villages did not share a unified system of measures; instead they were based on markets in Constance, Überlingen, Pfullendorf, and Ravensburg.

for borrowed grain. In 1625 Michel Lentz of Unterteuringen stated that Hailg owed him an old debt of 20 fl., now 60 fl. including eleven years of interest. These and other creditors settled in court for much lower sums.[232]

Among the 58 Amtmänner who held office between 1575 and 1625 there were at least 35, or about 60 percent, who at some point in their lifetimes held one or more properties in some form of tenure. One-third of all Amtmänner in this period held farms in annual lease, in addition to eight who held lifelong leases and four others with hereditary leases. Nine Amtmänner held more than one farm tenure simultaneously. Most tenants were wealthy and becoming more so over time, but there were differences among them. Four were millers and five were innkeepers. One of the hereditary properties had only 3½ acres, and two innkeepers held no land in tenure whatsoever. Thus, the tenant Amtmänner should not be viewed in sharp contrast to nontenant households or as a monolithic group.

Another 23 Amtmänner are not known to have held any farm tenure at all. For 18 of them, enough information is available to roughly describe their place within the spectrum of property and wealth. The men in this group are noteworthy for two reasons. First, they demonstrate that despite the domination of cereal agriculture, some villagers who were not farm tenants attained the highest local office. Second, as a result of their office, their economic backgrounds are well-documented compared to other nontenant households. They provide examples of the ways in which nontenants not only supported themselves, but in some cases numbered among the wealthiest village residents. Whereas tax lists, rent registers, and other records tend to neglect the nontenant households, these Amtmänner demonstrate the economic alternatives to farm tenures and large-scale grain production.

The untenured Amtmänner ranged in economic terms from modest to very wealthy. Many of them rose in economic status during their office terms, as did Mattheus Leub of Mimmenhausen (1610–1631). In 1603, before he became Amtmann, his property was valued at 805 fl. According to a rent register from that year he held four vineyard parcels, two meadows, and one Jauchert of arable in tenure from Salem. Earlier, he traded his house to the abbey for some land plus 191 fl. Lists from 1600 and 1607 called him a smallholder (Seldner). He sold a parcel here and there (1606, 1613, 1614) and borrowed 100 fl. in 1607 from Salem's legal counselor and later chancellor, Dr. Mattheus Klockh. Between 1612 and 1625, rent registers list him with 4–6½ acres depending on the year. When he died in 1631 his heriot was 15 fl., less than the value of a good horse, but his property was valued at 2,000 fl., more than that of the average farm tenant.

Jacob Klotz, the Amtmann of Weiler (1612–1624), was a modest householder with a wife and two children. In 1584 Klotz had purchased a house and garden for 100 lb. dn., half of it borrowed. The 1603 tax register listed his estate value as 193 fl. with no

[232] GLAK, 61/13327, 1625. Lentz received only a quarter of the debt he was owed, and his was the third suit brought against Hailg in that year alone. As for the burgher from Ravensburg, the Audience instructed him to be patient until the Sidelgericht made its decision.

farm. Firewood distribution lists from various years indicate he was a smallholder. He had at least six vineyard parcels by 1612 and bought 1½ Jauchert arable in 1622 for 120 fl., followed by another vineyard parcel for 230 fl. in 1624. When his wife died in 1630, Klotz was still alive but no longer in office. Her estate was valued at 450 fl., suggesting that the couple had accumulated some wealth, though they were still modest by the standards of other Amtmänner.

Martin Stett of Oberuhldingen (1587–1595) was one of the poorest nontenant Amtmänner. He was a householder for at least two decades before his appointment, with property worth only 42 lb. dn. in 1566 and 261 fl. by 1578. His wealth was probably somewhat greater by the time he took office, but according to a sampling of records, not by much. In 1590 he borrowed 200 fl. together with eight neighbors, listing his house as collateral. In 1593 he bought a small meadow parcel for 22 fl. He may have remained in office until his death in 1599, but if so, his activities have largely escaped the record. His death tax was only 4 fl.

Kinship among Amtmänner

In his studies of village headmen and rural elites in early modern Württemberg, Gerd Wunder found kinship to be a major factor for local officeholding.[233] Although he indicated that most headmen were wealthy and that wealth was important, kinship could be the decisive issue, so that even a modest member of an important officeholding family might be chosen for that reason. No one has provided a more compelling or better substantiated argument for the connection between kinship and political authority in the German countryside than David Sabean. His Neckarhausen studies demonstrate that kinship continued to play a dominant role well into the nineteenth century. He shows in great detail how the kinship matrix was socially constructed and changed over time, through shifting patterns of marriage alliance, godparentage, and links between certain groups of kin, especially cousins.

Kinship information for Salem's villagers prior to 1650 is sparse.[234] In the absence of information about godparentage, cousins, or even parents, our much more modest objective is to establish that kinship was a major factor in the practice of political authority in Salem's villages, that members of political families recognized and sought

---

233 Gerd WUNDER, Schwäbische Schultheißenfamilien, in: Zeitschrift für Agrargeschichte und Agrarsoziologie 9 (1961), pp. 203–210; idem, Bäuerliche Oberschichten im alten Wirtemberg, in: Bauernschaft und Bauernstand, 1500–1970: Büdinger Vorträge 1971–1972, ed. Günther Franz, Limburg an der Lahn 1975, pp. 137–152.

234 Parish records for Salem's villages start after 1648. The best sources for wives' names are the 1578 and 1593 tax lists and a list of the abbey's serfs from around 1600. The 1600 register was used for at least two decades, with marginalia added between 1594 and 1614. Besides these lists, the court, chancery, and Audience records are somewhat helpful for family information—including marriage agreements, death records, residence requests, manumissions, honorable birth certificates, and inheritance disputes.

to foster relationships among themselves, and that kinship was an important means of linking the political leaders of the various communities to one another.

Despite the source limitations, it is clear that a few politically active families held the majority of village leadership positions. Looking at last names alone, 17 families contributed over half (62 out of 116) of village headmen. Some families were primarily active in a single village, while others held offices in multiple locations.[235] The specific relationships between Amtmänner with shared surnames are not always known, but in some cases they can be positively identified as father and son. Laux Leub the elder and Laux Leub the younger served consecutively in Weiler, while Adam Ower the elder, Adam Ower the younger, and Jacob Ower the grandson all served in Grasbeuren. Jacob Schreiber and his son Georg both held office in Owingen.

Roughly half of Salem's Amtmänner served concurrent terms as territorial judges. When we look at shared surnames, the overlapping nature of these two offices becomes even clearer because the same political families who supplied most of the village headmen also contributed the territorial judges. In addition to the 60 Amtmänner who also served as Sidelrichter, another 32 shared a surname with at least one judge. In 92 out of 116 cases, therefore, Amtmänner either served as Sidelrichter or had family members who did. This astonishing concurrence does not even include relatives with different surnames. The pool of villagers chosen for local and territorial office was one and the same, and the political activities of village officials were rooted in family membership.

Kinship ties between office-holders with different surnames are much more difficult to establish but no less significant, because relationships were reckoned through women as well as men. In partible inheritance regions, both matrilineal and affinal kin could be extremely important.[236] The mothers of Salem's Amtmänner are mostly unknown, but the situation is a bit better with respect to wives. Among 81 known Amtmänner wives, 27 came from established Amtmänner families.[237] In other words, at least one in three had fathers, uncles, or other consanguineal relatives who served as Amtmänner, in most cases prior to the woman's marriage.[238] It was therefore a woman

---

235 Politically active families in a single village include the Aigens (Bermatingen), Buechmüllers (Urnau), and Stetts (Tüfingen). Those involved in several villages were the Billers, Hailgs, Leubs, and Villiebers. See Appendix 4.1.

236 Gerd Wunder found marriage alliances to be more prominent than the patriline in linking village headmen to one another in Württemberg. Idem, Schwäbische Schultheißenfamilien, pp. 209–210. Sabean's Neckarhausen studies provide excellent examples of the significance of female kin and affines in a partible region. Even in impartible regions, Sabean suggests that the link between maternal uncles and sisters' sons was extremely significant. Idem, Aspects of Kinship Behavior and Property in Rural Western Europe before 1800, in: Goody, Family and Inheritance, p. 100.

237 Surnames shared by Amtmänner and their wives include Biller, Hailg, Kurz, Langenstain, Leutin, Leub, Mangler, Mayer, Muettinger, Müller, Ower, Richel, Rogg, Schaitteckh, Schreiber, Sernatinger, Stengler, Storch, and Waibel.

238 All but five of these women had kinsmen who served as Amtmänner before their husbands.

who provided the link between families, and relations fostered with her kin may have facilitated the husband's rise to political office. Political connections were also established when two sisters or other female kin each married an Amtmann, making them in-laws by marriage. Twenty-six wives from eleven families linked Amtmänner in this way.[239] Finally, at least four women provided the link between eight Amtmänner by marrying two of them consecutively.[240] In all these cases, the wife's political connections helped her husband's career. Women played an especially important role in joining the village elites and political leaders of the territory together. Women who moved to their husbands' villages provided a critical link between different parts of the territory because they could draw on their relationships to kin and neighbors in both locations, bringing these relationships to bear for their husbands' careers and economic advancement as well as their own personal interests.[241]

Aspects of sociability and patron-client relationships involving Amtmänner and their neighbors are even more difficult to establish than those between Amtmänner and their kin. Still, a few general observations are in order. Amtmänner were frequently named as the witnesses to marriages, births, legal suits, and contracts of various sorts. They provided surety as guarantors for neighbors in cases of misconduct as well as financial obligations. Many Amtmänner were guardians for widows and orphans of no known family relationship, and several served simultaneously as churchwardens. On the one hand, individual Amtmänner would not have been chosen as political leaders had they lacked influence among their neighbors. On the other, the possession of such an important local office put them in a position to offer favors and punish offenses, which were means of further strengthening relationships while in office. The Amtmänner were involved in a great number of Audience petitions, often appearing on behalf of their neighbors.[242] It is hard to say whether such petitions were presented out of official duty, friendship, patronage, or some other reason, but they do demon-

[239] The eleven families providing wives for more than one Amtmann were: Biller, Dorner, Dreer, Hailg, Leub, Mäntz, Mayer, Meßmer, Schaitteckh, Schmidt, and Zürckh.

[240] Ursula Mäntzin was married to Martin Stett of Oberuhldingen around 1600 and to Andreas Villieber of Nußdorf until 1612. Agatha Müllerin survived her husband Georg Schreiber to marry Martin Stengelin, both of Owingen. When Amtmann Mattheus Leub of Mimmenhausen died in 1631, his widow Magdalena Zürckhin quickly married Balthas Diem of Leutkirch, who became Amtmann in 1632. Appolonia Küttin, the widow of Mattheus Burst (Owingen), remarried to Georg Donat (Grasbeuren). Adam Ower the elder (Grasbeuren) and Martin Richel (Neufrach) were both married to a Waldpurga Schaitteckhin, but their wives may have been different women who shared the same name.

[241] Sabean demonstrates how women in Neckarhausen utilized relationships outside the household in disputes with their husbands; see, for example, idem, Neckarhausen I, pp. 264–265.

[242] In a seven-year sample of Audience records, at least 56 petitions involved an Amtmann who made a request or appeared on behalf of some other individual. Most of these requests involved routine subjects (such as tenure conditions, alms, manumission, retirement, residency, marriage, and death taxes) offering the Amtmann no concrete personal benefits.

strate that the Amtmänner were involved in their neighbors' lives, assisting with the settlement of disputes and presentation of petitions. Occasionally, they were involved in ways that were less neighborly.

There were several cases of slander or verbal injury involving an Amtmann, two of which appear in the Audience records from 1611 and involved Christoph Langenstain, the Amtmann of Bermatingen. In the first incident, as the Amtmann stepped out of his house into the street, a drunken Jacob Mayer approached and insulted his wife. Langenstain denounced Mayer and demanded action against him.[243] The second incident likewise took place in the street. This time, the instigator (who was also drunk) called the Amtmann and another man scoundrels and thieves and said the actions of the entire community were useless ("*ain ganze Gemaindt seye khainnitz*").[244] Jacob Schreiber was another Amtmann who brought suit against two neighbors and complained of slander after they assaulted him with a pitchfork and accused him of working too closely with the Kaufmann and Großkeller.[245] In a fourth case, it was the Amtmann of Neufrach who caused the injury. According to Jacob Leub, Amtmann Martin Richel not only called him a scoundrel and a thief, he also accused his wife of being a notorious witch, publicly doubting whether Leub could control her.[246] Such incidents and denunciations demonstrate that the top village officials were as much involved in neighborly disputes as anyone, and their personal and official actions could be a source of criticism and animosity among neighbors.

Biographical Sketches

In closing, three personal narratives will provide concrete examples to illustrate key points. The first concerns the rise of a minor player through marriage alliances, followed by two others who were quite powerful and active in local politics.

Balthas Diem of Leutkirch was Salem's master cobbler in 1616 and he continued to carry the title of master throughout his life.[247] His ascent to the office of Amtmann (in Mimmenhausen, 1632) was achieved with the help of two marriages to influential

---

243 GLAK, 61/13370, 1611.

244 Christoph Langenstain seems to have been especially unpopular, if his conflicts with neighbors are any indication. On another occasion in 1619 he was the object of slander in his own home during a visit from Thoma Schmidtmaister of Mimmenhausen. Schmidtmaister's scathing verbal abuse included the comment that "many have been hung who had less grey hairs than Langenstain." Schmidmaister was imprisoned and fined 30 Reichsthaler despite the support of Mimmenhausen's Amtmann and his excuse that he had drunk too much wine. In another protracted court case, Jacob Grünenmayer of Kellerstobel accused Langenstain of bodily assault. He appealed the court decision, accusing Grünenmayer of libel. GLAK, 98/3200.

245 GLAK, 61/13327, 1630.

246 GLAK, 61/13370, 1611.

247 Besides millers and innkeepers, other nonagricultural occupations represented among Amtmänner include a baker, blacksmith, and bathhouse manager.

widows. Tax lists provide information about his parents, showing that he grew up in a modest, craftsman household. In 1578 he was the only child of the Neufrach cooper Christa Diem and his wife Agatha Schaitteckhin, whose total wealth was just 41 fl. By 1603 the family had grown to include five daughters, and their wealth had risen to 150 fl. Balthas Diem married Elisabetha Hailgin around 1608 and moved to Leutkirch where his wife held a hereditary lease, most likely a smallholding. In that year the abbey provided a new lease contract in Diem's name even though Hailgin had inherited the property from her first husband, Wilhelm Pfannenstil of Leutkirch, who left her nine children.[248] The new union produced at least two sons, Hans and Jacob. Balthas Diem was mentioned in a few chancery records, none of which suggest great wealth. When he borrowed 90 fl. from St. Margaretha's of Buggensegel in 1620 it was Abraham Fimppel, the innkeeper of Bermatingen, who mortgaged property on his behalf (suggesting he did not have extensive freeholdings).[249] In 1625 Diem was named together with Fimppel for a second time, when they jointly represented the wealthy Appolonia Hailgin of Pfullendorf in a legal suit involving the debts owed to her by several territorial residents. This court appearance confirms a kinship link to the innkeeper and the widow through Diem's wife: both he and Fimppel were married to Hailgins. Diem became an alternate member of the Sidelgericht in 1626, then a full member of the court in 1631. He also served as the Wespach hospital warden (*Armenpfleger*) in 1630 and 1632. His wife Elisabetha died in 1632, and the Audience protocol registered her heriot tax of seven gulden.

On the same date and in the very next entry, the Audience ratified the marriage contract between Diem and his second wife, Magdalena Zürckhin of Mimmenhausen. His first wife had been a good match, but this new wife was even better connected.[250] In addition to many influential kinsmen and kinswomen, Magdalena Zürckhin was the widow of Mimmenhausen's previous Amtmann, Mattheus Leub, and she still enjoyed close ties with the powerful Leub clan. The marriage agreement on 9 May 1632 specified that while both Diem and Zürckhin brought significant property to the union, the wife's portion was greater. If she died first, substantial portions would fall to her kin.[251]

248 Wilhelm Pfannenstil was the abbey's master cooper from 1573 until 1590 and in 1588 he became the Hofmeister in Constance. Other Pfannenstils held territorial office, including the Kaufmann Hans Pfannenstil in 1532 and the abbey's guestmaster Friedrich Pfannenstil in 1629.

249 Besides being the innkeeper of Bermatingen, Fimppel was a member of the territorial appeals court (*Hofgericht*) in 1615–1616, the head judge for Bermatingen's village court in 1629–1630, and the Hofmeister of Constance sometime before 1638. He became Amtmann of Bermatingen in 1632, the same year Diem became the Amtmann of Mimmenhausen.

250 Her father was Hans Zürckh, the tenant in Baufnang, and other Zürckhs held tenures in Mimmenhausen, Owingen, and Tüfingen. Among Magdalena's female kin were the wives of former Amtmann Andreas Villieber of Nußdorf, the Mimmenhausen innkeeper Galle Nihel, and the former Sidelrichter Urban Klaiber of Weildorf, by then a wealthy pensioner in Constance.

251 The children of her brother Christian and sisters Nothburga and Appolonia would receive 300 fl. and Hans Leub, her previous husband's brother, would receive 500 fl. GLAK, 61/13320, 1632.

If Diem died first, he could leave 200 fl. to whichever relations he pleased. Only a few months later, in December 1632, Balthas Diem was named in a chancery record as the Amtmann of Mimmenhausen. He had moved to a new village, married a new wife, assumed a new farm, and taken over the previous husband's office. For a cobbler, Master Diem enjoyed great social mobility over the course of his career, in large part because of the connections brought by his wives.

Christoph Langenstain of Bermatingen was an exceptional Amtmann, and not only because he held office for forty years (1592–1631). Langenstain was named in official records more often perhaps than any other abbey subject and he was extremely active in political affairs of all kinds. He was often referred to as Herr Amtmann, though not because he was a noble or even a large grain farmer. He was an abbey tenant and serf like most of his colleagues. In 1603, after he had served as Amtmann for a decade, the abbey offered him a new employment contract.[252] This nine-page document went into much greater detail than the norm. The contract widened Langenstain's responsibilities beyond local affairs and included extensive record keeping: he had to keep separate registers for financial accounts, fines and punishments, village wine sales, and guest services.[253] He was even responsible to assist the Pfister and bursar with the financial records from various administrative districts, examining, auditing, and justifying the records kept by other abbey officials and keeping such knowledge "secret to the grave." As his salary, Langenstain received the use of a house and twenty or so arable and meadow parcels plus grain, wine, firewood, and new clothes annually.[254] He was permitted to keep the fines from lesser offenses of not more than three shillings, and in view of his expanded duties, he was paid 25 fl. cash per year. By at least 1617 Langenstain had become a member of the Audience, and over the following years, he was one of that body's most regular participants.[255]

Christoph Langenstain was extremely wealthy, though not from grain agriculture or office perquisites. In 1603 his household was listed as the second-wealthiest in the territory (with 4,775 fl.), even though he held no farm other than the parcels associated with his office. By comparison, the estate inventory produced upon his death in 1632 shows a staggering level of wealth including extensive vineyards in Bermatingen and elsewhere.[256] His real estate in Bermatingen was worth 9,268 fl., and including all other property he had 16,335 fl. in land. His moveables were worth an additional

[252] GLAK, 98/233.

[253] Sections of his wine register survive in GLAK, 98/3198, 1603–1609.

[254] His probate inventory of 1632 describes his clothing. GLAK, 98/3204.

[255] The only other villagers to sit as members of the Audience were Valentin Mayer of Neufrach, who was a member on one occasion in 1623, and Johann Schentz, who was the abbey's forest supervisor and occasional member of the Audience for eight years before he became Owingen's Amtmann in 1633. Since regular lists of Audience members start in 1617, it is likely that Langenstain took part in its deliberations even earlier.

[256] GLAK, 98/3204. In Bermatingen he owned a freehold house with garden, orchard, and wine press worth 1,000 fl., a farm worth 1,830 fl., and vineyards worth at least 3,420 fl.

3,093 fl.[257] After the subtraction of debts, his net wealth was 21,405 fl.[258] This was an incredible sum for a territorial official by any standard of the time, whether noble or nonnoble.

As for family connections, Langenstain was born and raised in Kirchberg, Salem's grange on the lake near Hagnau.[259] Based on common surnames, his father Stoffel Langenstain and mother Agatha Rockhin were from local families. Both were Salem's serfs. His parents were wealthy, with 1,315 lb. dn. in 1566 and 1,902 fl. in 1578. Christoph had several siblings, including two brothers in Immenstadt and two in Kippenhausen. He married twice, first to Appolonia Hagenweilerin and then to Agatha Angerin. Based on their surnames, neither of which were shared by other territorial residents, both wives were outsiders. His first wife and three daughters, Maria, Anna, and Elisabetha, were free. Langenstain's probate inventory names the daughters' husbands, and it is no great surprise that each was a territorial outsider of high social standing: a legal doctor, a medical doctor, and Heiligenberg's Oberamtmann. This third husband was present at the signing of the Treaty of 1637 between Salem and Heiligenberg, and perhaps this marriage alliance helped to smooth relations between the neighboring administrations.

A search through the serial records turns up dozens of petitions, contracts, and legal suits naming Christoph Langenstain as a party, witness, guardian, or legal representative. He appeared on his own behalf, on behalf of his neighbors, and even for others outside his community. He also brought a number of reports and complaints about the misdeeds of others. His justice was strict, which is probably one reason the abbey trusted him with such great responsibility. Although Langenstain was named in too many petitions to mention, some examples from the Audience protocol give an idea of his activities. On behalf of neighbors, he negotiated death taxes (twice in 1624)

---

[257] Langenstain's probate inventory is of interest for the study of material culture. He was the wealthiest man in the territory by far, and his household possessions are fairly well described. Yet the absence of furniture, tablewares, and status objects suggests that the social presentation and material comfort of wealthy households was not so different from poorer neighbors. He had books, for example, but they were worth only 15 fl. There were also textiles, clothes, and metalwares in his inventory, but they are not as extensive or valuable as one would find in urban areas or in a later period. On the significance of the rise in household demand after 1650, see Jan de Vries, The Industrial Revolution or the Industrious Revolution?, in: Journal of Economic History 54 (1994), pp. 249–270; idem, Between Purchasing Power and the World of Goods: Understanding the Household Economy in Early Modern Europe, in: Consumption and the World of Goods, ed. John Brewer and Roy Porter, London 1993, pp. 85–132; idem, The Industrious Revolution: Consumer Behavior and the Household Economy, 1650 to the Present, New York 2008.

[258] He owed 3,862 fl. to various creditors and others owed him a total of 3,470 fl.

[259] Most but not all Amtmänner were born in the village where they held office. The above-mentioned Balthas Diem was another exception and a third was Johann Schentz, the Amtmann of Owingen in 1633–1635. Schentz was the territory's forest supervisor (*Waldvogt*) and became Amtmann after his predecessor resigned, with the commune's approval.

and requested alms (1599). He pledged surety for the payment of neighbors' manumission and emigration taxes (1630). He enforced the banishment of nonresidents and troublemakers from the village (1599, 1624). He shut down a bakery found to be selling bread beyond the territory (1630). He worked to fix ongoing problems with the village bathhouse. He mediated disputes between neighbors to avoid legal action (1624).

Other petitions concerned Langenstain's own commercial activities. In 1616 he requested compensation for sales taxes (*Abzug*) on vineyards he had purchased from an outsider in 1595.[260] He received permission to sell straw outside the territory in 1624 and 1629. When he was unable to collect as much grain as expected from the small tithe he had purchased, he requested a reduction of the price he had paid (this request was denied). In 1630 Langenstain proposed a parcel exchange with the abbey, and in 1631 he requested ratification of a land sale.

On several occasions the abbey relied on Langenstain's reports concerning matters of lordship, as when two parties proposed to exchange forest parcels and Langenstain was sent to inspect the properties (1630). When a subject had to appear before an outside court and requested legal representation (*Beistand*) from the abbey in 1613, Langenstain was chosen to accompany him. Langenstain also reported on neighbors' finances for manumission and heriot assessments (1600, 1624). The abbey asked Langenstain to order and enforce the peace in a family dispute over inheritance (1596). In 1611 he reported that two boys had discovered a large quantity of salt in the wine press that had been reported missing a few days earlier. In 1624 he reported the suspicious burial of a man and woman from Ittendorf, by a Heiligenberg official in a forest near Bermatingen. One thing stands out in all Langenstain's Audience petitions. None were submissions of grievances against the abbey on behalf of the commune or some other group, and few were requests for aid. Langenstain seems to have avoided the role of community spokesman. His activities, compared to those of other Amtmänner like Martin Richel, demonstrate a close alliance with the abbey. This may be why Langenstain's political career was so long and successful. It may also explain why he was the object of slander and insult on several occasions throughout his career.

Martin Richel, the Amtmann of Neufrach (1588–1616), is our final example. Like Langenstain, he spent a long term in office and was extremely active in political affairs. Unlike Langenstain, however, Martin Richel was a village insider who petitioned on behalf of his community and was extremely involved in neighborly affairs, taking sides and breaking the rules at times, getting into trouble along with his peers. He had strong family connections, mostly in the local community, including three kinsmen who served as members of the Sidelgericht. During his time in office there appears to have been a high level of social conflict in Neufrach, especially involving the commons and grazing disputes that pitted the village against its neighbors and split the community along internal lines. It is hard to say whether Neufrach's combative character was

[260] The vineyard was worth 1,030 fl. in 1595, with a ten percent tax of 103 fl.

the result of the community's own socioeconomic structure or a closer reflection of Richel's personality and leadership as the village headman. Either way, Richel's activities highlight the differences between him and Christoph Langenstain as village leaders and show the role he played in local disputes.

Martin Richel was a natural spokesman for his neighbors' complaints. He seemed to relish taking on the grievances of others, even representing nearby villages in delicate complaints against the abbey. For example, he petitioned in 1600 on behalf of the farm tenants of Neufrach, Buggensegel, and Weiler for the reinstatement of customary refreshments following carting services. He also asked the abbey to protect its subjects in Neufrach and Weiler from an outside lender who was trying to collect on predatory terms. In 1591 Richel requested permission for the community to turn a useless communal forest into a vineyard. After multiple requests the abbey agreed to the conversion of a small clearing two acres in size, but nothing more. Richel persisted in the following months, asking for more land and pointing out that two acres was not enough to support the community's needs. He raised the issue again in 1596. In that year he also tried to convince the abbey to give up its share of the crop from some arable land villagers had previously converted to hemp and flax with the abbey's permission.

The commons, and especially grazing rights, were a constant source of conflict in Neufrach. Richel was Amtmann in 1590 when the Audience investigated an illegal assembly by the Mayerschaft, allegedly to set wages.[261] Richel appeared with the village treasurers in 1591 to ask for the reinstatement of tenants' right to assemble. The Audience agreed, but limited their discussions to topics pertaining to the tenants. Richel was also the Amtmann in 1595 when a major dispute broke out over the number of animals each villager was permitted to keep. The result was a new grazing ordinance in 1596, created by the commune and ratified by the abbot, which specified a multi-tiered system based on the size of a tenant's farm. In 1613 the Amtmann reported one of the smallholders who spoke out against the agreement after the commune refused to amend it.[262] In 1605 Richel represented his community before the Sidelgericht in a commons dispute with Weiler. He repeatedly championed Neufrach's forest rights in 1599, 1600, and 1616.

With his many actions on behalf of the tenants, it comes as no surprise that Richel was one of the largest landholders in the village. In 1589 he acquired a six-year lease in exchange for a pension provided to his wife's stepmother, Ursula Mayerin, and by 1593 he had a large annual lease, possibly the same farm, with 37½ Jauchert in one field. In that year his gross wealth was 1,294 fl., his net wealth 764 fl., and his freehold property 260 fl. In 1599 he petitioned for a reduction of his manure rent from 15 to

---

261 See Chapter 3.

262 The smaller farm tenants complained that they should be allowed two additional oxen since they, too, had to plow fields and perform carting services. One of these smaller farmers was Andreas Richel, Martin's brother, but it was another man who got in trouble for swearing and criticizing the major tenants in public.

12 cartloads, in consideration of the fact he had converted two houses into one. By 1603 his situation had improved even further. According to the tax list his total wealth was 1,786 fl. and he had freehold worth 568 fl. in addition to the farm, now a lifelong lease. Not listed was the hereditary farm he took over from his father in 1602. In 1615 he purchased yet another hereditary farm in Weiler together with his niece's husband, the miller of Neufrach, and as a result of this transaction he was involved in a legal suit with Joachim Haimpolt, the seller and Oberamtmann of Ostrach. The purchase price, fully borrowed from Haimpolt, was 1,750 fl.

Richel was personally involved in his neighbors' interests and affairs on a much deeper level than the aloof Langenstain. The chancery records contain so many entries naming Richel as a pledge, marriage witness, property assessor, or guardian, that it is hard to keep track of them all. He was also active in the land and credit markets, individually and on others' behalf. In 1590 he borrowed large amounts of grain together with his neighbors on three occasions, presumably to sell to poorer villagers. Richel often bought and sold property, borrowed money, and carried loans as a legal guardian for orphans and widows. In 1600 he and the innkeeper took responsibility for repaying communal debts worth 220 fl. to a burgher from Meersburg. They in turn had to collect payments from their neighbors as best they could. Yet despite this apparent gesture of goodwill, Richel did not always get along with his neighbors. Only the year before, Richel complained about the same innkeeper for his refusal to sell wine according to custom, a case that ended in heated disagreement, swearing, and the innkeeper's incarceration. Also in 1599 Richel asked the abbey to appoint an official wine sales overseer to settle complaints and disorder in the village.[263] On at least two occasions, Richel was cited before the authorities for slandering his neighbors.

Richel's actions as a landholder and landlord caused dispute on numerous occasions. In 1606 the Audience penalized him for illegally building a new house instead of the permitted shed, after the community reported him and pointed out that he already controlled several hearths in the village. On another occasion (in 1600) a renter complained when Richel tried to throw him out of his house for unspecified reasons. The Audience sided with the renter, telling Richel to let the man stay in his house. In 1611 Richel was fined for selling straw and fertilizer outside the territory (in contrast to Langenstain, who requested permission to do the same). Also in 1611 Richel sold a parcel and got into trouble with the buyer for failing to properly disclose the rent.

As for his kin, the Richels were one of the most powerful families in Neufrach. Martin's grandfather Andreas was a Sidelrichter in 1572 with a large farm and hereditary smallholding. His father Hans was an alternate member of the court (1584–1591) who held a large farm as well as two hereditary smallholdings, one from his marriage to Martin's mother, Agatha Hailgin. The wealthy couple had property worth 2,006 fl.

---

263 "Amman von Neufra [Martin Richel] Pitt Inn namen der gemeindt daselbsten, man welle Inen wie von Altershero ein geschwornen einschennckher Verordnen, Dann es umb einschenckhen ein große Clag seye, ganng auch damit unordenlich zuo." GLAK, 61/13369, 1600.

in 1578. In 1580 Martin's father mortgaged 14 freehold vineyards to cover a loan to his in-law, Caspar Leub. Martin had at least four siblings, among them Andreas, another member of the Sidelgericht (1612–1624). Martin's first wife was Waldpurga Schaitteckhin, who may have been previously married to Grasbeuren's Amtmann Adam Ower.[264] Their eldest son Bartlin received a licentiate's degree in both laws and became a councilor and vice chancellor to the bishop of Eichstatt. Three of the younger children settled in Neufrach.[265] Martin's second wife Agatha Wiererin was an outsider, from Haresheim. Her kin are unknown, but she must have been wealthy: their 1615 marriage contract secured for her a child's portion plus 300 fl. in the case of Richel's death, as well as lifelong use of his hereditary tenure and retirement benefits to be provided by one of the stepchildren on the family farm. In addition to the Richels, who controlled many of the largest tenures in Neufrach over several generations, Martin's relatives belonged to the most important families in the territory: the Leubs, Hailgs, Schaitteckhs, Owers, Steckborers, Pfannenstils, Winters, Dreers, and Mayers. Martin Richel may not have been the most even-handed, model Amtmann, but he was deeply entrenched in the economic and social networks of his local community and the larger region.

4.9 Conclusions

Imperial tax registers present an extremely stable picture of territorial population, household wealth, and propertyholding during the second half of the sixteenth century (1566–1603). Since population was not rising and the large farms did not undergo greater fragmentation during this period, we must look elsewhere for sources of decline or social conflict in the villages prior to 1600. Wealth structure varied in individual villages, but in all communities there was an obvious division between the haves and the have-nots, as seen in the lack of middling households and in the large number of households in the lower wealth brackets. Despite these differences in wealth, petitions and legal suits do not provide evidence that village social life was characterized by bitter opposition between the farm tenants and smallholders, even in the early seventeenth century. The investigation of tenure, freehold property, inheritance practices, and supralocal markets in land and credit suggest several possible reasons for this.

---

264 Overlapping dates suggest their wives may have been different women with the same name. Even if not the same woman, they were probably close relatives, providing an affinal link between the two Amtmänner. There were many other powerful Schaitteckhs in Salem's territory, both male and female.

265 Daughter Magdalena married Hans Utz, who became the Amtmann after Martin Richel's death. Son Lorenz was involved in several property disputes with his stepmother and her two later husbands, Salem's master gardener Hans Hofmann and Georg Langenstain (probably the son of Buggensegel's Amtmann). Daughter Eva also married and remained in Neufrach.

The major landholders were the farm tenants, who were among the wealthiest households and were especially dependent on the abbey for both economic and political reasons. Yet wealth and tenure were only loosely related, in part because freehold property was widely available in small parcels. The diversified agrarian economy and a relatively open land market allowed for social mobility, with the accessibility of land permitting even poorer men and women to borrow money, buy land, and establish themselves in the community. Viticulture created a niche for smallholders and landless laborers, providing a viable alternative to large-scale grain agriculture. Communal initiatives to extend vineyards in a period of tightening resources created opportunities for untenured households through the intensification of labor. Freehold property was freely alienable and could be bought and sold, or passed along to heirs, according to the demands of the family life-cycle. Freehold property also weakened the extent and demands of landlordship and spurred economic development by encouraging local and regional market activity, especially in sales and loans as well as labor.

One of the key factors in the socioeconomic structure of Salem's villages was the combination of tenure by the lord's grace with partible inheritance of other family property. Tenure on one of the large farms was not guaranteed to any household, and the redistribution of property among various family members and even nonkin meant that property could not accumulate over generations in the hands of the richest families. Partible inheritance, characterized by the recombination of field parcels and division of houses, also limited the accumulation of property by some at the expense of others. The flexible timing of estate divisions made the younger generation dependent upon their elders, and it allowed for individual family circumstances.

Socioeconomic structure varied from village to village, with Nußdorf and Mimmenhausen providing examples of contrast. But just as the households of a village were interconnected by work and property and by social and family networks, so too were the territory's villages integrated on a regional basis. There was a high degree of geographical mobility, especially through marriage, but also for other reasons. Members of neighboring villages conducted business with one another including sales, loans, barter, marriage alliances, and labor. The Amtmänner not only stood between the community and the lord, they also bound the individual communities of the territory together, especially through their participation in the Audience and Sidelgericht, political organs that brought officials from the various communities together on a regular basis.

The Amtmänner acted as mediators between villagers and the abbot. They were in many respects privileged members of the community—wealthy, well-connected, and politically influential. Yet on the whole, the village headmen were not so different from their neighbors. They were integrated into socioeconomic life, locally and regionally, through land, wealth, marriages, patronage, and disputes. The Amtmänner were a fairly diverse group. They came from a variety of backgrounds, political orientations, social networks, and families. Some were wealthy tenant farmers and others were successful craftsmen. Some came from modest families but rose in fortune over the course of their careers, but a few fell into significant debt. Some were clearly the lord's men, while others boldly communicated villagers' grievances for redress before the Audience.

The socioeconomic structure of Salem's territory, local communities, and individual households had an impact on political development in the territory. This in itself is not an extraordinary statement. What must be established is the specific nature of that impact, and here we may have something more unusual. The general stability of the territorial population and its resources, the integration of villages and households, the position of women as major property-holders, and the continual redistribution of farms, parcels, and other property are all important factors. My earlier expectation was that this chapter would illustrate the nature of divisions within the village through the personal conflicts and social divisions among its members, presenting the limitations of the village commune and the wider community as a unified whole. This has turned out not to be the case, because fewer examples of grievance and discord involving social groups or class interests presented themselves than had been anticipated. There were certainly conflicts between individuals and communities, often involving communal and household resources such as forests and pastures, inheritance, and debts. I would not describe these disputes as systematic, however, or serious enough to prevent villagers from uniting around common interests. In fact, there is so little evidence of the village being torn apart by social difference or even personal enmity that I found I could not make these issues a central theme of this chapter as initially planned.[266] It may be simply the nature of the sources, but the view we are presented with is of stable and well-integrated local communities, whose members were not particularly discordant.

This chapter ends with a hypothesis, namely, that the low levels of conflict, especially involving entire villages and local social groups, allowed subjects to have a greater impact on territorial policy and development. Their participation in creating territorial policy and building political cohesion, rather than merely resisting the measures imposed by lords, can be seen especially in their Audience petitions and in the actions of their Amtmänner. Integration at the territorial level and shared legal customs also allowed subjects to have greater influence on legal practice, through the Sidelgericht. This court is the subject of the next chapter.

[266] Other conflicts between villages and villagers are addressed in Chapters 3 (commons) and 5 (legal suits).

Chapter 5: The Sidelrichter and Territorial Justice in Salem

Central to any understanding of political culture in Salem is the abbey's central court, known as the Sidelgericht. This institution is significant because of its unusual nature as well as for its lasting and weighty influence over territorial development. Here we will look in detail at Salem's central court and at its procedures, functioning, and members. The court's longevity and course of development can be explained through its utility in meeting the interests and objectives of various groups within the territory, not only litigants but also abbey administrators, resident elites, and the general body of subjects. This chapter describes the significance of Salem's judicial system for the territory's political development in the early modern period. It contributes also to an understanding of the complexity and diversity of legal and representative institutions, and of popular politics in early modern Europe.

In Chapter 2, we saw how the 15 peasant judges of Salem's central court objected to the abbot's alleged imposition of a new law code and new burdens that resulted in five years of conflict between them. The two sides engaged not with violence but with words and especially lawsuits, in which the discussion involved the sources of legal knowledge, the means used to interpret it, the right to change it, and relations between the abbey and its subjects. The outcome of that dispute in 1473 upheld subjects' right to resist their lord's unlawful actions and to sue him in a court of law. The settlement also guaranteed that the court staffed by 15 peasants would continue to interpret the law and settle disputes, specifically with regard to inheritance, property, and tenure. Furthermore, the decision restricted the abbot's unilateral legal authority: he could not impose new laws without the consent of thirty territorial representatives or imprison subjects for minor infractions.

In terms of the territory's legal development and relations between Salem's abbot and his subjects, the partnership agreement of 1473 served as a sort of constitution, a foundational document that set the legal parameters, opening the door to certain developments but closing the door on others. During the century after 1473 we catch glimpses of the court's activities and its members in the form of legal charters, resulting from the court's settlement of individual lawsuits.[1] Upon the judges' request in 1572, Abbot Georg produced a replacement copy of the 1473 agreement, which was by that time worn from a century of use. Suddenly in 1583, much fuller documentation allows for an investigation of the court's activities, its members, the individuals who sought its mediation, and their reasons for coming to court. In that year the Sidelgericht began to keep regular records of every session and every suit it heard.

1 GLAK, 4/4648 (1479), 4/1287 (1480), 4/2723 (1492), 4/2178 (1503), 4/2158 (1505), 4/2139 (1514), 4/4006 (1514), 4/4429 (1526), 4/5663 (1566), and 4/4627 (1578).

This chapter is concerned with the Sidelgericht, particularly in the fifty or so years starting in 1583. During this critical period of political development, the Sidelgericht occupied a central position not only from the practical and instrumental perspective of peacekeeping and settling conflicts but also on a symbolic and conceptual level. This chapter shows how the court functioned to connect the various parts of Salem's territory and build from them a common identity, a shared political culture based in the legal traditions of many villages and the participation of subjects from across the territory. Together in the courtroom they raised, argued, and rectified the contentious issues of everyday life. These small legal actions and their resolution brought the members of the territory together and strengthened bonds that were geographical, social, material, and cultural. The court did not merely penalize infractions and reconcile minor differences between territorial subjects, though these were its most basic activities. It also functioned to establish a territorial political awareness and even a broader notion of community on the basis of legal practices and norms that evolved out of the experiences, ideas, and difficulties of ordinary people. The participation of subjects at the court—as litigants and judges, bystanders and witnesses—had a powerful cumulative effect. The court served as the foundation for building a territorial polity from within.

The Sidelgericht appears unusual among legal tribunals of this period in several key respects.[2] First, its jurisdiction extended over the twenty or so villages and smaller hamlets belonging to the two central districts Under the Hills. Second, the court was composed of 15 judges who were all peasant subjects residing within the territory. Third, the Sidelgericht was one of the abbey's oldest secular institutions, established by the mid-fourteenth century if not earlier.[3] Fourth, during a period when many territories were undergoing a conspicuous transition from local and customary justice toward professional and centralized courts, the Sidelgericht continued to operate to a remarkable degree according to customary legal procedures and ideas conveyed primarily by villagers. Finally, this court was the primary support for the abbey's claims to imperial status and independent territorial authority.

Medieval courts of law were commonly composed of lay judges—that is, people without university degrees who were native to the community and who derived their primary income from some other occupation. They could be nobles or peasants but

---

2 This is not to suggest that the Sidelgericht was unique, however. Similar institutions may be found across Europe, including England, Franconia, Swabia, Switzerland, and elsewhere. Right in Salem's own backyard, Heiligenberg's territorial court was also composed entirely of peasant subjects; see GOETZ, Niedere Gerichtsherrschaft, pp. 73–74. Yet we are not well informed about such courts in the early modern period, in large part because sources are lacking. In this respect, too, Salem appears to be unusual.

3 The most significant early reference to the court is the royal privilege of 1354, but the abbey's jurisdictional rights are also mentioned in a 1224 privilege and in a legal charter from 1262. FEYERABEND, Chronik, p. 258; GOETZ, Niedere Gerichtsherrschaft, p. 98.

they were not lawyers or jurists with academic training. In the Middle Ages, even supraregional courts could be composed in part of peasants, especially in places lacking territorial towns or nobles.[4] In the villages, peasants commonly served as judges and they were among the local magistrates along with the headman and small council. Yet during the era of territorial statebuilding, beginning in the fifteenth century and increasingly over the course of the early modern period, lay judges were supplanted by professional jurists hired to serve territorial administrations. It was not only the judges who were replaced, however. Oral procedures were replaced by written ones, local customs by uniform, centrally imposed statutes and ordinances, and at the same time the basis of the law and for interpreting the law became more universal, more standard, in a word, more rational. This process resulted not only from the rise of territorial princes but also from a second early modern development, described as the "reception" of Roman law.[5] According to many older interpretations, the community's role of determining the law according to custom was gradually undermined by the centralization of justice according to the prince's standards and his hired jurists. Written procedure and foreign concepts of justice soon barred commoners from access to, let alone a leading role in, the interpretation of law.[6]

In Salem, the situation does not support such an explanation of legal development. The early establishment of a central court before the period of reception and statebuilding ensured a legal tradition that was customary yet unified at the territorial level. Unlike most village courts, which were absent in all but two of the central territory's settlements, Salem's Sidelgericht kept written records that have survived sporadically from the late fifteenth century and then much more regularly starting in the late sixteenth century. Yet early codification and centralization did not override villagers' legal customs or obstruct their participation in the territory's legal development. On the

---

4 SCRIBNER, Communities and the Nature of Power, p. 305; HOLENSTEIN, Bauern, pp. 20–21.

5 There is a large literature on the reception of Roman law in Germany. For an older, though still useful introduction in English, see Gerald STRAUSS, Law, Resistance, and the State: The Opposition to Roman Law in Reformation Germany, Princeton 1986. See also idem, ed., Pre-Reformation Germany, New York 1972; Franz WIEACKER, A History of Private Law in Europe, trans. Tony Weir, Oxford 1995; Wolfgang SELLERT, Zur Rezeption des römischen und kanonischen Rechts in Deutschland von den Anfängen bis zum Beginn der frühen Neuzeit, in: Recht und Verfassung im Übergang vom Mittelalter zur Neuzeit, ed. Hartmut Boockmann et al., Göttingen 1998, pp. 115–166; Diethelm KLIPPEL, Zur Geschichte der Gesetzgebung in der frühen Neuzeit: Eine Einführung, in: Gesetz und Gesetzgebung im Europa der frühen Neuzeit, ed. Barbara Dölemeyer and Diethelm Klippel, Berlin 1998, pp. 7–13.

6 This view continues to be widespread. See Karl Heinz BURMEISTER, Genossenschaftliche Rechtsfindung und herrschaftliche Rechtssetzung: Auf dem Weg zum Territorialstaat, in: Revolte und Revolution in Europa, ed. Peter Blickle, Munich 1975, pp. 177–178; Peter BLICKLE, Von der Leibeigenschaft zu den Menschenrechten: Eine Geschichte der Freiheit in Deutschland, Munich 2003, pp. 59–60; PROSSER, Rechtsaufzeichnungen, pp. 175–183; SCRIBNER, Communities and the Nature of Power, p. 305.

contrary, the central court was staffed by peasants who settled disputes between territorial subjects according to traditional methods, which not only provided them with an unusual degree of control over legal development, it also had broader political implications: territorial unification was not antipeasant or protoabsolutist.

One problem with the reception theory is that like many modernization theories it privileges signs of the new, failing to recognize or value threads of the old or the ways in which various legal mentalities interacted and became interwoven. The court records and other sources relating to territorial justice in Salem document the fact that peasant subjects maintained a strong influence over legal norms, yet this does not mean the court failed to evolve or that it did not incorporate a variety of needs and interests. The abbey's policies and objectives for territorial rule certainly also had an effect on the court, as seen in the records that were kept by the court secretary, a hired abbey employee. The court could not have flourished as it did without the lord's support, and the abbey had good reason to promote it. But first, before delving deeper into its multivalent uses and interactive processes, let us consider the court and its legal competence.

The Sidelgericht's major function was the administration of low justice—in other words, minor offenses generally punishable by fines.[7] Yet its legal competence and significance were much greater than its characterization as a small claims court might suggest. First of all, with very few exceptions, the abbot forbade his subjects to appear before any other court. According to official policy, therefore, the Sidelgericht alone punished offenses and settled disputes involving Salem's territorial residents. Second, the Sidelgericht heard civil suits between private parties as well as criminal cases prosecuted by the abbey. The latter pertained to actions committed against the abbey or the public welfare and were often categorized either as personal misconduct (*Frevel*), such as physical assault, or as statute violations (*übergangenes Gebot*), such as housing strangers.[8] An administrative official, usually the Kaufmann or Oberamtmann, prosecuted criminal suits on the abbot's behalf.[9] Third, as the territory's primary court, the Sidelgericht heard appeals and advised lower district courts on difficult legal matters from beyond the central jurisdiction. A 1558 statute from the northern Linzgau district Over the Hills stated that "cases concerning property rights, conditions of tenure, and other difficult matters should be referred to our gracious lord of Salem's Sidelgericht, as your

---

7 High justice belonged to Heiligenberg, though Salem tried to downplay this fact and prevent its subjects from appearing before the county court.

8 In practice, these categories were not strictly separate. Many infractions involved both personal misconduct and statute violations, and the prosecuted actions could be interpreted as crimes against the abbey or the public welfare, depending on one's perspective. Criminal suits, as well as other case types, are described below.

9 The Kaufmann, a salaried employee in the sixteenth century, normally prosecuted criminal suits until the middle of 1590. Starting in May of that year, following administrative restructuring, the Oberamtmann took over this role. Criminal suits occasionally specify that the Kaufmann or Oberamtmann legally represented the abbot, the entire abbey, the Großkeller, or the Pfister. Monks appeared infrequently in court and they did not prosecute crimes.

superior court, following the custom and ancient tradition of this court and according to previous agreement."[10]

The Sidelgericht also possessed significance beyond its judicial responsibilities. Each year the court published a list of annual prices for grain, straw, and manure known as the *Fruchten Anschlag*. Additionally, the agreement in 1473 identified the Sidelgericht as a representative body whose consent was required for the passage of new or revised territorial statutes. As indicated in Chapter 2, the Sidelgericht was associated with a tradition of resistance to lordship and with the protection of subjects' rights and freedoms against arbitrary demands. In some sense, the Sidelgericht fulfilled functions similar to those of *Landschaften*, the quasi-parliamentary assemblies found in other territories but absent from Salem's lands.[11]

Geographically, the Sidelgericht's jurisdiction stretched over all the residents of Salem's central district, regardless of their legal status or social backgrounds.[12] Even strangers from beyond the territory might find themselves summoned before the court, because it claimed authority over all offenses committed within its boundaries or involving its dependents, regardless of the opposing party's origins or identity. Nor was it unusual for outsiders (especially creditors) to act as plaintiffs, indicating both the difficulty of summoning Salem's subjects before outside courts and the wide network of social and economic relations that brought individuals together irrespective of territorial boundaries. Some plaintiffs' willingness to travel long distances to bring their cases before the Sidelgericht suggests that even they perceived the court to be of potential use. The appearances of villagers from beyond the territory for infractions such as wood theft and assault suggest, furthermore, that the tribunal was recognized past its own jurisdictional borders and that the abbey's backing gave it the power to summon and enforce rulings even against those who were not Salem's own.

As described in Chapter 1, Salem's royal privilege of 1354 established a link between its imperial status and the central court, and the document contained a clause requiring all disputes involving abbey subjects to be settled before this court and no other. Confirmed by a long series of emperors, the passage was often cited and interpreted as a prohibition against the use of outside courts. It featured in the abbey's oldest surviving statutes and oath formulas, and authorities attempted to enforce it through various means. Violation of the order was subject to a fine of five, ten, or even forty pounds.[13]

---

10 "Was auch Erblehen, lehen und Aigen, auch ander sachen euch zue schwer belangt, das sollen Ir für unsers Gnedigen herren von Salmanshweiler Sidel, alls Ewer obergericht, weisen, und daselbst Rechtferttigen laßen, alles nach gewonhait, altem herkhomen dis gerichts, unnd Auf Innhalt der vertrag." GLAK, 4/116. The Sidelgericht occasionally heard appeals from courts outside the central territory including those in Beuren (Heiligenberg), Einhard, Mainwangen, and Ostrach.

11 KUHN, Seehaufen, p. 114.

12 Clergymen, however, were exempt from the Sidelgericht and other secular tribunals. Residents from Bermatingen could request the transfer of cases against them to their own local court.

13 GLAK, 98/1546, 61/13315.

Subjects could not act as pledges or guarantors outside the territory, and even when summoned as defendants before the county court (which had authority over the most serious crimes), they faced stiff fines for appearing unless the abbey granted prior permission.[14]

In fact, however, the authorities' perpetual insistence on the Sidelgericht's absolute legal authority was a screen used to conceal the vulnerability of the abbey's broader claims.[15] Ultimately, such restrictions were impossible to enforce. Behind the fiction of full judicial exemption, the fact remained that Salem did not possess authority over high justice or other serious offenses before 1637.[16] This meant that criminal proceedings of greater severity were brought not before the abbey's Sidelgericht but before the county court (*Landgericht*) of Heiligenberg, whose claims to overlordship were the principal obstacle to Salem's autonomy throughout the abbey's history. Irreconcilable differences and competing claims between the two rulers were among the primary reasons for the Sidelgericht's significance to Salem and for its territorial lordship; they explain in large part the abbey's attempt to grant it the greatest possible latitude. The Sidelgericht was a critical institution for staking more general political claims. The abbot's assertions about the court's exclusive authority over his subjects were incongruous with the count's claims and with actual practice. Still, the court was a major foundation for Salem's assertion of territorial autonomy and an effective tool for eroding the count's powers from within.[17]

In reality, Heiligenberg's court of high justice was not the only exception to the Sidelgericht's legal authority. Also excluded were "spiritual crimes," violations against the church or common morality, including marriage disputes, sexual offenses, sorcery,

---

14 This put Salem's territorial subjects in the crossfire when they were summoned before Heiligenberg's court, as in 1602, when the spiritual council forbade two subjects to answer a summons on pain of a forty pound fine, with the recommendation that if the count imprisoned one of them, the abbey should retaliate with similar action: "Der Peurin Wie auch dem Dinßler, ist von Salem bei 40 lb. dn. straff nit zuershinen gebotten und diser beden halben vor Landtgericht durch Notarium protestirt worden laut Instruments. Und auff dem fahl deß Dinßlers nit ershei-nen, der Graf Ine Hernach beim Kopff nemen und beyfangen wurde, Ist ainhellig geshlossen, Dz ain Wegenfeng gethon werden solle." GLAK, 61/13315, 11 January 1602.

15 Or to cast it in more positive terms, the assertion may be seen as a symbolic self-representation of the abbey's authority and a reminder to subjects and competitors of the abbey's claim, even though everyone knew it was not enforceable. See SCHLUMBOHM, Gesetze, pp. 660–661.

16 Offenses of an intermediate grade, including assault with bodily injury (referred to in the sources as those involving "flowing wounds"), were divided between Heiligenberg and Salem according to location of the offense: inside the cloister, granges, and villages, they were under Salem's authority; outside settlement boundaries, they belonged to Heiligenberg.

17 The Sidelgericht provided the basis for many claims associated with territorial rule, including imperial tax collection, labor and military services, regulation of trade, imposition of tolls, control over forests and waterways, and rejection of the count's hunting parties. This led the legal historian Georg Goetz to observe that in the Linzgau, although territorial sovereignty arose from the union of high and low justice, low justice was the stronger of the two spheres. Idem, Niedere Gerichtsherrschaft, pp. 111–113.

and blasphemy. Two villages in the central territory had their own local courts.[18] Residents of Bermatingen even claimed exemption from the central court's jurisdiction by tenaciously defending the ancient legal customs of their own village court.[19] Moreover, informal means of conflict resolution were also available. Disputants could call on local officials or other neighbors to mediate, and the abbey's official policies encouraged such informal settlements. One sixteenth-century territorial statute stated that field damages caused by livestock should be settled by neighbors deemed acceptable to both parties.[20] The same statute added that if no such mediators could be agreed upon, parties could appeal to the Kaufmann, who would settle the conflict for a fee in the abbey's name. Another statute stated that trivial claims involving amounts of less than one pound should be settled by the village headman rather than the Sidelgericht.[21] By the late sixteenth century there were also other avenues for the resolution of conflict. At the Audience, subjects could address petitions directly to a panel of the abbey's highest-ranking territorial officials, who usually delivered a speedy resolution.[22] There was also the *Hofgericht*, the high court that heard appeals from the Sidelgericht and was composed of senior administrators, trained jurists, and the occasional villager.[23] Appeals to the *Hofgericht* were possible only in cases involving sums higher than ten gulden and they were heavily discouraged by expensive court fees, strict time limits, and special oaths.[24]

18 Records confirm the existence of a village court in Bermatingen throughout the period under study, and there are also lists of judges from the village court in Owingen (GLAK, 98/597). There is no indication of other village courts within the boundaries of the central territory, but there were courts in some of Salem's outlying districts including Schemmerberg and Ostrach.

19 Bermatingers did not take part in the dispute of 1468–1473, nor did the partnership agreement of 1473 apply to them. Although they claimed immunity from the central court, residents of the village did appear there both as plaintiffs and defendants.

20 GLAK, 98/1546.

21 Ibid. In fact, the Sidelgericht did hear both grazing offences and claims amounting to only a few batzen.

22 The Audience is further described in Chapter 6.

23 Records from the *Hofgericht* are extremely poor. Fragmentary records survive for only four sessions from the period 1615 to 1620 and can be found in GLAK, 61/13321. A handful of villagers normally served as alternate members and sometimes held the lowest-ranking seats. Despite the lack of records, scattered evidence indicates that the court was active over a longer period, though perhaps not on a regular basis. For example, Hans Bitzenhofer complained to the Audience in 1600 that his suit against Hans Hailg's heirs was still pending before the *Hofgericht*. The Audience declared that a meeting date should be set, which suggests that the court met infrequently. Mattheus Dreer of Mimmenhausen complained in 1631 that his appeal still had not been heard, since the *Hofgericht* had not met in such a long time. Hans-Martin Maurer (Ausbildung der Territorialgewalt, p. 182) noted that the *Hofgericht* in Ochsenhausen also met only when necessary or "from time to time."

24 Sidelgericht decisions appealed after a period of nine days were subject to penalties. Appeals procedures are mentioned in GLAK, 67/1782 and 98/1546.

We may conclude that there were many formal and informal alternatives to the Sidelgericht both within and beyond the territory, many of which were recognized and even encouraged by abbatial authorities.[25] The prescriptive measures of territorial statutes and oaths, requiring all legal disputes to be settled by the Sidelgericht, should not lead to the false impression that subjects actually brought all disputes before this court. Abbey officials' insistence on its exclusive jurisdiction had strategic and political significance that was not directed at the eradication of local and informal means of conflict resolution among subjects. Rather, their primary concern was to strengthen the abbey's claims to territorial independence from Heiligenberg. This made the Sidelgericht central to the interests of various groups within the territory, in ways that were not primarily oppositional.

5.1 Sources

One of the most extraordinary achievements of this peasant court was its production of detailed records for all cases heard between 1583 and 1654. The discovery of these serial records is what sparked my interest in Salem as a research topic, and they serve as the focus of this source-driven chapter. In some sense, they are the core of the entire study. The series is extensive, though discontinuous.[26] Its three thousand or so pages provide an impressive level of information, both quantitative and qualitative, about the economic, social, and legal foundations of this territory in the generations around 1600. The bulk of the court protocol consists of case descriptions and the basic format remains consistent over the entire period, with increasing detail over time. Illustration 5.1, Court Records from the Sidelgericht, provides example pages from two different years.

Responsibility for composing and keeping the court records was assigned to a court secretary or scribe (*Gerichtschreiber*), who was a salaried abbey official. Normally employed in the chancery office, keeping the court records was only a small portion of his duties. The records provide very little direct information about the secretary, but the handwriting indicates that the role of court secretary was not assigned to a single

---

25 In Bavaria, too, there were central governing bodies responsible for the judicial and extrajudicial settlement of conflict, and these coexisted alongside local alternatives, which the rulers often encouraged in order to stem the flow of complaints brought before the central court. See Renate BLICKLE, Laufen gen Hof: Die Beschwerden der Untertanen und die Entstehung des Hofrats in Bayern. Ein Beitrag zu den Varianten rechtlicher Verfahren im späten Mittelalter in der frühen Neuzeit, in: Gemeinde und Staat im Alten Europa, ed. Peter Blickle, Munich 1998, pp. 241–266.

26 Court records are missing for the years 1597–1604, 1606–1609, 1613–1614, and 1632–1645, but they survive for all other years from 1583 through 1631. There are also intermittent records from the years 1646–1648 and 1652–1654. GLAK, 61/13322–13329.

Illustration 5.1: Court Records from the Sidelgericht

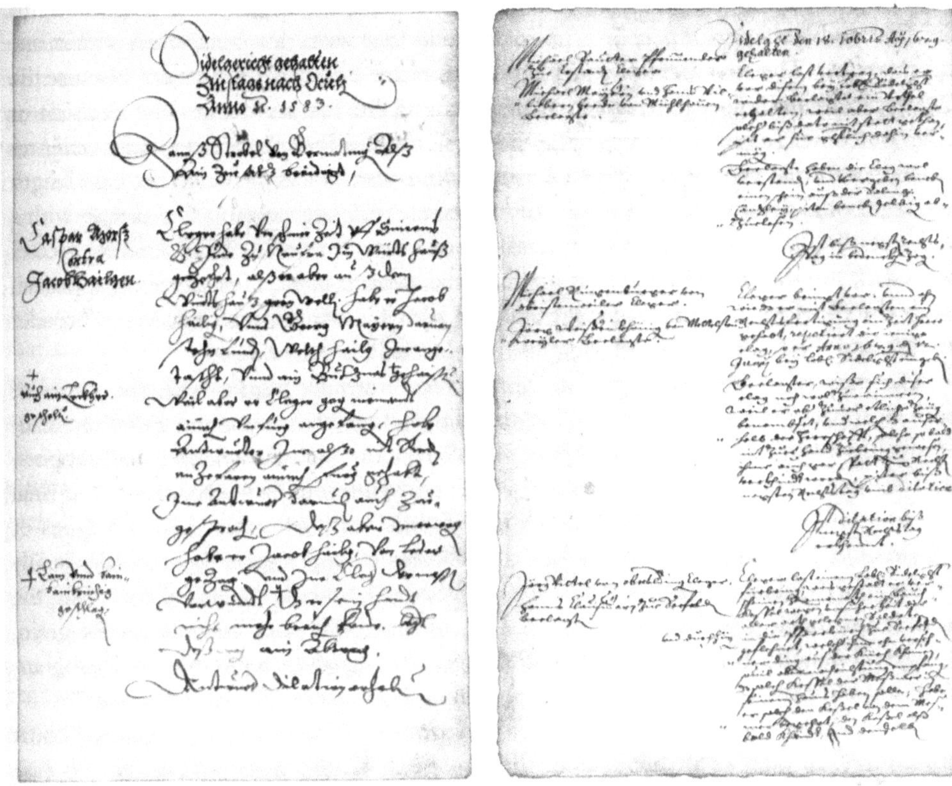

Example pages from 1583 and 1629
Generallandesarchiv Karlsruhe, 61/13322 and 61/13327

individual for long periods of time. The secretarial function could be fulfilled by any number of chancery officials who were not regular members of the court. We will return to the significance of the court secretaries below.

A survey of the entire record provides a broad overview of court activity, but for the purpose of statistical analysis, I have relied on a sample of records consisting of all cases heard during ten evenly spaced years.[27] This sample of cases allows us to measure the frequency and representativeness surrounding topics such as the subjects of dispute, litigants' geographical origins, gender, the use of witnesses and written evidence, the ratio of civil to criminal cases, and the duration of suits. The statistical data are augmented by examples taken from the surrounding years in a series of three-year clusters, an ap-

27 These include the first set of cases in 1583, followed by five-year intervals over the next fifty years: 1585, 1590, 1595, 1605, 1610, 1615, 1620, 1625, and 1630. There are no surviving records for 1600 or 1635.

proach that incorporates both quantitative and illustrative material.[28] This method of surveying the records in blocks around each major sample year grew out of a search for the first and last appearances for the many suits that were not completed within one calendar year. The first and last court appearances are especially important, because the first typically describes the subject of dispute and the last announces the decision or other outcome. Together, they provide the lawsuit's duration. Since many suits never resulted in a formal verdict, searching through three-year blocks provided the case length and additional details for only a minority of cases. Still, augmenting the sample with a wider reading of three consecutive years out of every five paid off by lending greater consistency to the findings and bringing unusual cases to light. This sampling approach made the court records more manageable and struck a compromise between a broader picture and the finer details, offering numbers as well as narratives.

The recorded entry for each court appearance normally begins with the names of both legal parties and their places of origin. Subheadings within the text guide the reader, distinguishing among various types of information such as opening and supporting statements, counterarguments, witness testimony, intermediate resolutions, and final decisions. Besides the case descriptions, the records routinely offer only two types of information. First, appearing at the start of each year's initial session, the records usually list the court's members in order of seat rank.[29] Second, toward the end of each year, the records list the annual *Fruchten Anschlag*, a list of territorial price equivalents for grain, straw, and manure. Starting in 1595, the Sidelgericht played an active role in setting annual values for these commodities and publishing them after each year's harvest.[30]

The court records contain no explicit description of legal norms or general court procedures. In fact, as already stated, their scope is for the most part limited to case hearings. More general, prescriptive rules of court procedure are found in the abbey's

---

[28] In other words, statistical information is based on the ten-year sample of cases with additional examples from the years 1584–1586, 1589–1591, 1594–1596, 1604–1606, 1609–1611, 1615–1616, 1619–1621, 1624–1626, and 1629–1631. There are no surviving records for 1582 or 1614.

[29] These lists include the names of court alternates (*Beisitzer* or *Zusätze*) and the court bailiff (*Gerichtsdiener* or *Gerichtsknecht*), but they do not reveal the identity of the court secretary.

[30] Such price lists are found in the court records for the following years: 1595, 1604–5, 1607, 1609, 1611–12, 1615–18, 1620–28, and 1631 (GLAK, 61/13324–13327). The court's responsibility for price-setting appears to derive from a complaint the entire commune of Owingen presented to the Audience on 16 Nov. 1595: "Since the assessment for straw, which they offer for sale to one another in the village, is set far too high, the honorable Sidelgericht should be the one to determine the price and tax." The first *Fruchten Anschlag* in 1595 notes, "This ordinance has been given to our gracious lord for ratification." The title for the 1605 list reads, "Tax and assessment made by the honorable Sidelgericht, concerning grain, straw, and manure." These brief descriptions demonstrate that the peasant judges were involved in setting territorial market prices as well as dispensing justice. It also suggests that the court fulfilled functions similar to the *Landschaften* in other territories, although I know of no territorial assembly responsible for setting annual commodity prices.

territorial statutes, as well as in two court reform measures introduced in 1566 and 1576. Like all normative sources, these documents reflect what "ought" to have been, especially since the reform measures were introduced to correct earlier abuses. Paired with these written guidelines, the day-to-day business described in the court records provides a good idea of how the court was supposed to proceed, how its actual practices did or did not reflect official policy, and how it evolved over time.

5.2 Court Procedures

As a court of law the Sidelgericht sat at regular intervals, normally once per month.[31] It met at the abbey's Upper Gate, located symbolically at the threshold between the convent and its territory. Court dates were announced in advance, and the bailiff summoned anyone obliged to attend. Whereas failure to appear before the court when ordered to do so could result in a stiff penalty of up to one pound, basic court fees started at the affordable rate of one shilling per party. Calling witnesses cost an additional one shilling each.[32] According to the 1566 reform mandate, hearings were to begin on summer mornings at six o'clock and during winter at eight o'clock, which for many litigants meant an overnight journey or a walk of one to three hours before sunrise.[33] Geographically, the Sidelgericht's jurisdiction covered a radius of roughly fourteen kilometers.[34]

The fifteen judges and four alternates (called *Beisitzer* or *Zusätze*) held office for renewable terms of one year.[35] Senior abbey officials including the prior, bursar, Großkeller, and Pfister were present at the opening session each January. Though the court records provide little specific detail about the opening session, it can be gathered from the occasional note that it began with a reading of the territory's two major law codes, the alte Jarbrief and the partnership agreement of 1473, followed by the ceremonial oath of office, sworn by each member of the court.[36] At the end of the year, either

---

31 In a sample of ten years, the number of sessions ranged annually between eight (1615 and 1620) and fifteen (1590 and 1595) with an average of ten.

32 GLAK, 98/1546, fol. 5v–6r. As for court fines, Barbara Schmidin and Ulrich Kretz were each charged one pound in 1585 for failure to heed a court summons. Schmidin excused herself, saying the summons had arrived at the last minute while she was away from home. In both cases the fine was reduced to half a gulden. GLAK, 61/13322.

33 This travel distance may help explain why Owingen and Bermatingen had their own village courts whereas other villages in the central territory did not. In 1593 the Audience approved the head judge's request for the Sidelrichter to receive wine with breakfast and lunch, and in 1615 the Audience agreed that on rainy days the abbey would provide fodder for their horses so the judges could ride to court. GLAK, 61/13369; 61/13371.

34 RÖSENER, Salem, p. 89.

35 Most judges served more than one year, however, and several were members for over 25 years.

36 Details about the opening session can be found in the court records from 1595, 1619, and 1646. Similar examples for the village courts of Bermatingen and Owingen are found in GLAK, 98/597.

after the closing session in December or before new judges began their service in January, the Oberamtmann or another abbey official relieved the previous judges of their oaths and questioned them about any irregularities or concerns that may have come up over the past year.[37] Other than these annual opening and closing rituals, the record suggests that the court was occupied entirely with case hearings.

Cases began with the plaintiff's initial statement and the defendant's response, which could be an admission or denial of guilt, countercharges, explanation, or request for postponement. Parties could present claims and evidence either orally or in writing.[38] Although parties were supposed to address the court through an approved legal spokesman or advocate (*Fürsprecher, Anwalt*), the records rarely refer to such representatives by name or otherwise.[39] In fact, even the legal actions of female litigants are often described in the court records as if she appeared in person and addressed the court herself, though this seems unlikely. The use of legal advocates was probably so ubiquitous that it required no special comment, and in any case, records were kept with few references to the legal advocate's mediating function.[40] Unless the defendant accepted the charges, disputes were rarely settled at the first hearing. Ensuing sessions involved the repetition and elaboration of arguments as well as the presentation of supporting evidence, submitted ordinarily in one of two forms: written documentation or oral witness testimony.[41]

The court's annual caseload varied from year to year. Chart 5.1 indicates the annual level of court activity in sample years according to three different estimates: the number of lawsuits, the number of pages, and the total number of court appearances (including

---

37 References to such inquiries are available for a number of years, but the judges' responses survive only from the year 1646, discussed below.

38 GLAK, 67/1782.

39 Arguments are usually recorded as if spoken directly by the litigants, and only a small minority of cases mention legal representation for either party. Yet in 1583, the court bailiff charged Hans Schaitteckh three shillings for speaking in court without a spokesman. Again in 1606 the court bailiff penalized Jerg Blanckh from Bamberg for speaking in court, against the prohibition: "Clagt habe nit durch sein fürsprechen sonder wider verbott Im gericht geredt seine Clagen selbsten fürgebracht, Clagt 3 ß dn." On 22 January 1629 the fine for speaking in court without an advocate was raised to three Reichsthaler after the judges pointed out to senior officials that many litigants were ignoring the prohibition. There are not enough references to advocates' names to offer any general conclusions about their identities or relationships to litigants, but they appear to have been territorial residents and not hired professionals.

40 Legal advocates are mentioned for all four lawsuits heard at a court session on 17 March 1620. What is interesting is that the person keeping the record that day was by his own admission not one of the regular court secretaries, he was merely filling in. Likewise, several entries in a row mention advocates on 5 May 1615. These references appear to have had more to do with recordkeeping anomolies than with the presence of legal advocates, which was rarely mentioned otherwise.

41 Oath-taking was also used occasionally as a form of proof. The use of evidence is described later in the chapter.

Chart 5.1: The Court's Annual Caseload

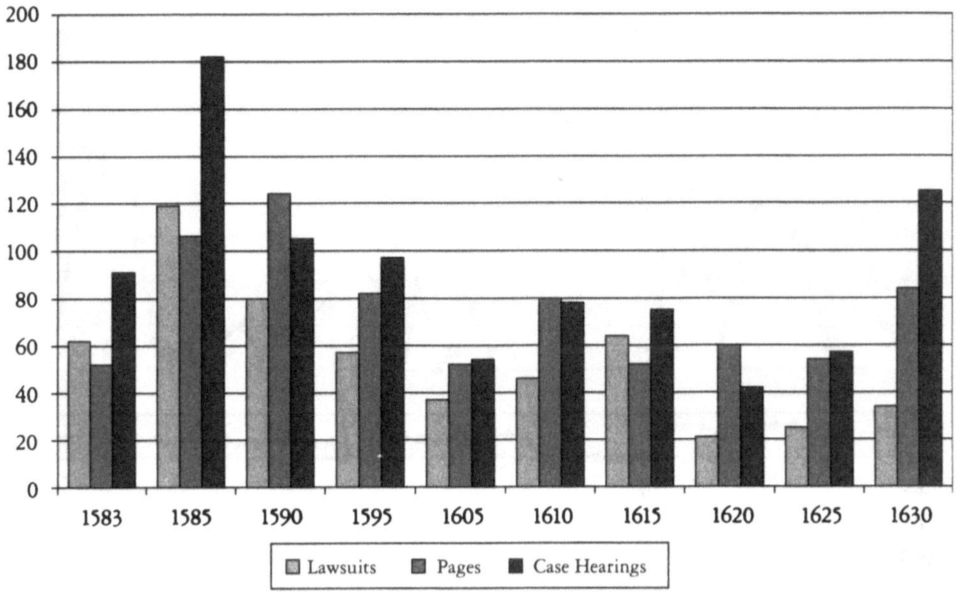

multiple appearances for many suits). The chart shows an especially high number of suits in 1585, and in 1630 there was a high number of court appearances compared to separate cases. Chart 5.2 provides a broader overview of the records for all years from 1583 until 1632.

The length of time and number of court appearances leading up to a final verdict varied widely from case to case. In criminal suits, a verdict was often reached immediately after the accused admitted to the charges and asked for mercy. Requests for birth certificates were always approved without the need for a second hearing. For most civil suits, however, the court reached a decision only after several months and multiple court appearances, if at all. Chart 5.3 shows the range in duration of suits from eight sample years.[42] More than a year after the initial hearing, a large proportion of cases (between 25% in 1605 and 75% in 1625) remained without a formal settlement.[43] Some of these "unfinished" cases were referred to other authorities (most notably the Audience) or settled amicably out of court, but many times the litigants failed to reappear for unknown reasons. Among settled cases, the average number of court appearances increased over time. As the chart indicates, 30% of all cases in 1630 ended with a verdict after six or more hearings, and 18% required more than ten hearings. The longest

[42] Case length is based on a search of three-year blocks. The sample years 1583 and 1615 are excluded because surrounding records are unavailable.

[43] Some cases classified as unfinished may have been eventually settled in court, but not within a year of the last known hearing.

Chart 5.2: Annual Court Activity (1583–1632)

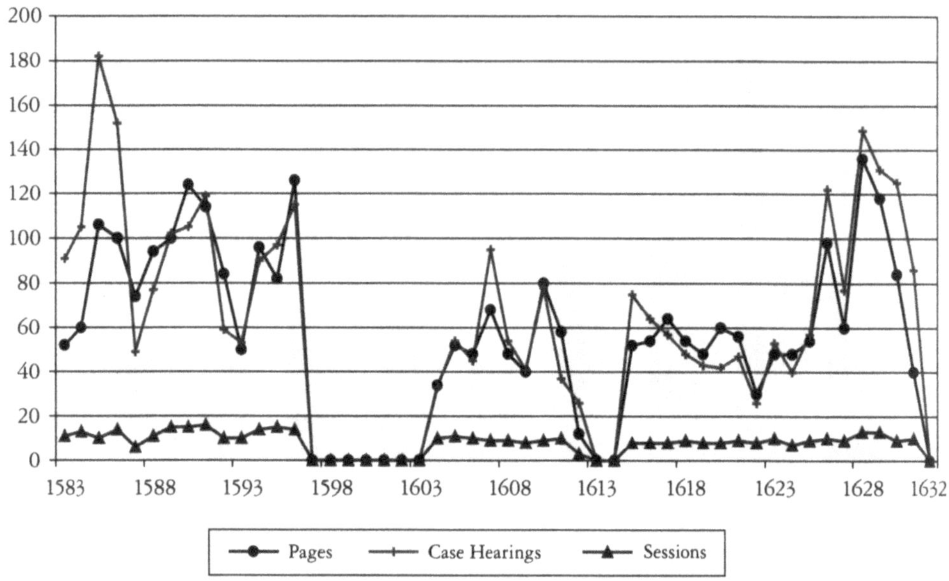

Chart 5.3: Number of Hearings per Case

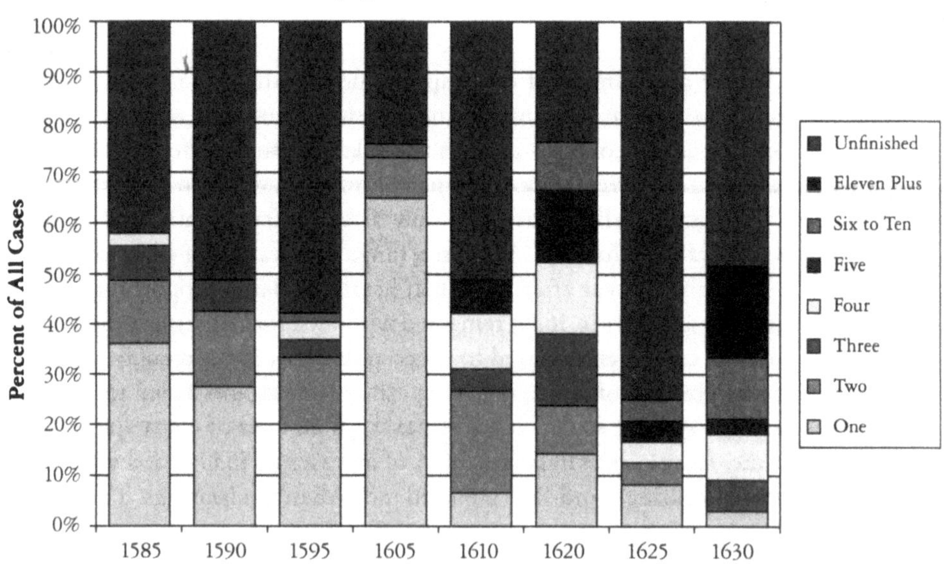

case from 1630, an inheritance dispute, was finally settled almost two years later, after twenty court appearances.[44]

Requests for postponement were a major cause of delay. Either party could request a deferral (*dilatio*), and the court rarely denied such requests. Defendants frequently asked for one at the first hearing, in order to prepare a response to the charges. Both plaintiffs and defendants used additional postponements to call witnesses or collect evidence, or when their advocate was unprepared. Requests for written copies resulted in further postponements, as did the presentation of witnesses, since depositions were made outside the public assembly. The postponement of a decision could potentially benefit the defendant, because each delay made it less likely that the plaintiff would continue to press his or her claims in court—following a deferral, a large percentage of cases never reappeared in court. Some delays do appear to have been intentionally obstructionist, yet repeated court appearances must have been frustrating for all litigants, as well as expensive. Postponements were especially hard on those from distant places, since they normally had to travel to the court for each hearing (or trust an advocate to capably represent them in their absence). On occasion, even when both parties pressed for a settlement, the court postponed its decision in order to deliberate further, request written documents, conduct an outside inquiry, or consult with legal experts. A decline in the number of separate cases toward the end of the period, starting around 1620, seems to coincide with several related factors: the increasing use of written documents, a rise in the average case length, the court's declining efficiency, and litigants' frustration with the process.

Yet until the 1620s, the Sidelgericht appears to have performed its functions capably and managed its large caseload with relative competence. To process all the cases—to listen to arguments, consider written evidence, hear witnesses, deliberate outside of court, produce copies, consult experts, initiate inquiries, and keep its own records—amounted to a considerable burden that was handled with surprising ability by a group of unpaid, nonprofessional peasant judges.

Finding and Declaring Judgment: The Umfrag and the Urteil

Following the presentation of legal testimony, the court retired for private deliberations in order to reach an *Urteil* (verdict). There was a period for discussion, and then the head judge initiated a process known as the Umfrag. First, the head judge posed a question. Then he called on each of the judges, one by one according to rank, to state his response. The Sidelrichter did not find the law without any instruction, however. Upon their sworn oath, the judges were admonished:

---

[44] Some of the unfinished cases were also of extremely long duration, most notably another inheritance suit heard 16 times between 1604 and 1606 before disappearing from the record without a decision.

> To be every man's judge, commonly and equally, the poor as the rich and the rich as the poor. You shall judge and speak the law according to your best understanding, as your conscience dictates, according to the custom and tradition of this Sidelgericht and according to the contents of both agreements, the old and the new. Have no regard for friendship or enmity, arrogance or prejudice, but instead for the godly law alone, and keep secret that which is to remain confidential, faithfully and without malice.[45]

Not only the final verdict but each of the court's intermediate decisions was subject to the Umfrag. Eventually, through a series of questions and responses, the law was "found" in favor of one party or the other. Characteristic of this process, the head judge decided on the relevant questions and their sequence, and the other members of the court spoke the law under his direction. With the exception of the head judge, the others were known collectively as the *Urteilsprecher*, or "speakers of judgment."

The head judge was also known as the *Stabhalter* (staff-bearer), and as such he represented the abbot's authority and that of the entire court. He was responsible not only for conducting the Umfrag but also for gathering the other judges' responses and composing from them a collective statement to be recorded in the official protocol and announced publicly to the court assembly. If the court was able to agree on a verdict, either unanimously or by majority opinion, the law would be declared as they had spoken it, without the head judge expressing his view. When the court was divided, however, it became the Stabhalter's duty to cast the deciding vote. The oath of office sworn by the head judge was slightly different from the one the Urteilsprecher swore. He, too, promised to treat the rich and poor, locals and strangers alike. In addition, he was instructed:

> To conduct the Umfrag without imposing judgment, and to consider therein nothing other than the pure law alone, according to your best understanding. And if it should occur that the judges are split in their judgment, then you shall follow the one that seems in your view closest to the law. You shall always judge and act according to the custom and tradition of this Sidelgericht and according to the contents of both agreements, the old and the new, faithfully and without malice.[46]

---

45 "Ir werdent schweren ... Jedermans gemain unnd gleicher Richter zusein, dem Armen alß dem Reichen, dem Reichen als dem Armen, Unnd Urtail unnd Recht sprechen, nach ewer besten Verstenndtnus, sovil ewer gewissen Weist, nach gewonhait unnd Herkhommen ditz Sidelgerichts, Unnd uff Innhalt baider bericht, New unnd alt, Unnd darInn weder freundtschafft, Veindtschafft, Muet nach Gaab Ansehen, sonnder Allain die göttlichen Gerechtigkhait, Unnd Zuverschweigen, waß Zuverschweigen ist, getrewlich und Ungevahrlich." GLAK, 67/1782, fol. 30v–31r.

46 "... auch getrewlich Unnd ohne alle Urtail umbzefragen. Unnd darInne gantz nichts anders anzesehen, Nach Ewer besten Verstendtnuß, Dann das Bloß Recht, Unnd ob dz were, Das die Richter In Iren Urtailen Zwayendt wurden, So offt dz beschicht, Das Ir dann der Urtail, Die Euch dem Rechten aller gleichest sein bedunckht, Verfolgen, Unnd In allweg Richten und Handlen wellendt, Nach ditz Sidelgerichts gewonhait Unnd Herkhommen, Und uff Innhalt der baider Bericht deß Newen, unnd Alten, getrewlich und ungevarlich." GLAK, 67/1782, fol. 30r–v. The old and the new was referred to the alte Jarbrief and the partnership agreement of 1473.

The oaths sworn by the Stabhalter and the Urteilsprecher identify several sources of legal knowledge that were used to reach a verdict. In addition to the two territorial law codes, the old and the new, the judges were expected to consider and follow the court's customs and traditions, conscience and understanding, the godly law, and the pure law alone. Both these oaths demonstrate that the Sidelrichter prevailed in their claim of 1470 that the law was found not in statutes alone but through the experience and knowledge of common people and their consultation of many sources. The oath formulas demonstrate that even the abbey continued to recognize these customary legal norms.

This process of finding and declaring the law, through discussion followed by a collective vote, reflected a communal understanding of what the law was and who could discover and apply it. The Stabhalter was necessary for the law's revelation, because only he could ask the questions. Likewise, only the Urteilsprecher could speak the law by submitting their responses. This separation of authority was typical of customary law, as was the belief that the law was properly identified, carried, expressed, and enacted through the community in dialogue with their lord.[47] The Stabhalter embodied the abbot's authority with his staff and was the conduit through which the law was publicly expressed, but he did not make or even interpret the law itself. The Urteilsprecher represented the legal experts of the community, in a tradition that was primarily oral and believed to live within each of its members. This dialogue between the symbolic representatives of lordship and community was grounded in tradition but continually updated, since the questions and answers were not always the same.[48] It was this process of exchange, the interaction itself, that formed the framework for a shared legal understanding. The method of reaching a final settlement by collectively finding the law, along with the fact that the judges were members of the community who stood between the abbot and his subjects, is one of the most important elements characterizing the Sidelgericht as a customary court.[49]

There was yet another actor whose participation was crucial in the process of declaring the law, and that was the court secretary. The court reform ordinance of 1566 emphasized the importance of recording the court's decision and reporting it fully and accurately to the interested parties. The following excerpt explains how the court's decision, the written record, and its formal proclamation were to be coordinated:

---

47 Compare, for example, the *Weisung*, a periodic process used to declare the laws according to questions posed by the lord and answered by his subjects, often at the village level. Gadi ALGAZI, Lords Ask, Peasants Answer, pp. 199–229; idem, Tradition als Gespräch der Ungleichen: Bauern und Herren in der spätmittelalterlichen Dorfversammlung, in: Eid und Wahrheitssuche: Studien zur rechtlichen Befragungspraktiken in Mittelalter und früher Neuzeit, ed. Stefan Esders and Thomas Scharff, Frankfurt 1999, pp. 191–210.

48 ALGAZI, Lords Ask, Peasants Answer, pp. 203–204.

49 See Bernhard DIESTELKAMP, Verwissenschaftlichung, Bürokratisierung, Professionalisierung und Verfahrensintensivierung als Merkmale frühneuzeitlicher Rechtssprechung, in: idem, Recht und Gericht im Heiligen Römischen Reich, Frankfurt 1999, pp. 263–5.

> When and however often an intermediate or final Urteil is issued, it should always be drawn up in writing after the Stabhalter has conducted his collective Umfrag, regardless of previous consultation, and in the absence of other parties. Then the Urteil should be recited carefully, and an Umfrag held once more. Afterward, the Stabhalter shall call the assembled parties to attention by announcing to them that the honorable Sidelgericht has reached a final decision (or otherwise come to a resolution), which has been written down and will soon be read aloud. Finally, the Urteil shall be proclaimed openly by the secretary or substitute, whichever is present at the time, along with a description of how its contents were conceived, determined, and issued; since in the past, the omission of such details has resulted in many shortcomings and disadvantages.[50]

Although the passage fails to indicate who should draw up the Urteil and read it back to the judges, the court secretary was the obvious choice. The court secretary was not directly involved in the process of reaching a verdict but his influence should not be underestimated, especially since he was responsible for the written record and because he, unlike the judges, was a salaried employee of the abbey who was in most cases not a native villager. Above all the regular members of the court, the secretary was indisputably the lord's man. The secretary was also extremely important because of his expertise with written documents. He facilitated the court's ability to communicate as well as preserve its decisions. He also enabled the court to keep up with the changing demands of litigants, who were increasingly interested in written forms of proof and the security records could provide. Potentially, the secretary brought knowledge and skills to the court that went far beyond reading and writing. Yet the phrase "the secretary or substitute, whichever is present at the time" suggests that the person occupying this position could vary from one session to the next, or at the very least, that someone else could just as easily perform the secretary's duties in his absence. Indeed, this vagueness and the lack of consistency in recordkeeping became a serious problem for the court in later years. The secretary was a key to the court's success.

The Urteil is sometimes written in the court protocol directly below litigants' statements. Often, however, a series of decisions appear at the very end of the session, following the judges' private deliberations on multiple cases. Decisions are always signaled by a separate heading, and they usually begin with an opening formula that contains a variation on the following words: "In the case between plaintiff A. and defendant B., the praiseworthy Sidelgericht, upon hearing the accusations and countercharges, written evidence and witness testimony, advice and legal council, declares the following." This same phrase, or something like it, was spoken aloud before the court assembly as an introduction to each verdict. Although the opening is extremely formulaic, it lists the specific forms of evidence the court considered in order to reach its decision.[51] This tells us, for example, whether the Sidelrichter consulted legal experts or consid-

50 GLAK, 67/1782.

51 Thomas HILDBRAND, Aktualisierung von Recht im Spannungsfeld von Eid und Schriftbeweis, in: Eid und Wahrheitssuche, ed. Stefan Esders and Thomas Scharff, Frankfurt am Main 1999, p. 176 n. 28.

ered written evidence. Such proclamations doubled as ritual recitations of the customary sources of legal knowledge, which reinforced the community's commitment to legal forms going beyond the written text. It also emphasized the fact that the decision came from the entire court.

In addition to stating judgment in favor of one party or the other, the court usually declared the specific amount of compensation to be paid, if any, by the losing party. If the defendant were found guilty, he or she might be required to pay the full amount claimed by the plaintiff or a reduced sum. Decisions in favor of the defendant occasionally required the plaintiff to compensate them for costs and damages associated with a frivolous complaint or false claims. The court also frequently assigned responsibility for legal fees to one or both parties. This practice avoided the need for further litigation in order to recoup court costs.

5.3 Litigants and their Lawsuits

As a court of law, the Sidelgericht offered litigants several practical advantages. It was relatively inexpensive, conveniently located, and reasonably efficient. It conducted its business in German and accepted evidence orally or in writing. Parties could rest assured that their disputes would be settled by respected neighbors or peers, whose legal training consisted of local knowledge and experience rather than a university education. Yet unlike village courts, the Sidelgericht supported social and economic networks across the territory by providing unitary legal standards, resolving conflicts between members of different communities, and offering a nonpartisan panel of judges representing the entire region.

Litigants had significant influence over the institutional development of the court, just as the court created and channeled opportunities for settling disagreements between neighbors and acquaintances. The types of problems individual litigants brought before the court, their decision to bring claims there in the first place, the types of arguments used, and the court's resolution or lack of one all bring us closer to the intersection between social and political experience. In order to better understand how the Sidelgericht worked, whose interests it protected, and how it responded to the community's demands, the following discussion focuses on the people who appeared in court and what brought them there.

Subjects of Dispute

What types of cases came before the Sidelgericht, and which were among the most common? To answer this question briefly, the Sidelgericht functioned mainly as a small-claims court. It heard minor civil disputes and criminal misdemeanors. Most private plaintiffs sought material compensation for damages caused by actions taken or responsibilities neglected by the defendant. Criminal suits prosecuted by the Oberamtmann or other abbey official typically sought payment of fines for offenses against statute, never imprisonment or corporal punishment. The great majority of claims therefore had an economic component, although this was not always the case and there were even a few court appearances that were unconcerned with disputes or infractions of any type—requests for documentation are the best example. According to Simon Roberts, "the very notion of 'dispute' may not be apposite if the court is just being used as a platform from which to tell people something. In cases of this sort, the objective may not lie in terms of judgment at all."[52]

It can be difficult to categorize all cases appropriately, let alone organize results in a way that is easily comparable to other case studies. As Katja Hürlimann points out in her study of Zurich's rural district courts, researchers have usually designed their own categories to fit the source data. At such an early stage in the research this is not an entirely bad thing, because closely tailored questions may bring out important peculiarities that a more general inquiry would hide. Here the classification of case types is based on the discovery of similarities among groups of cases.[53]

First of all, the cases are divided into two broad categories: civil and criminal suits.[54] Civil suits normally involved private individuals and pertained to damages for which the plaintiff sought compensation. Most criminal suits were prosecuted by abbey representatives, although a few cases brought by village communes or the court are also classified as criminal in the sense of offenses against public order.[55] Physical assault provides a good illustration of the difference between civil and criminal suits, because

---

52 Simon ROBERTS, The Study of Dispute: Anthropological Perspectives, in: Disputes and Settlements: Law and Human Relations in the West, ed. John Bossy, Cambridge and New York 1983, p. 23. For examples of how courts were used for purposes other than settling disputes, see Ulrike GLEIXNER, Rechtsfindung zwischen Machtbeziehungen, Konfliktregelung und Friedenssicherung: Historische Kriminalitätsforschung und Agrargeschichte in der frühen Neuzeit, in: Agrargeschichte: Positionen und Perspektiven, ed. Werner Troßbach and Clemens Zimmermann, Stuttgart 1998, p. 62.

53 Other classifications of case types may be found in Katja HÜRLIMANN, Soziale Beziehungen im Dorf: Aspekte dörflicher Soziabilität in den Landvogteien Greifensee und Kyburg um 1500, Zurich 2000, pp. 71–72, 300–301; Marjorie MCINTOSH, Autonomy and Community: The Royal Manor of Havering, 1200–1500, New York 1986, pp. 192–194, 206.

54 Engelberg Abbey's *Talgericht* also heard both types of cases, which were not distinguished as separate types in the medieval period. Heinz CATTANI, Entwicklung des Talgerichts von Engelberg unter Klosterherrschaft, Stans 1935, p. 12. See also GLEIXNER, Rechtsfindung, p. 62; HOLENSTEIN, Umstände der Normen, p. 20.

55 The court bailiff brought suit against individuals for failure to appear in court, and less commonly, for failure to address the court through an approved legal advocate. An example of a suit brought by the commune to protect the common welfare and punish a statutory offense is the complaint brought on behalf of the entire commune of Gebhardsweiler against Jacob Ower, who refused to open and close his meadow at the required times. The court ordered him to comply on 5 July 1605. Among criminal cases in the sample, there are five cases prosecuted by a commune or the court.

it is an action found in both categories. In civil cases, an individual plaintiff charged a defendant who had assaulted him or her personally. The plaintiff typically argued that the assault was unwarranted and requested compensation for resulting injury, damages, doctor's fees, or lost wages. When the abbey brought a criminal suit involving physical assault, however, it had nothing to do with personal injury. Instead, the charge was for fighting in general, which was both a transgression of the lord's commands and a threat to the public order. Criminal suits also targeted offenses against property rights, with resulting fines payable to the abbey rather than to the individual who had been harmed. Criminal suits were brought separate from, often in addition and as a result of, civil suits between private individuals. In addition to the two broad categories of suits between opposing parties, there were a handful of documentation requests from individuals seeking birth certificates or other records. Although such court appearances are not technically lawsuits, they are treated here under the umbrella of civil suits and considered alongside other requests for documentation.

There are a total of 169 criminal suits in the ten-year sample. Over half of them are described in the record according to the general categories of *Frevel* (personal misconduct) or *übergangenes Gebot* (statute violation). In many suits the Oberamtmann's accusation offers no further detail about the offense, but even from those cases that do provide specifics, the distinction between categories is not always clear.[56] Forest offenses were a common topic of criminal prosecutions, and sometimes a single action resulted in multiple charges with separate fees for each one. In 1615, for example, those found cutting or hauling wood from the forest against statute included Stoffel Rüedin of Rickenbach, accused of damaging trees and working on a holiday; Hans Müller of Mainwangen, for tree damage and violation of statute; and Peter Lüttberger the Nußmayer, for tree damage and personal misconduct. The vagueness of the record, and the difficulty of classifying infractions, is further indicated by the following entry from 1585, citing Andreas Klotz for multiple violations: "Charged four pounds for statute violation against Martin Mußel. Item one pound for misconduct against Peter Seckh. Item five pounds for housing strangers. Item five pounds for selling two chickens to idling soldiers, which is also prohibited."[57] On the whole, case descriptions provide good evidence about the most common types of infractions as well as for the fines associated with them. Among criminal suits that provide specific charges, the most frequent topics include fighting, swearing, breaking the peace, housing strangers, outstanding debts, illegal grazing, misuse of the commons, and petty wood theft. A breakdown of major case types is displayed in Chart 5.4.

56 *Frevel* most commonly referred to physical assault but it also applied to wood theft (*Holzfrevel*); *übergangenes Gebot* included statute violations such as housing strangers or illegal sales, but it also covered forest violations as well as failure to repay debts or obey the call to peace (Fridbot).

57 The record is from 29 June 1585. The Oberamtmann proved willing to reduce the first three charges, but not the fine for selling chickens to soldiers, which encouraged begging and theft among the able poor.

Chart 5.4: Types of Criminal Suits

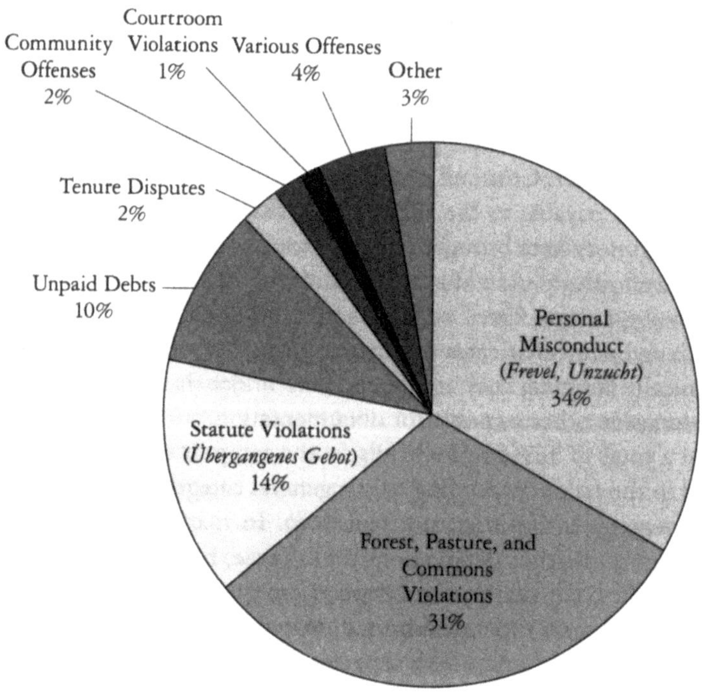

Chart 5.5 shows the primary subcategories among civil suits. The great majority, as previously stated, involve economic claims and especially various forms of debt.[58] In the ten-year sample there are a total of 373 civil suits, three-quarters of them concerned above all with monetary claims of some kind.[59] Financial compensation for damages derived from a wide variety of topics ranging from failure to repay a loan or deliver payment for purchased goods to property damage, wages, inheritance, or court fines. The types of economic claims within this general category are displayed in Chart 5.6.

58 For an interesting case study on debt in the royal manor of Writtel, see Elaine CLARK, Debt Litigation in a Late Medieval English Vill, in: Pathways to Medieval Peasants, ed. J. A. Raftis, Toronto 1981, pp. 247–279.

59 Among all 542 cases (criminal and civil), economic disputes between private individuals accounted for 51% of disputes. Hürlimann (Beziehungen, p. 72) found that 61% of cases from the district of Greifensee and 62% of cases from Kyburg concerned economic issues during the period 1480–1519, although she classifies only 6% and 13% respectively as cases specifically involving debt. Marjorie McIntosh found that debt cases accounted for somewhat over half of what she calls "personal actions" in Havering during the period 1352–1497. Idem, Autonomy and Community, pp. 192–194.

Chart 5.5: Types of Civil Suits

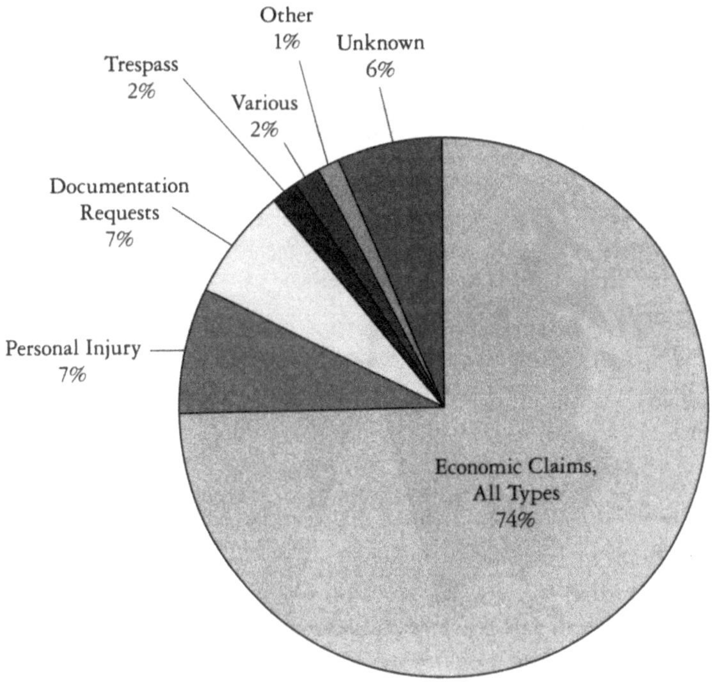

A second category of disputes, comprising 7.5% of all civil cases, concerns personal injury.[60] These include complaints about honor and verbal injury, physical assault, or a combination of the two. These cases also typically involve the demand for monetary compensation, but unlike cases in the category of economic claims, the payment of damages resulted from injuries that were not primarily economic in nature. Third, requests for documentation comprise 6.7% of all civil suits (including requests for birth certificates, which were not technically legal suits). Requests for birth certificates are an example of hearings initiated for reasons other than dispute or infraction, in which there was neither plaintiff nor defendant.[61] Besides appearances to obtain birth certificates, documentation requests fall under two types, each representing about 1% of all civil cases. First, there were suits citing the defendant's failure to provide writ-

60 Hürlimann found that 2% of cases in Greifensee and 9% in Kyburg involved personal offenses. This is low compared to other studies she consulted. Idem, Soziale Beziehungen, p. 74. Again, categorization may account for some differences. In Salem, many of the criminal suits classified as *Frevel* probably involved physical assault, yet they were not described further.

61 These cases were typically brought by young men and women who were planning to leave the territory. Approval, which was granted in all cases, required the testimony of two witnesses and payment of documentation fees.

Chart 5.6: Types of Economic Suits

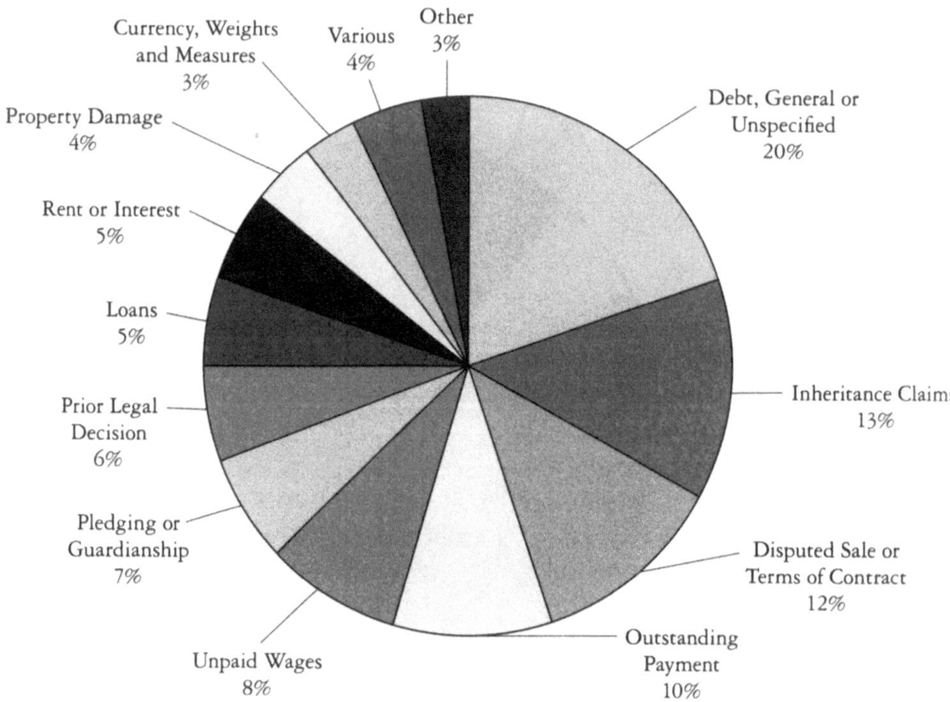

Chart 5.7: Litigants from Core Villages by Year

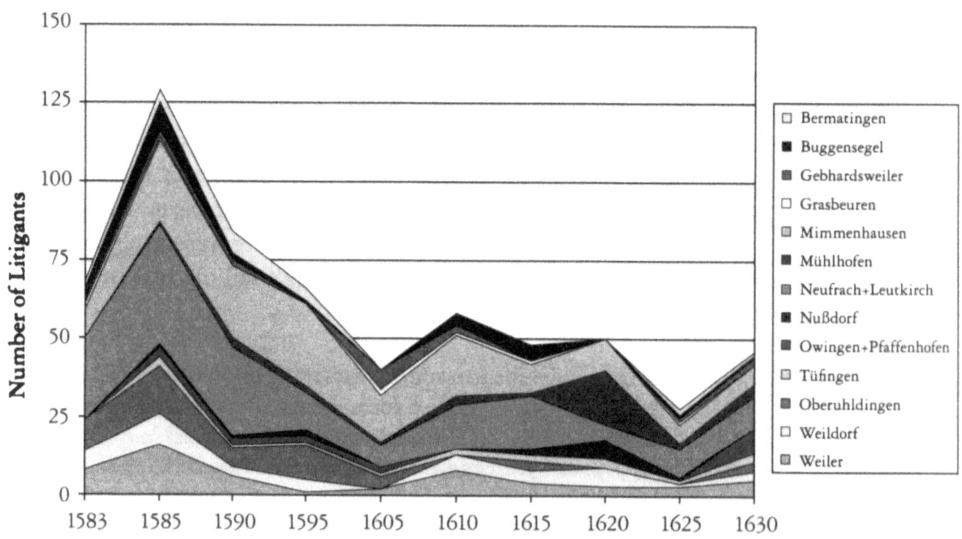

ten contract for a sale or loan; second, there were actions taken to obtain copies of decisions declared in previous court actions or requests for a previous decision to be read aloud before the court assembly. Only 1.6% of suits are classified as trespass, including unpermitted property use as well as the detainment of chattels (such as cows). Various complaints comprise another 1.6% of all cases. This category includes those with multiple subjects of dispute, in which no single complaint merits primary importance. For example, some cases involve both debt and insult, or physical assault and fines resulting from a previous decision, or trespass combined with property damage. "Other" subjects (1.3% of civil suits) refer to those that do not fit into any of the above categories—a broken marriage promise, for example, or the disputed ownership of a kettle. Finally, the category of unspecified suits (6.4%) include those with no stated subject as well as those that are illegible or unclear.[62] In the following discussion we will look at concrete examples of the various case types. Now, let us turn to the parties who appeared in court.

Litigants' Geographical Origins

Litigants came from all over the territory Under the Hills, from many places throughout the Linzgau, and from a few places beyond the region. Whether or not they resided within the court's jurisdiction, the great majority lived less than a day's walk from the abbey. There are 1,122 litigants from 97 different places in the ten-year sample, with 26 locations contributing five or more litigants.[63] Most parties, 617 of them, came from a core of 13 villages within the central territory. Chart 5.7 shows the number of litigants from these villages by year. Chart 5.8 lists the 83 other places, including hamlets and isolated farms near the abbey, cities or villages elsewhere in the Linzgau, and a few localities from beyond the county borders. One additional place contributed more litigants than any other, almost all of them plaintiffs: Salem Abbey, represented by the Oberamtmann (or Kaufmann), brought suit 164 times in the sample. Individual abbey officials (none of them monks) appeared as defendants in another five cases. Finally, 101 litigants are of unknown origins. For the geographical breakdown of all litigants, see Chart 5.9.

A comparison of opposing legal parties' geographical origins provides information about trade, social relationships, and regional mobility. Out of 291 civil suits where the origins of both litigants are known, 42 percent came from the same place, where-

62 Some cases are fragments for which the initial session could not be found in previous records. Since the subject of dispute is normally described in the first entry, such cases cannot be further categorized. Complaints submitted in writing are also difficult to categorize, since the record often fails to describe the subject or content of the texts.

63 For legal parties composed of multiple individuals from different places, each place has been counted once, resulting in a total number of litigants that is slightly higher than twice the number of cases in the sample.

Chart 5.8: Litigants from Places beyond the Core Villages

Location	1583	1585	1590	1595	1605	1610	1615	1620	1625	1630	Total
Adelsreute	3	0	1	0	0	0	0	0	0	0	4
Ahausen	0	1	0	2	0	0	0	0	0	0	3
Altenbeuren	0	0	0	1	0	3	1	0	0	1	6
Banzenreute	0	1	1	0	1	0	0	0	0	0	3
Constance	3	4	3	4	0	0	0	0	0	1	15
Daisendorf	0	0	1	1	2	0	1	0	1	2	8
Einhard	0	0	0	0	0	2	1	0	1	0	4
Forst	0	3	0	0	0	0	0	0	0	0	3
Frickingen	0	0	0	2	0	0	0	0	0	1	3
Haberstenweiler	0	0	0	0	1	0	0	0	0	1	2
Ittendorf	0	1	1	0	0	0	0	0	0	0	2
Jetkofen	0	0	0	0	0	0	0	3	0	0	3
Leustetten	0	0	0	1	0	0	1	0	0	0	2
Leveratsweiler	0	0	0	0	1	0	0	1	0	0	2
Lipperatsreute	0	0	1	0	1	1	0	0	1	0	4
Mainwangen	0	0	0	2	0	0	2	0	0	0	4
Markdorf	0	0	1	1	0	1	0	0	0	1	4
Meersburg	0	0	2	3	3	0	0	0	0	0	8
Nueßmayer	0	0	0	0	0	0	3	0	0	0	3
Ostrach	0	0	0	1	0	5	1	7	2	0	16
Pfullendorf	1	1	0	0	0	0	0	0	1	0	3
Ravensburg	0	1	0	0	0	0	0	0	1	0	2
Rickenbach	0	0	3	1	1	0	1	0	2	0	8
Rimperatsweiler	0	0	0	0	0	0	1	0	0	1	2
Seefelden	2	0	2	1	0	0	0	0	0	1	6
Siggingen	0	0	2	0	0	0	0	0	0	2	4
Sipplingen	0	0	1	0	0	1	0	0	0	0	2
Storen	0	0	1	2	0	1	0	0	0	0	4
Tafern	0	0	0	0	0	0	0	0	0	2	2
Tafertsweiler	0	0	0	0	0	0	0	10	0	0	10
Tepfenhard	0	2	1	0	0	0	0	0	0	0	3
Überlingen	2	1	5	2	0	0	0	2	0	0	12
Unterbach	0	0	1	0	0	0	3	0	0	0	4
Unterteuringen	0	1	0	0	0	0	0	0	1	0	2
Urnau	0	1	1	0	1	1	3	0	1	0	8
Wald	0	0	1	0	0	0	1	0	0	0	2
Wangen	0	0	0	0	0	0	0	0	0	2	2
Wendlingen	0	0	3	0	0	0	1	0	0	0	4
Wirrensegel	0	0	0	0	0	0	0	2	1	0	3
Wittenhofen	0	0	0	0	0	1	1	0	0	0	2
Wolketsweiler	0	0	0	0	0	0	9	0	0	0	9
Totals	11	17	32	24	11	16	21	25	12	15	184

Places contributing only one litigant in sampled years: Altheim, Baufnang, Berghof, Boshasel, Braitenbach, Brielholz, Bruggfelden, Burg, Durbheim, Elenweiler, Feldkirch, Hallendorf, Hederatsweiler, Heiligenberg, Hiltensweiler, Hohentwingen Amt, Honberg, Immenstadt, Katzental, Lorenz Spital, Madach, Maurach, Mendlishausen, Meßkirch, Ochsenbach, Ralzhof, Reutlingen, Riederßweiler, Roggenbeuren, Rohrdorf, Rotenbuhl, Schiggendorf, Schlagensweiler, Schwendi, Stadelhofen, Unteruhldingen, Walsberg, Wehausen, Werndorf, Wickhenweiler, and Wintersulgen.

Chart 5.9: All Litigants' Places of Origin

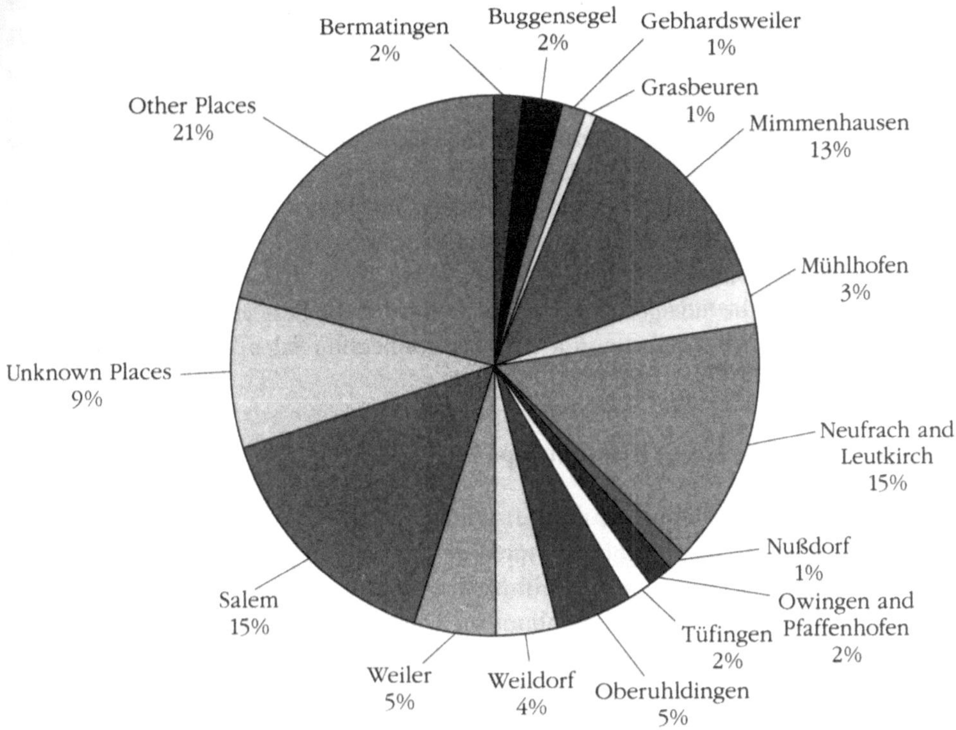

as 58 percent lived in different places. The percentage of cases involving residents of the same village is high enough to indicate that such internal conflicts frequently came before the Sidelgericht, but it is noteworthy that the majority of cases did not involve members of the same community. This is surely not because more conflicts involved nonneighbors, but because individual communes had other formal and informal means of conflict resolution. This resulted in the appearance of fewer internal conflicts before the court. We can conclude that the Sidelgericht was especially useful for resolving disputes between nonneighbors, those who did not share a local basis for settling disputes.

In her study of court records from two rural districts belonging to the canton of Zurich, Katja Hürlimann found similar percentages of cases involving members of the same locality. Her data suggest additionally that most conflicts involved litigants living within a five kilometer radius of one another.[64] Applying a similar method to the data

[64] Three-quarters of litigants in Hürlimann's sample came from inside the territory. The percentage of cases involving litigants from the same village ranged from 0–53% depending on location, and cases involving litigants from distances beyond five kilometers ranged from 9–24%. Idem, Soziale Beziehungen, pp. 136–141.

from Salem's court lends support to this conclusion. Among 168 civil suits between litigants who did not reside in the same settlement, 94 parties lived near one another whereas 74 others were separated by greater distances. If we then categorize all 291 civil suits according to relative geographical distance rather than village affiliation, we find that three-quarters of all litigants lived in close proximity while the remaining quarter came from places that were more than an hour's walk or ride away from one another. The many cases involving nonneighbors suggest a dense network of relationships across the territory and beyond its borders. They also suggest the central role of the Sidelgericht in guaranteeing and building confidence in such relationships. The enormous caseload involving debt is evidence of a lively exchange among territorial residents. Indeed, the Sidelgericht's records are one of the best sources of information concerning the dense socioeconomic network connecting Salem's villagers Under the Hills.

Socioeconomic Status and Relationships

The case descriptions frequently indicate a relationship between plaintiffs and defendants, who might be kin, neighbors, employer and employee, lender and borrower, or abbey and subject. Even when such information is given or can be inferred, however, we should not jump to conclusions about the causes of dispute, since our knowledge of the long history of relationships between individuals remains extremely limited.[65] Case descriptions occasionally mention disputes that had begun over a decade earlier. Neverteless, it would be of great interest to learn more about the socioeconomic context of interactions between plaintiffs and defendants.

It might be assumed that powerful members of the community would attempt to manipulate the court and its procedures for their own benefit and that they often succeeded.[66] It was certainly possible for territorial elites to press their interests through the court in various ways, not least because the members of the court were property-holders who likely shared many of the same values and attitudes. Legal decisions inevitably involved a personal element, such as the judges' evaluation of each party's reputation and reliability and the impression that one side had told the better story—not to mention a probable reluctance, in such an honor-based society, to side publicly against a powerful neighbor with whom one had regular contact.[67] Witness testimony provided elites with an additional advantage, because they were socially well connected

---

65 Achim Landwehr shows how individuals instrumentalized courts to punish their enemies, sometimes for reasons having little to do with the claims they brought before the court, thus translating personal conflicts into the discourse of law and lordship in order to pursue other objectives. Idem, Policey vor Ort, p. 67.

66 See GLEIXNER, Rechtsfindung, pp. 63, 66–68.

67 J. A. Sharpe, History of Crime in Late Medieval and Early Modern England: Review Article, in: Social History 7 (1982), p. 202.

and could call on a variety of solid witnesses. In addition, many local elites were related to the judges by blood or marriage.

In this context we might expect to find that the Sidelgericht functioned to enforce dominant legal and social norms, through which local notables could impose social discipline over their weaker neighbors and discourage "undesirable" behaviors. In fact, the court records provide surprisingly little evidence that decisions were found in favor of powerful litigants or that court business was dominated by the interests of the wealthy. The lesser members of the territorial community, as we shall see, also found many advantages in the Sidelgericht and contributed to its norms.

The tax lists from 1578, 1593, and 1603 facilitate the search for litigants' economic backgrounds, especially for those individuals involved in lawsuits during years immediately surrounding the property assessment dates. I initially searched tax registers for all litigants named in 1585, later adding the years 1590, 1595, and 1605.[68] The collection of information about the wealthiest and poorest litigants allows us to examine whether there is a correlation between an individual's wealth and the types of legal claims, or criminal offenses, with which he or she was involved. Using wealth information we can also compare the backgrounds of plaintiffs and defendants, to see if wealth made a difference in terms of the social constellation of disputes. In order to compare the court actions of wealthy and poor litigants, the following analysis is based on a sample of all cases from the aforementioned four years in which at least one legal party had property valued at over 1,000 fl. or less than 100 fl. The sample consists of 23 wealthy plaintiffs and 27 poorer plaintiffs, 35 wealthy defendants and 40 poorer defendants.[69] By year, the number of litigants is 55 in 1585, 28 in 1590, 25 in 1595, and 17 in 1605. There are 125 litigants in the sample.

The search for economic background information and the social constellation of disputes began, as already mentioned, with the year 1585. The findings based on this small sample suggest some very surprising conclusions. First, many litigants who appeared before the Sidelgericht were not wealthy by territorial standards. At least ten litigants in 1585 were members of the lowest tax bracket, with property worth less than 25 fl. in 1578. Second, poorer subjects commonly appeared in court not only as defendants but also as plaintiffs. A maid and a servant's wife both appeared as plaintiffs, one to report a verbal threat and the other to demand unpaid wages from a wealthy

68 This method resulted from a search for litigants' places of residence, which are frequently unspecified in court records from 1585. I was not only surprised to find so many of these litigants listed in the 1578 tax assessment, I was also struck by how many of them were extremely poor. This led to a search for wealth and property information for all litigants in 1585, which I later expanded to other years. The very rich and poorer litigants are the focus here, but it would be worthwhile to expand the comparison to include litigants from all wealth groups. Background information on 1585 litigants comes from the 1578 tax list, 1590 and 1595 litigants from the 1593 tax list, and 1605 litigants from the 1603 tax list.

69 There are more defendants than plaintiffs in both wealth groups because of the number of criminal prosecutions by abbey officials.

employer. Another eight plaintiffs in 1585 had less than 50 fl. in total wealth, and the claims of the poorest plaintiffs concerned a wide range of issues.[70] This is significant because it suggests that the court served much broader interests than those of local elites in their competition with one another or in the domination of lesser neighbors.

The cases involving wealthy litigants are no less surprising. First of all, at least three wealthy litigants in 1585 were acting as guardians, representing someone's interests other than their own. No case brought by a wealthy plaintiff in 1585 suggests rivalry or the attempt to humiliate an opponent, and no judgment in this sample appears to have been an act of social discipline carried out against lesser neighbors. Overall, wealthy litigants' subjects of complaint do not stand out as being unusual or different from the rest.[71] More interesting are the cases brought against wealthier defendants as well as the court's apparent tendency to find decisions against them, or at least not to find decisions in their favor. For example, the bathhouse manager of Neufrach accused Hans Richel, who was an alternate member of the court in 1585, of digging a ditch unlawfully across the plaintiff's land. Richel responded that the authorities had instructed him to do so, but the plaintiff persisted. No drainage ditch had been there ever before, he pointed out, nor did he want one now, since he collected water from above the bathhouse for his own use. He asked the judges to inspect the property, and after viewing it, the court decided against Richel. They not only told him to fill in the trench he had made, they also held him responsible for all court fees including the cost of their inspection. Most astonishing is the court's decision against Jacob Hailg, another member of the Sidelgericht and the Amtmann of Neufrach. His opponent accused him of owing a debt of just over three gulden. Hailg contested the charges, claiming his father had already repaid the debt. Nevertheless, the court decided in the plaintiff's favor and charged Hailg with court costs in addition. Without explicitly saying so, it appeared as if his own colleagues believed that Hailg, with property worth over 2,000 fl., would lie about only three!

70 The claims brought by poorer plaintiffs cover a wide variety of topics: wages and payment for services, requests for documentation (proof of honorable birth, proof of contract), personal injury resulting from tavern disputes, compensation for court fines, land rents, and unpaid debts.

71 Five such cases were minor debt claims. Two suits brought by Buggensegel's Amtmann, Michael Schaitteckh, appear to have been related and the defendant in each case was Stoffel Felder. The first involved property damages in a meadow and the second, initiated one month later, involved a brutal attack on Schaitteckh's daughters who were working in a meadow, presumably the same location mentioned earlier. Only one other case had a wealthy plaintiff not acting on someone else's behalf. He was Jacob Schreiber, the Amtmann of Owingen and second-ranking member of the Sidelgericht. Schreiber accused a neighbor of damaging his honor by saying he had bribed abbey officials. In a later hearing, Schreiber demanded to know whether another defendant had spread rumors that he was a dishonorable man. The court ordered an inquiry in the village, but no verdict is recorded.

If there were an attempt to discipline marginal groups within the community, we might expect to find a reflection of it in cases reported to and prosecuted by higher authorities. However, a comparison of defendants in criminal cases from 1585 offers no such suggestion. In that year the Kaufmann prosecuted 47 cases. The wealth or occupation of 29 defendants is known, and the accused represented a wide economic spectrum: seven came from destitute households (with less than 25 fl.), four were poor (25–99 fl.), five were smallholders (100–299 fl.), three were middling householders (300–499 fl.), four were prosperous (500–999 fl.), and four were very rich (1,000 fl. or more). Two others were innkeepers and presumably wealthy. Among these economic groups, the types of complaint were surprisingly equal in distribution. Lorenz Bürster, with 1,251 fl., was charged for assault inside the abbey walls, but so (in a separate incident) was Georg Haug, who had no property. Hans Klotz, with 1,559 fl., was charged with housing strangers, but so was Georg Rott with 455 fl. and Michel Duler with 94 fl. Several poorer defendants were charged for failure to repay seed loans (*Dingskorn*), but so were Georg Schaitteckh with 621 fl. and Hans Hörer with 1,053 fl. Fighting and general disregard for the lord's commands were common charges across the board.

As a result of these findings, I extended the search for wealth data to litigants from other years. Some topics of litigation involved wealthy and poor individuals in fairly equal numbers, as plaintiffs and as defendants. Still, slight differences can often be discerned. For example, two poor plaintiffs and a wealthy one demanded the outstanding payment of their inheritance portions. Three wealthy defendants but none who were poor were accused of failure to distribute inheritance portions. Individuals from all wealth groups appeared in court on charges of fighting. In one case two brothers, both destitute, were charged with fistfighting. In another, two wealthy men from Neufrach and Leutkirch were drinking together when the discussion turned to insults and physical assault. Poor Martin Erhart from Oberuhldingen accused the wealthy Jacob Ower from Banzenreute of assaulting him on the road for no reason as he was walking home. The defendant claimed it had been a misunderstanding—he thought the plaintiff was someone else. In fact, the sample includes yet another defendant on assault charges who claimed he had beaten a poorer plaintiff in the tavern, with a chair leg, by accident (see below). It is hard to say whether this excuse was a common one, or whether it was socially specific. In any case, assault seems to have been common to all social groups, among women and men. Another topic that involved defendants across the wealth spectrum was petty wood theft. The Oberamtmann charged one poor defendant in 1605 for taking firewood from an area other than that designated for his use; another poor defendant was accused of taking wood "against the prohibition." He protested that he had taken only one old stump. Jacob Ower, one of the wealthier individuals charged with forest violations in 1605, not only took wood from the vicinity of Leveratsweiler, he also encouraged others to do it.

Both wealthy and poorer litigants appeared as creditors as well as debtors. Yet differences between the two groups are apparent in the type of debt and the amount owed. For example, two debts involving wealthy litigants resulted from horse sales and another from the sale of wine. Two wealthy defendants were charged as the result of default by others, because they had provided surety for loans. Poorer plaintiffs demanded payment for wages or services on three occasions. One of them, Martin Morß of Neufrach, demanded wages of three Reichsthaler for his medical treatment of a young boy over the course of seven weeks. The defendant refused, since the boy was finally cured after his father resorted to a different healer. As defendants in debt litigation, the poor tended to owe small sums. In 1590 one woman had already settled the debts of her deceased husband when the creditor, poor Jacob Hagen of Bermatingen, suddenly remembered she owed him an additional eight kreuzer. The woman disputed the debt and brought him to court after he refused to settle amicably. Another widow appeared as a defendant when Claus Mayer of Neufrach came to report that he had lent her deceased husband a sum of less than three gulden while they were both serving as soldiers in France. Mayer demanded repayment of the debt as well as compensation for the six days he had spent caring for the dying man. Poor Veit Mägerlin of Weildorf was charged with half a gulden in wages for field labor and Hans Schneider of Bermatingen owed 13 batzen in locksmith's wages. The fact that such petty suits came before the court at all reinforces the fact that the barriers to litigation were extremely low. Basic court costs were minimal, and the burden of traveling to and appearing before the court must not have been too great if so many individuals were willing to bring suit for amounts of less than one gulden. Plaintiffs who chose to bring their claims to court instead of, or in addition to, other means of settlement were exercising choice.

There was a slight preponderance of poor over wealthy litigants in the sample, yet those with property worth less than 100 fl. also represented a much higher proportion of the general population—approximately five times the number of very rich householders. Thus, our acknowledgement that the number of poorer litigants is significant in volume must be tempered by the fact that wealthier subjects, viewed proportionally, were especially litigious. One reason they appeared in court so frequently is that they were presumably involved in many more daily transactions than lesser folk. Wealthy individuals, especially male householders, were active as buyers and sellers, borrowers and lenders, guardians, surety pledges, witnesses, and officials in the parish, village, or court. This made them more likely to become entangled in various types of dispute. There was yet another possible reason, however, suggested by the incidence of verbal injury and damages to honor. In Chapter 4, it was noted that several Amtmänner appeared before the court or Audience because of slander and verbal abuse charges. The sample of wealthy and poorer litigants confirms that the individuals involved in cases of honor, plaintiffs in particular, tended to be wealthy.[72]

---

72 Among the poorer litigants in the sample only Hans Merckh, the Bannwart of Owingen, appeared in court to defend himself against slander charges. The plaintiff Peter Kaiser (with 704 fl. in 1578, not listed in 1593) accused Merckh of remarking that Kaiser had bundled his own grain sheaves larger than the abbot's, insinuating that the plaintiff was trying to cheat the abbey. The case appears on 5 June and 3 July 1590.

In addition to five wealthy plaintiffs in the sample who appeared in court to defend their honor, two of their neighbors accused of defamation were also wealthy.[73] One of these suits was initiated in 1595 by Thoma Schmidtmaister of Mimmenhausen against the innkeeper's wife, Nella Owerin, and her supporters. On the day of a recent communal procession to the church in Seefelden, Schmidtmaister explained to the court, he had remained home to take care of some household business. He saw Christa Wuest's wife, who owed him some grain, and called her over to discuss it. Nella, whom he had reason to mistrust, spied them talking and soon the entire village was buzzing with gossip. Schmidtmaister brought suit to stop the rumors, but Nella responded that she had no feelings of malice against Schmidtmaister and would be interested to hear what others had been saying about him. Schmidtmaister demanded a village inquiry as proof of his claim, but no decision is recorded.[74]

Together, these suits involving rich and poor villagers present a general finding in stark contrast to the results of other studies, such as Edward Britton's Community of the Vill. According to Britton, plaintiffs from Broughton, England in the fourteenth century rarely came from poor and politically unconnected families, whereas individuals from all social groups were named as defendants.[75] He concluded that members of leading families frequently used the courts both to quarrel with other leading families and to bully their weaker neighbors, while poorer and poorly connected individuals rarely used the courts to press their claims. Marjorie McIntosh has come to a similar conclusion for Havering, also in England:

> Private suits focus on the activity of the manor's dominant families, leaving obscure the dealings of the poor and newcomers. Since the court's procedures were complex and stylized, the leading tenants who attended the court regularly and knew its methods well had a clear edge in their easy access to the law and ability to manipulate the forms to their own advantage.[76]

---

73 Besides those with over 1,000 fl. in wealth, another charge of verbal injury was brought by Georg Mayer, whose wealth of 921 fl. was not far below the others. When he tried to stop a fight between Bartle Hueber and the innkeeper's wife in Neufrach by calling for the peace in 1585, the defendant Hueber had ignored him saying that since Mayer was no honorable man, his Fridbot was without force. As a result of this suit, charges were later brought against the innkeeper's wife.

74 "Cleger Clagt, dz sich Neuerlich, Als uff Mittwoch vor Pfingsten, man Ain Creitzganng geen Seefeldt gehalten, sey er Thoma da hin bey der haußhaltung gewesen, Als aber er Christa Wiesten Weib ersehen, die Ime noch Ausstendig Korn zubezalen schuldig, darauff er Ihr gewunckhen, unnd sye der bezalung halber Angeredt, so bald solches die weiber ersehen, allerdinngs Inne gleich in bösem Argwon gehabt, Alls solte er nicht redlich sach treiben, und solchs Als bald Im dorff herumb getrochen. Anntr. Sagen sye Wissen nichts Args uff Ine noch, sye Wellen Auch gern die leit darumb hören, die solchs sagen wöllen. Cleger will sein clag beweisen, seind an die orth hingewisen, da dergleichen shmach sach hingehörig." 27 June 1595.

75 Edward BRITTON, Community of the Vill: A Study in the History of Family and Village Life in Fourteenth-century England, Toronto 1977.

76 MCINTOSH, Autonomy and Community, p. 191.

Katja Hürlimann admits it is difficult to identify the poorest litigants in her sample of cases from Zurich's rural districts. Still, she assumes the court was an instrument of power used by village elites and that the poor brought complaints mainly to protect their use rights.[77]

There are several possible reasons why the social character of litigation in Salem differed so markedly from patterns found in other premodern rural societies. The first is methodological, for Britton's social categorization (according to officeholding, not wealth) has drawn substantial criticism.[78] Beyond research methods (and theoretical approach), the divergence may be explained by the court's composition and procedures. Since the judges were knowledgeable in local custom, villagers may have felt more comfortable bringing conflicts before them than they would have before nonnative jurists or the salaried employees of the abbot. At least in theory, the Sidelgericht provided several safeguards against its abuse by elites and ensured the legal equality of all residents. No one was exempt from the court's authority, and the judges swore to consider the claims of serfs and freemen, rich and poor, neighbors and strangers, villagers and burghers equally and fairly. All judges were subject to an official inquiry at the end of each year that was directed specifically at uncovering impartiality. This, too, helped protect lesser folk from blatant discrimination. The court's low formal requirements and legal fees made justice accessible and affordable for ordinary subjects. Finally, the written record contained all the court's decisions and a description of the means used to find them, which held the court accountable to outside scrutiny and further encouraged impartiality.

Not surprisingly, men appeared in court far more often than women. Out of all 542 lawsuits in the ten-year sample, women appeared as litigants on 72 occasions. One unexpected finding is that the court record lists most women without reference to the legal guardians, advocates, or male relatives who surely spoke for them or at least accompanied them in court. Often the case descriptions are written as if the female litigant presented her own oral arguments. It is quite unlikely that women had the full legal competency this finding suggests, however. According to court procedure, both women and men were required to address the court through a legal spokesman. The most probable explanation is that women were accompanied in court by their legal guardians with such regularity that there was no need to comment on it.[79] Neverthe-

77 HÜRLIMANN, Soziale Beziehungen, p. 155; similarly GLEIXNER, Rechtsfindung, p. 67.

78 For a critique of Britton's methodology and approach, see Zvi RAZI, The Toronto School's Reconstitution of Medieval Peasant Society: A Critical View, in: Past and Present, 85 (1979), pp. 114–157. Britton classified litigants into four groups according to how many family members (based on surnames) were office-holders. Idem, Community of the Vill, p. 12.

79 Hürlimann (Soziale Beziehungen, pp. 155-156) came to the same conclusion with regard to records kept by the Zurich courts. Cattani (Engelberg, p. 51) believed that women could swear an oath in Engelberg's court and were represented there just like men, though the records do not provide evidence of their direct personal involvement as litigating parties.

less, women did appear personally in the courtroom and were not excluded from legal affairs. In 1583, for example, Melchior Klotz and his wife sued Melchior's father for the marriage portion he owed them. It is interesting that the record mentions the wife as a plaintiff concerning a marriage portion that was owed by her father-in-law to his son. In civil suits, women were most often involved in litigation against men, although five brought suits against other women. Women also appeared as members of joint legal parties, often with their husbands as in the above example. In criminal suits, the Oberamtmann occasionally charged small groups of women for fighting, verbal injury, or other misconduct. Other women were accused of grazing, grass collection, and forest offenses as well as drying crops or clothes in violation of the fire code.[80] Women also appeared in court as witnesses, and in this role they certainly did address the court in person rather than through a male representative. Among suits involving witnesses whose names appear in the protocol, 22.4 percent include at least one female witness. Though there is less evidence of women's actions in the courtroom than for men, these findings suggest that women could in fact play an active role in the legal process and have a direct influence over legal decisions. Furthermore, the subjects of dispute involving female litigants demonstrate that they took part in many of the same activities as men, including swearing, fighting, moneylending, selling, and entering legal agreements and business contracts.

Legal Argument, Objectives, and Strategy

As already indicated, the abbey's command that subjects bring disputes solely before the Sidelgericht was at best a symbolic gesture of authority. In reality, conflicts could be settled in a variety of ways—not only by courts, but also through amicable negotiation and compromise, informal mediation, formal arbitration, petitions to the Audience, or in other ways. A plaintiff's decision to bring a case before the Sidelgericht thus involved a choice. It entailed the weighing of possible risks and outcomes as well as surrendering control over the final settlement to the 15 judges, an ostensibly neutral third party.

Many of the civil suits brought before the Sidelgericht involved material damages, and so the most obvious explanation of why plaintiffs came before the Sidelgericht is that they sought financial compensation. Yet this is an over-simplification, because economic claims were frequently only the indicator of a much deeper issue. In addition, many private plaintiffs sought public confirmation of their positions or actions,

80 For example, Drina Hornstainerin of Lipperatsreute was charged in 1590 for grazing animals in a restricted area in Rickenbach. She claimed not to know the area was closed and excused herself, saying several maids had also grazed there and that the smith's daughter told them she had used the pasture many times. The fines were reduced from five pounds to two. Balthasar Klotz's daughter from Mimmenhausen was accused of shaking a pear tree in 1605, "as if it were her own." The Oberamtmann agreed to reduce the fines from one pound to only five batzen.

restoration of honor, an entry in the official record, or the assignment of blame to an opponent.[81] To understand why litigants chose the Sidelgericht and not some alternative form of conflict resolution, we must look deeper.

One reason many litigants brought suits was to have certain actions or statements officially registered.[82] This could be used to future advantage, as in 1595, when Hans Bitzenhofer asked the court to read aloud its earlier decision in his favor. The desire to have a complaint on record, or to avoid such a public form of rebuke, may help to explain why so many cases disappear from the protocol without settlement after only one or two court appearances.[83] Salem's court records do not indicate whether unfinished cases were officially withdrawn from consideration. Most likely, the opposing parties found an informal solution and simply failed to reappear. Sometimes, an entry in the record was settlement enough. In 1590 the former servant of Mimmenhausen's miller demanded wages and the defendant responded that there was no need to press legal charges, he would pay within the week.[84] In 1595 Simon Hermann tried to find out who had started the rumor he was a thief. When two defendants denied responsibility, Hermann asked for a written statement to that effect, and no further action was recorded. Hermann must have felt his reputation was sufficiently cleared. When Hans Hailg accused Michael App of taking ten wagonloads of manure they had agreed to share, and of using his shed without permission, App agreed to return the manure. As for the shed, App said he had three good witnesses to prove he had prior authorization to use it. Again, the case was closed. A guardian charged Jerg Lewlin in 1585 with a debt of more than five gulden. Lewlin acknowledged the debt but expressed hesitance to pay unless both guardians were present, to avoid confusion or the demand that he pay twice. At the next session, an entry stated that Lewlin had paid and the complaint was dropped. In this case, too, documentation was enough.

Customary norms, as well as those responsible for their custody, were resources to be used strategically and negotiated with.[85] The decision to bring formal legal action before 15 authority figures and a public assembly required careful tactics and an argument likely to convince both the judges and popular opinion. Sometimes one or both parties took great pains to justify their behavior, revealing something about the litigant's own values and those of their audience.[86] When legal arguments and counterarguments are recorded, they provide us with an idea of how individuals, and even

---

81 SABEAN, Neckarhausen I, p. 78; ROBERTS, The Study of Dispute, p. 23.

82 SABEAN, Neckarhausen I, p. 78; MCINTOSH, Autonomy and Community, p. 187.

83 MCINTOSH, Autonomy and Community, p. 198.

84 13 August 1590: "Andtworter Zaigt An, Er wol nit mit Ime Rechten sonder wol mit Ime Innerhalb Achttagen Abrechnen und bezahlen."

85 ROBERTS, Study of Dispute, p. 18; SABEAN, Neckarhausen I, p. 76.

86 Natalie Zemon DAVIS, Fiction in the Archives: Pardon Tales and Their Tellers in Sixteenth-century France, Stanford 1987. As Davis points out, the stories told in court were not necessarily truthful or untruthful, but either way, the construction and presentation of a narrative were important skills.

society more broadly, viewed behavior and misbehavior, rules and rule-breaking, the relevance of context, intent, personal honor, and other factors, which related to the designation of right and wrong and the assignment of compensation and blame. For example, in 1585 Veit Lamlin accused his neighbor, Agatha Hörerin, of chopping off his pig's back end and hind legs. Agatha's father responded for her: "All pigs should be kept either with the common herd or at home. This pig ran into their yard and gobbled up the chicken feed. Besides, the plaintiff had been able to butcher the pig and put it to his own use."[87] Despite his argument, the judges fined the defendant half a gulden; custom did not justify killing a neighbor's livestock for eating a few scattered grains in the barnyard. Still, the compensation was less than the value of a pig, suggesting the judges did not find Hörerin's actions entirely unjustified. In 1630 Thebus Stehelin appeared in court seeking to get out of an earlier legal decision that required him to pay the innkeeper twenty gulden in damages. He was hard of hearing, he explained, and did not know what had been said on his behalf. He suggested that the court should transfer responsibility to Bartlin Weißenkönig (possibly his former advocate or business partner) for being such a novice and doing a poor job representing him. The court disagreed, upholding its previous decision.[88]

Disputed property sales came frequently before the court, and explanations for wanting to back out of a deal provide interesting details about the determination of material value as well as the social norms regulating contracts. In 1610, for example, the butcher in Neufrach sued Christian Cammerer of Weildorf for refusing to pay the debt on a horse he had purchased. Cammerer defended himself with the "old horse" excuse: the seller had advertised it as a twelve-year-old, but it turned out to be twenty.[89] The court ordered the defendant to pay the full purchase price for the horse as well as half a gulden in damages.[90] In 1590 the court upheld another horse sale against a similarly reluctant buyer. On that occasion the defendant, Jorg Lang of Wendlingen, explained that he had traded horses with a dealer from Stetten and he wanted out of the agreement, since he had given one good horse for two that were completely worth-

87 Recorded on 4 June 1585. "Ant'r Es sej nit Weniger dz sein Tochter Ime solch schwein geclagter massen geschlagen, und dz auß denen Ursachen, Weil ain Jeder underthon solle seine schwein aintweders Under den Hirten schlagen oder daheim behalten. So sei es für sein Hauß geloffen und daselbst den Habern uff den er seinen huenern furgeworffen uffgefressen, Zue dem hab er Cleger solch schwein Vollends gemetzget und In seinen nutz verwendt."

88 19 February 1630. "Cleger last vortragen dz er und beclagter vor disem mit dem wirth von Neüfra einen Rechtshandel gehabt, weil aber er weisenkhönig desse ein anfenger gewesen, auch er wegen seines ublen gehörs die sach nit recht verstanden, pit er ihn wegen der 20 fl. so er dem würth geben soll, g'htlich zue absolvieren und solche gedachtem weisenkhönig als anfenger ufzuelegen." Perhaps not wanting to make the same mistake twice, Stehelin relied heavily on written arguments in another suit later that year.

89 This classic defense was found in several variations, for example, that the animal was sick, lame, blind, or ill-tempered.

90 Court records are from 15 November 1610 and 30 January 1611.

less. He was a young man, he said, and he had not understood the trade. The court required Lang to pay the outstanding debt in full, plus one gulden as compensation for damages.[91]

With land sales, undisclosed rents were one reason for dispute. Buyers sometimes sued for damages, refused to pay full price, or tried to back out of the deal altogether. When Lienhard Sickh bought a house from Claus Wuest and found that he owed the abbey six cartloads of manure instead of the two he was informed of, he brought the seller to court for damages.[92] The seller claimed he had always paid two cartloads but could not guarantee the rent would remain the same. The court required Wuest to pay compensation, and Sickh was stuck with the higher rent. In this case it remains unclear whether the abbey had recently tripled the rent and whether the seller knew this before the sale, purposely failing to mention it. In another case, the buyer of a land parcel in Mimmenhausen complained to the court that the seller had failed to disclose the tithe. He wanted the deal invalidated. Amtmann Mattheus Leub (who was also a Sidelrichter at the time) testified as a witness for the defense, pointing out that the tithe went without saying because all parcels in such places were subject to it as the plaintiff and everyone else knew.[93] The court agreed and charged damages to the plaintiff.

Another disputed sale involved the plaintiff Hans Albrecht of Ehingen and several unnamed persons from the communities of Neufrach and Weiler. Albrecht demanded payment for several Malter of grain they had purchased; the defendants objected the grain was of such poor quality that many had gotten sick and some were unable to work after eating it. They offered to pay something less. Despite three court appearances and several extended discussions of the evidence, no decision is recorded.[94] Such disputed property transactions required the court to sort out issues involving the determination of economic value and loss, breach of contract, accusations of trickery, and the subtleties of negotiating business contracts orally and in writing. These types of cases show how difficult it could be to determine a fair price and they demonstrate also the court's usefulness to litigants for airing their grievances and settling failed property transactions. The cases resulting from disputed sales surely represent only a small proportion of such transactions, but they offer interesting details, providing some indication of what types of business were conducted, by what means, and with whom.

Physical assault cases provide fascinating source material for several reasons. One is that peacekeeping was among the major functions of territorial governance and of the court. Jurisdiction over violence and bloodshed also involved the grey area between the

---

[91] The suit was decided in one appearance on 13 March 1590.

[92] This suit appeared in court on 6 February and 13 March 1590 with a decision at the second appearance.

[93] "Hierauff Zeûg geandtwurttet, Der Zehendt sey per se, unnd Ihme bekhlagten whol bewůßt, das gemainsglich ab allen güether, der Zehendten behöriger orthen geraicht werden solle." The case between Hans Maisterhans and Hans Schmidtmaister was decided on 22 August 1620.

[94] The case was heard on 12 February, 21 February, and 12 March 1591.

neighboring authorities of Salem and Heiligenberg. Litigants' justifications and witness testimony are sometimes recorded in great detail, and assault cases provide evidence about violence as well as attitudes toward it. The penalties for assault are noteworthy as an indicator of the sanctions and seriousness associated with violence, especially in comparison to property offenses.

Fighting broke out in a number of cases at the tavern. One such suit, from 1595, took place in Oberuhldingen. The plaintiff, Georg Legeler, sought damages from Hans Maag for hitting him in the head for no reason with a chair leg. The defendant acknowledged he had hit Legeler without cause but excused himself with the explanation that the blow had been intended for someone else. Witnesses testified that Maag had been fighting with Hans Storch until bystanders dragged the other man outside to cool off. Maag jumped up on a chair near the entryway and when Legeler walked in, oblivious of the whole affair, he received the blow to the head that was meant for Storch.[95] Maag's defense that he meant to hurt someone other than the plaintiff may have found some resonance, because after hearing the evidence, the court ordered Maag to pay the plaintiff three gulden instead of the ten Legeler demanded. When Maag brought suit against Hans Storch the following month to recoup the three gulden in fines, the court rejected his claims.

In another drinking incident from 1625, Martin Urnau shoved Georg Hermann down the stairs and stabbed him twice outside the Nußdorf inn. Urnau, the defendant, freely admitted to these actions but justified them in the context of long-standing hostilities. The dispute went back fourteen years, he said, to some business he and Hermann had conducted, in which there was an argument and insults directed at the defendant. Urnau, who had been traveling, had not seen Hermann again for years before the night of the recent assault. It was Hermann who renewed the dispute with insults. Tempers rose, and as the plaintiff prepared to leave the establishment, he slapped Urnau three times in the face. Urnau pushed Hermann in response, causing him to fall down the stairs. When Urnau proceeded to stab him below the staircase, he claimed, it was only because the plaintiff was threatening him with an open blade and he expected the same or worse. He was merely defending himself, in other words. He did not mean to hurt him badly, he was simply parrying blows and struck him a couple of times, but honorably. The record contains witnesses' names but no testimony or resolution of the conflict.[96]

---

95 Witness Burckhard Hailg of Oberuldingen testified: "Sagt wisse wol dz der beclagt Maag unnd Hanns Storch Ain Andern geshlagen, alls mann Aber denn Storchen hinaus gethon, beclagter Maag Alls bald uff Ain stuel gesprungen unnd Ain bain davon gebrochen, Inn dem der Cleger (so sonnst umb die sach nichts gewist) ohn Alles gefahr in die stuben Widerumb geganngen, welchen beclagter ersehen unnd strackh ohne Alle zuvorgegebne ursach, An den Kopf geshlagen." Recorded on 23 May 1595.

96 Recorded on 18 February and 18 March 1625.

Not only men but women, too, were accused on assault charges. In 1615 two women from Weiler were drinking at the Leutkirch inn when a dispute arose between them. The record describes a fistfight with hair-pulling and name-calling, including the insults whore and witch. Both women received reduced penalties of two and three gulden each.[97] In another incident Hans Kessler's wife fought both Andreas Erhart and his wife in the fields, using farm tools.[98] No case in the sample mentions spousal abuse, the most likely reason being that this form of "marital discipline" was deemed appropriate.[99] One suit, however, provides an interesting twist on the incidence of wife-beating. In 1585 Georg Lewlin sought compensation from Balthasar Fünfflin's wife for fines he owed the abbey as a result of beating her. He told the court she deserved it, and besides, her husband had asked him to do it. Fünfflin's wife retorted it was none of his business. It was up to her own husband to correct her misbehavior and not another man. The court asked each party to submit evidence, but the disputants did not return to court.[100]

The road was another location where physical assaults commonly took place. In comparison to fistfighting, hitting, scratching, or pulling hair, overtaking someone by force (*Überlauf*) was an especially serious charge. In 1610 Simon Lenz of Mühlhofen reported that as he was returning home from the annual market in Meersburg, Jacob Ower struck him in the head with a weapon, almost killing him.[101] The plaintiff demanded 66 fl. in damages. In another case the Oberamtmann brought suit against a man from Daisendorf for assaulting Jacob Hermann of Oberuhldingen on the road. The defendant had verbally assaulted the man, threatened him with a drawn weapon, and injured him in the presence of women.[102] The penalty of three pounds was reduced by half. The Oberamtmann also prosecuted Mattheus Wierer and Ulrich Hailg of Urnau for swearing and pulling a blade in 1615, during an altercation in the forest between Salem and Neufrach.

---

97 The incident appears in the record on 23 June 1615.

98 The Oberamtmann prosecuted both parties separately on 13 March 1590.

99 GLEIXNER, Rechtsfindung, pp. 69–70. Besides, marital disputes were spiritual offenses that would have been referred to an ecclesiastical tribunal such as the bishop's court in Constance.

100 "Clagt weil er Jüngst dem kauffman Umb dz er solch Weib auß gehaiß Ires aignen Manns Unnd Ir selbst höchster verursachung geschlagen, In straff erkhendt, Verhofft auß solcher verursachung sie solle Ine von solchem frefel entheben. Ant'rin Zaigt an Wie dz sie ainen Mann habe, Da sie Unrecht thue, soll er sie der selbig darumb straffen unnd nicht ain anderer Mann, Seie allso von Ime Cleger ungebürenderweiß geschlagen worden." Undated record from 1585.

101 "C.: Seye am Mörspurger Jarmarckht mit Hansen Heußlern haimbwerths gegangen, und auffm Weg gueter Ding geweßt, und Underwegen habe bekhlagter Ower Ihne angetroffen, und Ihme gleich ohn alleß versehen und ohnbeschuldter Dingen mit der Whär ainen hoch shädlichen straich In Kopff gegeben, und Ihne also auf den Todt verwundt, clagt derowegen für solchen seinen erlitnen schmertzen, versaumbnuß, und Artzetlhon, In allem per 66 fl." 7 December 1610. After five appearances, the court awarded the plaintiff 60 fl. in damages.

102 "Clagt vor 14 tagen habe beclagter Jacob Hürman von Oberuldingen, Alls er uf seinem haimbgehn gwest, mit gwertter handt überlofen, uber Ine zuckht, übel geschworen und Gottsgelestert, und damit etliche Weiber vorgewesen, hette er Ine verwundet." Recorded on 5 July 1605.

They blamed an unnamed peasant, riding by on his horse, for provoking the incident. At the time, they were all on their way home from the oath-taking ceremony at Salem to celebrate the recent election of Abbot Thomas Wunn.[103]

In cases such as these, decisions often hung on whether verbal insult incited the violence and on who had acted or spoken first. Some cases of physical assault resulted in serious injury, requiring medical attention or bed rest. One woman claimed damages from her attacker not only for her own injuries but also for her daughter's lost wages while she tended to her mother's bedside for ten days. Many records indicate that the beating resulted in bleeding, which is important since Heiligenberg had jurisdiction over "flowing wounds" outside village boundaries. Such descriptions may have been meant as an intentional challenge to outside authority. Assaults resulting in lesser damages, especially when both sides were conceivably at fault, came less often before the court as civil suits. Such cases, when brought to the authorities' attention, often resulted in criminal prosecution and additional fines. The Oberamtmann prosecuted Andreas Reuter of Mimmenhausen because he resolved a dispute involving "blood and lying" without reporting it.[104]

Conversely, criminal prosecutions sometimes resulted in civil suits. In 1615 the Oberamtmann charged two men with fighting on repeated occasions. First, Hans Utz of Neufrach had assaulted Hans Einhard of Leutkirch, leaving him bloody. Later, both men were involved in a fistfight. Upon their request the court reduced the charges, making Utz responsible for 1½ pounds and Einhard for ten batzen. On the same date, after one intervening hearing, Einhard brought a new suit against Utz claiming ten batzen in damages for court fines. He offered three witnesses, including the innkeeper and his maid, but no decision is recorded.[105]

In this case, Einhard had good reason for hitting back after his assailant beat him bloody in an earlier fight. Still, ten batzen was an extremely low penalty for fighting and the penalties for physical assault were surprisingly low in many cases—especially when compared to fines for other offenses such as wood theft, which could amount to over ten pounds depending on the infraction.[106] In 1591 the Oberamtmann accused Hans Huber's wife of taking produce from someone else's garden and assaulting another woman, perhaps on different occasions. For hitting and misconduct she was charged 12½ shillings, and for the vegetable theft she was charged one pound, almost

---

103 The suit appeared on 25 August 1615. Initial fines of two gulden each were reduced by an undisclosed amount.

104 "Habe sich umb ain bluet: und lugenfreffel gegen ainem zu Mimmenhausen Im wirtshaus ohnwissendt seins herrn oberambtmans vertragen." 8 June 1610.

105 Recorded on 10 March 1615.

106 According to more than one treaty with Heiligenberg, the abbey's court could not charge more than ten pounds in penalties for any infraction. By 1615, however, the abbot openly rejected this limit, and even earlier, higher fines may have been charged and recorded in the court protocol as a form of protest against restrictions on the authority of the abbot and his court.

twice as much as for the assault. The fines also seem lenient in the criminal suit against a man from Feldkirch (probably a local servant) for beating someone to the ground with his fists so that blood flowed, which he did for no reason at all during the night of Shrove Tuesday (*Fastnacht*) celebrations.[107] The initial fine of three gulden was reduced to twenty batzen. Perhaps the court and prosecutor saw drunken revelry as a good excuse for bad behavior, or perhaps fighting was simply more socially acceptable in certain situations than petty theft or property damage.

Criminal Suits

Just over thirty percent of all cases the Sidelgericht heard were criminal suits, prosecuted by district officials in the abbey's name.[108] These cases usually involved violations of the abbey's authority to command and prohibit (*Gebot und Verbot*). The sources refer to most of these offenses as *Frevel* or *übergangenes Gebot*, personal misconduct or statute violation. In some years there were few or no such criminal suits, but in others, abbey officials prosecuted dozens of cases at a single hearing. This irregularity, displayed in Chart 5.10, suggests that the abbey may have brought a large number of cases in order to set an example and curb disobedience at certain times when it was perceived to be a serious problem. Or perhaps local officials such as the Amtmann and the forest warden brought infractions to the attention of higher officials irregularly, in response to a specific inquiry or when they were looking to reinforce order. The record from 31 March 1615 supports this interpretation, when for example nine defendants in a row from Wolketsweiler appeared to answer for forest violations.

These criminal prosecutions by abbey officials, which in some years amounted to a large proportion of the court's entire caseload, might suggest that the Sidelgericht functioned primarily as the lord's preferred means of domination and resource extraction. A closer look reveals otherwise. The accused typically acknowledged their guilt immediately and asked for a merciful penalty. Many criminal suits were settled at the first hearing, in part for this reason. This is significant because in civil suits, a settlement at the first hearing was quite unusual. Defendants in noncriminal cases almost always requested a postponement or contested the plaintiff's charges.[109] Another significant finding is that in cases where the accused admitted fault, the penalties awarded in a final settlement were in most cases lower than the initial charges.[110] In fact, the

[107] "Habe verschiner Faßnacht Michael Sauttern nechtlicher weyl ohn alle Ursach, mit fausten zue boden unnd bluettrysendt geshlagen." Recorded on 23 June 1615.

[108] Abbey officials were plaintiffs in 164 out of 542 cases in the ten sampled years. Additionally, five suits involved violations of court procedure or communal rights.

[109] The only category of noncriminal court appearances that were routinely resolved at the first hearing were requests for the certification of legitimate birth.

[110] Twelve defendants in the sample of criminal suits were required to pay the full amount, compared to at least 72 who accepted reduced charges. In several criminal cases, the record states

Chart 5.10: Abbey Prosecutions by Year

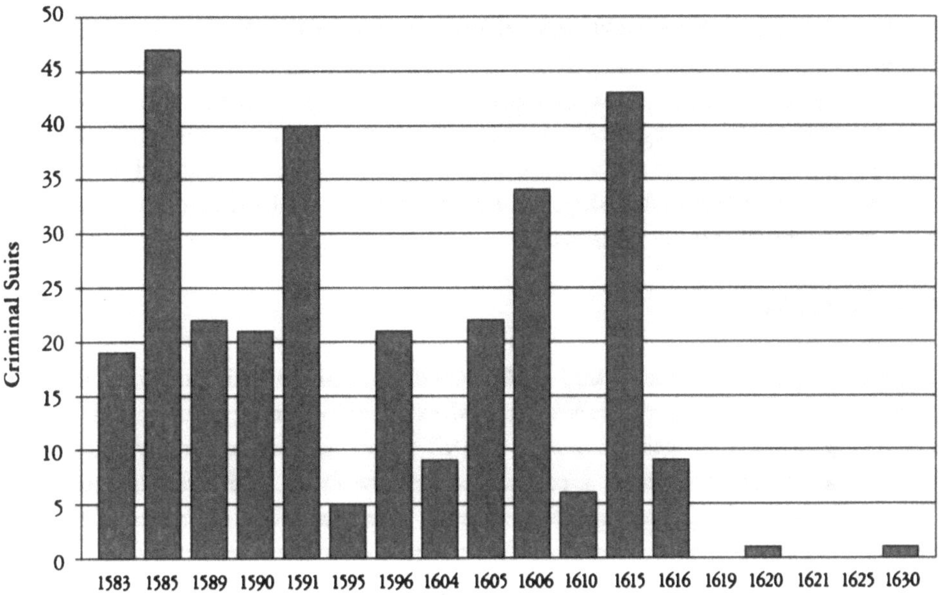

fines could be significantly lower, often half and sometimes only a third or quarter of the original claim. In other words, the Sidelgericht effected a compromise in which the defendant confessed guilt in exchange for a reduced penalty. The record often states explicitly that the parties "settled" or "agreed voluntarily" on a lower amount. For example, the Oberamtmann brought charges in 1615 against four men from Altenbeuren for cutting firewood in the abbey's forest. The initial charge for misconduct and forest damages was three Reichsthaler. The record states its decision: "Upon the intercession of the entire and honorable court, agreed at two gulden each." The court's mediation was useful to the abbey because it helped officials collect money from subjects and forced offenders to acknowledge the lord's authority. At the same time, the Sidelgericht mitigated the lord's demands, providing offenders an opportunity to negotiate a milder penalty. Moreover, not all of the accused admitted fault and not all criminal suits resulted in penalties. In one sense, the prosecutor's willingness to compromise actually strengthened the lord's authority because the demonstration of flexibility and mercy on his part afforded greater compliance and respect for the rules. Yet the fact that these cases came before the Sidelgericht at all demonstrates the limits of the abbey's authority.[111] Even when territorial statutes clearly stated the penalty for an offense, officials

that the complaint was settled amicably (*gütlich*), which suggests that the fines had been lessened by an undisclosed amount. In 58 suits no verdict is recorded, and three defendants were absolved of the charges.

111 Cf. SREENIVASAN, Ottobeuren, p. 27.

could not always simply demand the fines. They used the court, just like anyone else, to justify their claims and hold offenders accountable. They were willing to compromise in order to obtain a subject's acknowledgement of wrongdoing. The form of compensation abbey officials sought was perhaps more symbolic than financial, since a reduced penalty resulted not only in the defendant's admission of guilt but also in potential feelings of gratitude or obligation, which might be expressed in greater loyalty or better behavior in the future. Criminal cases suggest that the court functioned, even when used by representatives of lordship, to bring parties to a settlement, not to squeeze as much money from them as possible.

Forms of Evidence

Litigants relied on arguments and explanations to improve their positions and persuade the judges, but they also submitted evidence to the court as proof of their claims. Two forms of evidence were preferred over all others: witness testimony and written documentation. Some litigants used one form or the other, and a few offered both. Chart 5.11 shows the percentage of cases each year that relied on either of the two forms of evidence. This section considers the role of witness testimony and written documents in the substantiation of legal argument. It also examines how the presentation of evidence affected court procedure and the process of reaching a verdict.

Members of the court heard the oral testimony of witnesses in private, often between sessions, and the records provide inconsistent coverage of this evidence. Sometimes it is merely noted that "witnesses shall be heard," other times the names of witnesses are recorded, and in some cases the testimony itself is described in great detail, stretching on for pages. Such long descriptions of witness depositions are more common later in the period, but since records generally become more elaborate over time, it is difficult to tell whether witnesses actually appeared more often or if their testimony was simply recorded and preserved with greater regularity in later years. The fullness of description for witness testimony also seems to have depended in part on the individual scribe. Among sampled records, the years around 1595 appear especially detailed. The location and timing of depositions must have also made a difference in how and where they were kept.[112] An entry in the record from 1595 stated that the secretary would hear the witnesses at a time and place of his choosing.[113]

The depositions contained in the court records permit some general observations about the role of oral testimony as legal evidence. Transcriptions of witnesses' state-

[112] If witnesses were heard at the end of a regular court session, their actual statements may have been recorded in the court protocols, whereas testimony reported between sessions may have been heard by fewer judges and transcribed in a separate register or not at all.

[113] "Interloquendo geurthailt, ... das die gegenwertige Zeugen, über die eingelegte fragstuckh, nach gelegenhait des Herrn Secretarij uf zeit unnd mahlstatt, so Innen ernent würt, verhört werden sollen." 27 June 1595, suit brought by Jacob Mayer against Jacob Ower.

Chart 5.11: Litigants' Use of Evidence: Witnesses and Written Documents

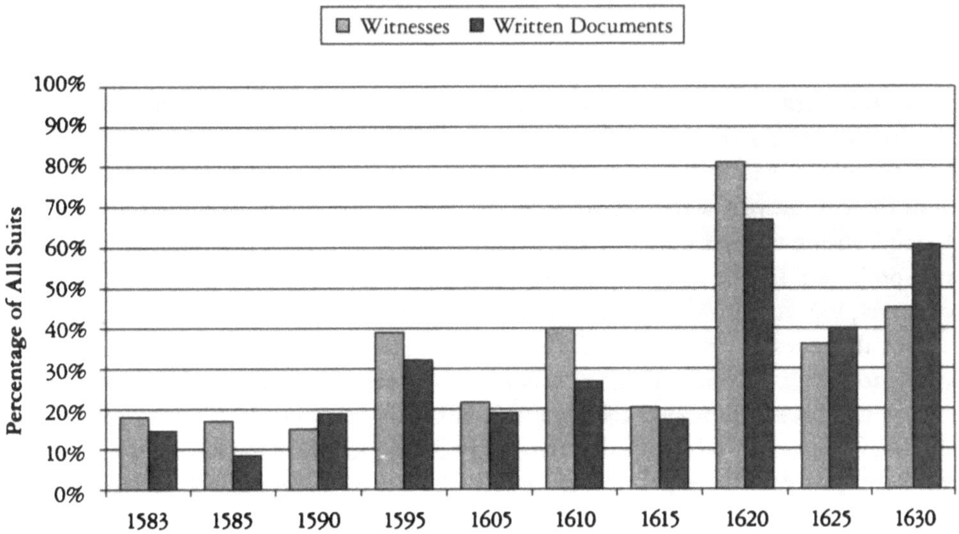

ments start out with the person's name, place of origin, and in some cases, age. Before the deposition began, witnesses were warned against perjury and they swore an oath to tell the truth. Witness testimony was heard in private, but it was not a matter of strict secrecy. Litigants could review transcriptions of witness depositions or even request a copy, produced at their own expense. Witnesses must have therefore directed their statements not only toward the court but also toward a larger audience, including the parties for and against whom they testified.

Persons in positions of authority such as Amtmänner, priests, and other officials were popular witnesses because their word was believed to hold greater weight than that of the average person. The age of witnesses was sometimes recorded for the same reason, because older people possessed greater authority, especially in cases involving knowledge of customs such as grazing rights or the location of boundary markers. In a 1605 boundary dispute between the communes of Grasbeuren and Gebhardsweiler, ten witnesses ranged in age from 50 to 85. Witnesses were chosen not only from among the senior members of the community, however. Disputants often named their neighbors and sometimes even family members as witnesses. Servants made occasional appearances, and women were called upon with surprising frequency. Out of 116 cases listing witnesses by name, 26 of them included at least one female witness. In 1630 nine women testified in one dispute over ownership of a cooking pot. In 1610 four women described the events leading up to a tavern dispute.[114] Even youths occasionally

[114] The cases were a 1630 dispute between Jorg Vittel and the sexton of Seefelden and a 1610 dispute between Jacob Senfft and Hans Zucktenmantel respectively; GLAK, 61/13327, 61/13326.

bore legal witness.[115] In Salem's territory, therefore, women and household dependents were held to be legally competent to the extent that they could take the oath and offer testimony. On the other hand, those who were believed to have a personal interest in the case, as well as those known to hold a grudge against one of the litigants, were considered unfit to offer testimony. The opposing party could petition the court to dismiss a proposed witness on these grounds.[116] When the former Amtmann of Nußdorf brought suit in 1615 against the entire commune, the court declared that since all of the commune's witnesses were biased, they would not be admitted or heard.[117] A single strong witness could be the deciding factor in a case, but multiple witnesses were preferred. In one case, the record noted above the decision that "the defendant's witnesses, four in number, spoke better than the plaintiff's."[118]

Not all witnesses provided useful information about the case, and some seemed unwilling to testify. "Knows nothing" was a fairly common response, suggesting that the witness had been summoned against his or her will—they would not have traveled to the abbey voluntarily to testify that they had nothing to add. One former witness, Michel Rennwarten of Ittendorf, showed his displeasure by suing the men who had called him to testify in an earlier suit. After taking the trouble to come all the way to court, he said, the court had not even heard his statement. The defendants denied responsibility, explaining that the hearing had been cancelled when their opponent, from Constance, failed to appear. The court ordered Rennwarten to give his testimony as promised (the other suit was ongoing) and told the defendants to compensate him for his trouble.[119] Despite the reluctance of some witnesses, many others offered testimony providing great detail about the circumstances, location, relationships, and various perspectives surrounding a case. The evidence of witnesses is of interest with respect to individual suits, but also for the insights it provides about everyday life, social relationships, personal stories, and the attitudes surrounding the incidence of conflict.

---

[115] In 1585, for example, a fourteen-year-old boy bore witness in Teiß Frey's suit against Barbara Schmidin for breaking a marriage contract. A young boy testified in 1620 on behalf of defendant Jacob Michel in a suit involving grain debt, despite the plaintiff's objections.

[116] On 12 May 1620 the defendant Martin Sathaas objected to one of the witnesses against him, calling him "*partheyish*." The court agreed (in an Umfrag) to dismiss the witness because of his relationship to the plaintiff: "Beschaidt, auf genomnen bedacht unnd gehabte umbfrag, ist erkhendt, das auff des bekhlagten begehren, der aine Zeug, freundtshafft halber nit verhört werden solle."

[117] "Beshaidt, Weyln die bekhlagte Gemaindt Nussdorff Partheyishe Gezeugen fürwenden, sollen solche nit admittirt unnd verhört werden." 28 September 1620. The charges involved villagers' failure to repair fences despite the order to do so, leaving the Amtmann personally responsible for resulting damages claimed by Mimmenhausen residents. According to the defendants, the Amtmann had entered an agreement without their knowledge.

[118] "Annt'rs Zeügen haben Ime (deren Vier geweßen) besser dann dem Cläger gesagt." The court's decision required the plaintiff to pay half a gulden in damages. 11 December 1595.

[119] Recorded on 29 June 1585.

Written documentation was the second major type of legal evidence. Litigants presented originals or copies of relevant material to the court, including sales contracts, tenure agreements, letters of credit, and previous court decisions.[120] Many persons apparently possessed their own collections of legal records, and some even kept their own accounts. Guardians, for example, submitted records as proof of how they had administered the property under their care.[121] Others, too, submitted personal accounts to the court as proof of payment or nonpayment. One of the most surprising submissions to the court was from a suit between Peter Seissing and Hans Leub over the use of a meadow in 1606. Leub, who had recently purchased some property adjacent to Seissing, brought five sales contracts to the court, the oldest of which was 96 years old! Parties without their own copies of written documents could refer to records kept by the chancery, bursar, or court. Even better, they could arrange for these record-keeping offices to provide copies. Occasionally, the judges ordered parties to support their claims by providing key documents or written statements at an upcoming court hearing.[122] The requirement that litigants should provide the court with written proof suggests that documentary evidence was readily available and familiar to many of Salem's village subjects.

Litigants used written documents in many different ways, most of which were voluntary. They could even present their opening arguments in writing. This became more common later in the period, and it had an unfortunate side effect: when a plaintiff submitted the charges in a separate written statement, the court records do not bother to describe them, and without the supporting documents, the subject of complaint is no longer discernable. Ironically, oral statements are more likely to have survived in the

---

[120] For example, the following specific documents are mentioned in a total of eleven suits from 1615: Geburtsbrief, Urkunde, Abzugs Steur und Schatzungs Zetteln, schriften und designationen mit A. B. und C. signirt, Urteilbrief, schriftliche Verantwortung, Abschrift, Kaufbrief, Geburtsbrief, zeugensag abschrift, Zettel, schreiben von der wittib, Kaufbrief, schriftliche versicherung, and Brief. Documents specifically mentioned in 1620 include: Brief und Sigel, Rechnungszettel, Kaufbrief, Zettel sub. no. 1, briefliche documenta, Teilungszettel cum annexa petitione, schrifftliche Clag sub lit. A., Clagbrief, Abschrift, Summarische Clag, gerichtsprotocol und zetteln, schrifftlicher Bericht, Heuratsbrief, and schriftliche Verantwortung.

[121] On 14 February 1595 the guardians for Simon Mußel's orphans submitted their debt register (*schulden Register*) to demonstrate that the stonemason Melchior Wuest still owed them four gulden for borrowed grain. On 13 May 1625 Bartlin Müller submitted an extract from his own private account book (*extractus seines shuldtbuechs*) in defense of his actions as a guardian, after the repayment of loans he had made went sour in the hyperinflation of the early 1620s. In response, the defendant Michael Ringenburger submitted "*ain Copia shuldtbriefs aus der Cäntzley verförtiget.*"

[122] For example, on 10 March 1615 the court told defendant Veit Villieber to bring his written response to the next hearing: "Ist interloquendo indicialiter decernirt, Dass bekhlagter Villieber biss zum negsten Gericht, Uber vorgeshribne clag, sich schrifftlich verfassen soll." On 30 September 1625 the court told Bartlin Müller to obtain written proof (*schrüfftlichen shein*) from the Oberamtmann and bring it to the next hearing, in order to demonstrate his payment on behalf of the plaintiff's widowed mother.

record than written ones. Litigants frequently requested personal copies of documents submitted by the opposing party, including written arguments, contracts, and witness depositions. A copy of the court's final verdict was a common request that could be used in several ways: it facilitated the future enforcement of a suit's outcome without having to refer to the court, it could be used as proof that a dispute had been settled, or it could be submitted as legal evidence in a later dispute. Copies were always produced at the expense of the person making the request.

Written documents played a central role in the suit brought by Conrad Müller of Storen against Martin Hornstain and Christian Beckh of Mainwangen in 1595. At the first appearance on 14 February, Müller submitted his claims in writing and the defendants requested a copy of the letter and a postponement.[123] At the second appearance, the plaintiff requested another postponement to prepare his case. At the third session on 7 May, Müller referred to his previously submitted written claim and the defendants submitted their own written defense. The subject of dispute was finally mentioned; it concerned the estate of Christian Beckh's deceased father and the responsibility to repay his remaining debts. On 23 May, the defendants submitted a previous Urteil and asked that it be read aloud.[124] The plaintiff requested another postponement and a copy of that decision. On 13 June, Müller submitted a letter of credit (*Schuldbrief*) along with a supporting document (*ein schrifftlich eingelegte beweiß articul*) naming guarantors for the outstanding sum, and in reply, the defendants pointed to the previously submitted Urteil declaring them free of the matter. The defendants also called four witnesses, each of whom commented on the accuracy of Müller's 16 "articles of proof." The testimony fails to elucidate the contents of the articles—most statements referred to each of the numbered articles as true, false, or beyond the witness's knowledge—but the priest of Mainwangen did state that Beckh's farm was an annual lease that had nothing to do with the inheritance. The priest also offered to tell what he knew about Article 15 in secret.[125] At the end of the final entry, the court declared its decision in favor of the defendants. The creditor from Storen was ordered to pay each of them ten batzen in damages.[126] The court records do not disclose many of the details of this lawsuit, but they do demonstrate both parties' reliance on several types of written evidence.

Plaintiffs sometimes appeared in court for the specific purpose of obtaining written confirmation of some action or agreement, or simply to acquire a document. The most common documentation requests were for certificates of honorable birth, which appear in small numbers in each of the sampled years, but there were many other rea-

---

123 "Cleger übergibt ainn shrifftliche Clag, Pit solche zuverlesenn. A. pit umb abshrifften und dilation."

124 The Urteil was from the village court in Mainwangen, located northeast of Salem not far beyond its territory.

125 "Denn 15. stellt er dem richter haimb."

126 Records relating to the case are found on 14 February, 7 March, 4 April, 9 May, 23 May, and 13 June 1595. At some of the hearings, claims against the two defendants appear separately.

sons. In 1630 two guardians brought Georg Mauch of Neufrach to court for defamation. The dispute had started when the two parties haggled over the price of a house Mauch hoped to rent, after which he complained to a neighbor that the guardians "lied like rascals and thieves." Mauch agreed to publicly retract his words but this was not enough for the guardians, who demanded a written apology. In the end, Mauch paid the chancery to produce a written statement restoring the plaintiffs' honor. Similarly, Simon Hermann of Mimmenhausen brought suit against his neighbor Blesi Bösch to clear his name after some money went missing and rumors spread that Hermann was the thief. Bösch, who admitted the recent loss, told the court he did not hold Hermann responsible. Hermann asked for a certificate declaring him beyond suspicion.[127]

In other suits, the defendant refused to comply with a plaintiff's demand before receiving a contract to secure their rights. In 1615 Agatha Dulerin of Neufrach demanded that Christian Betzlin pay the 110 fl. he owed her for a pension, otherwise she would stop providing benefits. Betzlin told the court he was still waiting to receive a written contract and he would not pay until she produced it.[128] Georg Bader complained in 1610 that Michel Rott still owed him over 9½ fl. from the sale of a house. Rott said he would gladly pay, but not without a copy of the sales contract. We can conclude from these examples that individuals valued written documents as forms of proof, kept them to provide future security, willingly paid for their own copies, and went to the trouble of appearing in court to secure them.

Since court procedure stated that arguments could be made orally or in writing, litigants' heavy reliance on documentation leaves the impression that they understood the importance of written records and knew how to use them effectively. Whatever their level of literacy—whether they kept records themselves, collected relevant copies, or simply knew that a supporting document existed—ordinary subjects grasped the power of the written word and did not hesitate to use it in support of their personal objectives.

Unsurprisingly, the use of written documentation increased dramatically over time, and the submission of as well as requests for written materials represented an enormous workload for the court. In 1620 as well as 1630, over sixty percent of all cases involved the submission of documents or requests for copies (see Chart 5.11 above). By 1630 it was not unusual for a single case to result in dozens of documents being submitted to and copied by the court. As shown in Chart 5.1 (above), the length of court records was also increasing compared to the number of separate cases. On average, the case descriptions were becoming longer and more complicated.

---

[127] The case appeared on 19 September and 30 October 1595, after Hermann brought suit unsuccessfully against another neighbor for spreading the rumor on 9 May.

[128] "B: sagt, Wann er darumben schrifftlichen versichert, wölle allßdann er seinem versprechen geleben unnd nachkhommen. Beshaidt, Sollen sich mit ainandern verainigen unnd brieff auffrichten lassen." 3 November 1615.

5.4 Obstacles to the Court in a Period of Decline

By the 1620s, the Sidelgericht was beginning to show signs of strain. During this decade the court continued to meet regularly and keep thoroughly detailed records, more complete perhaps than ever before. However, cases took much longer to settle on average than they had ten or twenty years earlier. The court had always granted a large number of postponements, frequently upon the defendant's request. Yet a growing number of delays were caused by the judges' own need for more time and information; also, it may be speculated, by the judges' need to consult outside legal authorities more often as cases became more complicated. There was a brisk traffic in written documentation, and the downside of all the submissions and requests for copies is that the court appears to have become increasingly clogged up by the enormous workload. There were complaints by litigants that their witnesses, named at a previous session, still had not been heard; others complained that the copies they had requested still had not been made; there were even cases in which both parties requested a decision, but despite their urging, the court declared yet another postponement. Another indication of the difficulties in this period is that several members asked, for the first time on record, to be relieved of their duties. Morale among the judges must have been extremely low.

Evidence suggests, however, that the difficulties facing the court were not simply the result of lay judges becoming overwhelmed by a greater amount and complexity of legal evidence. In fact, several factors contributed to the court's decline. Part of the problem was that the court did not have a consistent, full-time secretary or adequate staff to support its growing needs. Another issue was the social stratification and partisanship that characterized the period, and from which the judges were not immune. In this climate, skepticism toward the justice provided by local notables is understandable. Third, villagers in the 1620s and 1630s were facing problems much more serious than the court was equipped to solve. Perhaps for these reasons, more villagers chose to address their troubles directly to the abbey's senior officials in the form of Audience petitions.[129] This constellation of issues impeded the court's effectiveness, but it was a temporary situation. The struggles experienced by the court were symptomatic of a more general decline in the early seventeenth century.

One problem certainly promoting the decline was that there were more cases involving written documentation than ever before, while the number of separate docu-

[129] There are other reasons why the Audience may have become more attractive than the court, as suggested by Renate Blickle for Bavaria, where disputes were settled more frequently before the council than by the court in the early seventeenth century. An extrajudicial settlement resembled a compromise rather than declaring a winner and loser, which facilitated the return to a peaceful coexistence. Also, the decisions were faster and thus less expensive than lawsuits. Idem, Supplikationen und Demonstrationen: Mittel und Wege der Partizipation im bayerischen Territorialstaat, in: Kommunikation in der ländlichen Gesellschaft vom Mittelalter bis zur Moderne, ed. Werner Rösener, Göttingen 2000, pp. 285–289.

ments relating to each case was also on the rise. The enormous burden associated with keeping written documents begs the question of who was actually reading, writing, and copying all these materials. The earliest evidence of a court secretary is an employment contract from 1492 for a man named Christoph Ruff, nicknamed Stöltzlin, from the imperial city of Lindau. Stöltzlin agreed to a five-year term as the abbey's scribe (*Schreiber*), during which he would record whatever his lord (the abbot) and the abbey required. He promised specifically "To compile and produce myself, and not assign to any other scribe, that which is necessary for the business and cases brought amicably or legally before his grace, regardless of why or from whom they may come, as well as anything required by the judges of his grace's Sidelgericht or by the court in Bermatingen."[130] We can conclude from this agreement that the court secretary was a scribe employed by the abbey, whose responsibilities to the Sidelgericht were only a fraction of his duties. Even if the workload of a scribe was less arduous in 1492 than a century later, it is hard to believe that one individual could have produced all the legal documents required by the abbey and its courts. Seventeenth-century employment contracts demonstrate that keeping the court's records and attending court sessions continued to be just one small part of the secretary's duties.[131]

When the court was in session, the usual secretary was not always present. It is clear from the variations in handwriting that no single individual acted consistently as the court secretary. Sometimes the script lasted for only a few months or alternated back and forth between sessions. Four cases in a row were postponed in 1620 until the next session because of the secretary's absence.[132] The fact that the session took place at all and that written records were kept (in better handwriting than usual) suggests that the court did not require a specific individual to be present in order for court business to proceed. Still, the lack of consistency in recordkeeping was an issue, especially because the court considered individual lawsuits over multiple sessions.

In 1629, extremely frustrated by the chaotic state of affairs, the judges complained about the situation to higher officials. The note, recorded in the protocol, reads as follows: "The praiseworthy Sidelgericht has brought it to the proper attention of the officials here today at this court assembly in the name of his reverence, our gracious lord, by their

---

130 GLAK, 4/7618. For his services Stöltzlin received room and board, an annual salary of 18 fl., and two sets of clothes.

131 Employment contracts for chancery secretaries including Dr. Johann Wahl in 1624 and Georg Blaicher in 1641 mention court attendance in Article 5, among other duties: "Fünfftens dem Sidelgericht und andern Raths und Verhörstägen, zue reden an gesetzten und bestimbten tägen, sovil möglich selbst personlich beywohnen, dieselbe besitzen helffen, und darüber undershidliche Protocolla halten solle." GLAK, 98/240, 31 December 1624.

132 GLAK, 61/13326. The note after the first case on 17 March reads, "Weil man aber an begerte clag, dermahlen uß mangel des anderen gerichtshreibers, so fir dißmahl nit endthalben gewesen, nit bey handen, ist ain solches bis zum negsten Gerichtstag verschoben." Whoever wrote the entries on this date had better handwriting than the usual secretary, who returned for the next session on 12 May 1620.

suitable request, that from now on they wish to be granted a permanent court scribe, one who would be sworn in on the record as is proper. Sebastian Leub is thus appointed upon gracious ratification."[133] Despite the judges' explicit request for a long-term appointment, Leub appears to have moved on to other things shortly thereafter. His departure from the Sidelgericht, signaled three months later by a new hand, may have been an undesirable outcome from the perspective of the court. For the reader it is extremely fortunate, because the handwriting of his replacement was such an immense improvement. With the sharply increasing demand for written records during this decade, it is no wonder that court secretary was becoming a difficult position to fill.[134]

In the decades after 1629, despite the court's efforts to address problems with the secretary, the situation grew worse. In comparison to the long and detailed records of the 1620s, surviving records from the 1630s, 40s, and 50s are extremely erratic. After 1631 the records break off completely and do not resume again until 1646, leaving one to wonder whether the court continued to meet, and if so, how regularly. Were the records lost or were they kept at all?[135] Despite the treaty with Heiligenberg in 1637 awarding full jurisdictional authority to the abbey, the court does not appear to have been restructured until after the Thirty Years War, and meetings of the Sidelgericht remained sporadic during this difficult period. In 1638 Abbot Thomas I called an assembly of the court and expressed concern that order and discipline in the territory were declining.[136] He noted that many of the court's former members had died or gone away during the course of the war, but he urged the newly reconvened judges to do their best to hold sessions regularly, helping to restore peace within the territory.

Still the records do not resume until 1646, and then it is under the heading: "The reassembly of Salem's honorable Sidelgericht, which has been neglected for many years, held on 9 April, 1646." That same year, abbey officials conducted an inquiry among

---

133 "NB. Es hat ain Loblich Sydelgericht den herren beambten die der Gerichtsbesatzung In Namen deß Hochw. Unnßers Gnedigen Herrens beygewohnt gebürlich Ahngebracht unnd gebetten, daß man Ihnen hinfüro Ainen beständigen Gerichtsschreiber Verordnen unnd auff daß protocol gebürlich beaidigen wölle, unnd Ist darzue Auff Gnedige Ratification Verordnet Sebastian Leub." 22 January 1629.

134 Sebastian Leub, who was most likely an abbey subject from Weiler, is one of very few court secretaries who are known by name. Others include Georg Mantz from Biberach, a chancery secretary for three years ending in 1607 upon his resignation. Dr. Johann Wahl was the secretary in 1624. Georg Blaicher from Pfullendorf was the court secretary in 1627, appointed in 1641 as the abbey's head secretary. Johann Neuschell was named *Canzelist und Gotshaus Schreiber* in 1631 and *Gerichtschreiber* in 1634. Johann Conrad Stöb was listed as court secretary in 1636. Bartholome Stahel (or Stabel) held the title of *Ambt- und Gerichtschreiber* in 1646 and 1648. GLAK, 61/13327, 98/232, 98/240, 98/597, 98/3502.

135 The Thirty Years War explains much of the problem, since its full effects in the region coincided with the disappearance of court records. Sebastian Bürster's chronicle describes these years in detail.

136 GLAK, 98/597.

the Sidelrichter in an effort to determine the causes of past irregularities and reestablish court order. The questions posed to each of the judges were not in fact new. The procedure of asking judges to report on problems during the previous year before being sworn back into office was customary and can be found in several earlier texts.[137] The difference in 1646 is that each judge's responses are recorded below the questions. Two copies of their statements have survived, suggesting that multiple senior officials recorded and scrutinized them carefully.

The inquiry was conducted in a fashion similar to an Umfrag. Johann Hainrich von Pflaumern, abbey councilor and legal doctor, posed three separate questions to each of the judges in turn. First, "Have you noticed anything suspicious or partial as a member of the court, any impropriety or law that has not been followed?" Second, "Do you know if any of the judges has done anything dishonorable or troublesome?" And third, "Are any members of this court bound to one another by ties of friendship?" Most of the judges, who gave their answers in the presence of the entire group, merely repeated the information given by those before them or said they knew nothing. Yet details provided by the highest-ranking members who answered first and by dissenting judges further down the line offer important insights.

Only two men had specific responses to the first question, both pertaining to the court records. Judge number three responded simply, "Has no idea what has happened to the records."[138] The description of judge number nine's response was, "Knows nothing except that there were serious deficiencies relating to the records and the scribes."[139] It is curious that when asked about suspicious or improper behavior, partiality, and failure to observe the law, both judges framed their answers in terms of recordkeeping. It is unclear whether this was directly related to the topic of suspicion and impropriety or whether the judges intended to shift the focus of discussion to what they saw as the court's major problem. Either way, it is significant that both of them mentioned the records without being prompted to do so. Moreover, their conclusions about recordkeeping suggest slightly different problems. The first response indicates that the records had been kept but could no longer be found, whereas the second implies that records had been kept poorly or not at all, perhaps owing to troubles with the court secretary, who remained unnamed.

---

137 GLAK, 98/597. The judges from the two village courts were also questioned annually. The opening session for Owingen's court on 4 February 1625 provides a total of six questions posed to the judges, including "Ob khein freundtshafft, oder Partheyish Recht dieß Jahr gehalten." Another was "Ob khein Gerichtß verwanter durch empfangene mackhel zue diesem Gericht Untaugenlich worden."

138 "Wo die acta seien wiße er nit." GLAK, 61/13328, 9 April 1646.

139 "Wiße nichtß alß daß vor disen groser Mangel an den actis und gerichtshreibern ershinen seie." Ibid. Here, the second copy records a slightly different response: "Wiße nichtß alß daß vor disen vil an den acta und gericht schreiben seie hinderns gewesn." ("Knows nothing, other than that there were many hinderances to the records and the recordkeeping.") GLAK, 98/600.

The difficulties facing the court cannot be pinned entirely on the secretary or lack of one, however. There are also signs of division among the judges themselves. Their responses to questions two and three, which sought to elicit accusations against other members of the court, were mostly formulaic. Almost all the judges answered the second question by describing a quarrel between two of the court's members, Michael Heffelin and Andreas Michel, both of Neufrach. No one explained the source of the dispute, although judge number three said he had heard that one stole something from the other, and judge number fifteen offered to tell what he knew in private. In response to the third question, several Sidelrichter mentioned that Hans Kessler of Nußdorf and Hans Vogler of Owingen were in-laws. Kessler freely admitted to being Vogler's stepfather-in-law and asked to be dismissed from the court. Jacob Ower pointed out that he and Hans Georg Rauch were also distantly related. Although they had served together in the past, he "asked submissively to be relieved of this difficult burden."[140] The responses to this last question reveal several problems. First, three judges and one alternate were related to another member of the court, with the remaining judges divided in their opinion as to whether this posed a problem. In addition, it appears that some members were unhappy serving the court and did not want to be there. Yet despite their pleas and the customary kinship prohibition, the authorities retained the related judges as members of the court. As for Michael Heffelin and Andreas Michel, they were told to vent their disagreement and work things out at the next session. Meanwhile, two alternates would sit in their place.[141]

Sporadic court records after 1646 indicate that the Sidelgericht continued to meet and consider cases occasionally.[142] The last page of the volume, from 1654, contains no indication that the secretary knew this would be his last transcription. The record simply breaks off without explanation at the end of a case description. The court's decline over the period from roughly 1620 until 1654 is not terribly surprising. Missing records starting in 1632 may have been burned, plundered, or lost during the course of the Thirty Years War. As the abbot's 1638 letter and the initial session title from 1646 suggest, the court assembled infrequently for many years amidst the more general disorder. Yet the court's decline set in at least a decade before the full-blown effects of the war, which arrived in the early 1630s. Perhaps the best indication of the court's decline in the period after 1620 is that fewer cases were brought before the court, whereas during the same period, Audience petitions skyrocketed. As many obstacles beset the court, subjects increasingly brought their disputes before this body of senior abbey

140 "Bittet untertenig ihn dises shweren Lasts zu entlassen." Ibid.

141 There is no indication of this dispute's outcome, though neither man was named in the next list of judges, from 1650.

142 Records for the years 1646–1648 and 1652–1654 are mostly concerned with deceased debtors and bankruptcy auctions (*Gantsachen*), reflecting the difficulties of the war years. With the exception of 1646, records survive for only one or two hearings annually.

administrators—who declared their decisions with greater efficiency and according to the lord's favor, not according to the law as interpreted by fellow neighbors and subjects.[143] The Oberamtmann, too, stopped bringing suits before the court around 1620. The court was suffering an apparent loss of confidence, albeit temporarily.

In 1637, amidst the chaos and waging of war, Salem and Heiligenberg entered a treaty that ended centuries of dispute. Salem acquired full judicial authority within its lands, including high justice, in exchange for relinquishing certain properties and rights to Heiligenberg in the northern Linzgau. In 1637, however, because of the general situation, the abbey was in no place to immediately erect a new high court or reorganize its existing court system that was, as we have seen, in a serious state of decline. Because of the lack of court records during these years, it is unclear how or by what authority capital offenses were treated immediately following the agreement of 1637. What we do know is that sometime in the mid-seventeenth century, perhaps around the time the Sidelgericht's records finally ceased in 1654, a new high court was ultimately established.[144] This reconfigured court replaced the Sidelgericht and was known as the court of maleficence (*Malefitzgericht*) or of blood justice (*Blutgericht*). The history of this court is not the subject here, but it does provide key evidence that customary law began to flourish once again after the mid-seventeenth century.

The best proof of this comes from the lists of judges, including two from 1698 and 1716 as well as an earlier, undated list.[145] They demonstrate that the new court of blood justice was composed of many of the same individuals as before! This suggests that the Sidelgericht was not disbanded but transformed and renamed to emphasize its heightened significance. The first list, though undated, indicates the court's membership at an intermediary stage between the last known Sidelrichter of the 1650s and the members of the new court in 1698. On the undated list we find seven men who had been Sidelrichter between 1650 and 1652. The list from 1698 in turn contains two

---

143 It was the increasing complexity of local rural life and at the same time the loosening of traditional relationships that created sufficient space for the norms and policies of central authorities to take hold. In this case, evidence does not suggest that "law begins where friendship ends," but rather, that social strife led villagers to abandon the law in order to call on the lord's mercy, a move that was further reinforced by the magnitude of problems that could not be addressed by the court or their neighbors. See LANDWEHR, Policey vor Ort, p. 65; Rosi FUHRMANN et al., Supplizierende Gemeinden: Aspekte einer vergleichenden Quellenbetrachtung, in: Gemeinde und Staat im Alten Europa, ed. Peter Blickle, Munich 1998, p. 321.

144 The earliest known record pertaining to the new court is a description of procecures from 1669: "Forma wie man ein Malefitzgericht zue Salem halten solle." The document outlines the use of advocates, the presentation of evidence, the Umfrag, the role of the court secretary, and other matters. GLAK, 98/601. A reference to Johann Stengelin of Owingen as the last Stabhalter of the Sidelgericht indicates that the new court replaced the older one rather than creating an additional layer of justice above it. Yet Johann Stengelin did not step down: he became the first Stabhalter of the new high court. GLAK, 98/597, 98/1735.

145 GLAK, 98/597.

names also found on the earlier list, and in 1716, there were three who had been judges in 1698. Thus, the social continuity of the court was preserved as its membership gradually changed. The judges' geographical and family affiliations give additional support to this finding. In 1716, twelve of the fourteen judges were Amtmänner and they represented the communities of Adelsreute, Bermatingen, Buggensegel, Grasbeuren, Mendlishausen, Mimmenhausen, Neufrach, Nußdorf, Oberuhldingen, Owingen, Weildorf, and Weiler. One was a miller, another was an innkeeper, and all of the judges were villagers. Not only were the members of the new court chosen from the core villages of the territory, some of them represented the same families as in the past, including the Dilgers, Leubs, Stengelins, and Voglers.

The reorganization of the justice system after 1637 might have provided the opportunity to make a clean break, for the abbey to dispense with its peasant judges and their legal customs. Yet such a break did not occur. The establishment of the new court, which was really a reconfiguration of the old court under a new name and with expanded powers, requires us to reject the conclusion that the peasant judges and the customs on which the law was based had outlived their usefulness by the seventeenth century. This is because the revitalized court was composed of a similar circle of judges from the same villages and families who continued to declare the law throughout the territory, now with even greater legal authority than before.

5.5 Who Were the Sidelrichter?

Central to the court's significance is the fact that its members were peasant subjects drawn from various villages across the territory. Who were these men who served on the territory's central court and interpreted its law? Many of the questions in this section are similar to those asked of the Amtmänner in Chapter 4. Again, we will look at wealth, property, kinship, and officeholding in order to compare the judges with their neighbors and determine the extent to which these political elites shared group characteristics. In other words, did the Sidelrichter stand apart from other peasants as a separate ruling class or were they integrated members of their local communities, ordinary men who were not so different from other householders? Since they were among the primary mediators between the abbey and its subjects, we would also like to know what characterized their relationship to the abbey and whether there were certain qualities that made them good candidates for appointment and promotion within the abbey's service. As indicated in the previous chapter, these are ambitious questions for a study of common people during the generations around 1600.[146] It will be useful before moving on to the findings to describe the sample and method, including some limitations specific to the material and how they are accounted for.

---

[146] Chapter 4 describes the sources on wealth, tenure, and kinship.

Chart 5.12: Sidelrichter Lists with Gaps, 1471 – 1652

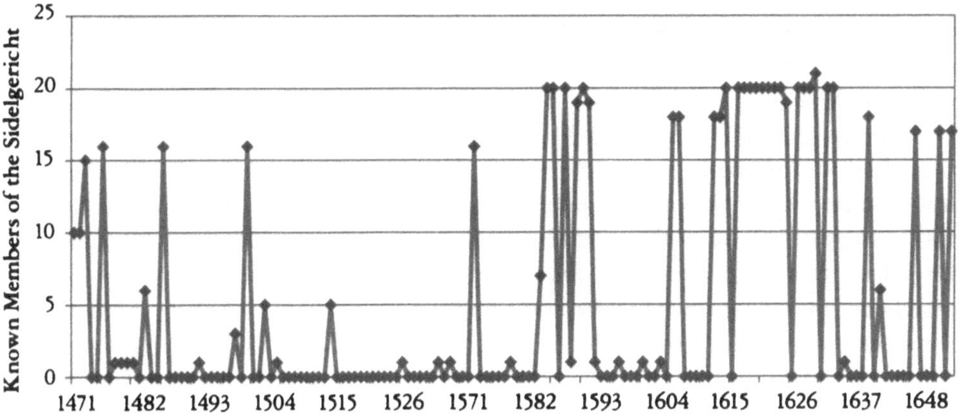

The biggest source limitation specific to our analysis of the Sidelrichter is that only a fraction of them are known by name. There are lists of judges in the court records, starting in 1583, but such lists are missing for several key years and sometimes for many years in a row. Additional lists are found in a separate dossier of miscellaneous judicial records, and these help fill some of the holes.[147] Still, as Chart 5.12 shows, lists are missing for 23 years between 1584 and 1632 including a stretch of 13 years from 1592 – 1604 as well as for many more years before and after these dates. Before 1583, judges' names are only intermittently available. Six lists survive from the period 1471 – 1500, but following a few scattered names found in legal charters from the early sixteenth century, there are no names at all from 1515 through 1565.[148] For most of the sixteenth century, there are enough records to establish the existence of the court but almost no mention of the judges. Finally in 1572 there is a full list of 16 judges, the first since 1500, and then another full list in 1584. Between 1584 and 1632 there are 26 lists, six of them before 1600 and another twenty afterward. At least four additional lists survive from the years after 1632, including 1638, 1646, 1650, and 1652. For the lists that are available, judges' names are listed in order of seat rank, which allows an investigation of the court's composition over time and of individual judges' career trajectories. The annual lists of names are especially useful because of their entirety: for each year they give the names of all members in rank order, which can be compared over time to other complete lists. The discontinuities cause several difficulties, including the lack of precise start and end dates for many judges. Yet a comparison of lists

[147] GLAK, 98/597 (with lists from 1612/1613, 1629, 1632, and 1638 among others).

[148] Legal charters containing individual judges' names (not full lists) include GLAK, 4/123, 4/124, 4/126, 4/130, 4/131, 4/316, 4/363, 4/368, 4/1136, 4/1287, and 4/2158; early court decisions, with some names, are found in GLAK, 4/1287, 4/2139, 4/2158, 4/2178, 4/2723, 4/4006, 4/4429, 4/4627, 4/4648, and 4/5663.

on either side of the gaps allows a partial reconstruction of the court's members during the missing years. Despite obvious source limitations, the available information is quite useful. Altogether, there are 164 known members of the court from the period 1471–1646.[149] Their names and dates of service are found in Appendix 5.1: Members of the Sidelgericht.

In order to focus the analysis where sources are available, I have clustered judges according to chronology and other criteria. For example, the majority of background information is available for those judges who served during the fifty years surrounding 1600, whereas little to nothing can be said about economic background and kinship for judges from a century earlier. For certain questions I narrowed the inquiry to "full members," excluding court bailiffs and alternates. For others, I compared judges from three distinct periods: 1471–1514, 1572–1596, and 1600–1638. I also paid closer attention to those judges who are named in multiple lists and less to those who became members after 1638. The sample will be specified as necessary if other than the complete list of 164 members.

Method of Appointment

First, we need to address this important but elusive question: by whom and through what process were the members of the court selected? The sources are indisposed to offer any concrete answers, even during the conflict leading up to the partnership agreement of 1473.[150] Three historians have approached this problem, each of them drawing different conclusions. Elmar Kuhn says that the abbot chose the judges himself.[151] Hermann Baier says the abbot chose the head judge, but he does not mention

---

[149] Judges who began terms in 1646 or earlier are followed into the 1650s, but those who became judges after 1646 are excluded from the list.

[150] In 1470, the Sidelrichter did mention in their opening statement before the bishop that "the abbey has the power to fill its court, called the Sidelgericht, with people of the abbey," but no specific reference indicated who chose the judges or how. GLAK, 4/120, fol. 2v. This is somewhat surprising, since similar conflicts in other territories led to a revision of the procedures used to choose the judges. In Marchtal, for example, a treaty in 1520 specified that all judges would come from the communes and that the abbot and communes would each choose half. In Engelberg, the appointment of judges was a repeated source of disagreement. Decisions in 1444 and 1469 specified that the abbot had the right to choose the judges but they had to be residents of the valley jurisdiction. In 1605 a new decision declared that Engelberg's abbot had the right to choose the head judge and four others; the remaining four were chosen from among twelve men recommended by valley residents. In 1619 the subjects complained that native people should be preferred as judges over newer inhabitants or outsiders. BLICKLE and HOLENSTEIN, Agrarverfassungsverträge, p. 104; CATTANI, Engelberg, pp. 38–42, 76–78.

[151] "Der Sidelrichter (später Stabhalter) und seine in der Regel 14 Urteils-Sprecher (im 17. Jhd. noch 4 Zusätze oder Beisitzer) sprachen Recht anstelle und im Auftrag des Abts und wurden von ihm jeweils für ein Jahr aus seinen Untertanen bestellt." KUHN, Mönche und Bauern, p. 54.

how the other judges were appointed.[152] According to Willi Schober, the abbot chose half the judges starting in the thirteenth century and the village communes chose the rest.[153] Unfortunately, none of these historians provides a source to support his statement. Though I have not found conclusive evidence one way or the other, there is one passage in the court protocol that seems to offer a suggestion. Using this example and other clues, I would respond to the question of court appointments not with an assertion but with a new working hypothesis.

The evidence comes from the opening court session on 15 January and the following session on 19 February 1619. First, a long entry on 15 January describes how the court was called to order in the presence of the prior, Pfister, bursar, and Großkeller, who were there on behalf of the abbot and in his name. One noteworthy detail the record provides is that the Oberamtmann, Joachim Vögelin, was the one who carried out the official procedures on that day of swearing the old judges out of office, questioning them, and swearing them back in for the upcoming year.[154] The second detail has to do with the replacement of judges. According to his inquiry, the record states, the Oberamtmann found that no new judges would be necessary except for one, to replace the deceased Georg Schreiber of Owingen. Without assigning any definite agency for the decision, the record states that Martin Stengelin was chosen (*erkhiest*) as the new judge.[155] After that the judges reassembled, the statutes were read aloud, and the Oberamtmann administered the oath to each of them. At the February session, another note before the start of case hearings referred to the choice of Martin Stengelin as the new judge. This time, it stated, the Oberamtmann proposed as he had at the previous court session that Martin Stengelin, who had been chosen to fill the vacant seat, should join the court as a new addition. According to the usual oath, he was sworn in.

These two passages indicate first of all that the abbot was not present for these discussions. Instead it was the Oberamtmann, the abbot's legal representative and criminal prosecutor, who questioned the existing judges about current conditions on the

---

152 "Organ dieser Gerichtsbarkeit war das Sidelgericht, das an der Klosterpforte tagte und in dem ein vom Abt eingesetzter Sidelrichter den Vorsitz führte." BAIER, Staat und Kirche, p. 133.

153 "Das Kloster hatte Einfluss auf die Besetzung des Sidelgerichts; anfänglich ernannte das Kloster selbst die Richter aus der Zahl der Gerichtsuntertanen in den verschiedenen Gemeinden; im 13. Jh. werden die 'Fünfzehn' zur Hälfte vom Abte und zur Hälfte von den Gemeinden—von den Salem gehörenden Dörfern—bestellt." Willi SCHOBER, Die Strafgerichtsbarkeit des Klosters Salem, JD diss., Freiburg im Breisgau 1926, p. 70. Among the three authorities cited, Schober is the least trustworthy. His study contains several inaccuracies and other such unsupported assertions.

154 Sources from other years indicate that the abbey's officials (*Amtsherren*) were collectively involved in the opening session's procedures of questioning the judges, reading statutes, and swearing in the members.

155 Other sources use the terms *erwählen*, *besetzen*, *anstellen*, and *verordnen* to describe how the judges assumed office. The emphasis of some of these verbs tends in the direction of appointment, others in the direction of election, but in no case do the sources mention the agency behind the choice of judges.

Chart 5.13: Judges' Places of Origin

Adelsreute	1
Ahausen	1
Altheim	1
Baufnang	2
Bebenweiler	2*
Bermatingen	25**
Bitzenhofen	1
Buggensegel	2
Forst	1
Grasbeuren	7*
Hagnau	1
Hedertsweiler	1
Hergisweiler	1
Lugenhof	1
Mendlishausen	1
Mimmenhausen	17*
Mühlhofen/Gebhardsweiler	1
Unknown Place	1

Neufrach and Leutkirch	22*
Nußdorf	14*
Oberhof	2
Oberuhldingen	6
Owingen and Pfaffenhofen	22
Ralzhof	1*
Rickenbach	1
Schwandorf	2
Tepfenhard	3*
Tüfingen	5*
Unteruhldingen	1
Urnau	3
Wälde	1
Wehausen	3
Weildorf	8
Weiler	7
Wendlingen	1
Judges Total	164
Places Total	169

* 5 judges who moved from one village to another are counted twice

court and nominated a new judge to fill the vacant position. Yet the Oberamtmann did not simply appoint the new judge. Instead, he suggested Stengelin to the court at the January session and repeated his proposal in February, as if the decision had not yet been finalized. My hypothesis is that new judges were nominated by the Oberamtmann or other representative of the abbot but that they were actually appointed through a dialogue involving senior officials and the sitting judges, followed by confirmation before the entire court. Furthermore, the Oberamtmann's initial nomination was surely influenced by information he received from the judges, for he was not as familiar as they were with all the leading villagers and their backgrounds. As for Martin Stengelin, he had no experience as a court alternate or an Amtmann. What he did have was a connection to Georg Schreiber, the deceased judge who was also the former Amtmann and village innkeeper. Stengelin, as we saw in Chapter 4, married Schreiber's wealthy widow and this is what seems to have launched his career. Around the same time he was chosen as a judge he also became the new Amtmann in Owingen. The choice of judges, therefore, seems to have been linked to social relations in the village. It also seems to have been a negotiated process that was perhaps the abbot's choice in theory but was in fact subject to information and advice received from judges and other vil-

Chart 5.14: Sidelrichter from Major Villages

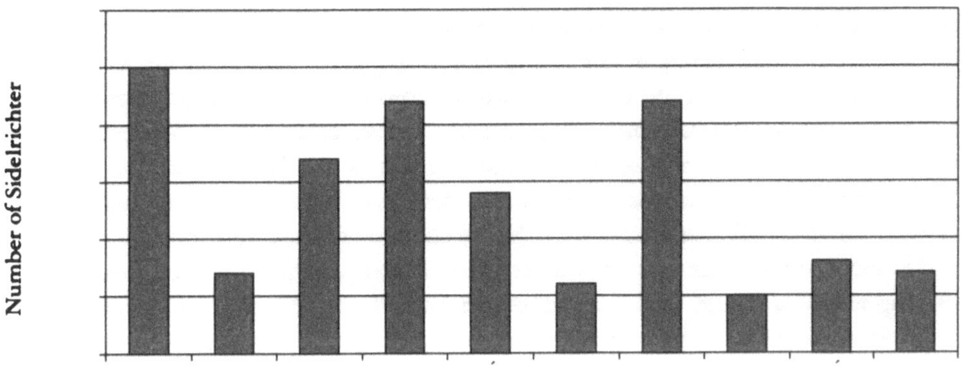

lagers. This hypothesis is also supported by evidence described below, including the servility status of judges, their places of origin, family affiliations, and the strong correspondence in officeholding between judges and village headmen.

Village Affiliation

Each of the court's members lived within a day's walk of the abbey. The great majority came from the larger and mid-sized villages of Salem's territory Under the Hills, but others came from the smaller hamlets and a few were from beyond territorial borders. Chart 5.13 shows all judges' places of origin and the number of judges from each locality. Chart 5.14 gives a breakdown among the ten villages contributing five or more judges to the court.

The villages of Bermatingen and Owingen contributed the highest number of judges over the entire period. Two factors may have contributed to the leading role of these villages. First, Bermatingen and Owingen both maintained their own local courts. This meant that members of these villages were more likely than others to possess the requisite skills for judicial officeholding. At least ten Sidelrichter were also members of the village court in either Bermatingen or Owingen, and two of them were simultaneously the local head judge. The second factor has to do with political geography. Incorporating the most respected members of outlying villages as judges on the central court helped to integrate these places within the territory's shared legal traditions and norms. If the head judge was from Bermatingen, this brought prestige to his village and made local people more aware of the central court, perhaps more likely to use and support it. If two or three judges came from Bermatingen, the effects were similar. Encouraging inhabitants of border areas to identify with the abbey's jurisdiction rather than their own local customs or, even worse, leaving them open to outside influence, may have been intentional policy or just common sense. Either way, it connected outlying areas to the center. Bermatingen's participation in the Sidelgericht is especially significant in this context, since it was the one village in the territory whose residents could claim exemption from it. The fact that judges from this village played a leading role on the court demonstrates that Bermatingers were not completely independent of the central court or territorial legal customs despite their judicial immunity. Other villages contributing many judges to the court were Mimmenhausen and Neufrach, both in close proximity to the abbey, and Nußdorf, on the lake near Überlingen. This broad distribution of judges suggests the sharing of legal authority (and responsibility) among the various parts of the territory.

Most of the judges lived within the central territory but there were exceptions, especially in the early period.[156] Within its own territorial boundaries, Salem claimed judicial authority over all inhabitants regardless of whose serfs they might be, or on whose land they might reside. For Salem to claim as its judges the jurisdictional subjects of another lord, the count of Heiligenberg in particular, was a bold rejection of that neighbor's territorial claims and a certain invitation for legal confrontation. A challenge to this practice came in 1509, and the arbitration settlement of that year specified that Heiligenberg and Salem could each use judges only from their own judicial sphere.[157] After 1509 almost all the Sidelrichter came from places belonging to Salem's jurisdiction, but not Hans Heffelin (1514) from Hagnau, Georg Ill (1572–1587) from Wälde, or Hans Hund (1632, 1638) from Wendlingen.

Wealth, Tenure, and Freehold

The wealth, tenure, and property statistics for Sidelrichter are quite similar to those described for Amtmänner in Chapter 4. This is true not only because both groups were among the village's political elites but also because so many individuals held both offices simultaneously. Instead of covering the same statistical information in repetitive fashion, this section seeks to build on the previous discussion and raise some new questions that are specifically relevant to the territorial judges.

156 Judges before 1509 came from Ahausen, Altheim, Bebenweiler, Bitzenhofen, Hergisweiler, Rickenbach, and Unteruhldingen. Although Salem did claim both land and serfs in these locations, all were outside its jurisdictional boundaries.

157 Heiligenberg, too, used village subjects to staff its territorial court. The decision by the abbot of Bebenhausen and two minor nobles, Conrad von Schellenberg and Wolfgang von Honburg, was as follows: "Uff solhs haben wir Sy, mit Irem wissen also vertragen, Das nun hinfuro der obgenant unser herr von Salem sin sidel unnd ander gericht, allain mit den Jhenen, so hinder Im in Sinen gerichten sitzen, besetzen sol, Deßglichen unser heren von Werdemberg, mit besatzung Irs landtgerichts und ander Irer gerichten ouch thun söllen, unnd also kain tail die so nit In sinen gerichten gesessen, mer zu Sinen gerichten, Es sige Landtgericht, Sidelgericht, oder anndere geRicht ervordern sölle." GLAK, 67/1431, fol. 48v.

In the preceding analysis of wealth distribution and propertyholding, we concentrated on the tax lists from 1578, 1593, and 1603, and these sources remain central to our inquiry. Many Sidelrichter are named in these registers, including some who held office at the time and others who held office in subsequent years. For our initial analysis we will focus on those judges who were full members of the court (not alternates) within six years of a tax assessment.[158] According to this criterion there are 17 judges each in the 1578 and 1593 lists and another 15 named in 1603. Later we will return to those judges found in tax lists more than six years prior to their careers on the court.

On the whole, the Sidelrichter were much wealthier than other villagers, though there was significant variation among them. In the top one percent of territorial households there were three judges in 1578, three in 1593, and two in 1603. The majority of judges were in the top five percent of wealth (eleven individuals in each of the three years), and just a few were below the top ten percent.[159] In all three lists only two judges, both in 1578, had property valued below the territorial average of 391 fl.[160] Of the three assessment years, average and median wealth among judges were highest in 1593.[161] Compared with the Amtmänner, Sidelrichter had higher average wealth, significantly higher in 1593. Not every Sidelrichter was extremely rich, but as a group they stood out from most of their neighbors.[162]

The landholding structure of Sidelrichter households was similar to that of Amtmänner. Actually, there was a slightly higher percentage of nontenants among the judges. In 1578, 8 out of 17 held a tenure of some sort and 6 of these were large farms subject to annual renewal. In 1593, 11 out of 17 held tenures, 9 of them annual leases, and in 1603, 10 of the 15 held tenures including 8 annual leases.[163] This left 9 judges in 1578, 6 in 1593, and 5 in 1603 who were without farm tenures. Freehold property is listed for most tenants in all three lists. In 1578 the average value was 1,256.8 fl. with

---

158 I chose six years as the cutoff in order to make the best use of the tax lists, since lists of judges are not available from 1578, 1593, or 1603. Full lists are available from 1572 and 1584, and these can be compared to property and wealth in 1578. Lists from 1605–1606 are compared to 1603 and lists from 1587 and 1589–1591 to 1593.

159 Six judges in 1578 were below the tenth percentile of wealth, and there were two each in 1593 and 1603. The top ten percent is roughly equivalent to the highest wealth bracket, those with 1,000 fl. or more.

160 The poorest judges in 1578 were Conrad Megerlin from Bermatingen with 184 fl. and Laux Leub the elder from Weiler with 264 fl.

161 Average wealth among judges was 1,754 fl. in 1578, 2,379 fl. in 1593, and 2,148 f. in 1603. Median wealth was 1,700 fl. in 1578, 2,187 fl. in 1593, and 1,952 fl. in 1603.

162 Average wealth among Amtmänner was 1,711 fl. in 1578, 1,327 fl. in 1593, and 1,686 fl. in 1603.

163 Besides the annual tenures in 1578 there were two lifelong leases, a hereditary lease worth 800 fl., a hereditary smallholding worth 250 fl., and a smallholding of unspecified lease type. In 1593 and 1603 there were two hereditary smallholdings, each worth 400 fl. Three judges held more than one property in 1578, but none did in 1593 or 1603.

a range of 178–3,038 fl. among 8 households; in 1593 the average was 922.7 fl. with a range of 250–2,750 fl. among 10 households, and freehold in 1603 averaged 1,028.2 fl. with a range of 0–3,570 fl. among 9 households. The size of farms, based on the number of parcels, was basically the same in 1578 and 1593.[164] Animal ownership among these same households in 1578 and 1593 averaged 303.9 fl. and 206.7 respectively.[165] It is interesting that although the value of freehold and livestock among tenants sank in 1593, total wealth among judges was significantly higher in that year. This is probably because of the great wealth possessed by the two extremely wealthy nontenants in 1593, which offset the decline among other households.

Net wealth is available for tenants in all three tax lists. Compared to the average tenant, net wealth among Sidelrichter was higher as well as more stable over time. In 1578, average net value among tenant Sidelrichter was 80.1% of gross wealth; in 1593 it was 86.1% and in 1603 85.5% of gross. Whereas several Amtmänner in all three lists feature among households with debts of over half their gross value, no Sidelrichter was so heavily indebted.[166]

A comparison of wealth among the tenants and nontenants indicates that the latter were not poorer on average. In 1578 the tenants averaged 2,600 fl. compared with 1,001.1 fl. for nontenants, but in 1593 and 1603 the situation was reversed: tenants in 1593 averaged 1,923.2 fl. and nontenants averaged 3,215.5 fl.; in 1603 the tenants averaged 2,003.5 fl. and nontenants averaged 2,438 fl. Subcategories of wealth are normally listed only for tenants, but in 1593, wealth categories are described for two nontenants, both of whom were Sidelrichter in or around that year.[167] These entries provide some insight on the wealth structure of very rich households without farms.

---

164 In 1578 the number of parcels in each field averaged 24.4 with a range of 12–40, and in 1593 there was an average of 25.3 parcels in one field with a range of 16–36.

165 These values are somewhat higher than for the Amtmänner, whose livestock values averaged 242.8 fl. in 1578 and 195.4 fl. in 1593. Livestock values for Sidelrichter ranged from 173 fl. to 398 fl. in 1578 and from 121 fl. to 347 fl. in 1593. No values are available for 1603.

166 The Sidelrichter with the highest recorded debt in the sample was Moritz Mayer of Tüfingen, who became a judge in the 1590s and remained on the court until 1629. In 1593 he had gross wealth of 1,185 fl. but only 834 fl. net, and in 1603 he had 1,435 fl. gross but only 745 fl. net, with debts reaching to almost half his entire property value. According to rent registers between 1612 and 1625 the situation did not improve. In 1612 he owed the abbey over seven Malter of spelt, which was close to a year's rent on his farm. In 1619 he still owed over five Malter and by 1625 he had been replaced by a new tenant, Martin Hailg, though by 1626 he held the court's second-ranking seat. His political rise, despite his debts, was probably facilitated by family connections. His father Andreas Mayer had been the head judge for many years before Moritz took his place.

167 Hans Hailg was a Sidelrichter from 1583–1591 and Hans Mayer was a Sidelrichter from 1585–1591. There are no lists available from the years 1592–1604, but both men were probably still judges in 1593. As of the last available list, Hailg was judge number four and Mayer was judge number ten.

First, Hans Hailg of Bermatingen and his wife Margaretha Dilgerin had six children and five servants in 1593. They had no farm, yet their gross wealth was 6,724 fl., the highest in the entire territory, and their net wealth was 4,289 fl. The greatest source of property value was their freeholdings, worth 4,600 fl. Livestock was worth 189 fl., about average among farm tenants, but their wine value was much higher than most (14 Fuder, worth 700 fl.), as was their cash and credit value (500 fl.). Viticulture appears to have been the major source of income for Hans Hailg's household, but he also had grain (in storage and in the field) worth 378 fl., so some of his freehold must have been arable. Household items had a combined value of 150 fl., clothing and textiles 115 fl., hay and straw 52 fl. The values for each of these property types were comparable to the most prosperous tenant households.

Hans Mayer of Bermatingen was the second nontenant listed in 1593 with property by subcategory, and he was only slightly less wealthy than Hans Hailg. His was the second wealthiest household in the entire territory with 5,005 fl. gross and 4,405 fl. net. He, too, was married with six children (but no servants), and like Hans Hailg he was Salem's serf with a wife and children belonging to Heiligenberg. He had no farm, but his freehold property was worth 3,950 fl. His values in other categories were somewhat lower than Hailg's, but his wealth was concentrated in the same categories. He had 5½ Fuder of wine worth 275 fl., cash and credit worth 330 fl., grain worth 253 fl., household items (25 fl.), clothing and textiles (40 fl.), hay and straw (19 fl.), and farm equipment (specified as casks and grape presses, 30 fl.). The tax list demonstrates that both households were heavily involved in wine production and market activity, in addition to the more traditional grain agriculture and animal husbandry on a smaller scale.

In addition to the Sidelrichter named in one of the tax lists, 17 are found in all three lists.[168] This allows us to consider changes in household wealth over time. A good example is Conrad Biller the younger from Oberhof. He was the son and namesake of another Sidelrichter, whom he replaced on the court sometime around 1592. The year after his appointment, his property value was 2,307 fl. and he held one of the largest farms in the entire territory. He was married with two children. Earlier, as a recently established young man listed in 1578, he had been married with one child on the same farm with property worth 1,832, so his wealth was increasing over time. By 1603 his property value had risen further, to 2,541 fl. with almost no debt—his net worth was 2,530 fl. Conrad Biller remained the head judge until 1616, the year he died. There is no significant property or wealth information about him after 1603, except that he retired in 1613 and arranged for his son Mattheus to take over the farm. Mattheus, too, eventually became a Sidelrichter, following the family's political tradition.

Many other Sidelrichter rose steadily in wealth over the course of their careers, including Mattheus Leub, Andreas Mayer, Adam Ower the younger, Severinus Rueff, and

[168] This number includes court alternates as well as several who were not in office at the time of all three tax assessments.

Mattheus Senfft. Others, however, reached a highpoint in wealth earlier in their careers and shed property as they moved into retirement. Adam Ower the elder (Sidelrichter from at least 1572–1591) is listed with 1,060 lb. dn. in 1566, 2,945 fl. in 1578, and 1,169 fl. in 1593. In 1578, when his wealth was greatest, he had a wife and eight children and he held a hereditary smallholding in addition to a large farm. By 1593, however, he was remarried and only two children remained at home. His recently established son of the same name, who would soon take his place on the court, had property worth just 305 fl. in 1593, but by this time the father had probably outfitted at least six children and was making plans for retirement. He died sometime around 1600. The same situation explains Laux Leub the elder's decline in wealth. He had property worth 1,061 lb. dn. in 1566, but by 1578 he had only 264 fl. and no farm. One of his five children was Elsa Leubin, whose husband Hans Mayer of Neufrach had property worth 661 fl. in 1578 and was a judge in 1584–1585 (around the time her father died). Another child was Laux Leub the younger, who joined the court in 1589 and had 1,278 fl. by 1593 including a farm. The father, though he was called the Amtmann in 1578 and was most likely still a member of the court, had obviously begun handing property down to his children.

At least five Sidelrichter changed villages during the course of their careers, and in two cases, the move marked a transition in wealth as well as political standing. Mattheus Senfft (judge from at least 1585–1606) started out in Tüfingen with a wife and one child, 766 fl. in property value, and no farm in 1578. Around 1589 he remarried and moved to Mimmenhausen, where he purchased a hereditary property for 400 fl. and became the new Amtmann.[169] His economic fortunes then improved dramatically: in 1593 his wealth had risen to 2,187 fl., and by 1603 he had 2,478 fl. He and his second wife had six children at home around 1600, and though he lost his position as the Amtmann, he probably remained a member of the court until his death in 1610.[170] Veit Claußmar is the second example, a Sidelrichter from at least 1583–1606 who was called the head judge shortly before his death in 1610.[171] In 1578 he lived in Grasbeuren and his wealth was 1,734 fl., though he had no farm. When he moved from Grasbeuren to Bermatingen in 1590, however, his wealth and seat rank declined considerably. His move was the result of a successful Audience petition for a vacant farm in Bermatingen. The house there had recently burned down, and the rebuilding costs may partly explain why his wealth was only 914 fl. in 1593.[172] In that year he was married with four children. By 1603 his wealth was even lower, despite rent registers describing the farm as having 42½ acres in the two productive fields. His gross wealth was 498 fl., net wealth

[169] Mattheus Senfft was introduced in Chapter 3 as the Amtmann in dispute first with Oberamtmann Johann Vogelin and then with the commune over grazing rights for horses.

[170] Senfft was a court alternate in 1585, and over the years his seat rank improved steadily from last place in 1587 to seat number eight in 1606. There are no lists of judges for 1607–1610.

[171] Claußmar was occasionally named as the acting Stabhalter during sessions when Conrad Biller was absent, but in fact, Biller remained the head judge until 1616.

[172] Claußmar's net wealth was 639 fl. and he had freehold worth 250 fl.

only 326 fl., and he had no freehold property. He had remarried since his first wife's death in 1599, so perhaps the decline in wealth reflected a recent partition among the four children. For whatever reason, his seat rank on the court also took a dive coinciding with his move to Bermatingen. During the 1580s he was listed as judge number six on four lists and then as judge number four in 1589, but in 1590 (the same year he left Grasbeuren) his seat dropped to fifteen and then rose only slightly to fourteen in 1591. Over the intervening period his rank climbed again, so that by 1605–1606 he held seat number 2, and he served occasionally as the acting head judge.

The tax lists provide most useful for judges who served during the late sixteenth century, but they also describe the households for some seventeenth-century judges at an earlier stage in life. Mattheus Lochmayer (1605–1622), for example, was an established householder long before he became a member of the court. In 1578 he was listed as a young man, married with one child, no farm, and property worth 681 fl. In 1593 he still had no farm and his property value had decreased slightly to 515 fl. Sometime after that, Lochmayer's wife and four children freed themselves from bondage to Kreuzlingen Abbey and became Salem's serfs. Perhaps for this reason, the family's fortunes began to improve. By 1600 Lochmayer had finally acquired a farm, a large one with 49 acres in two fields, and it was around this time that he became a judge. By 1603 he had 841 fl. and five children. His economic fortunes after 1603 are basically unknown, but he was well-off when he died in 1625, owing a hefty heriot tax of 30 fl. for the best horse. Another man who became a member of the court relatively late in life was Hans Weißenkönig of Neufrach, who was a court alternate from 1605–1616 but was listed as a householder as early as 1578. According to the three tax lists, he was a man with stable wealth and many children: in 1578 he had 960 fl., a farm, a wife and seven children; by 1593 his wealth decreased to 891 fl. and the number of children increased to ten. In 1603 he was back to 960 fl., the same as in 1578, and at least six of his eleven children had left home. It was around this time that he became a court alternate but his political position, like his wealth, never advanced. He remained a court alternate without promotion for over a decade.

Finally, it is worth reemphasizing that some of the wealthiest judges never acquired farm tenures. Among them was Andreas Villieber of Nußdorf (1584–1616), who had a house and five rented vineyard parcels around the time of the 1578 tax list, when he had 777 fl. in all property combined. By 1593, however, he had 2,205 fl. in wealth, and in 1603 he still had 2,100 fl., despite having no farm. He died in 1613 leaving a house worth 500 fl., but his other property is unknown. Steffan Muettinger of Oberuhldingen (1589–1606) was the smith, who purchased parcels here and there but never acquired a farm. Despite this, his wealth went from 457 fl. in 1578 to 2,416 fl. in 1593 and 2,040 in 1603. He retired and handed the smithy over to his son around the same time he became Amtmann, in 1603, after he had also served as a member of the court for several years. All his children were out on their own by the time he passed away in 1611. The most fabulously rich man in the territory was no doubt Christoph Langenstain (1590–1631), whose property was described in Chapter 4, but not far behind him were Hans Hailg (1583–1591) and Severinus Rueff (1605–1624), who like Langenstain were judges from Bermatingen.[173] Severinus Rueff appears less wealthy in the tax lists (1,150 fl. in 1593, 1,715 fl. in 1603), but it was later that his fortunes really took off. He was the head judge from 1617 until his death in 1626, and probably the only reason he never became Amtmann in Bermatingen is that Christoph Langenstain occupied the post for so long. The best evidence of Rueff's wealth comes from his widow's retirement agreement in 1631, in which she specified shares to seven sons and sons-in-law in return for lifelong care. Ursula Humline's property was worth 5,485 fl. (including her widow's share of Rueff's property and her own marriage portion of 1,250 fl.), and according to the retirement agreement, there had already been an estate division following Rueff's death. Her own property included 43 separate vineyard parcels, ranging in value from 70 fl. to 220 fl. To each of the seven children she distributed between four and eight vineyards.[174] These examples demonstrate that it was possible for households to acquire substantial land holdings without, or in addition to, farms held in tenure from the abbey.

Kinship

A first approach to the question of kinship among Sidelrichter is to look at the number of seats passed down through the male line. Such relationships are the easiest to establish because agnatic kin share the same last name. The comparison of all 164 judges' surnames yields 86 Sidelrichter—that is, slightly over half—who shared 28 common names. In many cases, no specific relationship can be recognized between individuals sharing surnames, and in some cases, there may not have been one. Some names are so common that they do not guarantee any close kinship tie. For example, the Hailgs headed 20 households in 1578 alone, with 105 individuals in seven different villages. Four Hailgs served as Sidelrichter, yet the relationships between them are unknown.[175] Several pairs of fathers and sons served consecutively as members of the court. We have already encountered some of them—Adam, Adam, and Jacob represented three generations of Owers in Grasbeuren. There were Hans and Veit Claußmar of Gras-

173 Hans Hailg's itemized property with an emphasis on wine and moneylending has already been mentioned, as well as the fact that he headed the wealthiest household in 1593. In 1603, his widow Margaretha Dilgerin was the wealthiest householder with 7,345 fl. including 5,500 fl. in freehold property.

174 GLAK, 98/4402.

175 In Bermatingen alone there were three household heads named Hans Hailg in 1578, including one who was a Sidelrichter. Another was the butcher with 576 fl. and the third had wealth of only 80 fl. Other common surnames represented by several Sidelrichter include Mayer (19 households in 1578 and 12 Sidelrichter in all years), Müller (13 households in 1578, 5 Sidelrichter), Schneider (10 households in 1578, 3 Sidelrichter), and Stett (10 households in 1578, 2 Sidelrichter).

beuren, Hans and Martin Möckhing of Owingen, Hans and Andreas Richel of Neufrach, Laux and Laux Leub of Weiler, Conrad Biller of Owingen and Conrad Biller of Oberhof, among others.

When two individuals shared the same name, it is not always easy to distinguish between them. Likewise, it is suspected in some cases that similar names in fact refer to the same individual.[176] Even when two men can be identified with certainty, it is often difficult to tell which data belongs to whom. Both the Conrad Billers and Adam Owers were definitely fathers and sons, and for a number of years there were two separate households headed by men of the same name. This confirms that they were not the same person, yet it is not always clear which man is intended when a reference is made to one or the other. Even the year of the father's retirement from the court and his son's appointment to replace him is difficult to pinpoint in these two examples.

Some powerful families had members residing throughout the territory (and beyond), and several of them contributed members to the court from more than one village. A good example is the Biller family, with two brothers and their two sons who served as Sidelrichter from Owingen, Oberhof, and Weildorf (though not all at the same time). Different members of leading families could hold local offices simultaneously in more than one village, yet the Sidelrichter were supposed to be unrelated to one another in order to encourage greater neutrality.[177] It was fairly common for a member of the court who died in office to be replaced immediately by a younger family member, and some families contributed judges over several generations in this way without missing a single year. Again, one of the best examples is the Biller clan.[178] The

[176] For example, there are three early Sidelrichter from tiny Wehausen with slightly different names: Polay Felder, called "Sogger," was a Sidelrichter in 1471–1473. Velin Sogger was a Sidelrichter in 1486. Finally, Peter Sogger was a Sidelrichter in 1500. Another case of uncertain identity concerns Hans Müller of Pfaffenhofen (1471–1473, 1480), Hans Müller "called Thomas" of Owingen (1503, 1514), and Hans Thoma of Owingen (1500). This time, tax listings for both Hans Müller and Hans Thoma from Owingen suggest separate identities. In a third case Veit Claußmar of Grasbeuren and Bermatingen turn out to be the same person, but this was unclear until the discovery of an Audience petition confirming that he moved from one village to the other.

[177] Distant relationships were sometimes overlooked, as the results of inquiries in 1640 and 1646 demonstrate. The ban on related judges does not specify what degree of kinship was prohibited, and this may have depended on the individual case.

[178] The continuity within family lines is conspicuous, especially when considering gaps in the record. Billers: Conrad the elder 1572–1591, Conrad the younger 1592–1616, Mattheus 1617–1631, Silvester 1631–1638, Mattheus 1646–1652. Dilgers: Hans 1614–1632, Andreas 1638–1678. Leubs: Laux the elder 1572, Laux the younger 1589–1612, Mattheus 1612–1631, Georg 1631–1652. Möckhings: Martin 1612–1628, Hans 1631–1632. Owers: Adam the elder 1572–1591, Adam the younger 1606–1632, Jacob 1638–1652. Stengelins: Peter the elder 1584–1606, Martin 1619–1631, Peter the younger 1638–1652, Johann (last Stabhalter of the Sidelgericht, then Stabhalter of the *Blutgericht* through 1698). Strobels: Michael 1572, Hans 1583–1616.

number of uncertain relationships among the Sidelrichter, even among agnatic kin, makes it hard to draw any firm conclusions about kinship. However, it appears that a number of leading families from throughout the territory had established a strong tradition of serving as Sidelrichter over generations and that kinship was a key factor behind many appointments.

Women are often the key to identifying relationships between men with different surnames. Fortunately for us, women in Salem's territory did not take their husbands' names when they married, so it is easy to identify their most basic kinship affiliation. In tax registers and serf lists, I was able to discover the names of 90 wives who were married to 66 members of the court, all of them in the period after 1575.[179] Of these wives, 42 shared surnames with at least one Amtmann or Sidelrichter, suggesting that they came from the same group of families. Although slightly over half of judges' wives came from beyond this close circle, the political interconnections are highly suggestive.

Wives also served to create kinship links between Sidelrichter in other ways. A comparison of last names yields 31 women who shared 13 last names with one another. Some of these women were sisters or other close kin. Sometimes such a tie can be identified with certainty, as in the case of the Sidelrichter wives Christina and Waldpurga Meßmerin, who were both Kreuzlingen serfs from Grasbeuren and the daughters of Ulrich Meßmer, one of the territory's wealthiest men with an estate value of 2,461 fl. in 1578. Their husbands, Mattheus Lochmayer and Simon Mußel, were both members of the Sidelgericht; in fact, they even sat on the court at the same time. These sibling-marriages were almost certainly strategic moves, creating a link between two Sidelrichter families and providing each with a wife of great wealth. When two Sidelrichter married women from the same family this established ties between the husbands, regardless of the family's other political connections.

At least four and perhaps five women married more than one territorial judge in succession. These women provided the link between multiple powerful husbands by marrying them consecutively and transferring the household wealth, status, property, and children of one to the other. We have already encountered several of them in Chapter 4, because their husbands were both Amtmänner and Sidelrichter. A new example is that of Franz Schaitteckh and Hans Dilger, both of whom married Agatha Barthin, the wealthy widow from Schwandorf. Her Sidelrichter husbands each bargained with the abbey to have their names added to her lifelong lease on one of the abbey's best farms. Later, each of them came into conflict with their stepsons over rights to the farm and other property. Appolonia Kuttin was identified earlier as the wife of Mattheus Burst and Georg Donat, both Amtmänner, but in fact she was also married previously to a third man, Stoffel Schneider, and all three husbands were Sidelrichter! The marriage contracts for her second and third marriages stipulated conditions to protect her

179 Several individuals in the sample married more than once, men more frequently than women, which is why there are more wives than husbands listed.

preexisting children. Urban Klaiber of Weildorf and Andreas Villieber consecutively married the same woman, Anna Zürckhin. Their spouse's sister also married two Sidelrichter (the Amtmänner Mattheus Leub and Balthas Diem, mentioned in Chapter 4), and what is particularly interesting in this case is that her two husbands were colleagues on the court for several years before one died and she married the other.

Many of the judges who served in the 1620s and 1630s are found as children in earlier tax records and serf lists. This provides us with their parents' wealth information and the names of family members, including mothers and siblings. For example, Martin Dulenkopf was the son of Franz Dulenkopf and Anna Urnauerin, who had property worth 2,160 fl. and two farms in 1593. Martin was one of nine children, and around 1600 his brother Veit was the innkeeper in Mühlhofen with 1,053 fl., another brother Jacob was married in Oberuhldingen with 985 fl. and a hereditary farm, his brother Christian was a monk in Alsace, and his other siblings were married in Gebhardsweiler, Grasbeuren, and Schiggendorf. One sister was manumitted. Veit Resstlin was the son of Jerg Resstlin and Margaretha Neckarin, who had property valued at 897 fl. in 1593. His father was the abbey's guestmaster and his brother was a monk in Salem. His mother's name suggests that he was also related to Abbot Vitus Nekher (1583–1587), a native son from Mimmenhausen. Michael Härlin was another judge whose brother was a priest. His parents Martin Härlin and Agatha Geigerin had 532 fl. in 1593. Among the mothers of other Sidelrichter were women from several prominent families: Agatha and Eva Schaitteckhin, Katharina and Waldpurga Leubin, Katharina Möckhingin, Agatha Hailgin, and Margaretha Billerin. Most Sidelrichter whose parents are known grew up in either prosperous or very rich households.

Kinship ties among Sidelrichter were uncovered and explicitly mentioned in two court inquiries conducted in 1640 and 1646. The record from 1640 contains four family tree diagrams followed by a recommendation by Salem's legal counselor, Dr. Johann Hainrich von Pflaumern. The family trees reveal that a total of six Sidelrichter were related to other members of the court, yet the counselor's opinion scrawled below the diagrams was that all six men should retain their seats, because "such in-lawships, and closer relationships as well, pose no impediment here."[180] He reminded the judges that "all voted together on the court, but if any one of them held an interest in a case, ... the interested parties should abstain and step back from the decision."[181]

---

180 Three of the four family trees were interlinked, demonstrating that two Sidelrichter and two court alternates were all somehow related to one another. The fourth family tree not only contained two sitting judges, the family had also contributed at least seven members to the court in less than a century.

181 "Dz solche Schwagershafften, und auch nähere verwandtshafften hierinnen kein hindernuß bringen, seind obspecificirte Personen alle mit einandtren beim Gericht gelassen, und darbei erinneret worden, dz sie samentlich ihre stimen beim Gericht geben aber allein daß interesse deß einen, ... die Interessirten billich abstehn und den abtritt nemen müessen." GLAK, 98/597.

According to the 1646 inquiry, as we saw earlier, four judges and alternates were related to others on the court. Still, abbey officials decided not to replace any of them, even though two clearly stated their wish to step down. The inquiries of both years demonstrate the abbey's willingness to tolerate related individuals on the court against the official prohibition, at least toward the end of the Thirty Years War, as long as they did not display open favoritism or factionalism. These examples suggest that kinship among Sidelrichter was a common problem toward the end of the period and that such ties ran deeper than they first appear.[182] The high level of intermarriage among Sidelrichter seems to have been characteristic of this period of instability and decline, or at least to have become a growing topic of concern. Yet it also appears that the interrelationships among judges were not an intentional strategy on their part to control the court. The lack of enthusiasm several judges expressed, some of them pointing to distantly related kin as an excuse to retire, suggests instead that it had become quite difficult to find candidates who were both qualified and willing to serve as judges. Furthermore, the situation in the 1640s was quite different from the one in the 1620s. We know from Sebastian Bürster's chronicle that the population along with the entire rural infrastructure that sustained it had been wiped out during the intervening decade. Evidence suggests that the circle of prominent families was narrowing over the course of the early seventeenth century in an attempt to create stability and secure property, and this tendency had unintended consequences for the court.

Officeholding

Most Sidelrichter did not come to the court without previous officeholding experience, nor were their political activities restricted to matters of justice. There is a strong correlation between village headmen and territorial judges: out of 164 Sidelrichter, 60 held both offices concurrently. Because of gaps in the lists, many individuals' exact start and end dates are unknown, but some men became Amtmann first whereas others were Sidelrichter first. Since 104 Sidelrichter are not known to have held the office of village headmen, it was obviously not a prerequisite for court appointment. Yet the fact that the title of Amtmann appears beside judges' names on official court lists suggests that the position was seen to be relevant, as indeed it was. For one thing, the headman was the abbey's local official and representative, which meant that unless he performed his duties poorly, he was backed by the abbot's confidence and trust. Second, the headman was accustomed to the responsibility of settling neighborly disputes and he was well informed about the history of personal conflicts in his village. Third, the headman was the person most often chosen to speak for neighbors in legal matters—as a guarantor,

182 Many of the relationships identified in 1640 involved circuitous cousin marriages. For example, Martin Stengelin's second wife Anna Billerin was the cousin of Mattheus Biller. Hans Vogler's wife was the cousin of both Stoffel Felder and Georg Weißenkönig. Stoffel Felder's uncle's wife was somehow related to Georg Leub, who was in turn the uncle of Georg Weißenkönig.

guardian, witness, or advocate. This increased his familiarity with legal customs and forms of legal presentation and procedure. Finally, most headmen were accustomed to the use of written documents, whether or not they could read and write.[183] Each of these experiences was important preparation for the responsibilities of court membership.

Another important training ground for future Sidelrichter was the position of court alternate (Beisitzer or Zusatz). The alternates, usually four in number, were nonvoting members of the court who observed the regular judges and played a supporting role. They were present at regular court sessions, took a formal oath of office, and may have taken part in some of the court's discussions. Perhaps they had other duties not mentioned in the sources, such as hearing witness testimony, collecting information for the court, advising litigants, or acting as legal advocates. Yet they did not participate in the Umfrag. When one of the fifteen seats fell vacant, an alternate often assumed the last seat while those above him advanced in rank. This was not automatic, however. It was possible to become a Sidelrichter without serving first as a Beisitzer, and some alternates never advanced to become full members of the court. At least four men remained court alternates for many years without promotion.[184] Still, about half of Sidelrichter appointed between 1585 and 1638 were listed previously as court alternates. Because of gaps in the record, the actual number is certainly somewhat higher.

The court posed no formal requirements in terms of previous experience, yet the majority of Sidelrichter held some sort of prior office, and many held offices simultaneously in the village or parish.[185] Although they were common subjects, unsalaried nonprofessionals without university training, the judges often had years of experience as court alternates and as village leaders. As members of the commune, the Sidelrichter were intimately familiar with relations and customs in the villages, both individually and collectively. This strengthened the link between local and territorial decisionmaking.

Term Length and Promotion

The Sidelrichter were appointed annually to the court. The entire court was sworn in before the year's first session and sworn out again following the last. Once appointed, however, most Sidelrichter served for several consecutive terms. Gaps in the record limit the discussion of term length and tend to underestimate the number of years judges spent in office. Still, the surviving lists make clear that most judges served for several years in

---

183 Many of them probably could read and write; see details in Chapter 3 about one Amtmann's recordkeeping duties and Chapter 6 for a discussion of village schools.

184 These were Hans Richel (1584–1591), Hans Weißenkönig (1605–1616), Andreas Richel (1612–1624), and Jacob Brem (1621–1629).

185 In addition to the Amtmänner, ten Sidelrichter were members of the village courts in Owingen or Bermatingen. Ten others were churchwardens, six were village treasurers, and represented once each were a forest warden, boundary guard, and commercial inspector (*Unterkäufer*). Overall, about half of all Sidelrichter held some concurrent local office.

a row, and some men served for extremely long periods of time. Sixty-three Sidelrichter served terms of ten years or more, nine for 25 years or more, and one individual was a member for 42 years! This suggests a pattern of career officeholding on the court.

Christoph Langenstain may serve to illustrate the careers of long-term Sidelrichter. Langenstain joined the court in 1590 and assumed the lowest-ranking seat. In 1591 he was listed again in last position.[186] Then comes a large gap in the sources, so we cannot be sure of his seat rank during the years 1592 to 1604. He probably continued to rise gradually, because by 1605, he had moved up to seat number six. In 1606 Langenstain experienced a minor demotion, moving down one seat to number seven. This fall in rank was only temporary, however, and according to the next available list in 1612 he had moved up to seat number four, where he remained for only two years before moving up again to seat number three in 1614 and seat number two in 1617. He continued to serve as the court's second-ranking member for the next eight years, even though he asked to be relieved from office in 1622. When Severinus Rueff died in 1626, Langenstain was promoted to the position of head judge. He continued to serve as Stabhalter for the next six years, until his death in 1631 or 1632.[187] Over the course of 42 years as a member of the court, Christoph Langenstain is named in 21 lists.

Langenstain is unusual for the fact that we know his start and end dates as a judge. There are 53 members who are known to have served for one year, but gaps in the surrounding lists mean they may have been judges for longer than that. In almost every case, judges listed only once appear in years surrounded by gaps: 1476, 1486, 1500, 1526, 1566, 1568, 1572, 1584, 1589, 1591, and 1638. For this reason, we are better off to focus our investigation of term length and promotion rate on a smaller sample of those judges who are known to have served for a number of years, let us say those found on five or more lists. Even within this smaller group of judges, we must not forget that time spent in office may have been longer than the records reveal, and gaps between lists mean that changes in seat rank are only partially available.

Nevertheless, the comparison of seat rank over time provides some instructive details about the promotion rate among Sidelrichter. Chart 5.15 illustrates the careers of 37 judges who are listed five times or more between 1572 and 1632. Viewed as a whole, this busy chart reveals several interesting patterns. Almost all the judges rose in rank over time, at an average rate of less than one up to four seats per year over an individual's entire career. Most changes in seat rank were in an upward direction, but there were also a few demotions, most of them minor. As the chart shows, demotions were clustered in certain years. Steep declines are found during the period 1587–1606,

[186] Langenstain is listed in 1590 as the last of 16 judges and in 1591 as the last of 15 judges. It was unusual for there to be 16 judges in addition to alternates, but the number of judges fluctuated slightly from year to year. There were only 13 or 14 Sidelrichter according to lists from 1605–1606, 1612–1613, 1629, 1631–1632, 1638, and 1646.

[187] Langenstain was still listed as head judge in 1631 but not in 1632, the year of his probate inventory and estate division.

Chart 5.15: Career Sidelrichter and Rising Rank, 1572–1632

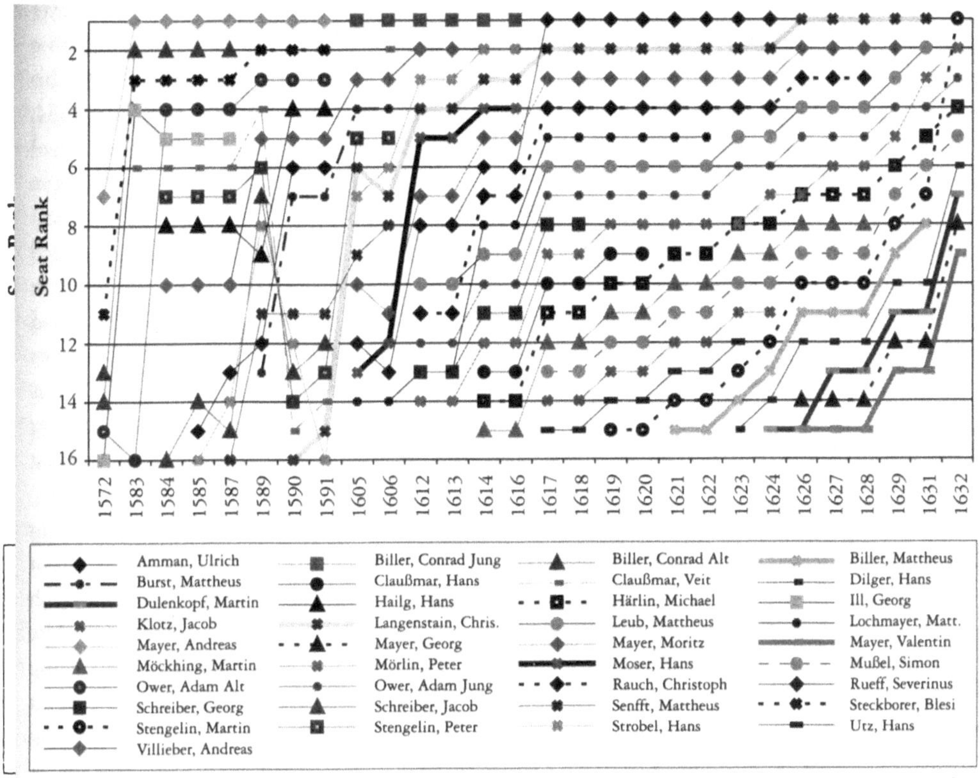

but only one demotion occurred in any other year.[188] Individuals were seldom demoted by more than one or two seats, nor were demotions long-lived, since most Sidelrichter rose again soon after the decline. The chart also shows that many Sidelrichter maintained the same seat rank for a number of years during the period 1616–1624. There were few major promotions and no demotions in these years. Then after 1628, promotions increased again both in the number of judges and in the speed of their advance. We can conclude that certain periods were characterized by a general halt in promotions, while others had much higher turnover rates. Overall, the great majority of Sidelrichter rose in rank over the course of their careers.

During this period, ten Sidelrichter experienced a total of twelve demotions at some point in their careers despite an overall upward trend in all but two possible cases. For most of these judges, minor demotion was followed by eventual promotion to a higher

[188] In 1590 and in 1606 there appears to have been a shake-up on the court, because four judges were demoted in both years. Other years of individual demotions include 1587, when two judges fell in rank; there was one demotion each in 1584, 1589, and 1605.

seat. For example, Laux Leub the younger fell from seat number eight in 1605 to seat number nine in 1606, but by 1612 he had moved up to seat number six. Moritz Mayer started at seat number ten in 1605, moved down to seat eleven in 1606, but then rose steadily up to seat number two over the course of a 25-year career. Exceptions to this general trend include Conrad Biller the elder, who was demoted three times in 1584, 1587, and in 1590, ending his career in 1591 only one seat higher than where he had begun in 1572.[189] Veit Claußmar experienced one of the most dramatic demotions in 1590 when he fell from seat four to seat fifteen, but in 1591, he moved up again to seat fourteen and finished off in 1606 at seat number two.[190] Steffan Muettinger was listed as a court alternate in 1589 and then as a judge in 1590–1591 and 1605–1606 (with a long gap in between). In 1590–1591 he held seat number nine, but by 1605 he had moved down to seat eleven, then in 1606 he moved back up to seat number ten. Since no lists are available from 1592 to 1604, or between 1607 and his death in 1611, it is uncertain whether this partial record accurately reflects his entire tenure, or whether his seat rank improved after 1606. We can conclude from the evidence of declining seat rank that demotions were unusual and short-lived.

The gradual promotions most judges experienced were evidently not contingent upon wealth, family, or officeholding. At the same time, promotions were not equal or automatic. Promotion appears to have been related in part to individual factors, such as performance, and to general trends, above all the staffing needs of the court. The latter may reflect the loss of judges to death or retirement, the difficulty in recruiting new members, or both. Based on what we know about the annual court inquiries, it is also possible that promotions and especially demotions resulted from other judges' reports to higher authorities.

Officeholding was most certainly a source of power and prestige but it could also be a burden, especially since appointments were renewed for such long durations. Several judges asked to be relieved from office, sometimes successfully but often not. In 1623 Mattheus Lochmayer was granted retirement at his request because of poor hearing and advanced age, and Mattheus Biller was replaced in 1631 when he pointed out that his stepfather was already a member of the court.[191] Severinus Rueff and Christoph Langenstain, both of whom eventually became head judge and served terms of 20 and 42 years respectively, each served for several years following their requests to step down. These and other requests for dismissal appear in the record only after 1620, suggesting that court service was increasingly viewed as an onerous duty and that filling the seats was becoming more problematic toward the end of the period. The situation

[189] Biller was replaced by his son of the same name in 1592, and since the father does not appear on the 1593 tax list, he most likely passed away in or shortly after 1591.

[190] Veit Claußmar's demotion, as noted earlier, coincided with his move from Grasbeuren to Bermatingen where he took over a farm and the responsibility to rebuild a house that had burned down.

[191] Mattheus Biller was reappointed to the court sometime before 1638.

does not suggest that certain elite families (or individuals) manipulated the court by intentionally monopolizing its seats, because even some of those in the highest-ranking positions and those who served the court alongside kin made it tactfully known that they wished to resign. Again, this raises the question of how and why judges were appointed to and dismissed from judicial service.

The Stabhalter

Fourteen men are known to have served as the Stabhalter during the years 1471–1646. All but one of those who served after 1583 (when lists become available in sequence) were members of the court before their promotion to head judge.[192] Most individuals worked their way up to the highest-ranking seat over several years. In other words, the Stabhalter was chosen from among the Sidelrichter, not from a separate pool. The head judge earned his position through previous experience and, we may assume, through his proven skills and reputation as a member of the court. When a Stabhalter died or otherwise vacated his seat, the second-ranking member might be chosen to replace him—but this was not always the case. Severinus Rueff, for example, was judge number six in 1616, but the next year he became the head judge, bypassing two others who outranked him. The same thing happened when Martin Stengelin jumped from seat eight to head judge in 1632, skipping ahead of four higher-ranking members who did not retire that year. Thus, promotion was not automatic. Merely outliving those in higher positions or establishing seniority was not a sufficient qualification for being chosen as the court's leading member.

Looking at the Stabhalter as a group, no characteristic stands out that might explain why certain members advanced to the court's highest seat over others. They were mostly wealthy, but not exclusively so, which reflects the findings for Sidelrichter overall. The wealthiest was Christoph Langenstain, with property worth 4,775 fl. in 1603.[193] Georg Mayer of Neufrach, on the other hand, had assets worth 921 fl. in 1578 and net wealth of only 499 fl. Geographically, the head judges also came from a wide spectrum of places. Four were from Bermatingen, two each from Neufrach, Nußdorf, Owingen, and Oberhof, and one came from Buggensegel, Mimmenhausen, and Tüfingen. Some Stabhalter had the benefit of family connections.[194] For others, however, no such relationships are evident. Professional experience or social connections may have

---

192 The only exception is Conrad Biller the younger, who replaced his father as a member of the court in 1592. Whereas Conrad the father held seat number twelve in 1591, Conrad the son immediately became the Stabhalter after the deaths of his father and the previous head judge, despite having no prior personal experience. The reasons for this unusual appointment are unknown.

193 By the time he died, his estate was much larger. See Chapter 4 and GLAK, 98/3204.

194 Conrad Biller was a member of the powerful Biller clan, and Martin Stengelin was related to this same family by marriage. Severinus Rueff had one son in the abbey and another was a local priest.

helped some Stabhalter—many were village headmen and one was a miller—but this does not appear to have been a determining factor. Finally, most of the Stabhalter were Salem's serfs. Yet the significant exception of Jacob Schreiber, who was a serf belonging to Petershausen Abbey outside Constance, demonstrates that servility status was not a limiting factor for officeholding one way or the other.

On the one hand, the absence of defining characteristics prevents any simple explanation of why these men were chosen to lead the territorial court. On the other, the surprising lack of conformity is in itself an important finding, because it suggests that the men who served as Stabhalter were not so different from the others. It is probably too much to say that any man could become Stabhalter by working his way up through the Sidelgericht, but the men holding this office came from diverse backgrounds and were not an overly exclusive group in terms of kinship, property, or wealth.

Servility

One of the Sidelgericht's most striking features is the fact that most but not all of its members were abbey serfs. They spoke the law over fellow serfs as well as free inhabitants and other lords' bondsmen. They also settled the claims of urban creditors and even criminal cases prosecuted by higher abbey officials. Given Salem's efforts to limit outside influence within the territory, especially in jurisdictional matters, it seems reasonable to expect that all territorial judges would have been the abbey's serfs. Otherwise, this would give enormous political power and responsibility to outsiders, including those who had sworn loyalty to some other lord. Since the Sidelrichter decided many types of disputes involving the abbey's own commands and prohibitions as well as topics relating to tenure, inheritance, debt, property sales, land use, slander, and assault, we would at least expect to find other lords' serfs excluded from this very important office.

Yet surprisingly, at least ten members of the Sidelgericht were free men or other lords' serfs either before or during their office terms.[195] Severinus Rueff and his family were all free in 1590, but a list of serfs from that year noted his wish to become the abbey's serf, and by 1593, he and his family had changed their status.[196] Hans Hailg and Mattheus Senfft had also been free in 1578, but by 1593, both had become abbey serfs.[197] Bartlin

---

[195] Tax lists from 1578 and 1593 provide the servility status of all men, women, and children (but not servants). Other lists of serfs and nonserfs, including unpermitted residents, are found in GLAK, 67/1774, 98/1560, 98/1568–1569, and 98/2300–2303.

[196] GLAK, 98/2303. Rueff was a Sidelrichter by 1605 but not in 1591, and since there are no lists from 1592 to 1604, it is possible that his voluntary enserfment had something to do with his court appointment.

[197] Whether the change in legal status came before or after their respective court appointments in 1583 and 1585 is unknown. Again, enserfment may have coincided with or smoothed the way for their later appointments as judges.

Müller and Hans Weißenkönig, who were former serfs of Weingarten and Heiligenberg respectively, both became Salem's serfs in 1594 prior to their court appointments. Others, though, were not the abbey's bondsmen even during the years they served as members of the court. There was Conrad Megerlin from Bermatingen, who belonged to the Constance cathedral chapter, and Hans Moser of Owingen, who was the bondsman of the Überlingen hospital. The smith Steffan Muettinger from Oberuhldingen remained free. Jacob Schreiber from Owingen, a Petershausen serf, was not only a Sidelrichter between 1572 and 1588, he became the court's head judge in 1588 despite no evidence that he ever submitted to the abbey's bondage. Finally there was Veit Resstlin, the court bailiff for fourteen years, who was born an abbey serf in Mimmenhausen but bought his freedom and become a citizen of Überlingen in 1604.[198]

The legal status of judges' wives is also extremely important. Not only did outside marriages result in territorial subjects who were not the abbey's serfs, it also meant that property would fall to outsiders after the bondsman's death, because the legal status of children followed that of their mothers.[199] At least 14 wives of Sidelrichter were not Salem's serfs according to lists kept between 1578 and 1614. Four of them, and perhaps more, became Salem's serfs at some point before or during their husbands' court terms, but there were others who never changed their legal status or that of their children. Among spouses and heirs of Sidelrichter were serfs belonging to Constance, Heiligenberg, Kreuzlingen, Überlingen, and Ulm. Five wives were free during the time their husbands served as judges. Evidence that the legal status of judges and their wives was not unimportant to the abbey is provided by the example of Hans Hailg and his wife, Margaretha Dilgerin. We have already encountered this couple several times, most notably as the wealthiest householders in 1593 and 1603. As previously stated, Hans became the abbey's serf sometime between 1578 and 1593 and became a judge in 1583. His wife, however, never gave up her status despite strong pressure from the abbey. In 1589 Hans Miller of Obersiggingen petitioned the Audience for the manumission of his wife and six children in exchange for a carpenter's wife and six children who resided in Birkenweiler but belonged to Heiligenberg. Instead, the Audience offered to

---

198 In 1619, the year after Resstlin's appointment as court bailiff, there was some disagreement in Mimmenhausen as to whether he should be permitted to graze animals there and whether he was an abbey serf. The Audience neglected to comment on his legal status in response to the commune's petition on the matter, stating only that he had been admitted as a resident. It is possible that Resstlin became a bondsman again after returning to the territory, and it appears that there was pressure for him to do so, mainly from the commune, who was ready to exclude him from grazing rights unless he were an abbey serf.

199 Christoph Langenstain's three daughters were free, following their mother, and each one married outside the territory. After their father's death, they inherited his significant property including vineyards in Bermatingen and elsewhere.

manumit Miller's family in exchange for the wife and six children of Hans Hailg.[200] Yet there is no sign that the Audience consulted Hailg's wife about this exchange or that she consented. According to lists from 1590 and 1594, she still belonged to Heiligenberg. What is clear is that the officials wanted Margaretha Dilgerin and her children to become the abbey's serfs and that for whatever reason this did not happen.

These findings suggest that the great majority of Sidelrichter were the abbey's serfs either by birth or through "voluntary" enserfment, along with most of their wives and children. However, the minority of Sidelrichter and their spouses who were not abbey serfs have extraordinary significance for our understanding of officeholding and the selection of territorial judges. In the absence of sources explicitly stating the methods of nomination, confirmation, and appointment to the court, the most likely assumption would be that the abbot exercised control over court appointments. Yet the occasional inclusion of a Sidelrichter who was another lord's bondsman suggests otherwise. If the choice had been the abbot's alone, it is doubtful that he would have chosen a serf belonging to a neighbor, especially a political competitor such as the count of Heiligenberg. From the evidence of judges who were not abbey serfs there arises the strong possibility that the community of subjects, the judges, or someone other than the abbot or his direct representative had some influence over court appointments. In any case, participation in territorial decisionmaking was not strictly limited to the abbey's own serfs.

Despite lingering uncertainties about how the judges were chosen or by whom, and about the factors that influenced their rate of promotion, what remains most significant is that all 15 Sidelrichter continued to be peasant subjects and villagers throughout the period. Even if the court's members were appointed solely by the abbot or his representative, it is highly significant for the territory's legal development, political foundations, and the settlement of conflicts that legal decisions were found collectively by prominent members of the community.

In sum, the Sidelrichter were mostly rich, mostly abbey serfs, and in many cases, Salem's tenants. Yet exceptions indicate that these are general tendencies, not strict rules. In the end, the data suggest that the Sidelrichter were eminent local leaders but not the exclusive members of a separate ruling class. In one sense, the judges were the abbot's men. Yet in another, just as in the case of the Amtmänner, they belonged to the village communities. The judges provide the point of connection between the two.

---

200 "Beschaidt. Darauff haben Ire Gl. bewilligt gedachts Millers Weib unnd Sechs Kinder Gegen Hannsen Hailgen zue Bermatingen Weib unnd auch Sechs kinder so Hailgenbergischen seyen Tauschweiß hinzegeben." GLAK, 61/13369, 7 December 1589. In 1624 the Audience proposed similarly to exchange Hans Jerg Rauch's wife Salome Owerin from Schiggendorf for a woman who was moving to Heiligenberg's jurisdiction. The record does not indicate the couple's consent to the exchange or whether it actually took place, but Rauch became a Sidelrichter sometime between 1638 and 1646.

5.6 Conclusions

This chapter has described the Sidelgericht through many specific examples. Now, it is time to draw some final conclusions. In many ways, territorial justice in Salem during the decades around 1600 was the fruition of peasant demands leading up to and confirmed by the partnership agreement of 1473. In 1470 the judges protested: "They wanted to make us into jurists—we were supposed to lay the roll open before us and speak the law as whatever its articles said, just as jurists do with the written laws that fill their books." Over a century later it was common subjects, native inhabitants of the territory, who continued to be the finders, guardians, interpreters, and practitioners of the law. The court also continued to operate according to many customary principles. The alte Jarbrief, the judges asserted in 1470, "is not a matter of law or any of the abbey's rights but a mere provision of statutes." Still over a century later it was commonly thought that law was found not only in books but also in the everyday practices, experiences, knowledge, and conscience of ordinary people, in what the community held to be right. Changing situations might bring the need for supplementary laws in the form of written statutes, but these were subject to the community's consent and did not override older customs. For the law was believed to come not from the lord's enactments but from the people's collective memory, innate common sense, and approval. It was not to be found on a piece of brittle parchment or paper, it was organic: it lived inside the people, changing and growing as they did. It emerged through ritual performance, in social contexts.

The Sidelgericht testifies to the continuing legal authority of ordinary rural people over their own everyday affairs, not only at the local level but also throughout the territory—even in interactions with outsiders, strangers, and higher authorities. The procedures of the Sidelgericht ensured that common subjects maintained an understanding of their legal rights and could defend them in a court of law. It not only gave them access to the law, it allowed them to act as participants and in some cases as the leading experts in the judicial sphere. In subtle or dramatic ways, they even helped to shape the law, as practices and norms evolved with the territory's growing needs and litigants' presentation of argument and evidence. The court's development had much to do with the topics of dispute brought before it.

Yet we must not interpret the Sidelgericht as the champion of peasants' legal values over those of the abbey. It is true that the judges of the late fifteenth century engaged in a concerted resistance movement against the abbot that resulted in a debate over fundamental aspects of lordship and raised important questions about the legal order. By the time serial court records began in 1583, however, signs of opposition between the abbot and his judges had subsided. In fact, the significance of the Sidelgericht is not to be found in the struggle between lord and subjects, old and new, customary and scholarly, native and foreign, or any other such oppositional forces. The Sidelgericht was successful because it was able to satisfy a variety of needs simultaneously, drawing support from interest groups who did not normally see eye to eye. For different reasons, the central court served the political objectives of the abbey and its subjects, as well as the more practical concerns of judges and litigants, plaintiffs and defendants, rich and poor. On the one hand, it boosted the abbey's claims to territorial authority both internally and externally. The court was its major instrument for warding off Heiligenberg's claims to overlordship and for consolidating authority over a uniform band of subjects. On the other hand, it upheld communal values, protected subjects' interests, and placed 15 peasant subjects in charge of legal interpretations and decisions. These judges, local elites who performed a mediating function between the abbey and the communes, came to identify more strongly with centralizing policies and institutions through their service, strengthening the ties between the abbey and its settlements, though not primarily on the lord's terms. The court facilitated the transfer of local communal values and experience to a broader geographical area and to the higher political echelons of the territory, just as it encouraged greater compliance and a more positive disposition among subjects toward the centralization of rule. Salem's territorial court supported a stronger and more unified polity by incorporating diverse needs, providing an institutional setting for communication and compromise, and encouraging peace and stability in everyday situations as well as on a more symbolic level.

If this chapter demonstrates one thing, it is that Salem's peasants remained political actors during the century after 1525. Common people were not shut out from territorial decisionmaking during this period, in spite of many hurdles. Territorial administration in Salem was characterized by a partnership between the abbey and its subjects. If we were to look at the legal sources alone, we could even call it a time of ascendancy for peasant values and popular political influence. The Sidelgericht fostered a consciousness among inhabitants that they were members of a common polity, one that was to be sure not entirely to their liking, but one that nevertheless took account of their own daily experiences and political demands. This study proposes that the success of governance owes as much or more to this sense of connectedness and membership among the people than to the more typical measures of statehood, such as exclusive jurisdiction, military power, bureaucracy, or political sovereignty. The court's inclusion of a broad spectrum of territorial inhabitants challenges preconceptions about the role of elites in the process of political formation. Indeed, in a period characterized by the growth of princely authority, the Sidelgericht provides the basis for a very different picture of who might govern whom. The following chapter will further develop the thesis that during this period of intensive political formation, often defined as "statebuilding," Salem's peasants maintained their influence at the territorial level.

Chapter 6: "Life Is Good under the Abbot's Crosier": Territorial Governance in Early Modern Salem

This chapter looks at how Salem's territorial authority was constructed from within. It brings together various elements of rule that are characteristic of the early modern period in Salem and elsewhere, including those that are usually associated with the interests of central princely authority and statebuilding: taxation, loyalty oaths, legislation, and defense. Yet the bundling of strands into a unitary territorial government need not be characterized in terms of statebuilding, or solely in terms of the actions and interests of the abbot and his chief advisors who ruled from the center. Territorial authority was strengthened and even centralized, but not at the expense of peasant subjects' political contributions or organizational methods. Villagers, too, contributed to certain aspects of governance through their own actions and interests: petitions, rent resistance, and professional mobility are topics demonstrating their influence on territorial development from below. Political developments in Salem did not result simply from a combination of elements promoted either by the abbey or its subjects and forged through opposition and settlements between them. Almsgiving, residency restrictions, and lay education show especially well how political policy and practice in early modern Salem adapted in response to underlying social conditions and changing needs in ways that were not always intentional. Governance arose from interactions among various territorial groups and negotiations involving shifting pressures. These included the interests of lords and subjects but were not limited to a binary opposition between such idealized social categories or to a set of conscious objectives held by one side or the other.

The dealings between territorial actors sometimes involved opposition and disagreement, but conflict and resistance were not the driving forces behind Salem's political development. Many interactions between the abbey and its subjects are better characterized by participation and inclusion, communication and compromise. Negotiation was a tool with mutual benefits, not because territorial groups shared identical interests, but because it opened dialogue and diffused conflict. Petitioning, for example, gave peasant subjects the opportunity to voice their opinions as well as the feeling that they were being listened to. For the abbey, a few concessions to the peasants and the willingness to hear their demands were a small price to pay for the legitimacy and respect for authority these actions reinforced. One reason conflict was not the primary basis of relations between rulers and ruled in Salem is that the fundamental concerns of each group were not at odds with one another.

As seen in Chapter 1, Salem's most significant political challenge was an external competitor, the count of Heiligenberg. In many areas of territorial policy, the abbey's primary concern was to secure its autonomy and possibly even expand its territorial authority at Heiligenberg's expense, though the decisions made often had greater impacts for the subject population than for Heiligenberg. In the villages, and from the peasants' perspective, much greater concerns arose from the increasing pressure to secure material resources and the need to stabilize social relations. Peasants recognized that territorial officials and administrative decisions could be used to their favor, and consequently, they called on higher authorities to help them settle neighborly disputes and overcome personal or collective hardships. Since the various interests were divergent but not necessarily oppositional, there was room for negotiation and even mutual advantage.

Material presented in Chapter 3 raises objections to the traditional interpretation of the German Peasants' War as a major turning point in peasants' political influence. Yet the sixteenth and seventeenth centuries continue to be seen as a period of declining popular involvement during which territorial princes strengthened their grasp over an increasingly centralized political authority by establishing stronger administrative structures, unitary law codes, central courts, regular taxation, and new policies to regulate the minute details of economic, social, moral, and religious life. Those rulers who successfully implemented these changes were better able to form the inhabitants of their territories into a common band of subjects who shared uniform legal status and obligations. Administrative development and recordkeeping gave central authorities greater access to local information and greater control over behavior and resources in the villages. These developments have been associated with the rise of absolutism at the expense of local community, social discipline at the expense of customary folk practice. According to Heide Wunder, the early modern period saw a shift from rule with peasants to rule over peasants.[1] Even Peter Blickle sees a decline in the peasantry's political power as expressed through communalism, a decline that was already underway after 1550 and irreversible by the end of the Thirty Years War.[2] Yet the period under consideration here is one of transition, in which absolutism was far from effected and no such outcome had been predetermined.

As this final chapter will show, peasants played a central role in Salem's territorial development, especially in the period after 1550. Support for this thesis can be drawn from studies of the late seventeenth and eighteenth centuries, the age of absolutism. In William Beik's study of absolutism and society in Languedoc, the French king's authority appears as less than absolute. True, Beik's interest is in demonstrating that power was shared with provincial nobles, royal officials, and other elites rather than peasant subjects, but the general approach is nevertheless useful. According to Beik, "historians have moved from viewing the state as a triumphant organizer of society to viewing it as a fragile organism struggling against a vast, turbulent society, and finally to the realization that forces in society were influencing, if not defining the very func-

---

1 WUNDER, Bäuerliche Gemeinde, esp. pp. 80–82, 112.

2 BLICKLE, Obedient Germans, p. 78.

tion of the state."[3] He argues that Louis XIV was successful because of his defense of ruling class interests, not his repression of provincial privileges. Local elites depended on a centralized government and demanded that it do its job better; the king gave them what they wanted. Royal officials were not simply the instruments of bureaucratic centralization, nor were they solely infiltrating the government with particularist demands and class interests. The interconnection of concerns and relationships among individuals and social groups, and their impact on institutional development, was extremely complex. Even the government of the Sun King served class interests and performed social functions. Beik sees absolutism as an extension and defense of feudal class interests, designed to keep the peasant masses in their traditional social position of subjection.

By contrast, André Holenstein's study of "good policing" argues that state government in eighteenth-century Baden focused on the improvement of local conditions and incorporated the interests of many groups, including peasant subjects. This was made possible by opening lines of communication and listening carefully to what was going on in the villages.[4] He, too, sees the strengthening of state power as serving local interests, not only because it served to increase the resources at the state's disposal, but also because it promoted subjects' welfare and adapted to existing social contexts. This required gathering information at the local level, and officials found the population ready and willing to report on certain local conditions at visitations, court sessions, inquiries, inspections, and through petitions. Both Holenstein and Beik suggest that even absolutism was not absolute, that early modern European governments were influenced, and indeed in many respects created, through the interactions and socioeconomic needs of the polity's members and subjects.[5]

Of course, peasants did not always participate in governance in the ways or to the degree they might have liked. Nor was their influence always intentional. Nevertheless, just as abbey officials demanded from peasants the surplus of their labor, peasants demanded certain things in return. Resistance and the threat of rebellion posed limits, as did their ability to pay taxes. The popular belief in the right of subsistence and the idea of the common good required district administrators to do more, not less, to protect territorial subjects. The abbot maintained the upper hand in relations with subjects but this did not preclude overlapping interests, bonds of reciprocity, even shared identities.

---

3 William BEIK, Absolutism and Society in Seventeenth-Century France: State Power and Provincial Aristocracy in Languedoc, Cambridge 1985, p. 17.

4 HOLENSTEIN, Gute Policey. For a concise summary of these themes, see idem, Umstände der Normen, pp. 1–46.

5 Among the many recent studies of the political interactions between center and periphery, see also CASTIGLIONE, Patrons and Adversaries; OGILVIE, The State in Germany, pp. 417–441; HINDLE, State and Social Change.

Authority over land, people, and justice (*Grundherrschaft*, *Leibherrschaft*, and *Gerichtsherrschaft*) were the three traditional pillars of medieval lordship. During the long sixteenth century they continued to serve among the foundations of Salem's political authority. New, however, was the combination of the three to serve a unitary, central power. Each component of rule assumed new functions in the early modern period and their combination created a cumulative effect greater than the sum of its parts.[6] These newer functions in the early modern period did not result from the interests of lords alone, but also out of pressures from below, as shown with respect to servility in Chapter 2, land tenure in Chapter 4, and justice in Chapter 5. During the long sixteenth century, additional strands were woven into the bundle of rights that constituted Salem's territorial authority. This chapter addresses those elements that best characterize political negotiation and development within Salem's central territory during the early modern period.[7] They include imperial tax collection, the loyalty oath, legislative authority, the Audience of petitions, collective grievances, military defense, residence restrictions, charity, education, and professional mobility.

6.1 Imperial Taxation

In 1470 Emperor Frederick III granted Salem the right to collect imperial taxes from its subjects.[8] This privilege was a mixed blessing. On the one hand, taxation became an important component of Salem's imperial status and territorial autonomy. It supported Salem's claim to stand directly under the empire without any mediating authority.[9] It even gave Salem the right to collect taxes from other lords' serfs and tenants living within jurisdictional boundaries.[10] On the other hand, the privilege of 1470 preceded a steadily increasing demand for cash to support the imperial wars in Italy and against the Ottoman Turks. As territorial rulers recognized, the new and heavy burdens imposed on subjects heightened the potential for popular uprisings because the assessments were uneven, arbitrary, and especially burdensome for common people. In

6 BLICKLE, Bauer und Staat, p. 117; HÖLZ, Krummstab und Schwert, pp. 86–87.

7 Other elements of territorialization could be emphasized. These choices reflect the availability of source material and concentrate on relations between lords and subjects.

8 GLAK, 4/752.

9 The privilege was explicit on this point: "Nachdem dasselb Closter unß und dem heiligen Reiche on Mittel zugehöret." The right to collect taxes (*jus collectandi*) was a deciding criterion and, according to Winfried Schulze, the most secure symbol of territorial sovereignty in the late sixteenth century. Idem, Türkengefahr, pp. 268, 282.

10 The privilege granted Salem the right to collect taxes from both "*Eigen Lutten*" and "*Hindersessen*." Not surprisingly, this issue continued to be an area of dispute between Salem and Heiligenberg. A settlement in 1502 upheld territorial principles for the collection of taxes in Salem's favor. GLAK, 67/1431.

many territories and for many aspects of government, imperial taxation did not bring greater stability.[11] The emperor's privilege in 1470 certainly did not make the abbey's subjects more willing to pay new taxes, as late fifteenth-century tax disputes in Salem demonstrate.

Salem's abbots, like other territorial rulers at the end of the Middle Ages, lacked the popular legitimacy necessary to suddenly raise such enormous funds from its subjects. Not only that, Salem's tax rate was extraordinarily high compared with other territories of its size. Abbey representatives persistently lobbied for a reduction of their tax assessment over the early modern period, with little success. When we consider the freedom from imperial taxation both Salem and its subjects previously enjoyed, and keep in mind the popular belief that the lord's duty was to protect subjects from external threats, it is obvious that imperial tax collection could be an imposing task. This section outlines the growing imperial tax burden during the long sixteenth century. It assesses the positive and negative consequences of imperial tax collection for the consolidation and legitimacy of Salem's territorial rule. Finally, it will show that abbey leaders were not free to demand whatever they wanted from their subjects. Although the peasantry bore a significant share of the burden, there were limits on what they could be asked to pay.

Winfried Schulze describes both quantitative and qualitative differences between the imperial tax assessments of the first and second halves of the sixteenth century.[12] During the earlier period, collections were sporadic and assessments relatively low. Tax debates at the Imperial Diet centered on how contributions should be allocated and collected.[13] The system of Roman Months strengthened the authority of territorial princes but was a major blow to the tax freedoms of commoners, many of whom had not paid imperial taxes in the past. The privileged estates often escaped taxation altogether, even as the Imperial Diet declared in 1548 that no one was exempt. After mid-

11 Schulze sees the war taxes in most cases as a stabilizing element for political and social order, but not in smaller territories such as Waldburg in Upper Swabia. In the South German lands, tax resistance was central to a chain of revolts between 1590 and 1614. Idem, Türkengefahr, esp. pp. 270–297; idem, Reichstage und Reichssteuern im späten sechzehnten Jahrhundert, in: Zeitschrift für Historische Forschung 2 (1975), pp. 54–55; idem, Oberdeutsche Untertanenrevolten zwischen 1580 und 1620: Reichssteuern und bäuerlicher Widerstand, in: Bauer Reich und Reformation: Festschrift für Günther Franz zum 80. Geburtstag, ed. Peter Blickle, Stuttgart 1982, pp. 120–147. For small territories like Hohenlohe, Robisheaux doubts imperial tax collection was an advantage. Idem, Rural Society, pp. 177–178.

12 SCHULZE, Türkengefahr, esp. pp. 78–80, 181, 189, 245–246, 262–263.

13 According to the system of Roman Months, each imperial estate contributed an individualized base rate multiplied by the number of months the Imperial Diet approved. Roman Months referred to the monthly cost of maintaining the imperial army. A head tax known as the Common Penny was used briefly as an alternative in the early sixteenth century. Ibid., pp. 179–190; idem, Reichstage und Reichssteuern, pp. 46–49.

century, the rate and frequency of imperial tax collections increased steadily.[14] Discussions at the Imperial Diet now focused on the tax amount rather than the distribution or method of collection. Some territorial rulers resisted new taxes, warning that their subjects would be unable to shoulder higher burdens and might be incited to revolt.[15] Many others took advantage of the Turkish threat to bolster their authority and some even charged their subjects more than was owed, keeping a share for themselves.[16]

In Salem, the first recorded tax dispute between the abbey and its subjects came only five years after the privilege of 1470. Imperial war taxes (*Raißsteur*) were not the only area of disagreement—also at issue were the abbey's right to command and forbid (*gebott und verbott*) and other unspecified "damages" (*schäden*) subjects had suffered. Yet the arbitrated agreement of 13 October 1475 addressed only the first of the three complaints; the others were left for some other time.[17] The decision of 1475 required all the abbey's people (*gotzhus lut*) to declare their wealth under oath and pay four pence per pound (1.7 percent of wealth) in military taxes. This judgment is significant in several respects. First, settlement by outside arbitrators avoided the escalation of conflict and lent legitimacy to the tax assessment. Second, it formed an important precedent for future tax collections without subjects' approval. Third, the objections and their resolution came early in the struggle over imperial taxes, before the onset of regular and heavy assessments. Finally, despite other grievances that might have been negotiated as part of a package deal, the decision put off these issues and dealt solely with the tax assessment. Since the settlement acknowledged Salem's right to demand military contributions without considering subjects' grievances in exchange, the terms appear to

---

14 The imperial tax levies from 1556–1603 were as follows: 16 Roman Months in 1556/7, 7 in 1559, 48 in 1566/7, 12 in 1570, 60 in 1576, 40 in 1582, 80 in 1594, 60 in 1597/8, and 86 in 1603. At 316 fl. per Roman Month during the period 1521–1680, Salem paid more than other abbeys (including Kempten), the bishop of Constance, or the count of Fürstenberg. SCHULZE, Türkengefahr, pp. 79–80. See also HÖLZ, Krummstab und Schwert, pp. 65 n. 23, 100; BAIER, Staat und Kirche, pp. 141–142; Karl BECKER, Salem unter Abt Thomas I. Wunn und die Gründung der oberdeutschen Cistercienser-Kongregation, 1615–1647, in: Cistercienser Chronik 48 (1936), pp. 166, 168.

15 This was not merely strategic argument for the purpose of tax evasion. During the period 1590–1614 there were uprisings relating wholly or in part to imperial taxes in many Austrian and Upper German territories, and lords were anxious that new taxes might lead to a more widespread movement similar to the one in 1525. SCHULZE, Türkengefahr, pp. 292–296; Idem, Reichstage und Reichssteuer, p. 54.

16 It was not uncommon for princes to collect double or even triple the amount required, and imperial lawyers tried to devise justifications for overtaxation in order to stem the flood of legal suits brought by subjects against their lords. In 1594 the Saxon chancellor accused a few princes of charging their subjects up to twenty times the total tax. SCHULZE, Türkengefahr, pp. 255–256, 273–274, 289; idem, Reichstage und Reichssteuern, pp. 51–52.

17 GLAK, 4/1139. The count of Heiligenberg and city councilors from Pfullendorf served as arbitrators.

have been a decided victory for the abbey. They circumvented the calling of a territorial assembly, which might have made demands of its own in return for war taxes.

The dispute over taxes was renewed in 1496, this time regarding the Swabian League assessment. Subjects again expressed opposition to the idea of paying taxes, but as in the earlier case, the two sides entered arbitration without calling a territorial assembly, adding further precedent for taxation without consent or the hearing of subjects' concerns in return for financial assistance.[18] The subjects' total burden of 401 fl. was seemingly bearable on this occasion, although the requirement that they pay just over half of Salem's 800 fl. assessment would lead to much greater burdens if a fifty-fifty split became the norm as taxes continued to rise.[19]

Salem's earliest surviving tax lists are not comprehensive. A comparison of names and the number of households in the early lists demonstrates inconsistencies, suggesting the difficulties of conducting tax assessments as well as a high level of tax evasion.[20] These incomplete lists do not allow a comparison of subjects' contributions against the abbey's total assessments. Several of them demonstrate, however, that subjects paid a percentage of their household wealth rather than a percentage of Salem's assessment.[21] This is significant, because the rate of household taxation did not rise at the same pace as the abbey's skyrocketing tax obligation. One tax list from 1516 presents an exception in two respects, showing the fluidity of tax collection methods in the early sixteenth century. According to this list, the abbey's subjects consented to pay half of the abbey's entire assessment over two years for a total of 700 fl.[22] Payments were listed by village rather than by household, suggesting that each community took responsibility for collecting the tax from its own members. The 1516 tax list thus appears to be unusual with respect to both consent and communal responsibility for collection.

18 GLAK, 4/365. The nobleman Hans Jacob von Bodman and Überlingen city officials arbitrated the settlement.

19 A fifty-fifty split was common among many imperial abbeys, and subjects in some territories paid even more. Armgard von Reden-Dohna, Reichsstandschaft und Klosterherrschaft: Die schwäbischen Reichsprälaten im Zeitalter des Barock, Wiesbaden 1982, p. 19.

20 Many of the descriptions are fragments and some are undated, but early tax lists are available for the years 1488, 1493, 1501, 1505, 1518, 1530, and 1557. See GLAK, 98/2006–2007, 98/2026. These dates do not correspond to those of imperial tax collections, probably because Salem's tax assessments were used for several years rather than created anew for each collection. For the dates and tax levels in this period, see Wilfried SETZLER, Kloster Zwiefalten: Eine schwäbische Benediktinerabtei zwischen Reichsfreiheit und Landsässigkeit. Studien zu ihrer Rechts- und Verfassungsgeschichte, Sigmaringen 1979, pp. 88–89. See also BAIER, Staat und Kirche, pp. 141–142; SCHULZE, Türkengefahr, pp. 79–80.

21 The tax rate was highest in 1488. At 2%, it was slightly higher than the amount set in 1475. The rate was significantly lower in the mid-sixteenth century, between 0.4% (1566) and 0.5% (1557) of household wealth. In 1578 it was 0.8%, 1593 1.7%, and 1603 1% of wealth. GLAK, 98/2006, 98/2016, 98/2024.

22 "Also haben sich die unterthan des gotzhus mit ainandern veraint ... so dann die Ubrigen vij c. lb. dn. haben die underthan bewilligt und zugesagt." GLAK, 98/2011.

In contrast to the late fifteenth century, there are no recorded tax protests and no tax revolts by Salem's peasants after the mid-sixteenth century.[23] In fact, when peasants organized to present collective grievances against the abbey in 1629–1630, imperial taxation was not even among the topics of complaint. This absence is noteworthy, considering the dramatic increase in the scale and frequency of assessments after 1550. Starting in 1566, Salem's tax lists became much more comprehensive as well as detailed. The tax lists from the second half of the sixteenth century, including the years 1566, 1578, 1593, and 1603, are much more accurate and valuable sources of wealth and population data than any previous lists. They show advances in recordkeeping and suggest a greater ability to enforce tax compliance as well as to collect other household information.[24]

Salem's tax record from 1566 began with a preamble (*Fürtrag*) explaining the reasons for the tax and the means for its enforcement.[25] It shows how the abbey explained and justified the tax to its subjects and describes the means used to coax or coerce subjects into acceptance. The 1566 text appears to have been a model for justifying later tax collections; the 1603 tax assessment, for example, followed it closely in wording and in structure. The 1566 preamble lists the officials responsible for overseeing the tax collection: the Pfister, Kaufmann, and secretary. We can imagine them standing before the assembled peasants as the text was proclaimed:

> It is now present and common knowledge how the gruesome and bloodthirsty villain, our terrible sworn enemy the Turk, in addition to the irretrievable tyrannical practices he has already cultivated, has once again personally and with unheard-of military strength invaded the kingdom of Hungary. And not only that, for he is also of the intention and ultimate plan to overrun our entire common fatherland, our Christian name and beliefs, and bring it all under his bestial power.[26]

---

23 Audience petitions rarely mention imperial taxes. In one of very few examples, the Amtmann of Weildorf asked in 1596 that the community be spared from war taxes (*Raißsteuer*), or at least receive a reduction, because so many of their cows had died that year. The Audience members replied they would have to think about it. In 1605 the treasurers of Owingen's confraternity asked to be spared from the tax since they had no property. Hans Claußmar of Grasbeuren reported in 1595 that Heiligenberg was demanding imperial war taxes from some property he had inherited in Unteruhldingen. The Audience told him to pay the tax, at least for the time being. None of these petitions suggest organized tax resistance. GLAK, 61/13369.

24 See Chapter 4; also BAIER, Bevölkerungs- und Vermögensstatistik, pp. 196–197.

25 GLAK, 98/2019.

26 "Nachdem nun mer Landkundig, wie das der grausam Wieterich und erschrockenlich Erbfeindt der Turckh, onerstettigt seiner vorgepflegnen Tyrannischen ubungen, abermalen mit unerhorter Höreßkrafft aigner person, nit allain das Kunigreich Hungern gewaltigclich uberzogen, Sonder auch endtlichs willens und vorhabens seye, unsern Christenlichen glauben und namen, auch gemaines Vatterland, ganz und gar auß zu reytten, und unndter seinen Vihischen gewalt zupringen." GLAK, 98/2019, fol. 1r–v.

This opening statement brought the threat home, calling on feelings of terror and Christian duty.[27] Next, the preamble shifted responsibility away from the abbey by emphasizing that the tax burden was shared equally by all members of the empire. It declared that the tax had been approved at the Imperial Diet by all the estates and that the abbey was merely following orders. No one was free from the tax, not clergy or laypeople, exempt or nonexempt, widows, orphans, or even servants.[28]

With the point made that the tax was indeed necessary and everyone obliged to contribute, the preambles of 1566 and later years moved on to enforcement. Subjects were required to itemize their property value according to a detailed inquiry. Accuracy of reporting was maintained above all by oath. In case the dire consequences of perjury were not enough, more immediate threats were added. Anyone who complained, resisted, or refused to comply would be charged twice the normal rate.[29] The 1603 preamble stated that if tax officials believed a subject had assessed his land or moveables below their worth, they could confiscate the property for the abbey's use and pay its stated value in return.[30]

An added justification for the tax in 1603 was the suggestion that subjects' own misdeeds and impiety were to blame for both the Turkish situation and the imperial tax burden. As was the case elsewhere in the empire, the Turkish threat served as a platform for demanding greater devotion, better behavior, and special prayers.[31] Local

---

27 Such strategies were not of the abbey's own invention. They had been previously discussed at the Imperial Diet and used throughout the empire to justify war taxes. SCHULZE, Türkengefahr, pp. 277, 299; idem, Reichstage und Reichssteuern, p. 45.

28 Added emphasis was given in 1603 to the nonexempt status of all subjects: "Daß yeder Obrigkait zuegelaßen sein solle, Alle Ire underthonen Gaistlich unnd Welltlich, sie seyen Exempt oder nicht Exempt, gefreyet, oder nit gefreyet, niemandt usßgenomen." GLAK, 98/2003. Very similar wording was used at the Imperial Diet in 1548; SCHULZE, Türkengefahr, p. 250.

29 This stipulation was introduced at the Imperial Diet of 1566; ibid.

30 "Wöllicher sein vermögen, an ligendem oder vahrendem guett, nit mit trewen, unnd in der Warhait, sonder mit trug unnd Aigennütziger hinderhalltung, und vershweigung deß Rechten werdts, Angeben wurden, Allso daß Ire G: oder dero verordnete erkhennen möchten, oder selbstwüsten, daß es Zue Ring angeschlagen worden, unnd ains andern oder beßern werdt were, So wöllen Jre G: Inen in diesem fahl vorbehallten haben, sollich guett in Angezaigtem werdt, Anzenemen unnd Irem Gottshaus einzeziehen und dem Inhaber oder besitzer nach seinem Anschlag darvon zelösen." GLAK, 98/2003, fol. 3v. An Audience petition from Ulrich Bawhoffer of Bermatingen in 1599 indicates this provision was already in effect before 1603. Bawhoffer told the Audience he would be happy to pay the *Raißgeld* if he were treated the same as other people. The Audience responded, "Ir Gl. wöllen nit daß die Amptleuth deßhalb in verdacht kommen Aber sy wollen Ime beim Aydt die güetter de novo schetzen lassenn, und nach dem es sich befindt, nach dem wöllen Ir Gl. sich wissenn zehalten. Wann er fehl, wöllen Ir Gl. die güetter ahn sich ziehen und Inn, Weib und kindt hinweisen." GLAK, 61/13369. This example is one of the only tax complaints found in the Audience records or elsewhere.

31 This emphasis on collective guilt also came directly from the Imperial Diet. SCHULZE, Türkengefahr, p. 277.

officials were instructed to make sure priests gave extra sermons on the importance of honorable actions and the consequences of sinful behavior. Bells were to be rung each day at noon calling residents to make special prayers for God's intercession in such terrible times.[32] The desire to limit dissent was most certainly the underlying context of another statement in the 1603 preamble, that the abbot was sheltering his subjects as much as possible and carrying a far greater burden than they:

> And now, if memory serves the reverend and spiritual Lord Peter Abbot ... then each of you, every abbey subject and inhabitant, has paid your imposed and required taxes in the past few years obediently and repeatedly. For this reason he would like to spare you further contributions as he has graciously spared you this past year. Yet unfortunately he cannot abstain from calling on you, whose tax contribution yields less than one-third of the abbey's total assessment ... Out of urgent need and the impossibility of meeting this high and heavy tax, we must again request and impose fair and dutiful assistance on you and all subjects and inhabitants of the abbey, as all other lordships and authorities are also doing at this time.[33]

A comparison of the abbey's total tax burden with the amount collected from residents supports the abbot's claim that subjects were spared from carrying the bulk of the assessment.[34] This practice was a departure from the norm in most territories, including those of other imperial abbeys.[35] One obvious reason for this difference is that Salem's tax rate was unusually high. Throughout the period 1521–1680 Salem paid 316 fl. per

---

32 "Daß alle oberkhaiten in Iren gebietten, deren Pfarrherrn unnd Predigern Anbevehlen sollen, von den Cantzeln daß volckh zur Bueß Beßerung deß Lebens und In brünstigen Andächtigen gepett zuvermahnen, daß auch deßwegen täglich, ... zue Mittags Zeiten, Ain sondere glockhen geleuttet werde. Allso ist hierauf Hochwolermellts unsers gnedigen herrn Ernnstlicher Bevelch und Mainung, Daß hinfüro diesem Puncten in Allweg mit fleiß unnd Andacht nach gesetzt und gelebt werde, Wie dann die Elltern und haußvätter Ire Kinder und Ehehallten dahin ermanen unnd weisen, dz sie Jeder Zeit, wann sollche glockhen geleittet werden, mit endtblöstem haupt und Kniend, den Allmächtigen Gott, umb abwendung diser straf mit Rechtem eyferigen gebett Anrüeffen und Pitten sollen." GLAK, 98/2003.

33 Ibid.

34 In 1566 the abbey collected approximately 1,412 fl. from villagers, compared with a total assessment of 15,168 fl. for 1566–1567. In 1578 the subjects in the two central districts owed 2,160 fl., compared with Salem's 1576 tax assessment of 18,960 fl. In 1593 Salem's total bill came to 25,280 fl. and in 1603 it was 27,176 fl., whereas subjects were assessed at 1.7% and 1% of wealth in the same years. Even with taxes collected annually at this rate (the 1593 tax was paid over four years), subjects' contributions were far less than the amount due. GLAK, 98/2016, 98/2026.

35 Kempten's subjects paid three-quarters of the assessment according to a 1526 agreement; in Brechtsgaden, Ochsenhausen, and Rottenmünster they paid two-thirds. Abbeys Elchingen, Roggenburg, Petershausen, and Wettenhausen off-loaded the entire assessment onto their subjects, and in Bavaria, subjects paid five percent of wealth twelve times in the years 1577–1593. According to Blickle, subjects without representation in territorial assemblies were much more likely to be overtaxed. Idem, Landschaften, pp. 328–9, 358, 510; SCHULZE, Türkengefahr, p. 285; REDEN-DOHNA, Reichsstandschaft, p. 19.

Roman Month, which was by far the highest base rate of any abbey after 1550. Even higher-ranking Kempten and the bishop of Constance paid much less.[36] During the 21 years of Abbot Peter II's reign (1593–1614) Salem paid a total of between 140,000 and 180,000 fl. according to various estimates, and during the Thirty Years War, the situation became even worse.[37] Salem's abbots and representatives at the imperial court tried repeatedly to obtain a reduction of the base rate, and in the eighteenth century Salem even offered to give up its imperial status in exchange for tax relief.

We might assume from Salem's extremely high tax rate that the abbey lacked political influence at the imperial court, interpreting its failure to negotiate a tax proportional to its size or similar to what other abbeys paid as a sign of weakness rather than strength. Salem's contemporaries and most historians have viewed the situation differently. Not only is Salem frequently identified as one of the wealthiest if not the wealthiest abbey in its region overall, Salem's properties and incomes were a source of envy among its peers. Armgard von Reden-Dohna makes an explicit connection between Salem's high tax rate, its sources of wealth, and the fact that subjects contributed less to the tax assessment than in other territories.[38] This is because Salem's wealth was primarily built not on the backs of tenant farmers but on its network of granges and urban properties, on large-scale grain and wine production paired with trade privileges, which supported an economic system and sources of income unrivaled by other abbeys.[39] Since Salem's tax assessment and the enormous wealth on which it was based did not correspond to the size of the subject population, abbey officials could not expect subjects to carry the bulk of the burden without the risk of provoking resistance. Instead, the abbey came up with most of the funds from its own treasury, taking out loans to cover the balance.

In terms of provoking resistance, the tax assessment of 1578 presents another interesting finding: in contrast to the texts from 1566 and 1603, legitimation strategies were conspicuously absent. Unlike the preambles to those lists, the text from 1578 barely mentioned the Turkish threat. It made no attempt to blame subjects for their sins and did not cite the abbey's poverty as grounds for requiring financial assistance. Yet the 1578 tax list is the most thorough and descriptive source of household wealth information for the entire period. Why did the abbey dispense with the usual justifications, and how was it possible to collect such details without the usual level of coercion?

---

36 In 1551 Kempten owed 152 fl. per Roman Month and the bishop of Constance paid 204 fl. Among imperial abbeys, Ochsenhausen paid the second highest rate of 128 fl. in 1595, followed by Weingarten with 120 fl.; most abbeys paid between 20 and 80 fl. HÖLZ, Krummstab und Schwert, pp. 65, 100.

37 BAIER, Staat und Kirche, p. 145; idem, Akten des dreißigjährigen Krieges, p. 134; FEYERABEND, Chronik, p. 249. According to tax receipts, Salem paid 169,542 fl. during the period 1576–1608 and 242,748 fl. in the years 1618–1629. GLAK, 98/2016.

38 REDEN-DOHNA, Zisterzienser, p. 55; idem, Reichsstandschaft, p. 19.

39 See Map 1.2, Salem's Regional Networks.

A hypothesis is that the abbey's leadership and social composition in 1578 made the usual justifications unnecessary. Listed at the top of the document were the names of the officials responsible for conducting the tax assessment, all of whom had close ties to the subject peasantry. Many were former abbey subjects, including the Pfister Veit Nekher (later abbot from Mimmenhausen), the Kaufmann Panthaleon Scherer (a serf from Neufrach), the Stabhalter and village headman Andreas Mayer (from Tüfingen), and the abbey secretary Johann Vögelin (from Mimmenhausen). The high level of detail in 1578, including information on servility, family size, servants, and additional subcategories of wealth for farm tenants, leads to the conclusion that the tax inquiries and responses were more elaborate than usual. The abbey's return to the 1578 tax list as the most accurate description of property after the Thirty Years War also supports this conclusion.[40] It appears that the abbey avoided new tax assessments in difficult economic times and relied on legitimation strategies above all when there was reason to expect tax resistance.

Returning to Winfried Schulze, the collection of imperial war taxes had several important consequences for territorial states and for the participation of common subjects in decisionmaking. Many of these consequences can be applied to the situation in Salem. First, the collection of imperial taxes on an ever-increasing basis was a test of the strength and survival of individual territories.[41] Yet for those able to manage the burden, imperial tax collections could actually be a source of power and consolidation. Regular taxation not only accustomed subjects to paying more but also forced them to take responsibility for things previously seen as lords' obligations—above all, defense.[42] Imperial taxes also strengthened the ruler's authority at the expense of territorial estates and subjects by invalidating their right to approve taxes, weakening the right of consent in general, and overriding earlier tax freedoms enjoyed by subjects.[43] Without the power to withhold taxes, the estates lost their leverage in other areas. Another way the imperial tax system reinforced territorial rule was by requiring greater administrative organization and written documentation. For Salem this was especially important. The imperial tax documents are the best surviving descriptions of the territory's population, households, and wealth. The energy invested in recording the wealth and tax obligations of each household yielded long-term benefits in the form of information about the economic structure and viability of the territory, its villages, and individual households.

---

[40] Individual tax assessments were used as the basis for repeated collections, not only because of the time and effort required to investigate and compile such a document, but also because new assessments could provoke widespread opposition. Assessments from 1651 and 1653 were already unusable by 1658, and according to Baier, the 1578 list remained a most useful reference in the mid-seventeenth century. Idem, Bevölkerungsbewegung, p. 68.

[41] SCHULZE, Türkengefahr, p. 268; idem, Oberdeutsche Untertanenrevolten, p. 145.

[42] SCHULZE, Türkengefahr, pp. 278–279.

[43] Ibid., pp. 243, 250–251, 264.

At the same time, however, the handling of imperial tax collection could diminish rulers' legitimacy in subjects' eyes.[44] The propaganda campaign at the imperial level and the justifications for tax collections in individual territories helped in part to avoid this problem. Yet many lords' fears of peasant revolts and the negative impact of taxation on their authority over subjects limited support for new taxes as well as their ability to collect them. In this sense, peasants did have some influence over taxation. In Salem, the right to tax was an extremely useful symbol of territorial authority and a source of imperial status, but it came at a heavy price. Salem's assessment was extremely high, so high that administrators dared not pass the entire cost off on the abbey's subjects. The collection of taxes was a privilege, but the duty to pay them was a burden to the abbey and its subjects alike, and Salem was in no position to overtax its dependents. The arbitration agreements, preambles to tax assessments, and large share paid from the abbey's coffers are all indications that there were limits to what the abbot could demand, even with imperial backing.

6.2 The Loyalty Oath

Oaths were sworn in Salem by many groups and on many occasions. Salem's archive contains oath formulas specific to various types of officials and employees, tenants, taxpayers, litigants, witnesses, students, serfs, and other groups. They are scattered in various files, sometimes attached to territorial statutes, or mentioned in employment and tenure contracts. The most important type of oath in the context of territorialization was the *Huldigung*, an oath of allegiance sworn to a new lord upon his election. In Salem, the loyalty oath was sworn by men from age fourteen and women from age twelve. The records relating to the Huldigung have been carefully collected in a single volume of over one thousand pages.[45] André Holenstein has written extensively on oath-taking in abbatial lordships and in comparative perspective.[46] He sees oath-taking as a ritual performance, a "constitution in practice" (*Verfassung in actu*):[47]

> The constitutional life of the territories in the Old Empire knew a periodic and recurrent process, which repeatedly brought lords and subjects together in one place to swear the oath, an act of exceptional legal and symbolic importance. These events, called "Huldigungen," were also

---

[44] Ibid., pp. 276–280.

[45] GLAK, 98/1547.

[46] André HOLENSTEIN, Die Huldigung der Untertanen: Rechtskultur und Herrschaftsordnung (800–1800), Stuttgart and New York 1991; idem, Äbte und Bauern; idem, Seelenheil und Untertanenpflicht: Zur gesellschaftlichen Funktion und theoretischen Begründung des Eides in der ständischen Gesellschaft, in: Der Fluch und der Eid: Die metaphysische Begründung gesellschaftlichen Zusammenlebens und politischer Ordnung in der ständischen Gesellschaft, ed. Peter Blickle, Berlin 1993, pp. 11–63.

[47] HOLENSTEIN, Huldigung, p. 512.

> customary in Upper Swabian monasteries since at least the fifteenth century. On this public occasion ... a reciprocal act of surety took place concerning the foundations of rule and good policy; in short, concerning the constitution of the community.[48]

According to Holenstein, the oath was central to relations of lordship. The texts associated with oath-taking permit us to view the basic elements of lordship at a set time and place.[49]

The earliest dated oath formulas pertaining to Salem's territorial subjects are from 1537, but undated texts and other evidence demonstrate that the oath was not new.[50] For example, an arbitrated settlement of 1478 between the abbey and Bermatingen endorsed the abbey's claim that Bermatingers, like all territorial inhabitants Under and Over the Hills, were required to swear the oath.[51] Included in the decision were full texts of the oaths sworn by serfs (*aigene Leute*) and other jurisdictional residents (*Hintersassen*), copied from an earlier document. The same oath formulas appear in 1537. In fact, the texts underwent very few changes during the long sixteenth century, leading to the conclusion that the oath was customary and formulaic and that it retained its shape over the long term. The preamble to the 1537 formulas stated that two copies had been cut from a single piece of parchment, half given to each party.[52] Since the peasants had access to the text, the abbey could not change the wording without notice.

The oath formulas sworn by Salem's dependents in the sixteenth century were short and simple, not a detailed list of all the lord's rights and expectations.[53] The earliest documents containing the oaths provide two formulas, one for the abbey's serfs and the other for nonservile residents of the jurisdiction.[54] A comparison of the two reveals

---

48 HOLENSTEIN, Äbte und Bauern, p. 244.

49 Ibid.; idem, Huldigung, esp. pp. 278–279.

50 Hans-Martin Maurer cites Salem's 1476 statute as one of the earliest references to abbatial Huldigungen. In fact, all his other examples are later: Schussenried 1480, Ochsenhausen 1498, Söflingen ca. 1500; the earliest actual oath formulas he provides are from Schussenried 1505, Ochsenhausen 1508, and Rot 1521. Maurer sees the appearance of oaths in a set ceremonial form around 1480 as significant because it coincided with territorialization and the leveling of status among dependents. Idem, Territorialgewalt, p. 186, esp. n. 157.

51 See Chapter 3; GLAK, 4/1687. Other early references to the Huldigung are found in documents relating to the Sidelrichter dispute as discussed in Chapter 2. The obligation of all adult serfs to swear the loyalty oath was also among the major themes of territorial statutes in 1476 and 1486, discussed below.

52 GLAK, 98/1547, fol. 32r.

53 In comparison, see Rot Abbey's longer oath formula in HOLENSTEIN, Äbte und Bauern, pp. 245–246.

54 The 1476 statute's description of *Hintersassen* as "alle und yegclich manns personen, so In siner gnauden Gericht Zwinng und Bann geseßn sind" contains no indication that such persons lacked membership rights in the commune, though this was a common definition of *Hintersassen* elsewhere; cf. Bierbrauer, Ländliche Gemeinde, p. 179.

several common elements. The oath taken by a *Hintersass*, the inhabitant who was neither serf nor tenant, read as follows:

> The *Hintersass* shall swear an oath to God and the saints to be obedient to commands and prohibitions, and to do everything a *Hintersass* is responsible to do for his lord, without infringement on the rights of his legal *Halßherr* with regard to servility and jurisdiction. If he has an issue or claim against my gracious lord and his gracious convent, their common people, inhabitants, or affiliates, no matter what the subject and as far as it occurred inside the abbey's jurisdiction, then he shall take his concern nowhere else than before the proper judge—that is, spiritual matters to the ecclesiastical courts and worldly matters to my gracious lord's tribunal of 15, faithfully and without harm.[55]

The oath taken by the abbey's serfs went like this:

> The *Aigenman* shall swear an oath to God and the saints to be the legal bondsman of my gracious lord and his gracious abbey of Salmansweiler, neither to alienate his body, property, or possessions from them, nor to accept any other lord or protection in any way. In addition, every serf will be obedient to commands and prohibitions as required by his lord. And if he has an issue or claim against my gracious lord or another lord of the convent, its serfs, or other inhabitants, whatever it may be, then he shall not take his claims anywhere else besides the proper judge in spiritual matters, or my gracious lord's tribunal in worldly matters, that is, the 15 of the Sidelgericht, faithfully and without harm.[56]

The brevity of these texts emphasizes the centrality of key elements. Jurisdictional rights received primary emphasis in both versions, with regard to obeying the lord's commands and prohibitions (*gebot und verbot*) as well as settling all disputes before the

---

55 "So wirdet der hindersaeß schweren, ainen ayd zu gott unnd den hailign, gebotten unnd verbotten gehorsam zů sin, und alles das zuthun, das ain hindersäß sinem herren schuldig ist, Doch allweg sinem rechten halßherren an siner Lybaigennschafft unnd gerechtigkait on schaden. Unnd was ouch ainer zu minem gnedigen herren, siner gnaden Convent herren, oder armen leuten, hindersaessen unnd zugewanndtn zusprechen hett, oder gewonne, Warumb das, unnd das sich dweil er Inn dess gotzhws gerichten Seßhafft gewesen were, gemacht unnd verloffen hett, Sol er sy nit wyther furnemen, noch beckhumbern, dann die gaistlichen vor Irem ordennlichen richter, unnd die weltlichen vor mins gl. herren stab, als vor den funfftzehnen getrulich unnd ongevarlich." GLAK, 98/1547, fol. 23v–24r.

56 "Der aigenman wirdt schweren, ainen aid zu got unnd den hailigen, mins gnedigen herren von Salmenschwyler unnd siner gnaden gotzhws, Recht aigen zu sin, sin lyb, hab unnd gut, dem selben minem gnedigen herren, unnd siner gnaden gotzhws, nit zu entpfrömden, noch dhain anndern herren, noch schirm, an sich nemen, dhains wegs, Sonnderbar Auch gepotth unnd verbotten gehorsam zu sin, Wie dann ain yeder aigenman sinem herren pflichtig und schuldig ist, Und was ainer zu minem gnedigen herren von Salmenschwyler, oder anndern siner gnaden Convent herren ald zu dess Gotzhws aigenleuten unnd hindersässen zu sprechen hette oder gewunne Warumb das were, Das er sy nit wyther furnemen noch beckhumbern soll, Dann die gaistlichen vor Ierem ordennlichen richter unnd die weltlichen Vor mins gnedigen herren Stab, als vor den funfftzehnen dess Sidelgerichts, getrulichen unnd ongevarlich." GLAK, 98/1547, fol. 23r–23v.

abbey's court. Clearly, the abbey claimed jurisdictional rights over *Hintersassen* just as over other territorial dependents. *Hintersassen* were free from any demands that would interfere with the rights of their *Halßherren*—this was most likely a reference to other lords' serfs and possibly to Heiligenberg's high justice.[57] By contrast, abbey serfs swore not to alienate themselves or seek outside protection. In addition to these clauses were references to less specific responsibilities. Common to both texts was the general promise to obediently perform any duties required from persons of their status. This can be seen as an insurance clause, covering other demands not specified in the oath.[58] Thus, the oath could potentially support novel requirements or the reinstatement of duties that had fallen into disuse.

Abbey dependents in the outlying districts also swore the Huldigung to Salem's abbot. There, too, abbey dependents swore either as serfs or as residents of the jurisdiction. Only slight differences in these formulas distinguished them from those of the two central districts. First, reference to "the abbey's court of 15" was changed to "the court in which they sit, and to which they lawfully belong."[59] Second, the oaths for outlying areas elaborated on the prohibition against the use of outside courts: "Moreover, they shall not take issues or claims before any other or foreign court."[60] Third, these oaths sometimes specified obedience to a particular district official of the abbey.

Many peasants belonged as serfs, tenants, and jurisdictional residents to more than one lord, so it was common for individuals to swear loyalty to several different authorities. This frequently led to disputes between neighboring rulers, since the promise to follow multiple lords' commands and perform certain duties for each of them involved conflicting claims and loyalties. The oaths taken by inhabitants of Salem's central territory and in other districts were related in particular to the struggle against Heiligenberg.[61] The importance of the oath for maintaining the lord's claims against outsiders

---

57 A *Halsherr* was a lord over life and limb (*Herr über Leib und Leben*). Alfred GÖTZE, Frühneuhochdeutsches Glossar, 7th ed., Berlin 1967, p. 114.

58 For example, the oath said nothing about marriage prohibitions. However, the clause stating that a serf should do whatever the lord required could certainly be used to reinforce this and other rules found in territorial statutes.

59 "In den gerichten, darin er gesessen, unnd dahin er zuo recht gehörig ist." GLAK, 98/1547, fol. 25v–26r. Some formulas stated both alternatives: they must use either the court of 15 or the court in which they sit.

60 "Unnd sy sunst, mit dhainen anndern, noch frömbden gerichten, nit wyther fürnemen noch beckhumbern sollen." Ibid., fol. 26r.

61 In 1502 the count of Heiligenberg opposed the oath Salem demanded from its tenants residing in the district Over the Hills, and the abbot invited the count or his officials to attend the ceremony to see for himself that the oath did not infringe on his rights. In 1509 the count of Heiligenberg brought legal suit against Salem, in part because of the oath requiring all abbey dependents to settle their differences before the abbey's court. The abbot defended the oath as ancient custom, supported by the royal privilege of 1354. The arbitrators upheld the abbey's oath, so long as Salem did not intend to claim high justice. GLAK, 67/1431.

suggests that oaths functioned not only to instill obedience in subjects. They also delineated or extended the lord's claims with respect to neighboring authorities. This function best explains why the majority of Salem's surviving oath formulas are from the outlying districts, because Salem was especially concerned with maintaining and documenting its rights in areas of overlapping authority where the abbey's rights were most tenuous.

The enormous volume of Huldigungen contains many copies of the oath formulas, some dated and others not. They allow us to look for changes in the wording and meaning of the texts in order to discover developments in the territorial "constitution," or the understanding of territorial lordship as formed through the ritual communication between an abbot and his peasants. One later addition was a clause requiring serfs and *Hintersassen* "to promote the lord's interests, to warn and protect against harm and dishonor."[62] This particular phrase, however, described such a basic element of loyalty and was so general that it did not represent any additional burden or provoke objections.[63] In fact, none of the versions of the two oath formulas from before the Thirty Years War contain any significant alterations in meaning or content. The major difference was the addition of a third, separate text.

In the earliest Huldigung texts there was no oath formula specific to tenants, though an early version does mention them in a margin note: "All those in possession of abbey tenures should receive the property for a period of time according to the terms of the tenure contract."[64] Only hereditary and lifelong leases, however, were normally subject to tenure contracts. The more numerous annual tenures resulted in no written agreements, long-term guarantees, or apparently, oath-taking. In later versions of the Huldigung, from Ehingen in 1546 and in the central territory by at least 1576, an oath formula for tenants with short-term leases appeared below those for serfs and jurisdictional residents.[65] The tenants' oath formula of 1576 went as follows:

> You who hold property from the abbey as *Hand-* or *Schüpflehen* will likewise swear, in the same way and form, that in the future you will give up your property every year, free and unencumbered by word or deed, according to the contents of the Jarbrief and the order of our gracious

62 "Alle zeit Iren nutz zufurdern, schaden und unehr zu warnen und zewenden." GLAK, 98/1547, fol. 27r–27v. This clause is not found in an earlier set of oaths (fol. 23v–24r).

63 Holenstein describes this phrase as both conventional and ubiquitous, a sign of the common underlying structure of lordship and shared understanding of its basic values and categories. Idem, Huldigung, pp. 278–279.

64 "Item alle die so lehengueter vom Gotzhus besitzen, sollen dieselben gueter lut der Lehen brieven zue Zytlicherweil empfahen." GLAK, 98/1547, fol. 32v, 1537.

65 Other versions of the tenants' oath are undated and were perhaps written before 1576. It is significant that the earliest dated oath formula for tenants comes from outside the central territory, because there it was the basis for claiming loyalty from those who were not abbey serfs or residents of its jurisdiction. In this way the oath helped extend political authority at the expense of neighboring rulers.

> lord or whoever speaks on the abbey's behalf. Whoever receives a renewal of his lease will occupy it, use and enjoy it in his own person. He will also work at all times honorably and according to the set schedule, make no material changes, handle and manage everything faithfully and without harm.[66]

Preambles to the oath formulas used by Abbots Peter II in 1595 and Thomas I in 1615 mention slight "improvements."[67] Yet a careful comparison of the oaths sworn by serfs and *Hintersassen* in these years reveals no changes in meaning. The two major oath formulas in 1615 were identical in content to those sworn in 1537. There were some additions to the tenants' oath, however. It was expanded after 1576 to cover not only single-year leases but also lifelong and hereditary leases. What was new about these additions was not the tenure conditions, which were clearly specified in general statutes as well as individual tenure contracts, but the requirement that they swear an oath alongside other territorial dependents at a general assembly. In other words, a minor change in the text reflected a more significant change in the performance and understanding of the oath. It integrated tenants into the territorial community and established their status as territorial subjects on the basis of landholding. The most significant changes over time were found not in the text of the Huldigung but in the context of its performance.[68] Three modifications to the performance of the oath highlight the sociopolitical context of the Huldigung in Salem as a form of personal allegiance enacted together with other subjects. These changes involved the location of the performance, the act of gift-giving, and the reciprocal promises made by the abbot.

One type of document found in Salem's Huldigung collection describes the itinerary for the abbot's riding circuit *(Umritt)* throughout his lands to receive the oath.[69] These documents list the times and places of villagers' assemblies as the abbot rode

---

66 "So werden Ir, die vom Gotßhauß mit handt oder Schupff Lehen belechnet seind, gleicher maß und gestalt schweren das Ir hinfüro gemeinlich Und sonderlich, alle Jar Järlichen nach laut unnd Innhalt deß Jarbrieffs Ewere gueter Alß Schupflehen, obgemeltem unserm gnedigen herrn oder wer deßhalb yeder zeyt von deß Gotßhauß wegen bevelch haben würdet, frey ledigclich von Mund unnd hand, wie sich solchs zethun gepürt Auffgeben, Und welchem die Widerumb Verlihen werden, Das der die in selbs Aigner Person besitzen nutzen unnd nießen, Auch yeder zeyt in gueten Ehren unnd rechten Zeit bewen, Wesenlich unnd in Allweg unverendert Innhaben, halten und Werben sollen und wöllen, Alles getrewlich und one geverde." GLAK, 98/1547, fol. 48r.

67 According to the dossier's title page, the oath formula for 1595 was recorded *"in verbesserter formb"* and in 1615 it was *"noch in vermehrt und Gebesserter formb."* GLAK, 98/1547, fol. 1v, 3v.

68 On the performance aspect of legal texts and their meaning in the context of public rituals, see Jeanette RAUSCHERT, Gelöchert und befleckt: Inszenierung und Gebrauch städtischer Rextstexte und spätmittelalterlicher Öffentlichkeit, in: Text als Realie, ed. Karl Brunner and Gerhard Jaritz, Vienna 2003; ALGAZI, Lords Ask, Peasants Answer; PROSSER, Rechtsaufzeichnungen, p. 190.

69 GLAK, 98/1547, fol. 44r–v (1576), fol. 64r–68v (1584), fol. 76r–77r (1590), fol. 89v–96r (1595), and fol. 41r–v (undated but presumably before 1576).

ceremoniously from place to place accompanied by his counselors.[70] Such itineraries are available for 1576, 1584, 1590, and 1595. They include one to three performances per day, occasionally scheduled as early as six o'clock AM.[71] The abbot did not visit every village. Instead, subjects from several neighboring villages or an entire district assembled in some central or convenient location.[72] The Huldigung took place at specific locations symbolic of the abbey's lordship in the community: "in front of the inn," "before the Amtmann's house," "by the abbey's granary," "at the wine press," "inside the administrative residence," or "in the great hall." Altogether, the abbot's rounds took seven to ten days to complete but were stretched out over a longer period.[73]

After the peasants swore their oaths, the abbot typically distributed wine or cash for buying drinks. Toasting to the new abbot raised the level of festivity and was in addition an important memory aid; the celebratory atmosphere and sociability following a new abbot's first visit could be recalled years later.[74] The ritual of the new lord providing drinks served multiple purposes. First, it emphasized the reciprocal nature of the oath. Second, the drink symbolically acknowledged the lord's authority and sealed the act as a form of contract.[75] Finally, the lord's gift was a token of his generosity and benevolence that could be emphasized more or less depending on time and location.[76] In 1576 Abbot Matthäus gave one or two gulden to each group of assembled peasants, barely enough to cover drinks.[77] In 1584 the abbot's gifts of cash and wine were of

---

70 In 1595 Abbot Peter was accompanied by the prior and two other monks, one professional notary, two witnesses, and a secretary. GLAK, 98/1547, fol. 85r.

71 In 1576 Abbot Matthäus arrived in Tüfingen at 6:00 AM, Nußdorf at 8:00 AM, and Oberuhldingen at 1:00 PM. The tight spacing of his schedule suggests the ceremony's brief duration. GLAK, 98/1547, fol. 44r–v.

72 In 1576 and 1584 the oath was sworn in Pfaffenhofen, Tüfingen, Nußdorf, Neufrach, Bermatingen, and Oberuhldingen (and in other places outside the central territory). Subjects assembled at each location from the surrounding villages. GLAK, 98/1547, fol. 44r, 64r.

73 In 1584 the schedule was as follows: 27 June Tüfingen, Pfaffenhofen, and Nußdorf; 28 June Neufrach; 7 July Schemmerberg; 10 July Unterelchingen; 13 July Ehingen; 29 August Bermatingen; 30 August Oberuhldingen; 4 September Rotenbuhel and Ostrach; 8 September Bachhaupten; 29 October Madach. GLAK, 98/1547, fol. 64r–68v.

74 Unlike other types of oaths, the oath to a new abbot was an irregular act that might not be repeated for decades, so memory rituals were extremely important, as they were for *Weisungen* centuries earlier. ALGAZI, Lords Ask, Peasants Answer, p. 213; PROSSER, Rechtsaufzeichnungen, p. 63.

75 Drinks were used to seal many other types of contracts such as sales or employment agreements, marriages, forgiveness of offenses against the community, and the acceptance of new residents. See Ann B. TLUSTY, Bacchus and Civic Order: The Culture of Drink in Early Modern Germany, Charlottesville 2001, chap. 6.

76 HOLENSTEIN, Huldigung, p. 467.

77 GLAK, 98/1547, fol. 41r–v. Forty subjects in Ehingen received 1 fl.; seventy subjects in Unterelchingen received 2 fl.; 120 subjects from Schemmerberg, Altheim, and Äpfingen received a total of 4 fl.; eight subjects in Jungingen received six batzen. The list does not mention any places in the central territory.

somewhat greater value.[78] Also noted in 1584 were gifts to the abbot from the outlying districts of Unterelchingen and Schemmerberg: a suckling calf and a cup worth 27 fl. In 1595 the value of the abbot's gifts to subjects in the outlying districts (but not those of the central territory) rose tremendously and for no specified reason.[79] This differential makes it appear as though the abbot hoped to buy the loyalty of certain dependents in 1595 by throwing them a good party and making a strong impression. The amount spent on the ceremony and specifically on drinks in different locations over time supports the hypothesis that the oath was part of a larger strategy of territorialization in areas where the abbey's authority was relatively weak and in a period when competition with external authorities had reached a critical point.[80]

A major change in venue followed the election of Abbot Thomas I in 1615. For the first time, instead of riding a circuit to receive the oath, the abbot required all the subjects Over and Under the Hills to attend a ceremony at the abbey. This change in location shifted the renewal of vows from the peasants' turf to their lord's home court. It emphasized the central authority of the abbot instead of his relationship to the various local communities. In addition, it permitted the entire convent to attend. This allowed for much greater ceremonial, not only because the abbey provided a backdrop for the fanfare, but also because the event brought together all the subjects from a much larger area.[81] To add to the splendor and festivity of the occasion, the territorial militia assembled for review.[82]

In return for the allegiance sworn by his subjects in 1615, Abbot Thomas offered a reciprocal promise to respect the traditions of the abbey and its subjects. According to the text, he proclaimed:

> In return, your grace has offered not only to abide by your good, old, and reasonable rights, privileges, customs, practices, and traditions, but also to act as a true father and ruler. In addition and no less, he will faithfully protect and execute the imperial and royal privileges, free-

78 GLAK, 98/1547, fol. 64r–68v. Subjects in Tüfingen received 2 fl., Pfaffenhofen 3 fl., Nußdorf 1½ fl., Neufrach 12 Eimer of wine, Bermatingen 10 Eimer of wine, Oberuhldingen 4 fl., Schemmerberg 4 fl., Unterelchingen 8 fl., and Ostrach 6 fl.

79 The highest payments included 35 fl. to Ostrach, 30 fl. to Schemmerberg, and 15 fl. to Unterelchingen. By contrast, gifts given to subjects in the central territory declined. Neufrach received 15 Viertel (quarters of an Eimer), Bermatingen 10 Viertel, Maurach 9, Pfaffenhofen 5, and Tüfingen 2 Viertel of wine. Compared with 1584, the amount given to some communities declined four-fold. GLAK, 98/1547, 1595, fol. 89v–96r.

80 It was in or around 1595 that Salem and Heiligenberg entered a legal suit before the Imperial Chamber Court in Speyer.

81 The oath continued to be performed at the abbey into the eighteenth century. A diagram from 1737 shows the careful attention paid by abbey administrators to the importance of space, designating where various groups should stand at an oath-taking ceremony in the garden. GLAK, 98/1547, fol. 522r. A picture showing the spatial arrangements at a ceremony from Neuenburg in 1786 is reproduced in HOLENSTEIN, Huldigung, p. 279.

82 GLAK, 98/1547, fol. 493r.

doms, and judicial exemptions, which past Roman emperors and kings who are up in heaven have generously granted and bestowed with special mercy to the abbey of Salmansweiler and its subjects and dependents for many centuries, and which will now be clearly read to you. Finally, he will act in accordance with all that has been customary since ancient times.[83]

This pledge may not have been new, for similar promises were made by the rulers of other territories in this period.[84] The text from 1615 is, however, the earliest surviving record of such an agreement in Salem. Its timing is especially important, because it was written in the context of the first ceremony held at the abbey rather than in the various local communities. The ceremonial location symbolized the centralization of rule, yet the addition of the abbot's reciprocal promise to respect his subjects' rights and customs warns against our interpretation of this ceremony as a step toward absolutism. Further evidence of the new text's significance is its continuing use into the eighteenth century.[85]

Oaths were extremely beneficial in a period when official enforcement measures were weak or lacking, because they promoted self-regulation and the internalization of behavioral norms.[86] Subjects were obedient to the lord's commands not only because they were compelled, but more importantly, because they swore before God that they would. Oaths were especially effective because they called upon religious belief, conscience, and anxiety about the afterlife. Oath-takers were frequently reminded of the serious consequences of perjury. Even the hand gesture had symbolic meaning: three raised fingers represented the holy trinity, while the bent thumb and little finger signified the subordination of body and soul before God.[87]

Peasants occasionally used the oath (or their rejection of it) to support their own interpretations of lordship. As we have seen, Salem's peasant judges renounced their oath of office in 1468 and walked out after detecting alleged innovations, an act of protest with long-term significance for territorial rule. During the German Peasants' War, rebel leaders including the Amtmann of Bermatingen required Salem's monks to swear a loyalty oath to them, initiating a legal and symbolic relationship in which the

---

83 "Dargegen dan Ihre Gl.: Erbüetig seind Eüch bey Ewern guoten allten vernunfftigen Rechten, gerechtigkaiten, gewohnhaiten, breüchen und herkommen, nit allein verbleiben zuolaßen, sonder auch allß ain getrewer vater unnd Oberkaitsherr, dabey sowol unnd nit wenniger auch bey den Kay: unnd Kön: Privilegien, Freyhaiten und gerichtß Excemtionen, dem Gottßhauß Salmansw: auch deßen underthonnen unnd zuo gewandten vor vil 100 Jahren, von den In Gott ruohenden römischen Kayßern unnd Königen miltig zuo sondern gnaden unnd guothaten, erthailt und gegeben so man Eüch Jezten verstendtlich verlesen würdet, würkhlich zuoschutzen unnd handtzuohaben, unnd alleß daß zuo laisten waß deßwegen von Alterß herkommen unnd gebreuchlich gewesst Ist." GLAK, 98/1547, fol. 160v.

84 HOLENSTEIN, Äbte und Bauern, p. 244.

85 There are at least three later copies of the 1615 formula, which was adopted in identical wording by Abbot Emanuel Sulger in 1680. GLAK, 98/1547, fol. 488, 490, and 494–495.

86 HOLENSTEIN, Huldigung, p. 248.

87 HOLENSTEIN, Seelenheil, p. 34.

peasants became, in a sense, the lords. Only in extreme cases was it necessary for subjects to oppose their lords with force, because a refusal of the oath dissolved the bonds between them just as effectively. Without the oath, the lord was unable to command obedience. The oath therefore gave subjects a certain degree of power within lordship. Each time a lord asked them to swear an oath, they were in a position to withhold it until their own demands were met.

If we interpret political developments in Salem on the basis of modifications to the oath, then we must conclude that the abbey's leaders were attempting to strengthen territorial identity among various groups of dependents, among them tenants and especially the residents of outlying districts where Salem's claims were tenuous. At the same time, the abbots made an effort to show respect for subjects' customs by retaining the oath in its original form and making reciprocal promises in return. Abbots displayed generosity by distributing gifts, especially to those least dependent on the abbey. The oath's development demonstrates the territorialization of authority, not over peasants but with peasants.

6.3 Legislative Authority

Two legal codes, by now familiar to the reader, formed the basis of Salem's political life and legal development during the long sixteenth century. The first was the alte Jarbrief, a customary law code of allegedly ancient origin that became the center of controversy during the Sidelrichter dispute starting in 1468. The second, the partnership agreement of 1473 (*der neue Bericht*), was the result of that dispute's arbitration. As mentioned in Chapter 3, it is in some ways surprising that the alte Jarbrief remained valid in the early modern period. After all, the Sidelrichter accused the abbot and his administrators of inserting innovative phrases and articles into a recently revised version of the text, and the settlement in 1473 modified and even nullified some of its provisions after five years of resistance. Yet over the course of the sixteenth century, the alte Jarbrief was reissued and introduced in several outlying districts where Salem acquired low justice, sometimes with supplemental articles thrown in.[88] During the same period, no new law codes, statutes, or ordinances appear to have been introduced on a general level in the central territory. This section seeks to provide an explanation of why this was so.

Although the alte Jarbrief contained specific provisions favorable to lordship, its customary nature also lent certain benefits to subjects in the central territory, especially over the long term. The continuing use of the alte Jarbrief supported the idea that old law and custom were the foundations of legal and political relations, that old law takes precedent over new, and that law which is found takes precedent over that which is created. Preference for the older law could serve in principle to hinder rulers' abilities

88 GLAK, 98/1546.

to create, determine, and interpret the law.[89] In fact, both documents provided specific guarantees for the continuing participation of peasant subjects in political development. First, they recognized the Sidelrichter as the people's representatives, whose consent was a fundamental requirement of all new legislation.[90] Second, they confirmed the Sidelgericht as the abbey's central court, guaranteeing that territorial justice would continue to be administered and interpreted by common subjects. Thus, both legal texts set a precedent for the community's active role in territorial law and justice.

The continuing influence of the territory's twin legal codes in the sixteenth century and beyond is readily apparent in sources such as the judges' oath formulas and the copiaries. In these collections of the abbey's most important legal documents, copies of the two texts appear sometimes on their own and elsewhere as an introduction to later ordinances.[91] In more than one example, an intermediate title between the alte Jarbrief and the newer articles states: "So much from the alte Jarbrief. The following commands and prohibitions have been composed and added to the foregoing from year to year according to occasion and necessity."[92] The preservation of the two foundational documents in multiple copies as well as continuing references to them in later centuries are strong signs of their enduring importance. Furthermore, keeping and referencing these texts was beneficial not only to the abbey or as symbolic reminders merely of the lord's authority. In 1572 the Sidelrichter asked Abbot Georg II to confirm the 1473 agreement and provide them with a new copy, since the seals on their original

89 Custom was not necessarily as old or rigid as might be assumed, however, nor was custom always aligned with subjects' interests against innovations that promoted lords' agendas. Simon Teuscher demonstrates that custom was a rhetorical tool in lords' arsenal of domination and territorialization during the later Middle Ages. In fact, appeals to custom were used as a legitimation strategy by various groups including peasants and lords, and custom provided cover for gradual change. The importance of custom for Salem's peasants in this case was that it supported their opposition to the lord's unilateral imposition of new demands. Peasants were not necessarily resistant to change, but as seen in Chapter 2, they rejected the idea that the abbot was the source of law.

90 The alte Jarbrief's preamble made this clear by stating the participation of the Sidelrichter in its creation. The settlement in 1473 required the consent of the Thirty (territorial subjects) prior to the enactment of any new legal codes or changes to the existing ones.

91 GLAK, 67/1429, 67/1431, 67/1478, 67/1782.

92 For example, "Sovil aus dem alten Jarbrieff. Volgendte bott und Verbott sind hernach von Jar zue jar nach gelegenhait jederzeit und ervorderung der noth aufgesetzt und den vorgehenden zuegethon worden." GLAK, 4/116, 1558, fol. 6r. Other ordinances refer to the 1473 agreement in similar fashion. In the 1476 statute, the participation of the Thirty in drafting the articles is specifically mentioned: "So volgend hernach die artickel die in verschinen Jaren, durch wilendt ainem herrn und abbt zu Salmanschwyler mit sampt synen gaistlichen amptt Luttn ouch domals den dryssigen namlich funffzechnn des sydelgerichtz und funffzechnn von den gemaindenn innhaltt des nuwenn berichts." See GLAK, 67/1478, fol. 13–14, 49, 51.

had been damaged.[93] The replacement document, produced 99 years after the treaty's creation, is proof of the text's continuing validity and its significance to the Sidelrichter who requested it.

Yet the alte Jarbrief and the partnership agreement did not address all types of behavior and could not inhibit the further development and elaboration of territorial law. Serfdom and the loyalty oath were among the topics of two agreements concluded soon after the partnership agreement, in 1476 and in 1486. These agreements, introduced in Chapter 3, clearly resulted from continuing disagreement over issues that remained ambiguous or unresolved after 1473. They are of special interest here because no general law codes have survived from the central territory for the remainder of our period and because these agreements are the last known references to statutory law involving the participation of the Thirty.

The agreements of 1476 and 1486 each consisted of four articles, with similarities in structure and content. Both documents began by listing the parties involved, including the top abbey administrators and the Thirty territorial representatives. The inclusion of the Thirty served to legitimate the agreements. It also reinforced the declaration in 1473 that all new legislation required consent. In both texts, the first article concerned the oath.[94] Both agreements also made specific reference to the alte Jarbrief and the neue Bericht, and both addressed questions arising from differences between them.[95] The underlying message was that where the two codes conflicted, the newer law should be followed.[96] Thus, they cemented the position of the partnership agreement and resurrected the alte Jarbrief as the twin pillars for future legal development. They treated the recent settlement as a supplement to the alte Jarbrief and not as its replacement.

For the outlying districts, abbey officials produced several new general ordinances during the long sixteenth century. But none of them, even documents bearing titles such as "Salem General Ordinance" or "Police Ordinances for the Subjects of Salem

---

93 GLAK, 4/135–136, 2 February 1572. Their concern with the decaying seals demonstrates that the peasant judges viewed the physical condition of the document as relevant to its validity, as Rauschert argues (Gelöchert und befleckt, pp. 163–164). The document's worn condition may also indicate its value as a physical document that was continually displayed and used rather than safely locked away.

94 The agreement of 1476 concerned the political duties and capabilities of male subjects: to swear the loyalty oath, command the peace, evaluate tenure disputes, and certify payments in kind. In 1486 the common theme was control over female serfs and their property—through the loyalty oath, heriot, and restrictions on widows' ability to remarry or alienate property.

95 At issue in 1476 were the terms of annual leasehold, and in 1486, the heriot tax owed by female serfs.

96 The gradual displacement of the old law by the new opened the door to legislative development, which could be detrimental to subjects to the extent that rulers monopolized legislative power and used it against subjects' interests. As previously noted, old custom was viewed in positive terms by lords as well as peasants and used by various groups as a rhetorical strategy. See, for example, the Mimmenhausen grazing dispute in 1603, described in Chapter 3.

Abbey," applied to the villages Under the Hills.[97] Many of the articles in these newer ordinances were based on earlier law codes; some followed the older provisions verbatim, down to the penalty amount. The various law codes were not, however, identical in organization or wording. Indeed, many of them lack any apparent topical arrangement, confirming the statements of some preambles that newer articles had been added over time as necessary. Sometimes articles were repeated even within a single document, giving the impression that it had been composed either by joining various law codes together without removing duplicate material or by jotting down articles in random order.[98]

It is tempting to assume that later ordinances from outlying districts were also valid in the central territory, especially since they address new areas of behavior and give greater detail.[99] This assumption, however, would be risky and careless. The early modern ordinances from Salem's outlying districts may or may not have had more general application, and they may or may not have been based on customs of the central territory such as the alte Jarbrief. The puzzle to be solved is, why are there no surviving legal codes of a general nature for the central territory during the long sixteenth century and what relationship, if any, existed between the written and unwritten laws of Salem's various districts?

One possibility is that early modern ordinances from the central districts were lost or destroyed. Yet it seems highly unlikely that ordinances would have survived only from other places, sometimes in multiple copies, and not from Salem's central territory—the largest, oldest, most profitable, best consolidated, and least contested of its rural districts. Besides, sixteenth-century sources such as the Sidelrichter oath formulas make no mention of newer laws. A similarly improbable hypothesis is that law in the central district remained essentially bound by custom to the two older law codes. It is certainly possible that no new general ordinances were recorded, but doubtful that there was no further legal development to address the major changes in the economy, population, social structure, and political organization that took place between 1473 and 1637.

---

97 The specificity of an ordinance to a particular district is revealed by references to specific places (imprisonment in Madach, or delivery of rent to Pfullendorf) and to outlying district officials (the Vogt of Mainwangen or the Oberamtmann of Ostrach), in titles stating the district of origin, and in introductory statements such as "this ordinance was written by Veitt Michel, Salem's Kaufmann in Ostrach." Examples include GLAK, 98/396 (1625 *Polizeiordnung*, from the Hegau), 4/368 (1500 *Weisthum*, Over the Hills), 4/116 (1558 *Gemeinden Statuten*, Over the Hills), and 65/11324 (1558 *Gebot und Verbot*, with oath formulas, Over the Hills).

98 This lack of organizational strategy was common in territorial ordinances of the time, as was the repetitiveness, according to Marc RAEFF, The Well-Ordered Police State: Social and Institutional Change through Law in the Germanies and Russia, 1600–1800, New Haven 1983, p. 49.

99 For example, the older law codes say nothing about morality and church attendance, drinking and swearing, forest ordinances, fire safety, village assemblies, rent collection, and so on.

There was simply too much development during this period for the old laws to have remained intact. Besides, the sixteenth century was precisely the period when the explosion of general ordinances and "*gute Policey*" began in other territories.[100]

This leads to a third possibility, that law evolved in the central territory without formal codification, whereas administrators in the outlying districts were compelled to record legal statutes. There are several plausible reasons why this might have been so. First, codifications and written records often reflect novel or unusual circumstances, especially in the early stages.[101] In a climate of hostility to innovation, lords risked popular resistance to new written laws; law codes were not, therefore, introduced without due cause and consideration. There was little reason to write down customary rules that had been in use for generations unless new conditions called for it. In the outlying districts, unlike the central territory, the abbey had no ancient legal tradition to fall back on and no written law codes. Whereas the abbey's early imperial and papal privileges recognized its older rights and properties, often listing them by name, the newly formed districts in places like Pfullendorf and Schemmerberg lacked such specific protections. Hence the need to establish written precedent. In such places, new law codes were especially useful for asserting and expanding claims against competing territorial powers.[102]

Irmtraut Eder has suggested that legislation often resulted from competition between lords rather than conflict between a lord and his peasants.[103] According to Eder, even medieval customals (Weistümer, usually assumed to reflect some point of intersection between communal and lordly interests) should be seen in the context of one lord's claims against another. Salem's careful preservation of numerous legal codes, in precisely those areas where authority was weak and prone to conflict because of overlapping claims, indicates that new legislation was a strategy specific to the regional

---

100 *Gute Policey* is a political concept founded in the early modern period. It refers to rulers' attempts to promote right social order and the common welfare by setting policies concerned with the everyday aspects of moral, economic, and social behavior. It has become a major field of research in recent years, and some see it as a new paradigm for understanding the early modern period. A good overview is provided by Andrea ISELI, Gute Policey: Öffentliche Ordnung in der Frühen Neuzeit, Stuttgart 2009. See also the extensive documentation of ordinances from this period in the ongoing project of the Max-Plank-Institut started under Karl HÄRTER and Michael STOLLEIS, eds., Repertorium der Policeyordnungen der frühen Neuzeit, Frankfurt 1996 (with ten published volumes by region as of 2010).

101 André Holenstein makes this point with respect to oath formulas, but it also holds true for other legal documents. Idem, Huldigung, pp. 222–223.

102 In this context, Simon Teuscher's comments about the territorialization of rights and the late medieval invention of custom through "oralization" are especially useful. Idem, Textualising Peasant Enquiries, pp. 239–251.

103 Irmtraut EDER, Weistümer als Dokumente der Territorialpolitik, in: Deutsche ländliche Rechtsquellen: Probleme und Wege der Weistumsforschung, ed. Peter Blickle, Stuttgart 1977, pp. 142–196. This argument is further developed by TEUSCHER, Erzähltes Recht; idem, Textualising Peasant Enquiries, esp. pp. 241, 245, 249.

situation. One reason for the lack of early modern legislation in the central territory may have been, therefore, that it was unnecessary because Salem's authority there was relatively secure.

Still, external pressures provide only half the explanation. We have already seen in Chapter 2 how new laws could provoke opposition among subjects and how internal conflicts could lead to new legal settlements. Either way, the lord could not legislate without notice and the enforcement of new legal codes could not proceed without consent. For a small ecclesiastical polity such as Salem, the question of why there were no general ordinances in a period of statebuilding may impose false assumptions or at least approach the issue from the wrong angle. Instead, we might ask: what incentives were there for the abbot to impose new laws? To this we may postulate that territorial custom, the Sidelgericht, the partnership agreement, the potential for opposition and the threat of revolt, and above all, the political organization of the village communes presented major disincentives. The abbot's failure to consult the Thirty and the lack of a territorial assembly (*Landschaft*) can be interpreted as a defeat for the territorial community and the principle of consent. Yet the evidence, or the lack of it anyway, confirms one of Karl Siegfried Bader's major findings: the local communes were largely left to regulate their own internal affairs and make their own decisions. The abbey was mainly concerned with its economic interests and legal privileges, not controlling the everyday lives and behavior of its peasants.

One way the abbot expressed his will was to address orders to his officials rather than his subjects. Abbots and other senior officials spelled out their expectations of the Amtmänner through several sets of detailed instructions between 1578 and 1599.[104] In many ways, it was easier to call all the lord's local stewards together in one room and emphasize to them the importance of their duties and the information they needed to provide. These face-to-face instructions, followed up with regular inquiries, put pressure on those individuals who had the greatest local influence and access to knowledge. Though this strategy was certainly less ambitious and had less symbolic value than declarations of new policy addressed directly to the general body of subjects, it avoided the confrontations this could potentially provoke. The solution was conservative, but effective enough.

New legislation addressed to the collective territorial residents Under the Hills was consequently limited. There were ordinances on many small, specific topics but no large, general law codes. Regulations sometimes resulted from voluntary or arbitrated legal settlements, such as the tax assessments of 1475 and 1496, or they were passed at the local level, such as the Bermatingen tavern ordinance of 1595.[105] Prescriptive

---

104 See Chapter 3; also GLAK, 98/233, 98/395, and 61/13369.

105 GLAK, 4/1139 (1475), 4/365 (1496), 4/1790 (1595). Other local legislation includes a 1585 forest ordinance for Madach, passed in the context of a dispute between Salem and the count of Nellenburg, and a 1596 grazing ordinance for Neufrach, which was ratified by the abbot but drafted

measures such as the abbey's guesthouse ordinance of 1625 and the Wespach hospital ordinance of 1626 did not directly concern abbey subjects and therefore did not require their consent or generate much attention.[106] Specialized ordinances from the mid-sixteenth century prohibited trade with Jews and set penalties for swearing and other blasphemous behavior. [107] Reform measures addressed the duties of Sidelrichter in 1566 and 1576.[108] A new chancery ordinance was proposed at a council meeting in 1624.[109] Directives on some specific topic were stated occasionally in the Audience records, often without any stated legitimation or consultation. Poor laws written in 1573, 1574, and 1623 were not based on common consent, instead citing the abbey's necessity and the common good as justifications.[110] New restrictions on forest use in 1602 referred to previous abuses by subjects and the declining state of the forests.[111] Regulations of inns and especially the wine trade were the subject of ordinances in 1605 and 1616 for the districts Under and Over the Hills.[112] According to communal grievances, the abbey introduced a straw ordinance in 1599 and a manure ordinance in 1626.[113] These examples suggest that the abbot and his administrators increasingly viewed their authority to command and forbid as being free from the principle of consent, especially when the issue of regulation involved the welfare of the abbey and its territory. The lack of general ordinances or declarations of the lord's legislative authority, however, suggest that such developments remained severely limited, in part because the concept of *gute Policey* and the intensive regulations this objective would entail did not correspond to the ruling style or interests of a Cistercian monastery any better than it did to the residents of its tiny territory.[114]

Audience meetings provided opportunities for informal policymaking. Individuals and groups of subjects presented petitions and this assembly of territorial administrators responded, usually by granting or denying favors and dispensations. The needs expressed by subjects sometimes resulted directly or indirectly in new policies. Abbey

by members of the community. GLAK, 98/371, 4/4628, and 4/4544. Wage limits were also set on a local basis—Neufrach and Mühlhofen in 1619, Mimmenhausen in 1594 and 1603. GLAK, 98/3480, 98/492, and 98/4419, fol. 246r–249r.

106 GLAK, 98/1717 and 98/1584.

107 GLAK, 98/597 and 98/1779.

108 See Chapter 5 and GLAK, 67/1782, fol. 34–43.

109 GLAK, 61/13315.

110 See below; GLAK, 98/59.

111 GLAK, 98/374.

112 GLAK, 98/3142.

113 These ordinances are mentioned in response to a petition from Buggensegel and formal grievances by Neufrach. GLAK, 61/13369, 98/3481.

114 Improving crop yields or facilitating rent collection was one thing, but establishing a "system of information and inspection" on the basis of legislation, visitation, denunciation, and many other measures in order to police everyday life in the villages and promote the general welfare (as characterized by eighteenth-century Baden) was quite another.

administrators occasionally used the Audience as a platform for announcing the abbot's decisions and instructions on particular matters. The Audience was a good place to declare official policies, since the meetings were well attended by village headmen. Still, the effectiveness of the lord's commands and prohibitions depended upon their enforcement by leaders in the local communities.[115] Without more formal codification, consent, or some form of legitimation, such policy declarations by the Audience were especially tenuous. Above all, the Audience was an effective institution for promoting communication between the abbey and its subjects. Many historians now recognize that the effectiveness of territorial policy in the early modern period depended much more on the ability to reach out to local communities through channels of communication than on the ability to centralize and monopolize power.[116] New regulations were most effective when they accomodated local circumstances and served the interests of the intended recipients as well as the ruler.[117]

6.4 Verhör: Audience of Petitions

The Audience was a periodic meeting of territorial administrators that assembled primarily to hear and respond to the petitions (requests and complaints) presented by abbey subjects.[118] Salem's Audience minutes (*Verhörprotokolle*) are one of the most revealing source collections for the study of lordship in general and subjects' demands in particular. In fact, the Audience records provide a level of detail and insight about a variety of different topics from villagers' perspective that is hardly imaginable, let alone to be hoped for, in premodern times. The Audience records provide all sorts of information, not only about subjects' most common needs and problems, but also about

115 On laws that were not implemented, see SCHLUMBOHM, Gesetze, pp. 647–663; cf. HOLENSTEIN, Umstände der Normen, pp. 42–44, with emphasis on the social context of selective implementation, a point also made by LANDWEHR, Policey vor Ort, pp. 50–51. On the Amtmann's role as mediator, see Chapter 3.

116 HOLENSTEIN, Gute Policey; BLOCKMANS et al., Empowering Interactions; OGILVIE, The State in Germany, pp. 167–202.

117 LANDWEHR, Policey vor Ort, p. 58.

118 Salem's *Verhör* was not a ruling council (*Rat*) or court (*Gericht*) but an "Audience" where petitions were heard. Records from the 1630s bear the titles *Verhör* and *Audientia* interchangeably, suggesting the English translation chosen here. By petitions, I mean the simple requests and complaints as well as formal grievances brought by individuals and groups for the lord's consideration, not the formal and collective submission of demands more characteristic of the modern period (see FUHRMANN et al., Supplizierende Gemeinden, p. 322 n. 302). These were most often presented orally in Salem. ***Bitten*** and ***klagen*** are the verbs most commonly used in the sources to describe petitioners' statements (as well as ***begehren, berichten, sich beklagen, halten, vorhalten***, and ***vorbringen***, among others). Elsewhere, the term *Verhör* applies to other types of assemblies; for example, Ottobeuren's *Verhör* protocol recorded all actions of the abbot's court. SREENIVASAN, Ottobeuren, p. 316 n. 127.

unusual situations. These records may be profitably approached from many angles, and elsewhere in this study they are used for various purposes: to investigate communal actions and grazing disputes in Chapter 3, tenure and inheritance petitions in Chapter 4, territorial residence and opposition to rents later in this chapter. Here, the focus is on the significance of the Audience for subjects' participation in territorial policy decisions and political development.

Over the past several years there has been a growing interest in the subject of "supplications."[119] The material from Salem differs from that of most other studies in that the requests were typically presented orally rather than in written form, yet the theoretical considerations and great value of such sources, described by Andreas Würgler, apply equally to Salem's Audience records. This collection is especially noteworthy because of its extensiveness and early start date, in 1583. Most research on supplications has concentrated on the eighteenth century.[120]

The Audience records are by far the most extensive serial source in Salem's archive. The volumes run from 1583 to 1802, filling tens of thousands of pages.[121] The Audience customarily met each Thursday or on Wednesdays preceding a holiday.[122] Sessions took place two or three times per month in practice, less during the busy harvest season, for an average of twenty times per year (1583–1640). The number of petitions in a single year ranged from 10 (1593) to 478 (1612), with the decade 1610–1619 providing the highest number of appearances.[123] See Chart 6.1. The Audience continued to

---

[119] Grievances have become a major research area since the 1998 appearance of BLICKLE, ed., Gemeinde und Staat, shortly after that editor's call for more attention to this critical yet understudied element of political and judicial culture in his conclusions to another collaborative work: Peter BLICKLE, ed., Resistance, Representation, and Community, New York 1997, p. 335. For an overview of the recent literature as well as the material's potential applications, see Andreas WÜRGLER, Bitten und Begehren: Suppliken und Gravamina in der deutschsprachigen Frühneuzeitforschung, in: Bittschriften und Gravamina: Politik, Verwaltung und Justiz in Europa (14.–18. Jahrhundert), ed. Cecilia Nubola and Andreas Würgler, Berlin 2005, pp. 17–52.

[120] The term *Supplikation* entered into German administrative texts around 1500, however, and the practice of presenting complaints before the lord was much older. According to Renate Blickle, the Bavarian *Hofrat* was a central governing body established in the mid-fifteenth century as the direct consequence of societal necessity and as a product of internal political development from below. Idem, Supplikationen und Demonstrationen, p. 274; idem, Laufen gen Hof, pp. 263, 265.

[121] GLAK, 61/13369–13488, 1583–1802. In order to gain an overview of the period, I constructed a core sample of all petitions from seven years: 1583, 1589, 1599, 1600, 1611, 1624, and 1630. This sample forms the basis for quantitative analysis, with supporting details provided by a more extensive reading of the years 1584–1588, 1590–1596, 1604–1606, 1613, 1616, 1618–1619, 1629, and 1631–1635.

[122] GLAK, 61/13315, 1602; 61/13374, 1635.

[123] There are records for each year between 1583 and 1640 with the exception of 1588. The only time a session was held at which no one appeared was in 1585. By decade, the average number of petitions heard annually was as follows: 48 in 1583–1589, 86 in 1590–1599, 159 in 1600–1609, 361 in 1610–1619, 278 in 1620–1629, and 202 in 1630–1639.

Chart 6.1: Audience Petitions, 1583–1640

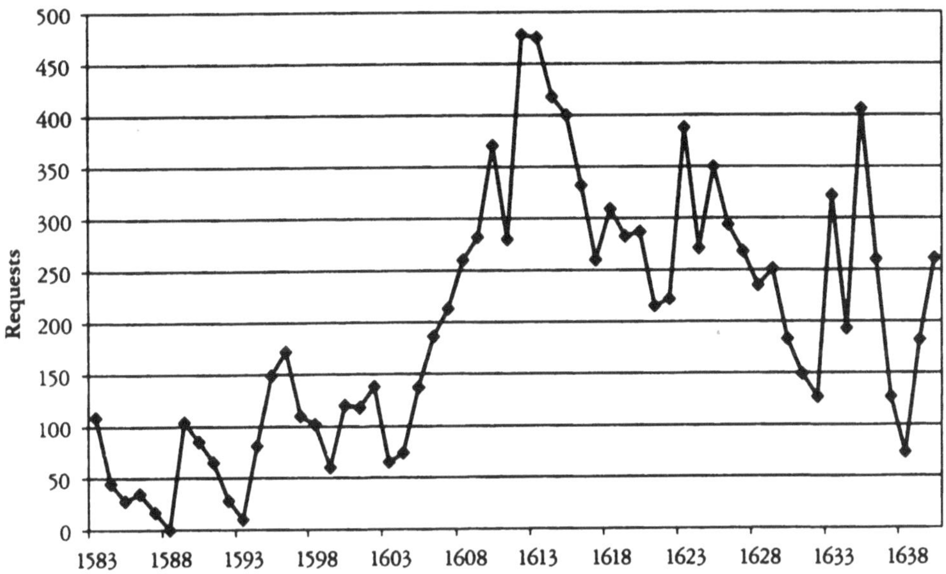

meet with relatively few interruptions even during the Thirty Years War, an indication of the effectiveness, stability, and importance of this institution to the abbey and its subjects.[124] The Audience records demonstrate that the abbey took subjects' petitions very seriously and dedicated enormous resources to having them heard. In fact, considering the hundreds of petitions presented each year, it is hard to comprehend how this group of the abbey's senior administrators found sufficient time to attend to other official business. Audience petitions were a driving force behind territorial policy.[125]

The Audience was composed of a fluctuating group of the abbey's highest monastic and secular officials, listed at the start of each session's minutes beginning in 1617. Between 1617 and 1634, the number of members ranged between two and eleven with an average of six. The most consistent participants in this period were the Pfister, Großkeller, chancellor, Amtmann of Bermatingen, Oberamtmann, bursar, prior, forest supervisor, and Vogt of Maurach (in that order).[126] Their titles or names are listed

124 There are large gaps in the record from the years 1632, 1634, and 1637–1639, corresponding mainly to periods when the entire convent fled to Überlingen or Constance. Punctuating a long period of silence from 1584–1586, the record stated on 29 January 1596 that no one appeared and on 30 October that the Audience had not assembled recently due to plague.

125 Cf. Würgler (Bitten und Begehren, p. 36), who cites the 872 written suplications presented to the ruling council of Hesse-Kassel in 1594 as evidence of "political agenda-setting."

126 Occasional members included various secretaries, the chaplain, assistant bursar, commissioner, subprior, and supervisor of guardians. Infrequent members included the rentmaster and administrators from Esslingen, Kirchberg, Schemmerberg, Stockach, and Überlingen.

Illustration 6.1: The Audience Protocol

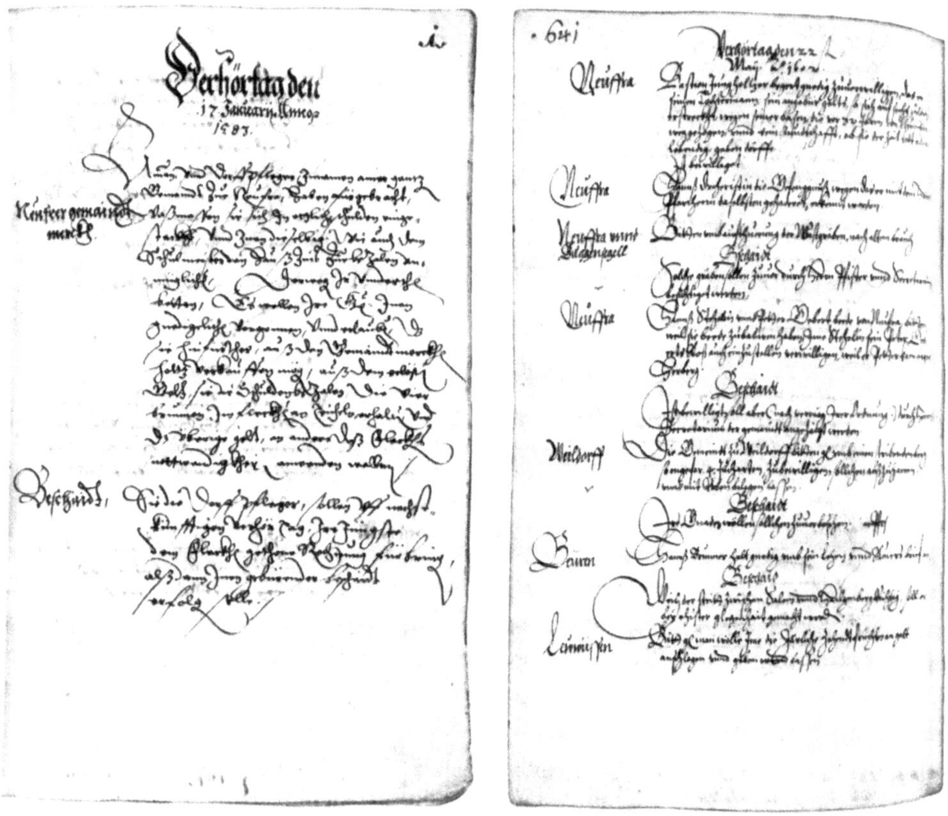

Example pages from 1583 and 1602
Generallandesarchiv Karlsruhe, 61/13369

in a loose hierarchy, with monastic officials above secular ones but with some variation in rank order within each category.[127] The abbot attended rarely, but the Audience sometimes postponed its decision to seek the opinion of "His Grace." Employment contracts for some lay officials list Audience attendance among their major responsibilities. For example, forest supervisor Johann Schentz was instructed in 1625 "to visit the Audience diligently and attend whenever possible, carefully recording any petition relating to his office as well as executing and carrying out the decision and command, loyally and without deviation or complaint."[128]

---

127 For example, the relative order of the Pfister, Großkeller, and bursar varied from one meeting to the next and so did that of the Oberamtmann, Amtmann of Bermatingen, and Vogt of Maurach.

128 GLAK, 98/216. The Oberamtmann, chancellor, and secretary were also required to attend whenever possible.

Chart 6.2: Subjects of Audience Petitions

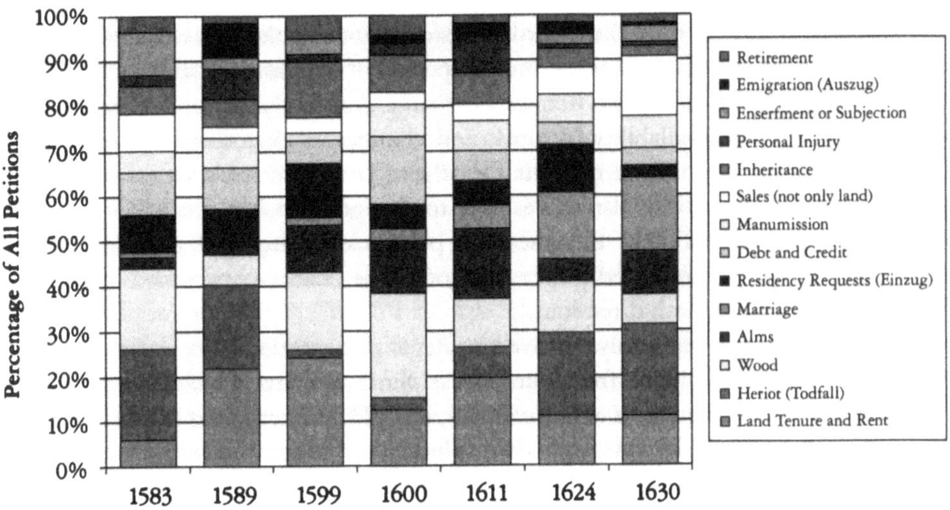

The Audience records were normally kept by a member of the chancery—the head secretary, chancellor, or one of many assistants. The handwriting confirms that not all sessions were recorded by the same individual. Entries typically begin with the person's name and place of origin, offset in the margin for easy reference. The petitions themselves, which were almost always presented orally, are typically summarized in a few sentences or brief paragraph with a decision (if any) at the bottom.[129] Illustration 6.1 provides two example pages from the Audience Protocol.

Chart 6.2 lists the most common topics of petition in sampled years, including the categories of firewood and lumber, land tenure and rents, alms, marriage, inheritance, death taxes, servility status (manumission and enserfment), territorial residence (entry and exit), property sales, credit and loans, and personal injury claims.[130] On the one hand, recurring topics of petition indicate what sorts of favors were commonly sought, what actions were limited by the abbot's authority to command and prohibit, and what exceptions to territorial policy were possible by special permission. On the other hand, the chart shows great variation over time in the topics brought before the Audience. The level of demand for resources was one factor behind petitioners' requests, yet no simple supply-and-demand explanation can fully account for the fluctuations. Changes in official policy or administrative organization sometimes played a greater role in the

---

129 Ironically, as is also true for the Sidelgericht, more is known about oral petitions than written ones. An entry from 1630 states without further detail that "both Hans Schmidtmeister and Georg Rundolt submit their claims in writing." GLAK, 61/13374.

130 This list of subjects is not exhaustive. The chart displays only requests involving the major identified themes, not the more infrequent and unusual topics of petition.

subjects of petition than the relative level of need. Alms requests, for example, were highest in 1611, high in the middle of the period, but low in the 1580s and especially low in 1624. The plague of 1611 may provide background for the high demand for alms in that year, yet the mid-1580s were another period of widespread sickness and death when few alms petitions appear. Requests for alms were likely influenced by attitudes toward begging, the availability of alms, and changes in eligibility requirements.[131] Fluctuations in the number of requests for other types of favors, such as wood, residency, and heriot reductions also correspond to changes in policy, recordkeeping, and administrative organization.[132] In some cases, policy clearly impacted petitions, whereas in others, petitions impacted policy decisions. The Audience provided the setting for communication in both directions.[133]

Although petitions certainly involved strategic presentation, they initiated a relatively open form of dialogue free from duress. Since petitioners voluntarily brought information to the attention of abbey officials, it could be interpreted by the Audience members (or by historians) differently than subjects' responses to an inquiry or inquisition demanding that they explain themselves or report on their neighbors.[134] Information about local conditions that accompanied petitioners' concerns served the interests of central administrators but could benefit subjects as well, to the extent that the abbey made an effort to address their needs and offer solutions. Occasionally, a subject's petition elicited the response that the abbey would soon draft a new policy to deal with the issue. For example, when the innkeeper in Oberuhldingen complained in 1595 that his wine sales were being undercut by local competitors who paid no excise taxes or innkeepers' fees, the Audience promised that a new wine ordinance would be forthcoming. When the Amtmann of Grasbeuren complained in 1594 about the foreign poor and the burden they imposed on the community, the Audience likewise promised to follow up with a new policy. In 1595 the commune of Owingen complained to the Audience that the standard prices for straw set by the abbey were too high, thus interfering with local trade. The next month, following the villagers' recommendation,

[131] The abbey passed a new alms ordinance in 1623 (for the first time since the 1570s), and this may explain why the number of petitions for alms dropped in 1624. See below; GLAK, 98/59, fol. 508–511.

[132] For example, the number of requests concerning death taxes was high in 1583, 1589, 1624, and 1630, but extremely low in 1599, 1600, and 1611. An entry in the Audience minutes from 1590 provides an explanation: "Note. The heriot shall no longer be recorded in this protocol, but rather, in its own separate register." Similarly, there are separate volumes of immigration requests (*Einzug*) for the years 1595 to 1613 (GLAK, 62/9264–9265).

[133] HOLENSTEIN, Gute Policey, pp. 300, 305; R. BLICKLE, Supplikationen und Demonstrationen, p. 268. Würgler points out that supplications could lead to the creation of central institutions and to a shift in administrative energies to focus on the topics raised by subjects. Idem, Bitten und Begehren, p. 37.

[134] WÜRGLER, Bitten und Begehren, pp. 26, 35.

the Sidelgericht assumed responsibility for establishing territorial commodity prices on an annual basis.[135] Even when the Audience provided no such direct response, the exchange of information about all sorts of topics such as the lack of housing, the problem of begging, the need for a priest, crop damages by wild game or bad weather, communal building projects, predatory lending, provisions for orphans, interference from county officials, property conditions, plundering by soldiers, and many other issues gave subjects the ability to influence territorial policy through the presentation of their needs and expectations.[136]

Audience decisions are not recorded with the same care or regularity as the petitions themselves. Some decisions may have been filled in later, as suggested by the many petitions followed by "B." for *Bescheid* (Decision) and a large blank space. One thing is clear, however: abbey administrators used the Audience not to apply the law but to impart favors where they chose. This could mean rewarding loyal service or attempting to win over powerful local men, encouraging economic growth or protecting the weak. For example, one Amtmann's request for firewood was granted along with the admonition to do his job well in the future.[137] A village teacher received a bonus because word of his diligence had reached the abbey. In 1624 several individuals sought a reduction of the death tax in recognition of loyal services performed for the abbey. The Audience granted a reduction in six cases and waived the tax completely in two others, but the heirs of two former employees had to pay in full. Audience decisions were formed on the basis of many socioeconomic factors and relationships we will never be aware of, yet the contents of this record offer a way to discover and partially reconstruct them. Subjects' requests and the Audience's responses substantiated and influenced as well as reflected relations of power within the territory.

Some types of Audience petitions overlapped with the topics considered by the Sidelgericht. These included assault and verbal injury, grazing disputes, complaints by communes against individual members, transgressions of the abbey's statutes, requests for birth certificates, debt collection, and the ratification of contracts. These areas of overlapping competency meant that individuals could appear before the body of officials they felt would be more receptive or likely to bring about the desired effect. Indeed, it appears that the choice of one decisionmaking body over the other depended less on the topic of complaint than the desired response. Some petitioners or plaintiffs approached one organ with a problem that would have been handled more appropriately by the other, and sometimes, they brought issues before both authorities in succession. The Audience occasionally declined to consider the petitioner's request

[135] All three examples are from GLAK, 61/13369.

[136] Cf. FUHRMANN et al., Supplizierende Gemeinden, p. 320.

[137] "Approved, but out of mercy and without any legal obligation … with the command that he should oversee his office with diligence." GLAK, 61/13369, 1594.

and recommended that he or she bring the issue before the Sidelgericht.[138] In general, the court's authority was to apply the law and hear suits between two parties involving damages. Requests for privileges or exemptions were better addressed to the Audience, which had greater latitude to grant or deny favors. The Audience also tended to make decisions more quickly and efficiently, which helps to explain why the number of petitions multiplied in the early seventeenth century, a period when the number of legal suits remained relatively flat.[139] The fact that so many subjects brought their grievances before the Audience and not the court demonstrates their willing involvement of territorial officials in personal and local concerns. Indeed, in this period they seemed to prefer the lord's mercy over their neighbors' judgment.

One of the most important functions of the Audience was its ability to diffuse conflict and avoid the escalation of protest through appeasement.[140] The successful petition, resulting in a favor or exception to the rules, obviously had a positive impact on relations between lord and subject and made the individual petitioner more likely to behave loyally and obediently in future words and deeds. Yet the right to petition was significant in and of itself, whether or not an individual took advantage of it and no matter what the outcome. It encouraged the belief among subjects that someone was actually listening to their problems or would listen in the future if a petition were made. It imparted the feeling that the abbot and his advisors were concerned with their personal situation. This gave subjects more reason to view the lordship in a positive light and to cooperate with official policies. The outlet for expressing needs and frustrations was a means of relieving tensions. Petitions usually brought a resolution to the problem without more serious actions being taken, and even in cases where a grievance was not resolved, the dialogue provided the abbey with a chance to address growing problems before they spun out of control. Recourse to the Audience diminished the likelihood that subjects would resort to more drastic alternatives. It also discouraged the development of territorial policies in isolation from subjects' expectations.

6.5 Growing Resistance to Land Rents

Not all Audience petitions were framed as requests for favors, however.[141] Some suggested that the abbey had ignored or even altered customary rights and obligations. In the early seventeenth century, rents provided a growing cause for grievance. Hans

---

138 The Audience referred petitioners to the Sidelgericht in 1583, 1600, 1604, 1605, 1611, 1613, 1624, and 1629 (not an exclusive list). The majority of these requests involved inheritance disputes, as discussed in Chapter 4.

139 WÜRGLER, Bitten und Begehren, p. 38; R. BLICKLE, Supplikationen und Demonstrationen, pp. 285, 289.

140 WÜRGLER, Bitte und Begehren, p. 38; FUHRMANN et al., Supplizierende Gemeinden, p. 320.

141 Cf. FUHRMANN et al., Supplizierende Gemeinden, p. 290.

Waibel asked for a rent reduction in 1611, pointing out that his father had paid only one pound cash plus three Eimer of wine, whereas his obligation was now four pounds and four Eimer. The abbey reduced his payment by one pound and suggested he give up his lease if he could not afford it.[142] In 1624 Simon Rainer from Birkenweiler complained that the grain rent (*Gulten*) had risen so high he could hardly manage. The Audience postponed its decision to consult the Pfister.[143] That same year Michael Tent of Tüfingen asked for a rent reduction on his vineyard plot, explaining that he could not afford it and would otherwise be forced to sell. The Audience told him he should report to the bursar his intent to let the vineyard go.[144] Hans Hund, the Amtmann of Wendlingen, asked forgiveness of the remaining twenty gulden he owed in entry fines, since his farm was no good and the rent had already increased by four pounds. His request was denied.[145] The Audience did not defend the lord's right to raise rents in any of these cases and it seldom granted rent reductions. Perhaps because abbey officials refused to discuss or even acknowledge rising rents, complaints in this area spilled out into collective grievances, expressed in the 1620s and 1630s by the tenant farmers of the entire Pfisteramt (to which we return below).

Many grievances were brought by entire communes or by other groups such as the farm tenants of one or more villages. In 1599, for example, the tenants of Neufrach, Buggensegel, and Weiler asked for the reinstatement of drinks, which they customarily received following carting services.[146] The entire commune of Weildorf complained about sharecropping in 1599, requesting the same treatment as Neufrach.[147] In a third petition that year, the commune of Buggensegel asked for the chaff left over from threshing the grain, according to custom.[148] The tenant farmers of Oberuhldingen and Seefelden asked for a reduction of their carting services in 1624, to which the Audience members replied they would have to think about it, "because their carting services are so short in comparison to others who must travel to Gehrenberg or Boshasel."[149] In 1629 the communities of Gebhardsweiler, Mühlhofen, and Oberuhldingen complained further that carting services were unevenly distributed. They asked the abbey to assign

---

142 GLAK, 61/13370, 1611.

143 GLAK, 61/13373, 1624.

144 Ibid.

145 Ibid.

146 GLAK, 61/13369. The Audience responded that laborers would receive their drinks but not before completing all services.

147 Ibid.

148 The Audience replied that straw would be given only in exchange for manure: "Wann sy thung werden geben, soll Ihnen daß Strow auch volgen, wa nit, sollen sy wie Andere deß strows in mangel stehn." When Buggensegel repeated its request a week later, the Audience responded that according to the new straw ordinance, villagers would receive a portion of straw in return for every 130 bundles of processed grain. GLAK, 61/13369.

149 GLAK, 61/13373. In 1629 the tenants making deliveries to Gehrenberg (near Markdorf) also complained about carting services. GLAK, 98/389.

an overseer and promised to be willing and obedient in return.[150] There were also complaints among the winegrowers. In 1620 the Amtmann and entire commune of Tüfingen petitioned for a reduction of the wine rent. Buggensegel and Weildorf requested the same.[151] In 1624 the vintners of Bermatingen asked the abbey to sell them some fertilizer, complaining that the farm tenants were swindling them with tiny bundles. They offered cash or wine in return, but the Audience gave no immediate decision.[152]

Meanwhile, the abbey's grain rents appear to have been not only highly variable from one farm to the next, they were also much more burdensome than elsewhere in the region.[153] Salem collected a percentage of the crop rather than a set amount from the large farms. The abbey's share, known as the *Landgarb*, was usually a third and sometimes half the harvest. This practice was established custom, even if tenants' resistance to it was new: rent registers from the early sixteenth century indicate that the abbey demanded a share of the crop from tenants throughout the period.[154] A comparison of these rent registers shows that the abbey's share did not increase over the long sixteenth century, but other types of rent—including eggs, chickens, house and hay taxes, and in some cases, manure—did rise significantly.[155] More important with respect to the Landgarb is that it was extended to previously exempt, smaller parcels. In Buggensegel, Owingen, Neufrach, and probably elsewhere, the abbey quietly changed the rent on smaller land parcels from a set price to a percentage of the harvest.[156] Before, it had been one of the advantages of smallholdings that they owed a low, set rent. Now, even households with a few plots of land paid the abbey a percentage of their yield, usually one-third, as ground rent. This extension of sharecropping resulted in many large and small producers owing dues (including taxes, tithes, rents, and interest payments) of over half their annual earnings. No wonder they were more concerned about the Landgarb and rising land rents than with imperial war taxes, which were normally one percent or less of assessed property value.

---

150 GLAK, 61/13373. The only response was that the Hofmeister of Maurach should submit a report.

151 GLAK, 61/13372.

152 GLAK, 61/13373.

153 See Chapter 4; cf. SABEAN, Power in the Blood, p. 5; SREENIVASAN, Ottobeuren, p. 137; HOLENSTEIN, Bauern, pp. 36–37.

154 Sharecropping was fairly uncommon in cereal agriculture, but according to Tom Scott, it was widely practiced in viticulture. Idem, Viticulture, 106.

155 See Chapter 4.

156 In Buggensegel, individual parcels were changed from a set rent to a share of the crop in 1602. A rent register of that year states: "Note. The Pfister's parcels, which have previously given a set rent, have been leased to the farm tenants and smallholders by his grace in 1602 for a third share of what the field gives." GLAK, 66/10419. The Audience record from 1595 describes the same occurrence in Owingen: "Note. The Keller's parcels in Owingen shall be leased in the future the same as those owing shares." GLAK, 61/13369. The Pfister and Keller parcels were small pieces of arable leased separate from the major farms. See BAIER, Bevölkerungsbewegung, p. 82.

In 1626 the farm tenants of Neufrach presented the abbey with a formal five-page list of grievances.[157] The subject of their complaint was the abbey's new policy regarding manure. It required tenants to reserve enough fertilizer to cover all fields owing a percentage of the crop before amending any private landholdings.[158] This was in addition to the manure they already paid as meadow rent and in exchange for firewood. According to tenants in Neufrach, the abbey's increasing demands for manure and the lack of space for grazing were ruining them. If the abbey did not address their grievances, they warned, they would not comply with the new order. Many of their complaints had to do with grazing rights, insufficient pasture, carting services, and the competing claims of smallholders and landless laborers. They also requested grain, expressing fears that with the repeated harvest failures and troop crossings they would run out of food before spring. There is no evidence of a settlement, and the allocation of fertilizer continued to be an issue in subsequent years. In 1632 the smallholders joined the farm tenants of Neufrach in a petition to dispense with the new manure ordinance.[159] The various individual and collective petitions described thus far provide insight on the economic situation as well as the reasons for farmers' growing resentment in the early seventeenth century.

Collective Grievances Against Sharecropping

On 11 April 1630 the farm tenants from Neufrach, Weildorf, Buggensegel, and Weiler collectively petitioned the Audience for a resolution of their grievances concerning sharecropping (the *Landgarb*), labor services (*Frondienst*), and ground rents (*Gülten*).[160] From the sound of it, these complaints were not new. The assembled officials declared they would state their decision the week after Misericordia, that is, three weeks after Easter. But the Audience protocol failed to mention the issue again until 12 December, when the peasants of the entire Pfisteramt (the district to which all four villages belonged) renewed their request: "The peasants (*Bauerschaft*) of the Pfisteramt humbly request a gracious response to the grievances they have recently presented in writing." The Audience members answered that they would take the matter into further consideration and impart their decision in due time.[161]

---

157 GLAK, 98/3481. The title page states that the document's author was Jacob Leub, a resident of Neufrach who may have been a secretary in Salem's treasury. (Another list of grievances from Neufrach's smallholders mentions Jerg Leub's brother, the treasury secretary. GLAK, 98/389.)

158 This policy addressed the practice of neglecting the lord's arable in favor of freehold (from which the lord did not claim a share of the crop) and vineyards (requiring heavy fertilization). The policy must not have been new, since Owingen tenants complained similarly in 1595.

159 GLAK, 61/13374.

160 Ibid., 1630.

161 Ibid. No similar grievances are mentioned in the protocol until 1634.

Were we to consider the Pfisteramt peasants' 1630 Audience petitions in isolation, they would appear as nothing special. Neither record provides a resolution, and the second one does not even mention the cause for complaint. Yet these two simple petitions grew out of many earlier, scattered grievances. They were hints of something bigger, a movement with a long history that united the tenants of an entire district, and extensive documentation provides a fuller picture. Written exchanges between villagers and abbey officials in the years 1629–1630 demonstrate subjects' mounting frustrations and a growing level of resistance in Salem's villages.[162] They allow us to see which burdens were, in the peasants' view, the major causes of economic decline. They provide evidence of increasing rents and services. They illustrate the administration's rationalizations and attempts to distract angry peasants from the main issues. They even show abbey officials' disregard for real economic hardship caused by harvest failures.[163] The resistance movement of 1629–1630 depicts the intricacies of negotiation between the abbey and its subjects.[164]

A short dossier contains five documents pertaining to the dispute, including six separate texts.[165] The way they are recorded leaves the time span between the texts uncertain, but they appear to have been used in the context of multiple Audience hearings. One of the texts refers to a meeting in which peasants huddled together with their Amtmänner to deliberate. Other texts name or refer to the abbot and eight senior abbey officials, presumably the Audience members. The negotiations between the abbey's representatives and the tenants of the Pfisteramt involved written documents but also face-to-face contact, dialogue, and even personal accusations. The first text, entitled "Summary of grievances by the praiseworthy abbey of Salmansweyler's peasants, or farm tenants, of Neufrach, Leutkirch, Weildorf, and Buggensegel," raises several issues in eight numbered points.[166] Major areas of grievance included carting services (which had doubled without the customary refreshments), house and hay taxes, and sharecrop-

[162] The documents described below are found in GLAK, 98/389.

[163] As in their response to other grievances, abbey representatives refused to admit increasing rents or service obligations.

[164] See also BAIER, Bevölkerungs- und Vermögensstatistik, pp. 211–212.

[165] GLAK, 98/389. The six texts include the peasants' initial list of grievances, the abbey's first response, the peasants' countergrievances, the abbey's second response, the peasants' additional grievances, and the abbey's final response. One document in the file is a compilation of five out of six texts, two contain the first three texts, and in the others, the fourth and fifth texts stand alone. All told, there are three copies of the first three texts, two copies of the fifth text, and one copy of the fourth and sixth texts. The documents are in different hands, and may have been written by or for various members of the Audience over the course of the dispute.

[166] "Summarishe Clagpuncten des Loblichen Gotshaus Salmanswyler Bauren, oder Mayer, zue Neufra, Leutkhürch, Weildorff und Buggensegel." GLAK, 98/389.

ping (the Landgarb).[167] There was no doubt about the tenants' chief complaint: "Lastly and above all else they complain against the Landgarb."[168]

The second text is a resolution passed by eight senior abbey officials and ratified by the abbot.[169] It bears the title: "Assessment. How best to deal with these peasants of Salmansweiler."[170] The points that follow contain several minor concessions of dubious value, including vague promises to limit demands for certain services (if possible) and the agreement to provide laborers with food and drink—but only after completion of the entire task and not to lazy, grumbling, or disobedient workers. The abbey recognized its obligation to provide seed corn as was customary, but failed to specify how much, which was the point of grievance. The officials carefully avoided the issue of rising house and hay taxes, changing the subject by offering concessions relating to a separate hay grievance (accusing the abbey of taking too many sheaves). They denied a general increase in rents, maintaining that each case was different, but promised to deal with tenants individually if they so desired. Those who complained against the manure tax could stop paying it, they suggested, if they did not need any firewood in return.

On the issue of sharecropping, the Audience refused any compromise whatsoever. Instead, the text devoted nine lengthy articles to why the abbey could not change its policies. The officials cited some of the usual reasons: sharecropping had been practiced for over one hundred years without complaint, and the abbey's share had not increased. Even a small reduction in grain rents would cause the abbey serious financial harm. It would lead other tenants to request similar reductions, which the abbey could ill afford with the rising costs of war taxes. It would take an enormous effort to change all the abbey's written registers and tenure contracts. In addition, since people always resist any sort of increase, temporary relief would be irreversible. Other points were more accusatory and deflected blame onto the petitioners individually and as a group. The officials insisted that hard times and successive harvest failures were not the result of sharecropping or the war. Rather, it was the fault of peasants' own farming practices and laziness. Manure was at the heart of the problem, and officials accused farmers of neglecting the abbey's land: "Whereas 15 acres of leased land should be fertilized annually, they do not add manure to a single one, or perhaps two or three acres at the

---

167 Other issues were harvest payments (*Schnittergeld*), the provision of seed corn, contested measures (the equivalence between one wagon and two cartloads), and other small payments (*Marckhengeld, Grabengeld*).

168 "Lestlich beshwähren süe sich am maisten wegen der Landgarb, so süe bis dato raichen müessen." GLAK, 98/389.

169 These abbey officials included Abbot Thomas Wunn, Prior Joachim Miller, Pfister Vito Huober, Joachim Beckhelhauben (monk, no title listed), Bursar Michael Riedinger, Chancellor Dr. Johann Wahl, the Stockach Hofmeister Joachim Vögelin, Amtmann Christoph Langenstain of Bermatingen, and Johann Maisterlin (no title listed).

170 "Guettachten. Wüe besagten Salmanshwylishen Bauren zue begegnen werden khundte." GLAK, 98/389.

most. As the common expression goes, manure is the best builder, and so the peasants yield barely 50 sheaves or so, whereas a properly fertilized acre could yield around 120 sheaves."[171] The officials singled out Jacob Wiggenhauser, Georg Hailg, Hans Fünfflin, Hans Schaitteckh, and Michael Ringenburger, each of whom had good farms and paid low crop shares, but "through their bad householding and extravagant lifestyles were ruined, and in some cases fell into bankruptcy."[172] The Audience members pointed to other groups—previous tenants, the small vintners, other communities with less fertile soil—who had cheerfully put up with the same or worse economic difficulties. The abbey's lengthy response and sharp reaction to farmers' grievances against sharecropping leaves no doubt about the issue's great importance and the intense feelings on both sides.

An internal memorandum from 16 March 1629, located in a separate file, shows abbey officials were in fact well aware of the rent increases. According to the title, it was written in response to complaints from Neufrach's tenant farmers.[173] Yet the text makes no mention of any grievances. Instead, it lists each of the large farms in the villages of Neufrach, Weildorf, and Buggensegel along with comparisons of the rents from 1629, 1620, and before 1620. The document confirms the abbey's claim that each farm was subject to different forms and levels of rent.[174] It also supports the peasants' accusations that in recent years their house and hay rents, entry fines, and share of harvest fees (*Schnittergeld*) had all risen significantly. The small tithe in Weildorf had increased as well, though this was not among the collective grievances.

The third text in the series of grievance documents, entitled "Remonstrance and protest of the farm tenants," describes the peasants' counterresponse. References to consultation, representation by village leaders, and exchanges of dialogue all indicate that the remonstrance was presented at a formal Audience hearing after abbey officials declared their initial response. In the secretary's words,

---

171 "Das wan Jahrlich 15 Jucharten Lehenacker getungt werden soltten, sie nit wohl einer acker, oder auf das maiste 2 oder 3 Juchert tungen: Worauß ervolgt, das weil der tung gemainen sprich wordt nach der beste bauman ist, die bauren uf sollicher ungetungter Juchert Ackers, kummerlich 50 oder ein wenig mehr garben bekommen, da hingegen aber uf einer recht getungten Juchert in die 120 garben geshniten werden khinden." GLAK, 98/389.

172 "Durch ihr unheuslichkait und vershwendish leben verdorben, und thailß gahr in die gant geraten." GLAK, 98/389. The administrators made no connection between the declining yields and the tenants' earlier grievances concerning manure.

173 "Memorial, Uber die beshwerden der Mayershafft zue Neuffra." GLAK, 98/3483.

174 For example, some tenants owed the third garb from all parcels while others owed the second garb on some parcels and the third garb on others. All farms in Weildorf were subject to the small tithe, but this was not mentioned for Neufrach or Buggensegel. Tenants in Neufrach and Buggensegel paid hay taxes by the wagonload, ranging from 0.55 to 1.10 wagonloads per meadow parcel (*Mannßmad*). GLAK, 98/3483.

> Afterward they [the peasants] took a pause to consult with their headmen, and through these leaders they made it known that they were indeed most humbly grateful for the graciously accommodating explanation of all points (except for the Landgarb). Yet because the Landgarb is their chief complaint, without the reduction of which no other remedy could be of use, it is their submissive request that their article concerning the Landgarb be graciously addressed as well.[175]

In the following statement we can detect a hint of sarcasm as the tenants tested officials' professed charity and generosity with a new request, one the abbey would not possibly be willing to consider:

> Upon which, if it is not possible to grant them any moderation or relief with respect to the Landgarb, and if the concessions made regarding the other grievances may be further extended, they would like to include this addition, so they can see that you [abbey officials] wish to gratify them wherever possible. Namely, they would like you to consider, as part of their grievances, the abolishment of entry fines on major farms. In addition, for those who have previously accepted such farms but not yet fully discharged such entry fines, the remaining debt should be forgiven. And if someone has already paid the entry fines in full, he should be reimbursed, at least in part if not entirely.[176]

After a second pause for consultation, the village Amtmänner returned to the refrain: only the Landgarb truly concerned them. Furthermore, if the Audience continued to deny their requests, they would appeal their cause directly to the abbot.[177] The abbey officials retorted that the abbot would certainly support their view against his tenants and warned that more complaints would likely result in the cancellation of previous concessions.

---

175 "Warauff sie mit ihren Ambtleuthen einen abstandt genommen und nach beshehner underredt, durch besagte Ambtleuth sich dahin vernemmen lassen, das sie sich zwar der gnedigen willfarigen erclerung uber alle Puncten (außer der landtgarb) underthonig bedanckhen, Allein weil sie mit der Landtgarb am maisten beshwehrt, ohne dem milterung ihnen nit geholffen seye, wan ihr underthönig Pit auch in disem Puncten der Landtgarb ihnen mit genaden zue begegnen." GLAK, 98/389.

176 "Uff Welliches ihnen ob außgefierte Puncten, warumb man in khain moderation oder milterung der Landtgarb bewilligen kinden, und die beshehne Wilfahr in Ubrigen Puncten mehrers exaggeriert und da bey diß angehenckt worden, damit sie sehen und Verspeuren kinden das man ihnen in moglichen fahlen zue wilfahren begehre, so wolle man auch in dem clag Puncten wegen der Ehrshätzen ihnen so weit begegnen, das wellicher einen haupt paw hinfiro thuen miessen, derselb des Ehrshatz befreit sein solle; Item wellicher shohn vor deme einen haupt paw gethon, und dan noch einen Ehrshatz geben hette, dem selben sollicher Ehrshatz wan er noch nit erlegt nach gesechen, oder da er erlegt were, wa nit in totum doch etwaß daran widerumb herauß gebn werden solle." GLAK, 98/389.

177 The abbot was apparently absent from this negotiation, but since his name heads the list of officials who drafted the abbey's earlier response (the second text), he must have been well aware of the peasants' grievances as well as involved in framing the abbey's official position.

The abbey's second response came on 31 May 1630.[178] It addressed not only the tenants of the four villages but the peasants of the entire Pfisteramt as well.[179] The order of articles was different than in the first response, but the issues remained basically the same, with the additional discussion of entry fines.[180] The biggest change was to address the Landgarb in the middle rather than at the end—an attempt, perhaps, to bury the main point where it would receive the least notice. In this version, in place of the nine points of emotionally charged rebuttal with respect to the Landgarb, the administrators gave this concise response: "In this it shall remain as before, for these considerable reasons alone: because it has been given since time immemorial, as all tenure contracts indicate. In addition, if we yield and allow any reduction of the Landgarb, other tenants will feel that they must also have a reduction, and therefore all tenure contracts and all other transactions would have to be changed at great cost and inconvenience."[181] There were other slight revisions but no further concessions.[182]

The fifth document in the series provides further elaboration of the peasants' grievances in six new articles.[183] They complained that the hay tax had been raised in recent years along with the chicken and egg tax. Fixed rents had been newly converted to a share of the harvest, for example in Neufrach, on one hundred separate parcels. The abbey contributed only one-seventh or one-eighth of the necessary seed corn, compared to the customary one-third to one-half. Additionally, the abbey's share of harvest

---

178 This was approximately six weeks after the peasants' Audience appearance on 11 April. It was obviously written after the first three texts, since it addressed entry fines in addition to the original grievances.

179 The title reads: "Ratshlag. Was gestalten den Bauren im Salmansweyler Pfister ambt wegen Ihren übergebenen Beshwerden geholffen werden könte." This confirms that the Audience entry from December 1630 concerning Pfisteramt peasants' complaints was indeed related to the others brought by Neufrach, Weildorf, Buggensegel, Leutkirch, and Weiler. On the back side of the document, only Neufrach is named.

180 The administrators promised that their legal advisors (*Rechtsgelehrten*) would consult the records to see how entry fines had been handled in the past.

181 "In diesem solle es beym vorigen verbleiben, und allein auß diesen erhöblichen ursachen, weilen solche vor unverdenckhlichen Jahren hero also gegeben worden, welches auch alle lehen und revers zue erkennen geben, undt darbey auch zue bedenckhen, dz andere Mayer, da mann Ihnen dergestalt weichen, und Etwas von denen Landtgarben thuen wollte, auch Einen nachzueg darinnen werden haben wolten, müessen auch dess wegen alle lehen und revers brueff und alle andere handlungen mit grosser ungelegenheit, und auf Ihren mehreren Costen anderst gemacht werden." GLAK, 98/389.

182 They elaborated on carting services, asserting that the customary annual meal was not the abbey's obligation and would be given only to subjects who were loyal, willing, and obedient. Lazy workers could expect only punishment. The officials again ignored the issue of rising house rents.

183 The title reads: "Verzaichnus Ettwelliche beshwernussen, der gesambten Mayern zue Neuffra, Weyldorff, und Buggensegel." According to one of the copies, abbey officials discussed these grievances on 8 July 1630.

fees was not enough to pay what the abbey's harvest workers were owed. The tenants also found the recent innovation of harvesting the abbey's share from each individual parcel to be extremely inconvenient. Finally, the abbey had not acknowledged their earlier grievance about rising house rents.

The officials offered no new concessions in their third, undated response.[184] First of all, they stated, many of the new grievances had already been settled in earlier actions and required no further discussion. On most of the points abbey officials insisted that their requirements had not changed.[185] They did address the Landgarb accusation, explaining that the hundred parcels in Neufrach had been joined with the larger farms at the peasants' own request, making them subject to the same terms as the rest of the farms to which they now belonged.[186] As for seed corn, the administrators admitted uncertainty as to exactly how much had been previously granted but promised to look into it. They refused to discuss house rents, repeating the position that each farm was subject to different terms and any disagreement would have to be settled on an individual basis.

Over the next few years, the Audience protocol made no mention of the Pfisteramt tenants' grievances or the Landgarb. The war hit especially hard in the early 1630s, which may explain the long silence, especially since the Audience met sporadically between 1632 and 1634 while the entire convent sought refuge in Überlingen and Constance. Several Neufrach widows asked in 1632 for forgiveness of death taxes; when Swedish troops burned the village in April, many of their husbands had been slain or burned in their homes. Then during the attack on Constance in 1633 and the siege of Überlingen in 1634, the region became a major battleground and soldiers were everywhere. At one point Bürster compared the scene to Judgment Day, it was as if the entire world had assembled there and every village and town was completely full.[187] During this period the Virgin Mary performed miracles to save the abbey church on three oc-

---

184 The title of the sixth and final text reads: "Beschaidt. Uber die fernere beshwärden der bawrn in dem Pfister Ambt."

185 They had always claimed hens and eggs, and harvest fees remained the same as before, abbey officials explained. (These might be waived in the future, they suggested, for certain farms and in exchange for other small fees.) As for accusations about harvest practices, abbey officials insisted the policies were both equitable and customary.

186 As Baier points out (Bevölkerungsbewegung, p. 82), small parcels of arable called "*Pfisteräcker*" or "*Kelleräcker*" were customarily subject to set rents rather than a share of the crop. These terms were less burdensome than the Landgarb and made such parcels especially desirable. They were sometimes leased along with the larger farms, or rented out to smallholders. The abbey's position here is suspect, because older farm descriptions often included individual parcels that yielded a set rent. It does not follow, therefore, that incorporating smaller parcels into the larger farms required a change in rent. As previously indicated, evidence demonstrates that Salem had already changed fixed rents to a share of the crop for individual parcels in Buggensegel (1602) and Owingen (1595).

187 WEECH, Bürsters Beschreibung, p. 35.

casions, but no one was there to protect the villagers, who had much greater concerns than the land rent.[188] It was not until late in 1634, after the Battle of Nördlingen on 5 September slightly reduced the immediate threat in the region, that villagers were able to take stock of the situation.[189] Then, the Audience protocol indicates a resurgence of collective grievances. In two separate petitions on 5 October, the tenants of Neufrach and Weildorf reported that they were no longer able to plow the fields without any horses. Abbey officials asked for patience. Later that same month, the Audience protocol noted that according to a written supplication, "the entire peasantry of the abbey" was requesting a resolution of their grievances. The officials continued to refuse any reduction of the land rent, citing previous decisions, but offered to waive the fees on straw and tenants' contribution to harvest workers' wages. The Audience also instructed village headmen to report at the next meeting which of their neighbors planned to continue farming and on what parcels. The bursar explained the following week that since many of the lord's best parcels lay fallow, the abbot had decided to let tenants exchange parcels—as long as they first reported it to the authorities and continued to pay the abbey what was owed.[190] When Buggensegel requested aid in November, the abbey asked the five major tenants to assess their farms including real and moveable property, rents, and debts. According to the report there were only a few cows and other animals left in the village; Balthus Schaitteckh alone estimated a personal loss of 1,000 fl. in horses. Each tenant reported large debts, increased hay rents, and grain rents of a third to half the crop. Each farmer concluded his statement by saying that the only way the abbey could possibly help would be to reduce the Landgarb.[191] Still on 21 March 1635 the abbey held out when the tenants of Neufrach, Buggensegel, and Weildorf collectively petitioned for seeds and other aid so they could plant their fields and attempt to make a new beginning.

---

188 Ibid.; BAIER, Akten des dreißigjährigen Krieges, pp. 129–162; GLAK, 61/13374. Bürster recounts the miracles on pp. 21, 42–45, and 49–50. Around the time of the siege in Überlingen, nearby Nußdorf fared badly; troops also set fire to Adelsreute, Owingen, Pfaffenhofen, Tüfingen, and Weildorf in 1634.

189 In November and December, for example, scores of petitions sought a reduction of the heriot tax.

190 "Herr P. Oberbursierer lasst alle Ambtleüth herein forderen und haltet Ihnen Vor, Wie daß Ihr Gnad. deß Hochwl: Unsers Gnedigen herren Praelatens gnediger befelch seie, Ihnen zuewissen zuemachen: Demnach Ihr gnadl: die beysorg tragen, Daß vil Ackherfeld uff ihren verliehnen höffen in der herrschafft, heürigs Jahrß, bekhanter laidigen Ursachen wegen, ohnbesambt bleiben: und es etwann Jehnige Pauren betroffen möchte, die besser felld, alß anndere, so sonnsten nit so guete hoff und güeter haben: Daß derowegen uß gl: verwilligung ainem jeden frey und erlaubt sein solle, fahls er dergleichen bessere güetter, alß er hatt, welche nit angeblüembt werden wolten, in erfahrung brächte unverhinderlich darein Zuefahren, dieselbige anzuesäen und seinen nutzen darinn zuesuechen: doch mit dem geding, daß Er dem Gotshauß darvon raiche, waß Jheniger shuldig were, so er pawte, deme der hoff verliehen." GLAK, 61/13374, 1634.

191 GLAK, 98/3275.

Finally, on 5 July 1635, there is a bit of evidence to demonstrate the peasants' eventual victory in the dispute over sharecropping.[192] An unassuming note in the Audience protocol describes the bursar's inquiry as to whether the abbot's reduction of the Landgarb from one-half to one-third and from one-third to one-fourth of the crop was intended to take effect immediately or after the next harvest. No response to his question is recorded, but it is enough to suggest that the peasants finally gained what they had persistently demanded. The reduction of the Landgarb in 1635 was a bittersweet reward, too late to be of much use for the remaining farm tenants, who by that time were barely scraping by and not paying their rent in any case.[193] Judging from the timing, the abbey's concessions probably had more to do with war damages than with five years of listening to tenants' complaints. Still, the reduction of the Landgarb was important in the long run because rents after the war remained at the new, lower level. This reduction would not have come about without the tenants' determined efforts. The final resolution of the Landgarb dispute is important for another reason as well: though it took several years of effort, the tenants of an entire district worked collectively and without resorting to violence. In the end, the abbey conceded significant and long-term rent reductions.

Despite heated disputes such as this one, there was a conspicuous lack of political violence in Salem's lands throughout the period under study. This fact calls our attention to Thomas Robisheaux's pertinent queries about the nature of "peasant unrest and the moral economy."[194] First of all, Robisheaux asks, why do violent revolts rarely break out in the weakest and most vulnerable territorial states? Their rulers hardly had the bureaucratic structures, the personnel, or the military forces to suppress resistance as the larger states could. Second, why were those peasants who were most vulnerable to the new pressures of the state often the least likely to protest publicly against the burden of new levies? In Salem, the Audience undoubtedly provides part of the explanation.[195] Through grievance procedures the abbey was able to diffuse tensions, grant selective favors, postpone decisions, offer vague promises, and deal with subjects individually before things got out of hand. In many cases the Audience provided concrete solutions to the problems subjects faced, but just as crucial was the general perception it was meant to

---

192 GLAK, 61/13374.

193 By 1635, the population was severely reduced and most of the fields were no longer cultivated. In that year the peasants of several villages decided to farm collectively in a central location, pooling their few plow teams and tools and taking turns doing the work and keeping watch. Pfullendorf donated some plow teams in 1637 to help Salem's subjects replant their fields after several years of neglect. WEECH, Bürsters Beschreibung, pp. 90–91, 93, 111; BAIER, Akten des dreißigjährigen Krieges, p. 147.

194 Thomas ROBISHEAUX, Peasant Unrest and the Moral Economy in the German Southwest, in: Archive for Reformation History 78 (1987), pp. 177–178.

195 Robisheaux describes a similar petitioning process in Hohenlohe, where the lord approved as many as 96% of wood and grain requests and answered most tenure and tax petitions favorably as well. Idem, Rural Society, pp. 171–173.

foster of the lord's benevolence. Especially for a small territory such as this one, personal appearances before the assembled representatives of rule were an important means of forging relationships, as for example when a positive response from the Audience laid the foundations for the petitioner's future obligations and loyalty. Furthermore, the Audience emphasized many elements of lordship that subjects valued most: protection, mercy, patronage, and reciprocity. There were obvious advantages for all sides.

6.6 Territorial Defense and the Schützengesellschaft

Owning a weapon and being prepared to defend one's homeland were citizenship requirements in many territories, for burghers and for peasants.[196] Citizen militias, separate from the imperial armies, were especially important for defending the region when regular troops were off fighting in distant lands. There are indications that Salem's male subjects were required to possess and bear arms even before 1525. By the late sixteenth century, local and territorial defense had become a major concern as well as a common duty.[197] The widespread introduction of muskets in the early seventeenth century led to advances in military preparedness and local organization.

In 1576 and 1587 the abbey kept detailed lists of the soldiers and weapons it could call on from each village. There were 581 and 628 soldiers respectively in the central territory.[198] The 1593 tax register describes the weapons carried by 491 householders (including five widows with weapons assigned to their farms), the most common weapons including axes (157), pikes and spears (137), and halberds (42).[199] These weapons were distributed across villages and socioeconomic groups, though armor (*Rüstung, Harnisch*) was typically listed only among wealthier households. Four men played drums, there was one piper, two had battle swords, and just one carried a firearm (*Büchse*). There were also 189 male taxpayers listed in 1593 as unarmed, with reasons supplied occasionally.[200] In 41 cases, the words "no weapon, not admitted, not sworn"

---

196 By executive order of the 1555 Imperial Diet of Augsburg, all imperial estates had to be ready to defend themselves against outside attack and to offer aid to their neighbors if necessary. See Manfred SCHECK, Von Schützen und Spießern: Das wehrhafte Vaihingen im Spiegel der Musterungslisten 1521–1633, in: Zeitschrift für Württembergische Landesgeschichte 52 (1993), pp. 137–153.

197 According to Salem's alte Jarbrief, the abbey claimed to inherit armor and weapons from male dependents who died without sons. In 1525, Salem's chronicler described the 10,000 peasant rebels assembled in Bermatingen as well armed. Tax assessments from 1578 and 1593 list armor and weapons as items of moveable wealth in peasant households. GLAK, 98/2026, fol. 2v, 6r.

198 GLAK, 98/1598–1599.

199 GLAK, 98/2050.

200 The sextons in three villages were exempt, along with all priests. One man still living with his mother was excused, as was another for physical incapacity. The abbey secretary and Oberamtmann were subject to taxation but not required to bear arms.

indicate villagers who were not legal residents or abbey subjects. For 108 others, the phrase "no weapon yet" states the expectation of future military service, perhaps from a new householder or youth who would soon join the ranks.

In 1610, 14,000 troops from Brandenburg-Ansbach marched across the region. Damages were minimal, but the incident led abbey leaders to make better defense preparations. For several years starting in 1611, Salem mustered all its troops annually in addition to semi-annual reviews of each district.[201] Abbey officials encouraged the creation of defense associations (*Schützengesellschaften*) in the various local communities, which functioned as "shooting clubs" with regular drill sessions and annual competitions to promote marksmanship and military skill. A 1612 shooting ordinance from the local association in Neufrach explained:

> Highest necessity requires a general military inspection, not only here but in all places under the abbey of Salmansweiler's authority. War veterans believe the musket to be the most useful weapon, but it is well known that many are completely inexperienced in the use of such weapons at this time. Therefore our gracious lord [etc.] has declared that target ranges are to be permitted throughout his jurisdiction and not only in Neufrach, where common shooting fellowships can be held so that musketeers can meet Sundays and holidays or at other times.[202]

Citizen militias were nothing new in 1611 but suddenly muskets, and shooting practice, became extremely popular.[203] According to correspondence between Salem and Heiligenberg, new target ranges appeared in Owingen and Pfaffenhofen as well as Neufrach in that year.[204] Abbey authorities encouraged marksmanship tournaments between villages and with other territories. An invitation to a shooting tournament in 1619, sent by Bermatingen to Mimmenhausen, said by way of introduction: "Certainly you are well aware of the gracious [etc.] authorities' earlier command that under the prevailing circumstances we must practice shooting and hold annual competitions at one of the three shooting ranges in Mimmenhausen, Neufrach, and Bermatingen to encourage

---

201 FEYERABEND, Chronik, p. 251.

202 "Dieweyl die höchst notturfft erfordert hatt, daß nit allain alhie, sonnder aller orthen, Alda daß Gottßhaus Salmanschweyler die Oberkhait hatt, Ain general Mussterung fürgenommen werden müessen, under annderm, denn Underthonen ufferlegten wehren, die Mußqueten die nuzlichisten bey denn verstendigen und krüegserfahrnen erachtet worden. Dieweyl aber wie offendtlich am tag, ettliche so Mußqueten ufferlegt, solliche zugeprauchen gannz unerfahren, sollen hiemit unnd Innßkhünfftig, nit allain zue Neüffra, sonnder aller In deß Oberkhaiten Zwing und Pännen, da Ihr Gnaden, der Hochwürdig, unnßer Gnediger herr, zeylstatten uffzerichten gnedig vergunnden und erlaubt, denn Mußqueten shüzen, alle Sonn- und feür- tag oder zue annderer Zeith, Alda dann gemaine Gesellschafft schiessen gehalten werden ..." GLAK, 98/3476, fol. 5v, art. 45.

203 Firearms were first introduced in the fifteenth century but caught on slowly because they were so cumbersome and inaccurate. According to Manfred Scheck the use of firearms in Württemberg increased slowly during the sixteenth century, then dramatically between 1608 and 1633. Idem, Schützen und Spießern, pp. 138, 146.

204 GLAK, 98/1616.

diligence, good practice, and experience among our marksmen."[205] At a new target range near the abbey, a shooting competition took place in 1626. The authorities donated 24 Reichsthaler for refreshments and the grand prize of an ox. For a tournament in 1628, Salem donated prizes including an ox, pig, and ram.[206]

In the early seventeenth century, heightened military concerns and the introduction of muskets and drills show up in various sorts of documents. The communes of Neufrach, Mimmenhausen, "and others" petitioned the Audience in 1611 for gunpowder and other supplies necessary to train with the recently assigned weapons. Similar requests followed in later years.[207] In 1612 Salem had 1,500 well-armed, uniformed men available for military service.[208] A 1613 list of judges from Bermatingen's village court was followed by the names of ten new residents and their weapons assignments, under the title: "Admitted to the commune and required to carry weapons as follows."[209] Further evidence appears in the form of marriage requests. Starting in 1616 and increasingly by the early 1630s, permission for residence or marriage became contingent upon military registration. Claus Neuenberger was admitted to Neufrach in 1616 and told to prepare for military service with his musket, rapier, and dress, "conforming in color and style to common practice."[210] A 1619 list of soldiers from Bermatingen names 121 men and their weapons.[211] In addition to general infantrymen there were a

---

205 "Eüch ist mer dann wolbewust was masen unnser genedige hoch erennde Oberkaidt bevelch, uß bewegenden ursachen vor disem mit Mussqeten zuoschiessen uferlegt worden, unnd Jerlich uf den drey Züllstadten, Mimenhausen Nifra unnd Bermatingen ain frey gesellenschiesen an ainem deren Orten zehalten An Ordnung gethon, damit den fleys deren Mussqutieren unnd guote Yebunng und erfarenhaidt zuo schiessen Contuniern unnd erspiren." GLAK, 98/1616.

206 GLAK, 98/1616, 27 Sept. 1626 and 15 Oct. 1628.

207 The Audience approved a grant of 15 fl. to Neufrach's 45 musketeers in 1611. In 1613 Mimmenhausen and Neufrach received twenty gulden, Bermatingen and Owingen ten gulden each. Officials approved contributions to all of Salem's local militias upon their request in 1616. GLAK, 61/13370.

208 FEYERABEND, Chronik, p. 251.

209 "In die Gemaindt daselbsten ufgenommen unnd beygesetzte Wehren uferlegt Worden Wie Volgt." GLAK, 98/597, 1613.

210 GLAK, 61/13370, 1616. Hans Müller's marriage to Anna Bursterin was also approved in 1616 with the reminder to prepare his "überwehr, Mußquet mit ihrer zuegehör, Rappier Schützenröckle von bestem tuech nach dem lindisch in der farb und form wie bräuchlich." New householders required to report for military service in the early 1630s included Christa Teuschel of Mimmenhausen, Peter Stett of Owingen, Mattheus Beckh and Hans Bart of Nußdorf, Michael Bommer of Neufrach, Martin Schilpin and Adam Jung of Nußdorf, Mattheus Ill of Owingen, Mattheus Fünfflin of Weiler, Jerg Meßmer of Oberuhldingen, and Hans Müller of Owingen. GLAK, 61/13374.

211 The document's title indicates that the authorities assigned a weapon to each resident: "Verzaichnuß dern von obrikait Jeden daselbsten ufgelegten weren." Weapons included muskets (65), pikes (34), short swords (9), pickaxes (4), and broad swords (3). Many entries describe the presence or absence of auxilliary equipment and its condition. For example, most pikesmen

commanding officer, standard-bearer, field surgeon, watchman, two drummers, and a piper. Three surviving lists from marksmanship competitions in this period record the names of participants from throughout the territory, along with their scores.[212]

An extremely revealing source is the aforementioned shooting ordinance from the local defense association in Neufrach. This document, containing 49 articles, appears to have been produced by the members and it was likely recorded by the society's own secretary (*Schreiber*). There is no mention of the society's origins, yet the 1612 ordinance proclaimed itself a renewal, hinting that the group's organization predated the abbey's recent policies promoting such activities. The ordinance expressed members' concerns that the abbey's new interest in military preparedness would result in the need for more powder and lead and in higher membership dues. It stated their desire that customary rules should remain in effect and be read aloud each year. This is significant, because it shows local defense associations did not develop solely in response to the abbey's urging. Protection was certainly a motivating factor, but the document suggests another reason for villagers' interest in associations for defense, or "shooting clubs"—like other sporting events, target practice and tournaments reinforced male sociability within and among various communities.

Sociability was an important aspect of the Neufrach shooting club. Article 19 of the ordinance stated that when the group shared a drink during shooting practice ("which no one should be forced to do"), they should save a glass for the commander (*Zeiger*) to be enjoyed afterward, in addition to his regular wages. Prizes for the top six scores provided performance incentives, with high honors accorded to the top two contenders.[213] Yet winning a prize was not the competition's primary goal. According to Article 37, those awarded first or second place could still compete in future events, but no one could take the top prizes more than once in order to give everyone a fair chance. In addition, the best marksman was required to give the commander two kreuzer. The winner of a "foreign" tournament was expected to provide drinks to all his comrades after their return home.[214] These regulations sought to promote friendly competition and military skill rather than envy and personal rivalries.

---

wore armor (*Harnisch, Rüstung*), while musketeers had special uniforms (*Schüzenrökhlj*, noted as absent in 11 cases). Muskets were usually listed "along with all accessories." Some weapons were described as deficient (*schlecht*) or missing (*manglet*). GLAK, 98/3202.

212 Participants in 1626 included 78 marksmen from Mimmenhausen, 31 from Bermatingen, 60 from Neufrach, 30 from Uhldingen, and 37 from Owingen. A second list from around the same period included 69 from Mimmenhausen, 22 from Weildorf, 20 from Tüfingen, and 12 from Grasbeuren. A third, undated list names participants from Mimmenhausen, Bermatingen, and Neufrach. Each list records individuals' performance on three target shots. GLAK, 98/1616.

213 First prize was either twelve batzen or four yards of fustian cloth. Fustian, a mix of cotton and linen, was a popular prize at races and tournaments; see GÖTZE, Frühneuhochdeutsches Glossar, p. 21; WEECH, Bürsters Beschreibung, p. 27 n. 1.

214 "Unnd ob man khünfftig ahn frembde orth zu Gesellen schiessen beruoffen, unnd man zuziehen geaintt wurde, Wöllcher dann daß erst bösst gewinnett, Soll Er der Gesellschafft so man

According to the Neufrach shooting society rules, membership was voluntary but not open to all. New members were admitted only at designated times, with non-members forbidden to participate or loiter around during shooting practice. The commander was expected to enforce these rules with fines, especially among the young servant boys, "to prevent any misfortune."[215] As a paid official, the commander had to attend all association meetings or find a substitute.[216] For others, attendance was voluntary unless the drillmaster (*Schützenmeister*) ordered everyone to appear.[217] No prizes were awarded if there were fewer than eight participants, and any who arrived late were ineligible to join. It was the commander's responsibility to judge the shots, and several articles regulated scoring. In case of disagreement, he should choose two impartial men to examine the target and make the call. When the association received an invitation to a foreign (that is, nonlocal) competition, the group would decide whether to attend by holding an Umfrag. Not everyone had to travel to such tournaments, but anyone who agreed to go and did not show up had to compensate the others with drinks.[218]

During the Thirty Years War, local organizations for defense temporarily broke down. According to Gabriel Feyerabend, the abbey discontinued its citizen militia and disarmed its subjects when large armies began crossing the region.[219] Yet other sources demonstrate that subjects continued to do what they could to protect their communities, the abbey, and even the city of Überlingen. The Amtmann of Weildorf reported in 1633 in the name of the entire commune that they had entered a mutual aid agreement with the neighboring village of Beuren (under Heiligenberg's jurisdiction) following

haimb khompt, Ain halb Vierttel Wein Zuverehren schuldig sein, Deßgleichen von Jedem frey Barchat Ain quartt, und soll diß uffs letst Gesellenschiessen, doch allweeg durch den Schreiber ordenlich auffgezaichnet werden." GLAK, 98/3476, fol. 4r, art. 34.

215 "Unnd soll der Zaiger ganz Niemandts, so nit zur Gesellschafft gehörig, besonnder Jung ungezogen gesindt mit Ihm hinauß lasßen, sonder sollches mit Ernst, zu verhüettung unglückhs, bey straff 3 ß dn. abschaffen." GLAK, 98/3476, fol. 3r, art. 26.

216 "Unnd so der Zaiger Ain oder mehr schießtäg versaumen und khainen ahn sein statt verordnen wurdt, soll Ihme doppelter lohn, bey abrechnung abgezogen werden." GLAK, 98/3476, fol. 2v, art. 18.

217 Article 13 stated: "Wann Innß khünfftig die geordnete Schüzenmaister die Schüzen uff ain ordenliche stundt durch den geschwornnen Zaiger, uff der Lauben zuerscheinen angekhündt würdt, Welcher ungehorsamb ußpleibt, soll ohne gnad allwegen umb 4 kr. unnachläßlich gestrafft werden, Wellich auch der Schreyber uffzaichnen soll." Article 12 made allowances for attending church consecrations, weddings, and other festivals. Since shooting practice and competitions were held on Sunday afternoons, there were often conflicting events.

218 An Umfrag was also used to determine punishments for foul language or behavior and to grant permission to use a borrowed weapon. Drinking fines were assessed for throwing another man's musket in anger, failing to remove the target after use, and for other offenses. GLAK, 98/3476, arts. 10, 14, 31, and 49.

219 FEYERABEND, Chronik, p. 251. Citizen militias in Württemberg also disbanded temporarily after the Battle of Nördlingen, when it became painfully clear that local peasants were no match for professional soldiers. SCHECK, Schützen und Spießern, pp. 149–150.

several recent attacks. The abbey ratified the arrangement.[220] That same year 400 peasant soldiers with reinforcements from Heiligenberg successfully protected the abbey against roving Swedish cavalry.[221] In 1634 several of Salem's subjects fell defending Überlingen and Sebastian Bürster, clearly no fan of the city, noted that peasants and soldiers did all the work to save it with little help from the townspeople.[222] Yet the bravery of volunteer militiamen could not stop the physical devastation and social dislocation of villages that followed. Not until after the war did signs of local defense societies start to reappear. Correspondence mentions Salem's *Schützengesellschaften* again in 1658, with growing documentation after 1660.[223] Eventually, a permanent garrison was established in Mimmenhausen to protect the abbey and its territory.

Salem's local shooting societies helped accomodate the abbey's military weakness, even if they were no match for professional soldiers during the war. They seem to have been a source of pride for both the abbey and its villagers in the early seventeenth century. Territorial defense in Salem was rudimentary compared with larger principalities, but it was also far less expensive and less burdensome to subjects, who organized regular drills and friendly competitions according to their own prescriptions. The organization of local and territorial defense is yet another example of a growing territorial identity built from below, based on complementary interests, social networks, and communal values.

6.7 Residency Restrictions and the Closure of the Village

Limiting the population of the village and the demands on its resources, especially by outsiders, were two concerns shared by abbey officials and community members in the decades around 1600. Individual residency petitions and Audience decisions from the period 1583–1635 demonstrate that growing concerns about overpopulation and tightening resources were resulting in greater restrictions on new residents and stricter enforcement of previously introduced policies. The restriction of new household formation is a process Govind Sreenivasan calls the "closure of the village."[224] In Salem, the abbey and the village communes used such restrictions to limit population growth and the division of wealth through the claims of outsiders and the poor. Growing restrictions on residency were above all an attempt to maintain stability in the village and

220 GLAK, 61/13374, 1633.

221 Bürster praised Salem's militiamen as good musketeers in 1633, assisted by 150 of Heiligenberg's poorly armed peasants carrying pig spears. On this occasion Salem offered bread and drinks to each one, and the peasants promised their future assistance. WEECH, Bürsters Beschreibung, p. 33.

222 Bürster described these incidents as he berated Überlingen for over two pages (for example: "Den pauren und redlichen, dapfern soldaten ist diese victoria zuezueaignen und nit den buorgern"). Ibid., pp. 46–48.

223 GLAK, 98/1616.

224 SREENIVASAN, Ottobeuren, p. 170.

to restrict resources for the use of certain households.[225] Limits on population growth before the Thirty Years War were imposed through preventative checks, which were socially rather than biologically constructed.

Throughout the long sixteenth century, outsiders needed permission to assume residence within the abbey's jurisdiction.[226] Both the abbey and the commune had good reasons for restricting the entry of new residents—especially those who were without property or desired skills, who would compete with established householders for limited resources, who were known for disorderly conduct, or who were not the abbey's serfs. From the petitions, clarifications, and responses found in the Audience records as well as more formal statements of territorial custom, permission from the abbey to reside in one of its villages appears to have been limited by three major conditions: wealth, servility, and communal consent.[227] These prerequisites are illustrated in the request made by Martin Erhart for his son-in-law in 1599. The Audience responded: "If his daughter's husband is able to provide a written certificate and charter [regarding his status and birth], demonstrate his wealth of fifty gulden, and be accepted by the commune, then His Grace would be satisfied to admit him."[228]

The first condition, financial resources, was usually satisfied by demonstrating wealth of at least fifty gulden. This minimum doubled to one hundred gulden around 1600, but the new standard took some time to implement.[229] According to Article 5 of a 1599 ordinance,

> Seeing how until now there has been a great deal of sexual misconduct among the servant youths as well as many imprudent marriages, which has been cause not only for common complaint and overcrowding but also for the constant deluge of requests from these people that the

---

[225] The Audience rejected one petition in 1624 from a young foreign worker who had insufficient property, with the added explanation: "sonderlich auch darumb, weil die gmeindt sonst übersetzt." GLAK, 61/13373.

[226] Residence generally implied not only permission to live within a certain settlement but also full rights as a member of the commune. Servants who were temporarily employed by established households often received permission to remain in the village for limited periods, but even they came under greater scrutiny in the early seventeenth century, especially if they were not abbey serfs and native to the territory. For example, the priest in Weildorf asked permission in 1624 to keep a servant who was a territorial outsider but had worked in the village for over twenty years. The Audience responded that the servant could remain until St. Jacob's Day and should then leave, despite the priest's claim that he could not find a replacement. Ibid.

[227] Individual entries rarely mention all three conditions, but they do appear in requests from all sampled years. The restrictions were probably invoked on a selective basis, depending on the petitioner's background and the abbey's willingness to have the individual as a resident subject. The conditions could be used to reject unwanted candidates or waived for others whom the abbey or commune preferred. Cf. ROBISHEAUX, Roral Society, p. 78.

[228] GLAK, 61/13369.

[229] In sampled Audience petitions from 1599, 1600, 1606, and 1611, fifty gulden remained the norm.

> abbey help them and administer alms, the communes are charged with the following: in the future, no one from outside the jurisdiction shall be admitted to a commune within the jurisdiction on the basis of marriage, unless he or she has property worth one hundred gulden, regardless of whether or not they are the abbey's serf. Rather, any resident who has married such an outsider, though they may well be a child born and raised in the village, shall be expelled from the jurisdiction along with their spouse.[230]

The Audience announced the increase from fifty to one hundred gulden again in 1615 as if it were new, and it was not until the years around 1624 that the measure was actually enforced.[231] The wealth requirement, it should be noted, primarily concerned territorial outsiders. It did not apply to abbey subjects wanting to move from one village to another or those who planned to marry a neighbor within the community. The Audience upheld this interpretation when it agreed in 1613 to permit a marriage between individuals from Bermatingen and Buggensegel. The wife was approved as a new resident of Bermatingen, even though she had very little property, "because the statute applies only to strangers from other lands."[232]

Servility was a second condition for aspiring residents. Newcomers were expected to become the abbey's serfs and swear a loyalty oath to the abbot. Audience decisions often required explicitly that the incoming spouse present a charter as proof of manumission before their admittance. Alternatively, the incoming spouse might offer or even request permission to become the abbey's serf in order to marry into the territory and become a legally recognized member of one of its communes. Two consecutive petitions in 1624, both from territorial residents, requested that the abbey accept them as its serfs so they could marry girls from another village.[233] These examples illustrate the continuing relevance of legal status in the early seventeenth century, but for different reasons than in 1473. Serfdom had developed new social and economic implications as the means of preferred access to resources in the abbey's villages, including communal membership, use of the commons, housing, marriage partners, farm tenures, employment, political office, and even welfare benefits such as bread alms.[234] In a period of tightening resources and demographic pressure, petitions for residence provide evidence to suggest why Salem continued to insist on serfdom and why it remained relevant even as servility was declining elsewhere.

Consent from the lord and commune was the third factor pertaining to residency. In some cases this requirement was specifically noted. For example, the carpenter Hans Hund from Urnau requested permission to marry a widow in Neufrach and move into her house. The abbey was agreeable but first told him to obtain the com-

230 GLAK, 98/395.

231 GLAK, 61/13370.

232 Ibid.

233 GLAK, 61/13373. One request was approved, the other denied.

234 According to tax lists between 1578 and 1603, serfs were wealthier than nonserfs on average as well as much more likely to hold farm tenures.

mune's support. A note in the record below indicated approval.[235] When the widow Barbara Michlerin of Tüfingen asked permission (through her father and the Amtmann) to marry a foreign serf who brought fifty gulden to the marriage, the Audience postponed its decision—not to demand that the man become the abbey's serf, but to hear the commune's opinion.[236] New residents were responsible for a small entry fee to both the commune and the lord, emphasizing the consent of all parties.[237]

The prosperous householders were perhaps especially wary of the growing number of poor strangers in the village because newcomers were a threat to their control of the farm tenures, held according to annual lease.[238] Restrictions on outsiders were also in the interests of poorer villagers, however, because new residents competed with them for housing, land, grazing rights, marriage partners, and labor opportunities. For example, in 1595 the Amtmann of Oberuhldingen complained in the name of the entire commune against a carpenter's assistant from Ravensburg, citing the overpopulation of the village and the fact that they already had enough carpenters. The abbey agreed that the man should move on.[239] It should not be assumed that the commune limited new residents solely in the interests of wealthy landowners and at the expense of poorer households. There were different reasons why village elites and modest householders supported residence restrictions, but in most cases they were in agreement with the abbey in their desire to limit the entry of strangers.

The abbey and the commune had different reasons for limiting residence, and they did not always agree on whom to admit. In some cases this caused tensions between them. There are even examples in which the commune rejected a candidate but the Audience overrode its opinion, as in 1594, when the son of Salem's brickmaker married a girl in Mimmenhausen and requested residence there. The commune registered their disapproval but the Audience granted permission anyway, citing the fact that he already

235 GLAK, 61/13374, 1630.

236 Though she had the Amtmann's support, his word did not stand for the entire commune. GLAK, 61/13370, 1611.

237 Bermatingen's entry fees of one pound to the commune and one pound to the abbey were higher than the five to ten shillings required by most villages. In 1609 Bermatingen raised its entry requirements further, following an Umfrag held in the village assembly. New residents were henceforth required to post a security deposit of fifty gulden, which would be returned after a probationary period of six months. At that time the entire commune would vote whether or not to approve the application for permanent residence. The abbot ratified this village statute in 1610, reserving the right to amend it in the future. GLAK, 67/1484.

238 Sreenivasan (Ottobeuren, p. 167) sees the closure of the village as an interest shared by village elites and territorial authorities but not by poorer households and yielding heirs. The restrictions left members of these groups unable to establish new households, forcing many of them to leave the village. Salem's residence restrictions targeting outsiders were a different situation, because they did not require poorer inhabitants of the village to leave. The measures were enforced mainly against territorial outsiders and only selectively against jurisdictional residents who wanted to marry into a neighboring village.

239 GLAK, 61/13369.

had half of a house in the village as well as employment at the abbey's kiln.[240] Michael Urnau from Nußdorf, who had married the Oberamtmann's maid, was permitted in 1605 to live with her in Mimmenhausen despite the commune's reservations, because his bride already had housing there. In 1624 a young man from Kempten requested permanent residence in Oberuhldingen, where he had lived for two years assisting the miller before marrying the miller's daughter. The commune objected, stating they did not want him or any others like him, even though he stood to inherit property worth 150 fl. and was a great help to his elderly father-in-law. The Audience approved his residence over Oberuhldingen's protests.[241] A more extreme case of disagreement comes from the village of Weiler. As described in Chapter 3, the Amtmann there called a village assembly that decided not to admit a man whose residence the abbey had already approved. This resulted in a denunciation by the disgruntled former Oberamtmann (who also lived in the village) and the Amtmann's removal from office. In other cases the Audience followed the commune's recommendation, as when a former resident returned from Bohemia in 1624 with a wife and three small children to rejoin the village of Owingen. The Audience denied them admission, noting the commune's opposition and the accusation that his wife was destructive to the common forests and fields.[242]

The majority of petitions for residence were the result of marriage or the intention to marry. The relationship between marriage plans and residency petitions changed in the early seventeenth century, reflecting greater restrictions on new residents combined with stricter controls over marriage. In sampled Audience petitions from before 1600, petitioners who wished to move because of their recent marriage or intent to marry simply declared this fact as grounds for permission, and requests to marry were extremely uncommon. By around 1611, however, many couples planning to establish new households requested permission for marriage and residence simultaneously. By 1624 it had become standard procedure to request the lord's permission prior to marrying. This was the case even when both spouses were territorial subjects and occasionally when the spouses were members of the same village. In 1624 several couples (who were not from the same village) were banished from the territory when it was reported that they had married and assumed residence without prior permission. Such harsh measures may help explain why so many other couples suddenly began requesting permission to marry, even when both spouses came from the same village.[243] These expulsions also suggest cooperation between local and territorial officials in restricting unwanted residents, since banishments often resulted from an Amtmann's report.

240 Ibid. Other examples of the Audience ignoring the community's wishes are found in 1599 and 1611.

241 GLAK, 61/13373.

242 GLAK, 61/13373.

243 To my knowledge there are no Audience decisions barring the marriage of couples who were both from the same village, but in at least two cases, poor couples were explicitly denied future alms.

Since the abbey had no other way of knowing who was living in the village or whether they were the abbey's serfs, local informants were critical to the enforcement of its policies. The involvement of Amtmänner and the rising number of petitions concerning residency and marriage show that at least some members of the commune, presumably its wealthier property-holders, were in support of such measures. In contrast to earlier limits on new residents from outside the territory, these new restrictions targeted native men and women without property.

The decision to admit or deny new residents fluctuated with changing policies and specific local conditions.[244] With the exception of 1624, the majority of residency petitions brought before the Audience in sampled years were approved. Despite hints in the early 1620s that policies restricting residence and marriage were starting to take hold, even against local couples, the situation had reversed itself by 1630. Because of the war and the rising insecurity in the region, families were fleeing rather than trying to settle there. Consequently, the few residency requests in 1630 were almost all approved. After 1630 it became increasingly difficult to secure good tenants who were willing to remain in the villages to maintain and protect the abbey's property, and by 1635, the abbey was willing to offer unprecedented concessions to keep its fields cultivated.

The strict controls on new household formation in the early seventeenth century are a reminder that demographic growth was not purely the result of biological factors. Government policies, as well as their successful implementation, depended on local support, which in turn resulted from specific socioeconomic pressures. The development of residency restrictions provides an example of how communities responded creatively and overcame difficulties according to an array of interconnected needs and interests, rather than helplessly falling victim to the conditions that have often been used to characterize the early seventeenth century as a period of crisis. In this situation, abbey authorities and various actors within the villages worked together toward similar though not identical goals, exhibiting a fair degree of cooperation. Finally, the role of servility status in limiting immigration and the enjoyment of material and communal resources during this period, rather than serving to restrict the emigration of people and resources, emphasizes the flexibility of serfdom and its hallmarks.

6.8 Poverty, Charity, and Social Welfare

The consolidation of authority in Salem's territory Under the Hills was a two-way process of negotiation that depended on communication between the lordship and its subjects. The success of territorialization depended on the willingness of local residents to cooperate, and this cooperation depended in turn on the willingness of abbey

[244] An entry in the Audience minutes from 1604 noted that although the potter's son-in-law from Severatsweiler and the cabinetmaker from Neuenburg were both admitted to Mimmenhausen, future requests should not be so easily granted. GLAK, 61/13369.

officials to meet certain expectations of their subjects. In a period of tightening resources, widespread poverty, and social dislocation, villagers' petitions demanded that the abbey step in to help them more, not less. The promotion of the common good and the preservation of the peasant household's basic necessities were interests all villagers shared, and they expected the abbey to protect them as best it could. By caring for the sick, elderly, orphaned, and especially the poor, Salem's officials played an important role in promoting the territory's social welfare, helping local communities, and cultivating good will among subjects. Salem committed a great deal of time, energy, and material resources to these tasks. Perhaps Salem was particularly dedicated to issues of social welfare because of its ecclesiastical identity, for the church was traditionally a major provider of charity. Yet this explanation only goes so far. In large part, Salem's efforts appear to have been a response to demands from below. It was also in the abbey's own interests to protect subjects from the effects of poverty, if for no other reason than to strengthen its tax base. Salem gave more alms to the poor than neighboring lords and even fed many poor subjects of Überlingen and Heiligenberg beside its own. These actions paid off, both with respect to communal and individual well-being, and in terms of legitimacy. Subjects were generally more willing to cooperate with the abbey when it displayed generosity and offered assistance to those who needed it most.

In the decades after 1600 the problem of rural poverty, and especially the issue of wandering beggars, was a growing concern in the Linzgau and elsewhere. According to the literature, early modern attitudes toward the poor as well as forms of charity shifted toward greater restriction, hostility, and a decline of personal relationships between donors and recipients.[245] According to this interpretation, territorial rulers and neighbors alike increasingly saw the poor as a threat to prosperity and stability, whose situation was no one's fault but their own. With the shift in prevailing attitudes, they were less likely than before to view the poor as Christ-like and charity as an opportunity to help others while earning personal redemption. Many feared the poor and believed that poverty spread sedition, sickness, and theft. Some historians see state-sponsored programs for poor relief in the early modern period as first attempts to subject the poor—especially beggars, homeless, and social deviants—to greater social discipline and control.[246] According to Claudia Schott's research on poverty and almsgiving in

---

[245] Robert JÜTTE, Poverty and Poor Relief, in: Germany: A New Social and Economic History, vol. 2, 1630–1800, ed. Sheilagh Ogilvie, London and New York 1996, pp. 389–390; RAEFF, Police State; ROBISHEAUX, Rural Society, pp. 69–70.

[246] The Reformation was a major catalyst for this shift, since princes and cities now took over the responsibility for alms from the charitable organizations affiliated with the church. It also severed the link between charity and salvation, leading to a decline in private charity. Irrespective of confessional difference, however, the problem of poverty was coming more and more under the supervision of territorial authorities. RAEFF, Police State, pp. 87–92. Against this view is Martin DINGES, Frühneuzeitliche Armenfürsorge als Sozialdisziplinierung? Probleme mit einem Konzept, in: Geschichte und Gesellschaft 17 (1991), pp. 92–101.

Salem, these objectives were never realized by abbey officials in part because they did not have the power or bureaucracy to enforce their will.[247] This section briefly evaluates these issues in the context of our larger themes of inquiry.

Poverty and charity had special political and social relevance in an ecclesiastical territory.[248] Requests for aid and the provision of alms tested and demonstrated the lord's commitment to key Christian and monastic values. The rising documentation of poor relief in Salem after the mid-sixteenth century reflects improvements in record-keeping, but it also suggests increasing concern on all sides as impoverishment spread and became a greater burden. Territorial policies and programs evolved in response to overwhelming individual need as well as the negotiation of various groups' appeals for protection and assistance.

A few statistics make clear the magnitude of the problem. According to tax lists, half of all households in Neufrach and Buggensegel and a third of those in Bermatingen were without property in 1505. At least one in four households was destitute in 1578, 1593, and 1603 with property worth 25 fl. or less. In 1630 an estimated eighty percent of the population consisted of smallholders and winegrowers, some of whom shared a house. A 1633 list designated three-quarters of all households as smallholders.[249] Records of almsgiving convey a similar impression. According to a letter written in 1575, the abbey distributed 5,000 loaves to the poor each week at a cost in grain of over 500 Malter.[250] In 1626 Salem's alms director, Sebastian Bürster, kept an account of semi-weekly bread distributions with a total of 241,521 loaves at a cost of 4,410 fl. for the year.[251] According to a 1628 list, the abbey supported 881 of its own needy subjects from various villages as well as 924 "foreign" poor.[252] These last figures suggest that territorial subjects receiving alms during the Thirty Years War made up almost one-quarter of all residents, while the total number of alms recipients including foreigners was equivalent to half the size of the entire territorial population.

The abbey supported the territorial poor in several ways. Most important was the "great alms," held each Wednesday and Saturday at the abbey's Upper Gate.[253] The

---

247 SCHOTT, Armenfürsorge, p. 9.

248 Peter HERSCHE, Intendierte Ruckständigkeit: Zur Charakteristik des geistlichen Staates im Alten Reich, in: Stände und Gesellschaft im Alten Reich, ed. Georg Schmidt, Stuttgart 1989; Franz QUARTHAL, Unterm Krummstab, pp. 282–283.

249 These numbers are based on GLAK, 98/2007, 98/2024, 98/2050, 98/2309, 98/2033, and BAIER, Bevölkerungsbewegung, p. 59. See also Chapter 4.

250 GLAK, 98/60.

251 SCHOTT, Armenfürsorge, pp. 30–32. The average weekly bread distribution was 4,645 loaves.

252 Ibid., pp. 28–29; GLAK, 98/59, fol. 18r. The poor belonging to neighboring territories and towns included 400 each from Heiligenberg and Überlingen as well as a few from Meersburg, Markdorf, and Lipperatsreute.

253 The Upper Gate (where the Sidelgericht also met) is specifically mentioned in the 1623 ordinance. Distributions sometimes took place at the Lower Gate, but not at the gate nearest to the bakery (*Pfistertor*); GLAK, 98/59 and SCHOTT, Armenfürsorge, pp. 14–15.

Pfister or Oberamtmann was sometimes present to keep order among the crowds, carrying a list of alms recipients to distinguish them from strangers and nonneedy subjects.[254] There were also several smaller alms distributions, including daily rations to a select group of local poor outside the abbey kitchen.[255] Bread was regularly distributed at other locations, such as Wespach hospital and the grange in Maurach.[256] Special alms were handed out on certain holidays, including St. Agatha's Day (5 February) and Maundy Thursday (three days before Easter). The abbey also granted favors to poor subjects on an individual basis, such as freedom from manumission or death taxes.[257]

Salem issued a series of ordinances on poverty and almsgiving, four of them from our period.[258] In the first, published in 1561, Abbot Georg II expressed concern that many of the semi-weekly alms recipients were not behaving in a deserving manner. Some of the poor were seen day and night in taverns, swearing and taking God's name in vain, while sitting around drinking wine.

> Not only do they squander these offerings godlessly, they show no gratitude whatsoever as they consume what is given and shared out of the will to honor God. Through their disgraceful actions and wastefulness, they wantonly condemn their wives and children to take up the beggar's staff. They should be ashamed to ask for such alms, but instead they simply say they have come for their bread, as if they had bought such provisions from the abbey for their maintenance, as if one were bound and obliged to give it to them.[259]

The abbot emphasized that only the eligible poor who acted honorably and were unable to support themselves would receive assistance. Although other lordships required the poor to wear identification badges, the abbot waived this requirement out of his "merciful and fatherly will." Still, alms would not be handed out indiscriminately. He directed the Amtmänner to list those who wished to receive alms so he could consider their requests.

---

[254] One list of alms-seekers from 1628 shows the kind of information and organization such documents contained. Names were grouped by village, and each entry was accompanied by notes on household size and the number of loaves. Margin notes described individuals' need, wealth, behavior, employment, legal status, and other criteria. GLAK, 98/59, fol. 13–18.

[255] SCHOTT, Armenfürsorge, p. 16.

[256] Evidence suggests that some subjects traveled to each distribution center. A note below the 1628 poor list stated: "Nussdorffer, Oberuldinger, Mulhoffer solten Maurach zuo friden lassen, und nit täglichen neben disem Almuosen erst nach dort hin lauffen und also shier ganz und gar durch die ganze wochen von dem Gottshauss leben, dan es gehet gar vil Almuosen aldort wegen diss zuo lauffen auff, alle wochen uffs wenigst – 200 brodt. Da doch vor disem offtermalen uber 40 oder 50 nit gebraucht worden." GLAK, 98/59, fol. 17v.

[257] For example, Caspar Sixt of Oberuhldingen received a begging permit for one year after his house burned down in 1590. Around ten percent of sampled Audience petitions were for bread alms, other forms of charity, or exemption from fees on account of personal poverty. Such requests ranged from 2 (1583 and 1589) to 42 (1611) annually.

[258] GLAK, 98/59; SCHOTT, Armenfürsorge, p. 18.

[259] GLAK, 98/59.

Abbot Georg II passed a second poor law on 26 September 1573, soon after entering agreements with Heiligenberg and Überlingen about almsgiving and the increasing burden of foreign beggars.[260] He repeated many of his earlier statements, complaining for example that many subjects still viewed semi-weekly bread alms as the abbey's duty and not as charity. He repeated his order that the poor stay away from taverns and inns and threatened to take away privileges from anyone who behaved undeservingly. The 1573 ordinance showed a greater concern with foreign beggars. It declared as its objective the protection of abbey subjects from harm caused by "foreign, unknown, wandering people." In the future all drifters, army deserters, beggars, and other idlers would be outlawed, banished, and denied any assistance.[261] In order to identify the poor, the abbot now introduced the badges he had explicitly forgone as unnecessary only twelve years earlier. Anyone requesting alms was required to wear their badge and appear at the specified place and time. There would be no more late handouts.

Less than one year later, on 5 June 1574, Abbot Georg II published a third ordinance: "A few points to be shared with the poor concerning weekly alms."[262] These additions were made "on account of momentous circumstances." Most notable was the declaration that from now on, alms would be given only to those appearing before the abbey gate, with their badges, at noon. "Therefore they should bring their children with them. Bread will not be sent home for those who do not appear in person."[263] Again, there were new restrictions on the foreign poor. Subjects of neighboring lordships should come only once a week, on Thursdays instead of the usual Wednesdays and Saturdays. They, too, had to wear identification badges. Other unknown strangers would receive nothing, as stated in the previous ordinance.

Almost fifty years passed before a new poor ordinance appeared in 1623.[264] This time, responsibility for keeping the registers of alms recipients shifted from the Amtmänner (who had previously submitted the lists) to the Großkeller and Pfister.[265] The ordinance eased certain restrictions on alms to poor residents but expressed greater

---

[260] The 1573 ordinance is found in GLAK, 98/59; see also SCHOTT, Armenfürsorge, pp. 10–11, 19. The agreement among the three lordships also occurred in 1573. Idem, p. 62.

[261] "Daneben die Ausslendishen frembden Arme Leuth, so weder in dess Gotsshaus Salmanssweyler, der Graueshafft heilligenberg, und der Statt Uberlingen, Hohen unnd Nidern Gerichten gesessen, noch begütet, dessgleichen die Gardtknecht, Landtstraiffer und andere faullenzende Personen und Bettler, abgeshafft, hingewisen, und Inen diss orts nichtzit gegeben werden." GLAK, 98/59, fol. 8r.

[262] GLAK, 98/59; SCHOTT, Armenfürsorge, p. 19.

[263] "Desshalben sie Ire kinder mit Inen bringen mogen, Dann wer nit Personlich Zugegen sein, demselben wirdet man das Brott nit heimschicken." GLAK, 98/59, fol. 9r.

[264] GLAK, 98/59, fol. 508–511; SCHOTT, Armenfürsorge, pp. 11, 19, 24.

[265] SCHOTT, Armenfürsorge, p. 24. This helps explain why so few petitions for alms were presented to the Audience in 1624 (see n. 131 above). The noticeable decline in that year is not an indication that alms were no longer handed out, but rather, that the Audience was no longer primarily responsible for such decisions.

concern with and even fear of wandering strangers.[266] The alms overseer was instructed to keep a watchful eye on strangers and exclude them if they became a nuisance. The Oberamtmann should be present if possible at alms distributions and station halberdiers for security near the Upper Gate. In case of food shortages, watchmen were to ride through the villages and isolated settlements day and night, protecting residents from wandering beggars. Householders were warned not to shelter anyone for more than one night and not to buy, sell, or trade poultry to strangers, which encouraged theft.

The evidence presented thus far supports Claudia Schott's argument that Salem's policies toward the poor were limited in many ways, by many interest groups, and by the lack of administrative tools or support necessary to meet such massive demand. Some of the behavioral regulations and penalties for actions such as public drinking and swearing could be interpreted under the rubric of social discipline. Yet the regulation of moral behavior and control over begging were hardly possible when abbey leaders were unable even to distinguish resident poor from strangers and handed out thousands of loaves at a time. When we augment the poor laws with other types of evidence from the period, it appears that changes in poor policy did not result from some overly ambitious plan to control the behavior of the destitute masses after all. As in many other areas of policy development, decisions at the territorial level were shaped by relationships with and pressures from two major groups: Salem's neighbors, primarily Heiligenberg, and its subjects in the local communities.

Abbey leaders were extremely concerned with how their charitable actions would be perceived by outsiders. The best demonstration of Heiligenberg's influence on abbey policy is perhaps a set of internal instructions dated 4 January 1575. The document was written in preparation for an upcoming meeting with the count, shortly after the ordinance limiting alms to foreign subjects.[267] The letter contained several justifications for the abbey's new restrictions. First, the author explained, there were the current food and wine shortages.[268] Second, almsgiving was getting out of control with the multitude of alms-seekers, the majority of whom demanded their daily bread as if it were their right and not an act of charity. Besides, the abbey's subjects were com-

---

[266] The ordinance qualified the 1574 statement that alms-seekers must appear in person. Semiweekly alms were also reinstated for an approved group of "foreign subjects," but only those who resided in Salem's territory Under the Hills. The 1623 text moderated its position toward wandering strangers by offering them any leftovers after distributions to registered families. GLAK, 98/59.

[267] This meeting most likely involved the abbot and the count, but it is unclear whether the document was written by the abbot or through some collaborative discussion among his close advisors.

[268] Things were so bad, the document attested, that even the monks' ordinary wine rations had to be discontinued and the abbey was importing grain at great cost. Hard times resulted in a much greater demand for alms, so that the abbey was distributing up to 5,000 loaves of bread per week. These shortages must have been the momentous circumstances cited in the 1574 ordinance. GLAK, 98/60.

plaining about the overwhelming demands of foreign beggars.[269] If these abuses were not corrected, the author worried, the abbey and its people would fall into destitution, decay, and disgrace. Yet he worried that any new limits would draw Heiligenberg's reproach. He pointed out that other lords had already introduced alms ordinances, causing beggars from the entire region to converge on the abbey. In conclusion, he expressed the hope that the count would not be upset or consider it unneighborly for the abbey to feed the count's needy subjects only once per week, "because whenever possible, in this and other matters, it would give the abbot and convent the greatest pleasure to gratify him [the count] before all other neighbors, and to consider his [subjects] before other poor people."[270]

Evidence also suggests that changes in poor policy came from the awareness of such great need in the decades around 1600, literally pressing its face up against the abbey gates. For example, when the Amtmann of Urnau requested alms for several poor villagers in 1590, the Audience approved his request and promised that a new alms ordinance would be issued soon. The shocking realization of such desperation among many villagers must have confronted abbey administrators at episodes such as an alms distribution in 1589, when the Pfister asked a woman from Weildorf to point out alms-seekers from Heiligenberg. Afterward, the Pfister reported, some of them waited for the woman and attacked her, beating her to the ground with an axe and showering her with verbal abuse.[271] In 1616 the bread overseer asked the Audience to require that the village headmen inform him whenever an alms recipient died, so that distributions would go to the right people.[272] Abbey officials were struggling simply to master the situation as hundreds of unfamiliar and hungry faces massed outside the abbey's gates.

Meanwhile, changing attitudes toward poor relief in the villages complicated the abbey's approach to almsgiving as religious charity, because others saw it as the lord's obligation to protect his dependents from poverty's effects. In 1594 the Amtmann of Grasbeuren petitioned the Audience in the name of the entire commune to complain about the continual molestation of villagers by cartloads of poor who were driven from one place to the next.[273] This was most certainly a reference to the common cus-

---

269 "Unnd uber diß Alles die frembden Armen leuth, von Allerlay Landtshafften unnd göginen heer, uf seinen Armen Hindersäßen tag und nacht gelegen, und die vil geblegt und beshwert haben." GLAK, 98/60, fol. 2r.

270 GLAK, 98/60, fol. 3r.

271 GLAK, 61/13369, 1589.

272 "Herr Brotamman begehrt bey verhör den Amptleüthen einzuebinden, das sye ihms anzaigen, wan ein mensch in ihren fleckhen und weylern sterbe, so das Armmueßen bey dem Gottshaus habe, es sey gleich das klain oder groß, damit er sich wem er das Armueßen geben soll, zu verhalten wiße." GLAK, 61/13370, 1616.

273 "Wie dz sie täglichen mit den Armen Leüten, so man Inen zuefüehr, hefftig beshwerdt, unnd also mit Irer fuehr steths behelliget, dz sie dardurch am hewen auch anderem übel verhindert werden." GLAK, 61/13369, 1594. His Grace promised to give the issue some thought.

Illustration 6.2: Beggars' Drive (*Bettelfuhr*)

By Hans Holbein the Younger, 1518
Wall fresco from the Hertenstein house, Luzerner Bürgerbibliothek

tom known as the *Bettelfuhr*, or "beggars' drive."[274] According to this practice, vividly depicted in a 1518 fresco by Hans Holbein the Younger, the poor were carted from place to place, allowing them to collect alms before moving on to the next stop. Sometimes the homeless poor were simply rounded up and dumped off elsewhere. See Illustration 6.2, Beggars' Drive. Buggensegel likewise complained in 1596 about the burden of having to drive the poor out of the village and requested an ordinance.[275] In 1624 the Amtmann of Owingen asked for permission to build stocks in the village, to better manage the "wandering, useless people."[276] Such examples indicate that local officials and entire communes were pressuring the abbey to do something about poverty's effects on local life.

Salem's commitment to charitable activities may have been higher than that of its neighbors. Charity was, after all, one of the founding ideals of the Cistercian Order. Yet the new regulations in this period and the abbey's response to the overwhelming level

---

274 Adalbert NAGEL, Die Bettelfuhr in Oberschwaben, in: Schriften des Vereins für Geschichte des Bodensees und seiner Umgebung 87 (1969), pp. 29–35, with references to the practice throughout Upper Swabia including Markdorf, Pfullendorf, and Heiligenberg.

275 "Meher Clagenn die vonn Buggensegel, Wie sy mit hinwegg fhüerung der Armen Leütthen so hoch beschwerdt werden, für andere dörffer, Pittenn umb ain Ordnung." GLAK, 61/13369, 1596. Yet another reference to the *Bettelfuhr* is found in the 1592 petition of Hans Mussel from Weildorf, who wanted to graze his new horse in the common pasture against the wishes of the community. The Audience told him he could keep a third horse if he would make it available for the abbey's use and agree to drive the poor out of the territory: "Er solle Auch mit seinen Rossen Wann es Vom Gottshauß begert würdt, zue Iren Wie dergleichen auch die Armen Leut hinweg zefieren schuldig unnd verbunden sein." GLAK, 61/13369, 1592.

276 No decision is recorded. GLAK, 61/13373, 1624.

of need expressed by its subjects demonstrate that policies toward the poor developed out of confrontations with the harsh realities of daily life in the world beyond the cloister, and from relationships between the abbey and its neighbors and subjects.

6.9 Education and Popular Literacy

Literacy and recordkeeping were skills more commonly found in Salem's villages than one might expect, even as early as the late sixteenth century. The evidence counters two widespread assumptions about education and the laity, first, that the Catholic Church was resistant to the idea of educating common people; and second, that village schools and lay education were not commonly established until later, starting in evangelical territories.[277] Salem's three-tiered system of schools within the territory and support for university attendance are evidence of the abbey's promotion of learning. Education was a springboard for the careers of monks and territorial subjects alike, and social and professional mobility in Salem cannot be understood without considering the role of education and the abbey's support for village schools.[278]

Audience petitions demonstrate the presence of schoolteachers in Salem's major villages in the late sixteenth and early seventeenth centuries.[279] Some schoolteachers were native to the area, including Georg Neher of Mimmenhausen, whose father petitioned at least twice for his son's appointment in their home village.[280] In 1630 the abbot's

277 Religious orders are often seen as hostile to the spread of learning among the laity. See Klaus SCHREINER, Laienbildung als Herausforderung für Kirche und Gesellschaft: Religiöse Vorbehalte und soziale Widerstände gegen die Verbreitung von Wissen im späten Mittelalter und in der Reformation, in: Zeitschrift für Historische Forschung 11 (1984), pp. 352–353. See also Gerald STRAUSS, Luther's House of Learning: Indoctrination of the Young in the German Reformation, Baltimore 1978.

278 On Salem and education, see Reinhard SCHNEIDER, Studium und Zisterzienser mit besonderer Berücksichtigung des südwestdeutschen Raumes, in: Rottenburger Jahrbuch für Kirchengeschichte 4 (1985), pp. 103–118; idem, Geschichte Salems, pp. 78–85; Thomas SPECHT, Die Beziehungen des Klosters Salem zur Universität Dillingen, in: Zeitschrift für die Geschichte des Oberrheins 59 (1931), pp. 272–292 (with a list of Salem's monks who matriculated between 1560 and 1622).

279 Earliest references to schoolteachers, found mostly in the Audience protocol, are from Neufrach (1583–1584), Mimmenhausen (1595, 1597, 1599, and 1601), and Bermatingen (1600, 1603–1604). There were also teachers in Leutkirch (1624), Owingen (1629), and Pfaffenhofen (1630). There may even have been instruction for girls, or a female teacher, as a disgruntled Audience petition from Mimmenhausen's teacher in 1624 suggests: "ob nit Ain Weibsbildt, so zue Grasbeüren ain zeitlang schuel gehalten, abzeshaffen?" GLAK, 61/13373, 1624.

280 The father, a shoemaker, also petitioned in 1613 on behalf of another son Jacob for a service appointment with the abbey, citing his education and singing experience. It is noteworthy that the shoemaker had two educated sons. GLAK, 61/13370.

kinsman, Jacob Wunn from Grasbeuren, was the schoolteacher in Pfaffenhofen.[281] Martin Brun was an outsider who married a local woman and asked to be accepted as a legal resident and abbey serf in 1584.[282] He taught for at least twenty years in Neufrach and later Bermatingen. Georg Blaicher from Pfullendorf petitioned the Audience in 1630 for the position of schoolmaster in Mimmenhausen.[283] He later became the abbey's overseer of guardians and was promoted in 1641 to abbey secretary. School buildings are also in evidence from the late sixteenth century. In 1595 the teacher in Mimmenhausen requested building materials to expand the classroom (*stubenn*), since there was not enough space for all the students. In 1613 he requested wood to build school benches and similar items.[284] In 1627 Abbot Thomas Wunn visited the building site in Mimmenhausen for a new school; by 1632 Owingen also had a schoolhouse.[285]

Salem's village teachers lived an extremely modest lifestyle, relying on the community and the abbey for the bulk of their support.[286] They were among the village smallholders, some without even sufficient housing.[287] In fact, the reason so many teachers are mentioned in the Audience protocol is that the abbey granted bread alms to supplement the meager wages paid by students' families. Each year they had to request

[281] GLAK, 61/13374. Jacob was most likely Thomas's older brother. Education ran in the family; in 1620 Jacob Wunn's two sons were absolved from further studies at the abbey's Stadthof in Constance. GLAK, 61/14334.

[282] Despite the support of Neufrach's Amtmann and priest, the abbey denied his request and told him he should first prove himself through good behavior. In the meantime, he could live in the village as long as he was employed there. GLAK, 61/13369, 1584.

[283] He, too, offered to become the abbey's serf. The abbey accepted on both counts. GLAK, 61/13374.

[284] GLAK, 61/13369, 1595; 61/13370, 1613.

[285] SCHNEIDER, Geschichte Salems, p. 84.

[286] In the very first petition recorded in the Audience protocol of 1583, the community of Neufrach requested permission to sell wood from the community forest in order to pay off debts and obligations including the schoolmaster's house rent. The community of Mimmenhausen granted their teacher the use of a common land parcel free of charge in 1597 and 1601 and gave him a wagonload of hay in 1613. Mimmenhausen's village accounts also list small sums paid to the teacher for his participation in religious celebrations, for example in 1594–1595: "Item für den Schuelmeister zalt an Creutzgengen und Jarstagen 1 fl. 3 bz. 8 dn." When the schoolteacher in Neufrach asked for a raise in 1622, the Audience suggested he ask each student for 15 kr. per quarter. Mimmenhausen's teacher was advised in 1624 to charge 30 kr. per quarter. Mattheus Sauter of Tüfingen petitioned for an appointment as schoolteacher in 1606. The Audience told him there was no money for a salary, but he was welcome to "hold school" if he could do so without the abbey's support. GLAK, 61/13369, 61/13373, 98/4419, 98/4420.

[287] In 1583 a village warden petitioned the Audience on behalf of Neufrach's teacher, who wished to move into the house of Georg Stobel, recently deceased—the teacher's own housing was inadequate. His request was denied, perhaps because the community had just admitted that they were already behind in paying the rent on his current housing (see the above footnote). When the Leutkirch teacher and his wife died in 1635, the abbey waived their death taxes since they had no property. GLAK, 61/13369, 61/13374.

a renewal of their bread rations, which gave abbey officials the regular opportunity to examine their performance. In 1611 Lorenz Schorch, the teacher in Mimmenhausen, asked for a continuation of the bread alms he had previously enjoyed. The Audience granted his request after an initial postponement to consult with the Großkeller. Later that year, Schorch left his post and was replaced by Georg Neher, who was granted bread on the same terms as his predecessor: one *zwaier* (two-pound loaf) daily. He was instructed to reapply for aid each year.[288] Apparently the bread was not enough to live on, because the new teacher soon returned to ask for two or three cartloads of firewood. He approached the Audience a third time to ask for a larger bread portion, "since he and his children could not get by on his earnings, especially in this time of dying when there are not many schoolchildren."[289] Neher made further bread requests in 1616, 1618, 1619, 1620, and 1624. Other teachers in the 1620s and 1630s received wine, vegetables, and grain. The abbey's contribution of bread and other provisions suggests an interest in educating local subjects.

Education was especially useful to the abbey for recruitment purposes. Since there was no highly developed bureaucratic apparatus or even an adequate number of officials to carry out administrative responsibilities, the ability of some villagers to read and keep basic accounts was especially valuable. The investment in lay education seems to have paid off, since it was not unusual for Amtmänner, treasurers, guardians, and innkeepers to keep written accounts. The education of subjects also prepared some of the most talented among them to join the abbey as novices.

Reinhard Schneider and others have already described the education of Salem's monks at various universities as well as in the abbey's gymnasium and higher *Studium*.[290] Here, it is worth briefly mentioning some of their findings. The abbey housed a secondary school, the gymnasium, which functioned primarily to recruit and train future novices.[291] Among them were area natives, some of whom served later in the abbey's administration.[292] The abbey also supported a school of higher learning, the Studium, which taught philosophy and theology as well as other subjects. Since there was no Cistercian seminary in the surrounding area, Salem's Studium was attended by visit-

---

288 The Mimmenhausen schoolteacher received the same bread rations in 1606. GLAK, 61/13369.

289 1611 was a plague year, and the Audience granted his request. GLAK, 61/13370.

290 SCHNEIDER, Studium und Zisterzienser, pp. 103–118; idem, Geschichte Salems, pp. 78–85; SPECHT, Universität Dillingen, pp. 272–292.

291 Course offerings included physics, logic, mathematics, music, handwriting (*Schönschreiben*), and foreign languages (Latin, Greek, Hebrew, and French). Visitation reports remarked favorably on the gymnasium in 1563, 1619, and 1673. SCHNEIDER, Geschichte Salems, pp. 83–84; Karl BRUNNER, Beiträge zur Geschichte des Klosterschulwesens in Baden, in: Mitteilungen der Gesellschaft für deutsche Erziehungs- und Schulgeschichte 14 (1904), p. 5.

292 See below. Other abbeys also founded schools for the education of boys. Cf. Louis LEKAI, Studien, Studiensystem und Lehrtätigkeit der Zisterzienser, in: Die Zisterzienser Ordensleben zwischen Ideal und Wirklichkeit, vol. 1, ed. Kaspar Elm et al., Bonn 1980, p. 168; Hermann Joseph PRETSCH, Klösterliche Dorfschulen – Kirche und Gesellschaft: Das Beispiel des Reichs-

ing scholars from other Cistercian houses as well as by the abbey's own novices and monks.[293] The abbots were personally responsible for overseeing the Studium, and several of them took an active role in the lessons. In fact, some of Salem's abbots were born in nearby villages and may have encouraged talented boys to continue their studies at the abbey.[294] In 1611 Salem was the first Cistercian abbey to establish its own printing press. Instructional materials were printed there, as were contributions to the abbey's rich library.[295] In the eighteenth century the Studium was divided into six classes, with a total of eighty to one hundred students.

Many of Salem's monks went on to attend various universities with the abbey's financial support. Salem's earliest students attended the University of Paris, where the Cistercians founded St. Bernard's College in 1245.[296] In the sixteenth century many of Salem's monks attended a growing number of German universities including Heidelberg, Freiburg, Ingolstadt, and above all Dillingen.[297] Between 1560 and 1622 at least sixty of Salem's monks studied at Dillingen, earning 29 bachelor's degrees in philosophy and 16 advanced degrees.[298] Many of these graduates went on to occupy leading

stifts Zwiefalten, in: Alte Klöster – Neue Herren: Die Säkularisation im deutschen Südwesten 1803, ed. Volker Himmelein and Hans Ulrich Rudolf, vol. 2.1, Ostfildern 2003, pp. 317–324; SREENIVASAN, Ottobeuren, p. 208.

293 Students came from the Cistercian abbeys Hauterive, Wettingen, Kaisheim, and Neuenburg. SCHNEIDER, Geschichte Salems, p. 83; idem, Studium und Zisterzienser, pp. 107, 117.

294 Abbots Johannes Scharpfer (r. 1494–1510) and Vitus Nekher (r. 1583–1587) were both patrons of education born in Mimmenhausen.

295 SCHNEIDER, Geschichte Salems, p. 84. Details about Salem's library in the sixteenth century are scarce, but by the secularization period it was one of the largest monastic libraries in Germany. According to an 1803 inventory there were over 60,000 printed books in addition to many costly manuscripts, later acquired by the University of Heidelberg. By comparison, Heidelberg's holdings in 1798 were only around 20,000 volumes. See Armin SCHLECHTER, ed., Vom Bodensee an den Neckar: Bücherschätze aus der Bibliothek des Zisterzienserklosters Salem in der Universitätsbibliothek Heidelberg, Heidelberg 2003; REDEN-DOHNA, Weingarten, p. 245; BECKER, Thomas Wunn, p. 174. See also the University of Heidelberg's digital library project, including an entire division of manuscripts from Salem.

296 Four of those who studied there later became Salem's abbots: Ulrich von Seelfingen, Konrad von Enslingen, Jodokus Necker, and Christian Fürst. SCHNEIDER, Geschichte Salems, p. 79; idem, Studium und Zisterzienser, p. 109.

297 Nineteen monks from Salem studied at Heidelberg between 1421 and 1522, including Abbots Ludwig Oschwald and Johannes Scharpfer. Salem also sent 19 students to Freiburg im Breisgau between 1496 and 1622 (mostly during the period 1547–1581), including four future abbots: Vitus Nekher, Stephan Enroth, Emanuel Sulger, and Stephan Jung. In addition, Vitus Nekher studied at Dillingen, Stephan Enroth at the Collegium Germanicum in Rome, and Stephan Jung in Vienna. SCHNEIDER, Geschichte Salems, p. 82; idem, Studium und Zisterzienser, p. 114.

298 According to Thomas Specht, 55 students from Salem matriculated at the university and a few others studied at the gymnasium there. He lists them all by name and matriculation date, along with details about their ecclesiastical careers. Idem, Universität Dillingen, pp. 274–275. See also SCHNEIDER, Studium und Zisterzienser, pp. 113, 115; REDEN-DOHNA, Weingarten, p. 247.

positions in Salem or elsewhere within the Order.[299] Dillingen's importance for Salem in the decades around 1600 is underscored by the fact that 31 out of 54 monks who elected Thomas Wunn in 1615 were among its alumni, many of them his classmates.[300] Of perhaps even greater interest for our purposes than the university attendance of monks is the finding that Salem occasionally sent laypeople to the university and funded their education. Among the names in Freiburg's matriculation lists, five from Salem were referred to explicitly as "*laicus*."[301]

The Cistercian Order produced few famous scholars or thinkers compared with some religious orders, and Salem was not especially known for its influential writers or intellectuals.[302] Nevertheless, education was highly valued within the abbey and found many practical applications. It is extremely significant that so many monks attended Dillingen, Freiburg, and other universities during the period 1550–1620, just as abbey officials were straining to produce the written records required for administrative advances and territorial consolidation. At least 14 of Salem's abbots were university educated, as were many of the abbey's higher territorial officials. Practical reasons also explain Salem's promotion of village schools and the gymnasium. By training and recruiting its brightest subjects, Salem was able to produce a highly skilled work force made up of territorial insiders who were both loyal to the abbey and knowledgeable about conditions there. Thomas Wunn is an excellent example of a peasant who rose to the abbey's highest office, which became possible only after he proved himself in the classroom as a young boy. Yet he was not alone. Education was an important factor behind the high level of social mobility and availability of various career paths enjoyed by Salem's subjects.[303] The resources Salem devoted to its schools, its library, and the students it sent to various universities demonstrate not only that the abbey valued education, but in addition, that it supported the education of its own subjects. Higher education was an opportunity for some local boys, and it was a factor for social and professional mobility within the territory. Education allowed some residents to exchange their role of subject for that of territorial administrator, monk, or lord.

---

299 Johann Muottelsee received a doctorate in theology there and was Salem's prior between 1609 and 1624. Benedict Staub received a doctorate in medicine and was later chosen as secretary of the Upper German Congregation. Thomas Wunn taught as a professor of philosophy at Dillingen before returning to Salem. Three who later served as abbot were Vitus Nekher, Christian Fürst, and Thomas Wunn: four more became abbots of other Cistercian houses.

300 SCHNEIDER, Geschichte Salems, p. 81. See also HÖLZ, Krummstab, p. 56.

301 All five came from Salem's central territory and matriculated in the 1550s. According to Schneider they may have been graduates of the abbey school who planned to become novices. Idem, Studium und Zisterzienser, p. 117.

302 LEKAI, Cistercians, pp. 227–247; Paul ZINSMAIER, Die Geschichtsschreibung des Zisterzienserklosters Salem, in: Freiburger Diözesanarchiv, n.s. 62 (1934), p. 1.

303 SCHNEIDER, Studium und Zisterzienser, p. 117.

6.10 Social and Professional Mobility

Many residents of Salem's central territory served the abbey in official capacities, from household servants and field laborers all the way up to the abbot and his closest advisors. In fact, one in three abbots in Salem during the early modern period was born an abbey subject.[304] The degree of social and professional mobility achieved by some of Salem's territorial subjects is remarkable in a period characterized by hierarchical social relations and lingering notions about the division of estates. The fact that peasants and monks ruled in the absence of nobles and burghers was not really so unusual, yet it defies common assumptions about early modern political organization. Salem provides an example of broadly based political inclusion involving small-scale, face-to-face, communal decisionmaking, where recruitment of local residents for administrative tasks built the territory from within and kept external interference to a minimum. The elevation of ordinary subjects to leadership positions did not slacken over the course of the sixteenth century. Indeed, there were more local residents at all levels of the territorial administration in the late sixteenth and early seventeenth centuries than in any earlier period.

Reinhard Schneider has described the social backgrounds of Salem's forty abbots and his findings suggest that social barriers within the monastery were extremely low, especially in the early modern period.[305] During the long sixteenth century, five out of fifteen abbots were Salem's own former subjects. Among the 22 who ruled after 1500, nine came from the surrounding villages.[306] Johannes Stantenant (r. 1471 – 1494) was most likely Salem's first peasant-born abbot.[307] He was elected in the midst of the conflict between the abbey and its Sidelrichter, a dispute he ended by signing the partnership agreement of 1473. The first territorial subject elected as abbot was his immediate successor, Johannes Scharpfer (r. 1494 – 1510). This ruler was the son of one of Salem's tenant farmers in Mimmenhausen. During his 16 years as abbot, Johannes II attended the Imperial Diet several times on behalf of the Upper German prelates and was a

304 This extraordinary fact was first pointed out by Armgard von REDEN-DOHNA, Reichsstandschaft, p. 30.

305 SCHNEIDER, Geschichte Salems, pp. 55 – 65. Appendix 6.1 lists all Salem's abbots by date.

306 Schneider says, "At abbatial elections, Salem's convent with its rural character apparently favored those capable people who came from the lordship's immediate vicinity and who remained closely connected to it throughout their ascent. They may have been valuable to the convent as trustworthy guarantors of Salem's interests." Idem, Geschichte Salems, pp. 56 – 57. See also REDEN-DOHNA, Reichsstandschaft, p. 30.

307 Johannes Stantenant was from Uffholz in rural Alsace and there is no evidence he was a noble. He had previously served as abbot in Lützel and may have been Salem's prior before his election, though some historians say he was called directly from Salem's mother house to become the new abbot. On Abbot Johannes I and the controversy over his election, see SCHNEIDER, Geschichte Salems, pp. 56 – 57, 64; FEYERABEND, Chronik, p. 180; STAIGER, Salem oder Salmansweiler, p. 122; Hermann GINTER, Kloster Salem, Karlsruhe 1937, p. 19.

member of the Imperial Governing Council (*Reichsregiment*) in 1500.[308] In this ruling council, Salem's peasant-abbot sat among twenty of the most powerful princes in the empire. Johannes II also established a new hospital (*Siechenhaus*) with attached chapel and a library with 39 glass windows.[309]

Another peasant-born abbot and former abbey subject was Abbot Johannes Fischer (r. 1534–1543) from Mimmenhausen. Among his accomplishments, Johannes III is remembered for defending the abbey against the bishop of Constance, who was determined to turn Salem into a dependent prebend.[310] This abbot's appeal to the emperor in 1541 resulted not only in the repudiation of the bishop's claims, but also in a privilege that placed Salem directly under the jurisdiction of the highest imperial courts, the *Reichskammergericht* and *Reichshofrat*.[311] According to Gabriel Feyerabend, Johannes III had a special affection for his subjects and was in return held by all in exceptionally high esteem.[312] Forty years later the convent elected Vitus Nekher (r. 1583–1587), the third abbot from Mimmenhausen who was also the elected director of the Upper Swabian College of Imperial Prelates.[313] Vitus Nekher was a learned man who studied at Dillingen and later Freiburg, mastering Greek as well as Latin. A patron of education, he sent young boys from the territory to study in Dillingen and elsewhere. He also promoted learning within the convent and enriched the abbey library with many scholarly books.[314] The serial records for the Audience, Sidelgericht, and chancery all began during his reign. Abbot Vitus died unexpectedly after only four years in office. Perhaps it was a tribute to him that the convent next elected yet another former abbey subject, Abbot Johannes Bücheler (r. 1587–1588) from Neufrach. Unfortunately, he died after only six months in office.[315]

The election of Abbot Thomas Wunn (r. 1615–1647) and his leadership provides the best example of social and professional mobility in Salem's history. See Illustration 6.3, Portrait of Abbot Thomas I Wunn. His achievements were impressive for any man, let alone the son of peasant subjects who was born a serf in Grasbeuren. Thomas I

---

308 BAIER, Staat und Kirche, p. 140.

309 GINTER, Salem, p. 23.

310 The dispute started in 1536. FEYERABEND, Chronik, pp. 214–15; STAIGER, Salem oder Salmansweiler, pp. 129–130; KALLER, Salem, p. 362.

311 STAIGER, Salem oder Salmansweiler, p. 130.

312 "Dieser würdige Abt halte für die Seinigen und seiner Unterthanen einer besondere Liebe, und wurde auch entgegen von allen ausserordentlich geliebt." FEYERABEND, Chronik, p. 213.

313 FEYERABEND, Chronik, p. 241; HÖLZ, Krummstab und Schwert, pp. 106–107; Ernst BÖHME, Das Kollegium der Schwäbischen Reichsprälaten im 16. und 17. Jahrhundert, in: Rottenburger Jahrbuch für Kirchengeschichte 6 (1987), pp. 286–287.

314 STAIGER, Salem oder Salmansweiler, p. 136.

315 Staiger says, "This man possessed an even greater spirit and was especially clever, so that one had reason to have high hopes; but man proposes, God disposes ... His death brought great sorrow, especially since he was still in the best years of his life. His sudden passing brought new evidence of man's frailty, a reminder that one cannot know the hour of one's death." Ibid.

Illustration 6.3: Portrait of Abbot Thomas I Wunn

By Jacob Carl Stauder, ca. 1720
From the Gallery of Abbots, International School at Salem

was among Salem's most celebrated early modern abbots, not because of his social origins but because of his long and colorful reign, his strong personality, and his distinguished achievements, which are especially notable because of the troubled times.[316] He not only steered his abbey through the many challenges of the Thirty Years War, he actually elevated the abbey's prestige in several key respects. First, he directed several ambitious building projects including a new prelature, renovated dormitory, quarters for novices and visitors, a warming room, granary, and the first three-story buildings.[317] Second, he was a major player behind the establishment of the Cistercian Order's Upper German Congregation, which brought together 62 abbeys and convents from the four South German provinces in 1624.[318] Thomas Wunn was elected as the Congregation's first president and thus became the overseer of all Cistercian houses in this vast region, responsible for conducting annual visitations, attending abbatial elections, and presiding over provincial assemblies.[319] In this role he traveled throughout Bavaria, the Swiss Confederation, Württemberg, and Alsace, both in war times (sometimes under military escort) and during periods of extreme illness.

316 See especially BECKER, Thomas Wunn, pp. 137–337.

317 The granary, or long house, was one of the few structures besides the church to survive the 1697 fire and it still stands today. Wunn's building projects took several years to complete. See GINTER, Salem, p. 32; STAIGER, Salem oder Salmansweiler, pp. 141–142; FEYERABEND, Chronik, p. 154; BECKER, Thomas Wunn, pp. 168–170; Karl OBSER, Zur Geschichte des Klosters Salem im 17. Jh., in: Zeitschrift für die Geschichte des Oberrheins 31 (1916).

318 The four were the Swabian, Franconian, Bavarian, and Swiss-Alsacian-Breisgauer provinces. Previous attempts to found an Upper German Congregation (as early as 1593, most notably in 1618) faltered mainly because of resistance from the General Abbot in Cîteaux and differences between members (especially Abbot Peter of Wettingen, who wanted a separate Swiss congregation). See Anton KOTTMANN and Markus HÄMMERLE, Die Zisterzienserabtei Wettingen: Geschichte des Klosters Wettingen und der Abtei Wettingen-Mehrerau, Wettingen 1996, pp. 166–174; SOMMER-RAMER, Zisterzienser, pp. 45–50; BECKER, Thomas Wunn, pp. 230–239.

319 LEKAI, Cistercians, pp. 133–134; SCHNEIDER, Geschichte Salems, pp. 44–46; SOMMER-RAMER, Zisterzienser, p. 49.

He also sent many monks and a donation of 250,000 fl. to reestablish Cistercian abbeys Bebenhausen, Königsbronn, and Herrenalb in Württemberg following the 1629 Edict of Restitution, an indication of Salem's size, leadership, and wealth.[320] Last but not least, Thomas signed a treaty in 1637 with the widowed countess Anna Maria of Heiligenberg, ending the centuries-long jurisdictional dispute between the two powers. As described in Chapter 1, this treaty recognized Salem's full jurisdictional powers and the legal and geographical boundaries of the abbey's central territory. In 1637 it was a peasant-born abbot who achieved for Salem its fully independent and unmediated status within the empire, a title claimed since 1354 but now for the first time fully justified.

Abbot Thomas ruled during an extremely turbulent time, and over the course of his long career he made many enemies as well as allies among his subjects, neighboring rulers, other abbots, and even his own convent. The abbot's involvement in responses to the Pfisteramt tenants' grievances in 1629–1630 demonstrate his unwillingness to yield to subjects' demands, and the level of grievance is itself a suggestion that they were unhappy with this peasant-abbot's policies, perhaps especially because they had higher expectations of an abbot they saw as one of their own. Amidst the constant troop crossings and quarterings, arson, plunder, starvation, and general devastation of the war years, Thomas I had to make difficult choices to protect the abbey, its monks, their properties, and subjects. The abbey's walls provided refuge for villagers on several occasions, and peasant militias defended it in return as best they could. Yet the entire convent and most of the abbey's administrators fled during the worst periods, and subjects' pleas for help were often denied or left unanswered because the abbey lacked the resources to provide plow teams, building materials, food, or loans, let alone protection from the soldiers.

Thomas's long absences from the territory and his involvements at the imperial court may have given rise to unpopularity within the convent.[321] Under increasing pressure from factions within the Upper German Congregation as well as his own abbey, and prevented from traveling by continuing health issues, Thomas tried to resign as the congregation's general vicar and as abbot on several occasions. On top of these problems, Abbot Thomas was the target of a defamation suit beginning around 1626. According to his accusers, Thomas acted in ways unfit for a monk—including drunkenness and familiarity with Protestants in Tübingen, dancing at a carnival celebration, and sexual relations with the duchess of Württemberg.[322] Testimony and correspon-

---

320 BECKER, Thomas Wunn, p. 168; SIWEK, Salem, p. 247.

321 In 1647 Abbot Thomas II was forced to submit to election conditions (*Wahlkapitulationen*), which the convent rarely imposed. According to Karl Becker, they provide greater insight about Thomas I's reign than about the convent's expectations of his successor, suggesting that Wunn had ruled with a heavy hand. Idem, Thomas Wunn, p. 176.

322 The scandal involved alleged misconduct during his visitations to Baindt and Bebenhausen, inspections of Salem's properties in Nürtingen and Reutlingen, and a stay at a health spa in Württemberg. The accusations were heard at the Imperial High Court (*Reichshofrat*) and by an

dence relating to the suit argue for Thomas's innocence and bring his personality to life. They also show the broad-based support as well as acrimony surrounding this abbot, with letters written by several abbots and ecclesiastical officials, the duchess of Württemberg, and Thomas himself.[323] The charges, resulting perhaps from jealousy over his power within the Upper German Congregation and from struggles with Heiligenberg, were eventually dropped.[324]

Thomas Wunn's rule as abbot warns us against making artificial distinctions between rulers and subjects, lordship and community. His ability to manage the challenges of the Thirty Years War, his unwillingness to bow to the pressures of his subjects or the count of Heiligenberg, and the contention surrounding his leadership in the Upper German Congregation are all reminders that common social origins were not necessarily a political impediment. In Salem even a peasant could become an imperial prelate, associate with other rulers, direct ecclesiastical assemblies, conduct visitations, and correspond with the emperor. Perhaps because of Thomas Wunn's unusual abilities, he also inspired intense opposition from peers and criticism from his subjects, all of which he weathered quite well.

Since local men from modest social backgrounds were so prevalent among Salem's abbots, it seems fair to postulate that many of the monks who elected them came from similar geographical and social origins, yet scarce documentation fails to substantiate the hypothesis.[325] Becoming a monk involved severing ties to the outside world and even assuming a new name, so the social origins of monks were deemed irrelevant and rarely mentioned in the sources.[326] Monastic officials are documented more frequently than other monks; still, their backgrounds are seldom described.[327] One source offer-

imperial commission headed by the abbot of Kaisheim. GLAK, 98/688 and 98/1965; BECKER, Thomas Wunn, pp. 163–164.

323 Thomas wrote personally to the emperor to proclaim his innocence and ask for support. The charges brought several abbots, ecclesiastical officials, and even the duchess to write letters in his defense. According to the duchess she did not see Wunn in Nürtingen or anywhere else. GLAK, 98/688.

324 BECKER, Thomas Wunn, p. 164.

325 Schneider addresses this problem repeatedly in Geschichte Salems, pp. 53–55, 57, 65. For example, "the single monk hardly ever appeared as an individual unless he held an office, an important one." Even compared to other Cistercians, Salem's documentation of members' names and social origins is bleak. The best sources of monks' names are documents relating to the certification of abbatial elections, in which notaries carefully listed all the monks who took part. Names from the sixteenth and seventeenth centuries are provided by LEODEGAR, Abtwahlen im 16. Jahrundert, pp. 98–106, and idem, Abtwahlen im 17. Jahrhundert, pp. 321–338.

326 SCHNEIDER, Geschichte Salems, p. 55, 57.

327 Bernard Mayer from Mimmenhausen was Großkeller in 1544, Jakob Biller of Owingen was assistant bursar around 1576, and Georg Moser also of Owingen was bursar and prior around 1610. Falling back on the peasant-abbots, Abbot Johannes Scharpfer had been the Großkeller, Abbot Vitus Nekher had been the Pfister and overseer of guardians, Abbot Johannes Büecheler

ing limited but suggestive evidence is a list of the abbey's serfs from around 1600.[328] The record names parents and their children, along with the whereabouts of family members no longer living at home. At least five families had sons who joined Salem's convent, including Sebastian Bürster of Neufrach who later chronicled the Thirty Years War.[329] Eight others were listed as priests, one was a Jesuit, and one was a member of Neuenburg Abbey in Alsace. Two more were noted simply as *gaistlich* (religious). Notably, twelve of the seventeen sons with clerical professions came from Mimmenhausen or Neufrach, villages close to the abbey with their own schools. It is even more difficult to discover the social backgrounds of Salem's laybrothers, but it is likely that common people including abbey subjects joined in large numbers.[330]

For various aspects of the territorial administration, the abbey depended on villagers who were not monks or laybrothers. Some of them were among the abbey's highest and most trusted salaried officials. One office frequently filled by villagers was that of Kaufmann, later replaced by the Oberamtmann.[331] Panthaleon Scherer, an abbey serf from Neufrach, was the Kaufmann between 1578 and 1589.[332] When the position was reconfigured and renamed in 1590 it was Johann Vögelin, a subject from Mimmenhausen, who first held office as the Oberamtmann (1590–1614). Vögelin then served as Hofmeister in Constance (1615–1621) before retiring as a burgher of that city.[333]

served as the bursar, and Abbot Thomas Wunn was the bursar and abbot-coadjutor before his election. GLAK, 4/237, 4/363, 4/2723, 61/13316, 61/13319, 98/1730, 98/2026; SCHNEIDER, Geschichte Salems, pp. 71–72; KUHN, Mönche und Bauern, p. 32.

328 GLAK, 98/1568–1569.

329 Sebastian Bürster held several administrative positions within the abbey including council member and Pfisteramt secretary (1624), alms overseer (1626), Pfister (ca. 1632), and *Brotkeller* (1635).

330 KUHN-REHFUS, Konversen und Pfründner, pp. 120–121; SCHNEIDER, Geschichte Salems, pp. 58–59; RÖSENER, Salem, p. 148; Louis J. LEKAI, The Cistercians: Ideals and Reality, Kent 1977, p. 340. The reported number of laybrothers hit an all-time low of only three in 1599, down from twelve in 1573–1574. There had been 180 laybrothers in 1311, and at the time of secularization there were 17. SIWEK, Salem, p. 29.

331 Early Kaufmänner include Hans Mayer from Mimmenhausen (1479) and Hans Pfannenstil from Neufrach (1538). Oberamtmänner came from the nearby towns of Constance, Aulendorf, and Zweifaltach, and from the villages of Weiler, Mimmenhausen, and Bermatingen.

332 Scherer raised a foster daughter during this period who later brought suit against him before the Sidelgericht for failing to return her inheritance portion when she reached majority.

333 Vögelin's employment contract from 1590 states explicitly that he was from Mimmenhausen. Earlier records name him as a scribe (*Schreiber* 1577 and 1584, *Cammerschreiber* 1582) and as the *Pfleger* in Esslingen. By at least 1608 he had become a burgher of Constance (GLAK, 4/63), where he continued to live after his retirement. In 1615–1616 he was an appeals court judge. The court records in 1625 call him Johann Vögelin the elder, burgher of Constance and former Oberamtmann (GLAK, 61/13327). GLAK, 62/9297 and 62/9299a contain his personal accounts from 1596 and 1599 relating to tax collection, both bearing his signature. Other documents signed by Vögelin are found in 98/2016 (1598) and 4/2744 (1577). Vögelin's excellent handwriting may be recognized in many other administrative documents.

He was succeeded as Oberamtmann by his son, Joachim Vögelin (1615–1622), who resided in Weiler and was also an Audience member (1618–1625). He later became Hofmeister of Stockach (1624–1638). The familiarity of individuals such as the Vögelins with local conditions and customs helped them to become successful and trusted territorial administrators.

Johann and Joachim Vögelin were not the only area residents promoted to offices in the outlying districts. One of the earliest known examples is Lienhard Gattenheimer from Grasbeuren, who in 1497 was the hospital director in Constance. Wilhelm Pfannenstil, a cooper from Leutkirch, was the Hofmeister in Constance (1588). So was Abraham Fimppel, the innkeeper from Bermatingen (prior to 1638). Andreas Müller of Bermatingen was the Hofmeister in Kirchberg and Hagnau between 1600 and 1630, Martin Lewolff of Oberuhldingen was the Hofmeister in Maurach shortly before 1616, and Hans Mayer of Oberuhldingen was the *Keller* in Nürtingen between 1583 and 1587. The lower-ranking members of Salem's appeals court *(Hofgericht)* were also villagers, including Abraham Fimppel of Bermatingen, Bartlin Müller of Leutkirch, Hans Rogg of Mimmenhausen, Jacob Senfft of Mimmenhausen, and Georg Holl of Nußdorf. At least three Amtmänner were occasional members of the Audience, including Christoph Langenstain of Bermatingen, who took part in over 300 sessions between 1617 and 1631.[334]

Chamber servants *(Cammerling)* Jacob Dreer of Mimmenhausen (1585, 1587), Lorenz Bürster of Neufrach (1589), Jacob Ower of Neufrach (until 1594), and Jeorg Buechmüller of Weildorf (1629) all came from prominent local families.[335] Jerg Moser of Owingen worked in the chancery office in 1598, Simon Klotz of Weildorf and Caspar Wuecherer of Mimmenhausen acted as head servant *(Oberknecht)* in 1610 and 1620 respectively, Severinus Cammerer of Mimmenhausen assisted the Pfister in 1623, and Valentin Mayer of Neufrach worked in the bursar's office in 1616. When the bursar's assistant, Sebastian Leub from Weiler, was reported to the Audience for severe misconduct in 1624, the officials expressed concern that if they relieved him from office immediately, the records would be thrown into disorder.[336] In 1620 the spiritual council *(Geistliches Rat)* decided that Georg Ower, from a prominent local family, could spend an hour each day in the bursar's office but he should also continue to work in the chancery office in order to learn proper script.[337]

---

334 The others were Valentin Mayer of Neufrach and Johann Schentz of Owingen.

335 Many chamber servants were wealthy. Jacob Dreer's daughter received an inheritance advance of 500 fl. plus moveables in 1589. Jacob Ower's estate was worth 2,600 fl. when he died in 1594. Lorenz Bürster died in 1595 as a smallholder without a horse, but his heriot was still substantial (7 fl.), and in 1578 his property was worth 1,250 fl.

336 GLAK, 61/13373, 1624. Sebastian Leub went on to hold several other offices including court secretary, Amtmann of Bermatingen, Hofmeister in Esslingen, and Oberamtmann. His bad temper and womanizing continued to cause problems in later years, not to mention his terrible handwriting. GLAK, 98/4402.

337 GLAK, 61/14334, fol. 1r–v.

Abbey gatekeepers, who controlled the flow of visitors and distributed alms to the poor, included Michel Locher of Weiler (1613), Lienhard Jerg of Tüfingen (1614), and Martin Moggilharzer of Tüfingen (until 1624). The Wespach hospital warden was usually an Amtmann or prominent member of one of the nearby villages, including Jacob Fünfflin, Caspar Schaitteckh, Jacob Klotz, and Laux Leub from Weiler, Blesi Steckborer of Weildorf, and Balthas Diem of Leutkirch/Mimmenhausen. Salem's guestmaster (*Gastmeister*) was usually a villager from Mimmenhausen: Simon Mussel, Lorenz Mussel, Jerg Resstlin, Hans Gaist, Friedrich Pfannenstil, and Jerg Lauterer held this position between 1580 and 1630. Each of these positions involved representing the abbey's authority and maintaining its boundaries, managing its resources, and keeping detailed written accounts.

It can be difficult to distinguish native villagers who became territorial officials from those who came from elsewhere but resided in one of Salem's villages.[338] For example, Michael Walraff served in many administrative positions between 1615 and 1626. He held a major farm tenure in Weiler and was involved in several disputes with neighboring villagers.[339] Joachim Haimpolt, the Oberamtmann of Ostrach, likewise held a farm in Weiler, a hereditary lease from St. Johann's of Constance that he sold for 1,750 fl. in 1615.[340] Secretary Bernhard Wagner lived in Neufrach and held property there, as did Dr. Johann Leutin, whose official titles between 1585 and 1625 included chamber secretary, councilor, and Hofmeister in Hagnau, Überlingen, and Ehingen. Johann Maisterlin owned freehold vineyards in Mimmenhausen and had kin in Beuren; between 1617 and 1631 he served as Oberamtmann, councilor, judge, Audience member, and Hofmeister in Überlingen and Maurach. Whether or not these men were native residents, many of Salem's territorial administrators lived with their families alongside other villagers. They enjoyed higher social status, but they were not distant figures cut off from everyday life in the village. They were involved in its business, religious life, conflicts, and social networks just like everyone else. With few

338 In 1633 the Audience instructed the Amtmann of Mimmenhausen that soldiers should be quartered in every household except those of the priest, chamber secretary, Oberamtmann, organist, barber, and cook, all of whom lived in the village. GLAK, 61/13374.

339 Walraff served as Oberamtmann, secretary, councilor and Audience member, Hofmeister in Madach and later Stockach. He was not a popular figure in the village. Besides his aforementioned denunciation of Amtmann Klotz, he also criticized the forest warden and requested exemption from customary labor services on account of his official duties. On several occasions in the 1620s, Walraff appeared as a defendant before the Sidelgericht for trying to repay the purchase price for his farm in bad currency. In 1629 the court bailiff took the extreme step of suing Walraff in the name of the entire court for his repeated interference in their affairs. He was also fined for speaking in court without an advocate. GLAK, 61/13327, 61/13373.

340 Joachim Haimpolt (or Haimpel) the elder was the Kaufmann of Ostrach in the late sixteenth century, and his son Joachim Haimpolt the younger was Oberamtmann of Ostrach in 1615. The son's succession to his father's property and office suggests this family's local roots, as does their 1603 property assessment of 1,633 fl.

exceptions they contributed community labor services, paid military taxes and rent, attended local assemblies, and swore the loyalty oath. They were householders with responsibilities similar to their neighbors and they were often abbey serfs; they bought and sold property, offered credit, held tenures, planted fields, went to church, and participated in communal life along with other villagers. Their activities on behalf of the abbey and as village residents blurred the lines between lordship and community.

It comes as no great surprise that Salem's subjects were especially prominent at the lower levels of the abbey's workforce, including servants, wage laborers, and craftsmen. These workers were not directly involved in territorial policy decisions, and arguably they may have lacked political significance, but from an economic perspective at least they were extremely important. Lists of abbey employees from 1481, 1593, and 1635 provide the names and wages of various groups of abbey employees.[341] In 1593 the abbey employed over 130 household servants, most of them listed by name.[342] In 1595 these employees swore a loyalty oath and so did all the abbey's craftsmen and masters in 1600.[343] Some masters came from elsewhere, but many were from the local area. Masons, coopers, locksmiths, saddlers, barbers, cooks, and carpenters were all employed on a long-term basis. Master craftsmen served the abbey's needs and also trained apprentices from the villages. A list of 74 workers in 1635 named craftsmen and apprentices, cooks and bakers, vintners, carters, fishermen, watchmen, gatekeepers, forest wardens, guestmasters, house servants, herdsmen, stall boys, messengers, and gardeners.[344] The majority of abbey employees headed households in nearby villages. For example, 84 of the 98 employees listed by name in 1593 are found in the tax list of that year and over half are found in three or more lists over the period 1578–1603. Some lived in poverty but a few had property worth several hundred gulden.[345] The nearby villages of Mimmenhausen and Neufrach were major contributors to the abbey's labor force.[346] Weildorf, too, supplied many workers. According to one

---

341 Hermann BAIER, Ein Sparerlaß aus dem Kloster Salem von 1481, in: Schriften des Vereins für Geschichte des Bodensees und seiner Umgebung 40 (1911), pp. 248–255; GLAK, 98/229 (1593), 98/1717 (1635).

342 GLAK, 98/229. Approximately 132 employees are listed, including 98 names and an additional 34 or more listed by title alone.

343 GLAK, 98/1547; 61/13369.

344 Many of them were also listed in 1634 among the thirty employees to whom Salem owed back wages. GLAK, 98/1717, 98/71.

345 For example, the master cabinetmaker Mattheus Mayer had 990 fl. in 1593, master baker Blasius Benthele had property worth 599 fl., the tile and brickmaker Michel Ortlieb had 202 fl., master tailor Hans Ruff had 363 fl., the cooper's assistant Christa Diem had 198 fl., fruitmaster Bastian Reuch had 195 fl., wagon driver Hans Lochmayer had 106 fl., and carter Balthas Haug had 193 fl. These and other abbey employees lived in the surrounding villages.

346 Nineteen employees were from Mimmenhausen, eighteen from Neufrach, ten from Weildorf, seven from Oberuhldingen, six from Tüfingen, and one each from Bermatingen, Owingen, Seefelden, and Weiler. Eleven other names were so common among villagers that their places

Audience petition from 1633, abbey servants made up half the population in that village.[347] Craftsmen and abbey servants frequently appeared before the Audience, where they sometimes received preferred treatment because of their service—such as pensions, permission to marry, approved residence, access to housing, and death tax reductions. Servants were often successful securing these types of favors for their kin as well. The abbey's household needs provided a living for smallholders and the landless, encouraged the development of specialized crafts and skills among villagers, and generally boosted the local economy. Abbey employment could also affect a person's status within the community (for better or worse), as well as provide consistent work, competitive wages, and the chance at further promotion or other favors.[348]

Some may view these lesser abbey employments as politically insignificant because they involved labor, not decisionmaking. This is, however, a matter of perspective. Workers including artisans, cooks, and household servants not to mention guestmasters, gatekeepers, and messengers represented the lord and enjoyed access to persons in higher positions of authority. Their proximity and relationships put them in a position to ask not only for personal favors but also to have an impact on territorial decisions, especially with respect to the concerns of daily village life. The impact of their words and deeds may have been indirect and even unintentional, yet their interactions and even their presence at the abbey had real political relevance.

The social background of Salem's abbots as well as monks, territorial officials, and abbey servants is noteworthy but not unique. Armgard von Reden-Dohna sees the role of abbey subjects within Salem's leadership as unusual among imperial abbeys.[349] Yet she also concludes that most South German abbeys were composed overwhelmingly of commoners, a fact deserving greater emphasis.[350] As the number of nobles enter-

---

of origin could not be positively identified.

347 "Ambtmann Von Weildorff bringt vor, daß sich die Gmaindt daselbsten verglichen, Weilen mann bej disen laidigen kriegsleüffen Potten haben müesse, Ihrer Zwen, so sich hierzue anerbietten, zuebesolden; Demnach aber fast der mehrer Thail zue Weyldorff Gotßhauß diener und darvon exempt sein wollen; Alß pitet er in Namen der Gmaindt, deß Gottshauß diener zur mittragung deß Costens anzuehalten. B. Sollen die Gotshauß diener [margin note: so Underthonen und gemeindtsleüth sein] schuldig sein, der gmaindt beschwerden und cössten helffen zetragen." GLAK, 61/13374, 1633.

348 According to serf lists from ca. 1600, the abbey employees Hans Bommer, Lorenz Bürster, and Jerg Schaitteckh all had sons in the convent. The pondmaster, Barthle Kraus, had one son who was a priest and two who had purchased their freedom. The cooper's assistant Christa Diem from Neufrach had a son who was an Amtmann and Sidelrichter. It is difficult to say whether there is any connection between the service of these fathers and their sons' professions, but the finding is interesting nonetheless.

349 REDEN-DOHNA, Reichsstandschaft, pp. 30–34.

350 Armgard von REDEN-DOHNA, Reichsklöster in Ostschwaben: Stand, Probleme und Aufgaben der Forschung, in: Suevia Sacra: Festschrift P. Fried, ed. Wilhelm Liebhart and Ulrich Faust, Stuttgart 2001, pp. 22–23. The Benedictine abbey of Zwiefalten was composed solely of non-

ing the abbeys dwindled in the later Middle Ages, most convents chose burghers as their leaders. Nor was Salem alone in electing peasants: Bebenhausen and Maulbronn were each composed mostly of burghers and peasants by the early fifteenth century, and both Cistercian houses elected nonnoble abbots by the later Middle Ages.[351] Not only Cistercians but Benedictines, too, increasingly admitted commoners and elected them as abbots starting in the fifteenth century. The long list of examples Hermann Tüchle provides, including Alpirsbach, Blaubeuren, Elchingen, Hirsau, Irsee, Ochsenhausen, Ottobeuren, St. Blasien, St. Gallen, St. Georgen, Weingarten, and Zwiefalten suggests that aristocratic Kempten, not Salem, was the exception to the rule.[352] Even Reichenau, a proud and prestigious abbey with extremely strict entry restrictions, was forced to admit burghers after its convent dwindled to only two members.[353] Female houses, tied longer and more closely to the interests of aristocratic families through their care for unmarried noblewomen, also began to accept nonnobles in the sixteenth century if not earlier.[354] Yet the social structure of early modern abbeys was not merely a response to declining membership. It resulted from practices of corporate rule, collective decisionmaking, the equal standing of members, and from the spiritual values of poverty, charity, humility, and labor. The abbeys demonstrate, as do free cities and rural republics, that absolutism was not the only possible course of early modern de-

---

nobles in the late eighteenth century, but it differed from Salem in that the burghers and peasants who made up its convent were recruited from other territories rather than the abbey's own subjects. PRETSCH, Klösterliche Dorfschulen, p. 317.

351 Jürgen SYDOW, Die Sozialstruktur eines mittelalterlichen Zisterzienserklosters, dargestellt am Beispiel der Abtei Bebenhausen, in: Rottenburger Jahrbuch für Kirchengeschichte 4 (1985), pp. 96–98; idem, Bebenhausen, pp. 80–85.

352 TÜCHLE, Süddeutsche Klöster, pp. 119–121. In Kempten, applicants had to demonstrate noble descent through 16 ancestors. Armgard von Reden-Dohna says, "If my view is correct, then Peter Blickle's research on the abbatial *Landschaften* has not considered the evidence of prelates' peasant origins and their resulting personal networks, which indeed relativized the opposition between abbey lordship and subjects. That may be because he proceeded from the princely foundation of Kempten, which possessed an aristocratic character." Idem, Reichsklöster in Ostschwaben, p. 23.

353 Einsiedeln, another aristocratic convent, accepted its first burgher novice in 1536. Komberg and Ellwangen both left the Benedictine Order to become *Chorherrenstifte* in order to maintain their aristocratic exclusivity and avoid Benedictine reforms that encouraged the admission of burghers. TÜCHLE, Süddeutsche Klöster, pp. 119–121.

354 Half of the female Cistercian houses in the German southwest lost their noble character by the early modern period, and even those that retained an aristocratic identity began to accept burghers by the sixteenth century. Maren KUHN-REHFUS, Die soziale Zusammensetzung der Konvente in den oberschwäbischen Frauenzisterzen, in: Zeitschrift für Württembergische Landesgeschichte 41 (1982), pp. 22–24; TÜCHLE, Süddeutsche Klöster, p. 122.

velopment in Central Europe. They also challenge the notion that the imperial church was monopolized by nobles and exclusively aligned with feudal-dynastic interests.[355]

The high level of social and professional mobility in Salem, manifested in the frequent election of peasant-abbots as well as the participation of subjects at all levels of the administration, had major significance for relations within the territory. The promotion of local subjects reflected the complementary goals and mutual interests of the abbey, the territorial community, and those individuals who rose through its ranks.[356] The timing of peasant subjects' rise to territorial leadership is also suggestive. It appears as no coincidence that the convent chose its first peasant-abbot in the late fifteenth century, at a high point in communalism's power and villagers' resistance, and as Salem boldly executed the consolidation of authority in its central districts. Furthermore, peasants' increasing representation among abbots as well as administrators in the period after 1525 demonstrates that in Salem, members of the peasantry maintained or even increased their role in territorial politics rather than declining in influence during the early modern period. The abbey's choice of leaders was based on a complex and flexible set of considerations that the sources rarely reveal, but one of the most important consequences of election from within was that any member could potentially rise to the top. If the abbey's members were mostly burghers and peasants, then it makes sense that they would prefer abbots and administrators from similar backgrounds, reflecting their own social composition, experience, and perspectives.[357]

---

355 This point is made emphatically by Reden-Dohna in several of her articles, especially Reichsstandschaft, p. 39; Zisterzienser, p. 52; Reichsklöster in Ostschwaben, pp. 22–23. By contrast, Peter Blickle equates the church with the nobility as sharing ruling values in opposition to those of workers and subjects. It is interesting to note, however, that the exact same values Blickle ascribes to common people—peace, common good, domestic necessity, and work, for example—were also among the highest positive values shared by Salem and other Cistercians. See Blickle's conclusions, in: Resistance, Representation, and Community, p. 332.

356 The objection could be raised that peasant-abbots acted as rulers, not subjects, and that territorial officials represented lords, not neighbors. While it may be true that the socially mobile were transformed by their achievement of higher authority and status, social mobility remains relevant to territorial stability and integration in two key respects. First, it reminded subjects of the possibilities of advancement and in some cases lent greater legitimacy to the regime, because peasants saw someone they recognized, perhaps someone from their own village, in a position of high status and authority. Second, the election or appointment of commoners to high offices suggests that those inside the convent or the territorial administration viewed the promotion and inclusion of common people as beneficial and desirable. Common social origins were not a barrier to rule.

357 The social origins of monks were theoretically irrelevant with respect to the order's ideals, and social ties were intentionally minimalized. Still, as Reinhard Schneider points out, issues of social background and stratification could not be completely disassociated from an abbey's collective attitudes, goals, and self-understanding. Idem, Geschichte Salems, p. 55.

6.11 Conclusions

This chapter has built on the material presented in earlier chapters to demonstrate the political significance of peasant subjects at the territorial level. In chronological terms, the investigation has focused on the decades before and after 1600, showing how villagers continued to participate in the political sphere in the generations after 1525. Central authority was growing stronger, but not at the expense of communal values or peasants' influence. The period brought many challenges, and may be characterized as an age of crisis, yet the problems rural society faced did not result in the collapse of the village commune or pave the way to absolutism. On the contrary, the difficulties encountered by the people of this era encouraged them to find new solutions. In spite of growing needs and tightening resources, individuals and groups representing diverse interests negotiated the way forward with generally positive results.

The consolidation of political authority at the territorial level was accomplished in Salem as elsewhere on two levels. In the first place, it involved the hardening of territorial boundaries against outsiders in physical, legal, and symbolic terms. In the second place, it involved the integration of all territorial subjects and the promotion of a shared identity through common laws, values, practices, and behavioral norms. Territorialization on both levels is clearly visible in many of this chapter's individual sections. For example, the collection of taxes, the performance of the loyalty oath, the extension of legal codes to outside districts, and the provision of alms to the poor all reflect the abbey's goal of limiting Heiligenberg's authority within its villages. The promotion of internal solidarity and cohesion can be seen especially in the local defense associations, closure of the villages to new residents, educational opportunities, and professional mobility available to subjects. In these examples, villagers and their local values were integrated at the territorial level and brought in line with the abbey's own interests. In other cases, groups of subjects found strength in collective opposition to the abbey's policies—the best example is to be found in their grievances, especially the Pfisteramt tenants' unified opposition to sharecropping.

In each of the areas presented in this chapter, abbey authorities demonstrated strong leadership and maintained a firm grasp on policy decisions. The abbey reminded its subjects on many occasions, such as when it required new tax assessments, administered the loyalty oath, denied rent reductions, or responded to Audience petitions, that it was the lord's place to decide, declare, and instruct. At the same time, however, each of these instances demonstrates that administrative decisions were informed by an awareness of subjects' needs and expectations. Although the abbot and his senior advisors made clear that they were the ones who made territorial policy decisions, their policies reflected their knowledge and understanding of local concerns. Policies without support from the general populace or from local officials were unenforceable. In other words, strong government was built upon legitimacy among subjects rather than the ability to bend villagers to its will. Without popular legitimacy and cooperation, government decisions could not take hold. In fact, certain sections of this chapter suggest that government policies, though made and declared by abbey officials, resulted directly from subjects' concerns and expectations. The Audience provides many examples of villagers' requests that not only informed central authorities of local conditions, they actually presented the material and framed the discussions that propelled territorial development. This interactive process reveals that subjects contributed more than we often recognize.

When we consider the usual political models of this period, statebuilding and the rise of absolutism, certain aspects of territorial governance in Salem look quite remarkable. Not only was the territorial ruler an abbot surrounded by monks, the social composition of the monastery and its territorial administration was decidedly nonnoble. Even more surprising was its regionalism: many of the abbey's members, officials, employees, and even abbots were recruited from the surrounding villages belonging to its central territory. Yet the finding that peasants and serfs participated in governance need not be interpreted as a weakness. In terms of territorial unification, both externally and internally, what better way to accomplish political consolidation than to incorporate and build on the loyalty of its own subjects?

The level of charity and social welfare provisions in Salem presents another aspect of territorialization that is rarely remarked upon. Salem not only distributed thousands of loaves of bread to its own subjects each week, it also included the paupers of neighboring territories. Here, too, measures taken were more than a reflection of Cistercian generosity or spiritual commitment. On the one hand, they were responses to the high level of demand in such difficult economic conditions and unsettled times. On the other, they bolstered the abbey's political legitimacy while providing a certain level of social security to the subject population. In a period of decline this was good for everyone, not just the poor.

Finally, it is worth emphasizing that Salem's peasant subjects participated willingly and enthusiastically in the process of territorialization, above all in the early seventeenth century. That is not to say the villages were filled with aspiring politicians or cheerleaders, yet they clearly invited territorial officials to weigh in on local affairs. They actively engaged them also in a dialogue about how things could be improved. In addition, their contributions demonstrate an ability to participate in territorial decisions and think beyond local boundaries. The Audience and the enormous number of requests, petitions, and grievances it heard on a weekly basis is truly an amazing source of information on many different topics. On the whole, the Audience records demonstrate more than any other source the active and voluntary participation of peasant subjects in a process that not only promoted a stronger central authority but also set an agenda for political development based on socioeconomic conditions and the needs of ordinary rural people. In an extremely difficult and challenging period, the polity continued to develop in Salem out of the experiences and expectations of its villagers, overseen by an elected abbot and his circle of advisors, reminding us that troubled times may also lead to strength and growth.

Summary and Outlook

Salem's peasant subjects continued to participate in shaping territorial policy and development over the long sixteenth century. Territorial authority became stronger but not at villagers' expense or counter to their interests. Their actions in and around the years 1473, 1525, and 1630 demonstrate that they were capable of collective action and resistance to the policies they opposed. Yet they eschewed violence and did not seek to overthrow the lord's authority, even in such periods of crisis. Instead, they preferred negotiation through the submission of grievances, arbitration, and legal settlements. Despite these and other examples of opposition, governance in Salem is not best characterized by conflict between the abbey and its subjects. It was a multidirectional bargaining process that involved shifting alliances, unequal partnerships, reciprocity, compromise, and even cooperation among various groups. The peasantry's political influence did not decline after 1525. This is chiefly because communal principles were integrated at the territorial level and because subjects were involved directly and indirectly in policy decisions and administration. It is also because local and territorial levels of government were not primarily at odds with or exclusive of one another. If anything, the challenges facing rulers and ruled in the decades around 1600 sharpened subjects' demands and lent greater weight to their contributions. In this context the actions of village elites and territorial mediators assumed new importance.

Political development in Salem's territory was characterized by the participation and influence of peasant subjects, but its particular style of rule resulted from a specific combination of factors. Some of the most important were the ecclesiastical nature of lordship, the territory's small size and location in an area of broadly dispersed authority, the abbey's relations to neighbors and the empire, and its administrative and social structures. Each of these factors brought important consequences including advantages as well as limitations. Some details of Salem's political framework were obviously tailored to its situation, yet this does not mean it has nothing to offer us. Salem's political achievements within its specific context demonstrate that there are indeed possible alternatives to the prevailing political models. Perhaps more important is the fact that Salem's political organization was much more typical of early modern German territories than has been recognized. The case of Salem contributes to our understanding of the possibilities and limitations of statebuilding in the early modern empire and of the complexity of relations between lords and subjects. It should be seen as an opportunity to observe the past more accurately in its own terms and on its own merits.

The abbey's central court, the Sidelgericht, functioned both to unify the territory and to incorporate the concerns of various individuals and groups. This court was the heart of the territorial community and at the same time the primary basis of the abbey's claims to imperial status. Its 15 lay judges, men chosen from each of the territory's major villages, interpreted the law according to a common discourse and shared social context.[1] Viewed from the perspective of institutional development as well as interpersonal relationships, the Sidelgericht served to combine elements of community and lordship and address the diverse needs of the abbey and its subjects. The court demonstrates that these ordering principles and interest groups were not fundamentally opposed to or exclusive of one another. In some ways, they were mutually advantageous. The court bolstered the abbey's territorial autonomy against external threats and at the same time gave peasant subjects a central role in the territory's legal development. It strengthened territorial authority but not at subjects' expense.

The members of this court, the Sidelrichter, were among the most important political actors in Salem's territory. They were not merely a buffer between center and periphery, between the abbey and its subjects. They occupied a central position of authority where many lines of power crossed, and they were members and representatives of many different groups. How their personal loyalties, social relationships, and local experiences played out depended on the particular attitudes and circumstances of each individual judge, but none belonged fully to the commune or the lord. Through their regular association, the judges shared concrete knowledge and built a broader perspective so that their decisions were informed by and involved with the symbolic participation of the territory's many parts. As the men who collectively settled conflicts and interpreted the law for the entire territory, the judges were involved simultaneously with the most mundane issues of local life and neighborly conflict and with the far loftier construction of a shared political culture and territorial identity. By listening to litigants, considering argument and evidence on various topics, discussing and seeking advice on difficult issues, consulting precedence and written statutes as well as reflecting on the context and their own consciences, they harnessed energy from many different directions. Through their hands, that energy was continuously converted from potential into current and usable forms of power that flowed back through the communal circuits. The judges did not determine the law, yet in a fundamental way it was expressed and actualized through them.[2] The fact that the Sidelrichter were unsalaried members of the various local communities, some serving concurrently as village headmen, had a major impact on the territory's political organization, integration, communication, and values. The Sidelrichter show how communal principles entered the sphere of territorial politics and how rule from the center stretched into each of Salem's villages.

Like the Sidelgericht, the Audience was a body of officials that met on a regular basis to hear, discuss, and decide on the problems territorial subjects brought before them. It, too, provided an institutional setting for the ventilation of grievances and resolution of conflict. It was a place where many different interests were expressed and

---

1 SABEAN, Power in the Blood, p. 29; KASCHUBA, Kommunalismus, p. 69.

2 HILDBRAND, Aktualisierung von Recht, p. 189.

a variety of needs met. The Audience contributed greater legitimacy to central rule, because the power to command and prohibit went hand in hand with the power to grant exceptions.[3] Dispensations made the rules more tolerable, while favors strengthened the bonds of respect, loyalty, and obedience. At the same time, the Audience communicated subjects' needs and expectations, putting pressure on territorial decision-making. Petitions made senior officials aware of problems in the village not only in the sense of monitoring but also because such regular, face-to-face interactions fostered empathy and understanding. Audience members spent hours each week hearing and responding to subjects' requests and grievances. This gave villagers the opportunity to determine the topics of political discussion and influence policy decisions, in the context of the Audience and more broadly. One of the most important conclusions to be drawn from this material is that subjects willingly invited authorities from beyond the village to address their concerns. Their demands contributed to the strength of central government and influenced the direction of its growth.

From these central institutions and the people who took part in them, a pattern emerges involving the discussion, negotiation, and collaboration of various individuals representing a diverse set of interests and positions within the territory. They suggest a high level of interaction and involve a complex integration of different perspectives that force us to reconsider traditional assumptions about the roles and relationships between rulers and subjects, center and periphery, lordship and community, rich and poor. The institutional forms provided by the Audience and Sidelgericht opened lines of communication within the territory. It was their ability to diffuse conflicts and incorporate various groups without silencing their demands that provided for a high level of political and social stability, thus providing examples of how a successful polity operates, develops, and sustains itself.

For the entire period during which this book was conceived, written, and revised, I have been surrounded by a majestic forest of mighty redwoods, the tallest trees on earth. For this reason, it may be especially appropriate to end with the metaphor of a tree, which has inspired social comparisons in many different cultures. If we imagine for a moment Salem's political organization as a tree, we can see that it had many different parts that performed distinctive functions and that each component was essential to the health and development of the whole. Like a tree, the territory had different layers, both horizontal and vertical, and the perspective changed according to one's place within it. The tree has its core of heartwood, containing the oldest memories of years past and holding the trunk solid, rigid, strong. There are the tiny tips of the smallest branches and roots, ever pushing outward in search of more space and available resources, constantly extending new growth. From the very top of the tree, where the leaves collect sunlight to create new forms of energy, the bird's-eye view stretches out for miles across the land. From the base of the tree, where the roots spread out to

---

3 HOLENSTEIN, Gute Policey, pp. 281-282.

hold the tree in place, collecting water and nutrients, a completely different impression forms. Cool and dark, with the branches rising up like spires into the filtered light and rain, it looks and feels like a holy cathedral. No less important is the bark, protecting the tree from external harm, or the living cells just beneath it, carrying food and water up and down and all around, connecting the parts and invigorating the entire system. Much of the tree's growth from a tiny sapling to an ancient tree is the result of internal processes. A fir cannot produce apples, and neither can it simply uproot itself and go elsewhere. The tree's origins and character set certain limits. Yet there are also environmental factors. Too many other trees may compete for sun and space, preventing its growth, though some neighboring trees provide protection as well as companionship, for the health of the entire forest and for the energy and diversity of life it generates. The tree may experience setbacks or come to a premature end if exposed to certain factors, such as natural disaster or human impact. Even a tree that has expired feeds back into the cycle of life, creating space and providing nutrients to help a new seedling find its way. The point, of course, is that each part is interconnected. One is not more important than the other, one cannot survive and flourish without the other.

In a woodcut by the Petrarch Master, made around the year 1520, a tree represents the social order. See Illustration 7.1. There are a cluster of occupants perched in the branches at various levels, generally rising in social rank, while down in the roots, two contorted peasants toil with the entire weight of the tree on their backs. Yet upon closer examination we cannot help but notice something unexpected. Up at the very top we discover two more peasants, one resting with his pitchfork by his side and the other one playing the bagpipes! How did these peasants manage to ascend so high, above all others, and what was the Petrarch Master trying to tell us? One possibility is that the peasants in the treetops had been lifted closer to God as a reward for their hard work and sacrifice, a belief in the spiritual value of labor the Cistercians might have shared. Another possibility is that the peasants had traded roles, climbing slowly in a process of social mobility by way of their knowledge, experience, and personal abilities as did Abbot Thomas Wunn and many others. A third possibility is that this unexpected image was meant as satire, a criticism of the social order and a commentary on its rigidity; or perhaps it was meant to call attention to those members who insist on defying their assigned places and roles. In any case, the image challenges us to think about the ways the various layers work together and what relationships exist between them, to appreciate the contributions of diverse members at multiple levels and to imagine the possibilities of a different social order. The Petrarch Master's tree asks us to reconsider the values we associate with high and low, large and small, leisure and toil. It offers an unusual perspective on how and why positions are assigned and ranked within the overall social structure.

This study advocates that we look at political development in the smaller territories and in the severely fragmented regions of the empire, which serve as an important counterpoint to the better-known examples of large princely states.

Illustration 7.1: The Tree of Society

By the Petrarch Master, ca. 1520
Two peasants toil among the tree roots and two others sit high above, resting and playing the bagpipes.
From the New York Public Library

The story of Salem's political structure and development is worth telling not only because it challenges linear notions of historical progress but also because, although they defy traditional models, it is suspected that Salem's experiences were not so uncommon as they may at first appear. Salem is important not because of its distinctiveness and thus incomparability, but because its political leaders and subjects struggled—with a large measure of success, I would argue—to meet the same challenges as other lordships, and in doing so combined common elements of rule in unexpected ways. The case of Salem is therefore helpful for understanding other imperial estates, especially in regions of dispersed authority such as the German Southwest, in ecclesiastical lordships, and above all in the free imperial abbeys. Salem presents us with some new and remarkable material for conceptualizing the possibilities of effective, small-scale political development in the early modern period.

Salem's territory was not an autonomous political unit, at least not before 1637. It was certainly not a state. Even after the treaty of the year, Salem's regime was inscribed within larger imperial structures and was never fully independent. Yet neither were other German territories fully sovereign states in this sense. Salem challenges us to view early modern political development in the Holy Roman Empire in terms of its diversity and possibility, to understand that there was not just one path or a single model of rule.

Appendix 4.1: Amtmänner (Village Headmen)

Adelsreute	
Hailg, Heinz	1502
Hailg, Melchior	1566, ca. 1578/80, 1581–1583
Hailg, Mattheus	1590–1611
Hailg, Jos	1614, 1629

Bermatingen	
Pfau, Lienhard	1468–1470, 1474
Aigen, Hermann	1479–1493
Aigen, Benedict	1515–1532
Hummel, Bartholome	1536–1557
Stob, Jorg	1566
Stenzel, Martin	1572
Schiesser, Leonhard	1576
Aigen, Hans	1577, ca. 1578
Rackh, Georg	1582–1587
Hailg, Hans	ca. 1587/9
Engler, Johann	1589
Langenstain, Christoph	1592–1631
Fimppel, Abraham	1632
Leub, Sebastian	1634, 1639, 1649–1652
Mayer, Hans	1636–1638, 1646

Buggensegel	
Mandler, Ulrich	1512/1514
Mangler, Hans	mid-16th century
Schaitteckh, Michael	1556–1587
Villieber, Hans	1589–1610
Langenstain, Jeorg	1611–1619
Rogg (Rockh), Hans	1624–1639

Gebhardsweiler	
Mayer, Claus	mid-16th century
Ower, Sebastian	ca. 1578/80, 1581
Rimelin, Ulrich	1593
Dulenkopf, Martin	1624–1631

Grasbeuren	
Wern, Hans	1528
Storch, Hans	1556–1557
Schenck, Hans	1566
Ower, Adam der Alt	mid-16th century, 1572–1599
Ower, Adam der Jung	ca. 1600, 1603–1629
Donath, Georg	1636
Ower, Jacob	1638–1639, 1646, 1653

Mimmenhausen	
Schlegel, Jorig	mid-16th century
Wuest, Michael	1566, 1572
Leutin, Hans	ca. 1578
Höltzlin, Bernhard	ca. 1578/80, 1581–1585
Wagner, Conrad	1587
Senfft, Mattheus	1589–1596, 1599
Maisterhans, Marx	1602–1607
Leub, Mattheus	1610–1631
Diem, Balthas	1632
Steeger, Christoph	1635
Rundolt, Georg	1637–1638, 1642

Mühlhofen	
Straus, Manning	mid-16th century
Leugker, Bastian	1572
Mayer, Solomon	ca. 1578/80, 1581
Sixt, Balthas	1590–1615

Neufrach	
Obermüller, Conrad	1505, 1512
Mayer, Georg	1566
Hailg, Jacob	ca. 1578/80, 1581–1587
Richel, Martin	1588–1616
Utz, Hans	1617–1623
Mayer, Valentin	1623–1632
Heffelin, Michael	1637–1638

Nußdorf	
Sernatinger, Jacob	1524, mid-16th century
Villieber, Veit	mid-16th century, 1566
Mayer, Georg	1568
Waibel, Hans	1572
Villieber, Andreas	ca. 1578/80, 1581–1613
Härlin, Michael	1613–1618
Holl, Georg	1619–1635
Kessler, Hans	1646–1648
Oberuhldingen	
Storch, Hans	mid-16th century
Urnau, Michael	1566–1581
Stett, Martin	1587–1599
Muettinger, Steffan	1603–1611
Urnau, Jacob	1611–1619
Winter, Hans	1620–1624
Rauch, Hans Georg	1626–1648
Owingen and Pfaffenhofen	
Kolb, Hans	1473
Kurz, Hans	1556, mid-16th century
Weber, Balthas	1566, 1572
Schreiber, Jacob	ca. 1578, 1579–1588
Burst, Mattheus	1588–1611
Schreiber, Georg	1612–1618
Stengelin, Martin	1620–1633
Schentz, Johann	1633–1635
Stengelin, Peter	1637–1662
Tepfenhard	
Stett, Steffan der Alt	1517
Stett, Hans	mid-16th century
Stett, Steffan der Jung	ca. 1578/80, 1581–1590
Stett, Jacob	1603
Amman, Ulrich	1608, 1620
Scheckh, Jacob	1638

Tüfingen

Velen (Voler), Hans	mid-16th century
Mayer, Andreas	1566–1589
Mayer, Moritz	1590–1629
Biller, Georg	1632

Urnau

Schlyen, Hans	1501
Müller, Hans	1525
Buechmüller, Jorig	mid-16th century
Buechmüller, Christa	1566–1591
Hailg, Georg	1600–1616
Speckher, Hans	1619–1624
Buechmüller, Jerg	before 1631
Wielat, Georg	1638
Hildebrand, Georg	1645

Weildorf

Cammerer, Hans	1566, 1572
Steckhborer, Blesin	ca. 1578, 1581–1598
Biller, Bartlin	1600–1611
Rauch, Christoph (Stoffel)	1611–1628
Biller, Silvester	1629–1638
Ziegler, Adam	1639

Weiler

Leub, Klainhans der Alt	1512
Schaitteckh, Caspar	mid-16th century
Leub, Laux der Alt	1572–1581, 1584
Leub, Bastian	1584, 1585
Bitzenhofer, Ursus	1585–1587
Leub, Laux der Jung	1589–1611
Klotz, Jacob	1612–1624
Ringenburger, Michael	1626–1627
Leub, Georg	1638, 1646

Appendix 5.1: Members of the Sidelgericht

* designates one or more missing lists before or after known series of dates.
G = Gerichtsdiener (bailiff), B = Beisitzer (court alternate), SR = Sidelrichter (judge), STH = Stabhalter (head judge)

Name	Place	Office Dates
Aigen, Benedict	Bermatingen	STH: *1526*
Aigen, Hermann	Bermatingen	STH: *1486–1505*
Amman, Ulrich	Bebenweiler; Tepfenhard	SR: 1585–1591*
Biller, Conrad der Alt	Owingen	SR: *1572–1591*
Biller, Conrad der Jung	Oberhof	STH: 1592–1616
Biller, Mattheus	Oberhof	B: 1617–1620 SR: 1621–1631 STH: *1640–1652*
Biller, Silvester	Weildorf	B: *1631 SR: 1632–1638*
Bluem, Mattheus	Oberuhldingen	B: *1646 SR: 1650–1652*
Brem, Jacob	Grasbeuren	B: 1621–1629*
Burckhart, Hans	Forst	SR: *1471–1473*
Burst, Hans	Owingen	SR: *1486*
Burst, Mattheus	Owingen	B: 1585–1587 SR: 1589–1606*
Burst, Michel	Nußdorf	SR: *1471–1483*
Cammerer, Hans	Weildorf	SR: *1572*
Chorher, Ulrich	Weildorf	SR: *1476*
Claußmar, Hans	Grasbeuren	B: *1612–1613 SR: 1614–1620
Claußmar, Veit	Grasbeuren; Bermatingen	SR: *1583–1606*
Diem, Balthas	Leutkirch	B: *1626–1629 SR: 1631–1632*
Dilger, Andreas	Raltzhoff; Bermatingen	SR: *1638–1652*
Dilger, Hans	Schwandorf	B: 1614–1622 SR: 1623–1632*
Donath, Georg	Grasbeuren	B: *1631–1632*
Dulenkopf, Martin	Mühlhofen; Gebhards-weiler	B: 1623 SR: 1624–1632*
Ellengast, Hans	Neufrach	SR: *1476*
Engler, Johann	Bermatingen	SR: *1589
Felder, Polay (called Sogger)	Wehausen	SR: *1471–1473*

Felder, Stoffel	Wehausen	B: *1640–1646*
Gaist, Hans	Mimmenhausen	G: 1622–1623
Gebhardt, Galle	Neufrach	G: 1617–1621
Hagen, Peter	Altheim	SR: *1500*
Hailg, Hans	Bermatingen	SR: *1583–1591*
Hailg, Jacob	Neufrach	SR: *1584–1589
Hailg, Jos	Adelsreute	B: 1632*
Hailg, Michael	Nußdorf	B: 1590–1591*
Haller, Jorg	Bermatingen	B: *1626–1631
Härlin, Michael	Nußdorf	B: *1612–1613 SR: 1614–1634*
Heffelin, Hans	Hagnau	SR: *1514*
Heffelin, Michael	Neufrach	B: 1632 SR: 1635–1646*
Hermann, Velin	Rickhenbach	SR: *1471–1473*
Holl, Georg	Nußdorf	B: 1629*
Höltzlin, Bernhard	Mimmenhausen	SR: *1584–1585
Hörer, Moritz	Mimmenhausen	SR: *1572*
Hummel, Hans	Bermatingen	SR: *1486*
Hund, Hans	Wendlingen	B: 1632 SR: 1638*
Ill, Georg	Wälde	SR: *1572–1587*
Kessler, Hans	Nußdorf	B: *1638 SR: 1646–1652*
Klaiber, Urban	Weildorf	B: 1587 SR: 1589
Klenckher, Hans	Pfaffenhofen	SR: *1476*
Klenckher, Jerg	Owingen	SR: *1500*
Klotz, Jacob	Weiler	SR: 1617–1624*
Knecht, Georg	Bermatingen	SR: *1638–1652*
Koch, Jacob	Tüfingen	SR: *1476–1500*
Kramer, Hans	Hedertsweiler	SR: *1483–1500*
Kraug, Hans	Hergisweiler	SR: *1476*
Langenstain, Christoph	Bermatingen	SR: 1590–1624 STH: 1626–1631
Leub, Andreas	Baufnang	SR: *1471–1486*
Leub, Georg	Weiler	B: 1632 SR: 1638–1652*
Leub, Klainhans	Weiler	SR: *1500–1514*
Leub, Laux der Alt	Weiler	SR: *1572*

Leub, Laux der Jung	Weiler	B: *1589–1591 SR: 1605–1612
Leub, Martin	unknown	B: *1646*
Leub, Mattheus	Mimmenhausen	SR: *1612–1631
Leutin, Hans	Mimmenhausen	SR: *1572*
Lewolff, Bernhard	Oberuhldingen	SR: *1476*
Lochmayer, Mattheus	Weildorf	SR: *1605–1622
Maisterhans, Marx	Mimmenhausen	B: *1605–1606*
Mandler, Ulrich	Buggensegel	SR: *1500*
Mayer, Andreas	Tüfingen	SR: *1572 STH: 1583–1591*
Mayer, Georg	Bermatingen	B: 1618–1624 SR: 1626–1632*
Mayer, Georg	Nußdorf; Neufrach	STH: *1568–1572*
Mayer, Hans	Bermatingen	B: 1585 SR: 1587–1591*
Mayer, Hans	Bermatingen	SR: *1638–1646*
Mayer, Hans	Mimmenhausen	SR: *1476–1486 STH: 1492*
Mayer, Hans	Neufrach	SR: *1584–1585
Mayer, Jerg	Bermatingen	SR: *ca. 1498–1514
Mayer, Moritz	Tüfingen	SR: *1605–1629*
Mayer, Peter	Bermatingen	SR: *1486*
Mayer, Peter	Tüfingen	SR: *1476*
Mayer, Valentin	Neufrach	SR: *1626–1632*
Megerlin, Conrad	Bermatingen	SR: *1584
Michel, M. Andreas	Neufrach	B: *1638 SR: 1646*
Möckhing, Martin	Owingen	B: *1612–1613 SR: 1614–1628
Möckhing, Hans	Owingen	B: *1631–1632*
Mörlin, Peter	Bermatingen	SR: *1612–1632*
Moser, Hans	Owingen/Pfaffenhofen	B: 1590–1591 SR: 1605–1616
Muettinger, M. Steffan	Oberuhldingen	B: *1589 SR: 1590–1606*
Müller, Conrad	Bermatingen	SR: *1486*
Müller, Conrad	Neufrach	SR: *1500*
Müller, Hans	Pfaffenhofen	SR: *1471–1480*
Müller, Hans called Thoma	Owingen	SR: *1503–1514*
Müller, M. Bartlin	Leutkirch	SR: *1612–1613
Mußel, M. Lorenz	Mimmenhausen	G: 1614–1616

Mußel, Simon	Mimmenhausen	B: 1614–1616 SR: 1617–1632*
Obermüller, Conrad	Neufrach	SR: *1503–1514*
Ower, Adam der Alt	Grasbeuren	SR: *1572–1591*
Ower, Adam der Jung	Grasbeuren	B: 1606 SR: 1612–1632*
Ower, Jacob	Grasbeuren	SR: *1638–1652*
Peter	Bebenweiler	SR: *1486*
Pfau, Hans	Bermatingen	SR: *ca. 1498*
Rackh, Georg	Bermatingen	SR: *1584–1587*
Rauch, Christoph	Weildorf	B: *1605–1606 SR: 1612–1628
Rauch, Hans Jorg	Oberuhldingen	SR: *1646–1652*
Resstlin, Veit	Mimmenhausen	G: 1618–1632*
Richel, Andreas der Alt	Neufrach	SR: *1572*
Richel, Andreas der Jung	Neufrach	B: *1612–1624*
Richel, Hans	Neufrach	B: *1584–1591*
Rogg, Hans	Buggensegel	B: 1629 SR: 1631–1632 STH: 1638*
Rosstock, Lienhart	Neufrach	SR: *1486*
Rueff, Hans	Nußdorf	SR: *1471–1500*
Rueff, Severinus	Bermatingen	SR: *1605–1616 STH: 1617–1624*
Rüthart, Georg	Owingen	B: 1629*
Rundolt, Georg	Mimmenhausen	B: *1638 SR: 1650–1652*
Schäflin, Conrad	Ahausen	SR: *1471–1486*
Schaitteckh, Franz	Schwandorf	B: *1589 SR: 1590–1591*
Schaitteckh, Hans	Mendlishausen	B: *1638 SR: 1650–1652*
Scheckh, Jacob	Tepfenhard	SR: *1638–1650*
Schlig, Hans	Urnau	SR: *1486*
Schmidtmaister, Hans	Mimmenhausen	B: *1638*
Schneider, Stoffel	Lugenhof (Owingen)	B: *1584
Schneider, Lienhart	Nußdorf	SR: *1476*
Schneider, Peter	Owingen	SR: *1476–1478*
Schöchin, Jerg	Bermatingen	SR: *ca. 1498*
Schreiber, Georg	Owingen	SR: *1612–1618
Schreiber, Jacob	Owingen	SR: *1572–1587 STH: 1588

Schuchmacher, Lienhart	Neufrach	SR: *1500*
Schwies, Rueff	Nußdorf	SR: *1476–1483*
Seboltin, Hans	Urnau	SR: *1476*
Senfft, Mattheus	Tüfingen; Mimmen-hausen	B: 1585 SR: 1587–1606*
Sernatinger, Jacob	Nußdorf	SR: *1500–1514*
Sogger, Hans	Weiler	SR: *1476–1483*
Sogger, Peter	Wehausen	SR: *1486–1500*
Steckborer, Blesi	Weildorf	SR: *1572–1591*
Stengelin, Martin	Owingen	SR: 1619–1631 STH: 1632–1634*
Stengelin, Peter der Alt	Owingen	SR: *1584–1606*
Stengelin, Peter der Jung	Owingen	SR: *1638–1652*
Stenzel, Martin	Bermatingen	SR: *1572*
Stett, Hainrich	Tepfenhard	SR: *1479–1583*
Stett, Hans	Bitzenhofen	SR: *1476*
Stöblin, Stoffel	Mimmenhausen	SR: *1486–1500*
Strobel, Hans	Bermatingen	B: *1583–1584 SR: 1585–1616
Strobel, Michel	Bermatingen	SR: *1572*
Syplin, Hainz	Weiler	SR: *1476*
Thoma, Hans	Owingen	SR: *1500*
Ulmer, Balthasar	Neufrach	SR: *1584
Urnau, Jacob	Oberuhldingen	B: *1612–1613
Urnau, Michael der Alt	Unteruhldingen	SR: *1500–1503*
Urnau, Michael der Jung	Nußdorf	B: *1605
Utz, Hans	Neufrach	B: 1617 SR: 1617–1623
Villieber, Andreas	Nußdorf	SR: *1584–1613
Villieber, Claus	Oberuhldingen	SR: *1500*
Villieber, Veit	Nußdorf	STH: *1566*
Vögelin, Sebastian	Mimmenhausen	B: *1626–1629 SR: 1631–1632*
Vogler, M. Hans	Owingen	B: *1640–1646*
Wagner, Conrad	Mimmenhausen	B: 1587*
Weber, Balthas	Owingen/Pfaffenhofen	SR: *1572*
Weißenkönig, Hans	Neufrach	B: *1605–1616

Weißenkönig, Georg	Neufrach	SR: *1640–1652*
Weißenkönig, Georg	Nußdorf	SR: *1638*
Wern, Ander	Neufrach	STH: *1471–1473*
Wielat, Georg	Urnau	SR: *1638*
Wuest, Martin	Owingen	SR: *1471–1473*
Wuest, Michael	Mimmenhausen	SR: *1572*
Zäh, Hans	Owingen	SR: *1486*
Ziegler, Adam	Weildorf	SR: *1646–1652*
Zürckh, Hans	Bauflang	B: *1584

Appendix 6.1: Salem's Abbots

Date	Name	Background Notes
1. 1138–1165	**Frowin**	Monk from Bellevaux, then Lützel.
2. 1166–1168	**Gottfried**	Monk from Lützel.
3. 1168–1175	**Erimbert**	Monk from Lützel.
4. 1175–1191	**Christian I**	No background information.
5. 1191–1240	**Eberhard I von Rohrdorf**	Rohrdorf by Meßkirch. High nobility.
6. 1240–1241	**Berthold I von Urach**	Urach. High nobility. Former abbot of Lützel.
7. 1241–1276	**Eberhard II von Wollmatingen**	Wollmatingen. Untitled noble.
8. 1276–1282	**Ulrich I Graeter**	Biberach. Burgher. Former Großkeller in Salem.
9. 1282–1311	**Ulrich II von Seelfingen**	Seelfingen. Untitled noble.
10. 1311–1337	**Konrad von Enslingen**	Enslingen. Untitled noble.
11. 1337–1358	**Ulrich III von Werdenberg-Sargans**	Werdenberg-Sargans. High nobility.
12. 1358–1373	**Berthold II Tutz**	Former abbot of Wettingen. Dr. and Prof. theol.
13. 1373–1395	**Wilhelm Schrailk**	Former abbot of Raitenhaslach.
14. 1395–1417	**Jodokus I Senner**	Ravensburg. Burgher. Former Großkeller in Salem.
15. 1417–1441	**Peter I Ochser**	Ravensburg. Burgher. Former Großkeller in Salem.
16. 1441–1458	**Georg I Münch**	Constance. Burgher.
17. 1458–1471	**Ludwig Oschwald**	Überlingen. Burgher. Dr. and Prof. theol. in Paris.
18. 1471–1494	**Johannes I Stantenant**	Uffholz (Alsace). Former abbot of Lützel. Possibly former prior in Salem.
19. 1494–1510	**Johannes II Scharpfer (Schürpfer)**	Mimmenhausen. Peasant and territorial subject.
20. 1510–1529	**Jodokus II Necker**	Überlingen. Burgher, son of the town secretary. Prof. theol. in Paris.

21. 1529–1534	**Amandus Schäffer**	Strassbourg. Burgher. Refugee monk from Alsace.
22. 1534–1543	**Johannes III Fischer**	Mimmenhausen. Peasant and territorial subject.
23. 1543–1553	**Johannes IV Precht**	Tübingen. Burgher.
24. 1553–1558	**Johannes V Michel**	Neufrach by Riedlingen. Former procurator in Schemmerberg.
25. 1558–1575	**Georg II Kaisersberger**	Wemding (Bavaria). Burgher.
26. 1575–1583	**Matthäus Roth**	Neufrach by Gamertingen. Former procurator in Pfullendorf.
27. 1583–1587	**Vitus Nekher**	Mimmenhausen. Peasant and territorial subject.
28. 1587–1588	**Johannes VI Bücheler**	Neufrach. Peasant and territorial subject. Former bursar.
29. 1588–1593	**Christian II Fürst**	Herbertingen by Saulgau.
30. 1593–1614	**Peter II Müller**	Schellenberg by Waldsee.
31. 1615–1647	**Thomas I Wunn**	Grasbeuren. Peasant and territorial subject. Prof. phil. Former bursar.
32. 1647–1664	**Thomas II Schwab**	Bechingen by Riedlingen.
33. 1664–1680	**Anselm I Muotelsee**	Mimmenhausen. Peasant and territorial subject. Prof. phil. in Wettingen.
34. 1680–1698	**Emanuel Sulger**	Neufrach by Riedlingen.
35. 1698–1725	**Stephan I Jung**	Koblenz. Son of a carpenter and abbey subject from Nußdorf. Former prior.
36. 1725–1745	**Konstantin Miller**	Constance. Burgher.
37. 1745–1746	**Stephan II Enroth**	Meersburg. Burgher. Prof. theol. in Salem.
38. 1746–1778	**Anselm II Schwab**	Füßen am Lech (Bavaria).
39. 1778–1802	**Robert Schlecht**	Wemding (Bavaria). Burgher. Former prior in Salem.
40. 1802–[1804]	**Kaspar Oexle**	Schönberg by Ravensburg. Son of an organ maker.

Glossary of Terms

Abzug departure, emigration; exit fines owed by those leaving the territory (cf. **Einzug**)

Aigen, Aigengüter (Eigen) personal, freehold property

Aigene Leute (Eigene Leute) serfs, bondsmen and women, persons belonging bodily to another

Agrarverfassungsvertrag agrarian constitutional agreement

Amtmann (pl. **Amtmänner**) village headman

Arme Leute, Armer Mann commoners, poor folk; the common man

Bannwart local forest and field warden

Bauer, Bauern peasant(s)

Beisitzer (or **Zusatz**) alternate member of Salem's court

Bericht, der neue an arbitrated agreement reached in 1473 between Salem's abbot and territorial judges, serving as one of two major territorial law codes (cf. **Jarbrief, der alte**)

Bursar abbey treasurer and high administrative official; a monk

Dorfpfleger village treasurer (usually two in number)

Einzug entry, immigration; fees owed by new residents to the abbey and local commune (cf. **Abzug, Erschatz**)

Erblehen hereditary land tenure

Erschatz entry fees paid by new tenants with lifelong leases (cf. **Einzug**)

Etter village boundary demarcated by a fence, wall, or hedge

Frevel personal misconduct, criminal misdemeanor subject to fines

Fridbot call for peace, the legally binding authority of a witness to forbid a violent act

Fruchten Anschlag annual list of values for grain, straw, and manure, issued by the Sidelgericht starting in 1595

Fürsprecher (or **Anwalt**) legal advocate, court spokesman

Gastmeister guestmaster, head of Salem's guesthouse

Gebot und Verbot the authority to command and prohibit

Gemeinde commune, community

Gericht court, tribunal; jurisdiction (the area under the lord's legal authority)

Gerichtsbarkeit judicial authority

Gerichtsdiener (or **Gerichtsknecht**) court bailiff

Gerichtsherrschaft lordship over courts of justice; the authority to declare the law and pass judgment

Gerichtsschreiber court secretary

Gotteshausleute abbey dependents, literally "the people of God's house"

Großkeller grand cellarer, a high administrative official and district supervisor; a monk

Großkelleramt district supervised by the Großkeller, including villages of the central territory primarily west of the Aach River

Grundherrschaft landlordship, political authority derived from property

Gut, Güter, Guetlin property, properties, smallholding (cf. **Hof**)

Heiligenpfleger (or **Kirchenpfleger**) churchwarden, treasurer (usually two, sometimes three in number)

Heiratsabrede marriage contract

Hintersass a dependent who is not the lord's serf, literally "one who sits behind" (the abbey's jurisdiction)

Hof (pl. Höfe) farm, large property (cf. **Gut**)

Hofgericht Salem's high court of appeals

Hofmeister a high administrative official and district supervisor; usually an abbey employee but sometimes a monk (see also **Pfleger, Vogt**)

Huldigung loyalty oath sworn to a new abbot

Jarbrief, der alte an old legal customal, one of Salem's two major territorial law codes and a subject of controversy in the years 1468-1473 (cf. **Bericht, der neue**)

Kaufmann high administrative official and abbey prosecutor until 1590 (cf. **Oberamtmann**), one for the central territory and another for the northern district near Ostrach; an abbey employee in the sixteenth century, formerly a laybrother

Kirchenvogtei ecclesiastical guardianship

Landeshoheit territorial sovereignty

Landgarb share of the crop owed to a landlord (sharecropping)

Landschaft territorial assembly of estates

Landvogt Imperial vice-regent or steward

Landvogtei Imperial lands and rights administered by the Landvogt (in Upper Swabia and in other regions)

Leibeigene Leute (see **Aigene Leute**)

Leibgeding retirement or pension agreement, a contract describing payment in return for benefits

Leibherrschaft lordship over serfs

Leiblehen form of land tenure granting use-rights for one or more lifetimes

Mayerschaft farm tenants, the major local landholders

Oberamtmann high administrative official and abbey prosecutor since 1590 (cf. **Kaufmann**); an abbey employee, of which there were two: one for the central territory and another for the northern district near Ostrach

Pfister master baker, a high administrative official and district supervisor; a monk, though formerly a laybrother

Pfisteramt district supervised by the Pfister, including villages of the central territory primarily east of the Aach River

Pfleger guardian (over a village, church, orphans, or widows); also a title referring to certain district administrators (see also **Hofmeister, Vogt**)

Raißsteuer Imperial military tax

Rat ruling council (in a village or the abbey); also counsel, advice

Recht right, law, or justice

Reichsprälatenkollegium College of Imperial Prelates in Upper Swabia (as well as on the Rhine), a political organization promoting collective interests at the regional and Imperial level

Schnittergeld fees relating to harvest expenses (wages), paid by the tenant (sharecropper) and the landlord

Schreiber scribe or secretary

Schützengesellschaft an association for defense

Schupflehen (or **Handlehen, Jahrlehen**) form of land tenure subject to annual renewal

Sidelgericht Salem's central court, responsible for civil suits and criminal misdemeanors

Sidelrichter the lay judges, usually 15 in number, who composed Salem's central court

Seldner smallholder, cottager

Spital charitable institution for the care of poor, sick, and elderly persons

Stabhalter staffbearer, the head judge

Stadthof (pl. **Stadthöfe**) urban property providing extensive legal and economic privileges, used as a market access point and warehouse, as well as an administrative center, guesthouse, and place of refuge

Todfall heriot or death tax owed by serfs

Übergangenes Gebot criminal offense, statute violation

Umfrag form of collective inquiry used to reach decisions

Umgeld (or **Ungeld**) excise tax, often associated with wine sales

Unter den Bergen Under the Hills, the basin between Lake Constance and the Heiligenberg Hills, a name associated with Salem's central territory

Urkunde legal charter, an official document sealed by witnesses and often used to substantiate rights or claims

Urteilsprecher (see also **Sidelrichter**) a term for all judges except the first; literally, "speakers of judgment"

Verhör the "Audience" of petitions, a regularly occurring assembly of territorial administrators to hear subjects' requests and grievances

Vogt (or **Obervogt**) guardian or district administrator (see also **Hofmeister, Pfleger**)

Vogtei guardianship (see also **Kirchenvogtei**)

Vogteifreiheit immunity from guardianship, an idea promoted by medieval Cistercians claiming to be directly under the emperor's protection and therefore exempt from the protection (and interference) of a noble guardian

Voraus advance, a small inheritance payment made prior to a full partition. Used to provision a child upon reaching majority, while postponing the payment of a full share

Waldvogt head forest steward, a high administrative official and abbey employee

Weistum, Weistümer a customary form of law, often written ("customal"), though originally thought to be an oral form of inquiry and recitation, performed in a formal assembly of lord and subjects. Salem's alte Jarbrief is one such document

Weisung the formal process of declaring the laws, performed as a series of questions posed by the lord and answered by his collective subjects

(The following terms are defined above in the Notes on Usage, Currencies, and Measures: Batzen, Eimer, Fuder, Hofstatt, Imi, Jauchert, Gulden, Kreuzer, Malter, Mannßmad, Maß, Pfennig, Pfund, Schoffel, Shilling, Stuck, Thaler, and Viertel.)

Bibliography

Primary Sources

Generallandesarchiv Karlsruhe (GLAK)

Section 4 Generalia/37, 114, 116, 119–124, 126, 128–131, 135, 363, 365–366, 368, 752, 755, 1136–1137, 1139, 1158–1164

Section 4 Specialia/1468, 1472, 1497, 1500, 1508, 1513, 1519, 1523, 1553, 1687, 1698, 1769–1772, 1790–1791, 1810–1811, 2116, 2127, 2139, 2153, 2155, 2158, 2178–2179, 2617, 2637, 2651–2652, 2654, 2657, 2710, 2712, 2715, 2718, 2723, 2732–2734, 3401, 3623, 3655, 3658, 3677, 3883, 3892, 3894–3895, 3900, 3902, 3910, 3988, 4023, 4258, 4267–2468, 4428–4429, 4528, 4530, 4533, 4544, 4627–4628, 4630–4631, 4648, 4728, 4741, 4746, 4922, 4965, 4972, 5016, 5087, 5154, 5616, 5661–5662, 5663, 5852, 5929, 5933, 5935, 5941, 5943, 7618–7619

Section 61/13315–13329, 13369–13374

Section 62/9264–9267, 9297, 9299a

Section 65/11324, 11519

Section 66/10311–10312, 10358–10359, 10367–10378, 10416–10419, 11285, 11290–11293, 11726

Section 67/1431, 1435, 1468, 1478, 1484, 1774, 1782, 1786

Section 98 Generalia/31–32, 59–60, 216–252, 329–331, 360, 371–377, 388–389, 395–396, 492, 525, 595, 597, 600–601, 646, 688, 804, 814, 1252, 1260, 1546–1547, 1553, 1560–1563, 1568–1569, 1584, 1616, 1717, 1720, 1723, 1729, 1732, 1741, 1779, 1987, 2003, 2006–2007, 2016, 2018–2019, 2023–2024, 2026, 2300–2305, 2309, 3139–3140, 3142

Section 98 Specialia/3198, 3200, 3202, 3204, 3275, 3310, 3376, 3427, 3432–3433, 3435, 3460, 3474–3476, 3481–3483, 3499, 3502, 3659, 3670, 3681, 4402, 4419–4424

Published Sources

BAIER, Hermann, ed.: Akten zur Geschichte des dreißigjährigen Krieges am Bodensee, in: Schriften des Vereins für Geschichte des Bodensees und seiner Umgebung 44 (1915), pp. 129–162.

—, ed.: Ein Sparerlaß aus dem Kloster Salem von 1481, in: Schriften des Vereins für Geschichte des Bodensees und seiner Umgebung 40 (1911), pp. 248–255.

Bauernkrieg am Bodensee, in: Quellensammlung der badischen Landesgeschichte, vol. 2, ed. Friedrich J. Mone, Karlsruhe 1854, pp. 118–133.

BAUMANN, Franz Ludwig, ed.: Akten zur Geschichte des deutschen Bauernkrieges aus Oberschwaben, Freiburg im Breisgau 1877.

FEYERABEND, Gabriel: Chronik des ehemaligen Reichs-Stiftes und Münsters Salmannsweiler in Schwaben, von seiner Entstehung bis zu seiner Auflösung, 2 vols., 1833 [unpublished manuscript, Universitätsbibliothek Heidelberg].

FRANZ, Günther, ed.: Quellen zur Geschichte des Bauernkrieges, Munich 1963.

FRANZ, Günther, ed.: Jacob Murers Weißenauer Chronik des Bauernkrieges von 1525, Sigmaringen 1977.

KLOCKH, Mattheus, ed.: Anticategoriae zwaier Fürnemmer deß Hayl. Röm. Reichsständen Hailgenberg und Salmansweyl wegen ihrer hincinde habenden und praetendirten Privilegien und Verträgen, 1616.

KUHN-OECHSELE, Hildegard and Elmar L. KUHN, eds.: Der Seehaufen im Bauernkrieg: Eine Quellensammlung, vol. 2/2, Friedrichshafen 1982.

SCHNEIDER, Walter, ed.: Zwei Todfall-Rodel der Reichsabtei Salem aus den Jahren 1594–1600 und 1608–1628, in: Schriften des Vereins für Geschichte des Bodensees und seiner Umgebung 90 (1972), pp. 77–110.

WEECH, Friedrich von, ed.: Sebastian Bürsters Beschreibung des Schwedischen Krieges 1630–1647, Leipzig 1875.

WEECH, Friedrich von, ed.: Codex Diplomaticus Salemitanus: Urkundenbuch der Cistercienserabtei Salem, 3 vols., Karlsruhe 1883–1895.

Secondary Literature

ABEL, Wilhelm: Agricultural Fluctuations in Europe: From the Thirteenth to the Twentieth Centuries, trans. Olive Ordish, London and New York 1980.

ALGAZI, Gadi: Lords Ask, Peasants Answer: Making Traditions in Late-Medieval Village Assemblies, in: Between History and Histories: The Making of Silences and Commemorations, ed. Gerald Sider and Gavin Smith, Anthropological Horizons Series 11, Toronto 1997, pp. 199–229.

—: Tradition als Gespräch der Ungleichen: Bauern und Herren in der spätmittelalterlichen Dorfversammlung, in: Eid und Wahrheitssuche: Studien zur rechtlichen Befragungspraktiken in Mittelalter und früher Neuzeit, ed. Stefan Esders and Thomas Scharff, Gesellschaft, Kultur und Schrift 7, Frankfurt am Main 1999, pp. 191–210.

AMMAN, Hektor: Untersuchungen zur Wirtschaftsgeschichte des Oberrheinraumes II. Das Kloster Salem in der Wirtschaft des ausgehenden Mittelalters, in: Zeitschrift für die Geschichte des Oberrheins 110 (1962), pp. 371–404.

ASTON, T. H. and C. H. E. PHILPIN, eds.: The Brenner Debate: Agrarian Class Structure and Economic Development in Pre-Industrial Europe, Past and Present Publications, Cambridge and New York 1985.

BADER, Karl Siegfried: Ausgewählte Schriften zur Rechts- und Landesgeschichte, vol. 2, Sigmaringen 1984.

—: Bauernrecht und Bauernfreiheit im späteren Mittelalter, in: Ausgewählte Schriften zur Rechts- und Landesgeschichte, vol. 2, Sigmaringen 1984, pp. 11–47.

—: Der deutsche Südwesten in seiner territorialstaatlichen Entwicklung, Sigmaringen 1978.

—: Die Entwicklung und Verbreitung der mittelalterlichen Schiedsidee in Südwestdeutschland und in der Schweiz, in: Ausgewählte Schriften zur Rechts- und Landesgeschichte, vol. 2, Sigmaringen 1984, pp. 226–251.

—: Das Schiedsverfahren in Schwaben vom 12. bis zum ausgehenden 16. Jahrhundert, in: Ausgewählte Schriften zur Rechts- und Landesgeschichte, vol. 2, Sigmaringen 1984, pp. 157–225.

—: Studien zur Rechtsgeschichte des mittelalterlichen Dorfes, vol. 1: Das mittelalterliche Dorf als Friedens- und Rechtsbereich, Weimar 1957.

—: Studien zur Rechtsgeschichte des mittelalterlichen Dorfes, vol. 2: Dorfgenossenschaft und Dorfgemeinde, Cologne 1962.

—: Territorialbildung und Landeshoheit, in: Blätter für deutsche Landesgeschichte 90 (1953), pp. 109–131.
BAIER, Hermann: Zur Bevölkerungs- und Vermögensstatistik des Salemer Gebiets im 16. und 17. Jahrhundert, in: Zeitschrift für die Geschichte des Oberrheins, n. s. 29 (1914), pp. 196–216.
—: Des Klosters Salem Bevölkerungsbewegung, Finanz-, Steuerwesen und Volkswirtschaft seit dem 15. Jahrhundert, in: Freiburger Diözesanarchiv, n. s. 62 (1934), pp. 57–130.
—: Die Stellung der Abtei Salem in Staat und Kirche, in: Freiburger Diözesanarchiv, n. s. 62 (1934), pp. 131–154.
—: Zur Vorgeschichte des Bauernkriegs, in: Zeitschrift für die Geschichte des Oberrheins 78 (1926), pp. 188–218.
BAK, Janos, ed.: The German Peasant War of 1525, Library of Peasant Studies 3, London 1976.
BECKER, Karl: Salem unter Abt Thomas I. Wunn und die Gründung der oberdeutschen Cistercienser-Kongregation, 1615–1647, in: Cistercienser Chronik 48 (1936), pp. 137–145, 161–179, 205–239, 328–337.
BEIK, William: Absolutism and Society in Seventeenth-Century France: State Power and Provincial Aristocracy in Languedoc, Cambridge 1985.
BENSING, Manfred and Siegfried HOYER: Der deutsche Bauernkrieg, 1524–1526, [Berlin 1965].
BERENBACH, Eduard: 800 Jahre Grafen von Heiligenberg, Donaueschingen 1931.
BERKNER, Lutz K.: Rural Family Organization in Europe: A Problem in Comparative History, in: Peasant Studies Newsletter 1 (1972), pp. 145–156.
—: The Stem Family and the Developmental Cycle of the Peasant Household: An Eighteenth-century Austrian Example, in: American Historical Review 77 (1972), pp. 398–418.
BIERBRAUER, Peter: Der Aufstieg der Gemeinde und die Entfeudalisierung der Gesellschaft im späten Mittelalter, in: Kommunalisierung und Christianisierung: Voraussetzungen und Folgen der Reformation, 1400–1600, ed. Peter Blickle and Johannes Kunisch, Zeitschrift für Historische Forschung, supplement vol. 9, Berlin 1989, pp. 29–56.
—: Bäuerliche Revolten im Alten Reich: Ein Forschungsbericht, in: Aufruhr und Empörung? Studien zum bäuerlichen Widerstand im Alten Reich, ed. Peter Blickle, Munich 1980, pp. 1–68.
—: Freiheit und Gemeinde im Berner Oberland, 1300–1700, Bern 1991.
—: Ländliche Gemeinde im oberdeutsch-schweizerischen Raum, in: Landgemeinde und Stadtgemeinde in Mitteleuropa: Ein struktureller Vergleich, ed. Peter Blickle, Munich 1991, pp. 169–190.
BINDER, Max: Zur staatlichen Geschichte des Linzgaues, in: Badische Heimat 23 (1936), pp. 64–67.
BLACK, Antony: The Commune in Political Theory in the Late Middle Ages, in: Theorien kommunaler Ordnung in Europa, ed. Peter Blickle, Schriften des Historischen Kollegs 36, Munich 1996, pp. 99–112.
BLICKLE, Peter: Arbeit, Alltag und Recht: Wandlungen in der Ochsenhausener Grundherrschaft an der Wende vom Mittelalter zur Neuzeit, in: Ochsenhausen: Von der Benediktinerabtei zur oberschwäbischen Landstadt, ed. Max Herold, Weissenhorn 1994, pp. 127–138.
—, ed.: Aufruhr und Empörung? Studien zum bäuerlichen Widerstand im Alten Reich, Munich 1980.
—: Bauer und Staat in Oberschwaben, in: Zeitschrift für Württembergische Landesgeschichte 31 (1972), pp. 104–120.
—: Bäuerliche Erhebungen im spätmittelalterlichen deutschen Reich, in: Zeitschrift für Agrargeschichte und Agrarsoziologie 27 (1979), pp. 208–231.

—: Bäuerliches Eigen im Allgäu, in: Zeitschrift für Agrargeschichte und Agrarsoziologie 17 (1969), pp. 57–78.
—: Begriffsverfremdung: Über den Umgang mit dem wissenschaftlichen Ordnungsbegriff Kommunalismus, in: Zeitschrift für Historische Forschung 22 (1995), pp. 246–253.
—: Communal Reformation: The Quest for Salvation in Sixteenth-Century Germany, trans. Thomas Dunlap, Studies in German Histories, Atlantic Highlands 1992.
—: From the Communal Reformation to the Revolution of the Common Man, trans. Beat Kümin, Studies in Medieval and Reformation Thought 65, Leiden and Boston 1998.
—: The Criminalization of Peasant Resistance in the Holy Roman Empire: Toward a History of the Emergence of High Treason in Germany, in: Journal of Modern History, supplement vol. 58 (Dec. 1986), pp. 88–97.
—, ed.: Deutsche ländliche Rechtsquellen: Positionen und Probleme der Weistumsforschung, Stuttgart 1997.
—: Economic, Social, and Political Background of the Twelve Articles of the Swabian Peasants of 1525, in: The German Peasant War of 1525, ed. Janos Bak, London 1976, pp. 63–75.
—, ed.: Gemeinde und Staat im Alten Europa, Historische Zeitschrift, supplement vol. 25, Munich 1998.
—: Grundherrschaft und Agrarverfassungsvertrag, in: Die Grundherrschaft im späten Mittelalter, vol. 1, ed. Hans Patze, Vorträge und Forschungen 27, Sigmaringen 1983, pp. 241–261.
—: Der Kommunalismus als Gestaltungsprinzip zwischen Mittelalter und Moderne, in: Studien zur geschichtlichen Bedeutung des deutschen Bauernstandes, Quellen und Forschungen zur Agrargeschichte 35, Stuttgart and New York 1989, pp. 69–82.
—: Kommunalismus: Begriffsbildung in heuristischer Absicht, in: Landgemeinde und Stadtgemeinde in Mitteleuropa: Ein struktureller Vergleich, ed. Peter Blickle, Historische Zeitschrift, supplement vol. 13, Munich 1991, pp. 5–38.
—: Kommunalismus, Parliamentarismus, Republikanismus, in: Studien zur geschichtlichen Bedeutung des deutschen Bauernstandes, Quellen und Forschungen zur Agrargeschichte 35, Stuttgart and New York 1989, pp. 191–211; translated as Communalism—Parliamentarianism—Republicanism, in: Parliaments, Estates and Representation 6 (1986), pp. 1–13.
—: Kommunalismus: Skizzen einer gesellschaftlichen Organisationsform, 2 vols., Munich 2000.
—: Landschaften im Alten Reich: Die staatliche Funktion des gemeinen Mannes in Oberdeutschland, Munich 1973.
—: Von der Leibeigenschaft zu den Menschenrechten: Eine Geschichte der Freiheit in Deutschland, Munich 2003.
—: Obedient Germans? A Rebuttal: A New View of German History, trans. Thomas A. Brady Jr., Studies in Early Modern German History, Charlottesville 1997; originally published as Deutsche Untertanen: Ein Widerspruch, Munich 1981.
—: Die politische Entmündigung des Bauern: Kritik und Revision einer These, in: Revolte und Revolution in Europa, ed. Peter Blickle, Historische Zeitschrift, supplement vol. 4, Memmingen 1975, pp. 298–312.
—, ed.: Politische Kultur in Oberschwaben, Tübingen 1993.
—, ed.: Resistance, Representation, and Community, Oxford and New York 1997.
—, ed.: Revolte und Revolution in Europa: Referate und Protokolle der Internationalen Symposiums zur Erinnerung an den Bauernkrieg 1525, Historische Zeitschrift, supplement vol. 4, Munich 1975.

—: Die Revolution von 1525, Munich 1975 [4th ed. 2004]; translated by T. A. Brady Jr. and H. C. Erik Midelfort as The Revolution of 1525: The German Peasants' War from a New Perspective, Baltimore 1981.

—: Studien zur geschichtlichen Bedeutung des deutschen Bauernstandes, Quellen und Forschungen zur Agrargeschichte 35, Stuttgart and New York 1989.

—: Unruhen in der ständischen Gesellschaft 1300–1800, Enzyklopädie deutscher Geschichte 1, Munich 1988.

BLICKLE, Peter and André HOLENSTEIN, eds.: Agrarverfassungsverträge: Eine Dokumentation zum Wandel in den Beziehungen zwischen Herrschaften und Bauern am Ende des Mittelalters, Quellen und Forschungen zur Agrargeschichte 42, Stuttgart 1996.

BLICKLE, Renate: Laufen gen Hof: Die Beschwerden der Untertanen und die Entstehung des Hofrats in Bayern. Ein Beitrag zu den Varianten rechtlicher Verfahren im späten Mittelalter in der frühen Neuzeit, in: Gemeinde und Staat im Alten Europa, ed. Peter Blickle, Munich 1998, pp. 241–266.

—: Supplikationen und Demonstrationen: Mittel und Wege der Partizipation im bayerischen Territorialstaat, in: Kommunikation in der ländlichen Gesellschaft vom Mittelalter bis zur Moderne, ed. Werner Rösener, Göttingen 2000, pp. 263–317.

BLICKLE-LITTWIN, Renate: Besitz und Amt: Bemerkungen zu einer Neuerscheinung über bäuerliche Führungsschichten, in: Zeitschrift für bayerische Landesgeschichte 40 (1977), pp. 277–290.

BLOCKMANS, Wim: Citizens and their Rulers, in: Empowering Interactions: Political Cultures and the Emergence of the State in Europe 1300–1900, ed. Wim Blockmans, André Holenstein, and Jon Mathieu, Farnham and Burlington 2009, pp. 281–291.

BLOCKMANS, Wim, André HOLENSTEIN, and Jon MATHIEU, eds.: Empowering Interactions: Political Cultures and the Emergence of the State in Europe 1300–1900, Farnham and Burlington 2009.

BLUM, Jerome: Internal Structure and Polity of the European Village Community from the Fifteenth to the Nineteenth Century, in: Journal of Modern History 43 (1971), pp. 541–576.

BÖHME, Ernst: Das Kollegium der Schwäbischen Reichsprälaten im 16. und 17. Jahrhundert, in: Rottenburger Jahrbuch für Kirchengeschichte 6 (1987), pp. 267–300.

BOUTON, Cynthia A.: The Flour War: Gender, Class, and Community in Late Ancien Régime French Society, University Park 1993.

BRADY, Thomas A. Jr.: German Burghers and Peasants in Reformation and Peasants' War: Partners or Competitors?, in: Between the Middle Ages and Modernity: Individual and Community in the Early Modern World, ed. Charles H. Parker and Jerry H. Bentley, London and New York 2002, pp. 33–51.

—: German Histories in the Age of Reformations, 1400–1650, Cambridge 2009.

—: Some Peculiarities of German Histories in the Early Modern Era, in: Germania Illustrata: Essays on Early Modern Germany Presented to Gerald Strauss, ed. Andrew Fix and Susan Karant-Nunn, Sixteenth Century Essays and Studies 18, Kirksville 1992, pp. 197–216.

—: Translator's Introduction: A New View of German History, in: Obedient Germans? A Rebuttal: A New View of German History, by Peter Blickle, Charlottesville 1997, pp. ix–xiv.

—: Turning Swiss: Cities and Empire, 1450–1550, Cambridge Studies in Early Modern History, Cambridge and New York 1985.

BRADY, Thomas A. Jr., Heiko A. OBERMAN, and James D. TRACY, eds.: Handbook of European History, 1400–1600, 2 vols., Leiden and New York 1994.

BRENNER, Robert: Agrarian Class Structure and Economic Development in Pre-Industrial Europe, in: Past and Present 70 (1976), pp. 30–75.

BRITTON, Edward: Community of the Vill: A Study in the History of Family and Village Life in Fourteenth-century England, Toronto 1977.

BRUN, Katherine: The Abbot and His Peasants: Building the Territorial State in Salem, 1473–1637, PhD diss., Berkeley 2008.

—: Ruling Class and Regime in an Ecclesiastical Territory: The Case of Salem, in: Politics and Reformations: Communities, Polities, Nations, and Empires. Essays in Honor of Thomas A. Brady Jr., ed. Christopher Ocker, Michael Printy, Peter Starenko, and Peter Wallace, Leiden and Boston 2007, pp. 359–380.

BRUNNER, Karl: Beiträge zur Geschichte des Klosterschulwesens in Baden, in: Mitteilungen der Gesellschaft für deutsche Erziehungs- und Schulgeschichte 14 (1904), pp. 1–6.

BRUNNER, Otto: Land and Lordship: Structures of Governance in Medieval Austria, trans. Howard Kaminsky and James Van Horn Melton, from the 4th rev. ed., Middle Ages Series, Philadelphia 1992.

BURMEISTER, Karl Heinz: Genossenschaftliche Rechtsfindung und herrschaftliche Rechtssetzung: Auf dem Weg zum Territorialstaat, in: Revolte und Revolution in Europa, ed. Peter Blickle, Historische Zeitschrift, supplement vol. 4, Munich 1975, pp. 171–185.

BUSZELLO, Horst: The Common Man's View of the State in the German Peasant War, in: The German Peasant War 1525: New Viewpoints, ed. Bob Scribner and Gerhard Benecke, London and Boston 1979, pp. 109–122.

BUSZELLO, Horst, Peter BLICKLE, and Rudolf ENDRES, eds.: Der deutsche Bauernkrieg, 3rd ed., Paderborn 1995.

BÜTTNER, Rudolf: Das Konstanzer Heilig-Geist-Spital und seine Besitzungen im Linzgau, PhD diss., Constance 1986.

CARL, Horst: Vom Appenzellerkrieg zum Schwäbischen Bund – Die Adelsgesellschaften mit St. Georgenschild im spätmittelalterlichen Oberschwaben, in: Appenzell – Oberschwaben: Begegnungen zweier Regionen in sieben Jahrhunderten, ed. Peter Blickle and Peter Witschi, Constance 1997, pp. 97–132.

—: Der Schwäbische Bund 1488–1534: Landfrieden und Genossenschaft im Übergang vom Spätmittelalter zur Reformation, Leinfelden 2000.

—: Der Schwäbische Bund und das Reich – Konkurrenz und Symbiose, in: Alternativen zur Reichsverfassung in der Frühen Neuzeit, ed. Volker Press, Schriften des Historischen Kollegs 23, Munich 1995, pp. 43–63.

CASTIGLIONE, Caroline: Patrons and Adversaries: Nobles and Villagers in Italian Politics, 1640–1760, New York 2005.

CATTANI, Heinz: Entwicklung des Talgerichts von Engelberg unter Klosterherrschaft, Stans 1935.

CHAYANOV, A. V.: The Theory of Peasant Economy, ed. Daniel Thorner, Basile Kerblay, and R. E. F. Smith, Madison 1986.

CHRIST, Günter: Selbstverständnis und Rolle der Domkapitel, in: Zeitschrift für Historische Forschung 16 (1989), pp. 257–328.

CLARK, Elaine: Debt Litigation in a Late Medieval English Vill, in: Pathways to Medieval Peasants, ed. J. A. Raftis, Toronto 1981, pp. 247–279.

DAHM, Georg: On the Reception of Roman and Italian Law in Germany, in: Pre-Reformation Germany, ed. Gerald Strauss, Stratum Series, New York 1972, pp. 282–315.

DAVIS, Natalie Zemon: Fiction in the Archives: Pardon Tales and Their Tellers in Sixteenth-Century France, Harry Camp Lectures, Stanford 1987.

DEES, Robert: Economics and Politics of Peasant Production in South Germany, PhD diss., Los Angeles 2007.

DEISSLER, Vikar: Die Geschichte von Bermatingen, Überlingen 1911.

de MOOR, Martina, Leigh SHAW-TAYLOR, and Paul WARDE, eds.: The Management of Common Land in North West Europe, c. 1500–1800, CORN publication series 8, Turnhout 2002.

de VRIES, Jan: Between Purchasing Power and the World of Goods: Understanding the Household Economy in Early Modern Europe, in: Consumption and the World of Goods, ed. John Brewer and Roy Porter, London and New York 1993, pp. 85–132.

—: The Economy of Europe in an Age of Crisis, 1600–1750, Cambridge and New York 1976.

—: The Industrial Revolution or the Industrious Revolution?, in: Journal of Economic History 54 (1994), pp. 249–270.

—: The Industrious Revolution: Consumer Behavior and the Household Economy, 1650 to the Present, New York 2008.

DEWALD, Jonathan: Pont-St-Pierre, 1398–1789: Lordship, Community, and Capitalism in Early Modern France, Studies on the History of Society and Culture, Berkeley 1987.

DIESTELKAMP, Bernhard: Verwissenschaftlichung, Bürokratisierung, Professionalisierung und Verfahrensintensivierung als Merkmale frühneuzeitlicher Rechtssprechung, in: Recht und Gericht im Heiligen Römischen Reich, ed. Bernhard Diestelkamp, Ius Commune, special issue 122, Frankfurt am Main 1999, pp. 263–275.

DINGES, Martin: Frühneuzeitliche Armenfürsorge als Sozialdisziplinierung? Probleme mit einem Konzept, in: Geschichte und Gesellschaft 17 (1991), pp. 92–101.

DILLMANN, Erika, ed.: 1200 Jahre Bermatingen, 779–1979, Bermatingen 1979.

DUGGAN, Lawrence G.: Bishop and Chapter: The Governance of the Bishopric of Speyer to 1552, Studies Presented to the International Commission for the History of Representative and Parliamentary Institutions 62, New Brunswick 1978.

EDER, Irmtraut: Weistümer als Dokumente der Territorialpolitik, in: Deutsche ländliche Rechtsquellen: Probleme und Wege der Weistumsforschung, ed. Peter Blickle, Stuttgart 1977, pp. 142–196.

EITEL, Peter: Handel und Verkehr im Bodenseeraum während der frühen Neuzeit, in: Schriften des Vereins für Geschichte des Bodensees und seiner Umgebung 91 (1973), pp. 67–89.

—: Die Rolle der Reichsstadt Überlingen in der Wirtschaftsgeschichte des Bodenseeraumes, in: Schriften des Vereins für Geschichte des Bodensees und seiner Umgebung 89 (1971), pp. 9–22.

EITEL, Peter and Elmar L. KUHN, eds.: Oberschwaben: Beiträge zu Geschichte und Kultur, Constance 1995.

ENGELS, Friedrich: The Peasant War in Germany, trans. Moissaye J. Olgin, New York 1926.

FORSTER, Marc: Catholic Revival in the Age of the Baroque: Religious Identity in Southwest Germany, 1550–1750, New Studies in European History, Cambridge and New York 2001.

—: Kirchenreform, katholische Konfessionalisierung und dörfliche Religion um Kloster Salem 1650–1750, in: Rottenburger Jahrbuch für Kirchengeschichte 16 (1997), pp. 93–110.

FRANZ, Günther: Der deutsche Bauernkrieg, 1st ed. Munich 1933; 9th ed. Darmstadt 1972.

—: Geschichte des deutschen Bauernstandes, vom frühen Mittelalter bis zum 19. Jahrhundert, Deutsche Agrargeschichte 4, Stuttgart 1970.

FRIED, Pankraz: Zur Ausbildung der reichsunmittelbaren Klosterstaatlichkeit in Ostschwaben, in: Zeitschrift für Württembergische Landesgeschichte 40 (1981), pp. 418–435.

FRIEDEBURG, Robert von: "Kommunalismus" und "Republikanismus" in der Frühen Neuzeit?, in: Zeitschrift für Historische Forschung 21 (1994), pp. 65–91.

—: Village Strife and the Rhetoric of Communalism: Peasants and Parsons, Lords and Jews in Hesse, Central Germany, 1646–1672, in: Literature and Theology 7 (1992), pp. 201–226.

FUHRMANN, Rosi: Dorfgemeinde und Pfründstiftung vor der Reformation: Kommunale Selbstbestimmungschancen zwischen Religion und Recht, in: Kommunalisierung und Christianisierung: Voraussetzungen und Folgen der Reformation, 1400–1600, ed. Peter Blickle and Johannes Kunisch, Zeitschrift für Historische Forschung, supplement vol. 9, Berlin 1989, pp. 77–112.

—: Die Kirche im Dorf: Kommunale Initiativen zur Organisation von Seelsorge vor der Reformation, in: Zugänge zur bäuerlichen Reformation, ed. Peter Blickle, Bauer und Reformation 1, Zurich 1987, pp. 147–186.

—: Kirche und Dorf: Religiöse Bedürfnisse und kirchliche Stiftung auf dem Lande vor der Reformation, Quellen und Forschungen zur Agrargeschichte 40, Stuttgart and New York 1995.

FUHRMANN, Rosi, Beat KÜMIN, and Andreas WÜRGLER: Supplizierende Gemeinden: Aspekte einer vergleichenden Quellenbetrachtung, in: Gemeinde und Staat im Alten Europa, ed. Peter Blickle, Munich 1998, pp. 267–323.

FUTTERER, Adolf: Die Geschichte des Dorfes und des Kirchspiels Billafingen im Linzgau, Singen/Hohentwiel 1970.

GEMEINDE OWINGEN, ed.: 1000 Jahre Owingen, 983–1983 [Festschrift], Owingen 1983.

GENICOT, Léopold: Crisis: From the Middle Ages to Modern Times, in: The Cambridge Economic History of Europe, vol. 1, ed. M. M. Postan, 2nd ed., Cambridge 1966.

GIERKE, Otto Friedrich von: Das deutsche Genossenschaftsrecht, 4 vols., Berlin 1868–1881.

GINTER, Hermann: Kloster Salem, Karlsruhe 1937.

GLEIXNER, Ulrike: Rechtsfindung zwischen Machtbeziehungen, Konfliktregelung und Friedenssicherung: Historische Kriminalitätsforschung und Agrargeschichte in der frühen Neuzeit, in: Agrargeschichte: Positionen und Perspektiven, ed. Werner Troßbach and Clemens Zimmermann, Quellen und Forschungen zur Agrargeschichte 44, Stuttgart 1998, pp. 57–71.

GOETZ, Georg: Niedere Gerichtsherrschaft und Grafengewalt im badischen Linzgau während des ausgehenden Mittelalters, Untersuchungen zur deutschen Staats- und Rechtsgeschichte 121, Breslau 1913.

GÖNNER, Eberhard and Max MILLER: Die Landvogtei Schwaben, in: Vorderösterreich: Eine geschichtliche Landeskunde, 2nd ed., ed. Friedrich Metz, Freiburg im Breisgau 1967, pp. 683–704.

GOODY, Jack, Joan THIRSK, and E. P. THOMPSON, eds.: Family and Inheritance: Rural Society in Western Europe, 1200–1800, Past and Present Publications, Cambridge and New York 1976.

GÖTTMANN, Frank: Die Bünde und ihre Räume, in: Recht und Reich im Zeitalter der Reformation: Festschrift für Horst Rabe, ed. Christine Roll, Frankfurt and New York 1996, pp. 441–469.

HEAD, Randolph C.: Early Modern Democracy in the Grisons: Social Order and Political Language in a Swiss Mountain Canton, 1470–1620, Cambridge Studies in Early Modern History, Cambridge 1995.

HERSCHE, Peter: Intendierte Ruckständigkeit: Zur Charakteristik des geistlichen Staates im Alten Reich, in: Stände und Gesellschaft im Alten Reich, ed. Georg Schmidt, pp. 133–149, Veröffentlichungen des Instituts für Europäische Geschichte Mainz, supplement vol. 29, Stuttgart 1989, pp. 133–149.

HILDBRAND, Thomas: Aktualisierung von Recht im Spannungsfeld von Eid und Schriftbeweis: Überlegungen zum rechtspraktischen Handeln im 15. Jahrhundert, in: Eid und Wahrheitssuche: Studien zu rechtlichen Befragungspraktiken in Mittelalter und früher Neuzeit, ed. Stefan Esders and Thomas Scharff, Frankfurt am Main 1999, pp. 163–190.

—: Herrschaft, Schrift und Gedächtnis: Das Kloster Allerheiligen und sein Umgang mit Wissen in Wirtschaft, Recht und Archiv (11.–16. Jahrhundert), Zurich 1996.

HINDLE, Steve: The State and Social Change in Early Modern England, ca. 1550–1640, New York 2000.

HOFACKER, Hans-Georg: Die Landvogtei Schwaben, in: Vorderösterreich in der frühen Neuzeit, ed. Hans Maier and Volker Press, Sigmaringen 1989, pp. 57–74.

HOLENSTEIN, André: Äbte und Bauern: Vom Regiment der Klöster im Spätmittelalter, in: Politische Kultur in Oberschwaben, ed. Peter Blickle, Tübingen 1993, pp. 237–262.

—: Bauern zwischen Bauernkrieg und dreissigjährigem Krieg, Enzyklopädie Deutscher Geschichte 38, Munich 1996.

—: "Gute Policey" und lokale Gesellschaft im Staat des Ancien Régime: Das Fallbeispiel der Markgrafschaft Baden(-Durlach), 2 vols., Frühneuzeit-Forschungen 9, Epfendorf 2003.

—: Die Huldigung der Untertanen: Rechtskultur und Herrschaftsordnung (800–1800), Quellen und Forschungen zur Agrargeschichte 36, Stuttgart and New York 1991.

—: Seelenheil und Untertanenpflicht: Zur gesellschaftlichen Funktion und theoretischen Begründung des Eides in der ständischen Gesellschaft, in: Der Fluch und der Eid: Die metaphysische Begründung gesellschaftlichen Zusammenlebens und politischer Ordnung in der ständischen Gesellschaft, ed. Peter Blickle, Zeitschrift für Historische Forschung, supplement vol. 15, Berlin 1993, pp. 11–63.

—: Die Umstände der Normen – die Normen der Umstände: Policeyordnungen im kommunikativen Handeln von Verwaltung und lokaler Gesellschaft im Ancien Régime, in: Policey und frühneuzeitliche Gesellschaft, ed. Karl Härter, Frankfurt am Main 2000, pp. 1–46.

HÖLZ, Thomas: Krummstab und Schwert: Die Liga und die geistlichen Reichsstände Schwabens, 1609–1635, Schriften zur südwestdeutschen Landeskunde 31, Leinfelden-Echterdingen 2001.

HÜRLIMANN, Katja: Soziale Beziehungen im Dorf: Aspekte dörflicher Soziabilität in den Landvogteien Greifensee und Kyburg um 1500, Zurich 2000.

IRSIGLER, Franz: Zu den wirtschaftlichen Ursachen des Bauernkriegs von 1525/26, in: Martin Luther und die Reformation in Deutschland: Vorträge zur Ausstellung im Germanischen Nationalmuseum Nürnberg 1983, ed. Kurt Löcher, Schriften des Vereins für Reformationsgeschichte 194, Nuremberg 1988, pp. 51–60.

ISELI, Andrea: Gute Policey: Öffentliche Ordnung in der Frühen Neuzeit, Stuttgart 2009.

JÄNICHEN, Hans: Der Rechtszug im Spätmittelalter am Oberen Neckar und im pfalzgräflich-tübingischen Bereich, in: Zeitschrift für Württembergische Landesgeschichte 15 (1956), pp. 214–241.

JUSTICE, Steven: Writing and Rebellion: England in 1381, The New Historicism 27, Berkeley 1994.

JÜTTE, Robert: Poverty and Poor Relief, in: Germany: A New Social and Economic History, vol. 2, 1630–1800, ed. Sheilagh Ogilvie, London and New York 1996, pp. 377–404.

KALLER, Gerhard: Zisterzienserkloster Salem, in: Helvetia Sacra, ed. Cécile Sommer-Ramer and Patrick Braun, vol. 3/1, Bern 1982, pp. 341–375.

KASCHUBA, Wolfgang: Kommunalismus als sozialer "Common Sense." Zur Konzeption von Lebenswelt und Alltagskultur im neuzeitlicher Gemeindegedanken, in: Landgemeinde und Stadtgemeinde, ed. Peter Blickle, Historische Zeitschrift, supplement vol. 13, Munich 1991, pp. 65–91.

KERN, Fritz: Kingship and the Law in the Middle Ages, trans. S. B. Chrimes, Studies in Mediaeval History 4, Oxford 1939.

KLIPPEL, Diethelm: Zur Geschichte der Gesetzgebung in der frühen Neuzeit: Eine Einführung, in: Gesetz und Gesetzgebung im Europa der frühen Neuzeit, ed. Barbara Dölemeyer und Diethelm Klippel, Zeitschrift für Historische Forschung, supplement vol. 22, Berlin 1998, pp. 7–13.

KOTTMANN, Anton and Markus HÄMMERLE: Die Zisterzienserabtei Wettingen: Geschichte des Klosters Wettingen und der Abtei Wettingen-Mehrerau, Wettingen 1996.

KUHN, Elmar L.: Der Bauernkrieg am See, in: Seegrunde: Beiträge zur Geschichte des Bodenseeraumes, ed. Dieter Schott and Werner Trapp, Weingarten 1984, pp. 19–52.
—, ed.: Der Bauernkrieg in Oberschwaben, Tübingen 2000.
—: Der Bermatinger Haufen, in: 1200 Jahre Bermatingen, 779–1979, ed. Erika Dillmann, Bermatingen 1979, pp. 81–103.
—: Mönche und Bauern: Herrschaften und Untertanen im Mittelalter, in: 1000 Jahre Owingen, 983–1983 [Festschrift], ed. Gemeinde Owingen, Owingen 1983, pp. 17–60.
—: Der Seehaufen, in: Der Bauernkrieg in Oberschwaben, ed. Elmar L. Kuhn, Tübingen 2000, pp. 97–139.
KUHN-REHFUS, Maren: Konversen und Pfründner in südwestdeutschen Zisterzienserklöstern, in: Das Zisterzienserkloster Bebenhausen: Beiträge zur Archäologie, Geschichte und Architektur, ed. Wilfried Setzler and Franz Quarthal, Stuttgart 1995, pp. 105–130.
—: Die soziale Zusammensetzung der Konvente in den oberschwäbischen Frauenzisterzen, in: Zeitschrift für Württembergische Landesgeschichte 41 (1982), pp. 7–31.
KUNKEL, Wolfgang: The Reception of Roman Law in Germany: An Interpretation, in: Pre-Reformation Germany, ed. Gerald Strauss, Stratum Series, New York 1972, pp. 263–281.
LANDWEHR, Achim: Policey vor Ort: Die Implementation von Policeyordnungen in der ländlichen Gesellschaft der Frühen Neuzeit, in: Policey und frühneuzeitliche Gesellschaft, ed. Karl Härter, Frankfurt am Main 2000, pp. 47–70.
—: Zwischen allen Stühlen: Lokale Amtsträger im frühneuzeitlichen Leonberg, in: Policey in lokalen Räumen: Ordnungskräfte und Sicherheitspersonal in Gemeinden und Territorien vom Spätmittelalter bis zum frühen 19. Jahrhundert, ed. André Holenstein, Frank Konersmann, Josef Pauser, and Gerhard Sälter, Frankfurt am Main 2002, pp. 95–109.
LAUFS, Adolf: Gerichtsbarkeiten und Rechtspflege im deutschen Südwesten zur Zeit des Alten Reiches, in: Bausteine zur geschichtlichen Landeskunde von Baden-Württemberg, ed. Günther Haselier, Eberhard Gönner, and Meinrad Schaab, Stuttgart 1979, pp. 157–174.
LEKAI, Louis J.: The Cistercians: Ideals and Reality, Kent 1977.
LEKAI, Louis J.: Studien, Studiensystem und Lehrtätigkeit der Zisterzienser, in: Die Zisterzienser: Ordensleben zwischen Ideal und Wirklichkeit, vol. 1, ed. Kaspar Elm, Peter Joerissen, and H. J. Roth, Cologne 1980, pp. 165–170.
LEODEGAR, Walter: Abtwahlen in Salem im 16. Jahrundert, in: Cistercienser Chronik 48 (1936), pp. 98–106.
—: Abtwahlen in Salem im 17. Jahrhundert, in: Cistercienser Chronik 48 (1936), pp. 321–338.
LIEBHART, Wilhelm: Die Reichsabtei Irsee im Kampf um die volle Landeshoheit 1551–1692, in: Das Reichsstift Irsee: Vom Benediktinerkloster zum Bildungszentrum. Beiträge zu Geschichte, Kunst und Kultur, ed. Hans Frei, Weißenhorn 1981, pp. 152–167.
LUEBKE, David Martin: His Majesty's Rebels: Communities, Factions, and Rural Revolt in the Black Forest, 1725–1745, Ithaca 1997.
LURIA, Keith: Territories of Grace: Cultural Change in the Seventeenth-Century Diocese of Grenoble, Berkeley 1991.
MAIER, Kurt-Erich: Geschichte des Linzgaudorfes Owingen: Eine Heimatgeschichte mit besonderer Berücksichtigung der Sozial- und Wirtschaftsgeschichte, Owingen 1964.
MARKGRÄFLICHE BADISCHE MUSEEN, ed.: Kloster und Staat: Besitz und Einfluss der Reichsabtei Salem, Tettnang 1984.
MAURER, Hans-Martin: Die Ausbildung der Territorialgewalt oberschwäbischer Klöster vom 14. bis zum 17. Jahrhundert, in: Blätter für deutsche Landesgeschichte 109 (1973), pp. 151–195.

—: Der Bauernkrieg als Massenerhebung: Dynamik einer revolutionären Bewegung, in: Bausteine zur geschichtlichen Landeskunde von Baden-Württemberg, ed. Kommission für geschichtliche Landeskunde in Baden-Württemberg, Stuttgart 1979, pp. 255–295.

MAURER, Helmut: Bäuerliches Gedächtnis und Landesherrschaft im 15. Jahrhundert: Zu einer oberschwäbischen "Kundschaft" von 1484, in: Recht und Reich im Zeitalter der Reformation: Festschrift für Horst Rabe, ed. Christine Roll, Frankfurt 1996, pp. 179–198.

MCINTOSH, Marjorie: Autonomy and Community: The Royal Manor of Havering, 1200–1500, Cambridge Studies in Medieval Life and Thought, 4th series, vol. 5, New York 1986.

MEDICK, Hans: The Proto-industrial Family Economy: The Structural Function of Household and Family during the Transition from Peasant Society to Industrial Capitalism, in: Social History 3 (1976), pp. 291–315.

MEDICK, Hans and David Warren SABEAN, eds.: Interest and Emotion: Essays on the Study of Family and Kinship, Cambridge and New York 1984.

METZ, Friedrich, ed.: Vorderösterreich: Eine geschichtliche Landeskunde, 4th ed., Freiburg im Breisgau 2000.

MIDELFORT, H. C. Erik: The Revolution of 1525? Recent Studies of the Peasants' War, in: Central European History 11 (1978), pp. 189–206.

MINK, Karl Heinz: Die St-Georgs-Pfarrei, in: 1200 Jahre Bermatingen, 779–1979, ed. Erika Dillmann, Bermatingen 1979, pp. 42–51.

MÜLLER, Walter: Freie Gotteshausleute: Zur Problematik ständischer Benennungen in Quellen des 14. bis 17. Jahrhunderts, in: Zeitschrift der Savigny-Stiftung, Germanistische Abteilung 92 (1975), pp. 89–104.

NAGEL, Adalbert: Die Bettelfuhr in Oberschwaben, in: Schriften des Vereins für Geschichte des Bodensees und seiner Umgebung 87 (1969), pp. 29–35.

NUBOLA, Cecilia and Andreas WÜRGLER, eds.: Bittschriften und Gravamina: Politik, Verwaltung und Justiz in Europa (14.–18. Jahrhundert), Berlin 2005.

OBSER, Karl: Zur Geschichte des Klosters Salem im 17. Jahrhundert, in: Zeitschrift für die Geschichte des Oberrheins 31 (1916), pp. 65–85.

OGILVIE, Sheilagh: Germany and the Seventeenth-Century Crisis, in: History Journal 35 (1992), pp. 417–441.

—: The State in Germany: A Non-Prussian View, in: Rethinking Leviathan: The Eighteenth-Century State in Britain and Germany, ed. John Brewer and Eckhart Hellmuth, Studies of the German Historical Institute London, Oxford 1999, pp. 167–202.

PARKER, Geoffrey and Lesley M. SMITH, eds.: The General Crisis of the Seventeenth Century, London and Boston 1978.

PFISTER, Christian: The Population of Late Medieval and Early Modern Germany, in: Germany: A New Social and Economic History, vol. 1, ed. Bob Scribner, London 1996, pp. 33–62.

PRESS, Volker: Kommunalismus oder Territorialismus? Bemerkungen zur Ausbildung des Frühmodernen Staates in Mitteleuropa, in: Die Bildung des frühmodernen Staates – Stände und Konfessionen, ed. Heiner Timmermann, Forum Politik 6, Saarbrücken-Scheidt 1989, pp. 109–135.

—: Oberschwaben in der frühen Neuzeit, in: Oberschwaben: Beiträge zu Geschichte und Kultur, ed. Peter Eitel and Elmar L. Kuhn, Constance 1995, pp. 101–125.

PRETSCH, Hermann Joseph: Klösterliche Dorfschulen – Kirche und Gesellschaft: Das Beispiel des Reichsstifts Zwiefalten, in: Alte Klöster – Neue Herren: Die Säkularisation im deutschen Südwesten 1803, vol. 2, ed. Volker Himmelein and Hans Ulrich Rudolf, Ostfildern 2003, pp. 317–324.

PROSSER, Michael: Spätmittelalterliche ländliche Rechtsaufzeichnungen am Oberrhein zwischen Gedächtniskultur und Schriftlichkeit: Untersuchungen am Übergang von analphabetischen zu skriptualen Überlieferungsformen im Blickfeld rechtlicher Volkskunde, Veröffentlichungen zur Volkskunde und Kulturgeschichte 47, Würzburg 1991.

QUARTHAL, Franz: Unterm Krummstab ist's gut leben. Prälaten, Mönche und Bauern im Zeitalter des Barock, in: Politische Kultur in Oberschwaben, ed. Peter Blickle, Tübingen 1993, pp. 269–286.

RABE, Hannah: Das Problem Leibeigenschaft: Eine Untersuchung über die Anfänge einer Ideologisierung und des verfassungsrechtlichen Wandels von Freiheit und Eigentum im deutschen Bauernkrieg, Wiesbaden 1977.

RAEFF, Marc: The Well-Ordered Police State: Social and Institutional Change through Law in the Germanies and Russia, 1600–1800, New Haven 1983.

RAUSCHERT, Jeanette: Gelöchert und befleckt: Inszenierung und Gebrauch städtischer Rextstexte und spätmittelalterlicher Öffentlichkeit, in: Text als Realie: Internationaler Kongress Krems an der Donau, ed. Karl Brunner and Gerhard Jaritz, Vienna 2003, pp. 163–181.

RAZI, Zvi: Family, Land and the Village Community in Later Medieval England, in: Past and Present 92 (1981), pp. 3–36.

—: The Toronto School's Reconstitution of Medieval Peasant Society: A Critical View, in: Past and Present 85 (1979), pp. 114–157.

REBEL, Hermann: Peasant Classes: The Bureaucratization of Property and Family Relations under Early Habsburg Absolutism, 1511–1636, Princeton 1983.

—: Peasant Stem Families in Early Modern Austria: Life Plans, Status Tactics, and the Grid of Inheritance, in: Social Science History 2 (1978), pp. 255–291.

REDEN-DOHNA, Armgard von: Problems of Small Estates of the Empire: The Example of the Swabian Imperial Prelates, in: Journal of Modern History, supplement vol. 58 (Dec. 1986), pp. 76–87.

—: Reichsklöster in Ostschwaben: Stand, Probleme und Aufgaben der Forschung, in: Suevia Sacra: Zur Geschichte der ostschwäbischen Reichsstifte im Spätmittelalter und in der frühen Neuzeit. Pankraz Fried zum 70. Geburtstag, ed. Wilhelm Liebhart and Ulrich Faust, Augsburger Beiträge zur Landesgeschichte Bayerisch-Schwabens 8, Stuttgart 2001, pp. 15–32.

—: Reichsstandschaft und Klosterherrschaft: Die schwäbischen Reichsprälaten im Zeitalter des Barock, Institut für Europäische Geschichte Mainz 78, Wiesbaden 1982.

—: Weingarten und die schwäbischen Reichsklöster, in: Die Territorien des Reichs im Zeitalter der Reformation und Konfessionalisierung, vol. 5, ed. Anton Schindling and Walter Ziegler, Katholisches Leben und Kirchenreform im Zeitalter der Glaubensspaltung, Münster 1993, pp. 232–254.

—: Die Zisterzienser im Schwäbischen Reichsprälaten-Kollegium, in: Rottenburger Jahrbuch für Kirchengeschichte 4 (1985), pp. 51–58.

—: Zwischen Österreichischen Vorlanden und Reich: Die schwäbischen Reichsprälaten, in: Vorderösterreich in der frühen Neuzeit, ed. Hans Maier and Volker Press, Sigmaringen 1989, pp. 75–91.

REDFIELD, Robert: Peasant Society and Culture: An Anthropological Approach to Civilization, The William J. Cooper Foundation Lectures at Swarthmore College, Chicago 1956.

REINHARD, Wolfgang: No Statebuilding from Below! A Critical Commentary, in: Empowering Interactions: Political Cultures and the Emergence of the State in Europe 1300–1900, ed. Wim Blockmans, André Holenstein, and Jon Mathieu, Farnham and Burlington 2009, pp. 299–304.

REYNOLDS, Susan: Kingdoms and Communities in Western Europe, 900–1300, 2nd ed., Oxford and New York 1997.
ROBERTS, Simon: The Study of Dispute: Anthropological Perspectives, in: Disputes and Settlements: Law and Human Relations in the West, ed. John Bossy, Past and Present Publications, Cambridge and New York 1983, pp. 1–24.
ROBINSON, Philip: Die Fürstabtei St. Gallen und ihr Territorium, 1463–1529: Eine Studie zur Entwicklung territorialer Staatlichkeit, St. Galler Kultur und Geschichte 24, St. Gallen 1995.
ROBISHEAUX, Thomas: Peasant Unrest and the Moral Economy in the German Southwest, in: Archive for Reformation History 78 (1987), pp. 174–186.
—: Rural Society and the Search for Order in Early Modern Germany, Cambridge and New York 1989.
RÖSENER, Werner: Agrarwirtschaft, Agrarverfassung und ländliche Gesellschaft im Mittelalter, Enzyklopädie Deutscher Geschichte 13, Munich 1992.
—: Bauernlegen durch klösterliche Grundherren im Hochmittelalter, in: Zeitschrift für Agrargeschichte und Agrarsoziologie 27 (1979), pp. 60–93.
—: Entwicklung des Zisterzienserklosters Salem im Spannungsfeld um normativer Zielsetzung und gesellschaftlicher Anpassung während des 12. bis 14. Jahrhunderts, in: Zeitschrift für die Geschichte des Oberrheins 133 (1985), pp. 43–65.
—: Peasants in the Middle Ages, trans. Alexander Stutzer, Urbana 1992.
—: Reichsabtei Salem: Verfassungs- und Wirtschaftsgeschichte des Zisterzienserklosters von der Gründung bis zur Mitte des 14. Jahrhunderts, Vorträge und Forschungen, Konstanzer Arbeitskreis für Mittelalterliche Geschichte, special issue no. 13, Sigmaringen 1974.
—: Südwestdeutsche Zisterzienserklöster unter kaiserlicher Schirmherrschaft, in: Zeitschrift für Württembergische Landesgeschichte 33 (1974), pp. 24–52.
RUDOLF, Hans Ulrich: Ende und Ausgang – Der Weingartener Vertrag und die Folgen, in: Der Bauernkrieg in Oberschwaben, ed. Elmar L. Kuhn, Tübingen 2000, pp. 199–232.
SAARBRÜCKER ARBEITSGRUPPE: Probleme der spätmittelalterlichen Leibeigenschaft in Oberschwaben, in: Zeitschrift für Agrargeschichte und Agrarsoziologie 22 (1974), pp. 9–33.
SABEAN, David Warren: Aspects of Kinship Behavior and Property in Rural Western Europe before 1800, in: Family and Inheritance: Rural Society in Western Europe, 1200–1800, ed. Jack Goody, Joan Thirsk, and E. P. Thompson, Past and Present Publications, Cambridge and New York 1976, pp. 96–111.
—: The Communal Basis of Pre-1800 Peasant Uprisings in Western Europe, in: Comparative Politics 9 (1976), pp. 355–364.
—: Family and Land Tenure: A Case Study of Conflict in the German Peasants' War (1525), in: The German Peasant War 1525: New Viewpoints, ed. Bob Scribner and Gerhard Benecke, London 1979, pp. 174–199.
—: German Agrarian Institutions at the Beginning of the Sixteenth Century: Upper Swabia as an Example, in: The German Peasant War of 1525, ed. Janos Bak, London 1976, pp. 76–88.
—: Kinship in Neckarhausen, 1700–1870, Cambridge Studies in Social and Cultural Anthropology, Cambridge and New York 1998.
—: Landbesitz und Gesellschaft am Vorabend des Bauernkrieges: Eine Studie der sozialen Verhältnisse im südlichen Oberschwaben in den Jahren vor 1525, Quellen und Forschungen zur Agrargeschichte 26, Stuttgart 1972.
—: Power in the Blood: Popular Culture and Village Discourse in Early Modern Germany, Cambridge and New York 1984.

—: Property, Production, and Family in Neckarhausen, 1700–1870, Cambridge Studies in Social and Cultural Anthropology 73, Cambridge and New York 1990.
—: Young Bees in an Empty Hive: Relations between Brothers-in-law in a South German Village around 1800, in: Interest and Emotion: Essays on the Study of Family and Kinship, ed. Hans Medick and David Warren Sabean, Cambridge and New York 1984, pp. 171–186.
SABEAN, David Warren, Simon TEUSCHER, and Jon MATHIEU, eds.: Kinship in Europe: Approaches to Long-Term Development (1300–1900), New York and Oxford 2007.
SABLONIER, Roger: Dorf im Übergang vom Hoch- zum Spätmittelalter: Untersuchungen zum Wandel ländlicher Gemeinschaftsformen im ostschweizerischen Raum, in: Institutionen, Kultur und Gesellschaft im Mittelalter. Festschrift für Josef Fleckenstein zu seinem 65. Geburtstag, ed. Lutz Fenske, Werner Rösener, and Thomas Zotz, Sigmaringen 1984, pp. 727–745.
SACHS, Petra: Leben und Wohnen in Owingen, in: 1000 Jahre Owingen, 983–1983 [Festschrift], ed. Gemeinde Owingen, Owingen 1983, pp. 62–101.
SCHECK, Manfred: Von Schützen und Spießern. Das wehrhafte Vaihingen im Spiegel der Musterungslisten, 1521–1633, in: Zeitschrift für Württembergische Landesgeschichte 52 (1993), pp. 137–153.
SCHINDLING, Anton and Walter ZIEGLER, eds.: Die Territorien des Reichs im Zeitalter der Reformation und Konfessionalisierung, vol. 5, Katholisches Leben und Kirchenreform im Zeitalter der Glaubensspaltung, Münster 1993.
SCHLECHTER, Armin, ed.: Vom Bodensee an den Neckar: Bücherschätze aus der Bibliothek des Zisterzienserklosters Salem in der Universitätsbibliothek Heidelberg, Heidelberg 2003.
SCHLUMBOHM, Jürgen: Gesetze, die nicht durchgesetzt werden – ein Strukturmerkmal des frühneuzeitlichen Staates?, in: Geschichte und Gesellschaft 23 (1997), pp. 647–663.
SCHNEIDER, Reinhard: Geschichte Salems, in: Salem: 850 Jahre Reichsabtei und Schloss, ed. Reinhard Schneider, Constance 1984, pp. 11–153.
—: Vom Klosterhaushalt zum Stadt- und Staatshaushalt: Der Zisterziensische Beitrag, Monographien zur Geschichte des Mittelalters 38, Stuttgart 1994.
—, ed.: Salem: 850 Jahre Reichsabtei und Schloss, Constance 1984.
—: Studium und Zisterzienser mit besonderer Berücksichtigung des südwestdeutschen Raumes, in: Rottenburger Jahrbuch für Kirchengeschichte 4 (1985), pp. 103–118.
SCHOBER, Willi: Die Strafgerichtsbarkeit des Klosters Salem, JD diss., Freiburg im Breisgau, 1926.
SCHREINER, Klaus: Laienbildung als Herausforderung für Kirche und Gesellschaft: Religiöse Vorbehalte und soziale Widerstände gegen die Verbreitung von Wissen im späten Mittelalter und in der Reformation, in: Zeitschrift für Historische Forschung 11 (1984), pp. 257–354.
SCHOTT, Claudia: Armenfürsorge, Bettelwesen und Vagantenbekämpfung in der Reichsabtei Salem, Bühl 1978.
SCHUBERT, Ernst: Fürstliche Herrschaft und Territorium im späten Mittelalter, Enzyklopädie deutscher Geschichte 35, Munich 1996.
—: Vom Gebot zur Landesordnung: Der Wandel fürstlicher Herrschaft vom 15. zum 16. Jahrhundert, in: Die deutsche Reformation zwischen Spätmittelalter und frühen Neuzeit, ed. Thomas A. Brady Jr., Schriften des Historischen Kollegs 50, Munich 2001, pp. 19–61.
SCHULZE, Winfried: Bäuerlicher Widerstand und feudale Herrschaft in der frühen Neuzeit, Neuzeit im Aufbau 6, Stuttgart-Bad Canstatt 1980.
—: Oberdeutsche Untertanenrevolten zwischen 1580 und 1620: Reichssteuern und bäuerlicher Widerstand, in: Bauer Reich und Reformation: Festschrift für Günther Franz zum 80. Geburtstag, ed. Peter Blickle, Stuttgart 1982, pp. 120–147.

—: Reich und Türkengefahr im späten 16. Jahrhundert: Studien zu den politischen und gesellschaftlichen Auswirkungen einer äusseren Bedrohung, Munich 1978.

—: Reichstage und Reichssteuern im späten 16. Jahrhundert, in: Zeitschrift für Historische Forschung 2 (1975), pp. 43–58.

—: Die veränderte Bedeutung sozialer Konflikte im 16. und 17. Jahrhundert, in: Der deutsche Bauernkrieg, 1524–1526, ed. Hans-Ulrich Wehler, Göttingen 1975, pp. 277–302.

SCHWARZMAIER, Hansmartin: Reichsprälatenklöster, in: Die Territorien im Alten Reich, vol. 2 of Handbuch der baden-württembergischen Geschichte, ed. Meinrad Schaab and Hansmartin Schwarzmaier, Veröffentlichung der Kommission für Geschichtliche Landeskunde in Baden-Württemberg, Stuttgart 1995, pp. 546–609.

SCOTT, Tom: Economic Landscapes, in: Germany: A New Social and Economic History, vol. 1, ed. Bob Scribner, London 1996, pp. 1–31.

—: Freiburg and the Breisgau: Town-Country Relations in the Age of the Reformation and Peasants' War, Oxford and New York 1986.

—: The German Peasants' War and the 'Crisis of Feudalism.' Reflections on a Neglected Theme, in: Journal of Early Modern History 6 (2002), pp. 265–295.

—: Medieval Viticulture in the German-speaking Lands, in: German History 20 (2002), pp. 95–115.

—: Society and Economy in Germany, 1300–1600, European Studies Series, Houndmills and New York 2002.

—: South-West German Serfdom Reconsidered, in: Forms of Servitude in Northern and Central Europe: Decline, Resistance, and Expansion, ed. Paul Freedman and Monique Bourin, Turnhout 2005, pp. 115–128.

SCOTT, Tom and Bob SCRIBNER, eds. and trans.: The German Peasants' War: A History in Documents, Atlantic Highlands 1991.

SCRIBNER, Bob: Communalism: Universal Category or Ideological Construct? A Debate in the Historiography of Early Modern Germany and Switzerland, in: History Journal 37 (1994), pp. 199–207.

—: Communities and the Nature of Power, in: Germany: A New Economic and Social History, vol. 1, ed. Bob Scribner, London and New York 1996, pp. 291–325.

SCRIBNER, Bob and Gerhard BENECKE, eds.: The German Peasant War 1525: New Viewpoints, London 1979.

SEA, Thomas: Economic Impact of the German Peasants' War: The Question of Reparations, in: Sixteenth Century Journal 8 (1977), pp. 74–97.

SELLERT, Wolfgang: Zur Rezeption des römischen und kanonischen Rechts in Deutschland von den Anfängen bis zum Beginn der frühen Neuzeit, in: Recht und Verfassung im Übergang vom Mittelalter zur Neuzeit, ed. Hartmut Boockmann, Ludger Grenzmann, Bernd Moeller, and Martin Staehelin, Göttingen 1998, pp. 115–166.

SETZLER, Wilfried: Kloster Zwiefalten: Eine schwäbische Benediktinerabtei zwischen Reichsfreiheit und Landsässigkeit. Studien zu ihrer Rechts- und Verfassungsgeschichte, Sigmaringen 1979.

SHEEHAN, James J.: What is German History? Reflections on the Role of the Nation in German History and Historiography, in: Journal of Modern History 53 (1981), pp. 1–23.

SHANIN, Teodor: Introduction, in: Peasants and Peasant Societies: Selected Readings, ed. Teodor Shanin, Penguin Modern Sociology Readings, Harmondsworth 1971, pp. 30–36.

SHARPE, J. A.: History of Crime in Late Medieval and Early Modern England: Review Article, in: Social History 7 (1982), pp. 187–203.

SIWEK, Alberich: Die Zisterzienserabtei Salem: Der Orden Das Kloster Seine Äbte, Sigmaringen 1984.
SOMMER-RAMER, Cécile: Einleitung: Die Zisterzienser, in: Helvetia Sacra, ed. Cécile Sommer-Ramer and Patrick Braun, vol. 3/1, Die Orden mit Benediktinerregel, Bern 1982, pp. 27–86.
SPECHT, Thomas: Die Beziehungen des Klosters Salem zur Universität Dillingen, in: Zeitschrift für die Geschichte des Oberrheins 59 (1931), pp. 272–292.
SREENIVASAN, Govind P.: The Peasants of Ottobeuren, 1487–1726: A Rural Society in Early Modern Europe, Past and Present Publications, Cambridge and New York 2004.
—: The Social Origins of the Peasants' War of 1525 in Upper Swabia, in: Past and Present 171 (2001), pp. 30–65.
STAIGER, Xavier: Salem oder Salmansweiler, Constance 1863 [2nd ed. Meersburg 2008].
STALNAKER, John C.: Towards a Social Interpretation of the German Peasants' War, in: The German Peasant War 1525: New Viewpoints, ed. Bob Scribner and Gerhard Benecke, London 1979, pp. 23–38.
STRAUSS, Gerald: Law, Resistance, and the State: The Opposition to Roman Law in Reformation Germany, Princeton 1986.
—: Luther's House of Learning: Indoctrination of the Young in the German Reformation, Baltimore 1978.
—, ed.: Pre-Reformation Germany, Stratum Series, New York 1972.
SYDOW, Jürgen: Die Zisterzienserabtei Bebenhausen, Germania Sacra, n.s. 16, Berlin 1984.
—: Die Sozialstruktur eines mittelalterlichen Zisterzienserklosters, dargestellt am Beispiel der Abtei Bebenhausen, in: Rottenburger Jahrbuch für Kirchengeschichte 4 (1985), pp. 93–102.
TEUSCHER, Simon: Erzähltes Recht: Lokale Herrschaft, Verschriftlichung und Traditionsbildung im Spätmittelalter, Campus Historische Studien 44, Frankfurt and New York 2007.
—: Textualising Peasant Enquiries: German Weistümer between Orality and Literacy, in: Charters and the Use of the Written Word in Medieval Society, ed. Karl Heidecker, Utrecht Studies in Medieval Literacy 36, Turnhout 2000, pp. 239–251.
THEIBAULT, John: Community and Herrschaft in the Seventeenth-Century German Village, in: Journal of Modern History 64 (1992), pp. 1–21.
TLUSTY, Ann B.: Bacchus and Civic Order: The Culture of Drink in Early Modern Germany, Studies in Early Modern German History, Charlottesville 2001.
TROßBACH, Werner: Südwestdeutsche Leibeigenschaft in der Frühen Neuzeit – eine Bagatelle?, in: Geschichte und Gesellschaft (1981), pp. 69–90.
TÜCHLE, Hermann: Süddeutsche Klöster vor 500 Jahren, ihre Stellung in Reich und Gesellschaft, in: Blätter für deutsche Landesgeschichte 109 (1973), pp. 102–123.
ULBRICH, Claudia: Leibherrschaft am Oberrhein im Spätmittelalter, Veröffentlichung des Max-Planck-Instituts für Geschichte 58, Göttingen 1979.
—: Oberschwaben und Württemberg, in: Der deutsche Bauernkrieg, 2nd ed., ed. Horst Buszello, Peter Blickle, and Rudolf Endres, Paderborn 1991, pp. 97–133.
VOGT, W.: Die Bodenseebauern und ihr Hauptmann Junker Dietrich Hurlewagen im grossen Bauernkrieg, Augsburg 1892.
WALLERSTEIN, Immanuel: The Modern World-System, vol. 2: Mercantilism and the Consolidation of the European World-Economy, 1600–1750, New York 1980.
WARDE, Paul: Common Rights and Common Lands in Southwest Germany, 1500–1800, in: The Management of Common Land in North West Europe, c. 1500–1800, ed. Martina de Moor, Leigh Shaw-Taylor, and Paul Warde, CORN Publication Series 8, Turnhout 2002, pp. 195–224.

WEBER, Edwin Ernst: Das nordwestliche Oberschwaben, in: Der Bauernkrieg in Oberschwaben, ed. Elmar L. Kuhn, Tübingen 2000, pp. 315–350.

WIEACKER, Franz: A History of Private Law in Europe: With Particular Reference to Germany, trans. Tony Weir, Oxford and New York 1995.

WIESNER, Merry: Family, Household, and Community, in: Handbook of European History, 1400–1600, vol. 1, ed. Thomas A. Brady Jr., Heiko A. Oberman, and James D. Tracy, Leiden and New York 1994, pp. 51–78.

WILLOWEIT, Dietmar: Rechtsgrundlagen der Territorialgewalt: Landesobrigkeit, Herrschaftsrechte und Territorium in der Rechtswissenschaft der Neuzeit, Forschungen zur deutschen Rechtsgeschichte 11, Cologne 1975.

—: Territorialstaat, in: Handwörterbuch zur deutschen Rechtsgeschichte, vol. 5, ed. Adalbert Erler and Ekkehard Kaufmann, Berlin 1998, pp. 146–151.

WOLF, Eric R.: Peasants, Foundations of Modern Anthropology Series, Englewood Cliffs 1966.

WRIGHTSON, Keith: Two Concepts of Order: Justices, Constables and Jurymen in Seventeenth-Century England, in: An Ungovernable People, ed. John Brewer and John Styles, London 1980, pp. 21–46.

WUNDER, Gerd: Bäuerliche Oberschichten im alten Wirtemberg, in: Bauernschaft und Bauernstand, 1500–1970: Büdinger Vorträge 1971–1972, ed. Günther Franz, Deutsche Führungsschichten in der Neuzeit 8, Limburg an der Lahn 1975, pp. 137–152.

—: Schwäbische Schultheißenfamilien, in: Zeitschrift für Agrargeschichte und Agrarsoziologie 9 (1961), pp. 203–210.

WUNDER, Heide: Die bäuerliche Gemeinde in Deutschland, Kleine Vandenhoeck-Reihe, Göttingen 1986.

—: Serfdom in Later Medieval and Early Modern Germany, in: Social Relations and Ideas: Essays in Honour of R. H. Hilton, ed. T. H. Aston, P. R. Coss, Christopher Dyer, and Joan Thirsk, Past and Present Publications, Cambridge and New York 1983, pp. 249–272.

WÜRGLER, Andreas: Bitten und Begehren: Suppliken und Gravamina in der deutschsprachigen Frühneuzeitforschung, in: Bittschriften und Gravamina: Politik, Verwaltung und Justiz in Europa (14.–18. Jahrhundert), ed. Cecilia Nubola and Andreas Würgler, Berlin 2005, pp. 17–52.

WÜST, Wolfgang: Geistlicher Staat und Altes Reich: frühneuzeitliche Herrschaftsformen, Administration und Hofhaltung im Augsburger Fürstbistum, Studien zur bayerischen Verfassungs- und Sozialgeschichte 19, Munich 2001.

ZINSMAIER, Paul: Die Geschichtsschreibung des Zisterzienserklosters Salem, in: Freiburger Diözesanarchiv für Kirchengeschichte 62 (1934), pp. 1–22.

ZITZLSPERGER, Hermann: Schlimme Zeiten, in: 1200 Jahre Bermatingen, 779–1979, ed. Erika Dillmann, Bermatingen 1979, pp. 105–111.

Index

C

K

L

U

V

W

Y

Z

FSC
www.fsc.org
MIX
Papier | Fördert
gute Waldnutzung
FSC® C083411

Kolibri 360 GmbH
Ferdinand-Jühlke-Straße 7
99095 Erfurt, Deutschland
produktsicherheit@kolibri360.de